CALCULUS

from Graphical, Numerical, and Symbolic Points of View

VOLUME 1

ARNOLD OSTEBEE AND PAUL ZORN
St. Olaf College

1995
PRELIMINARY
EDITION

SAUNDERS COLLEGE PUBLISHING
Harcourt Brace College Publishers

Fort Worth Philadelphia San Diego New York Orlando Austin
San Antonio Toronto Montreal London Sydney Tokyo

Printed in the United States of America.

This material is based upon work supported by the National Science Foundation under Grant No. USE-9053363.

Any opinions, findings, and conclusions or recommendations expressed in this material are those of the authors and do not necessarily reflect the views of the National Science Foundation.

Ostebee/Zorn: CALCULUS FROM GRAPHICAL, NUMERICAL, AND SYMBOLIC POINTS OF VIEW, VOL. I, 1995 Preliminary Edition

ISBN 0-03-010602-8

456 018 98765432

Contents

About this book: notes for instructors

This book aims to do exactly what its title suggests: treat calculus from graphical, numerical, and symbolic points of view. In this preface we elaborate briefly on what this means.

Philosophy

Several common threads run through *Toward a Lean and Lively Calculus*, *Calculus for a New Century*, discussions at many professional meetings, the report of the NCTM/MAA Joint Task Force on Curriculum for Grades 11–13, and the NCTM *Curriculum and Evaluation Standards for School Mathematics.* First, there is a consistent call for *leaner and more conceptual courses*, driven by and focused on central ideas. Second, there is a realization that courses should *reflect modern technology both in content and in pedagogy.*

A diagnosis. Many calculus courses, we believe, slight the conceptual foundations of the subject and overemphasize routine techniques—formal differentiation, antidifferentiation, convergence testing, etc. Analytic objects (integral, derivative, convergence, etc.) are represented and manipulated only algebraically (i.e., *via* symbolic manipulation of explicit elementary functions). For example, textbooks often treat limits, derivatives, and integrals—all *analytic* objects—only as *algebraic* operations on *algebraic* functions. We try to take a broader view.

Whether one views calculus as an introduction to pure mathematics or as a foundation for applications (or both!), the conclusion is the same—concepts, not techniques, are truly fundamental to the course. Whatever uses they make of the calculus, students need more than a compendium of manipulative techniques. The *sine qua non* for a useful command of the calculus is a conceptual understanding that is deep and flexible enough to accommodate diverse applications.

A prescription. Our key strategy for improving conceptual understanding is combining, comparing, and moving among graphical, numerical, and algebraic "representations" of central concepts. This strategy pervades and unifies our exposition. Bringing graphical and numerical, as well as algebraic, viewpoints to bear on calculus ideas is the philosophical foundation of our text. By representing and manipulating calculus ideas and objects graphically, numerically, and algebraically, we believe that students gain a better, deeper, and more useful understanding.

The role of technology

Combining graphical, numerical, and symbolic viewpoints in calculus can be forbiddingly time-consuming and distracting without technological assistance. With technology, these viewpoints become practically accessible; hence, we use technology freely. So should our students.

Having said this, we emphasize that we do *not* intend to "automate" or "computerize" the calculus. We regard computers and graphing calculators strictly as instructional *tools*—albeit very powerful ones—to facilitate the crucial combination of graphical, numerical, and algebraic viewpoints. Our text exploits the capabilities of these tools to help students focus on the ideas that lie at the heart of the calculus.

How much technology? What kinds?

This text freely uses and refers to numerical and graphical computations, but it is independent of any particular technology. Any of the familiar high-level products—*Mathematica, Maple, Derive*—are certainly sufficient, but hardly necessary. Many graphing calculators (e.g., the TI-81, 82, and 85, the HP-48G, etc.) and special-purpose microcomputer software packages are adequate.

Our use of technology is most conveniently described in terms of *functionalities*. The requirements for Calculus I and Calculus II differ somewhat:

Calculus I: Chapters 1–5 (the traditional content of Calculus I) draw freely on machine graphics; almost any up-to-date *form* will do. Most graphing calculators would suffice; so would almost any flexible microcomputer graphing program, such as *MasterGrapher* or *MicroCalc*.

Calculus II: To make the best use of the remaining (Calculus II—not covered in this volume) material, students will require access to a modest level of numerical computation (mainly for estimating analytic quantities: integrals, series, etc.) Many microcomputer software packages provide the necessary functionality; so do some programmable graphing calculators. In addition, access to simple symbolic operations (e.g., formal differentiation, Taylor series expansion) is desirable, but not strictly necessary.

Symbol manipulation and hand computation

Although we emphasize concepts and use technology freely, we by no means ignore symbol manipulations in general, or hand computations in particular. We take the symbolic points of view of our title fully as seriously as the graphical and the numerical. We cover, for instance, the usual techniques for formal differentiation and antidifferentiation. Why do we do so?

That machines can do calculus manipulations does not render by-hand operations obsolete. Some manipulative practice and skill builds and supports conceptual understanding. Hand computation illustrates concepts concretely, builds "symbol sense" (the algebraic counterpart of numerical intuition) and an ability to estimate, and gives students a sense of mastery. It does *not* follow, though, that harder, more baroque computational problems are necessarily better or more useful; we deemphasize them. Both research results and our own experience suggest that diverting some time and attention to concepts does little, if anything, to reduce students' hand computational facility.

Distinctive features of the text

Our text differs significantly from standard treatments. Here are some of these differences, together with some of our assumptions, goals, and strategies.

Combining graphical, numerical, and algebraic viewpoints. Throughout the text we insist that students manipulate and compare graphical, numerical, and algebraic representations of mathematical objects. In studying functions, for example, students manipulate not only elementary functions but also functions presented graphically and tabularly. In the context of formal differentiation, exercises ask students to apply the chain rule to combinations of functions presented in various ways. Graphical and numerical techniques, with error estimates, complement algebraic antidifferentiation methods. For series, routine convergence tests are emphasized less than finding—and defending—numerical limit estimates.

A mainstream course. Our main strategy—combining graphical, numerical, and algebraic viewpoints to clarify concepts and make them concrete—aims *explicitly* at mainstream students, who especially need such help. We regard a more conceptual calculus as also more applicable. To *use* calculus ideas and techniques, students must know what they are doing and why, not merely how. Thus, our text is appropriate for a general audience: mathematics majors, science and engineering majors, and non-science majors.

Concepts vs. rigor. Proving theorems in full generality is less valuable, we think, than helping students understand concretely what theorems say, why they're reasonable, and why they matter. Too often, fully rigorous proofs address questions that students are unprepared to ask.

Still, we believe that introducing calculus students to the idea of proof—and to some especially important classical proofs—is essential. We prove major results, but *emphasize* only those that we believe contribute significantly to understanding calculus concepts. In examples and problems, too, we pay attention to developing analytic skills and synthesizing mathematical ideas.

More varied exercises. However clear its exposition, a textbook's problems generate most of students' mathematical activity and occupy most of their time. Through the problems we assign, we tell students concretely what we think they should know and do.

Routine drills and challenging theoretical problems are standard in texts; ours includes some of both. More distinctive, though, are problems that fall *between* these poles:

- Problems that combine and compare algebraic, graphical, and numerical viewpoints and techniques.
- Problems that require "translation" among various representations and interpretations of calculus ideas (e.g., to interpret derivative information in terms of either slope or rate of change).
- Problems that use calculus as a *language* for interpreting and solving problems. Students are asked to translate problems into mathematical terms, solve these problems using the tools of calculus, and reinterpret mathematical results in the context of the original problem.

Strategies for better problem solving. Emphasizing problem solving is nowadays *de rigeur* in calculus textbooks; ours is no exception. What, concretely, does such an emphasis entail in content and strategy?

Conceptual understanding, we believe, is the weakest link in students' ability to solve nontrivial problems. Thus, *the goal of better problem solving skills is implicit in the goal of deeper conceptual understanding.* To that end:

- We use numerical and graphical methods both to improve students' understanding of concepts and to enlarge their kit of tools to solve problems. Students, we find, are surprisingly quick to master and apply elementary numerical and graphical methods, even error estimation.

- When technology is available, students are freed, indeed forced, to *analyze* the structure of a problem and *plan* a solution strategy. We emphasize general problem-solving strategies (reduction to more tractable subproblems, estimation, search for patterns, etc.) explicitly wherever we can.

- We provide a greater *qualitative* variety of exercises including problems that are posed more generally, problems that call for more synthesis, and problems that rely on a larger set of solution techniques. In this richer environment, we hope students will come to see mathematics as an open-ended, creative activity, not a rigid collection of recipes.

Advice from you

We appreciate hearing instructors' comments, suggestions, and advice on this preliminary edition. Our physical and e-mail addresses are below.

Many of the suggestions received from users of earlier versions of this text have been incorporated in this version. However, time constraints have prevented us from following up on all of these suggestions by the deadline for this preliminary edition. A later edition will more accurately reflect the feedback we have received.

Arnold Ostebee and Paul Zorn
Department of Mathematics
St. Olaf College
1520 St. Olaf Avenue
Northfield, Minnesota 55057-1098

e-mail: `ostebee@stolaf.edu` `zorn@stolaf.edu`

July, 1994

How to use this book: notes for students

All authors want their books to be *used*: read, studied, thought about, puzzled over, reread, underlined, disputed, understood, and, ultimately, enjoyed. So do we.

That might go without saying for *some* books—beach novels, user manuals, field guides, etc.—but it may need repeating for a calculus textbook. We know as teachers (and remember as students) that mathematics textbooks are too often read *backwards*: faced with Exercise 231(b) on page 1638, we've all shuffled backwards through the pages in search of something similar. (Very often, moreover, our searches were rewarded.)

A calculus textbook isn't a novel. It's a peculiar hybrid of encyclopedia, dictionary, atlas, anthology, daily newspaper, shop manual, *and* novel—not exactly light reading, but essential reading nevertheless. Ideally, a calculus book should be read in *all* directions: left to right, top to bottom, back to front, and even front to back. That's a tall order. Here are some suggestions for coping with it.

Read the narrative. Each section's narrative is designed to be read from beginning to end. The examples, in particular, are supposed to illustrate ideas and make them concrete—not just serve as templates for homework exercises.

Read the examples. Examples are, if anything, more important than theorems, remarks, and other "talk." We use examples both to show already-familiar calculus ideas "in action," and to set the stage for new ideas.

Read the pictures. We're serious about the "graphical points of view" mentioned in our title. The pictures in this book are not "illustrations" or "decorations." Pictures like this one–

Graph of $y = x\ \sin(1/x)$ **near** $x = 0$

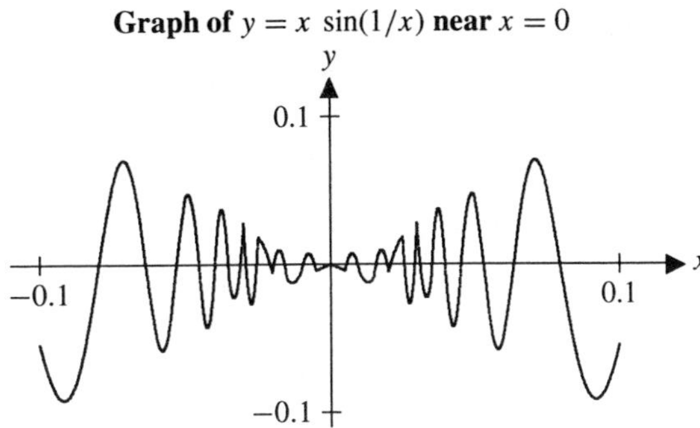

are everywhere, even in the middle of sentences. That's intentional: graphs are an important part of the language of calculus. An ability to think "pictorially"—as well as symbolically and numerically—about mathematical ideas may be the most important benefit calculus can offer.

Often they're put in margin notes, like this one.

Read with a calculator and pencil. This book is full of requests➥ to check a calculation, sketch a graph, or "convince yourself" that something makes sense. Take these "requests" seriously. Mastering mathematical ideas takes more than reading; it takes doing, drawing, and thinking.

Read the language. Mathematics is not a "natural language" like English or French, but it has its own vocabulary and usage rules. Calculus, especially, relies on careful use of technical language. Words like **rate**, **amount**, **concave**, **stationary point**, and **root** have precise, agreed-upon mathematical meanings. Understanding such words goes a long way toward understanding the mathematics they convey; misunderstanding the words leads inevitably to confusion. Whenever in doubt, consult the index.

Read the appendices. The human appendix generally lies unnoticed—unless trouble starts, when it's taken out and thrown away. Don't treat *our* appendices that way. Though perhaps slightly enlarged, they're full of healthy matter: reviews of precalculus topics, help with "story problems," proofs of various kinds, even a graphical "atlas" of functions. Used as directed the appendices will help appreciably in digesting the material.

Read the instructors' preface (if you like). Get a jump on your teacher.

In short: *read the book.*

A last note

Why study calculus at all? There are plenty of good practical and "educational" reasons: because it's good for applications; because higher mathematics requires it; because it's good mental training; because other majors require it; because jobs require it. Here's another reason to study calculus: because calculus is among our species' deepest, richest, farthest-reaching, and most beautiful intellectual achievements. We hope this book will help you see it in that spirit.

A last request

Last, a request. We sincerely appreciate—and take very seriously—students' opinions, suggestions, and advice on this book. We invite you to offer your advice, either through your teacher or by writing us directly. Our addresses appear below.

Arnold Ostebee and Paul Zorn
Department of Mathematics
St. Olaf College
1520 St. Olaf Avenue
Northfield, Minnesota 55057-1098

July, 1994

Chapter 1

Functions in Calculus

1.1 Functions, calculus-style

Calculus is a branch of mathematical analysis—the study of *functions*. Functions describe relationships among varying quantities; calculus helps us discover and quantify these relationships. But we're getting ahead of ourselves . . . .

Let's start from the beginning: What is a function? What functions are most important? Why?

Informally:

> *A function is a procedure*➻ *for assigning a unique output to any acceptable input.*

I.e., a recipe.

The most familiar functions are given by explicit algebraic formulas, like

$$f(x) = x^3 - 4x + 3 \qquad \text{and} \qquad g(x) = \frac{x^2 - 4}{x + 3}.$$

Such functions are easy to write down, easy to plug numbers into, easy to draw graphs of, and (as we'll see later) easy to differentiate and antidifferentiate.➻

We'll define these technical words soon.

Not every useful function comes equipped with—or even *has*—a convenient algebraic formula. Working with other-than-algebraic functions is an important theme of this course.

■ **Example 1.** Shown below are world population figures, in millions, over many centuries. [These data appear in materials produced by Project CALC, at Duke University.]

Human Population in Millions

year	0	1000	1650	1750	1800	1850	1900
people	100	200	545	728	906	1171	1608
year	1920	1930	1940	1950	1960	1976	1987
people	1834	2070	2295	2517	3005	4000	5000

The table shows what we expect: population grows "faster and faster" over time. *Plotting* the data shows this more clearly still:

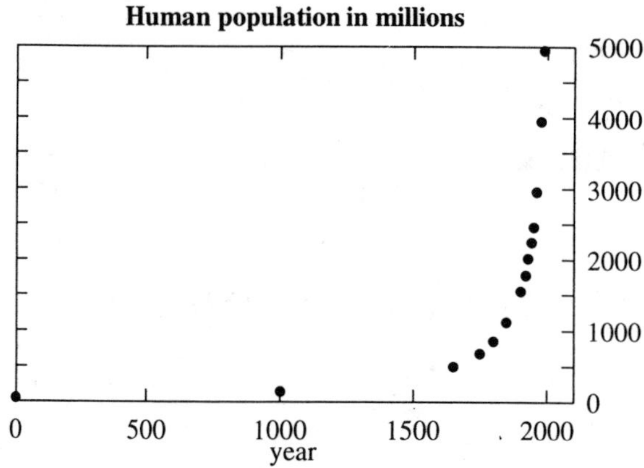

The graph is a **scatter plot**, consisting of a finite number of points, one per data item. Study it carefully to see how each point is plotted, and how each axis is used.

Times are inputs; populations are outputs.

What good would an explicit population formula be?

World population is certainly a function—at any time there's a corresponding population. But does the population function have some convenient *formula*? An answer would be well worth having!

Later we'll describe ways of choosing mathematical formulas that "fit" observed data with reasonable accuracy. The picture below, for instance, shows the graph of a mathematical function p, with formula

$$p(t) = 906e^{0.008(t-1800)}.$$

superimposed on the data. It seems to fit the data fairly well:

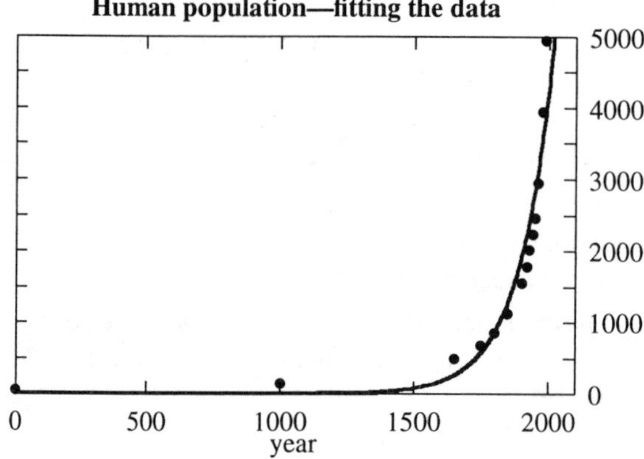

But we'll return to such matters at the end of this chapter.

Exactly how and why we chose this particular formula for p doesn't matter here. The various constants—906, e, 0.008, 1800—involved in the formula are called **parameters**. Choosing parameter values appropriately is part of the process called **curve fitting**. □

We'll define "continuous" rigorously later; here it's understood informally.

With such a formula we could predict the weather with perfect certainty.

■ **Example 2.** For any real number t, let $l(t)$ be the outside temperature, in degrees Celsius, t hours after midnight, January 1, 1994, in Northfield, Minnesota. This rule defines a function: To an input t (a time) l assigns an output $l(t)$ (a temperature). We'd expect l to be **continuous:** temperature varies smoothly, not by leaps and bounds. However, we don't expect l to be given *exactly* by a simple algebraic formula, now and forever. Nevertheless, we might reasonably try to *estimate* (or "model") l in some approximate or average sense. □

Functions without formulas

Functions like l, without explicit formulas, may seem strange or artificial. In one sense the *opposite* is true: most real-world functions are like the weather—messy, unpredictable, and imperfectly understood. The tractable, well-understood functions we use to model observed phenomena are, from this point of view, comparatively artificial. The real surprise is how successfully the basic mathematical functions model, and even predict, natural phenomena.

Example 3. Information about a function n is given in the table:

x	-3	-2	-1	0	1	2	3	4
$n(x)$	-4	-9	-1	0	1	8	3	-2

Our knowledge of n is, to say the least, incomplete. What's $n(100)$? For what inputs is n defined at all? Is the graph of n a smooth curve? Is there a secret formula for n?

The table alone doesn't say. (Incomplete information is common in practice, e.g., for experimental data.) More information would help. If, say, the table records the outside temperature x hours after midnight on January 1, 1994, then we'd expect $n(x)$ to be continuous and to accept non-integer inputs. To "model" the situation we might look for an explicit function that "agrees" with the data in the table. The complicated-looking polynomial function

As in the previous example.

$$p(x) = -\frac{152}{105}x + \frac{5}{72}x^2 + \frac{683}{240}x^3 - \frac{11}{144}x^4 - \frac{33}{80}x^5 + \frac{1}{144}x^6 + \frac{1}{70}x^7$$

is one possibility—it happens to produce the values given in the table. There's no guarantee, of course, that $p(x)$ gives "correct" temperature information for any other values of x. (Experimenting quickly shows that $p(x)$ can't possibly tell temperature for all time. For instance, $p(-10) = -98{,}251$—not a likely temperature even in Minnesota winter.) □

Example 4. Let m be the function shown graphically below.

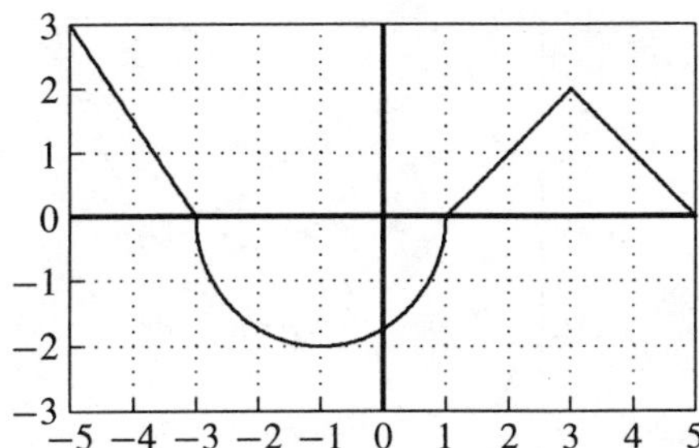

Some values of m, such as $m(-1) = -2$, are obvious even without a formula. Other values of m are less clear; $m(-2)$, for example, is *about* -1.7, but the exact value can't be determined from the graph.

As it happens, m can be represented algebraically, by a **piecewise-defined formula**: Because its graph consists of three line segments and a semicircle, the pieces are as follows:

Check our work.

$$m(x) = \begin{cases} -3x/2 - 9/2 & \text{if } -5 \le x \le -3 \\ -\sqrt{4-(x+1)^2} & \text{if } -3 < x \le 1 \\ x-1 & \text{if } 1 < x \le 3 \\ -x+5 & \text{if } 3 < x \le 5 \end{cases}$$

With the formula we can now find $m(-2)$ exactly:

$$m(-2) = -\sqrt{4-(-2+1)^2} = -\sqrt{3} \approx -1.732050808. \qquad \square$$

Patched-together functions. Functions like m, defined "in pieces," may seem unnatural and impractical. They are not. Computer-drawn graphs, for example, are usually made up of many short line segments or arcs—each described algebraically. The process of "splining" (i.e., joining properly chosen curves or line segments to form a single smooth curve) is based on elementary calculus ideas. Splines are used in computer-assisted design, engineering, and other applications.

Some functions are defined *only* in words.

Draw a picture to illustrate the situation!

■ **Example 5.** Let $V(x)$ denote the volume (in gallons) of water in a spherical tank, of radius 10 feet, when the depth is x feet. *Some* formula lurks here, presumably, but finding it is another matter. Even without an explicit formula we can answer questions like these:

- What volume of water is in the tank when the water is ten feet deep?
- Draw a rough graph of the function $V(x)$ for $0 \le x \le 20$. $\square$

Try it now. Is the graph of V a straight line? Why or why not?

■ **Example 6.** Hot days on the Oklahoma prairie generate strong up- and downdrafts. In the gondola of a hot air balloon, the altimeter needle swings. The function A (shown below) describes the altimeter readings over a certain period of time. Note the *units*: time t is measured in *minutes* and altitude $A(t)$ in *hundreds* of feet above sea level. (Central Oklahoma lies about 960 feet above sea level.)

The horizontal axis tells time, not distance, so the graph is not a "picture" of the balloon's flight. Or could it be?

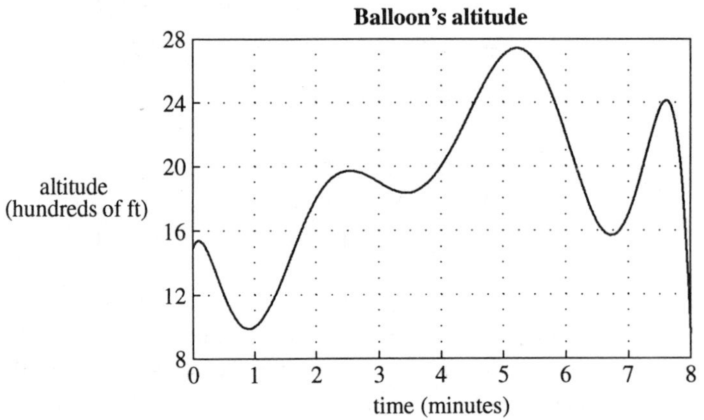

Reading velocity from the altitude graph. The graph of A tells a lot, directly, about altitude—when the balloon was highest, when it rose, when it fell, etc. But consider another, equally interesting question:

More interesting to the passengers, probably.

How fast *was the balloon rising or falling at time t?*

In other words, how does the balloon's **upward velocity** $V(t)$ vary with time?

What can the altitude graph tell us about the upward velocity? A lot:

- The *sign* of $V(t)$ tells whether the balloon is rising or falling at time t. Altitude *increases* as the balloon rises, so $V(t) > 0$ when the balloon is rising (e.g., in the interval $4 < t < 5$) and $V(t) < 0$ when the balloon is falling (e.g., if $2.5 < t < 3.5$).

- At $t = 1.5$ altitude grows *quickly* relative to time; the balloon is soaring upward. By $t = 2.4$ the balloon has leveled off. Some ups and downs follow, but at $t = 7.8$ things look bad. Altitude is plunging; so is the balloon.

- The vertical velocity $V(t)$ clearly depends on how *steeply* the A-graph rises or falls at time t. At $t = 6$, for instance, the A-graph is dropping, but how fast? How, in other words, might we estimate a value for $V(6)$?

  One approach is to focus on a *small* interval containing $t = 6$, such as $5.5 \le t \le 6.5$. A close look at the graph shows that

  $$A(5.5) \approx 27 \qquad \text{and} \qquad A(6.5) \approx 17\,.$$

  Over the one-minute interval $5.5 \le t \le 6.5$, therefore, the balloon drops about 10 vertical units, or 1000 feet. The **average velocity** over this interval, therefore, is around -1000 feet per minute. Since the graph looks nearly straight over this short interval, the velocity *at* $t = 6$ should not be much different:

  At the instant $t = 6$, the velocity is about -1000 feet per minute.

- The upward velocity $V(t)$ has an important and natural *graphical* meaning: at any time t, $V(t)$ is the *slope* of the A-graph at time t.

  Mathematical legalities arise in defining the slope of a curved graph. We'll deal with them carefully later; here, intuition is trustworthy.

  Just above we estimated that $V(6) \approx -10$. The graphical version of the same strategy runs like this: On a small interval near $t = 6$, the graph is almost straight. To estimate slope, therefore, any two nearby points should do. The line through (5.5, 27) and (6.5, 17), for instance, has slope

  $$\frac{17 - 27}{6.5 - 5.5} = -10,$$

  which agrees with our earlier estimate.

- By estimating the velocity $V(t)$ for *many* values of t, we could amass enough information to plot V. Doing so by hand is tedious; we used a computer:

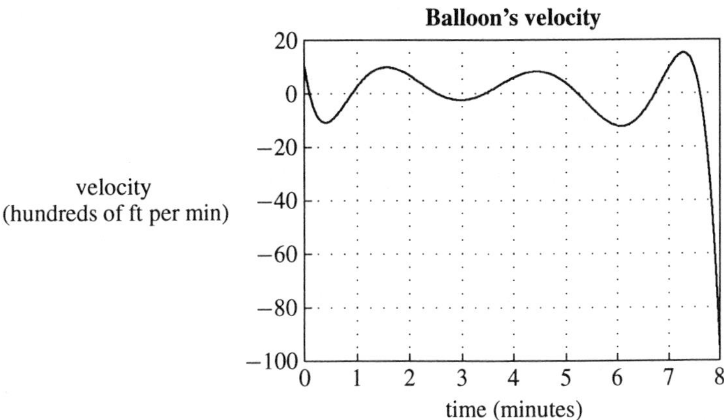

There's much to see in the new graph, but we'll content ourselves with a final observation: at $t = 8$, things look bleak. □

Functions from words

Mathematics is a language.

Because real-world problems usually come phrased in "natural" languages—French, say, or English—solving such problems must start with translation into the special vocabulary and grammar of mathematics. From paragraphs of ordinary prose come functions, variables, equations, operations, and the like.

Translation from English to French is not mere word-for-word replacement. An excellent translation respects French grammar, syntax, stylistic conventions, *and* vocabulary. A well-translated text captures the essence of the original.

Natural languages are suited to expressing nuance, emotional tone, and even ambiguity. Mathematical language is more straightforward. It emphasizes simplicity and precision, even in matters of depth and subtlety.

Nevertheless, the point made above applies—even more strongly—to mathematical language: to translate is to express the *essence*, not merely the form, of the situation. Distilling the essence of a problem, and expressing it mathematically, is the first—and often the largest—step toward a solution.

Calculus: the language of change. Different areas of mathematics are best suited to describe and predict different sorts of phenomena. Phenomena of *change* are the special province of calculus. Calculus offers both language in which to *describe* changing quantities and rules with which to *predict* their behavior. Functions are the basic objects of calculus, so translation for us will usually mean translation into functional language.

Cut on the heavy lines; fold on the dashed lines.

■ **Example 7.** To make a flimsy box from an ordinary $8.5'' \times 11''$ sheet of paper, cut squares from the corners and fold up the sides, as shown:

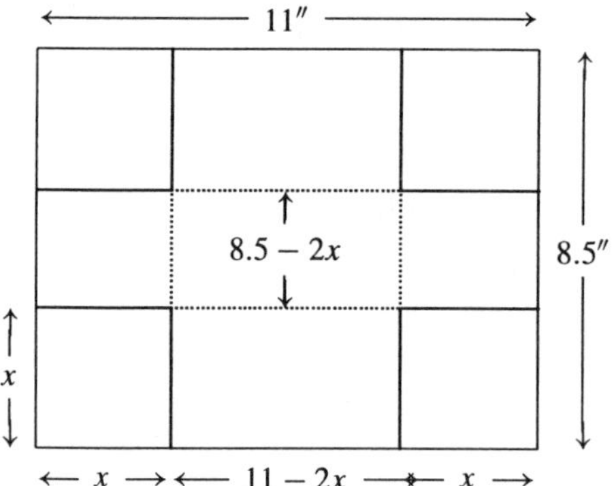

Which such box has the largest volume?

Solution: The volume V of the box depends only on the edge length—denoted by x—of the corners removed. In other words, V is a *function* of x. For any given x, V is easy to calculate algebraically:

$$V(x) = \text{length} \times \text{width} \times \text{depth} = (11 - 2x)(8.5 - 2x)x.$$

Notice that the formula makes sense, in context, only if all three factors are nonnegative—i.e., if $0 \le x \le 4.25$. In functional language, our problem is to find, among all feasible inputs x, the one that produces the largest possible output $V(x)$.

Notice our choice of horizontal range.

A graph shows how V varies with x:

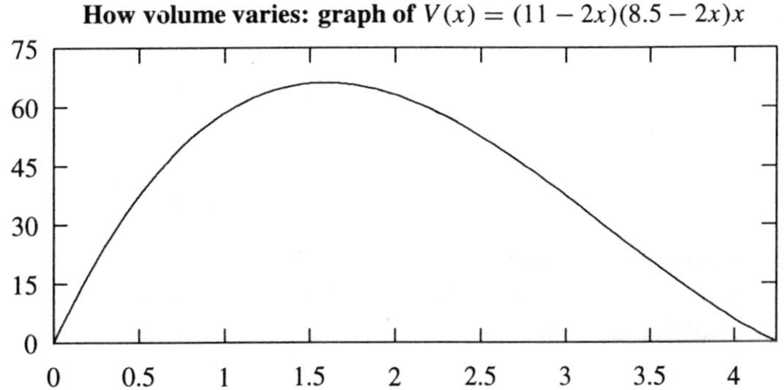

The maximum possible volume, apparently, is about 65 cubic inches; it occurs when $x \approx 1.6$ inches, i.e., for a box with dimensions $7.8'' \times 5.3'' \times 1.6''$.

By "zooming in" on the graph near $x = 1.6$ we can improve our estimates:

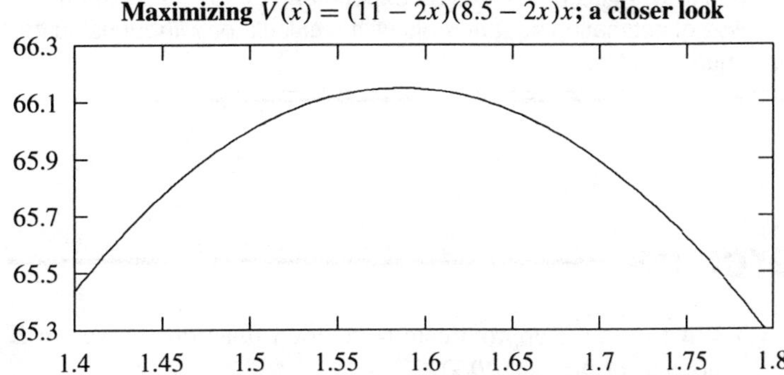

This sharper point of view suggests a maximum volume of about 66.1 cubic inches, achieved when $x \approx 1.59$ inches. (The dimensions then become $7.82'' \times 5.32'' \times 1.59''$.) With calculus methods, we could do better still. □

Just a bit better; for practical purposes, the results we found are probably adequate.

Functions approximating other functions

Sometimes it's useful to approximate one function with another.

■ **Example 8.** **(A polynomial approximation to the square root function.)** The polynomial function

$$p(x) = \frac{5}{16} + \frac{15}{16}x - \frac{5}{16}x^2 + \frac{1}{16}x^3$$

turns out to approximate the square root function $f(x) = \sqrt{x}$ closely near $x = 1$. Graphs show what this means:

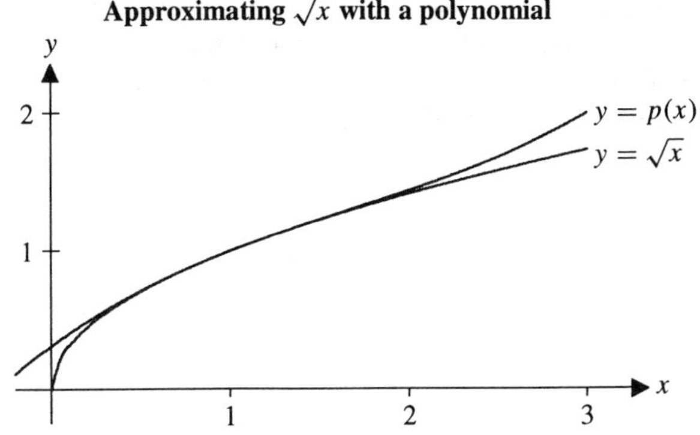

For $x < 0$, $f(x)$ is not even defined, so approximation is no longer an issue.

Near $x = 1$ the graphs are almost indistinguishable; elsewhere they pull apart. For example,

$$f(1.5) = \sqrt{1.5} \approx 1.22474 \quad \text{and} \quad p(1.5) \approx 1.22656$$

but

$$f(3) = \sqrt{3} \approx 1.73205 \quad \text{and} \quad p(3) = 2\,.$$

How we *chose* the polynomial p to approximate f must remain—for now—mysterious. Later in this book we'll learn to construct polynomials that approximate a wide variety of non-polynomial functions. □

Modern times. Years ago students learned paper and pencil techniques for computing square roots. Today we use calculators. Still the question remains: How does a calculator compute roots, and to what accuracy? As an experiment, try to find a systematic way of estimating square roots with a calculator *without* using the square root key.

Exercises

1. (a) What does the approximate population function p given in Example 1 predict for the year 2000?

   (b) What does it "predict" for the year 1000?

   (c) What does it "predict" for 1000 B.C.E.? ("B.C.E" means Before Common Era, aka B.C.)

   (d) Are these predictions reasonable?

2. (a) At what time was the balloon in Example 6 rising fastest? About how fast was this?

   (b) At what time was the balloon in Example 6 falling fastest? About how fast was this?

   (c) What happens at time $t = 8$?

3. Another possible way of depicting a balloon's flight graphically is to plot altitude vs. *horizontal position*, instead of altitude vs. *time*. Since westerly (i.e., west to east) winds prevail on the American prairie, a balloon above Oklahoma will often travel (ignoring vertical movement) due east. When this is so, it's natural to plot altitude against horizontal position, measuring the latter in *miles east of a starting point*. The resulting plot can be thought of as a "picture" of the balloon's flight.

   In this problem we consider the relationship, if any, between these two types of graph: *altitude vs. time*, as used in Example 6, and *altitude vs. position*, discussed just above. In particular, can the two types of graph possibly look the same?

   (a) Suppose that a *steady* 60-mph westerly wind blows. Draw an altitude vs. position graph. How are the two graphs related?

(b) Suppose that *no* horizontal wind blows. Draw a "picture" of the balloon's flight (i.e., an altitude-position graph). Do both types of graph make sense?

(c) What if an *easterly* wind blows? Draw a possible altitude-position graph. Does it look like an altitude-time graph?

4. Use the algebraic representation of m given in Example 4 to compute

(a) $m(-4)$

(b) $m(0)$

(c) $m(2.3)$

(d) $m(\pi)$

5. When you drive their compact car x miles, a certain rental company charges $f(x)$ dollars, where

$$f(x) = \begin{cases} 30, & \text{if } 0 \le x \le 100 \\ 30 + 0.07(x - 100), & \text{if } x > 100 \end{cases}$$

Describe this company's pricing policy in plain English. (Be sure to give economic interpretations of the constants 30, 0.07, and 100 that appear in the pricing formula.)

6. Find a piecewise-defined formula for each of the functions whose graphs are shown below. Each graph is made up of line segments and circular arcs.

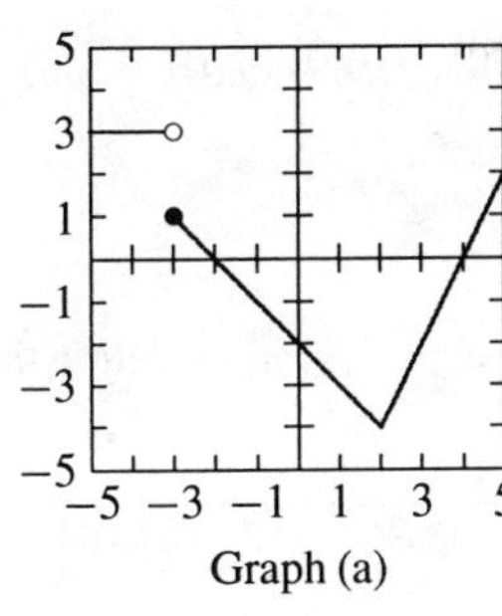

Graph (a)

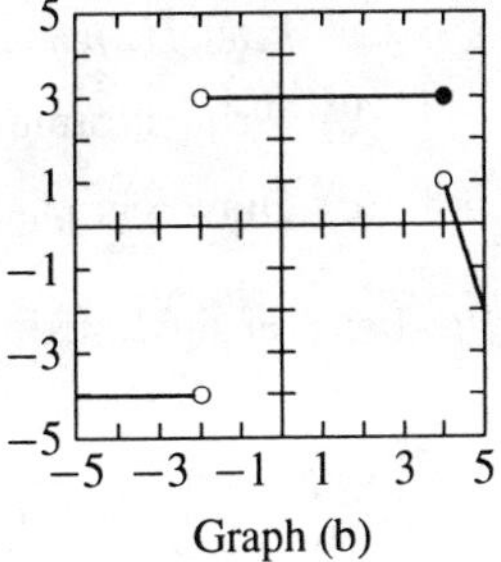

Graph (b)

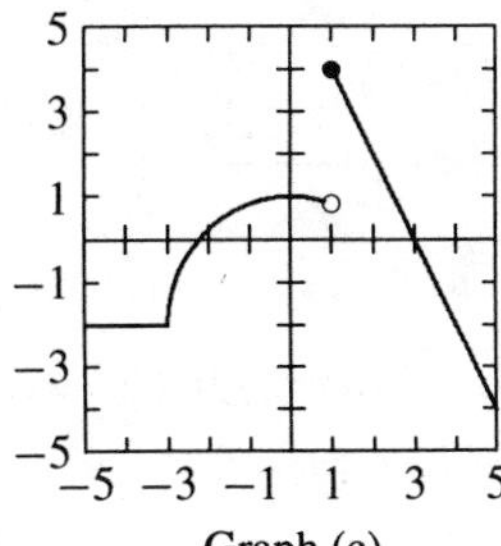

Graph (c)

7. Let $\ell(x) = 2x + 1$.

(a) Draw a graph of ℓ over the interval $[0, 5]$.

(b) Let $D(x)$ be the distance from the origin to the point $(x, \ell(x))$. Find a formula for $D(x)$. Sketch a graph of $D(x)$ over the interval $[0, 5]$.

(c) Let $A(t)$ be the area of the region bounded by the x-axis, the y-axis, $\ell(x)$, and the line $x = t$. Find a formula for $A(t)$. Sketch a graph of $A(t)$ over the interval $[0, 5]$.

8. Let f be the function defined by $f(x) = x^2$. Using f, define the function g by
$$g(x) = \text{the distance from } (0, 0) \text{ to } (x, f(x))\ .$$
For instance, $g(10) =$ the distance from $(0, 0)$ to $(10, 100) = \sqrt{10100}$.

   (a) Find $g(0)$, $g(-1)$, $g(1)$, $g(2)$, $g(500)$.

   (b) Write a formula for $g(x)$ in terms of x.

   (c) Draw a graph of g for $-5 \le x \le 5$.

9. Let f be the function defined by $f(x) = x^2$. Using f, define the function m by
$$m(x) = \text{the slope of the line from } (0, 0) \text{ to } (x, f(x))\ .$$
For instance, $m(10) =$ the slope from $(0, 0)$ to $(10, 100) = 10$.

   (a) Find $m(-1)$, $m(-2)$, $m(1)$, $m(2)$, $m(500)$.

   (b) Write a formula for $m(x)$ in terms of x.

   (c) Draw a graph of m for $-5 \le x \le 5$.

10. Let f be the function defined by $f(x) = x^2$. Using f, define the function j by
$$j(x) = \text{the slope of the ``secant'' line from } (1, 1) \text{ to } (x, f(x))\ .$$
For instance, $j(10) =$ the slope of the line from $(1, 1)$ to $(10, 100) = 11$.

   (a) Find $j(2)$, $j(1.1)$, $j(1.01)$, $j(0.99)$, $j(0.9)$, $j(0)$.

   (b) Write a formula for $j(x)$ in terms of x.

   (c) Draw a graph of j for $-2 \le x \le 2$.

11. Let f be the function defined by $f(x) = x^2$. Using f, define the function k by
$$k(x) = \frac{f(2+x) - f(2-x)}{2x}.$$
For instance,
$$k(0.1) = \frac{f(2.1) - f(1.9)}{0.2} = \frac{2.1^2 - 1.9^2}{0.2} = 4.$$

   (a) Find $k(-1)$, $k(-0.1)$, $k(0.1)$, $k(1)$, $k(1000)$.

   (b) Write a formula for $k(x)$ in terms of x.

   (c) Draw a graph of k for $-5 \le x \le 5$.

12. Let f be the function $f(x) = x^2 + 3x - 4$ and L the line that intersects f at the points $x = 2$ and $x = 2 + h$.

   (a) Find an equation of the line that intersects f at $x = -1$ and $x = 2$.

   (b) Find an algebraic expression for the *slope* of L. (The answer depends on h, of course.)

   (c) Use your answer to part (b) to find an equation of the line L.

   (d) Use your answer to part (c) to find an equation of the line that intersects f at $x = 2$ and $x = 2.003$.

(e) Use your answer to part (c) to find an equation of the line that intersects that curve at $x = 2$ and $x = -1$.

13. An open box is made by cutting squares of side w inches from the four corners of a sheet of cardboard that is 24 inches by 32 inches and then folding up the sides.

    (a) Express the volume of the box as a function of w. [HINT: Draw a picture.]

    (b) Estimate the value of w that maximizes the volume of the box.

14. Coffee mugs can be manufactured for sixty cents each. At a price of one dollar each, one thousand can be sold. For each penny the price is lowered, fifty more mugs can be sold.

    (a) Find a function that relates net profit and price.

    (b) What's the *best* price? [HINT: Graph the function from part (a).]

15. Express each of the following English sentences in mathematical notation using absolute values.

    (a) The temperature outside is within 5° (Fahrenheit) of freezing.

    (b) The temperature in that room is closer to $100^\circ F$ than to freezing.

    (c) The high temperature today is closer to yesterday's high temperature than yesterday's high was to the high temperature two days ago.

1.2 Graphs

Every equation in x and y has a **graph—the set of ordered pairs (x, y) of real numbers that satisfy the equation**. The graph of any equation of the form

$$(x-a)^2+(y-b)^2=r^2,$$

for example, is a circle. Associating an equation (an algebraic object) to a graph (a geometric object) is a powerful tool for understanding both.

With center (a, b) and radius r.

Graphs can be simple, complicated, or downright bizarre. Most graphs in calculus are of the everyday, $y = f(x)$ variety—almost every page of this book contains examples. Here, for a change, are some odder graphs:

■ **Example 1.** Below are the graphs of three equations: $x^2+y^2=-1$, $x^2+y^2=0$, and $x^2+y^2=1$:

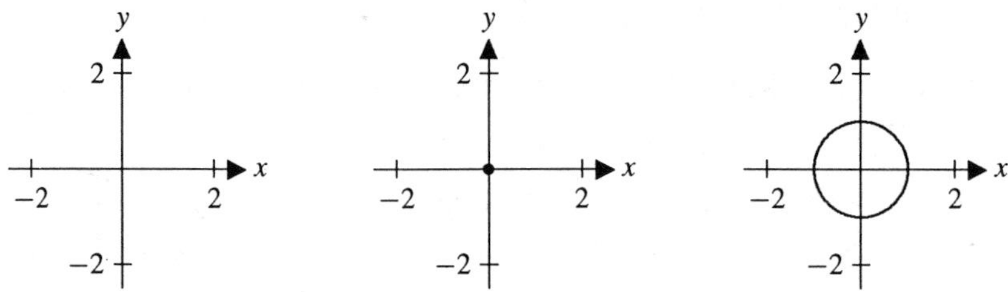

Is there some mistake? No; *no* pair (x, y) satisfies the first equation, so the first graph is *empty*. Only the origin $(0, 0)$ satisfies the second equation, so its graph is a single point. The third graph plays no tricks. □

Of real numbers.

Graphs of functions

The function $f(x)=x^2$ corresponds in the obvious way to the equation $y=x^2$, and hence to the familiar parabolic curve. In the same way, *every* function f corresponds to an equation $y = f(x)$, and therefore to a graph.

Not every equation (and, therefore, not every graph) corresponds to a function. Circles are obvious counterexamples: on a circle, most values of x correspond to two values of y.

> **Definition:** The graph of a function f is the set of points (x, y) that satisfy the equation $y = f(x)$.

In other words:

The graph of a function is the set of all points of the form $(x, f(x))$.

The "generic" picture looks like this:

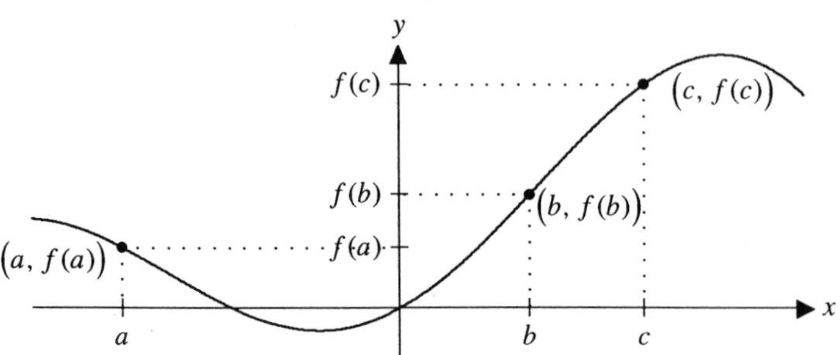

The graph of a function shows, geometrically, how the function varies over a range of inputs. Because calculus concerns precisely this question—how quantities vary with respect to each other—graphs play crucial roles throughout the subject.

Drawing the graph of a function given by an explicit formula, such as $p(x) = x^3 - 2x^2 + x - 2$, is an old, standard, and still important problem in elementary calculus. But other problems are just as important, especially now that machines draw graphs easily and accurately. Most important is to *understand* clearly what graphs say about functions, and how they say it.

A graph of this function appears below.

Not every machine-drawn graph is accurate . . . . More on this in the next section.

Drawing graphs is sometimes useful, but more interesting still is the connection between analytic properties of a function (e.g., whether it's increasing or decreasing) and geometric properties of its graph (e.g., whether it's rising or falling). Calculus tools unlock many such secrets.

Graphs—with and without formulas

Too much time and effort spent drawing graphs of nice functions with nice formulas can obscure an important fact:

Not every function has a nice formula—or any formula at all.

In real life convenient formulas are the exception. Having a formula amounts, in a sense, to knowing *everything* about a function. In this imperfect world, little is that certain.

■ **Example 2. (Function, formula, and graph.)** In the best possible circumstances we're given a function, its graph, *and* an explicit algebraic formula. Here, for instance, is a view of the graph of $p(x) = x^3 - 2x^2 + x - 2$.

Technically speaking, we see only part of the graph–the full graph is an infinite object.

Graph of $y = p(x)$

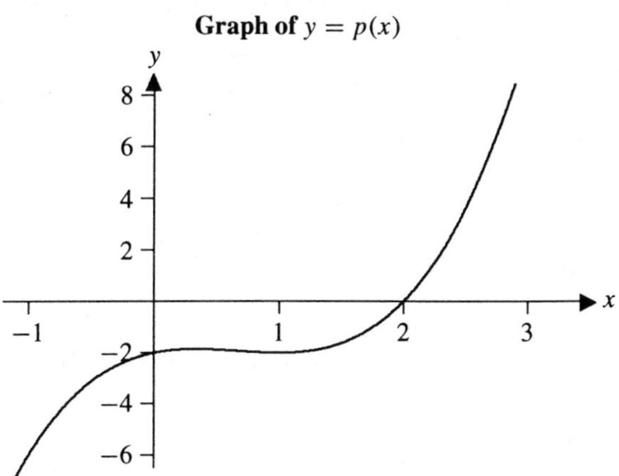

Observe:

A y-intercept. The graph intercepts the y-axis at height -2. In symbols: $p(0) = -2$.

No breaks. The graph shown is free of "jumps" or "breaks"—it can be drawn without lifting the "pencil." In mathematical language, the function p is **continuous** on the domain shown.

We'll define "continuity" carefully later on.

An x-intercept. The graph's x-intercept is at $x = 2$, so $p(2) = 0$. Factoring the formula shows the same thing:

$$p(x) = x^3 - 2x^2 + x - 2 = (x - 2)(x^2 + 1).$$

(The factored form tells us something more: $p(x) = 0$ *only* if $x = 2$.)

The graph rises as we trace it from left to right.

Where is p increasing? The graph of p *rises* from $x = 1$ to $x = 3$. In calculus language, the function p is said to be **increasing** for $1 < x < 3$. The picture ends at $x = 3$, so we can't tell from the graph alone what happens for larger values of x. In fact, it can be seen from the factored algebraic form of p that $p(x)$ increases for *all* $x > 1$. (Calculus methods we'll develop soon will show the same thing, more conveniently.) □

■ **Example 3.** **(A bare graph: no formula, no context.)** Below is a portion of the graph of a garden-variety calculus function f. No *formula* for f is given. Two "interesting" points are labeled.

Graph of $y = f(x)$

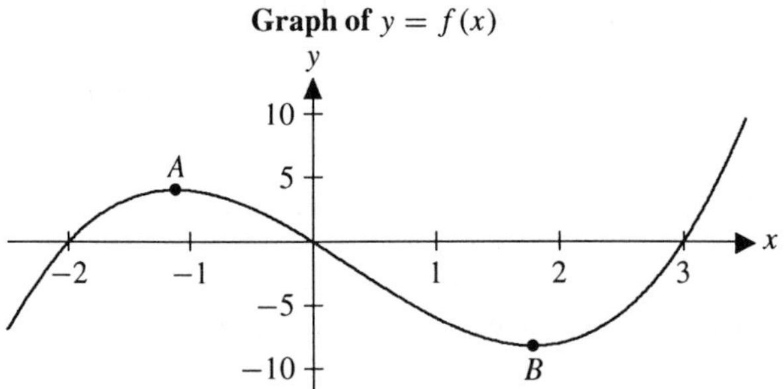

What can the graph tell us about the function f? What *can't* it say? Here are some samples:

- Because the point $(0, 0)$ lies on the graph, $f(0) = 0$. (Strictly speaking we should say $f(0) \approx 0$, since graphical data are always approximate. Here we'll trust our eyes.)

- Judging from the graph, $f(1) \approx -6$. To know whether $f(1) = -6$ *exactly*, we'd need more information.

- What's $f(10)$? The graph doesn't say. We might *guess* from the graph's general shape that $f(10)$ is some large positive number. Yet we can't be certain, from the graph alone, even that $f(10)$ exists.

- The points A and B correspond to **local maximum** and **local minimum values** of the function f. The coordinates of A—approximately $(-1.2, 4)$—imply that $f(-1.2) \approx 4$. Similarly, B's coordinates imply that $f(1.8) \approx -8$. Putting these data together, we might say (allowing for approximation errors) that $f(x)$ *increases* for $-2.5 < x < -1.2$, *decreases* for $-1.2 < x < 1.8$, and *increases* again for $1.8 < x < 3.5$.

Informally, high and low spots on the graph. We'll define these terms formally in the next chapter.

- For which values of x is $f(x) < -5$? One approach is to draw the *horizontal* line $y = -5$. This line hits the graph of f at three different points—near $x = -2.4$, $x = 0.7$, and $x = 2.5$. We'd estimate, therefore, that $f(x) < -5$ if either $x < -2.4$ or $0.7 < x < 2.5$.

  Two cautions are necessary: First, every number mentioned is only approximate. Second, we have no idea how $f(x)$ behaves for x *outside* the interval shown.

Do so now, with a ruler.

- Later, we'll define and study the slightly subtler idea of a graph's **concavity**. Concavity is a geometric property: the bowl of a spoon (in its usual position) is **concave up**; an umbrella (on a rainy day) is **concave down**. The f-graph, clearly, is concave *down* at the point A, and concave *up* at B. Somewhere *between* A and B, then, there must be an **inflection point**, where the

As rough synonyms, try "concave up" for "holds water" and "concave down" for "spills water."

Another term we'll define more precisely later.

direction of concavity switches. Where does this happen?

A close look shows that concavity changes *somewhere* between $x = 0$ and $x = 1$, but it's hard to be more precise than this. Soon, using calculus ideas, we'll see how to use the formula for p to locate inflection points precisely. □

■ **Example 4.** **(Graphs in context.)** [This example was drawn from *Calculus in Context*, a project of the Five Colleges consortium.]

In certain disease epidemics the affected population divides naturally into three groups: those *susceptible*, those *infected*, and those *recovered*. The epidemic's progress can be charted by observing how these populations vary over time. The three graphs below, labeled S, I, and R, show how the susceptible, infected, and recovered populations might vary over a 25-day period during a measles epidemic in a large school district.

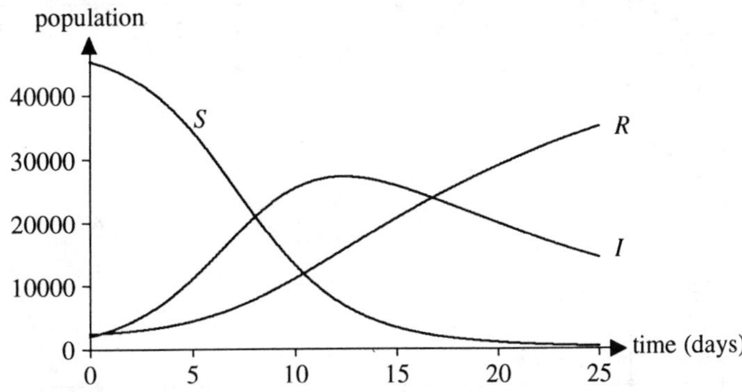

With these graphs, we can answer many questions about the epidemic:➻

Try to answer for yourself before reading the answers.

1. *How many children were in each population on day 10?*

   Reading the height of each graph on day 10 shows (allowing for estimation errors):

   susceptible ≈ 13,000; infected ≈ 26,000; recovered ≈ 11,000.

2. *On which day is the infected population largest?*

   The I-graph, and hence the infected population, peaks around day 12. (In calculus language, I assumes a local maximum value at day 12.

3. *When is the epidemic at its worst?*

   The answer depends on how we measure "badness." The number I of ill people is one reasonable measure. By this criterion➻ the "worst" day is around day 12.

   As we just saw.

   Another possible measure of "badness" is the number of people who fall ill on a given day. In our situation, to fall ill means to *leave* the susceptible population. From this point of view, the worst day occurs when the susceptible population *drops* most rapidly. A careful look at the S-graph suggests that this happens around day 7, where the graph points most steeply *downward*. (In calculus language, the day in question corresponds to an inflection point of the S-graph.) □

The entries should look familiar—cf. Section 1.1.

■ **Example 5. (Graphs from tabular data.)** Suppose we know only what this table tells about a function n:

x	−3	−2	−1	0	1	2	3	4
$n(x)$	−4	−9	−1	0	1	8	3	−2

How should we plot n? One problem is that *many* different functions "agree with n" (i.e., have the same values) for $x = -3, -2, \ldots, 4$. In graphical language, this means that many different possible graphs pass through the 8 data points.

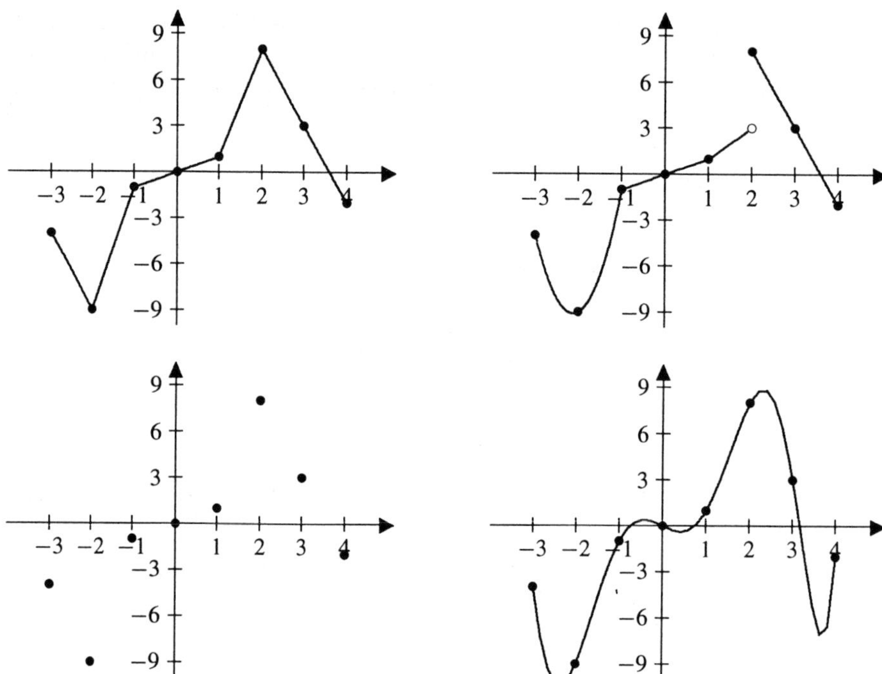

Is one of these graphs "right"? Without more information, we can't say. If we knew, say, that the function n represents outdoor temperatures, hour by hour, on a cold winter night, we might choose one as more likely than the others.

Which one?

Notice, in particular, the **discontinuity** in the graph at upper right. (The hollow dot indicates a "jump" at $x = 2$.) Physical experience says that air temperature varies continuously over time, so this graph seems unlikely to tell temperature. □

New functions from old: operations with constants

Creating new functions—and hence new graphs—from old is a recurring theme in calculus. There are many ways to "operate" on "old" functions to form new ones. The simplest such operations involve only **constant parameters**, attached in various ways to an original function. From the ordinary sine function, for instance, we can produce mutants like this one:

$$m(x) = 42 + 31 \sin\left(\frac{2\pi}{52}x\right).$$

In Section 1.6 we'll discuss a real-life application of the function above. Our present goal is more general: to understand how constant parameters affect *all* functions and their graphs.

Constant parameters

Given an "old" function f and a constant a, we can create such new functions as

$$f(x)+a, \qquad f(x+a), \qquad f(ax), \qquad \text{and} \qquad af(x).$$

How do these new functions differ from plain old f? How is the particular value of a involved?

Additive constants: vertical and horizontal translations

Given a function f and a constant a, consider the new functions g and h defined by

$$g(x)=f(x)+a; \qquad h(x)=f(x+a).$$

In each definition a is an **additive constant.**➻ Though similar in appearance, g and h are quite different: g is formed from f by adding a to *outputs* of f; h is formed by adding a to *inputs* of f.➻

If $a=0$, then $f=g=h$.

Read this sentence again; it's important.

Here are graphs of g for several values of a:

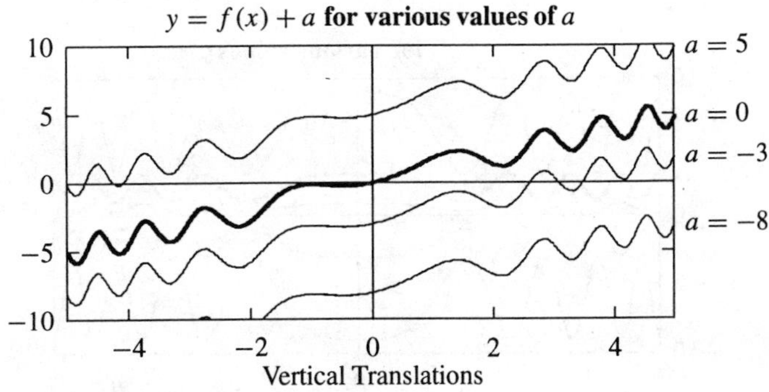

The graphs show how the value of a affects g:

> *The graph of $y=f(x)+a$ is the result of shifting the f-graph a units* upward.

In mathematics, moving an object without changing its shape is called **translation**; thus a's effect is a **vertical translation.**

The relationship between f and h is different. Compare *these* graphs:

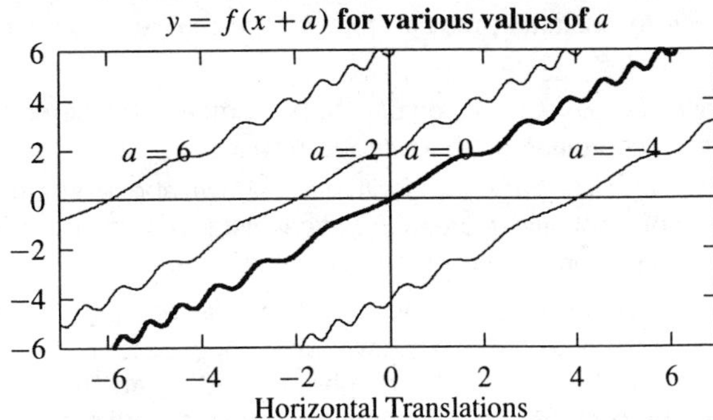

This time a causes a **horizontal translation**:

> *The graph of $f(x+a)$ results from shifting the f-graph a units to the* left.

Left? Not right? Yes, left. It might be surprising that the a in $f(x+a)$ moves the graph of f *left*, not right, To see why, consider the function $h(x) = f(x+2)$. Then $h(-2) = f(0)$, $h(-1) = f(1)$, $h(0) = f(2)$, etc. In effect, h has a two-unit "headstart" on f: whatever h does, f does the same two units *later.*

Multiplicative constants: stretching, compressing, and reflecting

Multiplicative parameters also make new functions from old. As before we start with a function f and a constant a, and form two new functions:

$$g(x) = af(x); \qquad h(x) = f(ax).$$

Notice that g results from multiplying f's *outputs* by a; h comes from multiplying f's *inputs* by a.

If $a = 1$, $f = g = h$.

Vertical stretching and reflection. Consider these graphs carefully:

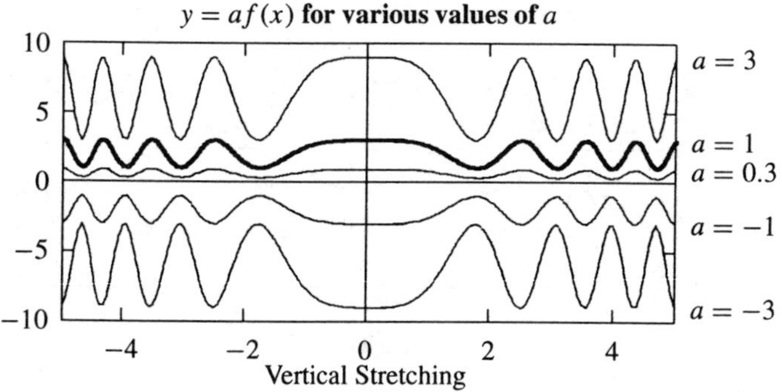

Vertical Stretching

The graphs show the effect of a on $g(x) = af(x)$: **vertical stretching** by a factor of $|a|$ and, if $a < 0$, **reflection** about the x-axis.

Stretching the language? Our use of such terms as "stretch," "compress," and "reflect" bears some comment:

- Stretching by a factor $a > 1$ is straightforward. The graph of $y = 3f(x)$, for instance, results from *tripling* the y-coordinate of each point on the f-graph.
- Stretching by *any* nonnegative factor a means the same thing: all vertical coordinates are *multiplied* by a.

  Notice that if $0 \le a < 1$, (as with $0.3f$, shown above) stretching by a factor of a actually *decreases* vertical distances. In such situations, we'll sometimes speak of "compressing" graphs.
- A *negative* multiplicative factor adds a *reflection* (about the x-axis) to the picture. The picture shows what happens for $a = -1$ and $a = -3$. In the simpler case, the graphs of f and $-f$ are "mirror images." The graph of $-3f$, by comparison, requires *both* a reflection *and* a vertical stretch, with factor 3, starting from f. (Order doesn't matter here. The graph of $-3f$ can be had either by reflecting the $3f$-graph or by 3-stretching the $-f$-graph.)

Horizontal stretching and reflection. The function $h(x) = f(ax)$ is formed by multiplying f's *inputs* by a. We just saw that multiplying *outputs* by a stretches the f-graph *vertically*. For similar reasons, multiplying *inputs* by a stretches or compresses the graph *horizontally*. The graphs below show h for several values of a:

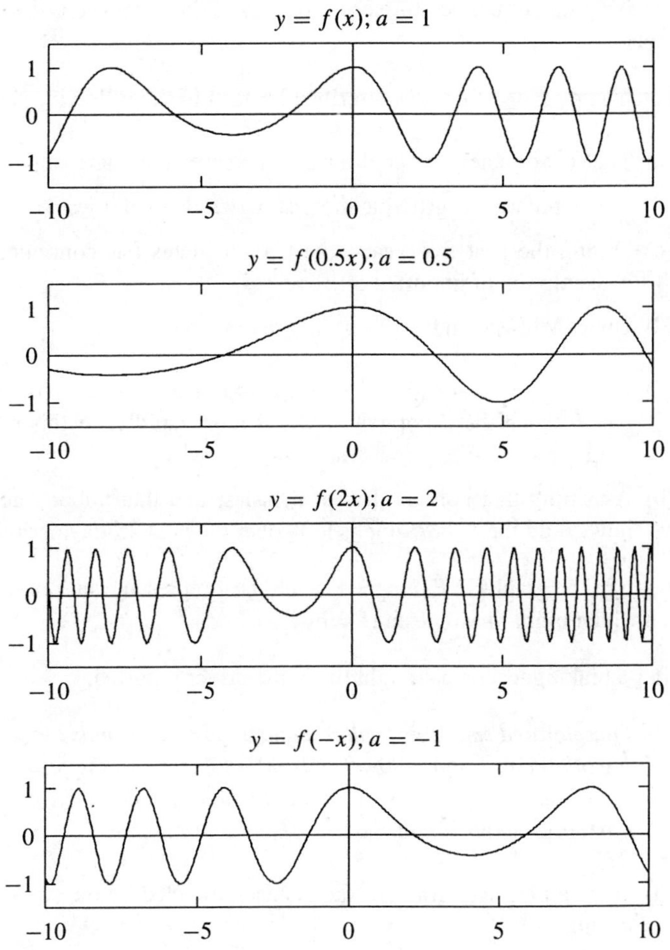

Notice the similarities—but also the differences—to vertical stretching:

- The graphs of $f(x)$, $f(2x)$, and $f(0.5x)$ show that if $a > 0$, the graph of $f(ax)$ is the result of *compressing* the f-graph horizontally by a factor of a (or, alternatively, *stretching* it by a factor of $1/a$).➻

- A *negative* value of a causes a *reflection*—about the *y-axis*, this time. The graph of $f(-2x)$, for instance, results from both compressing by a factor of 2 and reflecting about the y-axis.

Did you expect things to go the other way? If so, try this: If x measures time, then $f(x)$ is a quantity varying with time. From this point of view, the parameter $a = 2$ in $h(x) = f(2x)$ makes $h(x)$ vary twice as fast. Anything f does, h does in half the time.

Exercises

1. Consider the following sentence:

   The child's temperature has been rising for the last two hours, but not as rapidly since we gave her the antibiotic an hour ago.

   Sketch a graph of temperature as a function of time that is consistent with this scenario.

2. Sketch a graph of a function described by each of the following sentences.

   (a) The cost of a new car continues to increase at an increasing rate.

   (b) The population is growing more slowly now than it was five years ago.

   (c) During the past five years, the United States has continued to cut its consumption of imported oil.

   (d) Upper Midwest Industries profit growth slows.

3. (a) In Example 4 we asserted that the largest number of people fall ill on day 7, when the S-population drops most rapidly. Is this when I rises most rapidly? Why or why not?

   (b) Assuming that nobody dies of measles, and that nobody gets it twice, how could the S-I-R graphs look over the *next* 25-day period?

4. Which of the graphs in Example 5 would best represent outdoor temperatures on a winter night in Minnesota? Why?

5. After a braking test on a straight track, the driver reported:

   I accelerated smoothly from rest and within 15 seconds I was cruising at 60 mph. About 90 seconds into the test I hit the brakes. The car decelerated, but I was unable to stop in time. I hit the crash barrier at about 5 mph.

   (a) Draw a plausible graph of the distance traveled by the car as a function of time.

   (b) Draw a plausible graph of the car's speed as a function of time.

   (c) Draw a plausible graph of the car's acceleration as a function of time.

   [NOTE: Your graphs for parts (a)–(c) should be consistent with each other.]

6. An airplane takes off from one airport and, 45 minutes later, lands at another airport 300 miles away. Let t represent the time since the airplane took off, $x(t)$ the *horizontal* distance traveled, and $y(t)$ the *altitude* of the airplane at time t minutes after takeoff.

   (a) Draw a plausible graph of $x(t)$.

   (b) Draw a plausible graph of the plane's ground speed as function of time.

   (c) Draw a plausible graph of $y(t)$.

   (d) Draw a plausible graph of the plane's vertical velocity as a function of time.

7. Look at the hemispherical water tank sketched below.

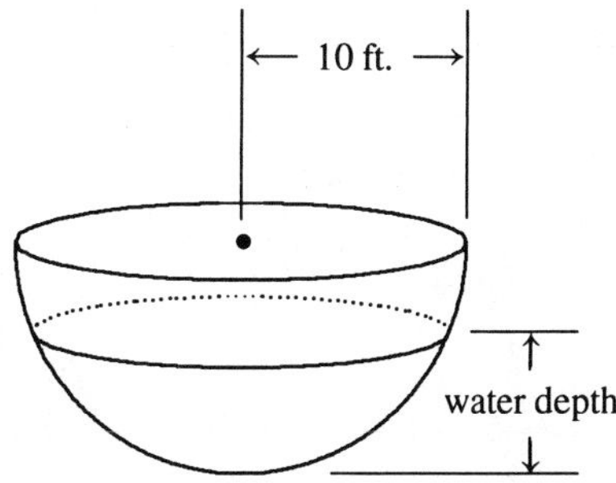

Let the letter D represent the *depth* of the water in the tank and let V be the *volume* of the water in the tank. Regard *volume* as a function of water *depth*.

(a) What is $V(0)$?

(b) What is $V(10)$?

(c) Which of the following graphs is most likely to be the graph of $V(D)$? Explain your reasoning.

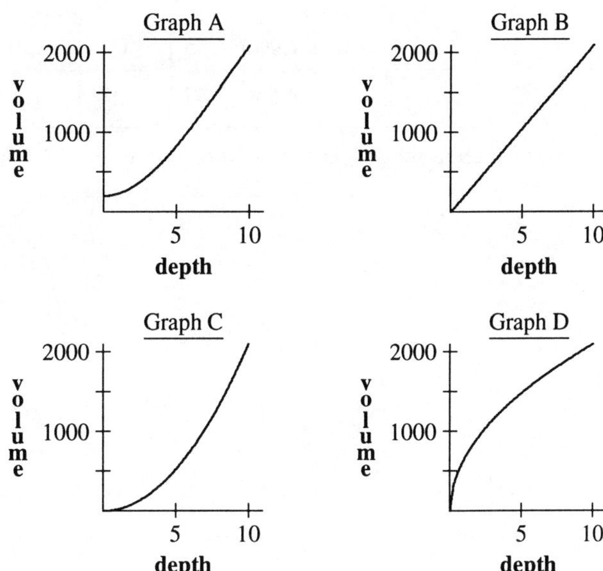

8. Tami, a chemistry major, took a class in glass blowing. Her first creation was a vase, quite irregular in shape. A good experimental scientist, Tami gathered the following data relating the depth (in cm) and volume (in ml) of water in her vase:

depth	2	4	6	8	10
volume	19	23	39	51	68

(a) Use Tami's data to sketch a graph of the volume of water in the vase as a function of the depth of the water in the vase.

(b) Use Tami's data to sketch a graph of the depth of water in the vase as a function of the volume of the water in the vase.

(c) What is the geometric relationship between the graphs you created for parts (a) and (b)? What does this relationship imply about the functions described by these graphs?

9. The graph of a function f is shown below. Use the graph to complete the table below. (Estimate as necessary.)

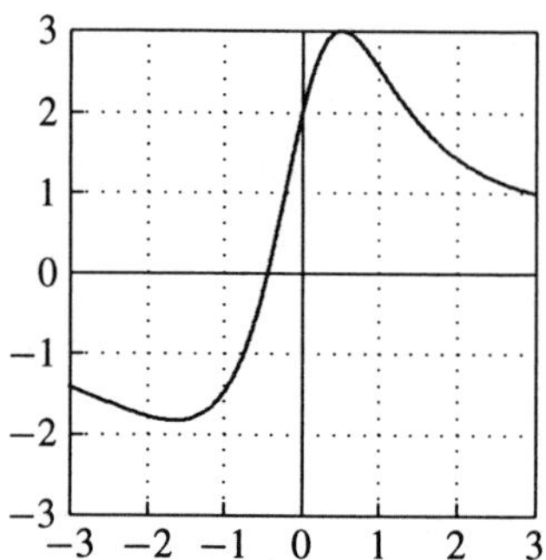

	x	$f(x)$
(a)	-2	
(b)	0	
(c)	1	
(d)		-1
(e)		2

10. Sketch graphs of $y = x^2 + 4$ and $y^2 = x + 4$ on the same set of axes.

11. Consider the following data about a function f that is defined for all x in the interval $[0, 5]$.

x	0.10	1.00	1.75	3.00	3.50	5.00
$f(x)$	2.83	8.53	2.47	-1.92	-1.63	-3.54

(a) Which of the graphs below might represent f?

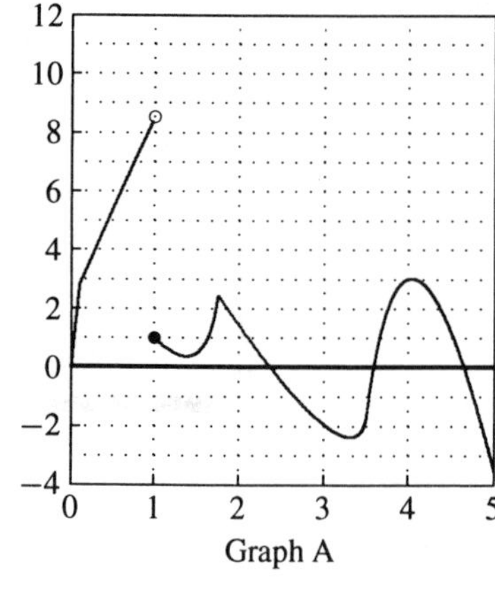

Graph A

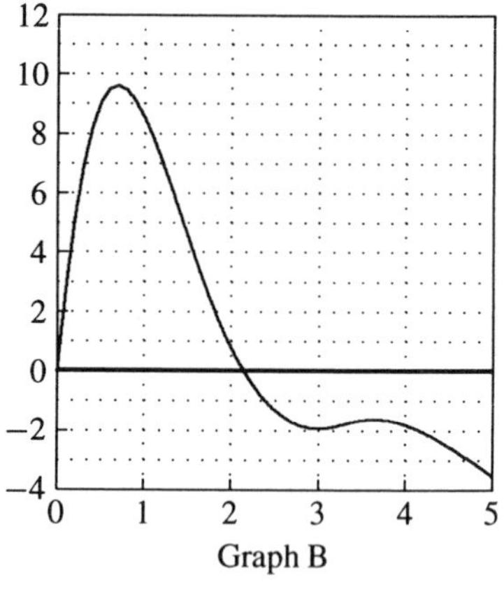

Graph B

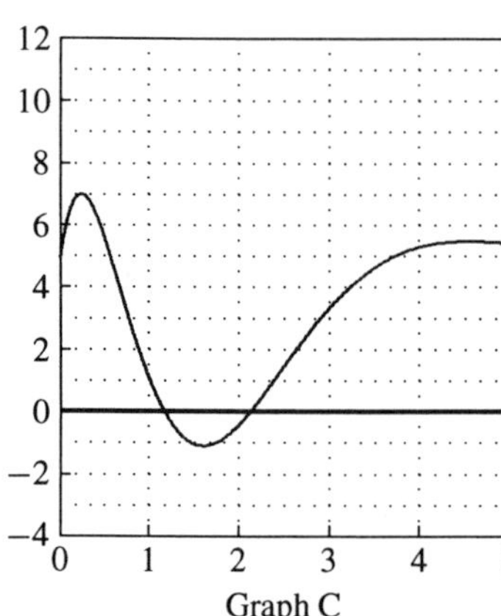

Graph C

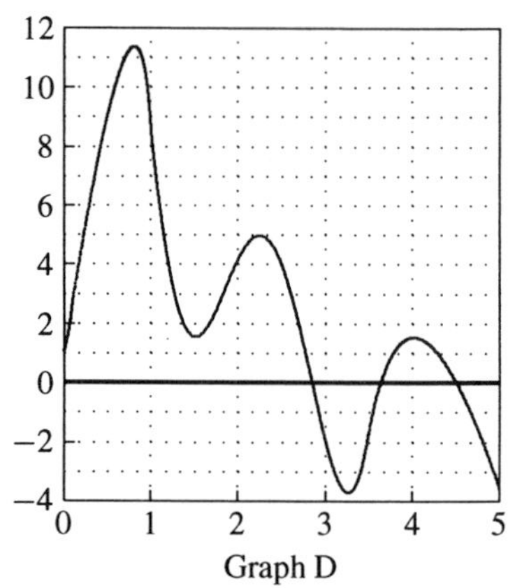

Graph D

(b) Describe each of the graphs above using appropriate mathematical terminology. Your description should include all the significant features of each graph (e.g., maxima, minima, roots, etc.).

12. The graph of a function f is shown below. Several points of interest are labeled.

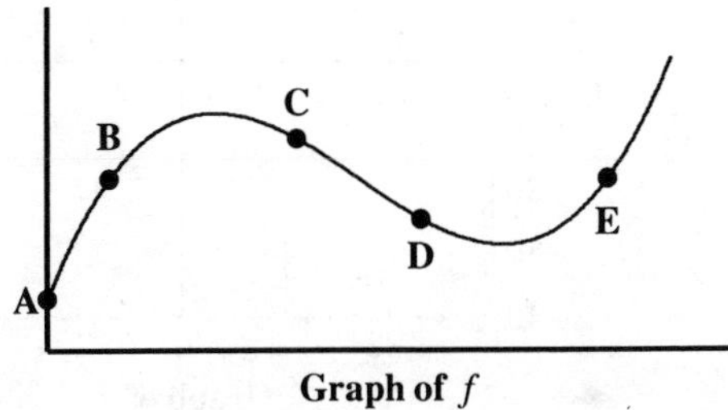

Graph of f

(a) Between which pair of labeled points is f increasing? Decreasing?

(b) Between which pair of labeled points is f concave up?

(c) Between which pair of labeled points does f have an inflection point?

(d) Between which pair of labeled points does f have a local maximum value? A local minimum value?

13. The graph of a function f appears below.

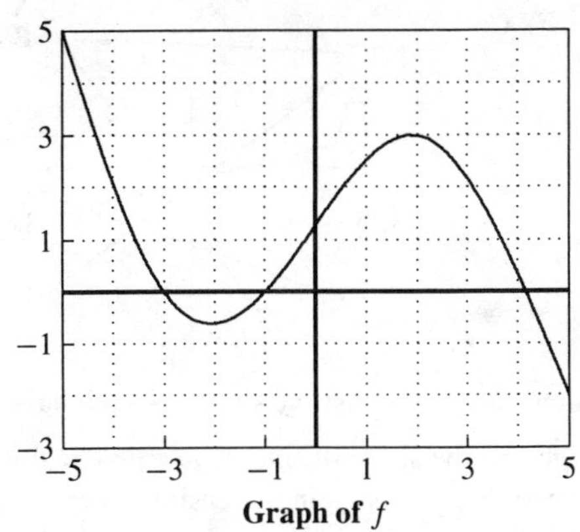

Graph of f

(a) Estimate the endpoints of the largest interval over which f is increasing.

(b) Estimate the endpoints of the largest interval over which f is concave up.

(c) Estimate the x-value at which f has a local minimum.

14. Sketch the graph of a function f that has *all* of the following properties:

(i) f is continuous on the interval $[-5, 5]$.

(ii) f is concave up on $[-5, -1]$.

(iii) f has a local minimum at $x = 2$.

15. Use the graph of f shown below for each of the following problems. (There is more than one possible answer to each.)

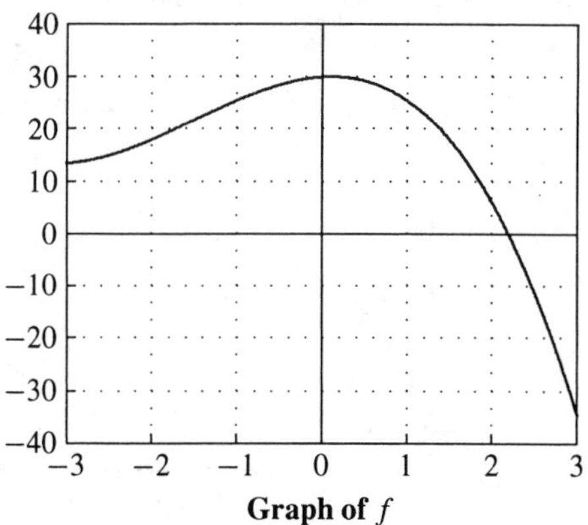

Graph of f

(a) Find a number L such that $L < f(x)$ when $x \in [2, 3]$.

(b) Find a number U such that $f(x) < U$ when $x \in [2, 3]$.

(c) Find a number L such that $L < f(x)$ when $x \in [-2, 1]$.

(d) Find a number U such that $f(x) < U$ when $x \in [-2, 1]$.

(e) Find an interval over which $-10 \leq f(x) \leq 20$.

(f) Find an interval over which $|f(x) + 10| \leq 20$.

16. Use the sketch below to answer each of the following questions.

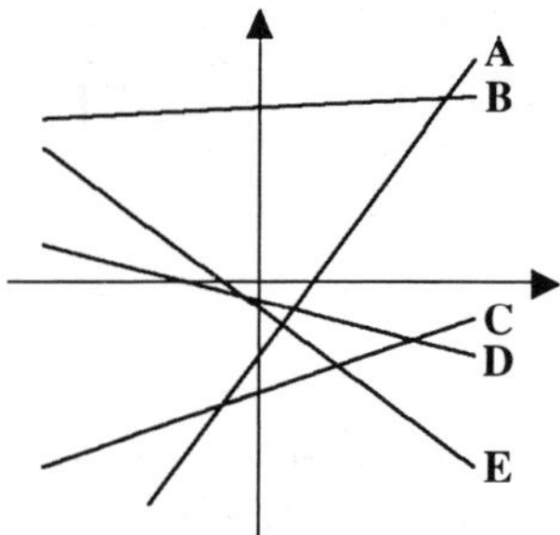

(a) Which lines have positive slope? Which have negative slope?

(b) Let m_A be the slope of line A, m_B be the slope of line B, etc. Rank the numbers $m_A, \dots, m_E$ in increasing order.

17. The figure below shows the line $y = mx + b$.

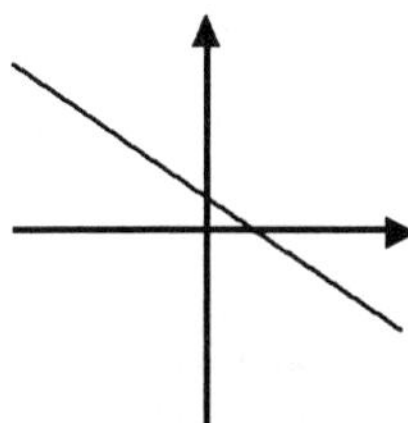

Sketch the following lines on a copy of the figure above. (Be sure to identify each line.)

(a) $y = mx - b$
(b) $y = -mx + b$
(c) $y = -mx - b$

18. Let L_1 be the line through (0, 0) and (2, 1), and let L_2 be the line that passes through (0, 0) and (3, 7). For which values of m does the line $y = mx$ lie "between" the lines L_1 and L_2?

19. Suppose that the graph of a function g lies between a line A, with slope 2, and a line B, with slope -1, for all $x > 2$, as shown below:

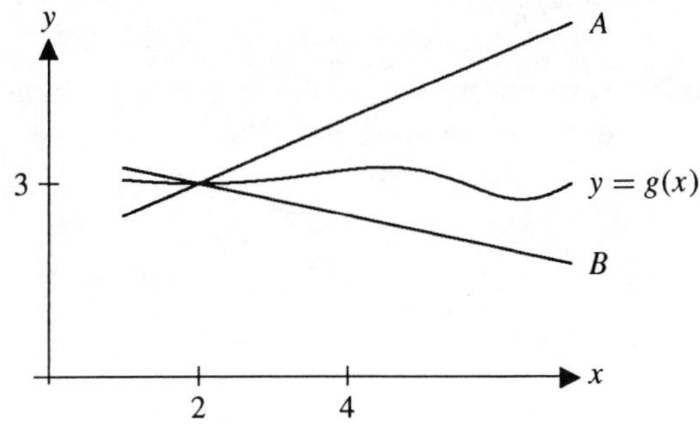

(a) Find an equation for the line A.

(b) What is the height of the line B at $x = 3$?

(c) Find numbers L and U such that $L < g(4) < U$ (i.e., find upper and lower bounds on the value of $g(4)$).

20. Let g be the function shown graphically below.

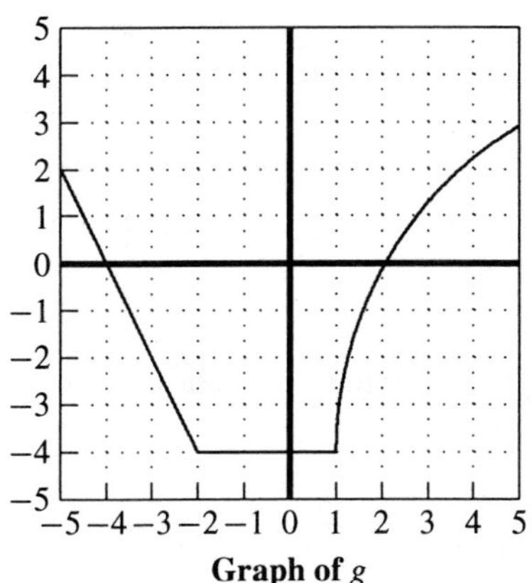

Graph of g

Sketch a graph of each of the following functions.

(a) $f(x) = g(x) + 1$

(b) $f(x) = g(x + 1)$

(c) $f(x) = g(2x)$

(d) $f(x) = 2g(x)$

(e) $f(x) = -g(x)$

(f) $f(x) = g(-x)$

(g) $f(x) = -2g(-x)$

(h) $f(x) = 3g(x - 2) + 1$

21. Describe (in a sentence or two) the geometric relationship between the graphs of each pair of functions below.

(a) $f(x); \quad f(x - 2)$

(b) $f(x) - 2; \quad f(x - 1) + 3$

(c) $h(x) = f(x + 1); \quad h(x - 1)$

1.3 Machine graphics

Graphics—the ability to represent mathematical objects geometrically—is the most important advantage mathematical computing offers.

Without computing, graphs can be tedious, if not impossible, to draw. Computing makes graphs, and the insights they offer, easily accessible. In this section we illustrate some of the power—and a few of the pitfalls—of computer graphics.

Graphical computing comes in many forms. Hardware ranges from handheld calculators to supercomputers. Software varies from simple plotting programs to sophisticated graphical environments. Plotting commands may be given by typed instructions, calculator keystrokes, mouse clicks, or in more exotic ways. The *Maple* command

```
plot( sin(x), x=-5..5 );
```

produces a graph something like this:

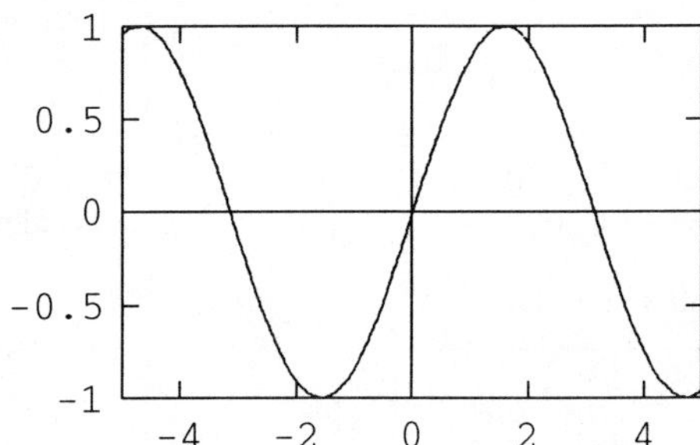

The *Mathematica* command

```
Plot[ Sin[x], {x,-5,5} ]
```

gives a similar result.

All such differences aside, several important ideas and terms apply across the board. Learn them well. They have to do not just with quirks of computing, but also with the essence of functions and graphs themselves.

The viewing window

The sine curve shown above is incomplete. It shows what happens for $-5 \le x \le 5$, but the sine function undulates merrily on forever.➻ Strictly speaking, we see only *part* of the sine graph, not the graph itself.

In both directions.

We're not that fastidious—we'll usually say "graph," not "piece of the graph." But the point remains: partial pictures are all we can expect. The full graph of a function may be infinitely long, so no finite picture can show all of it.

The term **viewing window** describes what *is* shown. In the graph above, for instance, the viewing window is the rectangle

$$\{(x, y) \mid -5 \le x \le 5, \quad -1 \le y \le 1\}.$$

(In **product notation** we'd denote the same rectangle by $[-5, 5] \times [-1, 1]$.)➻

*The square brackets in $[-5, 5]$ indicate a **closed** interval—one that contains its endpoints. See Appendix A for more on intervals and interval notation.*

The viewing window is the "product" of two intervals, one horizontal and one vertical. We'll call them, respectively, **xrange** and **yrange**. In computer jargon, *xrange* and *yrange* are **plotting parameters**. (The term **xdomain** might be more accurate than **xrange**; alas, it's never used.)➻

The next section has more details on domain and range.

No standard jargon. The names *xrange* and *yrange*, though suggestive, aren't standard; there *is* no standard terminology. Other common names include *hrange, vrange, inputrange*, and *outputrange.*

Six views of the sine function

Believe it or not.

The appearance of a graph depends—sometimes startlingly—on the viewing window. Here are six views of the *same* function:

Graph 1: $y = \sin(x)$

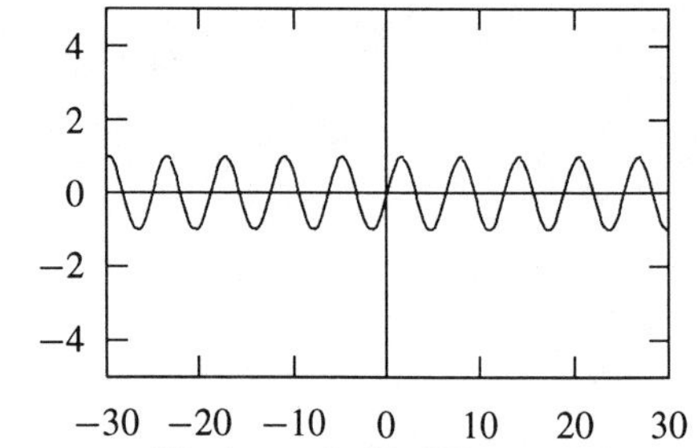

Window $= [-30, 30] \times [-5, 5]$

Graph 2: $y = \sin(x)$

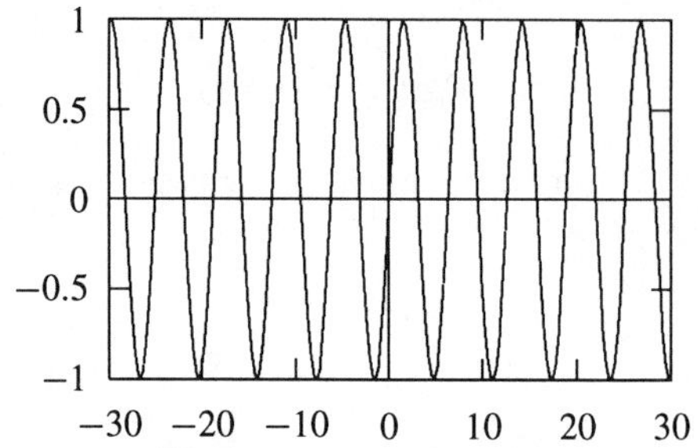

Window $= [-30, 30] \times [-1, 1]$

Graph 3: $y = \sin(x)$

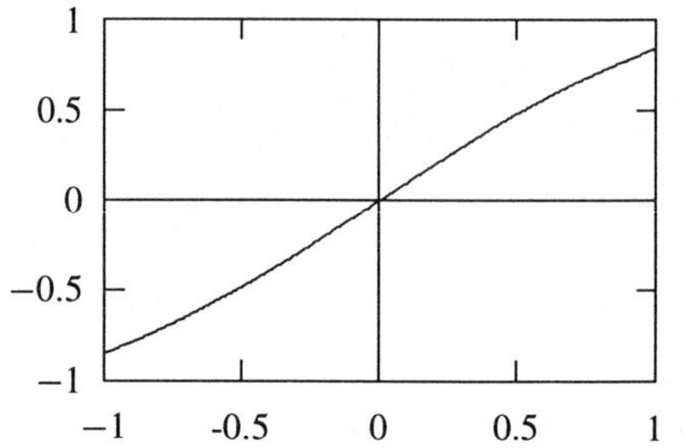

Window $= [-1, 1] \times [-1, 1]$

Graph 4: $y = \sin(x)$

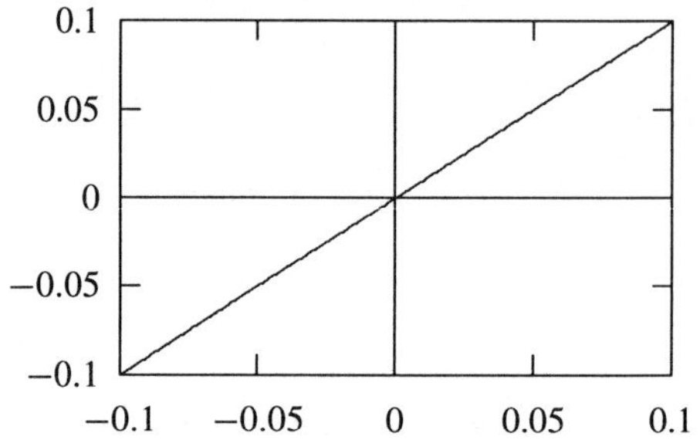

Window $= [-0.1, 0.1] \times [-0.1, 0.1]$

Graph 5: $y = \sin(x)$

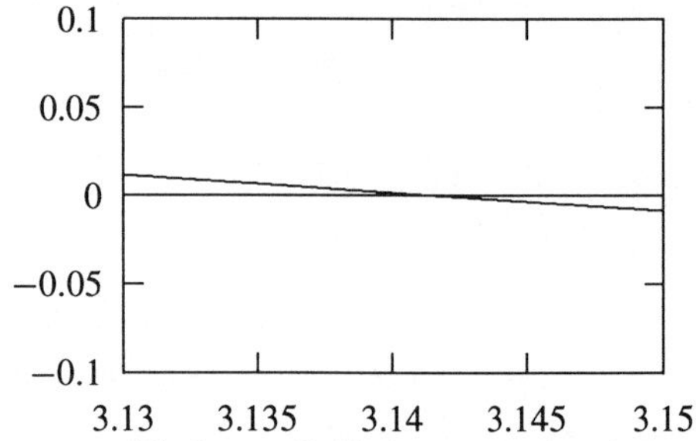

Window $= [3.13, 3.15] \times [-0.1, 0.1]$

Graph 6: $y = \sin(x)$

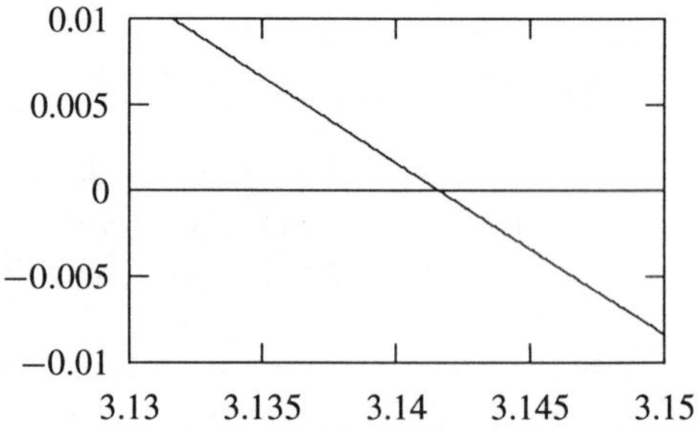

Window $= [3.13, 3.15] \times [-0.01, 0.01]$

Calculator, computer, sharp stick, etc.

A graph's *shape* depends—strongly—on the viewing window. Therefore every graphing device must somehow let the user choose the viewing window, whether with typed commands, mouse clicks, movable crosshairs, etc.

Who decides? Some devices try to *guess* what the user wants to see. For example, in the *Maple* and *Mathematica* commands

```
plot( sin(x), x=-5..5 );
Plot[ Sin[x], {x,-5,5} ]
```

xrange is specified explicitly, but *yrange* is not; the programs somehow choose *yrange*. Leaving choices to the machine may be the right thing to do, especially for complicated functions. If the machine chooses poorly, the user can always intervene. Here's the bottom line: Whether specified explicitly or chosen automatically, the viewing window strongly affects the appearance of a graph.

Plotting jargon

On paper, all six windows on the sine graph are about the same size and shape—about 1 inch by 1.75 inches. The differences reflect various choices of aspect ratio, center point, etc. A few technical words are handy in describing such differences:

Scale: Measures the *size* of horizontal or vertical units on a graph. The horizontal and vertical scales on Graph 4 are 10 times as large as those on Graph 3.

Zooming in: The result of *enlarging* the scale, by a **zoom factor**, in one or both axis directions. Graph 4 results from zooming in on Graph 3, with zoom factor 10 on each axis. (Horizontal and vertical zoom factors may differ.)

Zooming out: The result of *shrinking* the scale in one or both axis directions. Graph 3 comes from zooming out from Graph 4; both zoom factors are 10.

Aspect ratio: Measures the relative sizes of horizontal and vertical units. The viewing window $[-1, 1] \times [-3, 3]$ has aspect ratio 3:1—horizontal units are three times as large as vertical units. Aspect ratios matter especially when plotting objects like circles, for which the relative size of units matters.

Sample size; connecting dots

An unbroken curve has infinitely many points, but plotting devices can handle only finite data sets.➻ Therefore any physical graph can only *approximate* the "true" graph of a function.

On any machine, the number of "pixels" limits the accuracy of a graph.

This limitation raises➻ fascinating metaphysical questions, but it's seldom serious for the everyday functions of elementary calculus. For most functions, 100 data points will produce a passable graph. For really simple functions ➻ even fewer data points suffice.

For those interested in such things.

Lines, for example.

How to lie with computer graphics

A good way to understand almost anything is to try to break it.➻ It's fun, and easy, to fool even sophisticated plotting devices. Let's try.

Don't try this at home. The policy applies only to software, not to hardware.

Plotting devices use various strategies for drawing (apparently) "continuous" curves. The simplest devices simply plot one data point per horizontal pixel.➻ On machines with many pixels, this strategy is impractical; some way of "connecting the dots" is needed.

A "pixel"—picture element—represents one "dot" on a computer screen.

One simple strategy is to plot, say, 101➻ equally-spaced points, join them with line segments, and hope for the best. This usually works fine, but not always. Look

Why 101? Because 100 equal subintervals have 101 endpoints.

what happens to the sine graph in a huge viewing window:

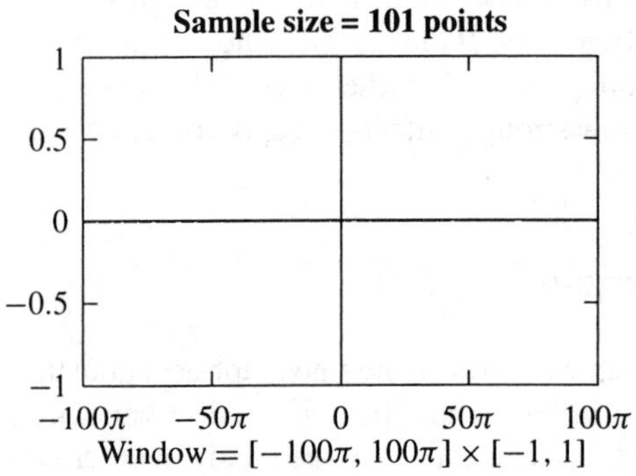

The graph is just the x-axis. See it?

The graph is clearly wrong. The curve $y = \sin(x)$ actually oscillates *100 times* over the *xrange* shown. What went wrong?

Nothing—the plotter did as it was told. The interval *xrange*, $[-100\pi, 100\pi]$, was cut into 100 equal pieces, and the sine function was sampled at the end of each piece. By unlucky accident, each sample point fell at a multiple of 2π, where the sine function is zero. Our plotting sample was too small, and too regularly spaced, to represent adequately the function's complicated behavior. The moral should be clear:

See page 391 for a truly nasty function.

Distrust large windows and ill-behaved functions.

Luckily, problems with sample size are uncommon in calculus applications. Many "smart" plotting devices recognize sticky situations and adjust sample sizes accordingly.

Cautions

Machine graphics should be viewed skeptically. Various surprises are possible; not all are the machine's fault. Here are some pitfalls to avoid:

Too few data: Plotting functions with irregular or ragged graphs may require many, many data points. Using smaller windows (i.e., zooming in) sometimes helps.

Awkward windows: Let $f(x) = x^{10} - x$. By simple algebra, $f(0) = 0$ and $f(1) = 0$, so the graph of f crosses the x-axis at $x = 0$ and at $x = 1$. Does the machine-drawn graph agree? Here's a look; the machine chose its own *yrange*:

The notation $1e + 07$ means 1×10^7, or 10 million.

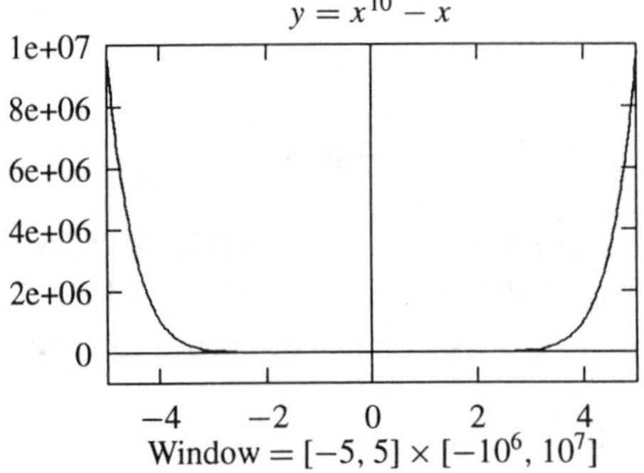

The graph shows disappointingly little near $x = 0$. The tenth power is at fault. Even for modest values of x, $f(x)$ is gigantic. To show everything, *yrange* must be correspondingly huge. As a result, all but the grossest behavior disappears.

Here's the same function in a smaller window:

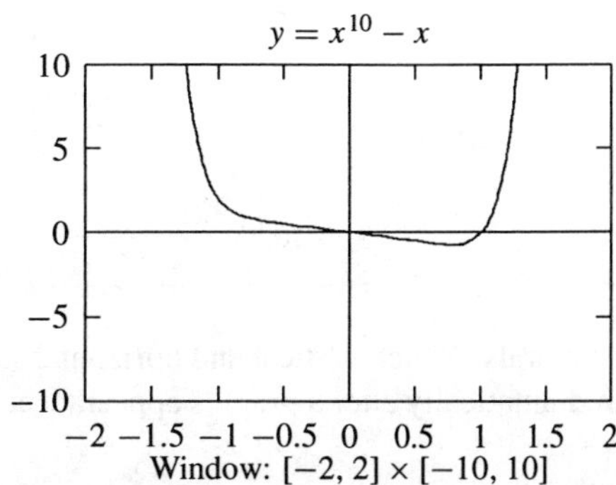

Which graph is better depends—literally, in this case—on one's point of view.

In this case there really is no good choice of window.

Scale effects: Different scales can give wildly different views of the same graph. Here are two views of the function $y = x + \sin(200x)/200$, the second a 10-fold magnification of the first.

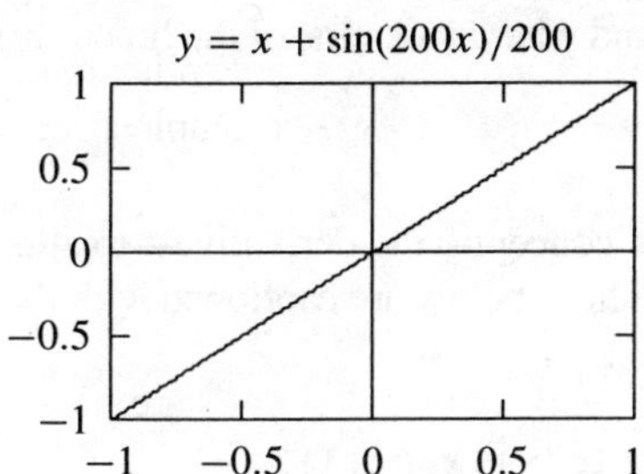

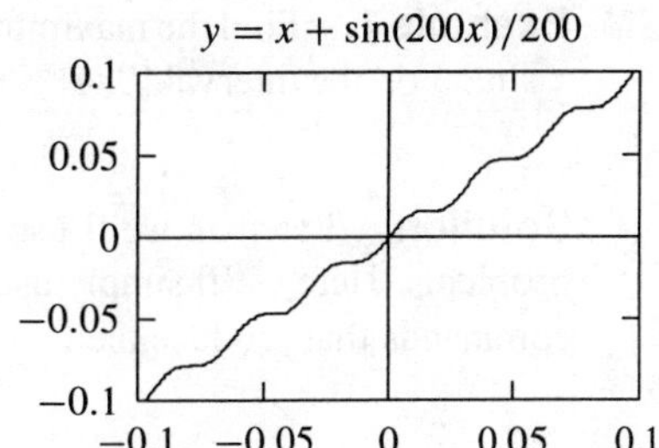

Notice the differences: The first graph looks almost straight; it's a slightly wiggly version of the line $y = x$. In the second graph, with smaller values of x, the rapid oscillations of $\sin(200x)/200$ produce a wiggly result. The moral: Viewing the same graph from different scales can show different aspects of a function's behavior.

Compared to x, the second summand, $\sin(200x)/200$, is small so it has little effect.

Slippery slopes: Shouldn't the line $y = 10x$ look steeper than the line $y = x$? Yet the graphs below look (almost) identical:

The lines have slope 10 and 1, respectively.

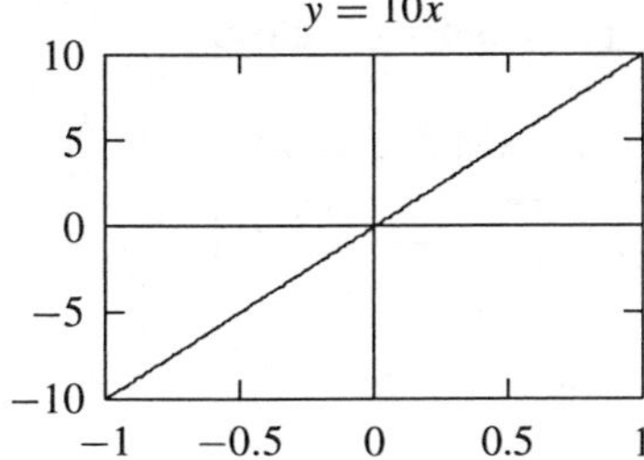

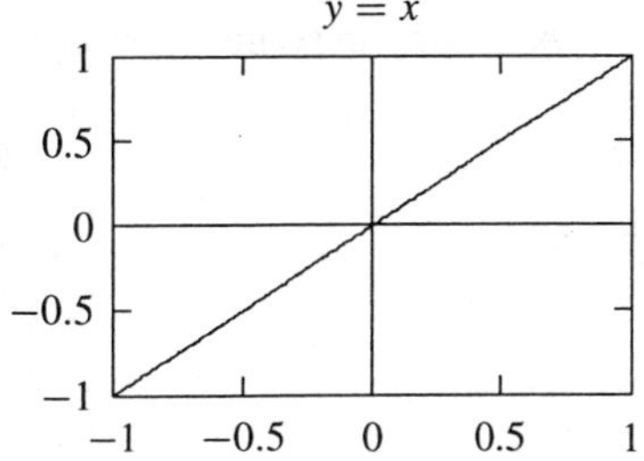

The apparent anomaly arises from different choices of *yrange*, i.e., different scales, for the two graphs. Our plotting device chose *yrange* just large enough to fit the plotting data. Plotting both lines in the *same* window

One curious effect of this policy: all lines with positive slope "look the same": all go from lower left to upper right.

gives a very different view:

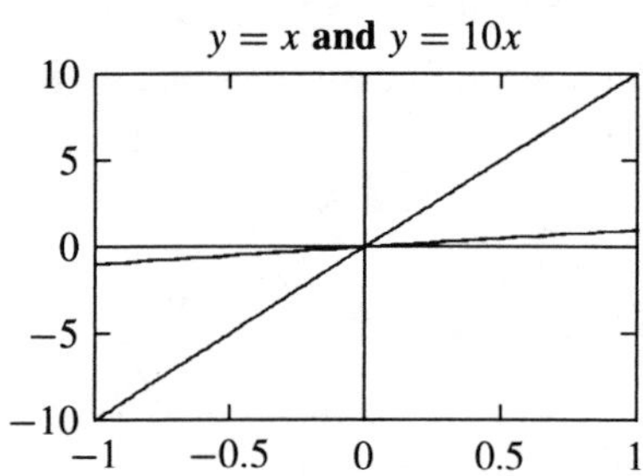

The morals: Watch vertical and horizontal scales carefully. Changing either can dramatically alter a graph's appearance.

Machine graphs in calculus

Or is it an obsession?

Mostly simple ones.

Despite our preoccupation with graphs, we'll spend relatively little time *drawing* graphs by hand. We'll draw *some* graphs, but we'll relegate most of that generally laborious work to machines. We'd rather read graphs and understand what they say about functions.

■ **Example 1.** Find the maximum value, and where it occurs, of the function $f(x) = x\sin(x)$ on the interval $[0, 4]$.

Solution: Later on we'll use a calculus concept—the derivative—to attack such problems. Here we'll simply use graphs. Those below are captioned with the *Maple* commands that produce them.

`plot(x*sin(x),x=0..4);`

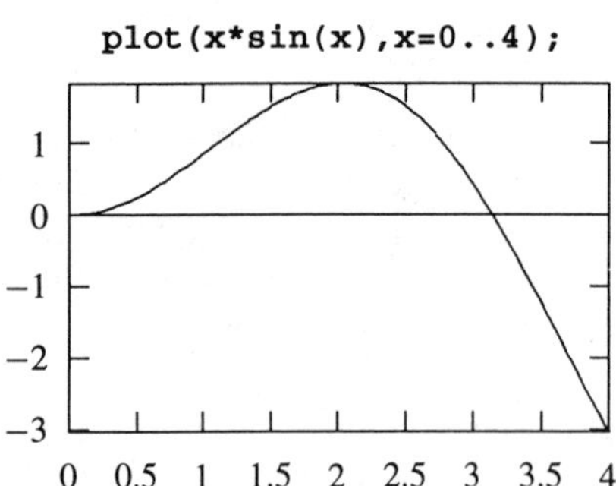

A maximum seems to occur around $x = 2$. Let's look more closely:

`plot(x*sin(x),x=1.8..2.2);`

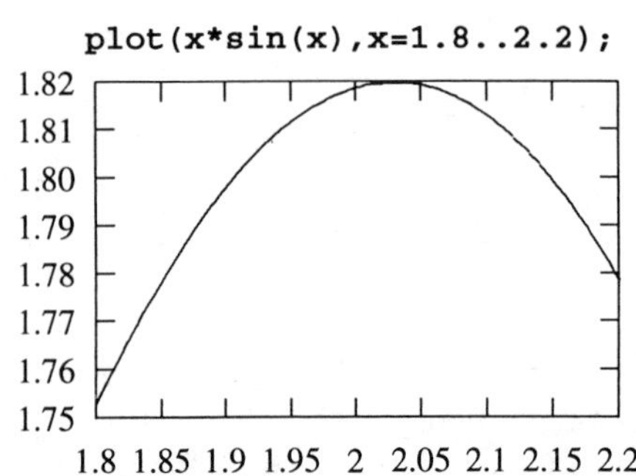

and still more closely:

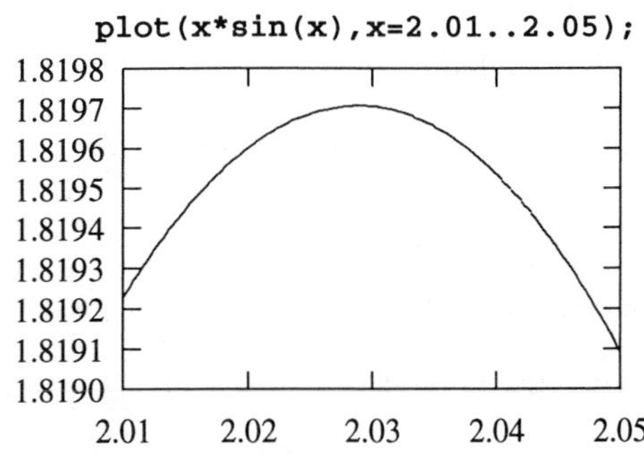

Conclusion: The maximum value is about 1.8197; it occurs near $x = 2.03$. □

■ **Example 2.** For x near 0, the function $p(x) = x - x^3/6$ is a good approximation to the sine function.➟ *How well* does p approximate the sine function on $[-1, 1]$? On $[-2, 2]$? For which values of x can we be sure that $p(x)$ differs from $\sin(x)$ by less than, say, 0.001?

We'll discuss later how to find simple functions, like p, that approximate more complicated functions, like the sine function.

Solution: First, we'll compare the graphs➟ of $p(x)$ and $\sin(x)$ for x in the interval $[-2, 2]$.

Which is which? How can you tell?

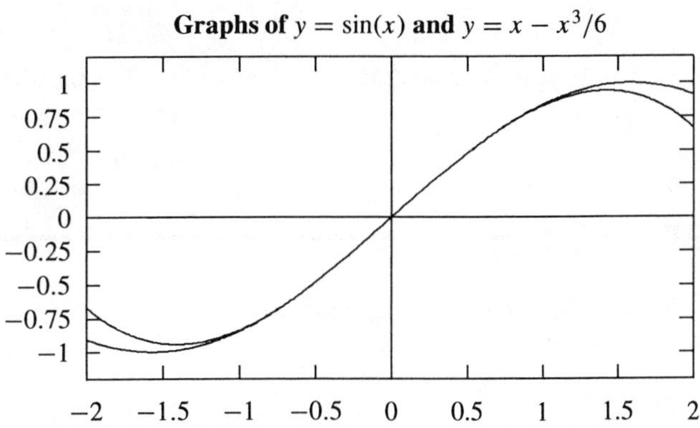

For $-1 \le x \le 1$ the approximation is good; there is little visible difference between the graphs. Things deteriorate when $|x| > 1$; by $x = \pm 2$, the graphs are far apart.

How might we *measure* how well one function approximates another on a given interval? One way is to find the *largest* difference, positive or negative, between the two functions on the given interval. On $[-1, 1]$, for example, we could graph the **error function** $p(x) - \sin(x)$:

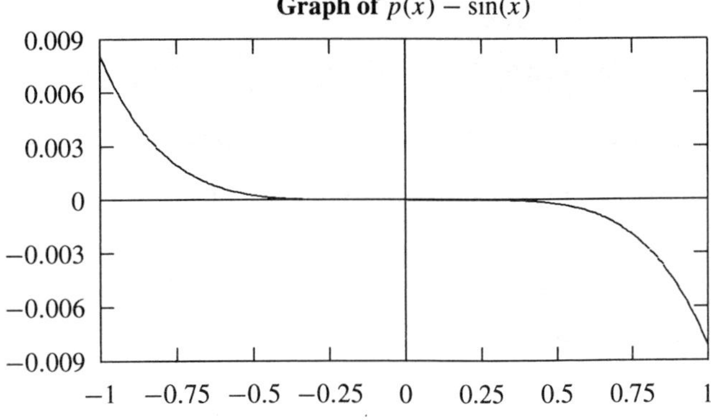

The graph shows that for x in $[-1, 1]$, the difference between the two functions is never more (in absolute value) than 0.009. In other words:

On $[-1, 1]$, $p(x)$ *approximates* $\sin(x)$ *with error no worse than* 0.009.

Not bad; for x in this interval, we could almost safely forget the SIN button on our calculators.

The remaining question asks:

For which values of x *is* $|p(x) - \sin(x)| < 0.001$*?*

Again a graph gives the answer:

Graph of $p(x) - \sin(x)$: a closer look

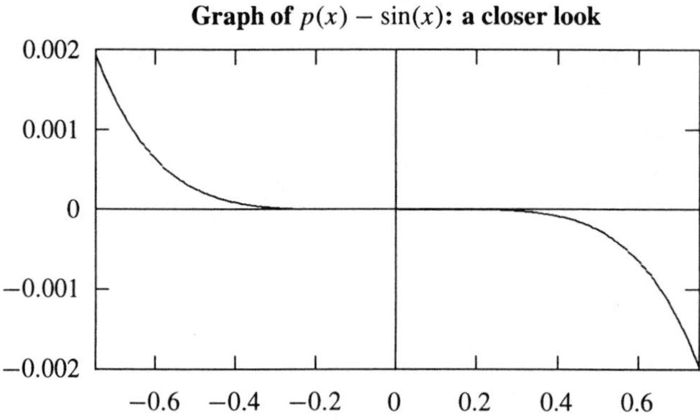

Conclusion: $p(x)$ approximates $\sin(x)$ with error less than 0.001 if $|x| < 0.65$. □

Exercises

NOTE: The exercises in this section require *some* form of plotting technology. Almost any form will do; the main requirement is some ability to choose viewing windows (e.g., by zooming).

1. In each part below, experiment to find a window in which the graph of $y = \sin(x)$ has (approximately!) the given shape or appearance. Express answers in the form $[a, b] \times [c, d]$.

   (a) A horizontal line.

   (b) A diagonal line from lower left to upper right.

   (c) A diagonal line from upper left to lower right.

   (d) A vertical line.

   (e) A rounded letter V.

2. Repeat the previous problem, using the graph of $y = \cos x$.

3. Repeat the previous problem, using the graph of $y = x^2$.

A number r is a root of a function f if $f(r) = 0$. Use a grapher to find (approximately, if necessary) as many roots as you can of each function in exercises 4–8 below. (Report answers to two decimal places.)

4. $f(x) = x^2 - x$

5. $f(x) = x - \sin x$

6. $f(x) = x - \cos x$

7. $f(x) = x - \tan x$

8. $f(x) = 2^x - x^2$

9. In this section we discussed the fact that $\sin(x) \approx p(x) = x - x^3/6$ for x near 0. Another, simpler, approximation to the sine function says that for x near 0, $\sin(x) \approx \ell(x) = x$. In this problem we pursue this latter approximation a bit further.

   (a) Complete the following table; report answers to two decimal places.

x	$\sin(x)$	$\|x - \sin(x)\|$	x	$\sin(x)$	$\|x - \sin(x)\|$
-1			1		
-0.5			0.5		
-0.1			0.1		
-0.01			0.01		

   (b) We said earlier in this section:

   On $[-1, 1]$, $p(x)$ *approximates* $\sin(x)$ *with error no worse than* 0.009.

   Does the same statement apply to $\ell(x)$? If not, what number could replace 0.009?

   (c) We *also* said:

   $p(x)$ *approximates* $\sin(x)$ *with error less than* 0.001 *if* $-0.65 < x < 0.65$.

   Find an interval $(-a, a)$ on which $\ell(x)$ approximates $\sin(x)$ with error less than 0.001.

10. Use the sketch below to answer each of the following questions.

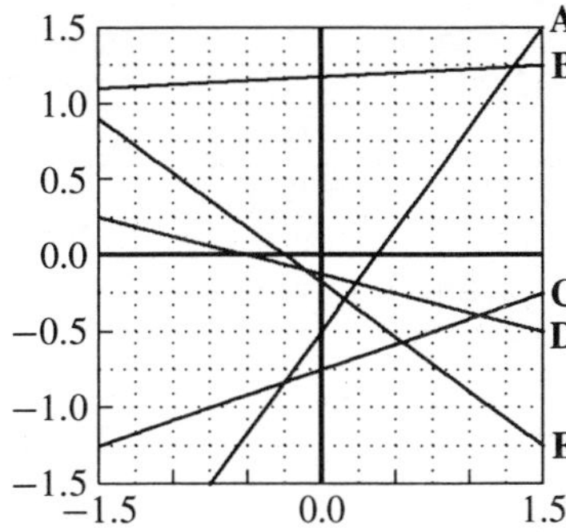

   (a) Do any lines have slope greater than 1? If so, which?

   (b) Where do lines **C** and **D** intersect? Justify your answer.

11. Use the sketch below to answer each of the following questions.
[HINT: This is *not* the same graph as in the previous exercise.]

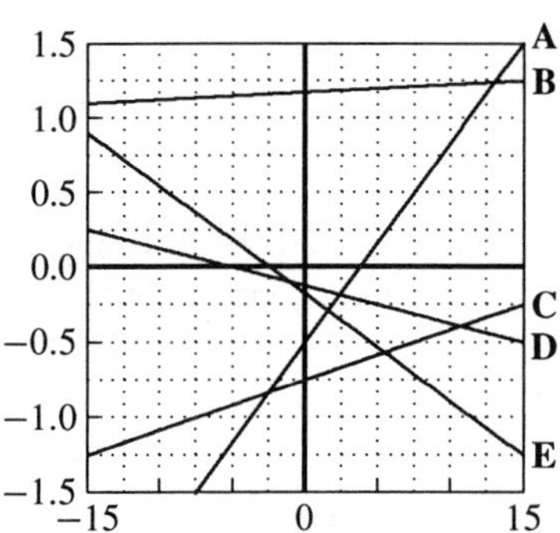

(a) Do any lines have slope greater than 1? If so, which?

(b) Where do lines **C** and **D** intersect? Justify your answer.

12. Use the sketch below to answer each of the following questions.
[HINT: This is *not* the same graph as in the previous exercise.]

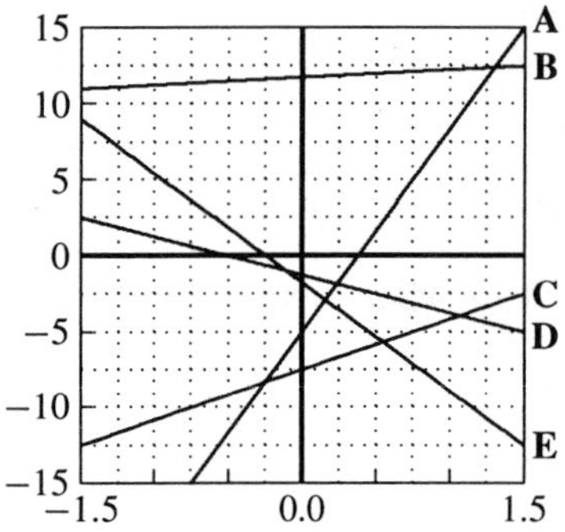

(a) Do any of the lines have slope greater than 1? If so, which ones?

(b) Where do **C** and **D** intersect? Justify your answer.

Graphs of most calculus functions "look straight at small scale." (Graphs 4, 5, and 6 in this section illustrate what this means for the sine function.) For each of the functions in exercises 13–18 below, find a window centered at the given point in which the graph of the given function looks like a straight line.

13. $y = x^2$ at $(2, 4)$

14. $y = -x^3 + 3x^2 - 4x + 2$ at $(1, 0)$

15. $y = \cos(x)$ at $(0, 1)$

16. $y = \cos(x^2)$ at $(0, 1)$

17. $y = \cos(x^2)$ at $(5, \cos(25))$

18. $y = \cos(x^2)$ at $(10, \cos(100))$

For each function f below, use graphics to estimate the maximum and minimum values of $f(x)$ when $-10 \le x \le 10$.

19. $f(x) = \sin(x)$

20. $f(x) = x + \sin(x)$

21. $f(x) = \dfrac{x}{x - 11}$

22. $f(x) = x^2$

23. $f(x) = 2^x$

24. $f(x) = 2^x - x^2$

1.4 What *is* a function?

What exactly *is* a function? We've already seen many examples, given by formulas, by words, by graphs, and by tables. With these examples as fodder, it's time to ruminate on the *general* idea of function.

Five examples

Any suitable definition of function covers a lot of ground. Functions appear in many guises; they can be described, formally or informally, in various ways. In what follows, we'll refer repeatedly to five example functions, at various levels of strangeness:

f $f(x) = x^2 + \frac{3}{x}$

g $g(t) =$ the world human population t years A.D.

h $h(u) = \begin{cases} 1 - u & \text{if } u \le 0 \\ u^2 & \text{if } 0 < u < 2 \\ 42 & \text{if } u \ge 30 \end{cases}$

j the function given by the graph below:

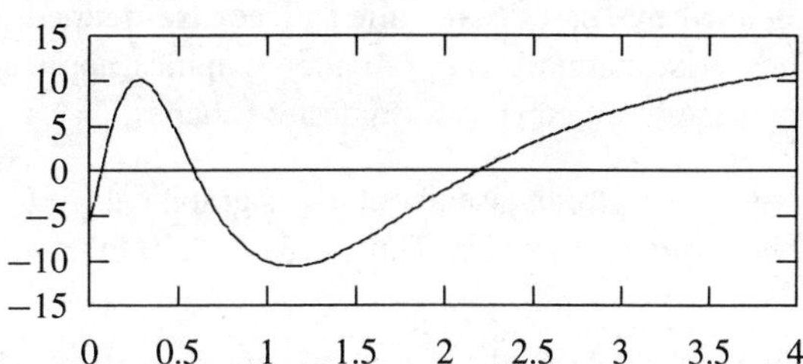

k the function given by this table:

n	−3	−2	−1	0	1	2	3	4
$k(n)$	−4	−9	−1	0	1	8	3	−2

These disparate functions have little in common except the property of *being* functions, to which we now turn.

The definition at last

Definition: A function is a **rule** for assigning to each member of one set, called the **domain**, *one* member of another set, called the **range**.

The definition uses three key words: **rule**, **domain**, and **range**. We'll discuss each separately.

Rule

A function accepts an input and—somehow—assigns an output. The **rule** describes *how* this assignment is made. For our example functions:

f The rule is a simple, explicit, algebraic "recipe": *Given a real number* x*, compute* x^2+3/x. To 5, for example, f assigns the number $f(5) = 5^2 + 3/5 = 25.6$.

g To a number t, say $t = 1992.23$, g assigns the world population at exactly that time, measured in years. Thus, imaginably, $g(1992.23) = 5{,}678{,}901{,}234$.

Admittedly there's trouble here: world population is *never* known exactly, and there's certainly no convenient *formula* available. Nevertheless, g makes perfectly good sense as a function. At any time t, there is one and only one population $g(t)$—whether or not we can compute it.

Notice, finally, that although the rule for f tells how to *calculate* outputs, the rule for g only *describes* outputs.

h The rule for h involves "cases"—different inputs are treated differently. Thus

$$h(-5) = 1 - (-5) = 6$$

because the input -5 satisfies the *first* "case" of the definition, but

$$h(175) = 42$$

since the input 175 satisfies the *third* case.

Functions defined by "cases" are called **piecewise-defined**, or **multiline functions**. They arise naturally in computer graphics applications, where "pieces" of curves are fit together to form desired shapes.

We discuss this process, called "splining" in Section 4.5. For a preview, glance at the pictures there.

j The rule for j—like everything else about j—is graphical: $j(x)$ *is the height of the graph at horizontal position* x. Thus, $j(3) \approx 7$, $j(1) \approx -10$, and $j(10)$ is not defined.

As with any function defined by a graph, values of j can be read only approximately. Despite this "inexactness" there's plenty to learn from graphs. Approximation is everywhere in the real world.

k We have *only* the table to use. Here is k's "rule": *for any* n *in the top row,* $k(n)$ *is the entry below* n. Thus, $k(-2) = -9$, $k(2) = 8$, and $k(42)$ is undefined.

Such a "rule" hardly seems to deserve the name. It gives no hint of *how* outputs are determined. Are we hiding some secret formula for k? No; sometimes a table contains *all* we know of a function. We might, with effort, find a formula or curve that "fits" tabular data, but deciding whether our formula is "right" would require more information.

See, e.g., Example 5 in Section 1.2.

A variable by any other name. For most of our functions we gave names—x, t, u, n—to our input variables. This was for convenience; the particular names don't matter. For example, the rules

$$f(x) = x^2 + \frac{3}{x} \quad \text{and} \quad f(z) = z^2 + \frac{3}{z}$$

define exactly the same function.

Domain

A function's **domain**, denoted $\mathcal{D}$, is its set of "acceptable" *inputs*. For our example functions:

f The algebraic rule $f(x) = x^2 + 3/x$ makes good sense *unless* $x = 0$. Hence, the domain of f is the set $\mathcal{D} = \{x \mid x \neq 0\}$.

g The rule $g(t) =$ "the world human population t years A.D." makes sense for *any* real number. Hence the domain of g can be taken as $(-\infty, \infty)$, the full set of real numbers.

The inputs t for which $g(t)$ can be reasonably known or estimated are, of course, more restricted. Conceding something to reality we might arbitrarily restrict our domain to the set $[-5000, 2100]$.

h By its multiline definition, h accepts as input any real number u *except* those for which $2 \leq u < 30$. Therefore the domain of h is the set $\{x \mid x < 2 \text{ or } x \geq 30\}$ or, in interval form, $(-\infty, 2) \cup [30, \infty)$.

j Acceptable inputs to j lie in the interval $[0, 4]$. (In computerese, the domain is the *xrange*.)

k Any function described by a table has a *finite* domain.➻ The domain of k has just 8 members: $\mathcal{D} = \{-3, -2, -1, 0, 1, 2, 3, 4\}$.

A table has only finitely many entries!

"Natural" domains. In practice, function domains are seldom stated explicitly. In this case➻ the "default" is the **natural domain**—the set of inputs for which the rule makes sense. For a function like f, given by an algebraic formula in x, the natural domain is the set of values of x for which the formula makes algebraic sense.

The most common case in calculus courses.

Range

A function's domain is its set of allowable *inputs*. The **range** is the corresponding set of *outputs*. In symbolic language:

If f has domain $\mathcal{D}$, then the range of f, denoted $\mathcal{R}$, is the set $\{f(x) \mid x \in \mathcal{D}\}$.

The number 42 (to pick one at random) lies in the range of a function F➻ if some input to F produces the output 42 (i.e., if for some number x, $F(x) = 42$). For example, 42 *is* in the range of the function $F(x) = \sqrt{x}$, but *not* in the range of the function $G(x) = -x^2$.➻

Why F, not f? Because we used f above.

Which input to F gives output 42? Why isn't 42 in the range of G?

Reading a function's range from its graph. *Defining* a function's range is simple; *calculating* it—especially by hand—can be difficult. Graphs can help. ➻

The number 42 lies in the range of F, for instance, if and only if the *horizontal* line $y = 42$ hits the graph of F *somewhere*. For *any* function F:

If viewing windows are chosen properly.

The range of F is the set of y-values at which a horizontal line hits the F-graph.

Here's a more illuminating way of saying the same thing:

Let lights shine horizontally, *from both left and right, on the graph of F. The range of F is the* shadow *thrown by the graph on the vertical axis.*

The picture below shows the "shadow" (or **horizontal projection**) cast by the sine graph on the vertical axis:

The range of $y = \sin x$ is $[-1, 1]$ — the shadow knows

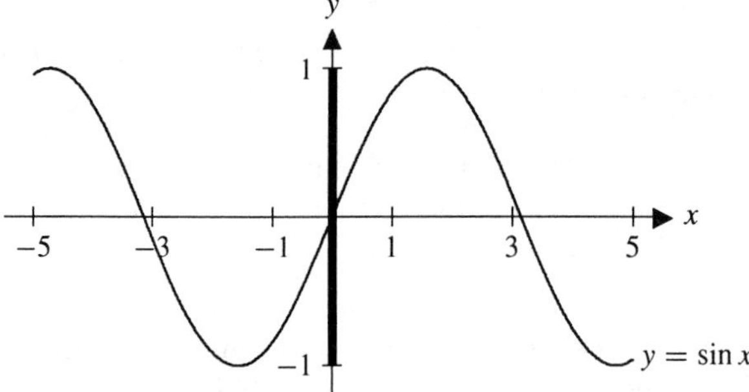

Finding ranges of our example functions. We'll use both graphical and algebraic methods to calculate the ranges of our example functions:

f The domain of f is $\mathcal{D} = \{x \mid x \neq 0\}$, so the range of f is $\mathcal{R} = \{x^2 + 3/x \mid x \in \mathcal{D}\}$. That's easy to write, but what, exactly, does $\mathcal{R}$ contain? Does $\mathcal{R}$ contain the number -2345.678, to choose one at random?

Here's a graph:

Graph of $f(x) = x^2 + 3/x$

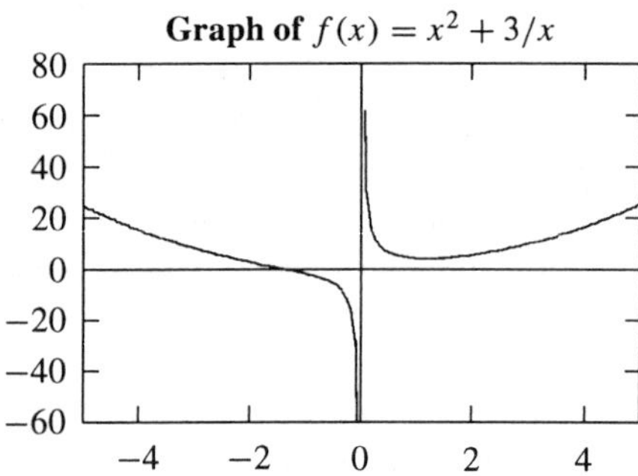

It suggests that *all* reals lie in the range: f seems to "hit" every real value at least once. Our random number -2345.678, in particular, seems to be the output for some input just to the left of zero. To estimate *which* x gives $f(x) = -2345.678$, let's look in another window.

To see why, imagine the graph's shadow on the vertical axis.

Do you agree that inputs just to the left of zero produce large negative outputs?

Graph of $f(x)$—a closer look

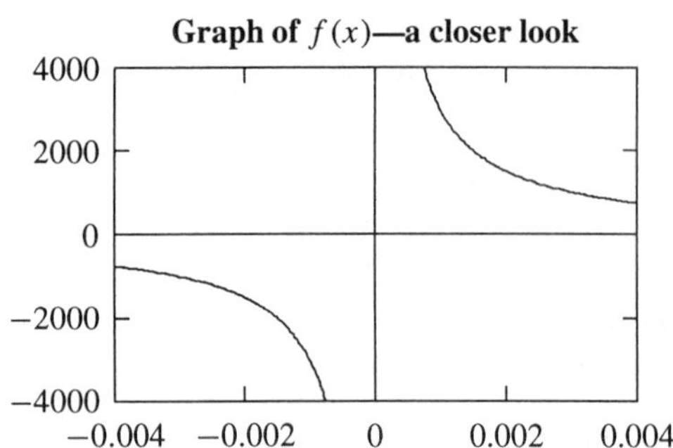

This graph suggests that $f(x) = -2345.678$ if $x \approx -0.0015$.

g By definition, g's range is the set of all world populations, for all time. This is clearly *some* set of non-negative integers; saying much more is almost impossible.

h The domain of h has three pieces. To find the range, we'll decide what each domain piece contributes separately, and then assemble our answers.

1. The output formula $1 - u$ holds when $u \leq 0$. As u varies from 0 through negative values, $1 - u$ covers the interval $[1, \infty)$. Thus, the range of h contains the interval $[1, \infty)$.

Convince yourself of this; it's easy but important. A graph should help.

2. For $0 < u < 2$, $h(u) = u^2$. As u varies from 0 to 2, u^2 ranges from 0 to 4. Thus the range of h contains the interval $(0, 4)$.
3. For $u > 30$, $h(u) = 42$. Thus the third domain piece contributes the one-member set $\{42\}$ to the range.

Putting the pieces together, we find that the range of h is

$$\mathcal{R} = [1, \infty) \cup (0, 4) \cup \{42\} = (0, \infty).$$

Notice that this union is "redundant"—the first two intervals overlap, and the "singleton" $\{42\}$ adds nothing new. This redundancy reflects the fact that some members of the range are "hit" more than once.

j The j-graph shows that the set of values "hit" by j is the interval $[-11, 11]$.

From graphs alone we can only estimate.

k The output set of k is the second row of k's table:

$$\{-4, -9, -1, 0, 1, 8, 3, -2\}.$$

The range of k, like its domain, is a finite set.

Domain and range—a machine's view. Computers and calculators can't escape issues of domain and range when plotting functions. Here's a machine-drawn plot of the function $p(x) = \sqrt{x^2 + 2x}$:

Graph of $p(x) = \sqrt{x^2 + 2x}$

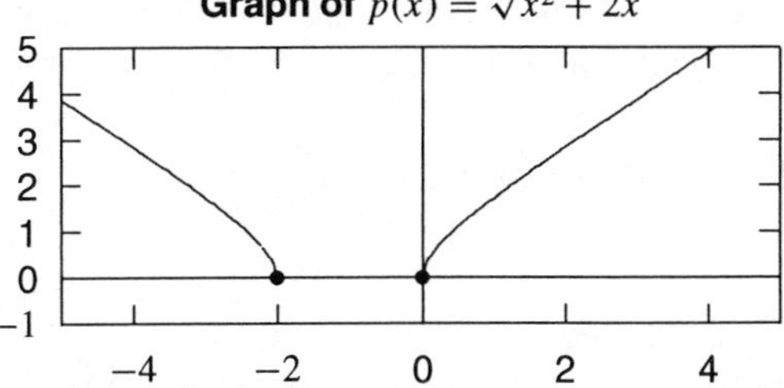

The gap from $x = -2$ to $x = 0$ is there for good reason: the **natural domain** of p *omits* this interval. The picture also suggests (but, being finite, can't *prove*!) that the range is $[0, \infty)$. With algebra, we could verify both of these observations.

The definition of function: reprise

A function is a package with three chief parts: **rule**, **domain**, and **range**.

The **rule** can be given in various ways—as an algebraic formula, as a graph, as a table, as an English description, etc. However it's given, the rule must not be ambiguous. To each element of the domain the rule associates exactly *one* element of the range.

The **domain** and **range** of a function f are, respectively, its input and output sets. The **natural domain** of f is the set of inputs for which f's rule makes sense. In calculus, both range and domain are usually sets of real numbers.

Elsewhere in mathematics, domains and ranges may be sets of vectors, matrices, functions, complex numbers, or more exotic objects.

Bounds

If $f(x) = x^2/(1+x^2)$, then for *any* real number x, $0 \le x^2 < 1+x^2$, so $0 \le f(x) < 1$. The graph shows the same inequalities:

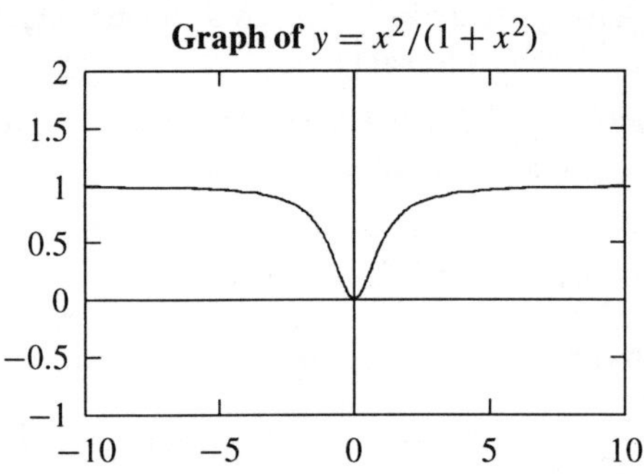

In mathematical language, the function f is said to be **bounded above** by 1 and **bounded below** by 0, and the bounds hold for *all* real numbers. The formal terminology is sometimes convenient:

> **Definition: Upper and lower bounds.** Let f be a function, m and M real numbers, and I a subset of the domain of f. Suppose that for all x in I
>
> $$m \le f(x) \le M.$$
>
> Then m is a **lower bound** for f on I, and M is an **upper bound** for f on I.

Notice that the definition does *not* require that m or M be "best possible" bounds. For the function above, for instance, $m = -1$ and $M = 2$ are legitimate lower and upper bounds.

The idea of **bounding** a function—finding or estimating how large or small a function's values can be—is important mathematically and in applications. Maximizing profit functions, for instance, generates intense practical interest.

In applications, estimating bounds is often the best that's possible.

Example 1. Find upper and lower bounds for $f(x) = x^2/(1+x^2)$ on the interval $2 \le x \le 7$.

Solution: We saw above that $0 \le f(x) < 1$ for *all* real numbers x—including those in the interval [2, 7]. Thus 1 and 0 are valid upper and lower bounds.

Can't we do better, however, now that we're looking only at a *subset* of f's domain? We can indeed; here's an appropriate graph:

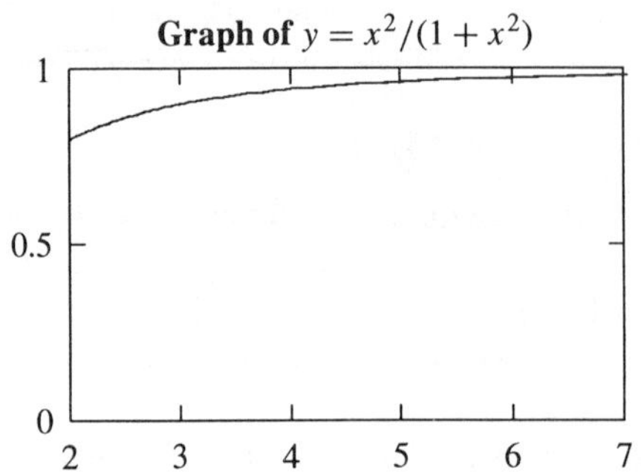

The graph shows that f *increases* from $x = 2$ to $x = 7$, so

The formula shows the same thing. Do you see how?

$$f(2) = 0.8 \le f(x) \le 0.98 = f(7).$$

In mathematical language: on the interval $[2, 7]$, f is bounded above by 0.98 and bounded below by 0.8. □

■ **Example 2.** Let j be the function given at the beginning of this section. Find *upper* bounds for j on the intervals $[0, 2]$ and $[0, 4]$.

Solution: The graph shows➽ that if $0 \le x \le 2$, then $j(x) \le 10$. If $0 \le x \le 4$, then $j(x) \le 11$. □

Allowing for estimation.

■ **Example 3. (Estimating a bound.)** Find upper and lower bounds for $n(c) = 2c/(1 + 5c^2)$ on the interval $[0, 1]$.

Solution: Finding a lower bound is easy. Since $n(0) = 0$ and $n(c) > 0$ when $c > 0$, 0 is the best possible lower bound.➽

Here, "best" means "greatest."

How about an upper bound? To find one we need to know how n behaves as c moves through $[0, 1]$. Does n increase, decrease, or do some of both? From the formula alone it's hard to say. As c moves from 0 to 1, both the numerator and the denominator *increase*, so the total effect on the fraction is ambiguous.➽

The two effects tend to cancel each other.

To *estimate* how large $n(c)$ can get, we'll decide first how *large* the numerator can be, then how *small* the denominator can be. For c in $[0, 1]$, the numerator—$2c$—can't exceed 2. Similarly, the denominator—$1 + 5c^2$—never falls below 1. Therefore the inequality

$$n(c) = \frac{\text{numerator}}{\text{denominator}} \le \frac{2}{1}$$

holds for all c in $[0, 1]$, so 2 is an upper bound for n on $[0, 1]$.

Is 2 the *best* possible (i.e., least) upper bound?➽ Not likely, given our rough and ready method. Here's a graph:

This time, "best" means "least."

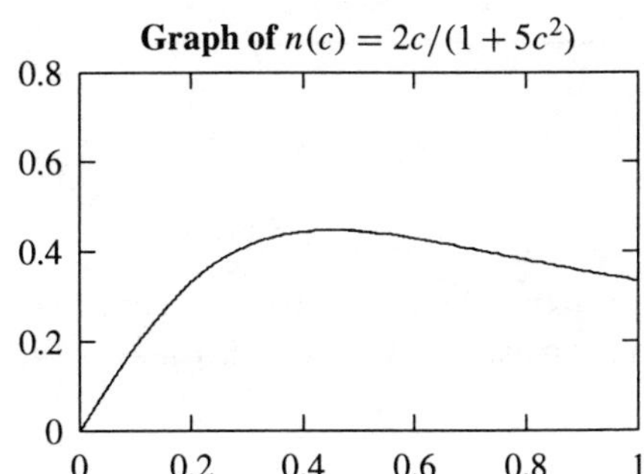

It shows that we can do *much* better: 0.5 is an upper bound for n on $[0, 1]$.

In the ballpark. Our algebraic estimate (2) in Example 3 was unnecessarily large. Nevertheless, such ballpark estimates are surprisingly useful in calculus. Finding the *least* upper bound or the *greatest* lower bound is often less important than finding *some* reasonable bounds.

Odd functions and even functions: graphical symmetry

Like certain numbers.

Certain functions are said to be either **odd** or **even**. These properties, though defined symbolically, are easily recognized graphically. First, the symbolic definitions:

> **Definition:** A function f is **even** if $f(-x) = f(x)$ for all x in its domain; f is **odd** if $f(-x) = -f(x)$.

■ **Example 4.** If $f(x) = x^2$, then

$$f(-x) = (-x)^2 = x^2 = f(x),$$

so f is *even*. If $g(x) = x^3$, then

$$g(-x) = (-x)^3 = -x^3 = -g(x),$$

so g is *odd*. The function $h(x) = x + x^2$ is *neither* even nor odd, because

$$h(-x) = -x + (-x)^2 = -x + x^2 \neq \pm h(x).$$

□

Graphs and symmetry

For functions like f, g, and h above, evenness or oddness are easily checked by algebraic manipulations. But what about the function $k(x) = \sin(x)$, which has no algebraic formula. To decide whether k is even, odd, or neither, let's look at the graph. To see how $k(x)$ and $k(-x)$ are related, we'll choose an *xrange* centered at $x = 0$:

Graph of $y = \sin x$: symmetric about the origin

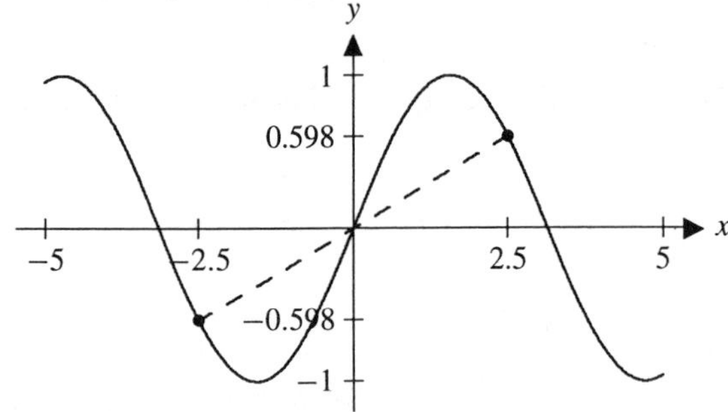

The graph's **symmetry about the origin** means that for any input x, $k(-x) = -k(x)$—just what it means for k to be odd. If, say, $x = 2.5$, the bulleted points show that

$$k(2.5) = \sin(2.5) \approx 0.598 \qquad \text{and} \qquad k(-2.5) = \sin(-2.5) \approx -0.598\,.$$

In general: *A function f is odd if and only if the graph of f is symmetric about the origin.*

Evenness is equivalent to another form of symmetry. See the exercises.

Periodic functions: repeating patterns

See the graph above.

The sine function is called 2π**-periodic**, because it "repeats" itself on every interval of length 2π. (So do the other basic trigonometric functions; we'll review them soon.) Any function is called **periodic** if it repeats itself on intervals of any fixed length.

Periodic functions: the graphical view

Here are graphs of three periodic functions, f, g, and h:

Graphs of three periodic functions

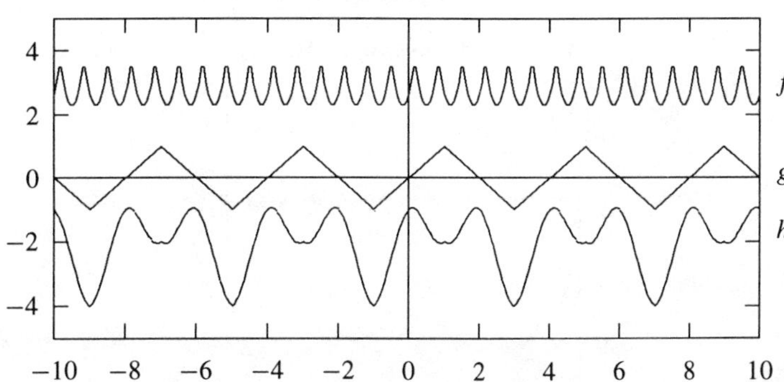

Each function's graph repeats some basic shape, over and over. How *often* a periodic function repeats itself depends on the **period**, i.e., the (horizontal) length of the basic repeating shape. It's easy to see from their graphs that g and h above have period 4. Reading the period of the wigglier f is trickier. One way to avoid seasickness is to count that f completes 30 "cycles" from $x = -10$ to $x = 10$, an interval of length 20. Thus f has period $20/30 = 2/3$.

Again, this is a graphical approximation—but a good one.

Periodic functions: the symbolic view

Periodicity can be defined symbolically:

> **Definition:** A function f is **periodic with period** P if the equation
>
> $$f(x + P) = f(x)$$
>
> holds for all x in the domain of f.

On the graph. If, say, $P = 3$, then the functional equation says that $f(x + 3) = f(x)$. What does this mean about the graph of f?

The equation says that $f(1) = f(4)$, $f(1.5) = f(4.5)$, $f(2) = f(5)$, $f(2.5) = f(5.5)$, etc. Thus, for *any* x the height of the graph at x is the same as the height of the graph at $x + 3$.

A shift to the left. For *any* function f, the graph of $y = f(x + P)$ is the result of shifting the graph of $y = f(x)$ a distance of P units to the *left*. From this point of view, the periodicity equation $f(x + P) = f(x)$ means:

We discussed graphical translation in Section 1.2.

The graph of f doesn't change if it's shifted P units to the left.

Convince yourself of this for each graph above.

Many periods. Because the sine graph repeats itself on intervals of length 2π, it *also* repeats itself on intervals of length 4π, 6π, 8π, etc. Thus, technically speaking, $2\pi, 4\pi, 6\pi, \ldots$ are *all* periods of the sine function. In practice, this ambiguity seldom matters; we're usually interested only in the smallest positive period.

■ **Example 5.** Below are graphs of

$$f(x) = \frac{\sin x}{3} + 3 \quad \text{and} \quad g(x) = (\sin x)^2 + \sin(x).$$

Which is which? *Why* is each function 2π-periodic?

Two periodic functions: $f(x) = \frac{\sin x}{3} + 3$, $g(x) = (\sin x)^2 + \sin(x)$

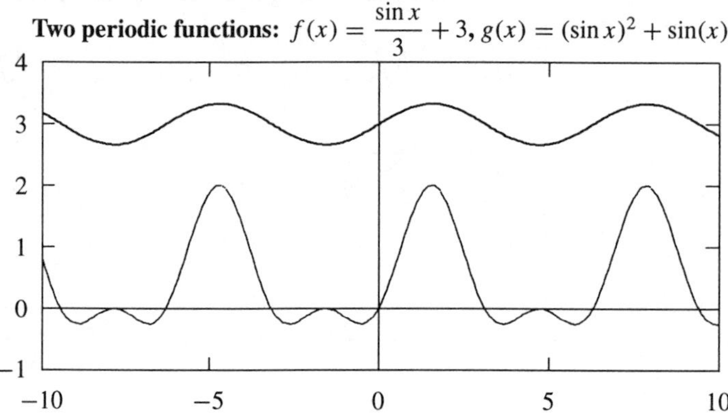

Solution: The upper graph is f—it's formed by compressing the sine curve vertically and translating it 3 units upward. The lower graph, therefore, is g.

Both functions look 2π-periodic. So they are: they "inherit" the sine function's periodicity. A symbolic calculation shows how:

Like the sine curve itself.

$$f(x+2\pi) = \frac{\sin(x+2\pi)}{3} + 3 = \frac{\sin x}{3} + 3 = f(x);$$
$$g(x+2\pi) = \left(\sin(x+2\pi)\right)^2 + \sin(x+2\pi) = (\sin x)^2 + \sin x = g(x). \quad \square$$

Functional language: names, nicknames, uses, and abuses

Everyday speech is a rich mixture of formal and informal language, names and nicknames, careful descriptions and vague allusions. The *common* things of daily life—friends, places, college courses, etc.—are likeliest to attract nicknames, verbal shortcuts, and aliases.

In calculus, functions are the commonest objects of all. Mathematical language, true to form, offers various ways of talking about functions, some clearer and more precise than others. Some linguistic tips follow.

Function vs. value. It's sometimes important to distinguish between a **function** and the **value of a function.** The sentence

Consider the function $f(x) = x^2$.

may seem clear, but it blurs the distinction between f—a function—and $f(x)$—a value of f. It would be technically clearer (though less euphonious) to say

We won't always be this fastidious.

Consider the function f defined by $f(x) = x^2$.

Composite functional expressions. If f is defined by $f(x) = x^2$, then it's clear what's meant by such expressions as $f(3)$, $f(z)$, and $f(-13/2)$. **Composite expressions**, like

$$f(x+3), \qquad f(-x), \qquad \text{and} \qquad f\big(f(x)\big)$$

need more care.

To make sense of them it helps to think of f as an **operator** or **procedure**: f accepts "anything" and returns its square. Thus

$$\begin{aligned} f(x+3) &= (x+3)^2 = x^2 + 6x + 9; \\ f(-x) &= (-x)^2 = x^2; \\ f(f(x)) &= \left(x^2\right)^2 = x^4. \end{aligned}$$

Functions vs. expressions. The statement

The range of $x^2 - 6x$ *is* $[-9, \infty)$.

is intelligible, but the *expression* $x^2 - 6x$ is used—not quite correctly—to describe a *function*. A scrupulously correct version of the statement preserves this distinction:

> *Let* f *be the function defined by* $f(x) = x^2 - 6x$. *The range of* f *is* $[-9, \infty)$.

Functions differ from expressions in subtle but important ways. For example:

- Not all functions are defined by symbolic expressions. Of the five functions that started this section, only two were so defined.➡ *Which two?*

- Several *different* symbolic expressions may define the *same* function. The following three expressions are equivalent:

  $$x^2 - 6x; \qquad \frac{x^2 - 6x}{\sin^2 x + \cos^2 x}; \qquad \frac{x^4 - 6x^3 + x^2 - 6x}{x^2 + 1}.$$

  Any one of them could define f.

- Functions don't care about variable names; expressions do. For example,

  $$x^2 - 6x, \qquad t^2 - 6t, \qquad \text{and} \qquad P^2 - 6P$$

  are different expressions, but all could define the same function.

Computers know the difference. Computer programs *insist* on the distinction between functions and expressions. In *Maple*, for example, the command

```
f := x^2 - 6*x ;
```

defines `f` only as an expression. To define f as a *function*, we could type

```
f := x -> x^2 - 6*x;
```

The latter form isn't pretty, but it's explicit: `f` is defined as an **operator** that assigns to any input x the output $x^2 - 6x$.

Exercises

1. Find the domain and range of each of the functions shown graphically below.

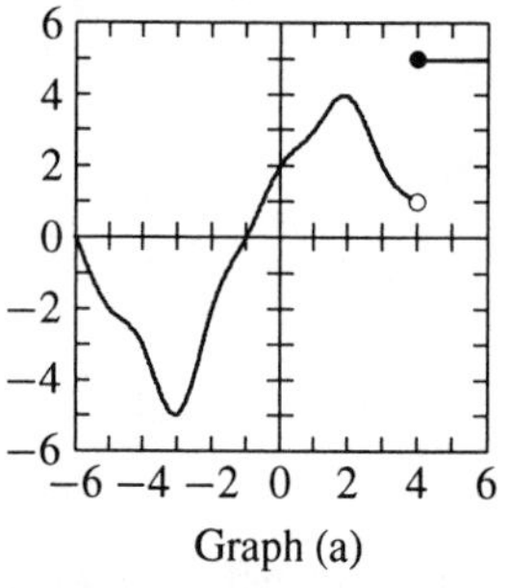
Graph (a)

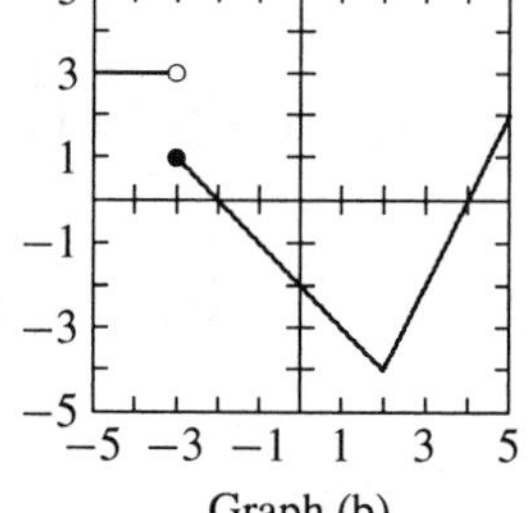
Graph (b)

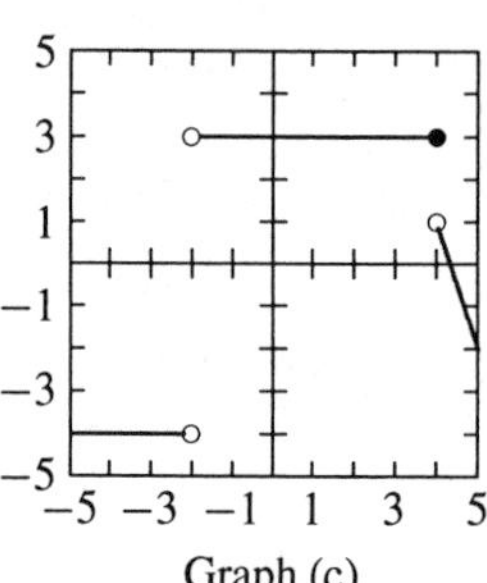
Graph (c)

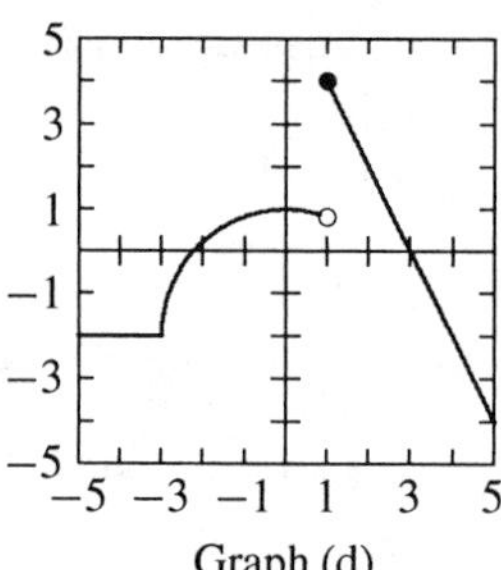
Graph (d)

2. Sketch the graph of a function that has the specified domain and range.

   (a) domain: $[-10, 10]$
   range: $\{4\}$

   (b) domain: $[-3, 2) \cup (3, 5)$
   range: $[1, 4)$

   (c) domain: $[-5, 5]$
   range: $(-6, -1] \cup [0, 5]$

   (d) domain: $[-3, -1] \cup [0, 2]$
   range: $[0, 3] \cup [4, 6]$

3. Find the natural domain of each of the following functions.

   (a) $f(x) = \dfrac{1}{(x-1)(x+2)}$

   (b) $g(x) = \dfrac{x+2}{x-1}$

   (c) $h(x) = \sqrt{x+2}$

   (d) $r(x) = \dfrac{1}{\sqrt{(x+2)(1-x)}}$

   (e) $s(x) = \dfrac{1}{\sqrt{(x+2)(x-1)}}$

   (f) $t(x) = \sqrt{\dfrac{1-x}{x+2}}$

4. Find the natural domain and the range of each of the following functions.

   (a) $f(x) = \sqrt{(x+3)(x-3)}$

   (b) $g(x) = x^2 + x - 2$

   (c) $h(x) = x^3 - |x|$

   (d) $j(x) = \sqrt{4 - x^2}$

   (e) $k(x) = \left(2x^3 + 5\right)^{2/3}$

5. Suppose that water is flowing into a cubical tank and that each side of the tank is ten feet.

   (a) Write a formula for V, the volume of water in the tank, as a function of d, the depth of water in the tank.

(b) What is the domain of V? What is the range of V?

(c) Write a formula for d as a function of V.

6. For each set below, find a function defined by a single algebraic expression that has that set as its natural domain. [EXAMPLE: The function $f(x) = \sqrt{(x-1)(x+3)}$ has the set $(-\infty, -3] \cup [1, \infty)$ as its domain.]

(a) $\{x \mid x \neq -1 \text{ and } x \neq 3\}$

(b) $[-1, 3]$

(c) $[-1, \infty)$

(d) $(-1, 3)$

(e) $(-\infty, -1) \cup (3, \infty)$

(f) $[-1, 3)$

7. Many precalculus textbooks discuss the **vertical line test** for determining whether a curve is the graph of a function: "A curve is the graph of a function only if each vertical line $x = k$ intersects the graph at most once." Explain why this test works.

8. Indicate which of the following curves are graphs of functions.

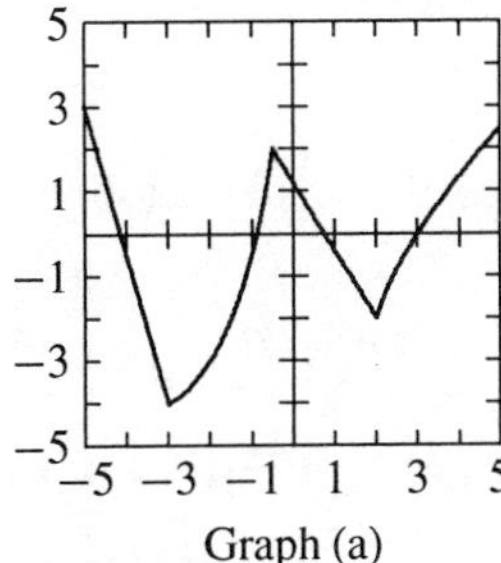

Graph (a)

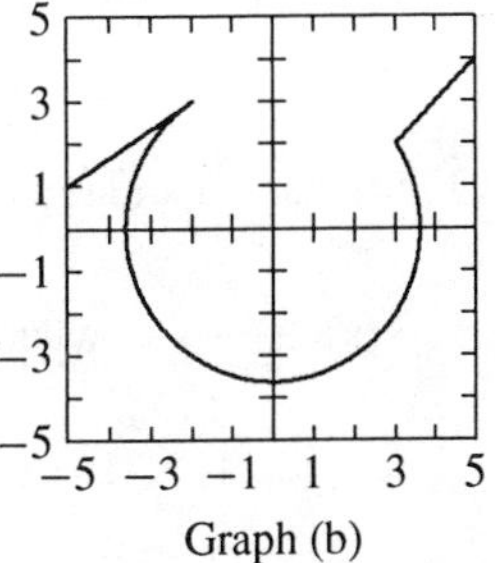

Graph (b)

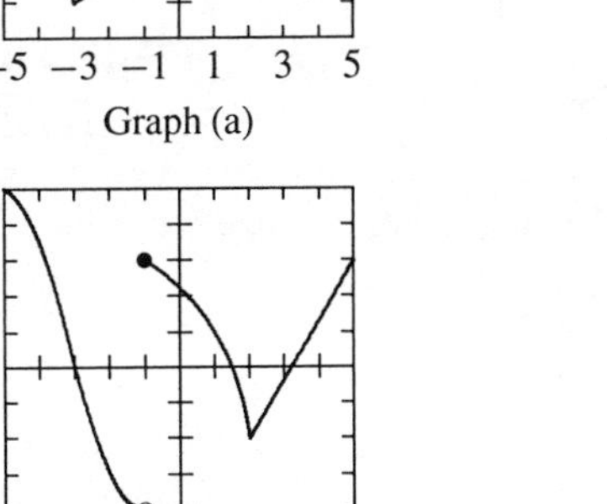

Graph (c)

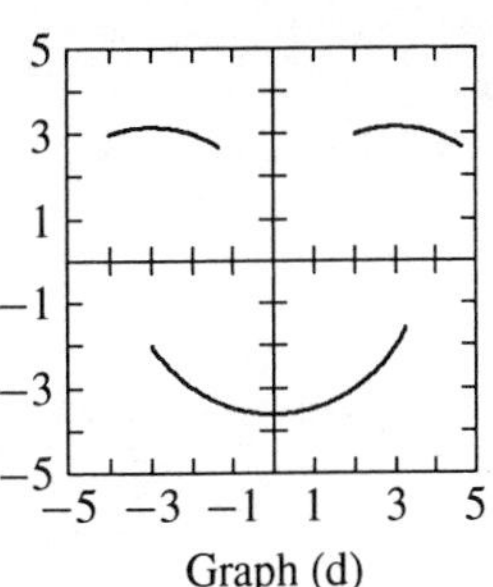

Graph (d)

9. Sketch the graph of each of the following piecewise-defined functions, then find the domain and range of each.

(a) $f(x) = \begin{cases} 0 & \text{if } x \leq -1 \\ 3x - 2 & \text{if } 1 < x < 1.5 \\ x^2 & \text{if } 1.5 \leq x < 2 \end{cases}$

(b) $f(x) = \begin{cases} 0 & \text{if } 0 \leq x < 1 \\ -2 & \text{if } 1 \leq x < 2 \\ x & \text{if } 2 \leq x \end{cases}$

(c) $f(x) = \begin{cases} \dfrac{1}{2 - x} & \text{if } x < 0 \\ \sqrt{1 + 4x^5} & \text{if } x > 1 \end{cases}$

10. For each of the following functions, find an interval on which the given bound holds. [HINT: Look at graphs.]

    (a) $f(x) = 3x - 2$; $|f(x)| < 8$
    (b) $g(x) = \dfrac{x}{x^2+4}$; $0.1 < g(x) < 0.3$
    (c) $h(x) = 2x^3 - 4x^2 + 5x - 6$; $|h(x) - 5| < 10$

11. Find upper and lower bounds on the value of each of the following functions over the specified interval.

    (a) $f(x) = x + 3$; $[-2, 5]$
    (b) $g(x) = x^2 - 2$; $(-4, 1)$
    (c) $h(x) = 1 - 3x^2$; $|x| < 2$
    (d) $j(x) = \dfrac{3}{x}$; $|x - 4| < 1$
    (e) $k(x) = \left(3x^2+1\right)^{-1}$; $|x + 2| < 0.5$
    (f) $m(x) = \dfrac{x}{x^2+3}$; $[-5, -1]$

12. Let $f(x) = \dfrac{x^2}{1+x^2}$. Show that $1/2 \le f(x) \le 1$ when $|x| \ge 1$. [HINT: Show that $1 + x^2 < 2x^2$ when $|x| \ge 1$.]

13. Find upper and lower bounds on the value of each of the following expressions.

    (a) $\dfrac{2}{x+3}$ when $5 \le x \le 7$
    (b) $\dfrac{1}{x^2+3}$ when $-\infty < x < \infty$
    (c) $\dfrac{1}{|x|+4}$ when $-\infty < x < \infty$
    (d) $\dfrac{x^2+2x+10}{x^2+2}$ when $|x| < 2$

14. Indicate which of the following functions are even, which are odd, and which are neither.

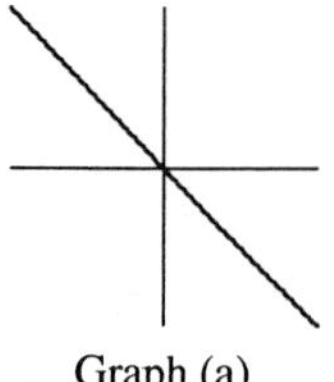

Graph (a)

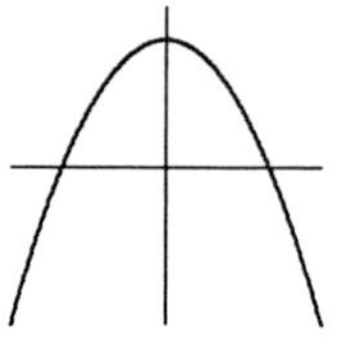

Graph (b)

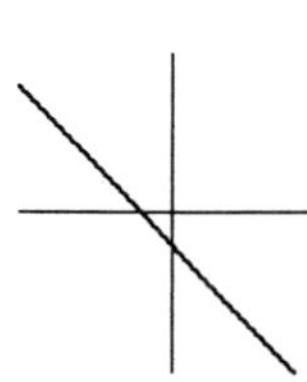

Graph (c)

Graph (d)

15. Indicate which of the following functions are even, which are odd, and which are neither. [HINT: Look at graphs of these functions.]

    (a) $3x^4 - 5x^2 + 17$
    (b) $12x^7 + 6x^3 - 2x$
    (c) $|x|$
    (d) $|x + 4|$
    (e) $x^4 + |x^3| - 2$
    (f) $4x^3 - 7$

16. The graphs of odd functions are symmetric about the origin. What geometric property characterizes *even* functions?

17. Suppose that f is an *odd* function whose domain includes zero. Explain why $f(0) = 0$ must be true.

18. Can a function be *both* even and odd? [HINT: Consider constant functions (i.e., functions of the form $f(x) = c$).]

19. Each of the graphs below shows a portion of the graph of an *even* function over the interval $[-5, 5]$. Complete these graphs.

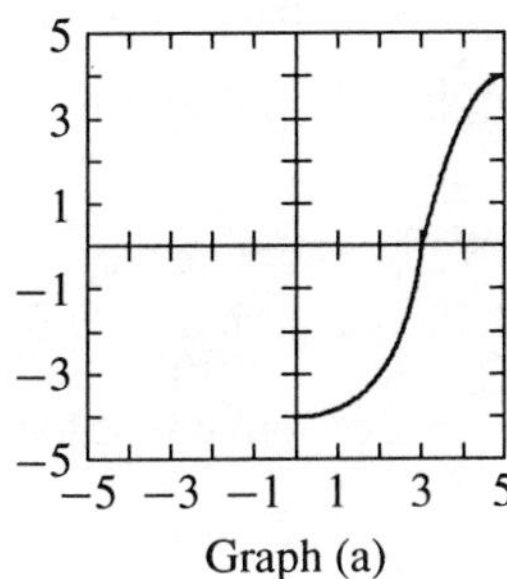

Graph (a)

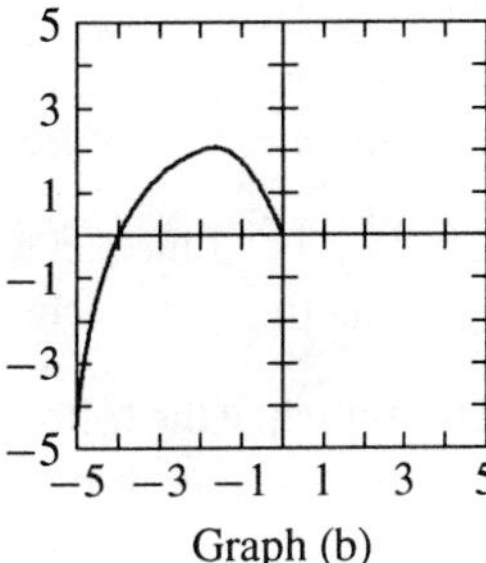

Graph (b)

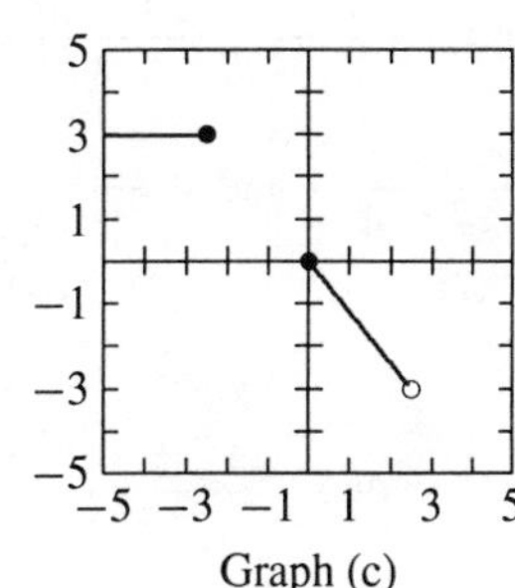

Graph (c)

20. Which of the graphs in the preceding problem could be a portion of the graph of an *odd* function over the interval $[-5, 5]$? Complete these graphs.

21. Recall that the sine function is 2π-periodic. In each part below, use a plot of the given function over the interval $[-5, 5]$ to decide whether it's periodic, and if so, to find its period.

(a) $f(x) = |\sin(x)|$

(b) $f(x) = \sin(|x|)$

(c) $f(x) = \left(\sin(x)\right)^2$

(d) $f(x) = \sin(2\pi x)$

22. The cosine function, like the sine function, is 2π-periodic. In each part below, first decide (e.g., by graphing) whether the given function is periodic, and if so, find its period. Then, for those that are periodic, give a symbolic argument like that in Example 5, page 46, that supports your claim.

(a) $f(x) = |\cos(x)|$

(b) $f(x) = \cos(|x|)$

(c) $f(x) = \left(\cos(x)\right)^2$

(d) $f(x) = \cos(2x)$

23. Suppose that f is a periodic function with period 1/2 and that

$$f(2) = 5, \qquad f\left(\tfrac{9}{4}\right) = 2, \qquad \text{and} \qquad f\left(\tfrac{11}{8}\right) = 3.$$

Evaluate each of the following:

(a) $f(0)$

(b) $f\left(\frac{1}{4}\right)$

(c) $f\left(\frac{3}{8}\right)$

(d) $f(-3)$

(e) $f(1000)$

(f) $f(x+5) - f(x)$

24. Let f be a function with period P, i.e., $f(x+P) = f(x)$. Show that $2P$ is *also* a period of f. In other words, show that $f(x+2P) = f(x)$. What does this mean graphically?

25. If f is a function with period P, then $P/2$ need not be a period of f. Draw a function f for which 2 is a period but 1 is not a period.

26. Which of the following pairs of algebraic expressions define the same function? Justify your answers.

(a) $x - 4$ and $\dfrac{2x^3 - 8x^2 + 3x - 12}{2x^2 + 3}$

(b) $\dfrac{3}{2x+1} - \dfrac{x}{x^2+4}$ and $\dfrac{x^2 - x + 12}{2x^3 + x^2 + 8x + 4}$

(c) $\dfrac{4x^2 + 3x - 7}{x}$ and $\dfrac{4x^4 + 3x^3 - 3x^2 + 3x - 7}{x^3 + 2x}$

(d) $\dfrac{x^2 + 2x + 1}{x - 1}$ and $\dfrac{x^3 + 4x^2 + 5x + 2}{x^2 + x - 2}$

1.5 A field guide to elementary functions

Elementary functions

An **elementary function** is one built from certain legal basic "elements," using certain legal operations. For example, the function

$$f(x) = \ln\left(\frac{\sin(2x)}{1+3x^4}\right)$$

is elementary because it is constructed (by addition, division, composition, etc.) from basic function "elements": the sine and natural logarithm functions, powers of x, etc.

Despite their name, elementary functions need not be trivial or simple-minded. Many different buildings can be built from standard sizes of brick. For the same reasons, elementary functions come in enormous variety.

What "standard" means for bricks is partly a practical matter,➡ but mainly a matter of choice. Our choice of functional "building blocks" is just as practical, but much less arbitrary. The basic elementary functions of calculus have proved themselves useful throughout mathematics and its applications.

Twice as long as wide, not too heavy to lift, etc.

A pictorial field guide

This section contains brief descriptions, with pictures, of various elementary functions. Like any field guide, this one emphasizes identification, classification, and basic behavior, rather than detailed study of its subjects. More details on each species of function met here can be found later in this book or in the Appendices.

Function families

Like birds or plants, the building-block functions of calculus fall naturally into "families"—far fewer, fortunately, than for birds or plants! We'll name just three:

Algebraic functions: Their rules involve only *algebraic* operations, such as these:

$$f(x) = x^2 + \frac{3}{x}; \qquad g(x) = \frac{x^2+3}{1+\sqrt{x}}.$$

Exponential and logarithm functions: Their rules involve exponentials or logarithms with various bases, such as these:

$$h(x) = 2^x; \quad k(x) = e^x; \quad m(x) = \log_2 x; \quad n(x) = \ln x.$$

Trigonometric functions: The *sine*, *cosine*, and *tangent* functions, together with their descendants the *secant*, *cosecant*, and *cotangent* functions.

Hybrids

Like some plants, the basic calculus functions "hybridize" freely, combining in various ways to produce new elementary functions. How functions combine, and how their descendants' traits reflect their own, is an important theme throughout this book. In this section, though, our main concern is with the basic building-block functions themselves.

Algebraic functions

An **algebraic function** is one defined using only the ordinary algebraic operations: addition, multiplication, division, raising to powers, and taking roots.

Roughly speaking, algebraic functions are those even the simplest calculator can handle.◂ If, say, the function f is defined by the algebraic rule $f(x) = x - 3\sqrt{x+1}$, then checking with a calculator that

$2.98 buys such a machine; trigonometric, exponential, and logarithm functions start a little higher.

$$f(1.7) = 1.7 - 3\sqrt{2.7} \approx -3.229$$

requires nothing fancier than the arithmetic and square root keys.

Polynomials

Polynomials are the simplest algebraic functions; their rules require only multiplication and addition.◂ (To review basic facts about linear, polynomial, and rational functions, see Appendix D.)

Positive integer powers of x can be found by repeated multiplication.

Definition: A **polynomial** in x is an expression that can be written in the form

$$a_0 + a_1x + a_2x^2 + a_3x^3 + \ldots + a_nx^n,$$

that is, a sum of *constant* multiples of *nonnegative integer* powers of x.

■ **Example 1.** Each of the expressions

$$5x+2, \qquad -x+5x^{17}, \qquad \text{and} \qquad (x+3)(\pi x^{17}+7)$$

is a polynomial in x.◂ None of

Use algebra to write the last example in standard form.

$$3-\frac{1}{x}, \qquad \sqrt{x}, \qquad \text{and} \qquad \frac{x+3}{\pi x^{17}+7}$$

is a polynomial. □

Polynomials as functions. The polynomial *expression* $2x^3+5x$ corresponds naturally to the *function* $p(x) = 2x^3+5x$. Any function defined by a polynomial expression is called a **polynomial function**. In practice the technical distinction between *polynomial* and *polynomial function* seldom matters; we'll use the terms interchangeably.

Domain and range. Because polynomials involve only multiplication and addition, they accept *all* real numbers as inputs. In other words, every polynomial function has the same *natural domain*: all real numbers.

Polynomials' *ranges* vary drastically. The range of $p(x) = 10$ is $\{10\}$, a set with just one member. By contrast, the range of $q(x) = x^2+3$ is $[3, \infty)$, an infinite interval. The range of $r(x) = x^3 - 2x^2$ is not obvious from the formula, so we'll look at the graph. Here, together, are graphs of p, q, and r:

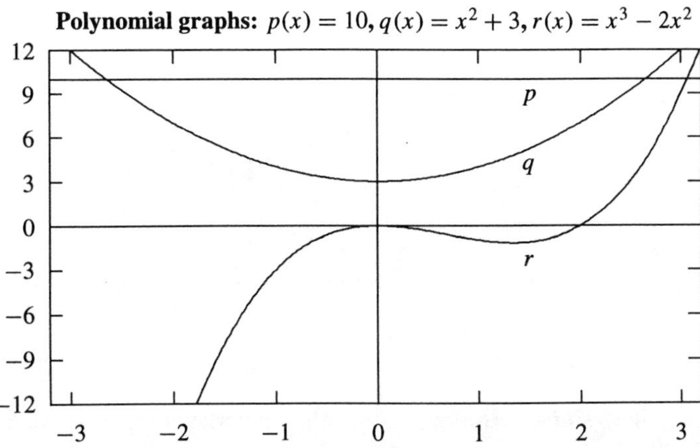

Notice:

Blowing up and down. The picture suggests that $r(x)$ "blows up" (tends to ∞) as $x \to +\infty$, and that $r(x)$ "blows down" (tends to $-\infty$) as $x \to -\infty$. Our impression is correct; for *any* polynomial, the term with the *largest power of x* determines what happens as x tends to plus or minus infinity. (For $r(x)$, the x^3 term "dominates".) Thus $r(x)$ assumes *all* real values, and its range is $(-\infty, \infty)$.

Plotting r in a larger window would show this even more clearly.

We'll show this soon, using limits.

Point of view. How *any* graph looks depends strongly on how the plotting window is chosen. Polynomials are no exception. Here are two more views of the same three polynomials:

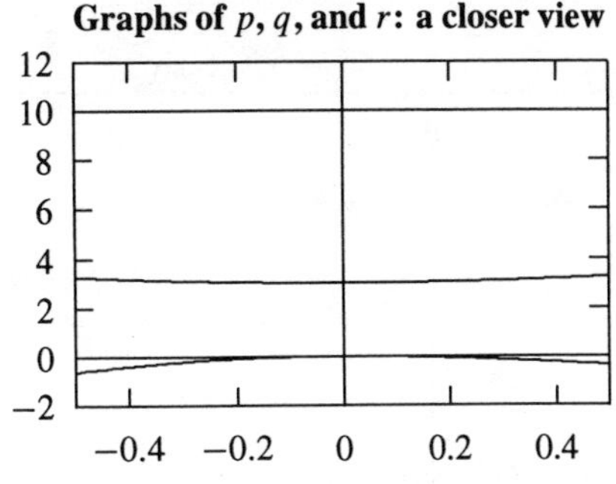

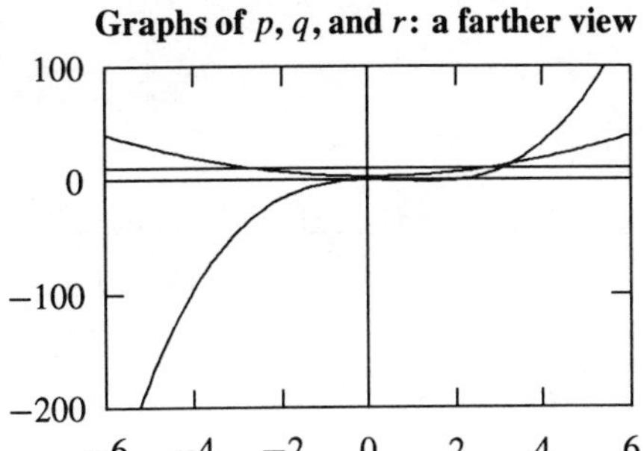

In the last picture the huge vertical scale makes p virtually disappear.

No breaks. Polynomial graphs are everywhere "continuous" and "smooth"—they have neither breaks or kinks. As we'll see soon, this reflects the fact that polynomials are among the simplest, best-behaved functions from the calculus point of view.

Lines and linear functions. The very simplest polynomials are constants, such as $p(x) = 10$. The simplest *interesting* polynomials are **linear functions**—polynomials that involve nothing higher than the *first power of x*. Each of the following expressions defines a linear function:

$$\ell_1(x) = 2x + 3; \quad \ell_2(x) = 2(x - 3) + 3; \quad \ell_3(x) = 2x + 1; \quad \ell_4(x) = -2x + 2.$$

Graphs of linear functions are, of course, *lines*:

Lines: $\ell_1(x) = 2x + 3$, $\ell_2(x) = 2(x - 3) + 3$, $\ell_3(x) = 2x + 1$, $\ell_4(x) = -2x + 2$

Each line's **slope**, y**-intercept**, and other important properties can be "read" from its equation.

I.e., highest power of x with a nonzero coefficient.

Which is which?

Quadratics and cubics: characteristic shapes. Graphs of **quadratic** and **cubic** polynomials—those with degree two and three—have standard shapes, called **parabolas** and **cubic curves**. Here are three quadratics:

Three quadratics: $q_1(x) = x^2$, $q_2(x) = -4x^2 + 4$, $q_3(x) = 2x(x + 2)$

Which is which? Check for yourself.

Here are three cubics:

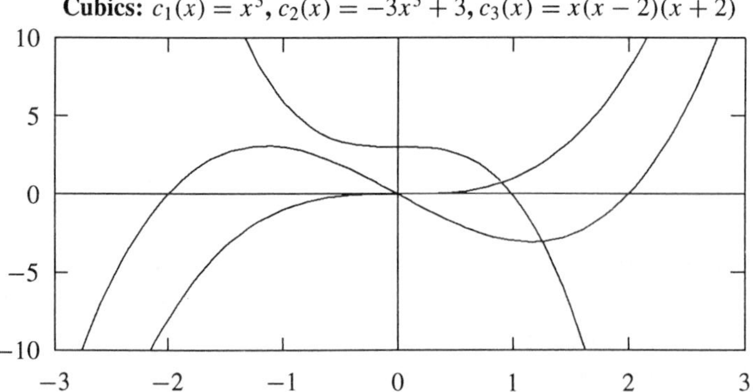

Polynomials in general: many shapes. Linear, quadratic, and cubic polynomials have characteristic shapes, but polynomial graphs in general can take almost any smooth, unbroken shape. Some shape restrictions *do* exist. For instance, a polynomial of degree n can have at most n **roots**; this means, graphically, that a polynomial graph can have at most n x**-intercepts**. (In particular, a polynomial function can't be periodic.)

Rational functions

Adding or multiplying two polynomials creates a new polynomial.➻ *Dividing* two polynomials➻ doesn't (usually) give another polynomial; it gives a **rational function**. Formally:

Is this really obvious? Think about it; try some examples.

I.e., finding their **ratio.**

> **Definition:** A **rational function** is a function whose rule can be written as the quotient of two polynomials.

■ **Example 2.** Each function below is rational:

$$f(x) = \frac{1}{x}; \quad g(x) = \frac{x^2}{x^2+3}; \quad h(x) = \frac{2}{x} + \frac{3}{x+1}.$$

The function $m(x) = \sqrt{x} = x^{1/2}$ is not rational because it involves a *fractional* power of x.

The function h may look suspicious. It's certainly the *sum* of two rational functions, but is h *itself* rational? The answer is yes, because we can *rewrite* $h(x)$ in the form:

$$h(x) = \frac{2}{x} + \frac{3}{x+1} = \frac{2(x+1)}{x(x+1)} + \frac{3x}{x(x+1)} = \frac{5x+2}{x(x+1)} \qquad \square$$

Graphs of rational functions

Rational functions➻ have an important new feature: the possibility of **horizontal** and **vertical asymptotes.**

Unlike polynomials.

■ **Example 3.** Consider the rational function

$$r(x) = \frac{x^2}{x^2-1} = \frac{x^2}{(x-1)(x+1)}$$

and its graph:

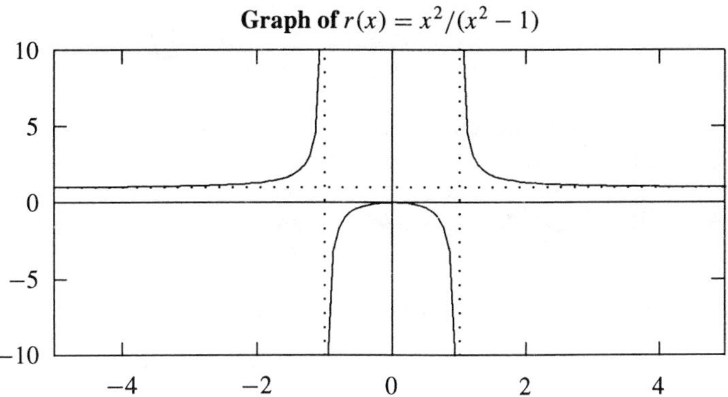

Asymptotes are straight lines toward which a graph "tends." Soon we'll study asymptotes and their relations to limits. Technicalities temporarily aside, it's already evident that this graph has three asymptotes: the *vertical* lines $x = -1$ and $x = 1$, and the *horizontal* line $y = 1$.

Where the *vertical* asymptotes come from should be clear: They correspond to real **roots** of the denominator.➻

It's natural to expect trouble where a denominator vanishes. It may be less obvious from the formula how the function misbehaves.

The *horizontal* asymptote (the line $y = 1$) reflects r's "long run" behavior. It shows how r behaves for large positive and large negative inputs. Specifically, the asymptote shows that $r(x)$ approaches 1 as x approaches plus or minus infinity. Manipulating r's formula shows why:

$$r(x) = \frac{x^2}{x^2 - 1} = \frac{(x^2 - 1) + 1}{x^2 - 1} = 1 + \frac{1}{x^2 - 1}.$$

The graph of r falls toward the asymptote.

As x tends to plus or minus infinity, $1/(x^2 - 1)$ remains positive, but tends to 0; hence $r(x)$ approaches 1 from *above.* Tabulating values of r for inputs with large absolute values gives similar information:

"Long-run" values of $r(x) = x^2/(x^2 - 1)$

x	10	100	1000	10000	...
$r(x)$	1.01010101	1.00010001	1.00000100	1.00000001	...
x	−10	−100	−1000	−10000	...
$r(x)$	1.01010101	1.00010001	1.00000100	1.00000001	...

□

Other algebraic functions

Polynomials and rational functions involve only the standard arithmetic operations: addition, subtraction, multiplication, division, and raising to *integer* powers. "Other" algebraic functions include ones like these—

$$f(x) = \sqrt{x}, \qquad g(x) = \sqrt{x + \sqrt{x}}, \qquad \text{and} \qquad h(x) = \sqrt{\sqrt[3]{x^2 + 1} + x^{6/7}},$$

that involve n^{th} roots. As we'll soon see, calculus methods and ideas apply just as readily to these "other" algebraic functions as to polynomials and rational functions.

These "other" algebraic functions do pose one new problem: finding output values. To illustrate, compare the functions

$$m(x) = x + \frac{5x + 2}{x(x + 1)} \qquad \text{and} \qquad f(x) = \sqrt{x}.$$

A calculator has no trouble, of course.

See the graph on page 7.

It's easy to compute, even by hand, that $m(2) = 4$. Finding $f(2) = \sqrt{2}$ to any respectable numerical accuracy is harder, at least by hand. Even here, calculus can help. As we said in Section 1.1, calculus can help us choose polynomial functions that closely approximate the square root function.

Exponential and logarithm functions

Section 1.6 contains a thoroughly practical application: using exponential functions to study how inflation affects college tuition.

If any aren't familiar, review the Appendices now!

Exponential and logarithm functions are among calculus's most important and most practically useful functions. Understanding these functions requires, first of all, a familiarity with the *algebra* of logarithms and exponentials. Quick reviews of the necessary algebraic basics appear in Appendices E and F. Most basic of all are these key facts:

How logs and exponentials are related. For a positive base b and real numbers x and y,

$$y = \log_b x \iff x = b^y.$$

This relation between logarithms and exponentials is crucial to understanding both types of function; we'll study it carefully below. In particular, we'll use this relation to *define* logarithm functions using exponential functions.

Important properties of logs and exponentials. We'll use freely and repeatedly these key properties:

$$b^x b^y = b^{x+y} \qquad (b^x)^r = b^{xr}$$
$$\log_b xy = \log_b x + \log_b y \qquad \log_b(x^r) = r\log_b x$$

(Note: In each line, b must be *positive*. In the top two equations, x and y can take any real values. In the second two, x and y must be *positive*. For many more details, see the Appendices.)

Exponential functions

> **Definition:** An **exponential function** is defined by an expression of the form
> $$f(x) = b^x,$$
> where b, the **base**, is a fixed positive number.

Each of the expressions

$$2^x, \quad 4^t, \quad \left(\tfrac{1}{2}\right)^z \quad \text{and} \quad e^x$$

defines an exponential function. (The base is fixed; the exponent varies—hence the name.) *None* of the expressions

$$x^2, \quad z^3, \quad (w+1)^{15}, \quad x^\pi$$

defines an exponential function, because each involves a *fixed*➻ power of a *variable* base.

Not variable.

Base e. Among all exponential functions, the one with base e turns out to be especially useful and convenient. (The fact that e is usually the "default" base on scientific calculators attests to that base's special importance.) The number e is irrational; its decimal expansion begins $e = 2.71828182\ldots$. What *makes* base e special—for both exponential and logarithm functions—will become clearer soon, when we study derivatives.

The function $f(x) = e^x$, with base e, is often called the **exponential function**➻ or, sometimes, the **natural exponential function**. Alternative notations➻ include

Calling it the exponential function *is a bit unfortunate—other functions are also exponential.*

Parentheses are often omitted with such named functions as sin, cos, ln, *and* exp.

$$\exp(x), \qquad \exp x, \qquad \text{and} \qquad e^x.$$

Graphs of exponential functions. Graphs of several exponential functions appear below. The rule for each is of the form b^x—only the base b varies. Points of special interest are shown "bulleted."

Exponential functions with various bases

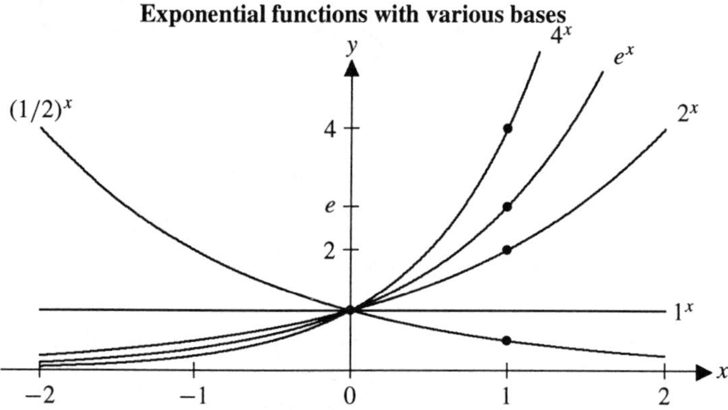

Observe:

Why not $b \leq 0$? Appendix E gives details.

Legitimate bases. If $b > 0$, then the expression b^x makes sense for any real number x. Thus any *positive* base b defines a sensible exponential function. (In practice, $b = 2$, $b = e$, and $b = 10$ are by far the most useful.)

Domain and range. Exponential functions accept *all* real inputs, so all have *domain* $(-\infty, \infty)$. The graphs show that unless $b = 1$, the *range* of the exponential function $f(x) = b^x$ is $(0, \infty)$.

Shapes. The shape of an exponential graph depends on the base b:

The larger the value of b, the faster b^x increases.

(If $b < 1$, b^x *decreases*. If $b = 1$, then b^x is a constant function.)

A common point. *Every* graph of the form $y = b^x$ passes through the point $(0, 1)$. In the language of functions:

If $f(x) = b^x$ then $f(0) = b^0 = 1$.

How do the graphs reflect these facts?

The input $x = 1$ is also of interest. For any function $f(x) = b^x$, $f(1) = b^1 = b$.

Learn the word "monotonic"—it's a convenient shorthand for a longer-winded phrase.

Exponential functions are monotonic. All exponential functions $f(x) = b^x$ are **monotonic,** i.e., either nonincreasing everywhere or nondecreasing everywhere. In graphical language:

What happens if $b = 1$?

If $b > 1$, the graph of $y = b^x$ is everywhere rising. If $0 < b < 1$, the graph of $y = b^x$ is everywhere falling.

Faster and faster. Perhaps the most important calculus property of exponential functions concerns *rates* of growth:

If $y = b^x$, then the rate of change of y is proportional to y itself.

This property of exponential functions is more subtle than those above. It can be seen only qualitatively in the graphs. The graph $y = 2^x$, for example, rises *faster* as it rises *higher*. We'll return to this idea later, after having studied rates of growth more carefully.

Exponential and power functions: they're not the same

The expressions 2^x and x^2 are typographically similar, but the resemblance ends there. They define entirely different functions, and their graphs show it:

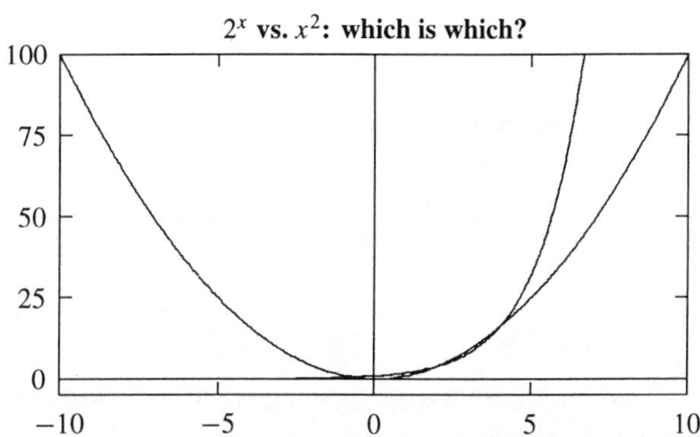

Note some differences:

Asymptotes. The graph of $y = x^2$ has no horizontal asymptotes. The graph of $y = 2^x$ has the line $y = 0$ as a horizontal asymptote, corresponding to the limit $\lim_{x\to-\infty} 2^x = 0$.

Or vertical ones.

More is true: *Every* exponential function $y = b^x$ (with $b > 0$ and $b \neq 1$) has the line $y = 0$ as a horizontal asymptote. By contrast, *no* power function x^b (with $b > 0$) has a horizontal asymptote.

If $b < 0$ then $y = 0$ is a horizontal asymptote.

Comparing rates of growth. As $x \to \infty$, both

$$x^2 \to \infty \qquad \text{and} \qquad 2^x \to \infty.$$

However, 2^x blows up much, much *faster* than x^2. Graphs can only begin to suggest how quickly 2^x outruns x^2.

To put the difference more dramatically let $f(x) = x^2$ and $g(x) = 2^x$. Then $f(1000)$ dollars might buy a starter home in Hollywood, but $g(1000)$ is (more or less) the number of molecules in the universe. For even larger inputs, and larger values of b, the differences are even greater.

Logarithm functions

Exponential and logarithm functions come in pairs: an *exponential* function with base b corresponds to a *logarithm* function, denoted $\log_b$, with the *same* base. The table below collects values of one such "matched pair" of functions, here with base $b = 2$. The values illustrate the correspondence between exponential and logarithm functions.

This works for any positive base b except $b = 1$. Why not $b = 1$? See below.

Notice the "mirror symmetry" in the table.

Exponential and Logarithm Function Values

Values of 2^x

x	-2	-1	0	1	2	3	10	13.288
2^x	1/4	1/2	1	2	4	8	1024	10000

Values of $\log_2 x$

x	1/4	1/2	1	2	4	8	1024	10000
$\log_2 x$	-2	-1	0	1	2	3	10	13.288

The formal definition makes the correspondence between logarithm and exponential precise:

> **Definition:** The **logarithm function with base b**, denoted
>
> $$f(x) = \log_b x,$$
>
> is defined by the condition
>
> $$y = \log_b x \iff b^y = x.$$

Each of the expressions

$$\log_2 x, \quad \log_4 x, \quad \log_{1/2} x, \quad \text{and} \quad \log_e x$$

Recall: $e \approx 2.718$.

In print and on calculator buttons.

defines a logarithm function with some base b. The logarithm function with base e is called the **natural logarithm function**; it's usually denoted by

$$\ln(x) \qquad \text{or} \qquad \ln x.$$

Graphs of logarithm functions. Graphs of logarithm functions with various bases appear below. (Exponential functions with the sames bases were plotted above—compare the pictures.) Interesting points are shown bulleted.

Logarithm functions—various bases

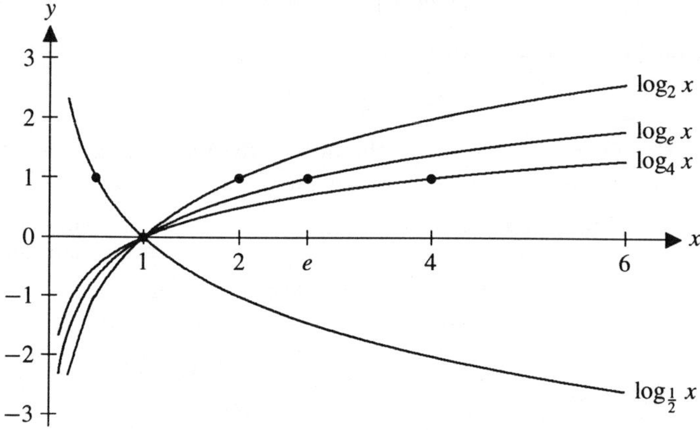

Pun intended.

Not surprisingly, properties of logarithm function graphs reflect analogous properties of exponential function graphs.

Why not $b = 1$? Because $1^y = 1$ for all $y > 0$—Appendix F has more details.

Legitimate bases. Any positive number b *except* $b = 1$ can be used as base for a logarithm function. (In practice, as for exponentials, $b = 2$, $b = e$, and $b = 10$ are most useful.)

Domain and range. The graphs illustrate that for any suitable base b, the logarithm function accepts *positive* inputs; outputs take on *all* real values. Thus every logarithm function has *domain* $(0, \infty)$ and *range* $(-\infty, \infty)$.

Growth rates. As for exponential functions, each graph's shape depends on b. This time, the *larger* the value of b, the more *slowly* $\log_b x$ increases. (If $b < 1$, $\log_b x$ *decreases.*)

Graphs of exponential functions rise *faster and faster* as x increases. Graphs of logarithm functions have a different (but related!) property: they rise *more and more slowly* as x increases.

A common point. The graph of every logarithm function passes through $(1, 0)$.
In functional language:

If $f(x) = \log_b x$ *then* $f(1) = \log_b 1 = 0$.

Similarly, for any $b > 0$, $f(b) = \log_b b = 1$.

Which point was "common" to exponentials?

Logarithm functions are monotonic. Every logarithm function is **strictly monotonic.** If $b > 1$, the graph of $y = \log_b(x)$ *rises* everywhere. If $0 < b < 1$, the graph *falls* everywhere.

I.e., either strictly increasing everywhere or strictly decreasing everywhere.

There is no logarithm function for $b = 1$.

Exponential and logarithm functions as inverses

The condition

$$y = \log_b x \iff x = b^y.$$

means that a logarithm function and an exponential function with the same base are **inverses** of each other.

We'll return to the idea of inverse functions in Chapter 3.

■ **Example 4.** For any base b, $f(x) = b^x$ and $g(x) = \log_b x$ are inverse functions. What does this mean if $b = 10$ and $x = 100$? What if $x = 5$?

Solution: That the base 10 exponential and logarithm functions are inverses means that $y = \log_{10} x \iff x = 10^y$. For $x = 100$ this says that

$$y = \log_{10} 100 \iff 100 = 10^y.$$

Since the second equation holds only when $y = 2$, it follows that $\log_{10} 100 = 2$.

What if $x = 5$? As any calculator knows, $\log_{10} 5 \approx 0.6989700041$. In this context, the inverse property says that $5 = 10^{0.6989700041}$—your calculator should agree. □

Does it? Exactly?

Inverse functions: the graphical view. The base e exponential and logarithm functions exp and ln are inverses. The same holds for base 2. The following graphs show what this means geometrically.

aka e^x and $\log_e x$

Logarithm and exponential functions are inverses

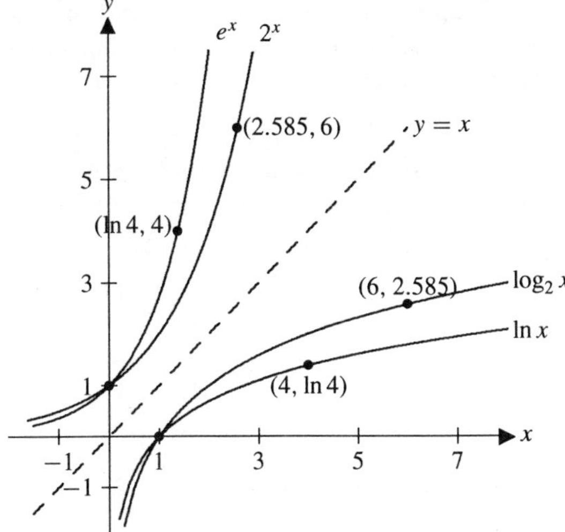

The graphs of inverse functions are symmetric with respect to the line $y = x$.

The picture suggests, too, why the base e is special. Look carefully:

To make the picture look right, we used horizontal and vertical units of equal size.

At the points $(0, 1)$ *and* $(1, 0)$ *the graphs of* $y = e^x$ *and* $y = \ln x$ *are parallel to each other and to the line* $y = x$.

The other two graphs don't have this property. At the moment, this property of e may seem unimportant, but it will soon prove surprisingly useful.

Logs or exponentials: which are simpler? The equation

$$y = \log_b x \iff x = b^y$$

can be taken to *define* the function $\log_b(x)$ in terms of the intuitively simpler exponential function b^x. To see that $\log_4 1.38703096913 \approx 0.236$, for example, we could check that $4^{0.236} \approx 1.38703096913$.

Does this approach to logarithms make sense? Are exponential functions really simpler than logarithm functions? In a strict logical sense, no: knowing either implies knowing the other. Intuitively, though, exponentiation is probably simpler than finding logarithms—just as squaring is simpler than finding square roots.

Defining logarithm functions *via* exponential functions is not the only possibility. The reverse strategy (to start with logarithms—defined without any reference to exponentials—and proceed to exponentials) is sometimes used. Although perhaps less intuitive, this approach can skirt troublesome technicalities.

Trigonometric functions

In geometry, sines, cosines, tangents, and other trigonometric quantities are defined as ratios of lengths of sides of right triangles. Here our point of view is different: we study sines, cosines, and other trigonometric objects as *functions* in their own right, connecting them only occasionally to right triangles. (For a review of trigonometric basics, see Appendix G.)

Why trigonometric functions matter

The most important property of the trigonometric functions—sine, cosine, tangent, etc.—is their repetitive, or **periodic**, behavior. The famous undulating graphs of the sine and cosine functions reflect this wave-like character:

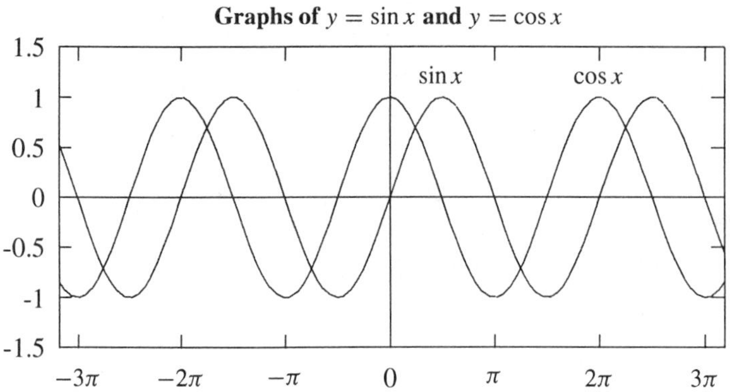

As always, the viewing window shows only part of the graph. In this case, what's shown is enough: the *full* graphs of the sine and cosine functions repeat the same pattern infinitely often.

Trigonometric functions defined: circular functions

For calculus purposes it's best to think of trigonometric functions in terms of circles, not triangles. The simplest circle—the **unit circle**—has radius 1 and center $(0, 0)$. In the uv-plane, the unit circle's equation is $u^2 + v^2 = 1$.

Calling it **the** *unit circle is a bit sloppy; many different circles have radius 1. But everyone does it.*

Using u and v here "saves" x and y for use below.

Imagine a point P, moving *counterclockwise* around the unit circle, starting from the **east pole** $(1, 0)$. As P moves endlessly around the unit circle, many related quantities vary as well: the u-coordinate of P, the v-coordinate of P, the slope of the segment from P to the origin, and others. *All* the trigonometric functions can be derived from these varying quantities. (For this reason, the sine and cosine functions are sometimes called **circular** functions.)

> **Definition:** For any real number x, let $P(x)$ be the point reached by moving x units of distance counterclockwise around the unit circle, starting from $(1, 0)$. (If $x < 0$, go clockwise.) Then
>
> $$\cos(x) = u\text{-coordinate of } P(x)$$
> $$\sin(x) = v\text{-coordinate of } P(x).$$

Here's the important picture:

It's worth many words; look carefully.

Defining $\sin x$ **and** $\cos x$

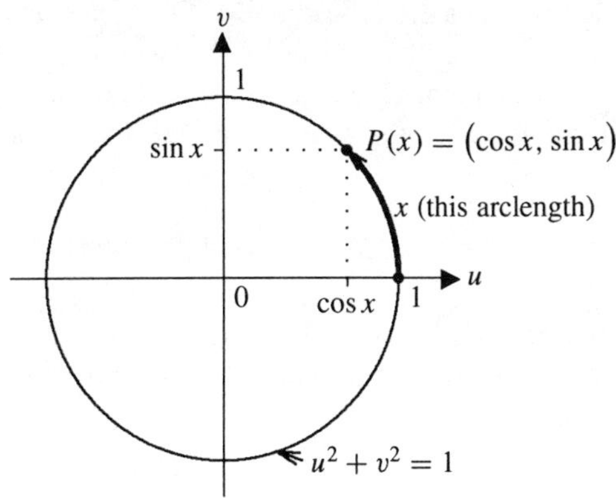

Simplest properties of the sine and cosine functions

Combining the definitions, the picture, the sine and cosine graphs, and a little reflection makes many properties of the sine and cosine functions evident.

Evident? Really? Mathematicians use words like "evident," "clear," and "trivial" in peculiar ways. "Evident" does not mean "immediately obvious," or "This stuff is transparent to everyone with the slightest aptitude for mathematics. If it isn't clear to you, go away and never come back." "Evident" really means "not difficult to convince oneself of with sufficient time and effort."

Domain and range. For *any* real number x, $\cos(x)$ and $\sin(x)$ are the coordinates of $P(x)$, the point x units of distance, measured counterclockwise, from $(1, 0)$. Thus *every* real number x is a legal input; the domain of both the sine and cosine functions is $(-\infty, \infty)$.

Recall: if $x < 0$, measure clockwise.

How do their graphs reflect this fact?

As our peripatetic point $P(x)$ circumnavigates the unit circle, its u- and v-coordinates fluctuate, but only between -1 and 1. Therefore, both functions share the same range: the closed interval $[-1, 1]$. In other words, for all x,

$$-1 \le \cos(x) \le 1 \qquad \text{and} \qquad -1 \le \sin(x) \le 1.$$

Famous values. The table below collects some important values of the sine and cosine functions:

Check some!

Famous Sines and Cosines

x	0	$\pi/2$	π	2π	$-\pi/2$	$\pi/4$
$P(x)$	$(1,0)$	$(0,1)$	$(-1,0)$	$(1,0)$	$(0,-1)$	$(\sqrt{2}/2, \sqrt{2}/2)$
$\cos(x)$	1	0	-1	1	0	$\sqrt{2}/2$
$\sin(x)$	0	1	0	0	-1	$\sqrt{2}/2$

Odd and even. It follows from the definition and the symmetry of the unit circle that the sine function is odd and the cosine function is even. In symbols:

How do their graphs show this?

$$\sin(-x) = -\sin(x) \qquad \text{and} \qquad \cos(-x) = \cos(x).$$

Trigonometric functions are 2π-periodic. For any real number x, the points $P(x)$ and $P(x + 2\pi)$ are identical. Therefore, both the sine and cosine functions repeat themselves, as the graphs show, on each interval of length 2π. In math-speak: the sine and cosine functions are **2π-periodic**. In symbols:

Do you see why? [HINT: What's the circumference of the unit circle?.]

$$\sin(x + 2\pi) = \sin(x) \qquad \text{and} \qquad \cos(x + 2\pi) = \cos(x).$$

A famous trigonometric identity. For any real number x the point $P(x) = \big(\cos(x), \sin(x)\big)$ lies on the unit circle, so the coordinates of P must satisfy the defining equation $u^2 + v^2 = 1$. Therefore

$$\left(\sin x\right)^2 + \left(\cos x\right)^2 = 1.$$

Equations like this one, that relate various trigonometric functions to each other, are called **trigonometric identities**. Many trigonometric identities exist; for more information, see the Appendix G.

(No parentheses?) Trigonometric, exponential, and logarithm expressions are often typeset without parentheses. For example,

$$\sin(x), \quad \ln(x), \quad \sin x, \quad \text{and} \quad \ln x$$

are all syntactically correct, but the last two are typographically standard. When confusion seems likely we'll use parentheses.

No algebraic formulas. Might the sine and cosine functions have simple algebraic formulas? Alas, no: trigonometric functions are known to be **transcendental**, i.e. they *can't* be written as algebraic combinations of powers, roots, sums, products, etc.

On the other hand, the trigonometric functions are far from mysterious; they've been studied, tabulated, and used for centuries. Even cheap calculators produce highly accurate values of these functions. How do they do it? Stay tuned . . .

Other trigonometric functions

Four additional trigonometric functions are defined in terms of the sine and cosine functions.

Definition: For real numbers x,

$$\tan x = \frac{\sin x}{\cos x} \qquad \cot x = \frac{\cos x}{\sin x}$$

$$\sec x = \frac{1}{\cos x} \qquad \csc x = \frac{1}{\sin x}$$

Pieces of the graphs of these functions appear below. Pieces are enough: like the sine and cosine functions, these repeat on every interval of length 2π. (In fact, the tangent and cotangent functions turn out to repeat even on intervals of length π. Appendix G explains why.)

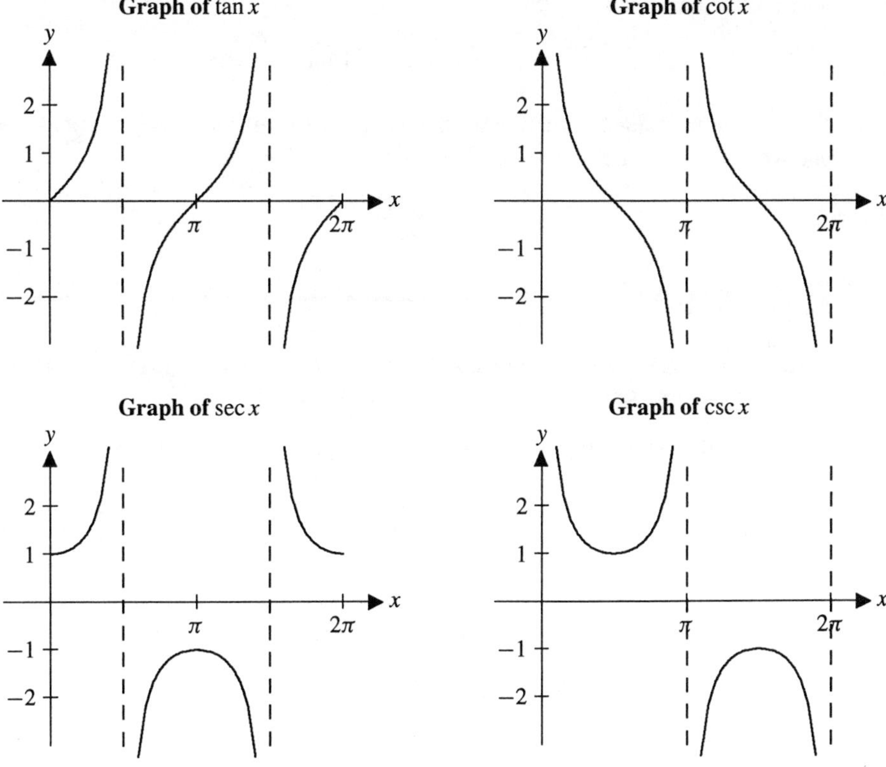

Properties of the "other" trigonometric functions

As legitimate children of the sine and cosine functions, the tangent, cotangent, secant, and cosecant functions inherit certain properties from their parents, but have their own personalities too.

Domains and ranges. Because the sine and cosine functions are defined for *all* real numbers, the "other" trigonometric functions are also defined for all real numbers *except* those at which a denominator is zero. The domain of the cosecant function, for instance, consists of all real numbers that *aren't* integer multiples of π.

As their graphs show, the range of the tangent and cotangent functions is $(-\infty, \infty)$—*all* real numbers are possible outputs. Outputs from the secant and cosecant functions, by contrast, must have absolute value greater than one. Thus, in interval language, the secant and cosecant functions have range $(-\infty, -1] \cup [1, \infty)$.

Asymptotes. The tangent, cotangent, secant, and cosecant functions all have vertical asymptotes. The asymptotes of the tangent function are discussed in detail below.

Functional properties. The following properties of the "other" trigonometric functions follow directly from their definitions. Each holds for all inputs t in the given function's domain:

Convince yourself carefully of each one, using only the definitions and the properties of the sine and cosine functions. Then observe how the graphs reflect each property.

- $|\sec x| \geq 1$
- $|\csc x| \geq 1$
- $\tan(-x) = -\tan x$
- $\sec(-x) = \sec x$

The tangent function, the unit circle, and slope. Like the sine and cosine functions, the tangent function has an important, pleasing *geometric* interpretation in terms of the unit circle:

$$\tan x = \frac{\sin x}{\cos x} = \text{slope of the line from the origin to } P(x).$$

Interpreting the tangent function as slope shows, for instance, why $\tan(\pi/4) = 1$, and why $\tan x \to \pm\infty$ as $x \to \pi/2$.

Exercises

1. Let (x_1, y_1) and (x_2, y_2) be points on the line $y = -2(x-1)+3$. If $x_1 < x_2$, what can be said about y_1 and y_2? How do you know?

2. Let (x_1, y_1) and (x_2, y_2) be points on the line $y = 3(x+1)-2$. If $y_1 < y_2$, what can be said about x_1 and x_2? How do you know?

3. Do the points shown in the table below lie on a line? If so, find an equation of the line. Justify your answers.

x	5.2	5.3	5.4	5.6	5.9	6.5
y	27.8	29.2	30.6	33.4	37.6	46.0

4. Do the points shown in the table below lie on a line? If so, find an equation of the line. Justify your answers.

x	0	1	3	6	10	15
y	0.000	0.785	1.249	1.406	1.471	1.504

5. (a) Give an example of a polynomial of even degree that defines an even function.

   (b) Does *every* polynomial of even degree define an even function? Why or why not?

6. Find an algebraic expression for a rational function that has *vertical* asymptotes at $x = -1$ and $x = 2$, and that has the line $y = 3$ as a *horizontal* asymptote. (Check your answer by graphing.)

7. Suppose that the lines $y = 3$ and $y = -3$ are horizontal asymptotes of a continuous function f and that f has no vertical asymptotes.

   (a) Explain why f cannot be a polynomial function.

   (b) Can f be a rational function? Justify your answer.

8. Find the domain and range of each of the following functions.

   (a) $\sin(3x - 1)$

   (b) $\sqrt{\cos x}$

   (c) $\sqrt[3]{\sin x}$

   (d) $1 + 2\cos(3x)$

   (e) e^{x^2}

   (f) $\ln\left(x^2\right)$

   (g) $\exp\left(x^3 + 1\right)$

   (h) $\ln\left(x^3 + 1\right)$

   (i) $\exp\left(x^2 - 8x + 15\right)$

   (j) $\ln\left(x^2 - 8x + 15\right)$

9. Let $f(x) = \ln(2 + \sin x)$.

   (a) Evaluate $f(0)$, $f(\pi/6)$, and $f(\pi/2)$ using a calculator.

   (b) What are the domain and range of f?

   (c) Is f even? Odd? Neither? Justify your answer.

   (d) Is f periodic? If so, find its period. If not, explain why not.

10. Which of the following functions is even? Odd? Neither? [HINTS: One way is to examine a graph of each function. Another, better, way is to use the facts that *sine* is an odd function and *cosine* is an even function.]

    (a) $\sec x$

    (b) $|\cos x|$

    (c) $|\sin x|$

    (d) $1 + \cot x$

    (e) $\cos x + \sec x$

    (f) $\sec x + \csc x$

11. By looking at graphs, find the period of each of the following functions.

(a) $\cot x$
(b) $\sec x$
(c) $\csc x$
(d) $\cos^2 x$
(e) $|\sin x|$
(f) $\sin(2x)$
(g) $\sin(x/2)$
(h) $|2\cos x|$

12. Let $f(x) = \ln(x^3)$ and $g(x) = \ln(x^2)$.

(a) What is the domain of f?
(b) Explain how to obtain the graph of f from the graph of $y = \ln x$.
(c) What is the domain of g?
(d) Explain how to obtain the graph of g from the graph of $y = \ln x$.

13. Suppose that $y = 20x + 1$ is an equation of the line that intersects the curve $y = b^x$ at $x = 0$ and $x = 4$.

(a) Find the number b.
(b) What is the slope of the line that intersects the curve $y = \log_b x$ at $x = 1$ and $x = 81$?

14. Each of the four functions graphed below is described by an algebraic expression having *one* of the following forms:

(i) $f(x) = Ax + B$
(ii) $f(x) = Ax^2 + B$
(iii) $f(x) = A\cos x + B$
(iv) $f(x) = \cos(Ax) + B$
(v) $f(x) = A\sin x + B$
(vi) $f(x) = \sin(Ax) + B$
(vii) $f(x) = 3^{(x+A)} + B$
(viii) $f(x) = \log_2(x + A) + B$

where A and B are real numbers.

For each graph below, decide which expression corresponds to that function and find appropriate numerical values for the parameters A and B. Explain each choice in a sentence or two.

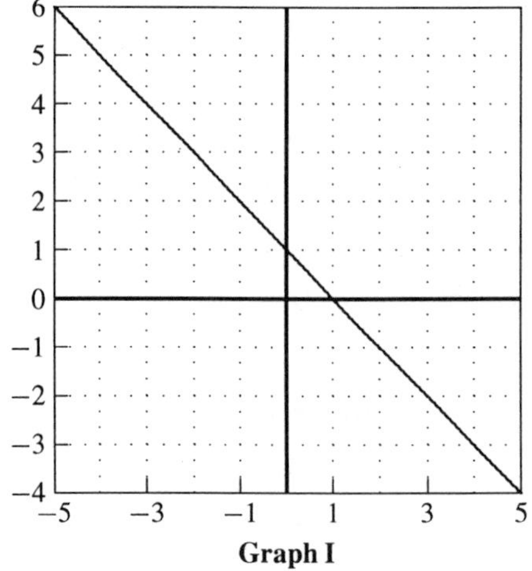

Graph I

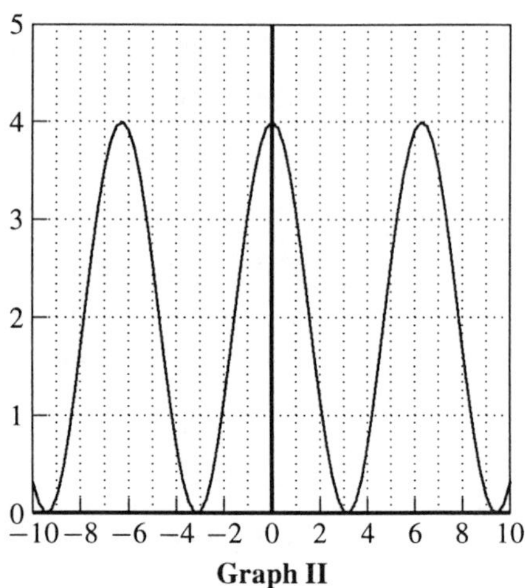

Graph II

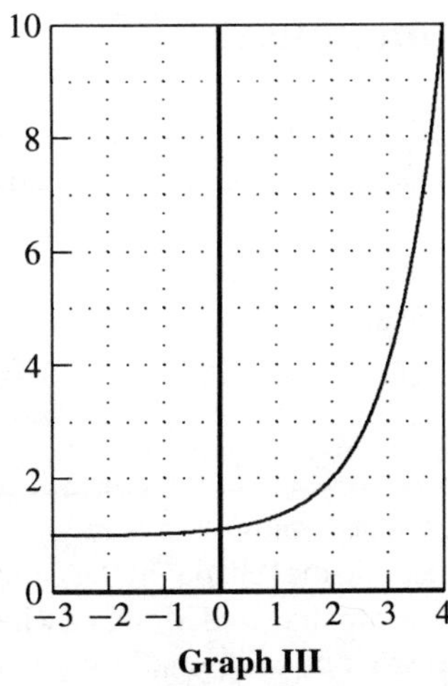

Graph III

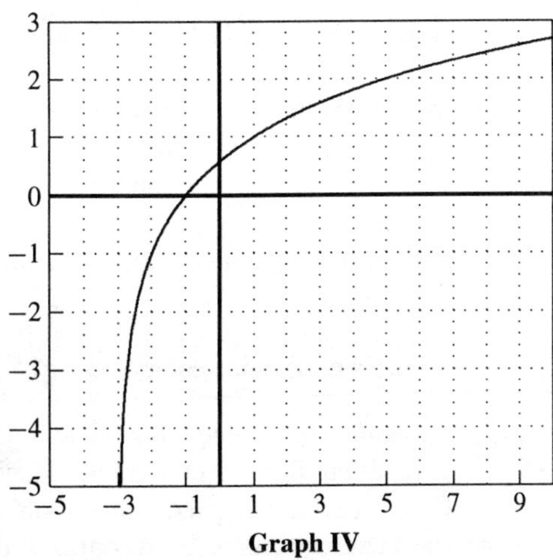

Graph IV

15. Each statement below shows that the sine function is *not* a polynomial. Explain why.

    (a) The equation $\sin x = 0$ has infinitely many solutions ($x = n\pi$ is a solution for every $n \in \mathbb{Z}$).

    (b) The sine function is bounded below by -1 and above by 1 (i.e., for every x, $-1 \leq \sin x \leq 1$).

1.6 Modeling with elementary functions

Why do the basic elementary function families—algebraic, exponential, and trigonometric—deserve their starring roles in calculus? What makes these particular functions uniquely valuable and important?

One answer is entirely practical: Elementary functions can be used to "model" real-world phenomena. We'll illustrate with several examples.

What is mathematical modeling?

To *model* a phenomenon—the U.S. Consumer Price Index, snowshoe hare and fox populations in the Arctic, gravitational forces on spacecraft, the "shape" of the Golden Gate Bridge, heating requirements in Minnesota, demand for hard red Montana wheat, risks and benefits of birth control drugs, varying weights of one-pound loaves, the progress of AIDS, Big Mac prices over the years—mathematically is to *describe* or *represent* the phenomenon quantitatively, in mathematical language.

All mathematical models have two important features:

Simplification: No model, mathematical or not, reproduces every property or aspect of the thing modeled. Every model necessarily *simplifies*, more or less, the reality it describes. A useful model is simple enough to permit calculations, but detailed enough to capture the *essence* of the phenomenon modeled.

Prediction: A useful mathematical model must do more than describe already-observed behavior: It should also help us predict or understand the behavior in question.

The process of mathematical modeling involves three steps:

Description: describing a phenomenon in mathematical language, using mathematical ingredients: functions, variables, equations, etc.

Deduction: deducing mathematical consequences of the mathematical description.

Interpretation: interpreting mathematical results in the language of the phenomenon under study.

Polynomials, rational functions, and the physical world

Polynomials and rational functions are among the simplest functions, because they're built using only the familiar arithmetic operations. Despite their simplicity, these functions nicely model a surprising number and variety of real-world physical phenomena.

Addition, multiplication, subtraction, and division.

Parabolic trajectories. What sort of path (or **trajectory**) does a "projectile" (a thrown baseball, say, or an airborne high jumper) describe during its flight from the ground into the air and back again? The general shape—some sort of "arch"—is clear enough, but how can we describe the trajectory mathematically? Is it a parabola? Part of a circle? One arch of a sine curve? Here are curves of all three types:

A semicircle, a parabola, and a sine curve: is one a trajectory?

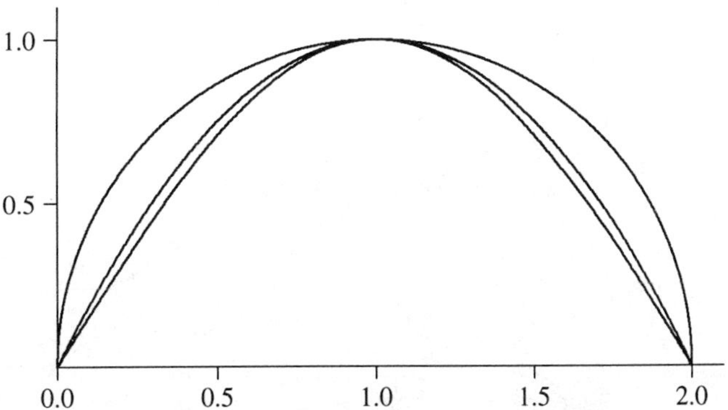

All three curves *look* possible at first glance, but only one is correct. It's a striking fact of mathematical physics that under "ideal" conditions a projectile influenced only by the force of gravity follows a *parabolic* trajectory. Later, using calculus tools, we'll be able to explain exactly *why* this fact holds. For now we'll *assume* it, in the following form:

Actually, one is less convincing than the other two. For more, see the exercises.

E.g., ignoring wind resistance, glider effects, and other stray forces.

Fact: Suppose that a projectile leaves the origin with initial velocity v_0, aimed along the line $y = mx$, and influenced only by gravity. The projectile's trajectory is a parabola, given by the quadratic equation

$$y = mx - \frac{g}{2v_0^2}(1 + m^2)x^2.$$

(g is the (constant) acceleration due to gravity.)

We'll use the formula in several ways, but first note:

Initial angle. The projectile's line of aim can be described either by its *slope* m, as above, or by the *angle* θ the line makes with the positive x- axis. In this case, $m = \tan\theta$, and the trajectory equation becomes

Is it clear that $m = \tan\theta$? For more, see the exercises.

$$y = x\tan\theta - \frac{g}{2v_0^2}(1 + \tan^2\theta)x^2.$$

Units. The formulas above "work" only with consistently-chosen units of measurement. If x and y (which measure horizontal and vertical distance) are measured in feet, and v_0 in feet per second, then $g = 32$ feet per second per second. If, instead, x and y are measured in meters and v_0 in meters per second, then $g = 9.8$ meters per second per second.

■ **Example 1.** A pitcher standing at the origin throws baseballs along the positive x-axis, always with initial velocity 128 feet per second, but aiming along various lines $y = mx$. Describe the possible trajectories.

About 87 miles per hour—typical in the major leagues.

Solution: In present units, $v_0 = 128$ and $g = 32$, so a trajectory with initial slope m has the form

Check that we've worked out the constants correctly.

$$y = mx - \frac{1 + m^2}{1024}x^2 = -\frac{1 + m^2}{1024}x\left(x - \frac{1024m}{1 + m^2}\right).$$

Here are trajectory curves for many values of m:

The equations make sense in context only when $y \geq 0$, of course.

Baseball trajectories

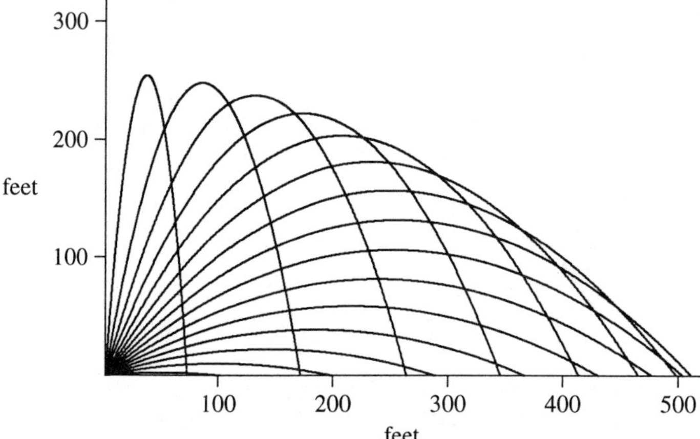

Observe:

Various shapes. Every trajectory parabola begins at the origin. Depending on its initial slope m, a trajectory may be either tall and narrow or short and squat. As the picture shows, balls that fly farthest have trajectories somewhere *between* these two extremes. In the next example we'll discuss how to maximize the ball's horizontal range.

Check our work.

Back to earth. When a ball hits the ground, its trajectory function is zero. As the formulas above show, each trajectory parabola has *two* roots: $x = 0$, where the ball starts, and

$$x_{\max} = 1024\frac{m}{1+m^2},$$

where the ball lands. (If, say, $m = 1$, then $x_{\max} = 1024/2 = 512$ feet.)

A parabola is symmetric about the vertical line through its vertex.

At the peak. Knowing $x_{\max}$ lets us find $y_{\max}$, the ball's height at its peak. The symmetry of parabolas means that every trajectory peaks exactly *halfway* from $x = 0$ to $x = x_{\max}$, i.e., at $x_{\text{middle}} = 512m/(1+m^2)$. This value of x gives the ball's maximum height for any given m:

$$y_{\max} = 256\frac{m^2}{1+m^2}.$$

□

■ **Example 2.** Consider again the situation of Example 1. With what initial slope m should the ball be thrown to rise as high as possible? What initial slope gives the maximum possible "range?"

And we'll hope that our calculations agree . . .

Or, equivalently, $\theta = 45$ degrees.

Solution: We'll start with common sense. Intuition says that to throw a ball as *high* as possible it should be aimed straight up. To throw as *far* as possible, we want a trajectory that's neither too tall nor too flat: setting $m = 1$ seems a reasonable compromise.

To check these guesses algebraically, we'll consider two functions of the initial slope m. For any given slope $m \geq 0$, let $f(m)$ be the peak *height* attained, and $g(m)$ the horizontal *distance* traveled. As we showed above, f and g can be written as functions of m:

Both f and g are rational functions of m.

$$f(m) = 256\frac{m^2}{1+m^2}; \qquad g(m) = 1024\frac{m}{1+m^2}.$$

Plotting f and g suggests answers to our questions:

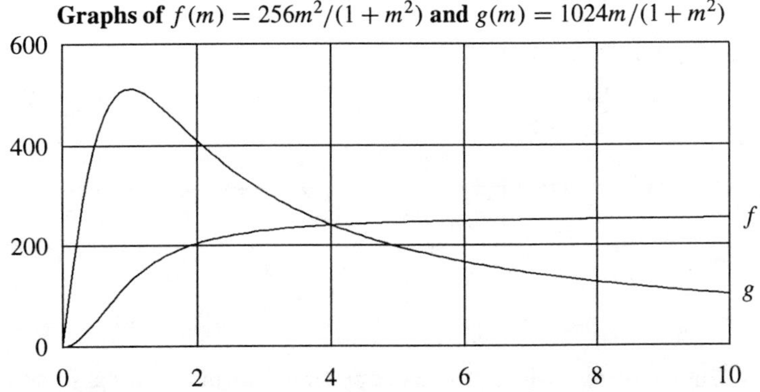

As its graph suggests, the height function f increases with m. Specifically, as $m \to \infty$,

Note the horizontal asymptote.

$$256\frac{m^2}{1+m^2} \to 256.$$

In baseball terms: As the slope m gets larger and larger (and the line of aim approaches the vertical), the ball's maximum height approaches 256 feet.

The g-graph suggests (as we guessed above) that the range function peaks at or near $m = 1$, where $g(1) = 512$ feet. Using ideas from calculus we'll soon be able to show this rigorously, by calculation. Until then, graphical evidence will do. In baseball terms: *For maximum range, aim the ball 45 degrees above the horizon.* □

See the exercises for an algebraic approach to the same problem.

Do real baseball players obey this rule? Do shot-putters?

Exponential functions, college tuition, and growth with interest

Exponential functions model phenomena that grow, like undisturbed bank accounts, "with interest." A fable will illustrate.

Ingrid and Eric. Ingrid was born on Labor Day, 1991. Her family is poor, but her wealthy Uncle Eric is determined that Ingrid should someday enroll at St. Lena College, where he himself attended. To this end, Eric resolves to pay Ingrid's first-year comprehensive fee at St. Lena. (After a year, Eric thinks, college students should fend for themselves.) If all goes well, Ingrid will enter St. Lena on Labor Day, 2010, her 19th birthday.

Eric's problem. Uncle Eric, ever prudent, wants to deposit the money *now*, at Ingrid's birth. Tax-sheltered 19-year bonds are available, paying 8% annually. Eric wants to cover Ingrid's first-year fee, but not trips to Fort Lauderdale or other foolishness. How much should he deposit now? Would \$14,300—the 1991 fee at St. Lena—be enough?

The crucial question, of course, is St. Lena's fee in the year 2010. Uncle Eric can't hope to *know* it 19 years ahead, but perhaps he can *estimate* it, based on past history. He starts by collecting St. Lena annual fee information, dating back to 1961 when the fee was \$1575. Looking for a pattern, he plots these data. (For convenience, he lets $t = 0$ correspond to the year 1960.)

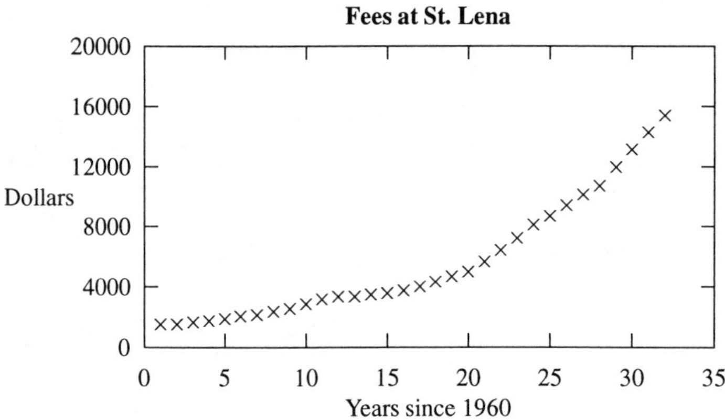

"Hmmm," thinks Eric, "looks exponential to me. Might some exponential-type formula 'fit' these data? If so, I could use the formula to *estimate* St. Lena's fee in 2010."

Uncle Eric fits a curve. Curious, Uncle Eric tries plotting functions of the form

$$f(t) = ae^{bt},$$

for various constants a and b, along with the fee data. Rusty on theory, Eric relies on trial and error. Eventually, he settles on the function

$$f(t) = 1350e^{0.07606t},$$

based on this graph:

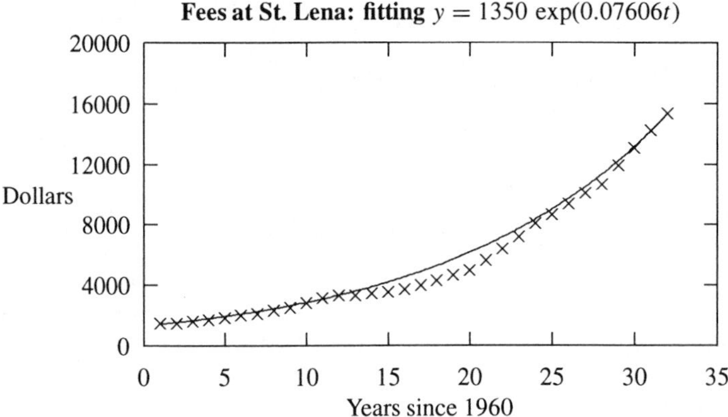

The year 2010 corresponds to $t = 50$.

"A nice fit," thinks Eric. "If this keeps up, in 2010 I'd expect St. Lena to charge about

$$f(50) = 1350\,e^{0.07606 \cdot 50} \approx 60527.91.$$

What books will cost in 2010 we leave to the reader's imagination.

What the heck—I'll make it a round \$60550; the kid will need something for books."

Uncle Eric plans ahead. How much should Eric deposit for Ingrid *now?*

Well, 8% interest, compounded annually, means that on each Labor Day, Ingrid's *old* balance is multiplied by 1.08. In functional language, let $P(t)$ denote the value of the deposit after t years; then the initial deposit—still to be determined—is $P(0)$. Here's what happens over time:

$$\begin{aligned} P(1) &= P(0) \cdot 1.08 \\ P(2) &= P(1) \cdot 1.08 = P(0) \cdot 1.08^2 \\ P(3) &= P(2) \cdot 1.08 = P(0) \cdot 1.08^3 \\ &\vdots \\ P(t) &= P(t-1) \cdot 1.08 = P(0) \cdot 1.08^t \end{aligned}$$

Now we can solve for $P(0)$, the initial deposit. We want $P(19) = P(0) \cdot 1.08^{19} = 60550$, so

$$P(0) = \frac{60550}{1.08^{19}} \approx 14030.17.$$

How it ended, and the moral. Uncle Eric put $14,030.17—not quite this year's fee—into 19-year bonds. Baby Ingrid, though still an infant, looks already like college material.

The fable hints at an important—the *most* important—use of exponential functions: modeling the behavior of quantities that grow (or shrink) under the influence of "interest." Financial quantities most familiarly exhibit such behavior, but so do others: populations, radioactive masses and many more.

We'll revisit exponential growth in Chapter 4.

Do models describe or predict? With a little mathematics and lots of hindsight, we could "fit" the St. Lena tuition's *past* behavior as well as we like. For example, it's possible (although messy) to find a polynomial function, of degree 30 or so, whose graph "hits" every one of the 31 points plotted above. Such a function might be said to *describe* the past, but must it also accurately *predict* the future?

No!

How accurately *any* mathematical model can be expected to predict behavior is a difficult and subtle question. The answer depends on many factors, some non-mathematical: the nature and complexity of the phenomenon being modeled, the reliability and validity of the observed data, and other factors.

Trigonometric functions: modeling weather

Minnesota weather is famous for its wild swings. Averaged over many years, however, even the weather becomes surprisingly predictable. Weather phenomena are by nature periodic, so it's natural to use trigonometric functions in weather models.

Temperature in Minneapolis. Plotting average weekly temperatures in Minneapolis produces a familiar shape:

From U.S. Weather Service data. Notice the horizontal scale—the "year" starts around March 21.

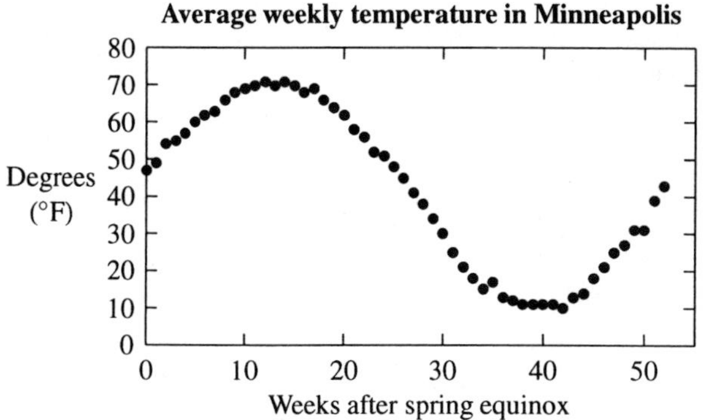

Although the plot *resembles* a sine curve, the unembellished formula $y = \sin x$ clearly doesn't "fit" the data:

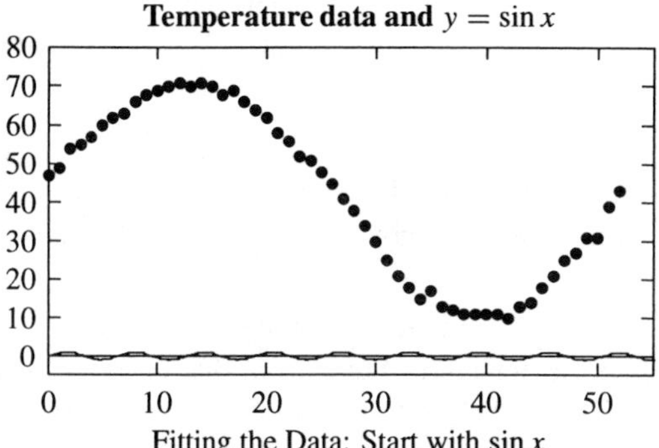

Fitting the Data: Start with $\sin x$

Unpromising as the graph above may seem, we'll persevere. Weather varies periodically (In an average sense, at least.) so it's reasonable to expect some **sinusoidal function**

$$a \sin(bx + c) + d$$

to "fit" our data, at least approximately. Our problem, then, is to choose appropriate values for a, b, c, and d.

A close look at the temperature scatterplot tells a lot:

A vertical center. The temperature data are *vertically* centered around 42 degrees Fahrenheit. An appropriate sinusoid, therefore, should be lifted 42 units up. We'll try $d = 42$.

High and low temperatures. The maximum and minimum temperatures—72 and 11 degrees respectively—suggest a vertical variation of about (*There's no shame in the word "about"—mathematical modeling is an inexact science!*) 31 degrees Fahrenheit in each direction. This argues for stretching the sine function vertically with factor $a = 31$.

Stretching the period. The period for temperature data is 52 weeks; the sine function's period is 2π. To match things up we'll have to *stretch* the sine curve horizontally, with factor $52/(2\pi)$. Setting $b = 2\pi/52 \approx 0.12083$ has this effect.

No horizontal shift. The scatterplot suggests that *no* horizontal shift is needed: the sinusoid seems to "start" at the left. Thus we'll set $c = 0$. (*We arranged this by starting our one-year period in spring. This does no harm. Had we insisted on an ordinary calendar year we would have needed a non-zero horizontal shift, i.e., a non-zero value of c.*)

Combining these observations argues for selecting the sinusoid

$$y = 31 \sin\left(\frac{2\pi}{52}x\right) + 42$$

as our best guess to fit the data. The remaining plots show the effects of adding these parameters one by one to the basic sine function.

Setting $d = 42$ produces a vertical shift:

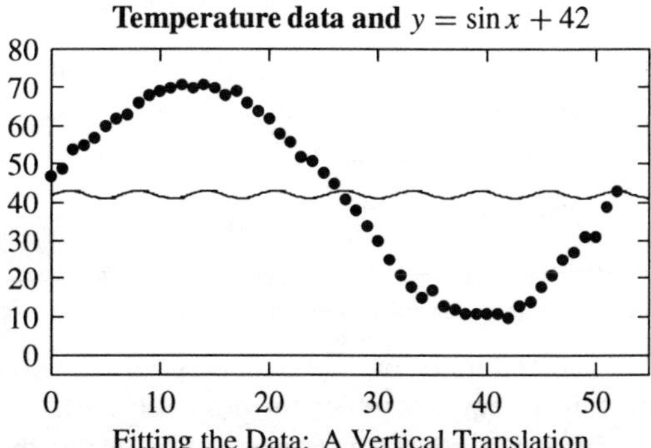

Fitting the Data: A Vertical Translation

Far too flat; setting $a = 31$ turns up the "amplitude":

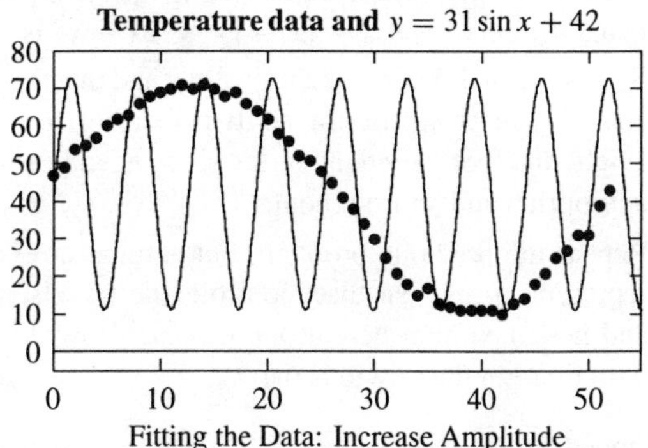

Fitting the Data: Increase Amplitude

We're wiggling too fast; including $b = 2\pi/52$ stretches the period:

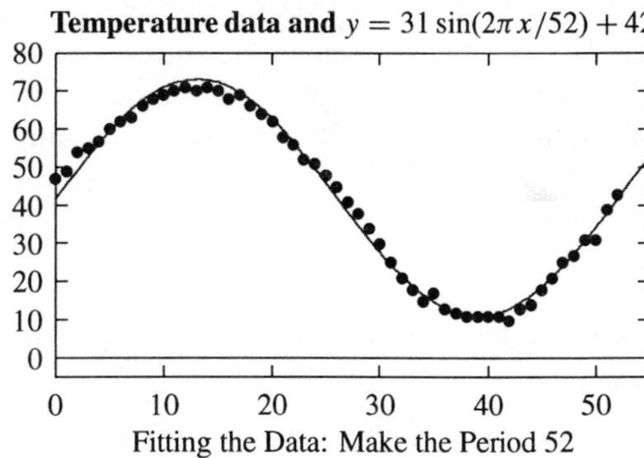

Fitting the Data: Make the Period 52

Much better.

■ **Example 3.** Predict the mean temperature in Minneapolis on December 31.

Solution: December 31 falls 40 weeks and 5 days (i.e., 40.71 weeks) after the spring equinox. The formula predicts a mean temperature of

$$42 + 31 \sin\left(\frac{2\pi}{52} \cdot 40.71\right) \approx 11.7^\circ \mathrm{F}.$$

□

Exercises

1. Consider again the three curves in the picture on page 73. (The curves are candidates for trajectories of an ideal projectile.)

   (a) The three curves have three points in common. Assign these points the coordinates $(0, 0)$, $(1, 1)$, and $(2, 0)$, respectively. In this system, the three curves have equations

   $$y = \sqrt{1-(x-1)^2}, \quad y = 1-(x-1)^2, \quad \text{and} \quad y = \sin\left(\frac{\pi}{2}x\right).$$

   Which curve has which equation? How do you know?

   (b) The *angle* a trajectory curve makes with the ground (i.e., the horizontal axis) is the angle at which the projectile is "fired." Estimate these angles (in radians) for the three curves shown. Using the result, explain why the semicircle *cannot* be a trajectory curve.

   (c) The Fact on page 73 says that among the three candidate curves, only the quadratic curve $y = 1-(x-1)^2 = 2x - x^2$ is a trajectory.

   Suppose that this curve *is* a trajectory, and that the x- and y-units represent *feet* (so the projectile travels two feet horizontally and has maximum height one foot). Find the initial slope m and the initial velocity v_0. (Use appropriate units throughout.)

   (d) Repeat the previous problem, but assume now that the x- and y-units represent *meters* (so that the projectile travels two meters horizontally and has maximum height one meter). How do your answers compare with those in the previous part?

2. We claimed in this section that if θ is the angle from the positive x-axis to the line $y = mx$, then $m = \tan\theta$. Explain why, using the right triangle with vertices $(0, 0)$, $(1, 0)$, and $(1, m)$.

3. All parts of this problem refer to the situation of Example 1, page 73. In particular, assume throughout that a ball thrown from the origin with initial slope m and initial velocity 128 feet per second follows the trajectory curve

   $$y = mx - \frac{1+m^2}{1024}x^2.$$

   (a) Show that the ball lands at $x = \dfrac{1024m}{1+m^2}$ feet. (The ball lands where $y = 0$.)

   (b) Let m be given. At what value of x is the ball highest? (Since the trajectory is a parabola, the vertex occurs halfway between the x-intercepts.)

   (c) Let m be given. How high is the ball at its "peak"? (Use the previous result.)

   (d) Use results of the previous part to complete the table below:

m	0.1	0.5	1.0	2.0	10.0	
peak height						255.9

   (e) A ball thrown *straight up* with initial velocity 128 feet per second rises 256 feet. Give an informal reason why, using results from the previous part.

4. In Example 2 we claimed that if $g(m) = 1024m/(1+m^2)$, then $g(1) = 512$ is the largest possible value of g. Equivalently, $m = 1/2$ is the largest possible value of $m/(1+m^2)$.

   Prove the latter claim by justifying each step below:

$$\begin{aligned} 0 \le (1-m)^2 &\implies 0 \le 1 - 2m + m^2 \\ &\implies 2m \le 1 + m^2 \\ &\implies \frac{m}{1+m^2} \le \frac{1}{2}. \end{aligned}$$

5. **(The danger zone.)** A curious bird flies over the baseball field of Example 1. The bird wants to see what's happening—but also to avoid thrown balls. How high must the bird fly to be safe? (If you find this scenario unconvincing, then try this: what shape should the stadium's roof have to avoid being hit by thrown balls?)

   The answer depends, of course, on x: the bird's danger zone is tall for x near zero but gets shorter as x takes larger and larger positive values; for sufficiently large x, the bird is safe even on the ground.

   The bird's danger zone is defined by still *another* curve. Here's the picture:

   Baseball trajectories and their upper envelope

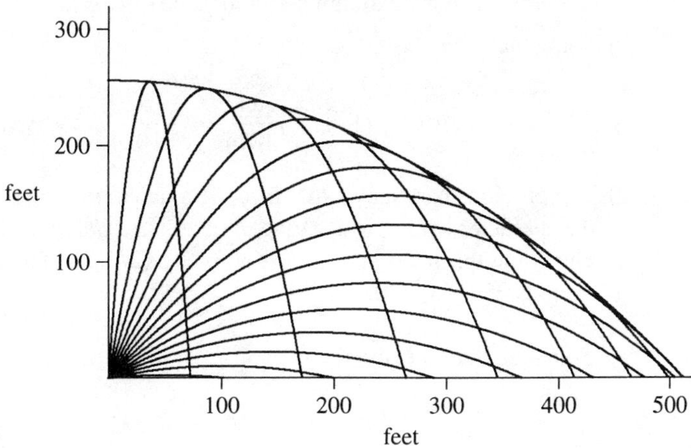

   The curve on top is called the **upper envelope** of our family of baseball trajectories. In this problem we'll study the upper envelope curve.

   (a) We said in Example 2: (i) a ball thrown straight upward at 128 feet per second rises to 256 feet; (ii) the maximum horizontal range for any trajectory is 512 feet. Use these facts to label the x- and y-intercepts of your upper envelope curve.

   (b) The upper envelope curve *looks* like half a parabola, but *is* it really parabolic? If so, its equation must be of the form $y = a - bx^2$, for some constants a and b. Use this fact and results from the previous part of this problem to find numerical values for a and b.

   (c) (This part requires a graphing calculator or other plotting technology.) Using your results from the previous part, plot the parabola $y = a - bx^2$ and the trajectory curves for $m = 0.5$, $m = 1.0$, $m = 2.0$, and $m = 4.0$— all on the same axes. Use the window $[0, 600] \times [0, 300]$. Does your picture suggest that you've chosen the upper envelope curve correctly? Why or why not?

6. The previous problem gives convincing graphical evidence that the upper envelope curve for the baseball trajectories is (like the trajectories themselves) a parabola. A rigorous proof of this fact requires some careful algebraic manipulation. Provide one, using the outline below.

   (a) Let $q(t) = at^2 + bt + c$ be a quadratic polynomial in t; a, b, and c are constants, with $a \neq 0$. Show that $q(t)$ can be written in the form
   $$q(t) = a\left(t + \frac{b}{2a}\right)^2 + \left(c - \frac{b^2}{4a}\right).$$
   Conclude from this (explain your reasoning) that the parabola $y = q(t)$ has its *vertex* at $t = -b/2a$.

   (b) Let u be the function whose graph is the upper envelope for the baseball trajectories. We want to show that for any fixed x_0 between 0 feet (the minimum horizontal range) and 512 feet (the maximum range), $u(x_0)$ is given by a quadratic expression in x_0. (We'll use x_0 rather than x to emphasize that—for now—x_0 is a *fixed* number.)

   Let $h(m)$ denote the height at x_0 of the trajectory curve with initial slope m. Explain:

   $u(x_0)$ is the maximum possible value of $h(m)$.

   (c) Show that for $m > 0$,
   $$h(m) = mx_0 - (1 + m^2)\frac{x_0^2}{1024} = -\frac{x_0^2}{1024}m^2 + x_0 m - \frac{x_0^2}{1024}.$$

   (d) The previous part shows that $h(m)$ is a quadratic function of m. Since the coefficient of m^2 is negative, h takes a *maximum* value at its vertex. Show that this maximum occurs at $m = 512/x_0$, and that the maximum value is $256 - x_0^2/1024$.

   (e) Conclude that $u(x_0) = 256 - \dfrac{x_0^2}{1024}$, so the upper envelope is indeed a parabola.

7. According to Uncle Eric's model, St. Lena's tuition doubles every X years. What is X? Why?

1.7 Chapter summary

Chapter 1 is a general introduction, and fly-by overview, of some of the objects, ideas, uses, and techniques of calculus.

Functions: more than formulas. The most important idea in Chapter 1 is that of **function**. We expect that most readers will be familiar, from pre-calculus experience, with functions like this one—

$$f(x) = x^2 + \frac{3}{x} + \sqrt{x}$$

that are **defined by formulas**. Such functions will indeed play important roles in this book. More characteristic of Chapter 1, however, are functions defined in *other ways*: by graphs, by tables, in words, etc. An important goal of this book is to understand calculus ideas from graphical and numerical (as well as algebraic) points of view. In real-world practice, moreover, functions seldom appear ready-made as formulas.

Graphs: pictures of functions. Formulas, even simple ones, give little sense of how a function behaves for various inputs. **Graphs**, by contrast, are ideally suited for this purpose. Graphs give functions a *geometric*, not just symbolic, meaning. Graphs, best of all, show how functions *vary*—when they rise, when they fall, when they're concave up or down, etc. All of these properties are crucially important in calculus itself, but even more so in applications of the subject.

Machine graphics. With machines—computers and calculators—*drawing* accurate graphs becomes easy. What remains is the good stuff: *interpreting* what graphs say. Doing so is an unending refrain throughout this book.

Using machines effectively to plot functions requires some care—things can go wrong—and some familiarity with newfangled jargon: **xrange**, **yrange**, **plotting windows**, **aspect ratio**, etc. Such niceties are discussed in Section 1.3.

Functions, formally. Truly understanding "function" means understanding the idea's three main parts: **rule**, **domain**, and **range**. Section 1.4 treats such things, with many examples. The variety is important: seeing function ideas and terminology in various settings helps clarify what they mean in *any* setting.

A field guide to elementary functions. Section 1.5 introduces the cast of leading functional characters in calculus. Many of the functions we'll treat in calculus are **elementary**—"built" by combining members of the leading function families: algebraic, trigonometric, exponential, and logarithm functions. We meet these function families only briefly in Section 1.5. Many more details about each family appear in the Appendices and in later sections.

Exercises

1. Suppose that f is a function such that $-2 < f(x) < 8$ for all x in $[-5, 5]$. Indicate whether each of the following statements must be true, might be true, or is false. Justify your answers.

   (a) $f(-5) = -2$
   (b) $f(1) < 17$
   (c) $f(0) > 1$
   (d) $f(10) < 8$
   (e) $-10 < f(4) < 12$
   (f) $|f(-4)| < 9$
   (g) $|f(3) - 4| < 7$
   (h) $|f(-2) + 5| > 1$
   (i) -10 is a lower bound for f on $[-5, 5]$
   (j) 100 is an upper bound for f on $[-5, 5]$

2. Let f be the function whose graph appears below.

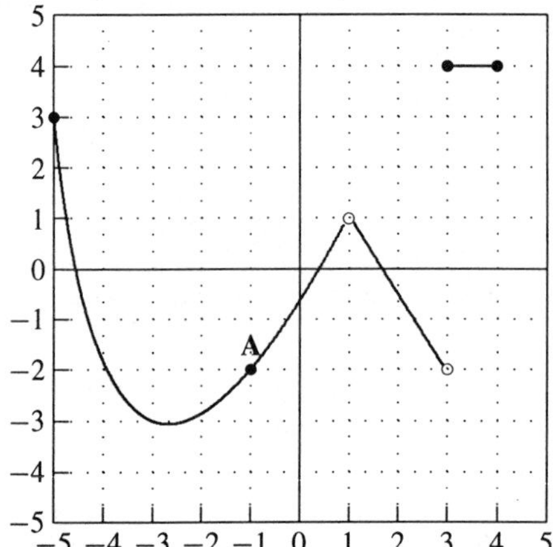

   (a) What is the domain of f?
   (b) What is the range of f?
   (c) Find (i.e., estimate) $f(-4)$, $f(0)$, and $f(3)$.
   (d) Is f even, odd, or neither? Justify your answer.
   (e) Is -1 an upper bound for f over the interval $[-4, -1]$? Justify your answer.
   (f) Find a lower bound for f over the interval $(1, 3)$
   (g) The line tangent to the graph of f at **A** has slope 1. Find an equation of this line.

3. Let f be the function graphed below.

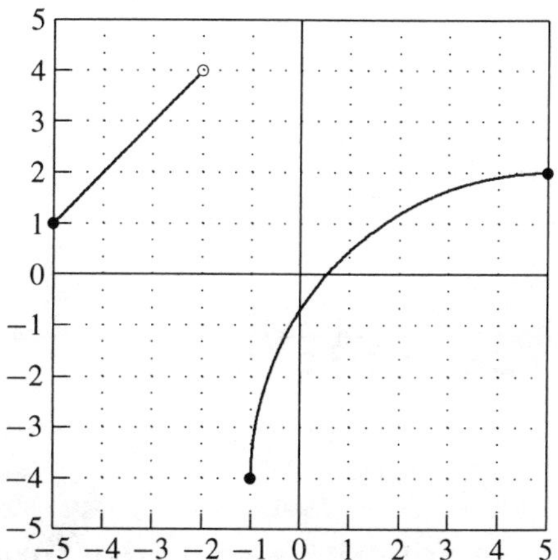

(The graph is made up of a line segment and a quarter-circle.)

(a) What is the domain of f?

(b) What is the range of f?

(c) Find a symbolic representation of f (i.e., an algebraic formula).

(d) Find $f(-4)$, $f(-2.5)$, and $f(0)$ *exactly*.

(e) Find upper and lower bounds on the value of f over the interval $(0, 4)$.

(f) Find a and b such that $|f(x) - 2| < 1$ if $a < x < b$.

(g) Find a and b such that $|f(x) + 2| > 2$ if $a < x < b$.

4. Let g be an *even* function with domain $\mathbb{R}$ (the set of all real numbers). Furthermore, suppose g has the values shown in the table below.

x	-5	-3	-2	1	4
$g(x)$	-1	0	-4	2	1

(a) Sketch the graph of such a function g over the interval $[-5, 5]$. (NOTE: There are infinitely many correct answers. Your graph need only be consistent with the information given above.)

(b) Find an equation of the secant line passing through the points $(-3, g(-3))$ and $(1, g(1))$.

(c) Assume that the slope of the line tangent to the graph of g at $x = -2$ is 3. Find an equation of this tangent line.

5. Find a formula for a function g with ***all*** of the following properties:

(i) The domain of g is $\mathbb{R}$.

(ii) The range of g is $[-2, 8]$.

(iii) g has period π.

(iv) $g(2) = 3$.

Chapter 2

The Derivative

2.1 Amount functions and rate functions: the idea of the derivative

Calculus is the mathematics of change. The immense practical power of calculus derives from its ability to describe—and predict—the behavior of changing quantities. Falling apples, orbiting spacecraft, growing populations, decaying radioactive materials, rising consumer prices: all can be modeled using the calculus of change.

The name itself isn't very descriptive, unfortunately. There are many ways to "derive" one function from another.

The calculus tool that makes all this possible is called the **derivative function.** In coming chapters we'll spend a lot of time and effort studying how to define derivative functions formally and how to calculate them symbolically. In the process, various subtleties and puzzles will inevitably arise.

Nevertheless, the basic idea behind derivatives is quite simple: *the derivative function f' measures the rate of change of a given function f.* Though sometimes disguised, this basic principle lies behind all our calculations and applications of the derivative.

This section is about the *idea* of derivative functions—not formal definitions or computational techniques. The relationship between f and f' is our main theme: the idea of f' as the rate function derived from f; how graphs of f and f' are related; what each function says about the other.

The derivative as a rate function

Any function f can be used to build new functions, "derived" in one way or another from f. Starting with $f(x) = \sin(x)$, for instance, we can concoct all sorts of new functions. The rules

$$g(x) = \sin(2x), \quad h(x) = \sin(x + \pi/2), \quad \text{and} \quad k(x) = \frac{\sin(x + 0.1) - \sin x}{0.1}$$

How are the graphs of f, g, h related?

all define "relatives" of f; the possibilities are endless.

Among all the possible functions one might derive from a given function f, the derivative function f' is unquestionably most important. Here's an informal description:

> **Definition: (The derivative as rate function.)** Let f be a function of x. Define the new function f' by letting $f'(x)$ denote the **instantaneous rate of change** of f at x. The function f' is called the **derivative**, or **rate function**, of f.

(We'll use "derivative" and "rate function" interchangeably to describe f'; when we do, we'll call f an **original function** or an **amount function**.)

We'll revisit and refine our definition of derivative in later sections.➻ First, however, we'll try out the ideas of rate function and amount function on the road.

We'll have to say, for instance, exactly what "instantaneous" means, mathematically.

Rates, amounts, and cars: the prime example

Moving cars provide the most familiar setting for comparing rates and amounts; cars nicely illustrate most of the basic ideas and even some of the subtleties. Here's a typical situation, stripped to essentials:

> *At noon on October 1, 1994, a car enters Interstate 94, heading east, from the State Capitol exit in Bismarck, North Dakota. For several hours, the car moves—sometimes east, sometimes west—at varying speeds.*

To put things in functional language, let's define some symbols:

t : the elapsed time, measured in hours, since a reference time $t = 0$;

$P(t)$: the car's position at time t, measured in miles *east* of a reference point at time t;

$V(t)$: the car's *eastward* velocity at time t, measured in miles per hour.

Here are possible graphs of the position and velocity functions:

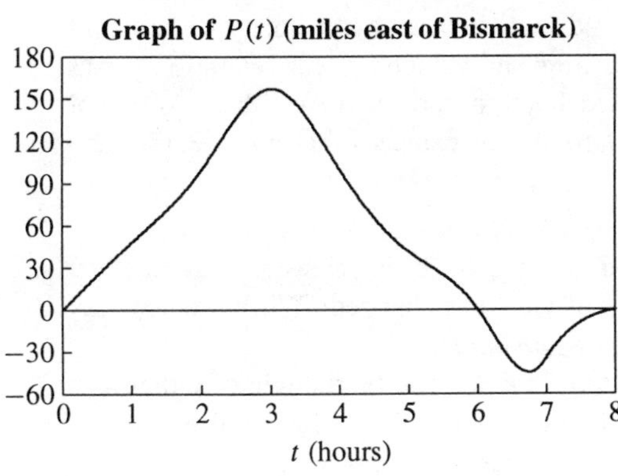

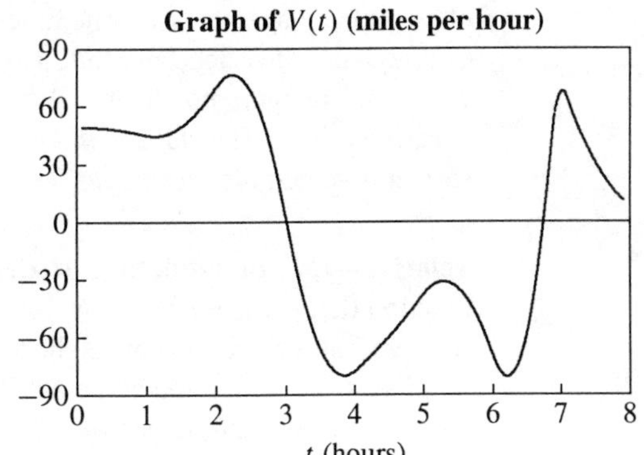

There's a lot to see:➻

Watch for several uses of the prime notation.

Points of reference. Choosing a reference time and reference point is entirely up to us. We could have used, say, the moment in the year 800 when Charlemagne was crowned Emperor of the West as our reference time, and downtown Glendive, Montana, as our reference point. But those choices seemed artificial, so we chose noon on October 1, 1994, and the State Capitol exit in Bismarck.

Position and velocity as functions of time. Once we've specified the necessary reference points and units of measurement, P and V become usable *functions* of t; at any sensible input time t the car has a well-defined position $P(t)$ and velocity $V(t)$. For example, the statements

$$P(2) = 100 \quad \text{and} \quad V(2) = 70$$

mean that at 2 pm, the car is 100 miles *east* of Bismarck, moving *east* at 70 mph.

Amount *vs.* rate. It's natural to think of P as an **amount function** and V as the associated **rate function**.➻ For any time t, $V(t)$ tells the *instantaneous rate of change of position with respect to time*. In symbols: $V(t) = P'(t)$.➻

The units—miles and miles/hour, respectively—support this view.

Or, simply, $P' = V$.

Positive and negative values. Both P and V can take either positive or negative values. The statements

$$P(6.5) = -40 \quad \text{and} \quad V(6.5) = -60$$

mean that at 6:30 pm the car is 40 miles *west* of Bismarck, traveling *west* at 60 mph. When $P(t) > 0$, the car is *east* of the State Capitol. When $V(t) > 0$, the car is headed *eastward.*

Maybe the driver missed his exit and still hasn't noticed it.

Equivalently, the P-graph is rising.

Position *vs.* distance, velocity *vs.* speed. Our functions describe the car's **position** and **velocity**. Why not use the more familiar terms **distance** and **speed**?

The difference is technical, but important. In physical language, distance and speed connote *nonnegative* quantities. Position and velocity can take either positive or negative values, so they can convey information direction.

Speedometer dials, for instance, contain no negative numbers.

East or west, in this case.

What the speedometer tells; what it doesn't. Speedometers can't tell direction, so a speedometer reading of 45 mph at $t = 1$ means that $V(1) = \pm 45$. The speedometer reading, moreover, is an **instantaneous speed**. It means that in the unlikely event that the car maintains the same speed for an hour, 45 miles will be covered.

Which is it really, 45 or -45?

Did the Bismarck driver behave this way?

Acceleration—another rate. Velocity, like position, has its *own* rate function. In physical language, this new rate function—the rate of change of velocity with respect to time—is called **acceleration**. Like position and velocity, the acceleration varies with time. In symbols: $A(t) = V'(t)$. Acceleration, too, can take either positive or negative values. The statement $A(2) > 0$, for instance, means that at $t = 2$, the car's eastward velocity is *increasing.*

Do the graphs support this?

Velocity—rate or amount? It depends ... Above we viewed V as the *rate* function derived from P. Now our point of view has changed: When we consider acceleration, velocity becomes the associated *amount.*

Here's the moral and some advice: Any function can be thought of either as a rate or as an amount, depending on the situation. To avoid confusion, think of rate functions and amount functions together, as inseparable pairs.

Units of velocity and acceleration. Every rate, properly understood, is the rate of change of *something* with respect to *something else.* The proper *units* for measuring rates depend both on what quantities are varying and on the units used to measure those quantities.

In the current setting, velocity is the rate of change of position (measured in *miles*) with respect to time (measured in *hours*), so the unit of velocity is *miles per hour.* Acceleration is the rate of change of velocity with respect to time, so its appropriate unit of acceleration is *miles per hour per hour*—the ratio of the unit of velocity to the unit of time.

Acceleration is sometimes expressed in other units, such as miles per hour per second.

Rate functions in other contexts

The ideas of amount function and rate function are intuitively natural when applied to physical quantities, such as distance and velocity, but the ideas of rate and amount make good sense in any context. *Any* function f can be thought of as an amount function: to an input t, f assigns the "amount" $f(t)$. How one interprets f' as a rate depends on context. If $f(t)$ is the *position* of a moving object at time t,

The variable name t suggests variation in time, but this is only an aid to intuition; mathematically, rates need not involve time.

The units of f' depend on the situation, too.

then $f'(t)$ is the *velocity* at the same time. If $f(t)$ represents *altitude*, then $f'(t)$ represents *rate of ascent*. If $f(t)$ represents the varying *value* of a bank deposit, then $f'(t)$ represents the *rate*, at time t, at which money flows into the account.

Even if f is a "pure" mathematical function—unattached to cars, balloons, money, or anything else—the idea of a rate function still makes good sense. To see how, notice that in each instance above, f' measures how fast *outputs* from f grow with respect to *inputs* to f. The same idea applies to "pure" mathematical functions: If f is *any* function, and $y = f(x)$, then $f'(x)$ represents the rate, at x, at which y grows with respect to x. The statement $f'(3) = 5$ means, for instance, that when $x = 3$, outputs from f increase 5 times as fast as inputs to f.

The derivative graphically: f' as a slope function

What does the derivative mean *geometrically*? How do the graphs of f and f' reflect the amount–rate relationship?

Slope is the key idea that link graphs to rates. By its very definition, slope is a rate of change, i.e., the *ratio*➸ of two changes Δy and Δx. Specifically:

'Rate" and "ratio" have common roots.

> *The slope of the f-graph at any point $(x, f(x))$ is the instantaneous rate of change of f with respect to x.*

In a nutshell:

> **Definition: (The derivative as a slope function.)** Let f be any function. The **derivative** function f' is given graphically by the rule
>
> $$f'(x) = \text{the slope of the } f\text{-graph at } x.$$

Like our first informal definition of derivative, this one needs—and will get—plenty of refinement and discussion.➸ First let's see what the definition means.

We'll have to say, for instance, precisely how to calculate a graph's "slope at a point."

Derivatives of linear functions

It's easy to find derivatives of *linear* functions.

■ **Example 1.** Let f be the *linear* function

$$f(x) = 3x + 1.$$

Explain—graphically and in terms of rates—why the derivative is the *constant* function

$$f'(x) = 3.$$

Solution: The graph of f is a straight line, so its slope—at *any* value of x—is 3. In symbols: $f'(x) = 3$ for all x. Here are graphs of f and f':

Graph of $f(x) = 3x + 1$

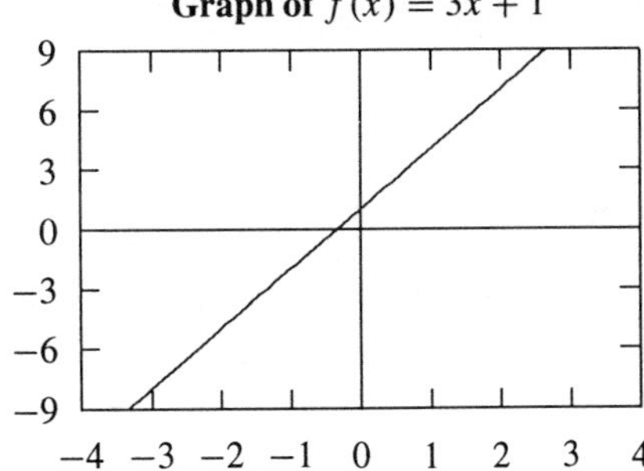

Graph of $f'(x) = 3$

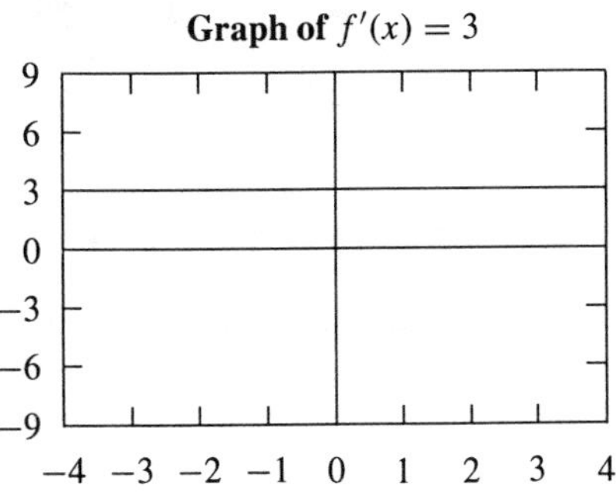

Let's put things in rate language. That f is linear, with slope 3, means that the f-graph always rises 3 times as fast as it runs. In other words, f increases at the constant rate of 3 y-units per x-unit. □

The example illustrates a general fact:

Fact: For any linear function $f(x) = ax + b$, the rate function is the *constant* function $f'(x) = a$.

The slope of a graph at a point: tangent lines

For straight lines slope is simple: a line has only one slope, and any two points suffice to compute it. But what is the slope of *any* graph at a point? How is such a slope measured?

Perhaps **the** *key idea.*

Finding the slope of a *curve* at a point is a key idea of calculus. That curves are, well, curvy, makes things trickier. In this section we'll take a first graphical look at the problem; in the next section we'll return to it in more detail.

The slope of a *curve* at a point P can be thought of as the slope of a certain *line* through P (called the **tangent line at** P) that "fits" the curve at P. Equivalently, the tangent line at P "points in the direction of C." In car talk:

The phrases in quotes are intuitive descriptions, not formal definitions. We'll give the latter in the next few sections.

If the driver lost control at P the car would—literally—go off on a tangent.

> *The curve is a highway, seen from above. A car, headlights blazing through fog, follows the road. When the car is at point P, its headlights point in the direction of the tangent line at P.*

Using these intuitive ideas, one can usually draw tangent lines with reasonable accuracy, and estimate their slopes. Here are short segments of tangent lines at several points along a curve:

Examples of tangent lines

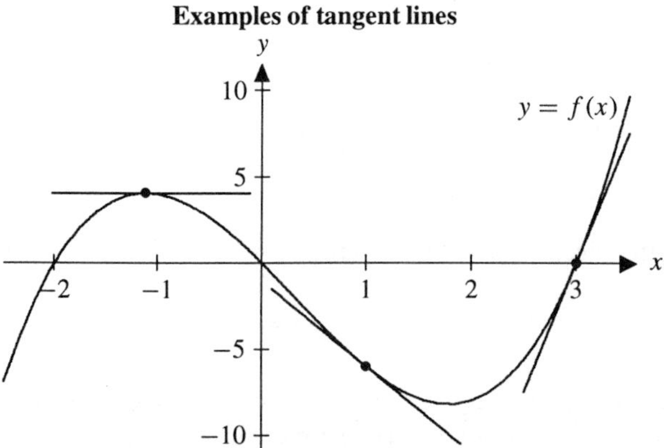

The leftmost tangent segment, at about $x = -1.1$, looks approximately horizontal. In function notation: $f'(-1.1) \approx 0$.

Relating amount and rate functions

How are an amount function f and its rate function f' related to each other? What can either function tell about the other? These questions are at the heart of calculus. We'll revisit them often, in graphical, numerical, and symbolic forms. The rest of this section begins the discussion.

The racetrack principle: fast dogs win

Here's a safe bet:

> *If dogs f and g start together and dog g* always *runs faster than dog f, then dog g* always *leads, and therefore wins the race.*

This so-called **racetrack principle**, appropriately rephrased, is surprisingly useful. The first step is to interpret it as a property of rate and amount functions. Here's one way to do so:

Terminology due to J.J. Uhl, U. of Illinois.

> **Fact: (The racetrack principle.)** Let f and g be functions defined for all x in $[a, b]$, and suppose that $f(a) = g(a)$. If
> $$f'(x) \le g'(x)$$
> for all x in $[a, b]$, then
> $$f(x) \le g(x)$$
> for all x in $[a, b]$.

Note:

Fair start. Requiring that $f(a) = g(a)$ means that f and g "start together" at $x = a$.

Rates of growth. The condition that $f'(x) \le g'(x)$ means that f "grows no faster" than g for $a \le x \le b$.

Never ahead. The conclusion means that f "never outruns" g for $a \le x \le b$.

Strict inequalities. A "strict" version of the racetrack principle also holds: If $f(a) = g(a)$ and $f'(x) < g'(x)$ for x in $[a, b]$, then $f(x) < g(x)$ for x in $(a, b]$.

In the strict version, $<$ replaces $\le$.

The racetrack principle is especially simple and useful when either f' or g' is a *constant* function.

■ **Example 2.** Let f be a function such that (i) $f(0) = 0$; and (ii) $f'(x) \le 2$ when $x \ge 0$. Show that $f(1) \le 2$.

Solution: Informally speaking, (ii) means that for $x \ge 0$, $y = f(x)$ grows no more than *twice* as fast as x. Thus as x increases one unit (from $x = 0$ to $x = 1$), $y = f(x)$ increases no more than two units (from $y = 0$ to $y = 2$).

The racetrack principle restates the same idea more formally. To apply it, let $g(x) = 2x$. Since g is *linear*, with slope 2, g' is *constant*: $g'(x) = 2$. Thus $f(0) = g(0)$ and $f'(x) \le 2 = g'(x)$, so the racetrack principle says that for $x \ge 0$, $f(x) \le g(x)$. Setting $x = 1$ gives $f(1) \le g(1) = 2$. □

Recall: If $f(x) = ax + b$, then $f'(x) = a$.

More safe bets: racetrack variants

The basic racetrack principle—that faster dogs pull ahead—can be restated in several other useful forms by changing the conditions slightly. In the three variants below, we no longer assume that dogs f and g start together. Each principle appears first in words, then in symbolic notation.

Does each word version seem reasonable? Do the symbols really say the same thing?

Photo finish. In words: If dogs f and g *finish* together, then the faster dog cannot have been ahead at any time.

In symbols: Suppose that $f'(x) \leq g'(x)$ for $a \leq x \leq b$ and $f(b) = g(b)$. Then for $a \leq x \leq b$,

$$f(x) \geq g(x).$$

Faster means farther. In words: If dog f runs *no faster* than dog g, then dog f runs *no farther* than dog g from time a to time x—regardless of where each dog starts.

In symbols: If $f'(x) \leq g'(x)$ for $a \leq x \leq b$, then

$$f(x) - f(a) \leq g(x) - g(a).$$

for $a \leq x \leq b$. (Note that $f(x) - f(a)$ and $g(x) - g(a)$ represent, respectively, the net changes in f and g from time a to time x. In racing terms, $f(x) - f(a)$ and $g(x) - g(a)$ are the net *distances* covered by dogs f and g from time a to time x.)

Equal speeds, equal distances. In words: If two dogs equally fast from time a to time b, then the distance between them remains constant.

In symbols: If $f'(x) = g'(x)$ for $a \leq x \leq b$, then for some constant C, $f(x) - g(x) = C$ for $a \leq x \leq b$.

C represents the constant distance between the dogs.

■ **Example 3.** Suppose that $f(0) = 3$ and $f'(x) \leq 2$ for all x. What can be said about the values $f(2)$ and $f(-4)$? Interpret the result graphically.

Solution: We'll apply the racetrack principle with $g(x) = 2x + 3$—we chose this g because (i) $g(0) = f(0) = 3$; and (ii) $g'(x) = 2 \geq f'(x)$. To estimate $f(2)$ we'll use the ordinary racetrack principle on the interval [0, 2]. It says:

Why is $g'(x) = 2$? Because g defines a line with slope 2.

$$f(0) = g(0) \text{ and } f'(x) \leq g'(x) \implies f(2) \leq g(2) = 7.$$

To estimate $f(-4)$ we'll use the photo finish version on the interval $[-4, 0]$. It says:

$$f(0) = g(0) \text{ and } f'(x) \leq g'(x) \implies f(-4) \geq g(-4) = -5.$$

Everything above can be understood geometrically. Here are possible graphs of f and g:

Racing functions: graphs of f and g

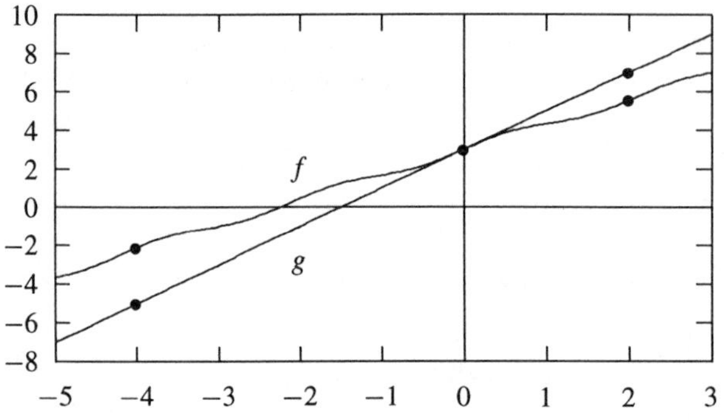

As the picture shows, f and g "agree" at $x = 0$, and f never rises faster than g. As a result, says the racetrack principle, f lies *above* g *before* $x = 0$, and f lies *below* g *after* $x = 0$. □

Compare, e.g., the points at $x = -4$ and $x = 2$.

Derivatives in action: using rate and amount functions

Many real-world phenomena naturally involve rate and amount functions; derivatives are just what's needed to describe and predict their behavior. To show derivatives in action, we end this section with some first illustrations. As above, *calculating* derivatives is deferred for later.

Free fall without air resistance

A moving object is said to be in **free fall** if it is affected *only* by gravity. Other possible forces—air resistance, engine thrust, etc.—are assumed to play no role.

Gravity exerts the same (constant) downward acceleration on all falling objects, regardless of their size, weight, initial velocity, or other characteristics. Galileo Galilei (1564–1642) is supposed to have discovered this fact by tossing various objects from the Leaning Tower of Pisa and noticing that all landed at about the same time.

Can air resistance be ignored? Air resistance does matter in practice. Parachutists depend on it for survival; cannonballs fall faster than, say, live chickens. *What* Galileo dropped isn't known—indeed, the whole Pisa story seems unlikely, with all those tourists milling around below. For physical reasons, air resistance is usually negligible for small dense objects moving at moderate speeds, as when a coin falls to the floor.

A falling object has, at any time t, a certain height $h(t)$, velocity $v(t)$, and acceleration $a(t)$. Given appropriate measurement scales for time and distance, h, v, and a are all functions of t, and the derivative relations $h' = v$ and $v' = a$ hold.➡ Galileo's discovery that an object in free fall has *constant acceleration* says, symbolically, that $a(t) = g$, or, equivalently, that

I.e., v is the rate function of h; a is the rate function of v.

$$v'(t) = g$$

for some constant g.➡ In the English system of measurement, $g \approx -32$ feet per second per second. (In the metric system, $g \approx -9.8$ meters per second per second.)

g is for gravity.

Formulas for distance and velocity. In the late 1600's Isaac Newton used Galileo's discovery to derive his *laws of motion*. Newton reasoned, for instance, that if (as in free fall) the acceleration function $a(t)$ is *constant*, then the velocity function must be *linear*.➡

We reasoned similarly above, when we said that if a function is linear, then its derivative is constant.

Suppose that at time $t = 0$ seconds an object is h_0 feet above "ground" level, and has *upward* velocity v_0.➡ Newton's laws of motion imply rather simple formulas for $h(t)$ and $v(t)$, the functions for altitude (in feet) and (vertical) velocity (in feet per second):

$v_0 > 0$ means that the object rises initially, perhaps by having been thrown upward.

$$h(t) = h_0 + v_0 t - 16t^2; \qquad v(t) = v_0 - 32t.$$

With these formulas➡ we can answer many questions related to free fall.

Consider: why are the minus signs present?

■ **Example 4.** Could a major league pitcher throw a ball to the 276-foot ceiling of the Hubert H. Humphrey Metrodome, home of the Minnesota Twins?

Solution: Yes—assuming free fall conditions, at least. Fastball pitchers throw with an initial velocity of around 95 mph, or 140 feet per second. If a ball is thrown upward, from an initial height of 6 feet, the formulas above say that

$$h(t) = 6 + 140t - 16t^2; \qquad v(t) = 140 - 32t.$$

Why?

Height is greatest at the instant when upward velocity is zero,← that is, when

$$v(t) = 140 - 32t = 0 \iff t = \frac{140}{32}.$$

Check the calculation.

At that time,←

$$h\left(\tfrac{140}{32}\right) = 312.25 \text{ feet},$$

higher than the Metrodome's ceiling. Graphs of h and v appear below:

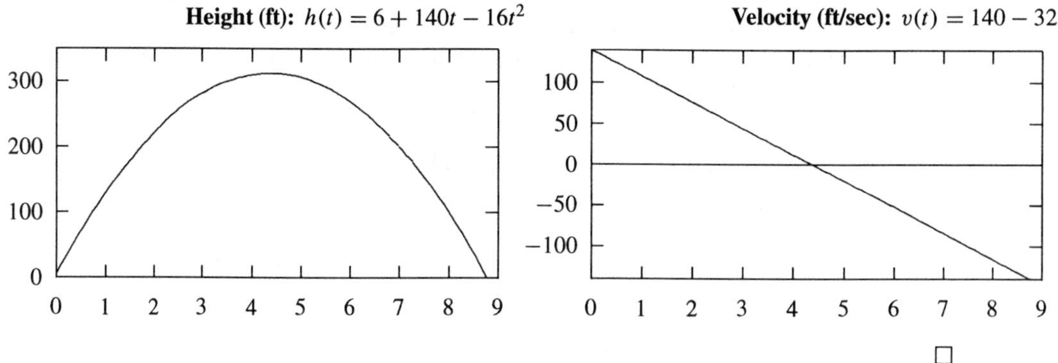

□

Falling with air drag

It's an observable fact of physics that when small, dense objects (e.g., baseballs) fall at moderate speeds, the deceleration due to air drag is (approximately) proportional to the *square* of the velocity. In prime notation this fact says that

$$v'(t) = g + kv(t)^2$$

for some constant k. (The numerical value of the proportionality constant k depends on physical factors—smoothness of the object, air density, and others. For a falling baseball the value $k \approx 0.003$ is reasonable.)

Differential equations

Any equation that involves derivatives is called a **differential equation**, or just **DE**. Each of the following—

$$f'(x) = 3; \qquad v'(t) = g + kv(t)^2; \qquad f'(x) = f(x)$$

is a DE. A **solution** to a differential equation is a *function* that satisfies the differential equation.← (As we saw above, $f(x) = 3x + 1$ is one solution to the first differential equation above. We'll see solutions to the others later.)

Note: A solution to a differential equation is a function, not a number.

Many of the most important applications of the calculus—physical applications, especially—involve posing problems as differential equations and then finding and using solutions.

■ **Example 5.** On an outing with Dad, Bud and Sis play catch on the observation deck of the IDS tower in Minneapolis. To Dad's horror their baseball slips over the edge, squarely beaning a lawyer on a lunchtime stroll along the Nicollet Mall, 600 feet below. What happens next?

Solution: Thanks to air drag Dad is sued for personal injury, not manslaughter. Here's why.

Without air drag, Newton's free-fall model applies, so

$$v'(t) = -32, \qquad v(t) = -32t, \qquad \text{and} \qquad h(t) = 600 - 16t^2.$$

Taking air drag into account leads to another differential equation:

$$v'(t) = -32 + 0.003v(t)^2.$$

Solving this differential equation symbolically is hard. We won't try, but only show graphs of the functions v and h that apply if air drag is taken into account. In the pictures below, the solid curves show the effect of air drag; the dotted curves ignore it. Notice, for example, the difference between the two velocity graphs. Ignoring air drag, the ball accelerates at a constant rate. Taking account of air drag gives a more realistic result: as the ball gathers speed, its acceleration tapers toward zero.

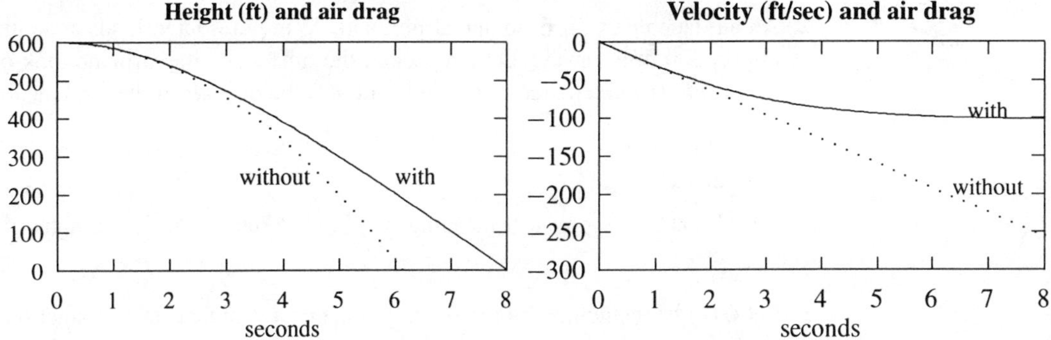

The two velocity curves show the advantage (to Dad and the lawyer) of air drag. *With* air drag the ball hits the lawyer at about 100 feet per second (i.e., about 68 mph)—unpleasant, certainly, but a slow pitch by major league standards. *Without* air drag the ball would be traveling more than twice as fast when it lands. □

Of course, it might also then have missed the strolling lawyer.

Understanding the universe. The idea of derivative is among the most important and powerful in all of mathematics—indeed, in all of human history. The concept of derivative, more than any other, distinguishes the calculus from other branches of mathematics, and accounts for the great power of the calculus to describe, and therefore predict, physical phenomena.

Planetary motion is one such phenomenon. In the early 1600's Johannes Kepler discovered by observation that the orbit of Mars is an ellipse; he suggested the same about other planets. Isaac Newton, using his early theory of calculus, demonstrated all this (and more) mathematically toward the end of the 1600's. As George Simmons puts it[a]:

> Newton's enormous success revived and greatly intensified the almost-forgotten Greek belief that it is possible to understand the universe in a rational way. This new confidence in its own intellectual powers permanently altered humanity's perception of itself, and over the past 300 years almost every department of human life has felt its consequences.

---

[a] *Calculus with Analytic Geometry*, McGraw-Hill, 1985, p. 547.

Exercises

1. Interpret each sentence below as a statement about a function and its derivative. In each case, indicate clearly what the function is, what each variable means, and appropriate units.

   (a) The price of a product decreases as more of it is produced.

   (b) The increase in demand for a new product decreases over time.

   (c) The work force is growing more slowly now than it was five years ago.

   (d) Health care costs continue to rise, but at a slower rate than three years ago.

   (e) During the past two years, the United States has continued to cut its consumption of imported oil.

2. An airplane takes off from one airport and, 45 minutes later, lands at another airport 300 miles away. Let t represent the time since the airplane took off, $x(t)$ the *horizontal* distance traveled, and $y(t)$ the *altitude* of the airplane.

   (a) What is the physical meaning of $x'(t)$? Sketch plausible graphs of x and x'.

   (b) What is the physical meaning of $y'(t)$? Sketch plausible graphs of y and y'.

3. Let $G(v)$ be the number of miles per gallon that a vehicle gets as a function of its speed, v, in miles per hour. Interpret the statement $G'(35) = 0.4$ in plain English using terms such as gas mileage and speed.

4. A company must budget for research and development of a new product. Let x represent the amount of money invested in R&D and T be the time until the product is ready to market.

   (a) Give reasonable units for T and x. What is T' in these units?

   (b) What economic interpretation can be given to T'?

   (c) Would you expect T' to be positive or negative? Explain.

5. The height of a ball (in feet) t seconds after it is thrown is given by $h(t) = -16t^2 + 38t + 74$; its (upward) velocity at time t is $v(t) = -32t + 38$.

   (a) From what height was the ball thrown?

   (b) What was the ball's initial velocity? Was it thrown up or down? How can you tell?

   (c) Was the ball's height increasing or decreasing at time $t = 2$?

   (d) At what time did the ball reach its maximum height? How high was it then?

   (e) How long was the ball in the air?

6. The graph of a function f is shown below. Rank the values of $f'(-3)$, $f'(-2)$, $f'(0)$, $f'(1)$, and $f'(4)$ in increasing order.

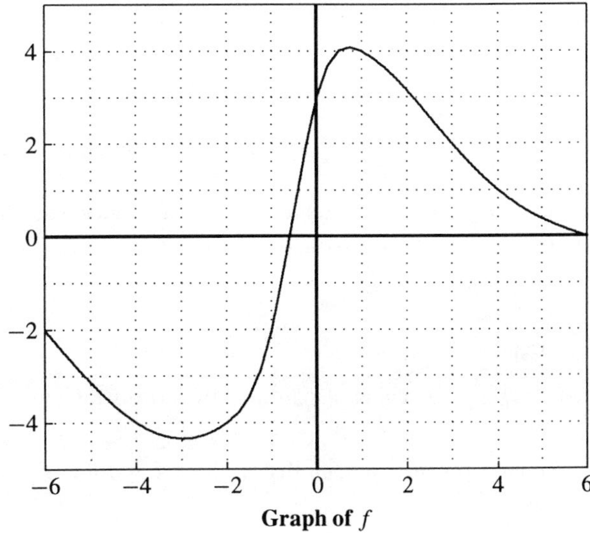

Graph of f

7. Suppose that $f(x) = x^3 - 5x^2 + x - 1$ and that $g(x) = x^3 - 5x^2 + x + 4$. Explain why $f'(x) = g'(x)$ for every x. [HINT: How are the graphs of f and g related?]

8. Suppose that $g(x) = f(x) + 3$ and that $f'(x)$ exists for all x.

   (a) Explain how the graphs of f and g related.

   (b) How is the graph of g' related to the graph of f'? Explain.

   (c) If $f'(1) = 5$, what is $g'(1)$?

   (d) Let $h(x) = f(x) + k$ where k is a constant. How is the graph of h' related to the graph of f'?

9. Let $f(x) = \sin x$ and $g(x) = \cos x$. Explain why the graph of g' is the graph of f' shifted $\pi/2$ units to the left. [HINT: $\cos x = \sin(x + \pi/2)$.]

10. Let $g(x) = f(x + 3)$ and suppose that $f'(x)$ exists for all x.

    (a) Explain how the graphs of f and g related.

    (b) How is the graph of g' related to the graph of f'? Explain.

    (c) If $f'(2) = 4$, what is $g'(-1)$?

    (d) Let $h(x) = f(x + k)$ where k is a nonzero constant. How is the graph of h' related to the graph of f'?

11. Suppose that $g(x) = 3f(x)$ and that $f'(x)$ exists for all x.

    (a) Explain how the graphs of f and g related.

    (b) How is the graph of g' related to the graph of f'? Explain.

    (c) If $f'(-1) = 2$, explain why $g'(-1) = 6$.

    (d) Let $h(x) = kf(x)$ where $k > 0$ is a constant. How is the graph of h' related to the graph of f'?

    (e) Let $j(x) = kf(x)$ where $k < 0$ is a constant. How is the graph of j' related to the graph of f'?

12. Suppose that f is periodic with period 5 and that $f'(x)$ exists for all x. Explain why f' is also a periodic function with period 5.

13. Suppose that $f'(3) = -2$.

    (a) Assume that f is an *even* function. Explain why $f'(-3) = 2$. [HINT: Give a graphical argument.]

    (b) Now assume that f is an *odd* function. What is $f'(-3)$?

14. Let $f(x) = 5$, $g(x) = x$, and $h(x) = -2x$. Evaluate $f'(11)$, $g'(-53)$, and $h'(37)$.

15. Let $f(x) = 3x + 2$ and $g(x) = 3x - 4$.

    (a) Evaluate $f'(0)$ and $g'(0)$.

    (b) Give a graphical explanation of the fact that $f'(x) = g'(x)$ for all values of x.

    (c) Find a function h such that $h(1) = 2$ and $h'(x) = f'(x)$ for all values of x.

16. Suppose that $f'(x) = 1$ for all x. Find an algebraic expression for $f(x)$ assuming that

    (a) $f(0) = 2$.

    (b) $f(1) = 2$.

    (c) $f(0) = -2$.

    (d) $f(-1) = -2$.

17. Suppose that $f(a) = b$ and $f'(x) = c$ for all x. Find a algebraic expression for $f(x)$.

18. Suppose that $f(x) = x - 2$ and $g(x) = 4x + 1$.

    (a) Plot graphs of f and g on the same axes.

    (b) Show that $f'(x) \le g'(x)$ for all values of x.

    (c) Show how the racetrack principle implies that $f(x) \le g(x)$ for all $x \ge -1$.

    (d) What does the racetrack principle say about the relationship between the numbers $f(x)$ and $g(x)$ when $x \le -1$?

19. Suppose that f and g are defined on the interval $[a, b]$, that $f(a) = g(a)$, and that $f'(x) \le g'(x)$ for all x in $[a, b]$.

    (a) Use car talk to explain why $f(b) \le g(b)$.

    (b) Suppose that $f(b) = g(b)$. What does this imply about f' and g'?

20. Suppose that f and g are defined on the interval $[a, b]$, that $f(a) = g(a)$, and that $f'(x) \le g'(x)$ for all x in $[a, b]$. Use the basic racetrack principle to show that $f(x) - f(a) \le g(x) - g(a)$ for all x in $[a, b]$.

21. Suppose that $f(1) = -2$ and $f'(x) \le 3$ for all $x \in [-10, 10]$.

    (a) Show that $f(2) \le 1$.

    (b) Show that $f(5) \le 10$.

    (c) Show that $f(0) \ge -5$.

(d) Is $f(9) < 31$? Justify your answer.

(e) Is $f(-5) > -23$? Justify your answer.

(f) Could $f(4) = 8$? Justify your answer.

(g) Could $f(-7) = -25$? Justify your answer.

(h) Could $f(8) = -25$? Justify your answer.

(i) Let $g(x) = 4x + 3$. Compare the numbers $f(7)$ and $g(7)$.

22. Suppose that $f(1) = 3$ and $f'(x) \geq 2$ for all $x \in [0, 5]$.

    (a) Show that $f(4) \geq 9$.

    (b) Show that $f(0) \leq 1$.

    (c) Let $g(x) = x + 1$. Compare the numbers $f(3)$ and $g(3)$.

23. Suppose that $f(2) = 1$ and $-4 \leq f'(x) \leq 3$ for all $x \in [-10, 10]$.

    (a) Find upper and lower bounds on the value of $f(6)$.

    (b) Find upper and lower bounds on the value of $f(-5)$.

24. Suppose that $f(1) = 2$ and $f'(x) \leq -3$ for all $x \in [-5, 5]$.

    (a) What does the racetrack principle imply about the value of $f(4)$?

    (b) What does the racetrack principle imply about the value of $f(-2)$?

25. Suppose that $f(0) = 2$ and $|f'(x)| \leq 1$ for all $x \in [-5, 5]$.

    (a) Find upper and lower bounds on the value of $f(1)$.

    (b) Find upper and lower bounds on the value of $f(-3)$.

26. Suppose that $f'(x) \leq 0$ for all $x \in (2, 7)$. Explain why $f(3) \geq f(6)$.

27. Suppose that $f'(x) > 0$ for all $x \in (2, 7)$. Explain why $f(4) < f(5)$.

28. The graph of the derivative of a function f is shown below. Use the graph of f' and the racetrack principle to answer the following questions about f. [NOTE: The graph of f is not shown.]

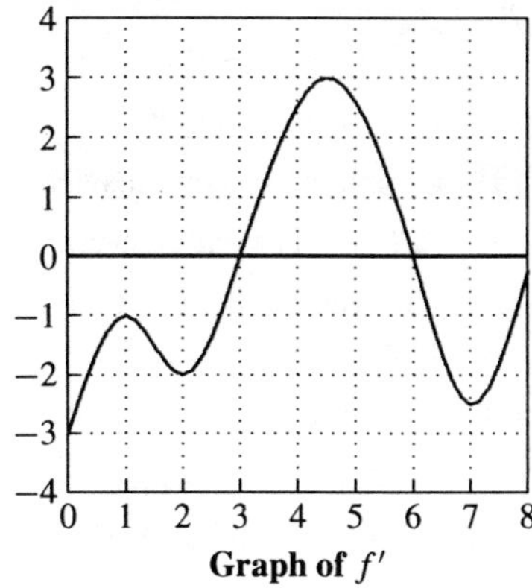

Graph of f'

(a) Explain why $f(5) - f(4) > 2$.

(b) Is $-6 < f(2) - f(0) < -2$? Justify your answer.

(c) Show that $-5 < f(2) - f(0)$.
[HINT: $f(2) - f(0) = (f(2) - f(1)) + (f(1) - f(0))$.]

(d) Which is larger: $f(3)$ or $f(6)$? Justify your answer. [HINT: Use part (a).]

(e) Which is larger: $f(0)$ or $f(3)$? Justify your answer.

29. The graph of the derivative of a function g is shown below. Use the graph of g' and the racetrack principle to answer the following questions about g. [NOTE: The graph of g is not shown.]

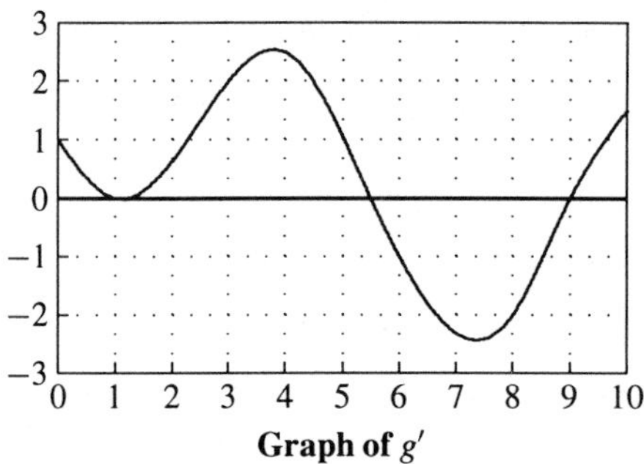

Graph of g'

(a) Is $g(2) < g(5)$? Justify your answer.

(b) Is $g(6) > g(8)$? Justify your answer.

(c) Rank the five numbers 0, 1, $g(2) - g(1)$, $g(8) - g(7)$, and $g(9) - g(8)$ in increasing order.

(d) Rank the four numbers $g(0)$, $g(1)$, $g(3)$, and $g(5)$ in increasing order.

30. Suppose that $f(-1) = -2$ and that f' is the function shown below. Use the racetrack principle to answer the following questions about f. [NOTE: The graph of f is not shown.]

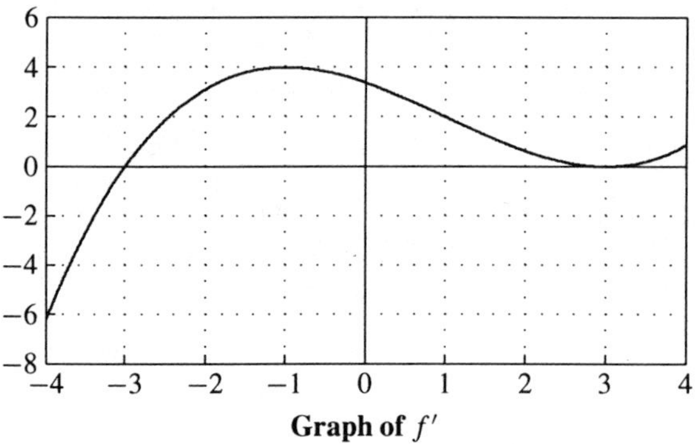

Graph of f'

(a) Could $f(3) = -6$? Justify your answer.

(b) Could $f(3) = 2$? Justify your answer.

(c) Show that f achieves its largest value in the interval $[-4, 4]$ at $x = 4$. [HINT: Show that $0 < f(-4) - f(-3) < 6$ and $f(1) - f(-2) > 6$.]

(d) Where in the interval $[-4, 4]$ does f achieve its smallest value?

31. Suppose that k is a real number and that f is a function such that $f'(x) \leq k$ for all x in an interval $[a, b]$. Show that $f(x) \leq k(x - a) + f(a)$ for all x in $[a, b]$.

32. The converse of the racetrack principle says that if $f(a) = g(a)$ and $f(x) \leq g(x)$ for all $x \in [a, b]$, then $f'(x) \leq g'(x)$ for all $x \in [a, b]$. Show that this statement is not true in general by giving graphical examples of functions f and g that satisfy the hypotheses of the statment but not its conclusion.

33. (a) Suppose that $f'(x) \leq 0$ for all $x \in [a, b]$ and $f(a) = c$. Use the racetrack principle to show that $f(x) \leq c$ for all $x \in [a, b]$.

    (b) Suppose that $f'(x) \geq 0$ for all $x \in [a, b]$ and $f(a) = c$. Use the racetrack principle to show that $f(x) \geq c$ for all $x \in [a, b]$.

    (c) Use parts (a) and (b) to prove that if $f'(x) = 0$ for all $x \in [a, b]$, then f is a constant function on the interval $[a, b]$.

34. Suppose that $f'(x) = g'(x)$ for all $x \in [a, b]$. Use the previous problem to show that there is a constant C such that $g(x) = f(x) + C$ for all $x \in [a, b]$. [HINT: If $h(x) = f(x) - g(x)$, then $h'(x) = 0$ for all $x \in [a, b]$.]

2.2 Estimating derivatives: a closer look

Writing $x = a$ helps "fix" our attention at a single point of the domain.

In the previous section we described the derivative function in terms of rates and slopes. Given a function f and an input value $x = a$,

$f'(a)$ is the instantaneous rate of change of f with respect to x at $x = a$.

In graphical language:

$f'(a)$ is the slope of the f-graph at $x = a$.

This brief section is—literally—a closer look at the derivative at a point. By "zooming in" on a function or its graph near an input value $x = a$ we'll be able to estimate numerical values of f'; we'll also see more clearly what the derivative means, both graphically and numerically.

Estimating $f'(a)$: the slope of a graph at a point

For a line, finding slope is a routine matter. For a curve, the idea of slope at a point is a little more subtle, but a lot more interesting.

Tangent lines

Remember the headlights-through-fog analogy? See page 90.

The slope of a curve at a point P can be thought of as the slope of the curve's **tangent line at** P, i.e., the straight line through P that, roughly speaking, "points in the direction of the curve" at P. This description, although vague by strict mathematical standards, is perfectly adequate to illustrate the idea. For nearly all calculus functions, moreover, it leads reliably to good derivative estimates.

■ **Example 1.** Let $f(x) = x^2$. Use tangent lines to estimate $f'(1)$ and $f'(-1.5)$. Interpret the results as rates of change.

Do you agree they're reasonable?

Solution: Here's the graph of f, together with reasonable candidates for tangent lines at $x = 1$ and $x = -1.5$:

Graph of $f(x) = x^2$ and two tangent lines

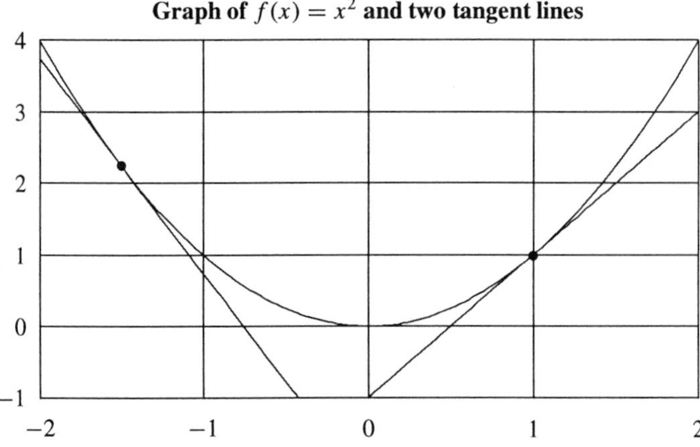

Check our estimates.

We can now estimate the slope of each tangent line directly from its graph. The line at $x = 1$, for instance, seems to rise 2 units as it runs 1, so its slope is 2. Similarly, the tangent line at $x = -1.5$ seems to have slope around -3. We conclude:

$$f'(1) \approx 2; \qquad f'(-1.5) \approx -3.$$

In the language of rates of change, the results mean: (i) at $x = 1$, y is *increasing* twice as fast as x; (ii) at $x = -1.5$, y is *decreasing* three times as fast as x. □

Zooming in to estimate slope

Drawing a straight tangent line on a curved graph is one way to estimate the graph's slope at a point. The strategy works because near the point of tangency, the graph and the tangent line are almost indistinguishable.

Another strategy—likely to be more convenient, given modern plotting technology—is to "zoom in" on the point in question, perhaps repeatedly, until the graph *itself* looks like a straight line. Once the graph looks straight, it's easy to estimate the slope.

■ **Example 2.** Let $f(x) = x^2$, as above. Estimate $f'(1)$ again, this time by zooming.

Solution: Zooming in successively on the f-graph near $(1, 1)$ gives these results:➻

Note the plotting windows.

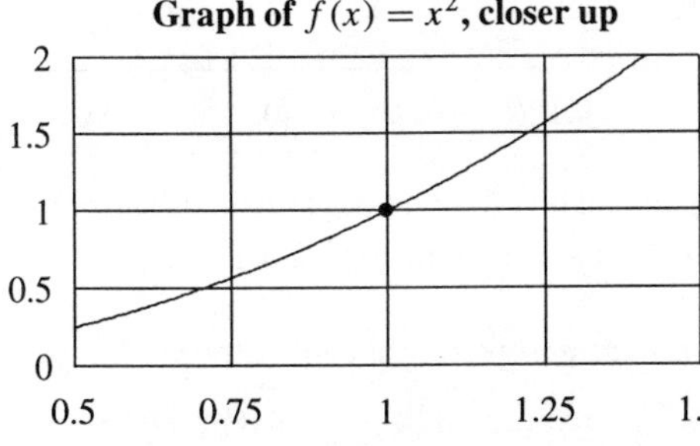

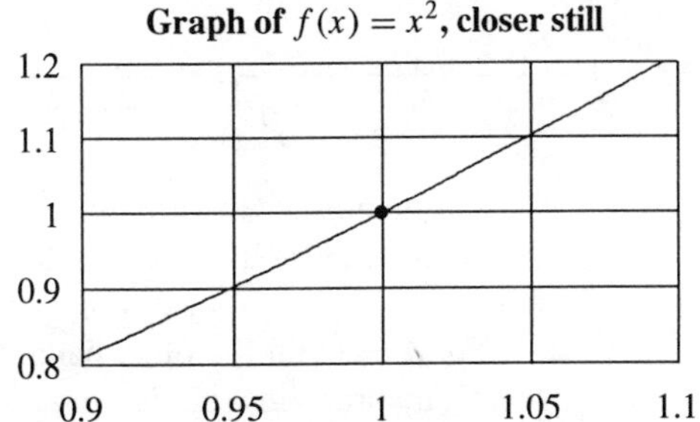

In the last picture, the graph looks virtually straight; its slope seems to be 2.➻ □

Check the estimate; use the grid.

When zooming works: local linearity. Remarkably, the zooming-in-to-estimate-slope strategy illustrated above almost always works. Zooming in on the graph of almost any calculus function f, at almost any point $(a, f(a))$, eventually produces what looks like a straight line with slope $f'(a)$. A function with this property is sometimes called **locally linear** (or **locally straight**) at $x = a$.➻ Local linearity says, in effect, that f "looks like a line" near $x = a$, and therefore has a well-defined slope at $x = a$.

These aren't formal definitions, just descriptive phrases.

The previous example showed that $f(x) = x^2$ is locally linear at $x = 1$ and $x = -1.5$. Now let's try zooming in on a trigonometric function.

■ **Example 3.** Is $f(x) = \sin x$ at $x = 1.4$ locally linear at $x = 1.4$? What does the answer say about f'?

Solution: Here are two views of the sine graph near the target point $P = (1.4, \sin 1.4) \approx (1.4, 0.9854)$:

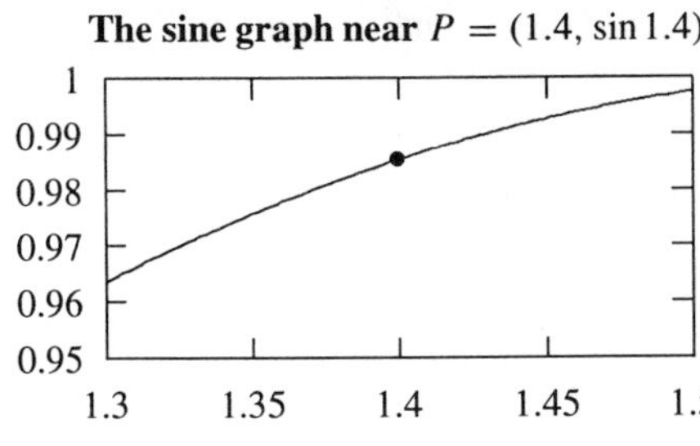

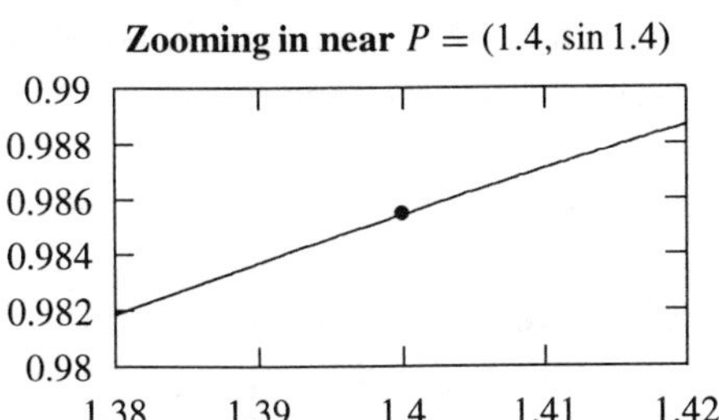

In the second window the sine graph is almost straight. To estimate the slope at P we can use any two points from the graph. Using $x = 1.38$ and $x = 1.42$, we found (approximately, of course) a slope of 0.17.➻ In function notation: $f'(1.4) \approx 0.17$.□

Do you agree?

When zooming fails: local non-linearity. Not every function is locally linear everywhere. A "kink" in a graph can't be "smoothed out" by repeated zooming in. At such a point the derivative doesn't exist, and our model of slope breaks down.

■ **Example 4.** Let $f(x) = |x|$. Does $f'(0)$ exist? Does $f'(a)$ exist if $a \neq 0$?

Solution: Here's the result of zooming near the origin:

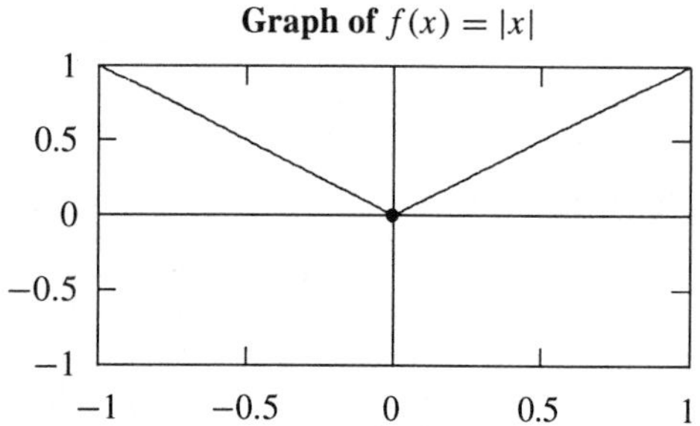

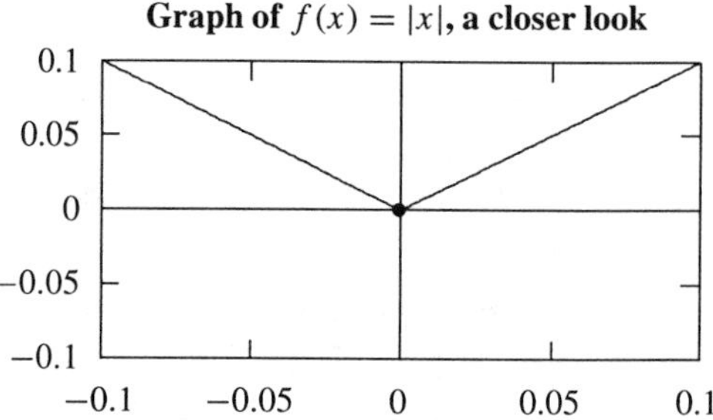

There's no mistake in the pictures. Zooming in had no effect on the kink at the origin. Zooming again would make no difference; that kink is there to stay, and $f'(0)$ doesn't exist.

For $a \neq 0$, on the other hand, the graph is *already* straight (with slope ± 1), so there's no problem with derivatives:

$$f'(a) = 1 \text{ if } a > 0; \; f'(a) = -1 \text{ if } a < 0.$$

In words: $f(x) = |x|$ is not locally linear at $x = 0$, but is locally linear elsewhere.□

Zoom factors and distortion. Throughout this section, "zooming in" means "zooming in with equal zoom factors in both directions." Requiring equal zoom factors is more than a technicality. Zooming repeatedly with *different* zoom factors can so distort the picture that all information is lost.

Consider, for example, the kink at $x = 0$ on the graph $y = |x|$, as in Example 4. Zooming in repeatedly—but *only* in the x-direction (e.g., with zoom factors 4 in x and 1 in y)—gradually flattens the vee. Eventually, the graph looks horizontal. Try it.

Plotting the rate function

Zooming in or drawing tangent lines to the graph of f lets us estimate $f'(a)$ for various values of a. By pooling such information we can *plot* the derivative function. The results are sometimes surprising.

Because our slope results are estimates, the plot is only approximate. But so is every plot.

■ **Example 5.** For $f(x) = x^2$, plot $f'(x)$. Then guess a formula for $f'(x)$.

Solution: In Example 1 we estimated that $f'(1) = 2$ and $f'(-1.5) = -3$. From the symmetry of the graph $y = x^2$, a few more values come easily:

About the y-axis.

x	-1.5	-1	0	1	1.5
$f'(x)$	-3	-2	0	2	3

Plotting these points suggests that the graph of f' is a straight line with slope 2, i.e., that $f'(x) = 2x$.

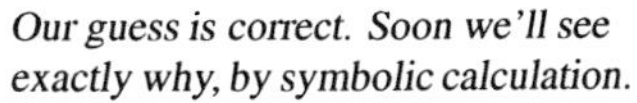
Our guess is correct. Soon we'll see exactly why, by symbolic calculation.

The graph of f'

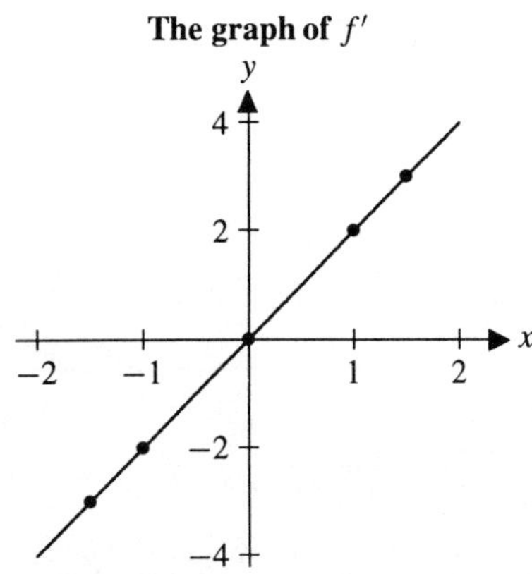

□

What's natural about e^x? Applying the same technique to the **natural exponential function** produces a real surprise—one that helps explain why the adjective "natural" fits.

■ **Example 6.** Let $f(x) = e^x$. Use tangent lines to plot f'; then guess a formula for f'.

Solution: Here's a graph of f (shown dotted); at several points, small segments of tangent lines (shown solid) are drawn:

Tangent segments to the graph of $f(x) = e^x$

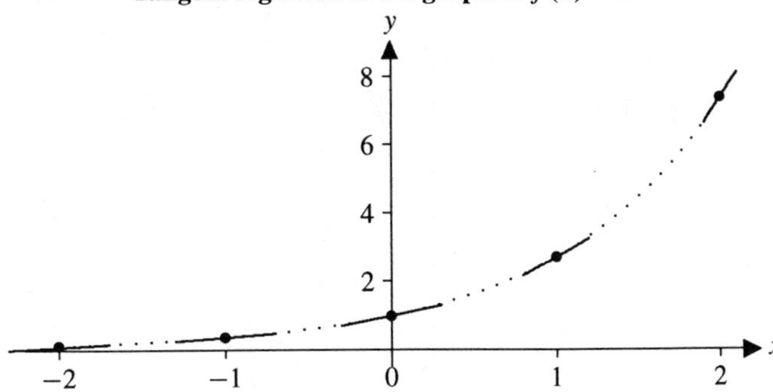

Using a ruler one can estimate the slope of each tangent segment. Several such results (rounded to one decimal place) are tabulated below.

Check some table entries yourself. Are they plausible?

The derivative of e^x—graphical estimates

x	−2	−1	0	1	2
y	0.135	0.368	1.000	2.718	7.389
slope at (x, y)	0.1	0.4	1.0	2.7	7.4

Plotting the slope data (with a smooth curve through the points) gives a striking result:

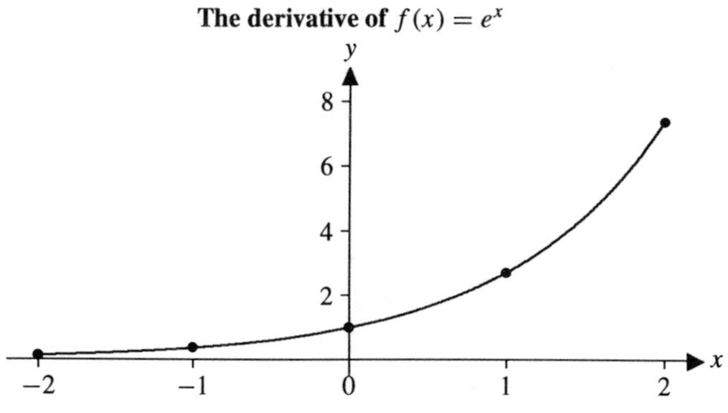

We'll prove this symbolically later.

Judging from the graphs, f and f' are identical! They *are* identical:

If $f(x) = e^x$, then $f'(x) = e^x$. The natural exponential function is its own derivative.

In other words: $f(x) = e^x$ solves the **differential equation** $f'(x) = f(x)$. This remarkable property makes the natural exponential function one of the most important and useful in all of mathematics. □

Exercises

1. Graphs of a function f and its derivative f' are shown below.

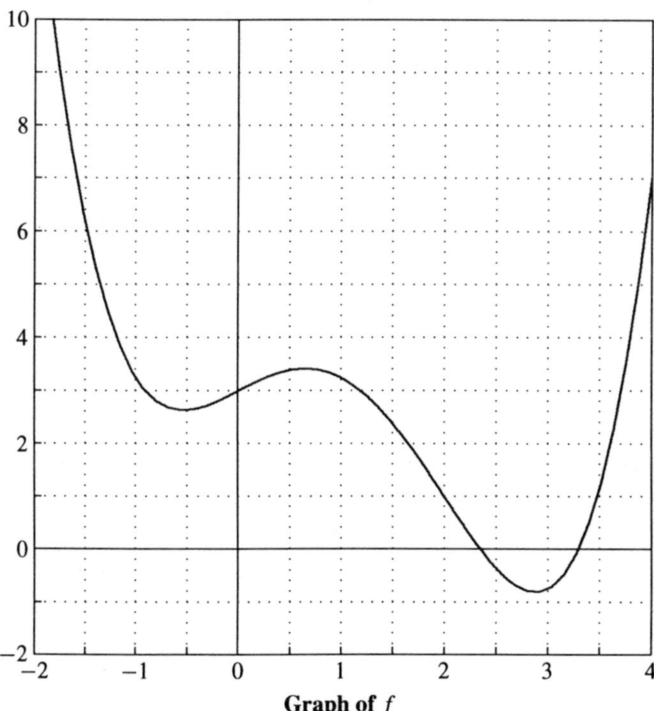

Graph of f

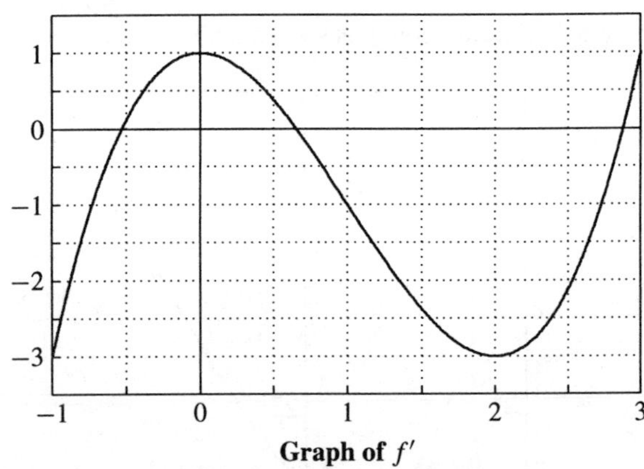

Graph of f'

(a) Draw short segments of the lines tangent to f at $x = -1$, $x = 0$, $x = 1$, $x = 2$, $x = 3$, and $x = 3.5$ on the graph of f.

(b) Estimate the slope of each of the tangent lines you drew in part (a).

(c) Are your answers in part (b) consistent with the graph of f' shown above? Explain.

(d) Find equations for the lines tangent to f at $x = -1$, $x = 0$, $x = 1$, $x = 2$, and $x = 3$.

2. The graph of a function f is shown below.

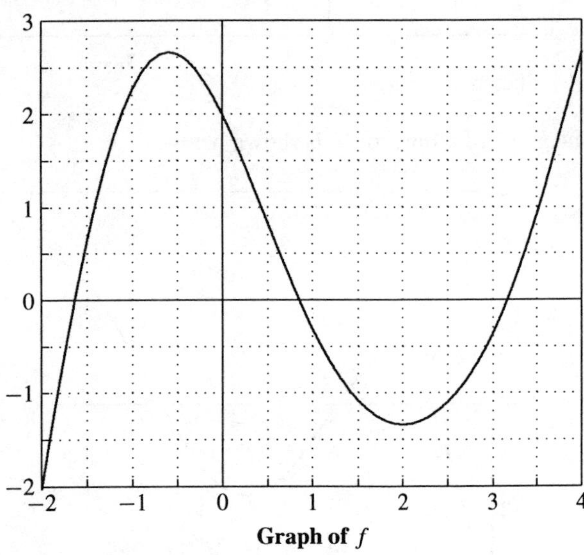

Graph of f

(a) Fill in the missing entries in the table below. [NOTE: Because f is given graphically, your answers will be estimates. However, your answers should approximate the exact values within ± 0.5.]

x	-2	-1	0	1
$f'(x)$	6.0			-2.0
x	2	2.5	3	4
$f'(x)$				3.5

(b) Use your answers to part (a) to sketch a graph of f'.

3. The graph of a function f is shown below.

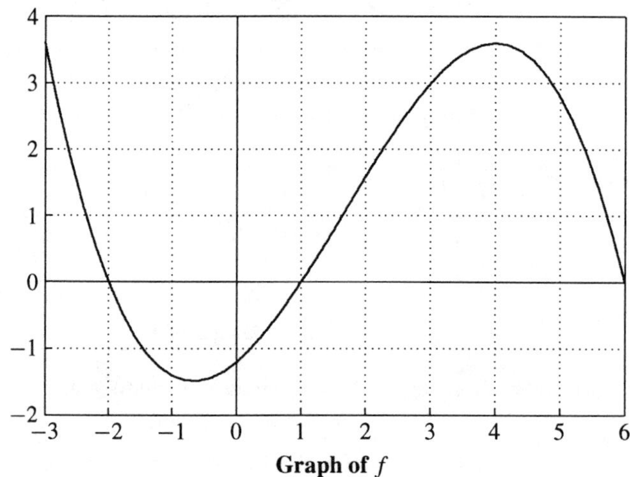

(a) Fill in the missing entries in the table below.

x	−3	−2	−1	0	1
$f'(x)$	−4.9			0.8	
x	2	3	4	5	6
$f'(x)$		1.1			−4.0

(b) Sketch a graph of f'.

4. The graph of a function f is shown below.

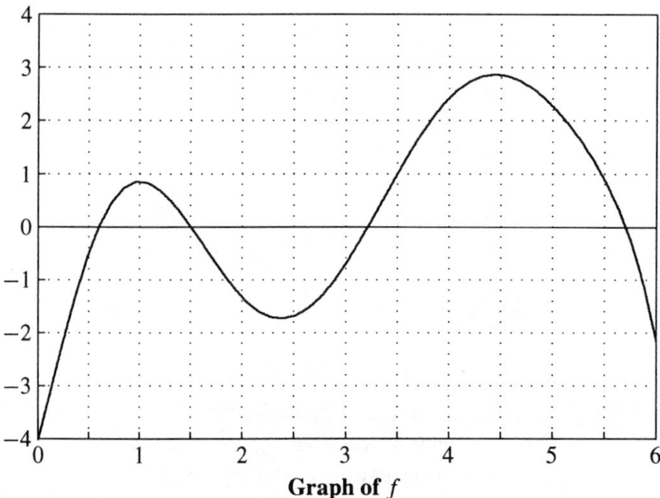

(a) Check the entries in the table below and replace any that are erroneous with reasonable estimates.

x	1	2	3	4	5	6
$f'(x)$	0	2	6	3	−2	42

(b) Sketch a graph of f'.

5. The graph of a function f is shown below.

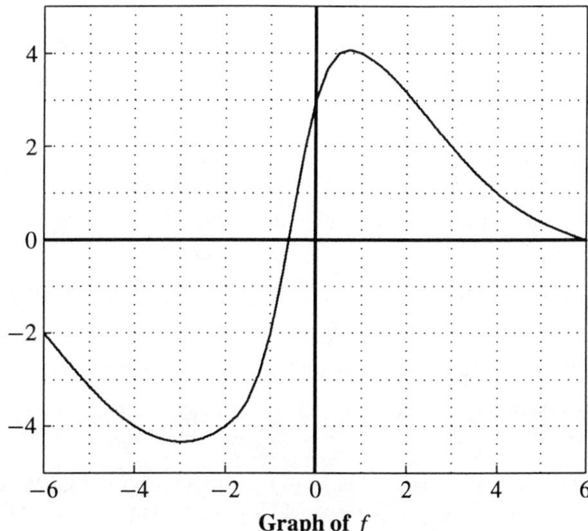
Graph of f

(a) Estimate $f'(-5)$, $f'(-3)$, $f'(-1)$, $f'(2)$, and $f'(4)$.

(b) Sketch a graph of f'.

6. Let f be the function whose graph is shown below.

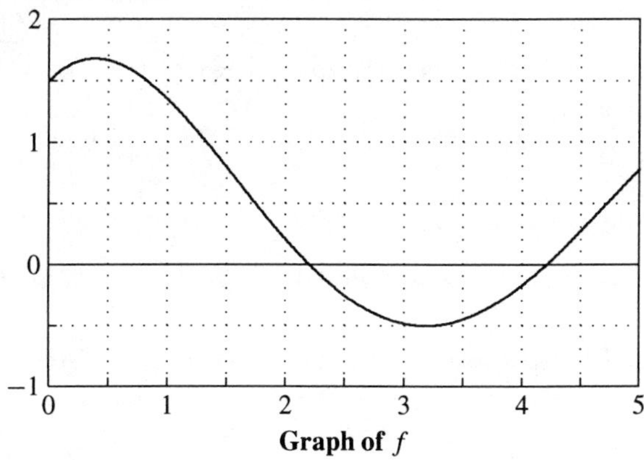
Graph of f

(a) Estimate $f'(0)$, $f'(1)$, $f'(2)$, $f'(3)$, $f'(4)$, and $f'(5)$.

(b) Use your results from part (a) to sketch a graph of f'.

7. Let $f(x) = x^2$.

(a) Use zooming to estimate $f'(0)$, $f'(1/2)$, $f'(1)$, $f'(2)$, and $f'(3)$.

(b) Use your results from part (a) to sketch a graph of f' over the interval $[-3, 3]$. [HINT: Why is $f'(-1) = -f'(1)$?]

(c) Use your results from parts (a) and (b) to guess an algebraic formula for $f'(x)$.

8. Let $f(x) = \sqrt{x}$.

(a) Use zooming to estimate $f'(1/4)$, $f'(1)$, $f'(9/4)$, $f'(4)$, $f'(25/4)$, and $f'(9)$.

(b) Use your results from part (a) to sketch a graph of f' over the interval $[0, 9]$.

(c) Why is $f'(-1)$ undefined? Why is $f'(0)$ undefined? What is the domain of f'? [HINT: Look at a graph of f.]

(d) Use your results from part (a) to guess an algebraic formula for $f'(x)$. [HINT: Evaluate $1/f(x)$ at $x = 1/4$, $x = 1$, $x = 9/4$, $x = 25/4$, and $x = 9$.]

9. Let $f(x) = x^3$ and $g(x) = x^{1/3}$.

(a) Use zooming to estimate $f'(0)$, $f'(1/2)$, $f'(1)$, $f'(3/2)$, and $f'(2)$.

(b) Use your results from part (a) to sketch a graph of f' over the interval $[-2, 2]$. [HINT: Why is $f'(-1) = f'(1)$?]

(c) Use your results from parts (a) and (b) to guess an algebraic formula for $f'(x)$.

(d) Estimate $g'(-1)$ and $g'(1)$.

(e) Why is $g'(0)$ undefined? What is the domain of g'? What is the domain of g?

(f) It can be shown that $f'(4) = 48$. Use this fact to find $g'(64)$. [HINT: How are the graphs of f and g related? The point $(4, 64)$ is on the graph of f and the point $(64, 4)$ is on the graph of g.]

10. Let $f(x) = 1/x$.

(a) Use zooming to estimate $f'(1/4)$, $f'(1/2)$, $f'(1)$, $f'(2)$, and $f'(3)$.

(b) Use your results from part (a) to sketch a graph of f' over the intervals $[-3, 0)$ and $(0, 3]$. [HINT: Why is $f'(-1) = f'(1)$?]

(c) Use your results from parts (a) and (b) to guess an algebraic formula for $f'(x)$.

11. Let $f(x) = e^x$.

(a) Use zooming to estimate $f'(-1)$, $f'(0)$, $f'(1)$, $f'(1.5)$, and $f'(2)$.

(b) Use your results from part (a) to sketch a graph of f' over the interval $[-1, 2]$.

(c) Use your results from part (a) to guess a formula for $f'(x)$. [HINT: Evaluate $f(x)$ at $x = -1$, $x = 0$, $x = 1.5$, and $x = 2$.]

12. Let $f(x) = \ln x$.

(a) Use zooming to estimate $f'(1/10)$, $f'(1/5)$, $f'(1/2)$, $f'(1)$, $f'(2)$, and $f'(5)$.

(b) Use your results from part (a) to sketch a graph of f' over the interval $[0, 5]$.

(c) Use your results from part (a) to guess a formula for $f'(x)$.

13. Let $f(x) = \sin x$.

(a) Use zooming to estimate $f'(0)$, $f'(\pi/6)$, $f'(\pi/4)$, $f'(\pi/3)$, $f'(\pi/2)$, and $f'(\pi)$.

(b) Use the symmetry of the sine function and your answers from part (a) to estimate $f'(2\pi/3)$, $f'(3\pi/4)$, and $f'(5\pi/6)$. Check your answers using zooming.

(c) Use your results from parts (a) and (b) to guess an expression for $f'(x)$.

14. Let $f(x) = \cos x$.

(a) Use zooming to estimate $f'(0)$, $f'(\pi/6)$, $f'(\pi/4)$, $f'(\pi/3)$, $f'(\pi/2)$, and $f'(\pi)$.

(b) Use your results from part (a) to guess an expression for $f'(x)$.

15. (a) Zoom in on the graph of $y = e^x$, near the point $(0, 1)$, until the graph looks like a straight line. What's the slope of this line?

(b) Zoom in on the graph of $y = \ln x$, near the point $(1, 0)$, until the graph looks like a straight line. What's the slope of this line?

16. The previous problem explains (partly) why base e is special. The italicized statement on p. 64 holds *only* for exponential and logarithm functions with base e. For other bases, a slightly different relation holds between the slope of $y = b^x$ at $(0, 1)$ and the slope of $y = \log_b x$ at $(1, 0)$. Let's "discover" this relationship for $b = 10$.

(a) Zoom in on the graph of $y = 10^x$, near the point $(0, 1)$, until the graph looks like a straight line. (This is the "tangent line" to the graph of $y = 10^x$ at $(0, 1)$.) Find the slope as accurately as possible.

(b) Zoom in on the graph of $y = \log_{10} x$, near the point $(1, 0)$, until the graph looks like a straight line. (This is the "tangent line" to the graph of $y = \log_{10} x$ at $(1, 0)$.) Find the slope as accurately as possible.

(c) How are the slopes in the previous two parts related to each other? What "variant" of the italicized statement referred to above holds in this situation?

17. In Section 1.5 we claimed:

If $y = b^x$, then the rate of change of y is proportional to y itself.

In this problem we explore this claim.

(a) By zooming in, estimate the slope of the tangent line to the graph of $y = e^x$ at $x = 0$, $x = 1$, and $x = 2$. Are your results consistent with the statement above? With what constant of proportionality?

(b) By zooming in, estimate the slope of the tangent line to the graph of $y = 10^x$ at $x = 0$, $x = 1$, and $x = 2$. Are your results consistent with the statement above? With what constant of proportionality?

18. (a) Sketch the graph of a function f that is consistent with these data:

x	-2	-1	1	2
$f(x)$	1	-1	-1	2
$f'(x)$	-3	0	-1	-2

(b) Sketch the graph of a function g that is consistent with these data:

x	-2	-1	1	2
$g(x)$	1	-1	-1	2
$g'(x)$	1	0	-1	-2

19. The line tangent to f at $(5, 2)$ passes through the point $(0, 1)$. Find $f(5)$ and $f'(5)$. Justify your answers.

20. Suppose that the line tangent to the curve of $y = f(x)$ at $x = 3$ passes through the points $(-2, 3)$ and $(4, -1)$. Find $f(3)$ and $f'(3)$.

21. The line tangent to the curve $y = f(x)$ at $x = 2$ has slope -1 and crosses the x-axis at $x = 5$. Find $f(2)$ and $f'(2)$.

22. Suppose that the line tangent to the curve $y = f(x)$ at $x = -2$ is described by the equation $y = 4x + 3$. Find $f(-2)$ and $f'(-2)$.

23. The graph of the derivative of a function f appears below. [NOTE: The graph of f is not shown.]

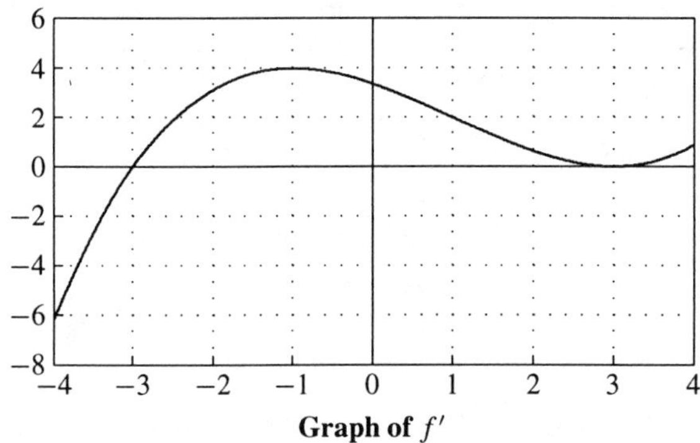

Graph of f'

(a) Suppose that $f(1) = 5$. Find an equation of the line tangent to the graph of f at $(1, 5)$.

(b) Suppose that $f(-3) = -6$. Find an equation of the line tangent to the graph of f at $(-3, -6)$.

Exercises 24–32 concern a function f whose derivative, f', is the function shown below. [NOTE: The graph of f is not shown.]

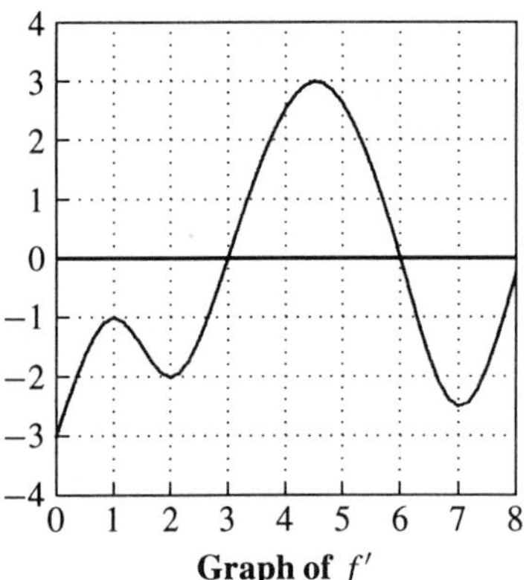

Graph of f'

24. Explain why each of the following *cannot* be the line tangent to the curve $y = f(x)$ at $x = 1$: (i) $y = x + 1$; (ii) $y = 3$; (iii) $y = -2x - 1$; (iv) $y = 2x$.

25. Which of the following could be the line tangent to the curve $y = f(x)$ at $x = 6$: (i) $y = -5$; (ii) $y = 6(x + 1)$; (iii) $6y = 2 - 3x$; (iv) $y = -6x$; (v) $y = 6x + 1$?

26. Find the equation of a line that is parallel to the line tangent to the curve $y = f(x)$ at $x = 4.5$.

27. Suppose that $f(0) = 1$. Explain why $y = -2x + 3$ is *not* the line tangent to the curve $y = f(x)$ at $x = 2$.

28. Suppose that $f(0) = 1$. Explain why $y = -2x - 1$ is *not* the line tangent to the curve $y = f(x)$ at $x = 2$.

29. Let $\ell(x) = f'(5)(x - 5) + f(5)$.

    (a) Is $\ell(6)$ greater than, less than, or equal to $f(6)$? Justify your answer.

    (b) Is $\ell(8)$ greater than, less than, or equal to $f(8)$? Justify your answer.

30. Let $g(x) = -3x + f(0)$.

    (a) Explain why $g(1) < f(1)$.

    (b) Is $g(2) < f(2)$? Justify your answer.

    (c) Is $g(8) < f(8)$? Justify your answer.

31. Let ℓ be the line tangent to f at $x = 1$.

    (a) Is $\ell(2) \leq f(2)$? Justify your answer.

    (b) Is $\ell(0) \leq f(0)$? Justify your answer.

32. Let ℓ be the line tangent to f at $x = 7$.

    (a) Is $\ell(8) \leq f(8)$? Justify your answer.

    (b) Is $\ell(6) \leq f(6)$? Justify your answer.

    (c) Is $\ell(2) \leq f(2)$? Justify your answer.

33. The graph of the derivative of a function g is shown below. [NOTE: The graph of g is not shown.]

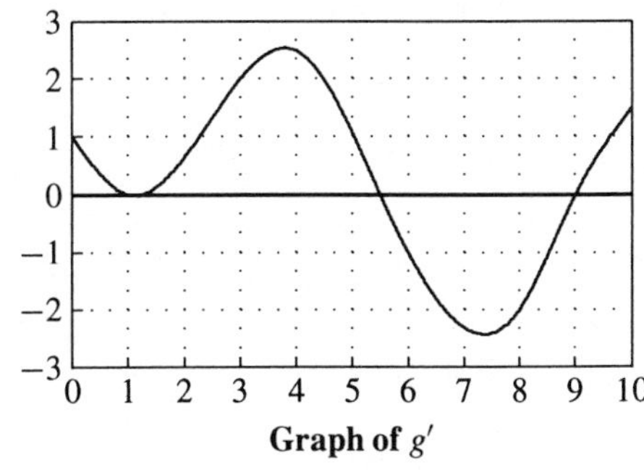

Graph of g'

    (a) Suppose that $g(3) = 11$. Find an equation of the line tangent to g at the point $(3, 11)$.

    (b) Let ℓ be the line tangent to g at $x = 2$. Is $g(5) \leq \ell(5)$? Is $g(1) \leq \ell(1)$? Justify your answers.

    (c) Let h be the line tangent to g at $x = 6$. Explain why $g(x) \leq h(x)$ when $6 \leq x \leq 8$.

    (d) Let h be the line tangent to g at $x = 6$. How do the values of $g(x)$ and $h(x)$ compare when $0 \leq x \leq 6$? Justify your answer.

34. Suppose that $f(2) = 4$ and $f'(x) = \sqrt{x^3 + 1}$ for $x \geq -1$.

    (a) Find an equation for the line tangent to f at $x = 2$.

(b) Let ℓ be the tangent line from part (a). Does $\ell(0)$ overestimate or underestimate $f(0)$? Justify your answer.

(c) Does $\ell(3)$ overestimate or underestimate $f(3)$? Justify your answer.

For each pair of functions in exercises 35–40 below, the constant A can be chosen so that $f'(x) = Ag(x)$ for every x in the domain of g. Find this value of A.
[HINT: Examine graphs of f and g.]

35. $f(x) = x^3, \quad g(x) = x^2$

36. $f(x) = \sqrt{x}, \quad g(x) = x^{-1/2}$

37. $f(x) = \sin x, \quad g(x) = \cos x$

38. $f(x) = \cos x, \quad g(x) = \sin x$

39. $f(x) = e^x, \quad g(x) = e^x$

40. $f(x) = \ln x, \quad g(x) = 1/x$

2.3 The geometry of derivatives

The geometric relationship between a function f and its derivative f' is easy to state:

> For any input a, $f'(a)$ is the slope of the line tangent to the f-graph at $x = a$.

This statement—innocuous as it appears—is one of the most important in this book. The next two sections explore its meaning and implications.

And much of this book.

Graphs of f and f': an extended example

Graphs of a function f and its derivative f' appear below. (For the moment, no *formulas* are given—or needed. We'll return to these functions symbolically at the end of the next section.) Three "interesting" points are labeled on each.

But don't peek.

Corresponding points (e.g., A and A') have the same x-coordinate.

Graph of f

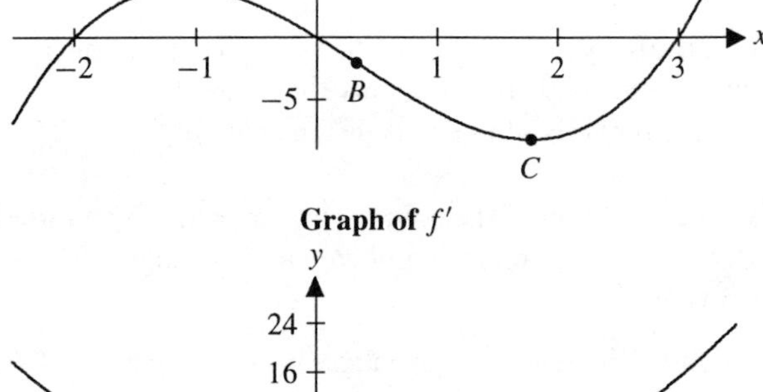

Graph of f'

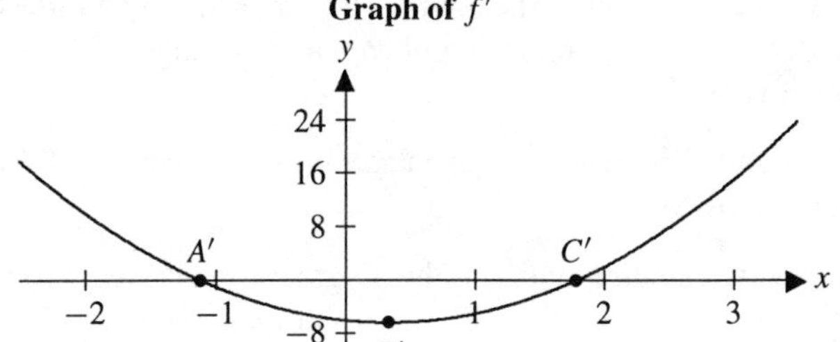

A first look

We've only asserted—not proved—that f' has the graph shown. Tools we'll develop in later sections will let us *show* this; here we'll just assume it.

The f'-graph tells how *slopes* of tangent lines to the f-graph behave. At B, for instance, the f-graph seems to have slope around -6; for this reason, the f'-graph has height -6 at B'.

Check carefully for yourself.

First let's observe several straightforward geometric relationships between the two graphs, introducing some useful new terminology in the process.

The sign of f'. The graph of f rises to the left of A, falls between A and C, and rises again to the right of C.

The *sign* of $f'(x)$ determines whether the line tangent to the f-graph at x points up or down. At A' and C' *f' changes sign.* Thus at A and C, f itself changes *direction.*

A' and C' correspond to roots of f'.

In the long run . . . The graph suggests that f "blows up" to the right of C, and "blows down" to the left of A. In geometric terms: As $x \to \infty$, the graph of $f(x)$ rises *more and more steeply.*

What happens over the same intervals on the f' graph? To the right of C', f' is *positive and increasing*. To the left of A', f' is *positive and decreasing*.

Stationary, maximum, and minimum points. The points A and C, with approximate coordinates $(-1.1, 4)$ and $(1.8, -8)$, where the graph is *horizontal*, are obviously of interest. They mark, respectively, high and low points of the graph.

We'll improve these guesses below, by symbolic methods.

The situation looks clear, but to avoid later confusion, it pays here to be extremely picky with the language—especially about the distinction between inputs to f (called "points") and outputs from f (called "values").

Here, in full detail, is the situation at $A \approx (-1.1, 4)$. The domain point $x = -1.1$ is called a **local maximum point** of f; the corresponding output—$f(-1.1) \approx 4$—is called a **local maximum value** of f. At C the situation is similar: $x = 1.8$ is a **local minimum point** of f, and $f(1.8) \approx -8$ is the corresponding **local minimum value** of f. The x-coordinates of both A and C are called **stationary points** of f. (We say **local**—rather than **global**—because elsewhere in its domain f may assume both larger and smaller values.)

$C \approx (1.8, -8)$.

See below for careful definitions of all these terms.

The corresponding points A' and C' occur where the f'-graph crosses the x-axis (i.e., at roots of f').

Any more stationary points? Are A and C the *only* stationary points of f? The picture doesn't say. It shows only the interval $-2.5 \le x \le 3.5$; additional stationary points could lie outside this interval.

Concavity and inflection. The point B, near $x = 0.3$, is an **inflection point** of f: at B, the f-graph's **direction of concavity** changes, from **concave down** to **concave up.**

Recall: "Holds water" and "spills water" are rough synonyms for "concave up" and "concave down."

The point B has another special geometric property: At B, the graph of f points *most steeply downward.*

The corresponding point on the f'-graph, B', is easier to see—it's a local minimum point. Later we'll use this property and some algebra to find the *exact* location of B.

Locating B or B' precisely by magnifying either graph doesn't work very well—viewed closely, both graphs look like straight lines.

What f' says about f

Interpreting the derivative function f' in terms of the slopes of tangent lines on the f-graph has many important geometric implications. We summarize several below.

Nicely-behaved functions. Many ideas in this section depend on both f and f' being reasonably "nice" or "well behaved." "Nice enough" means, roughly, that neither f nor f' displays sudden jumps or breaks. Any function f whose derivative function f' is continuous (i.e., without "breaks") is nice enough for us. Fortunately, most calculus functions *are* "nice" in this sense. As we proceed we'll see more of what "nice" means, and why it matters.

Increasing or decreasing?

A function f **increases** where its graph rises and **decreases** where its graph falls. The following definition captures these natural ideas in analytic language:

From left to right!

> **Definition:** Let I denote the interval (a, b). A function f is **increasing** on I if
>
> $$f(x_1) < f(x_2) \text{ whenever } a < x_1 < x_2 < b.$$
>
> f is **decreasing** on I if
>
> $$f(x_1) > f(x_2) \text{ whenever } a < x_1 < x_2 < b.$$

(If $f(x_1) \le f(x_2)$ for $x_1 < x_2$, then f is **nondecreasing** on I; if $f(x_1) \ge f(x_2)$ for $x_1 < x_2$, then f is **nonincreasing** on I. In either case, f is **monotonic** on I.)

In these definitions, $\le$ and $\ge$ replace $<$ and $>$.

The derivative detects whether a function increases or decreases on an interval I.

> **Fact:** If $f'(x) > 0$ for all x in I, then f increases on I. If $f'(x) < 0$ for all x in I, then f decreases on I.

This fact certainly *sounds* reasonable. To say that $f'(x) > 0$ means that the tangent line to the f-graph at x points *upward.* With any luck, so should the f-graph itself. Racetrack language makes the fact seem even simpler: if dog f has *positive* velocity, then dog f always runs *forward.*

See page 91 for more on the racetrack principle.

Plausible as the fact sounds, proving it rigorously requires one of calculus's "big theorems."

The mean value theorem—we'll see it later.

Behavior at a point. Functions are often said to increase or decrease *at a point.* To say, for example, that f **increases at** $x = 3$ means that f increases on *some* interval—perhaps a small one—containing $x = 3$. Now we can restate the fact above as follows:

Here, too, we're assuming that both f and f' are free of discontinuities and other naughty behavior.

> **Fact:** If $f'(a) > 0$, then f is increasing at $x = a$. If $f'(a) < 0$, then f is decreasing at $x = a$.

At $x = 1$, for instance, $f'(1) < 0$. The fact says—and the picture agrees—that at $x = 1$ the f-graph is decreasing.

Derive carefully. The previous fact's **converse** reads like this: *If f is increasing at $x = a$, then $f'(a) > 0$.* Tempting as it is, the converse is *false.* The next example shows why.

■ **Example 1.** Where is the function $f(x) = x^3$ increasing? Where is $f'(x) > 0$? What happens at $x = 0$?

Solution: As its graph shows—

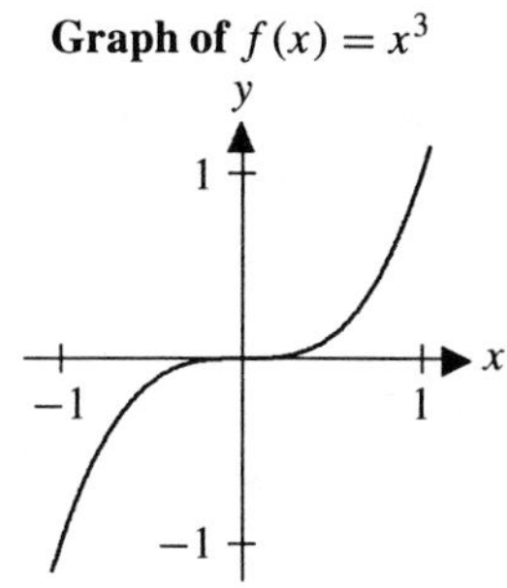

the function $f(x) = x^3$ increases *everywhere.* The graph shows, too, that $f'(x) > 0$ if $x \ne 0$, but that $f'(0) = 0$. □

Imagine tangent lines.

The derivative of an increasing function. What *can* be said about f' where f increases? This:

> **Fact:** If f increases at $x = a$, then $f'(a) \geq 0$; if f decreases at $x = a$, then $f'(a) \leq 0$.

The derivative of an increasing function must be *nonnegative*, but not necessarily *strictly positive*.

Maximum points, minimum points, and stationary points: formal definitions

The point A on the first graph in this section corresponds to a **local**, but not a **global**, maximum value of f. Using such technical language successfully requires clear definitions.

See page 115.

Look carefully to see why.

> **Definition:** Let f be a function and x_0 a point of its domain.
>
> - x_0 is a **stationary point** of f if $f'(x_0) = 0$.
> - x_0 is a **local maximum point** of f if $f(x_0) \geq f(x)$ for all x in some open interval containing x_0. The number $f(x_0)$ is a **local maximum value** of f.
> - x_0 is a **global maximum point** of f if $f(x_0) \geq f(x)$ for all x in the domain of f. The number $f(x_0)$ is the **global maximum value** of f.
>
> (Local and global **minimum points** are defined similarly.)

Several linguistic subtleties deserve brief mention:

Points vs. values. Local and global maximum *points* are *inputs* to a function; local and global maximum *values* are the corresponding *outputs*. The difference, although important, is sometimes blurred in informal speech. (The first sentence of the next paragraph is impeccably correct on this score.)

Local vs. global. At a *local* maximum point, a function f may or may not assume a *global* maximum value. Minimum points, too, may be local, global, or both.

Extreme values. The word **extremum** (plural **extrema**), which means "either maximum or minimum," is a convenient shorthand. We'd say, for instance, that for the function f at the beginning of this section, both points A and C correspond to **extrema** of f.

Finding maximum and minimum points

Geometric intuition says that at a local maximum point or local minimum point, a smooth graph must be "flat." More succinctly:

See A and C on the graphs above.

> **Fact:** On a smooth graph every local maximum or local minimum point x_0 is a stationary point—i.e., a root of f'.

This fact has immense practical value. To find maximum and minimum values of f, the fact says, we can limit our search to *roots* of f'. Each such root is a stationary point and therefore, possibly, a maximum or minimum point. (But not a sure thing—a stationary point may be only a "flat spot" in the graph.)

The next example shows how to sort out all the possibilities.

See the previous example: $f(x) = x^3$ has a "flat spot"—but not a maximum or minimum—at $x = 0$.

An important one.

■ **Example 2.** The graph of a function f' appears below—the f-graph is *not* shown.➻ Three points of interest are shown bulleted. Where, if anywhere, does f have local maximum or local minimum points? Why?

For now.

Graph of f'

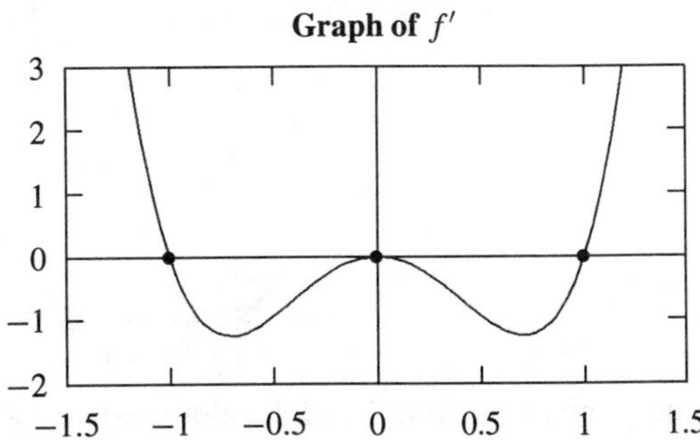

Solution: The three bullets on the graph—at $x = -1$, $x = 0$, and $x = 1$—represent *roots* of f' and therefore correspond to *stationary points* of f. What type of stationary point is each one: a local maximum, a local minimum, or just a flat spot?

The key to deciding is to check the *sign* of f' just before and just after each stationary point. We'll take each root of f' in turn:

At $x = -1$**.** Just *before*➻ $x = -1$, $f'(x) > 0$. Therefore (by a Fact above) f *increases* until $x = -1$. Just *after* $x = -1$, $f'(x) < 0$, so f *decreases* immediately after $x = -1$. This means that f has a *local maximum* at $x = -1$.

I.e., to the left of.

At $x = 1$**.** Consider values of x near $x = 1$. The graph shows that if $x < 1$, $f'(x) < 0$; if $x > 1$, $f'(x) > 0$. Thus, reasoning as above, f *decreases* before $x = 1$ and *increases* after $x = 1$. This means that f has a *local minimum* at $x = 1$.

At $x = 0$**.** This time the graph shows that $f'(x) < 0$ *on both sides* of $x = 0$. Thus f must decrease before *and* after $x = 0$, so $x = 0$ is *neither* a maximum nor a minimum point—just a flat spot in the f-graph.

Here, at last, is a possible f-graph. It agrees with everything we said above:

Graph of f

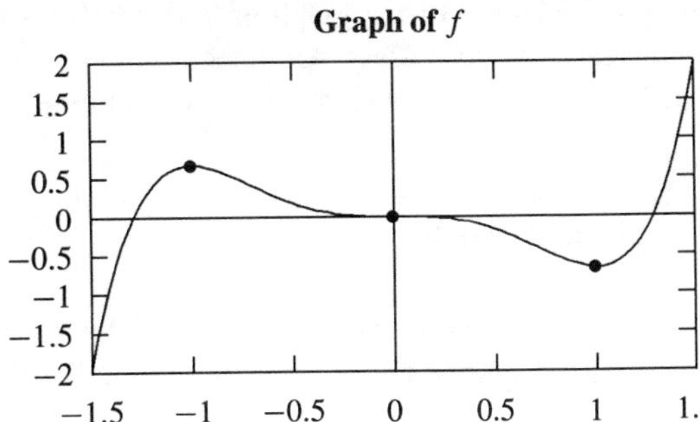

□

Let's summarize what we know about stationary points.

> **Fact: (First derivative test.)** Suppose that $f'(x_0) = 0$.
>
> If $f'(x) < 0$ for $x < x_0$ and $f'(x) > 0$ for $x > x_0$, then x_0 is a *local minimum point*.
>
> If $f'(x) > 0$ for $x < x_0$ and $f'(x) < 0$ for $x > x_0$, then x_0 is a *local maximum point*.

The next example shows what happens on a *crooked* graph.

*At $x = 0$ this function is **not** nice in the sense discussed above.*

■ **Example 3.** The function $f(x) = |x|$ has a local (and global) minimum point at $x = 0$, but not a stationary point. The graph shows why:

$f(x) = |x|$: a local minimum at $x = 0$

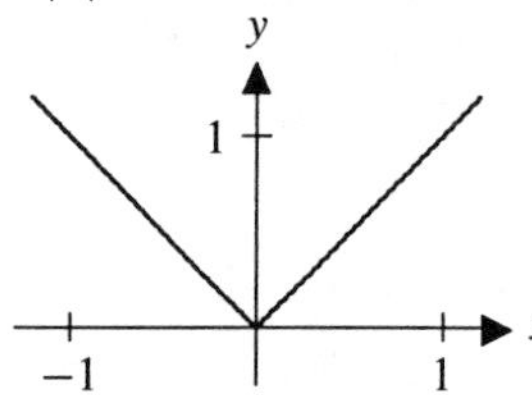

At $x = 0$ the graph has a "kink," and therefore *no* tangent line, and no well-defined slope. □

Concave up or concave down?

So far we've described concavity and inflection points informally, in graphical language. Here's a formal analytic definition:

> **Definition:** The graph of f is **concave up** at $x = a$ if the slope function f' is increasing at $x = a$. The graph of f is **concave down** at $x = a$ if f' is decreasing at $x = a$. Any point at which a graph's direction of concavity *changes* is an **inflection point** of the graph.

Look again.

The graphs of f and f' on page 115 illustrate everything:

Concave down. To the left of B the f-graph is *concave down*; To the left of B' the f'-graph is *decreasing*.

Concave up. To the right of B the f-graph is *concave up*; To the right of B' the f'-graph is *increasing*.

An inflection point. B is an inflection point of f; f' has a minimum point at B'.

Finding inflection points from the graph of f'

The direction of concavity of the graph of f depends, as the definitions show, on whether f' increases or decreases. An inflection point occurs, therefore, wherever f' *changes direction* i.e., wherever f' has a local minimum or a local maximum.

■ **Example 4.** Discuss concavity of the sine function. Find all inflection points; explain results in derivative language.

Do you agree? Are the roots of f' where they "should" be?

Solution: It's a fact—we'll show it carefully later—that if $f(x) = \sin x$, then $f'(x) = \cos x$. The graphs certainly make the claim plausible:

Graph of $f(x) = \sin x$

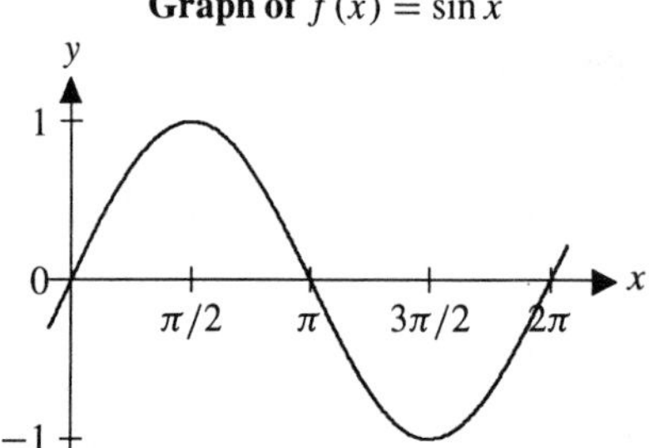

Graph of $f'(x) = \cos x$

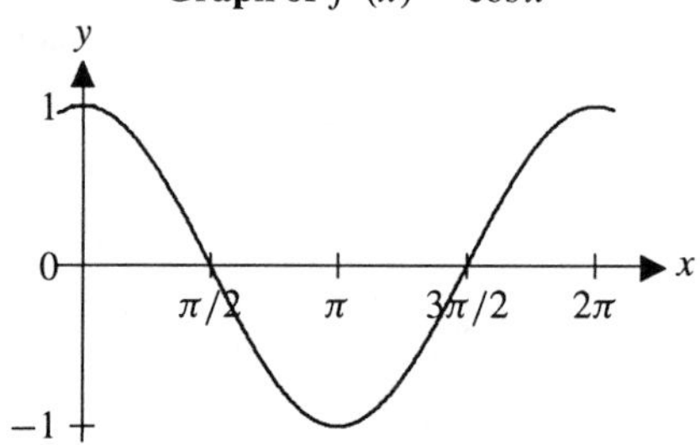

Notice:

Stationary points. f has *stationary points* (a local maximum point and a local minimum point) at $x = \pi/2$ and at $x = 3\pi/2$—exactly the roots of f'.

Global, too, in this case.

Increasing or decreasing? f *increases* on the intervals $(0, \pi/2)$ and $(3\pi/2, 2\pi)$—on the same intervals, f' is *positive*.

Concavity. f is *concave down* on $(0, \pi)$—where f' decreases—and *concave up* on $(\pi, 2\pi)$—where f' *increases*. In fact, f illustrates *every possible combination* of increasing/decreasing and concavity behavior.

Inflection points. f has an *inflection point* at each multiple of π—precisely where f' assumes a local maximum or local minimum. □

A sample problem

Here's a problem in the spirit of this section.

■ **Example 5.** The graph of the *derivative* of a function f is shown below.

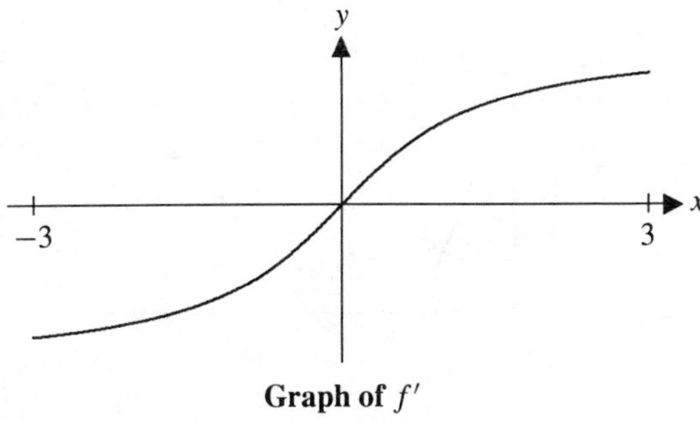

Graph of f'

(a) The equation $f(x) = 0$ can have *at most* two solutions in the interval $[-3, 3]$. Explain why.

(b) Explain why f *cannot* have two roots in the interval $[0, 3]$.

(c) Suppose that $f(0) = 1$. How many solutions does the equation $f(x) = 0$ have in the interval $[-3, 3]$? Explain.

Solution: Because f' is negative on the interval $(-3, 0)$ and positive on the interval $(0, 3)$, f itself must *decrease* on $(-3, 0)$ and *increase* on $(0, 3)$. Therefore f has a local *minimum* at $x = 0$, and no other stationary points. Therefore

(a) The graph of f is "U-shaped", so it can intersect the interval $[-3, 3]$ in at most two places.

(b) The graph of f *increases* on the interval $(0, 3)$, so it can cross the x-axis no more than once.

(c) If $f(0) = 1$, then f has *no* roots in the interval $[-3, 3]$, because f has its *minimum* value at $x = 0$.

□

Exercises

1. The graph of a function f is shown below. Several points are labeled.

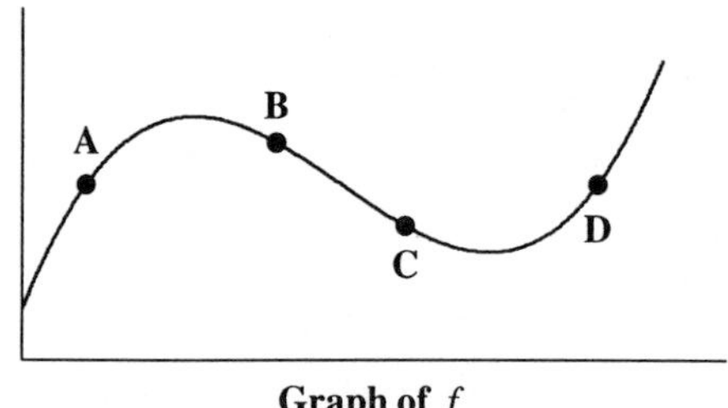

Graph of f

(a) At which labeled points is f' positive? Explain.

(b) Between which pairs of labeled points does f have a stationary point?

(c) Between which pair of labeled points does f have an inflection point?

(d) Between which pair of labeled points is f' increasing?

(e) Between which pair of labeled points does f' achieve its minimum value?

2. The graph of a function f is shown below.

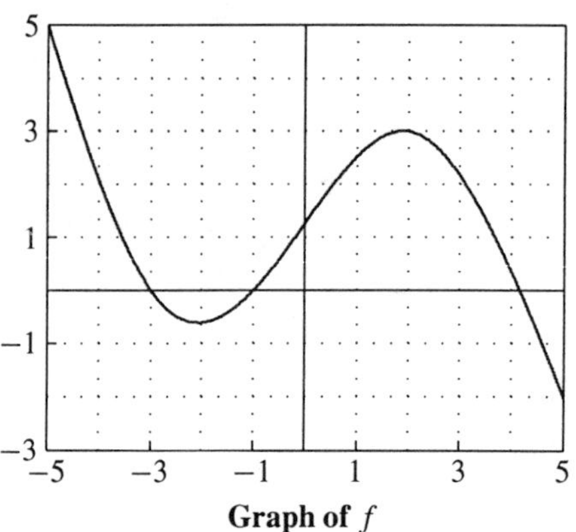

Graph of f

(a) On which intervals is f' negative? Positive?

(b) On which intervals is f' increasing? Decreasing?

(c) Where does f' achieve its maximum value? Estimate this value of f'.

(d) Where does f' achieve its minimum value? Estimate this value of f'.

(e) Sketch a graph of f'. [NOTE: Your sketch should be consistent with your answers to parts (a)–(d).]

3. The graph of a function f is shown below

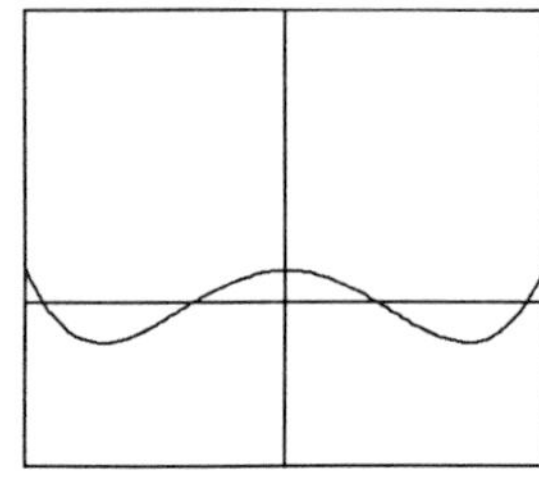
Graph of f

Which of the following figures could be the graph of f'? For each graph that you did *not* select, explain why it can't be the graph of f'.

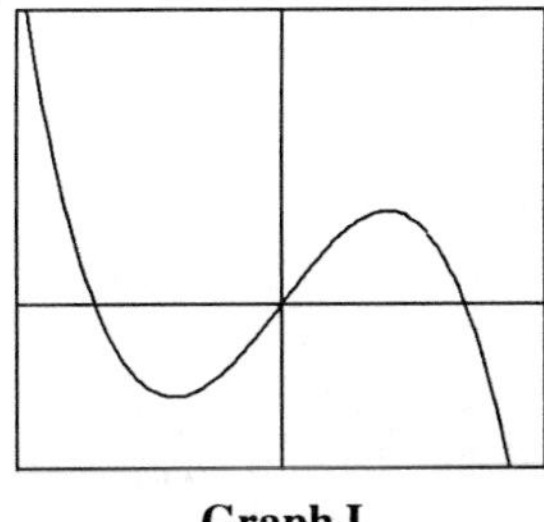

Graph I

Graph II

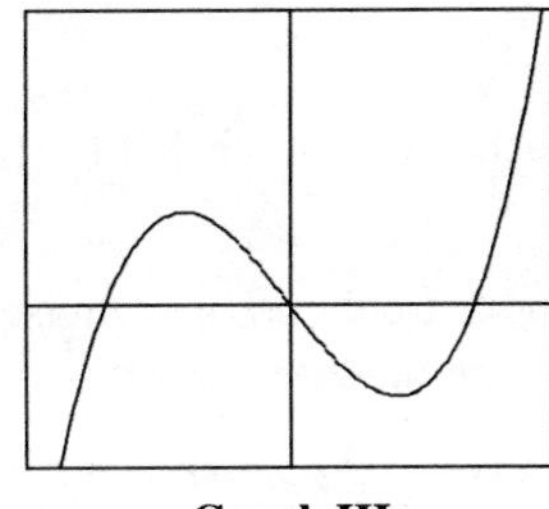

Graph III

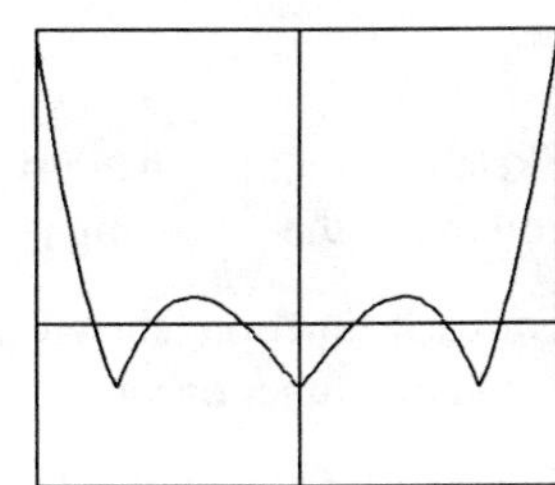

Graph IV

4. In the left-hand column below are graphs of several functions. In the right-hand column—in a different order—are graphs of the associated *derivative* functions. Match each function with its derivative. [NOTE: The scales on the graphs are not all the same.]

(a)
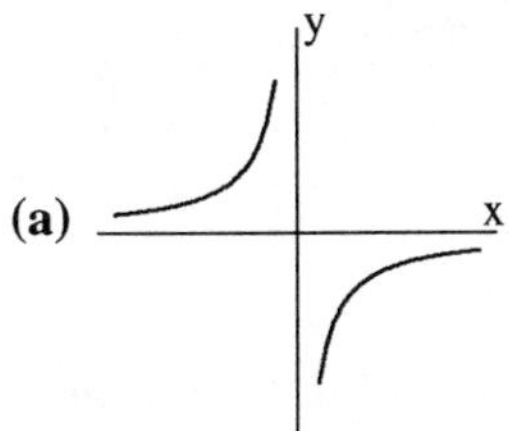

(i)
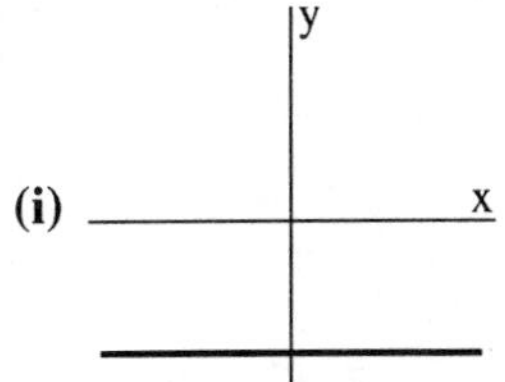

(b)
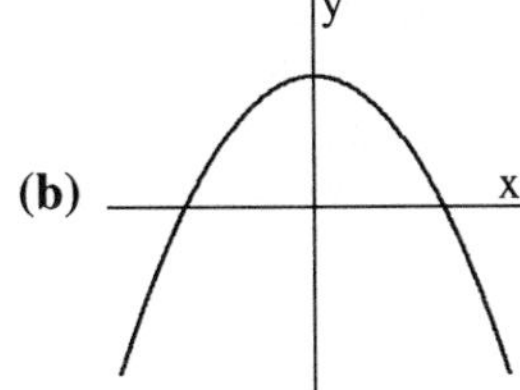

(ii)
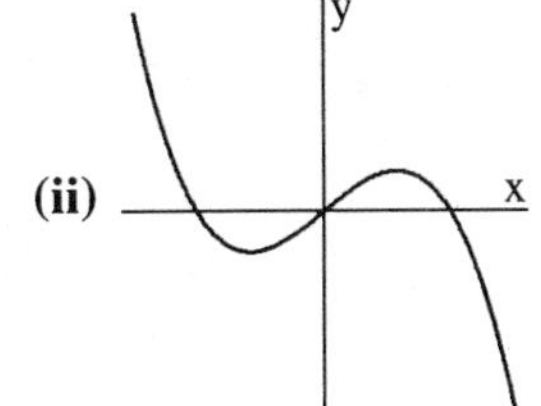

(c)
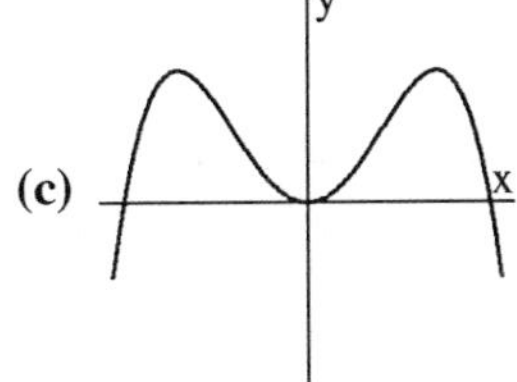

(iii)
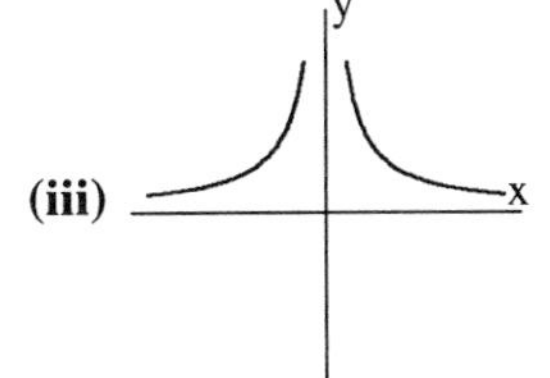

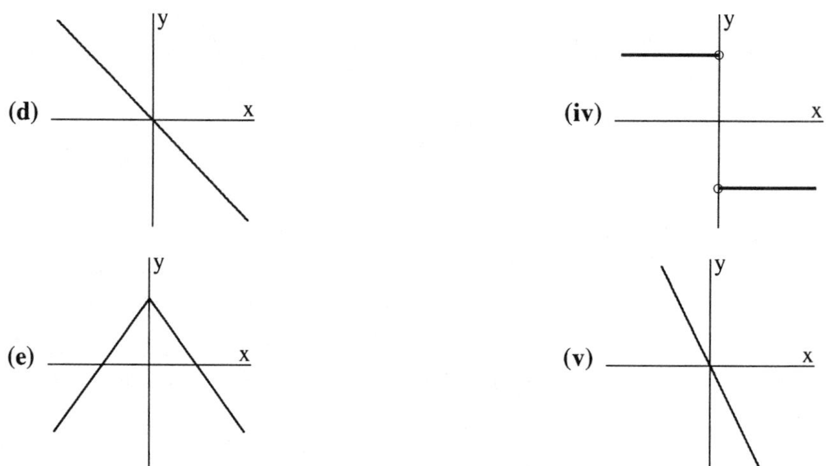

5. Sketch a graph of the derivative of each function labeled (i)–(v) in the right column of the preceding problem.

6. For each function labeled (a)–(e) in the left column of Exercise 4, sketch the graph of a function whose *derivative* is the function shown.

7. Graphs of f, f', and g (not the derivative of f) are shown below. Which is which? Explain how you can tell.

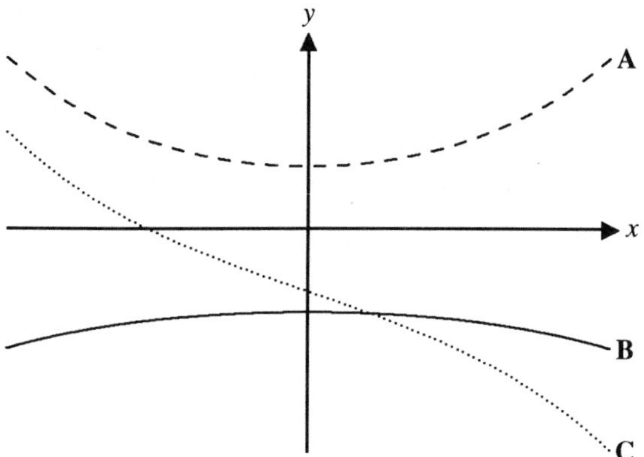

8. Graphs of f, f', and g (not the derivative of f) are shown below. Which is which? Explain how you can tell.

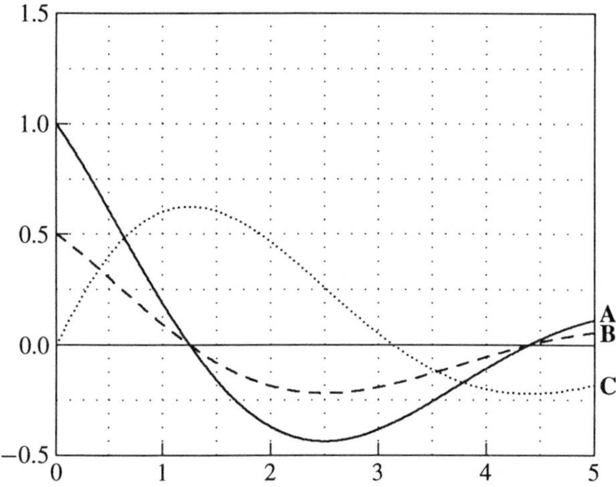

9. (a) Sketch the graph of a function f for which $f(x) > 0$ and $f'(x) > 0$ for all x.

   (b) Sketch the graph of a function g for which $g(x) > 0$ and $g'(x) < 0$ for all x.

   (c) Give formulas for functions f and g with these properties.

10. (a) Sketch the graph of a function f for which $f(x) < 0$ and $f'(x) > 0$ for all x.

    (b) Sketch the graph of a function g for which $g(x) < 0$ and $g'(x) < 0$ for all x.

    (c) Give formulas for functions f and g with these properties.

11. The graph of the derivative of a function f is shown below. Use the graph of f' to answer the following questions about f. [NOTE: The graph of f is not shown.]

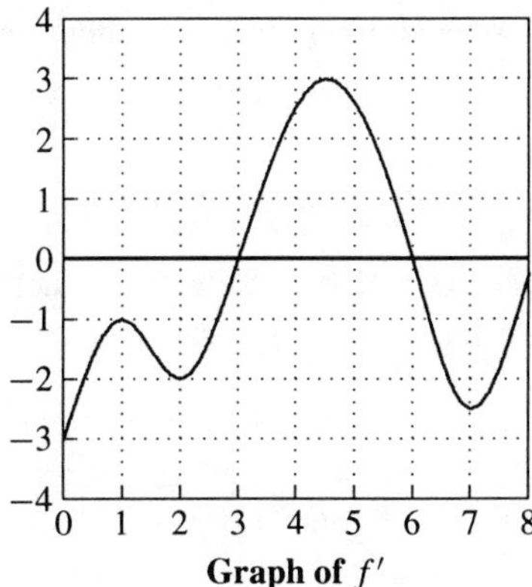

Graph of f'

   (a) On which intervals is f increasing? Decreasing?

   (b) Where does f have a stationary point?

   (c) Where does f have a local maximum? A local minimum?

   (d) On which intervals is f concave up? Concave down?

   (e) Where does f have a point of inflection?

   (f) Where does f achieve its maximum value on the interval $[0, 2]$? Its minimum value?

   (g) Where does f achieve its maximum value on the interval $[3, 6]$? Its minimum value?

   (h) Assume that $f(0) = 0$. Sketch a graph of f. (Your graph need only have the right general shape.)

   (i) How does your answer to part (h) change if $f(0) = 5$?

12. Suppose that $f(3) = -1$ and that f' is the function graphed in the previous problem.

    (a) Let ℓ be the line tangent to f at the point $(3, -1)$. Find an equation for ℓ.

    (b) Explain why ℓ lies below the curve $y = f(x)$ near $x = 4$.

    (c) Does ℓ lie above or below the curve $y = f(x)$ near $x = 2$? Justify your answer.

13. The graph of the derivative of a function g is shown below. Use the graph of g' to answer the following questions about g. [NOTE: The graph of g is not shown.]

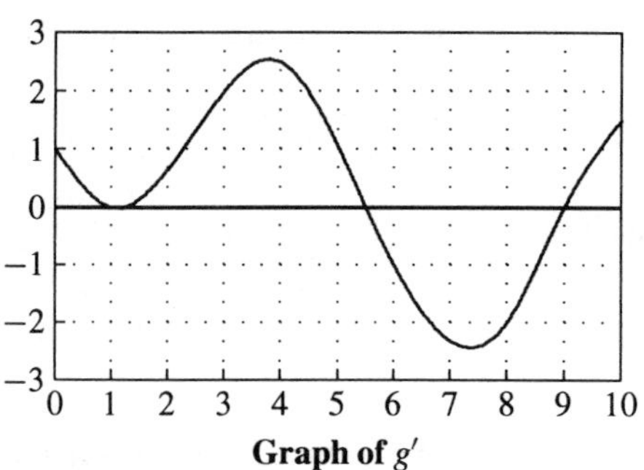

Graph of g'

(a) Where does g have stationary points?

(b) Where does g have local maxima? Local minima?

(c) The graph of g' has a local maximum at $x = 3.8$ and a local minimum at $x = 7.4$. What do these facts say about the graph of g?

(d) Is g concave up or concave down at $x = 5$? At $x = 8$? Justify your answers.

(e) Suppose that $g(0) = 0$. Sketch a graph of g.

14. The graph of the derivative of a function f appears below. [NOTE: The graph of f is not shown.]

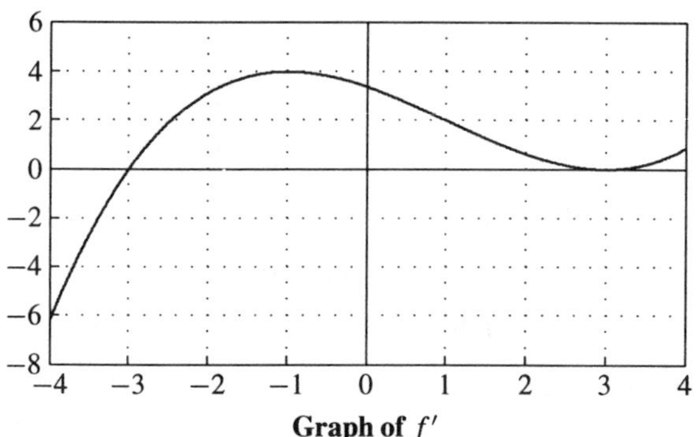

Graph of f'

(a) Where does f have stationary points?

(b) Where does f have local maxima? Local minima? Points of inflection?

(c) Is f concave up or concave down at $x = 1$? Justify your answer.

(d) Sketch the graphs of *two* functions that could be f.

15. The graph of the *derivative* of a function f is shown below.

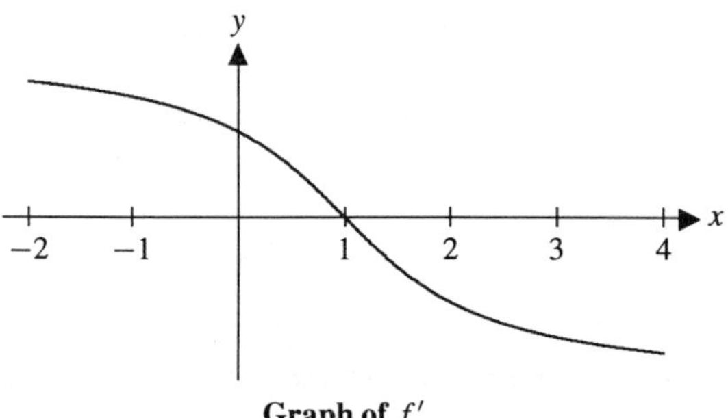

Graph of f'

(a) Where in the interval $[-2, 4]$ is f increasing? Where is f decreasing? Why?

(b) Where in $[-2, 4]$ does f have a stationary point? Is it a local maximum, a local minimum, or neither?

(c) Describe in words the general shape of the f-graph over the interval $[-2, 4]$.

16. Suppose that the derivative of a function f is $f'(x) = x + 2$.

(a) On which intervals, if any, is f increasing?

(b) At which values of x, if any, does f have a local maximum? A local minimum?

(c) On which intervals, if any, is f concave down?

(d) Sketch a graph of f.

Repeat the previous exercise for each of the following derivative functions. (Report approximate answers to two decimal places.)

17. $f'(x) = (x-2)(x+4)$

18. $f'(x) = (x-2)^2(x+4)$

19. $f'(x) = (x+1)^2(x-2)$

20. $f'(x) = (x^2+9)(x+6)$

21. $f'(x) = (x^2-9)(x+3)$

22. $f'(x) = \dfrac{1}{x^2+1}$

23. $f'(x) = \dfrac{x-2}{x^2+5}$

24. $f'(x) = \dfrac{x+1}{\sqrt{x^2+1}}$

25. $f'(x) = \dfrac{x^2+2}{\sqrt{x^4+8}}$

26. $f'(x) = e^{-x^2}$

27. $f'(x) = (9-x^2)e^{-x/4}$

28. $f'(x) = \ln(1+x^2)$

29. Let $f(x) = e^{\sin x}$. How many roots does f' have in the interval $[0, 2\pi]$? Where are they located? Justify your answers.

30. Suppose that the following information is known about a function f:

(i) f is positive on $[-7, 8]$

(ii) f is increasing on $[-2, 3]$

(iii) f is decreasing on $(4, 10)$

(iv) f' is decreasing on $[-3, 6]$

(v) $f'(4) = 0$

(vi) f has an inflection point at $x = 7$

(a) Explain why f has a local extremum at $x = 4$. Is it a local maximum or a local minimum?

(b) Where is f concave down?

(c) Where is f' nonnegative?

(d) Rank the four values $f'(4)$, $f(5)$, $f'(6)$, and $f(7)$ in increasing order.

(e) Sketch the graph of a function f with these properties.

2.4 The geometry of higher-order derivatives

As before, "nice" means that all the derivatives in question exist and have "continuous" graphs.

"Differentiate" means "find the derivative of."

The derivative of a nice function f is *another* nice function f'. Given the many uses of f', the next step is natural: *differentiate again*. The resulting function, denoted f'', is called the **second derivative** of f. Like f', the second derivative f'' carries useful information about f. What information? How do we read it?

Prime advice. With several functions (f, f', f'', etc.) in the picture, it's easy to lose one's bearings. One organizing principle helps:

> *The derivative of* any *function tells whether, and how fast, that function increases or decreases.*

We defined concavity in terms of f' in the last section.

If, say, $f''(a) > 0$, then f' is *increasing* at $x = a$. It follows, therefore, that f must be concave *up* at $x = a$.

What f'' says about f—concavity revisited

The graph of f is concave up or down at $x = a$ depending on whether f' is increasing or decreasing at $x = a$. The principle above, applied to f', reads like this:

> *If $f''(a) > 0$, then f' increases at $x = a$. If $f''(a) < 0$, then f' decreases at $x = a$.*

This leads to a useful test for concavity:

> **Fact:** The graph of f is concave *up* where $f'' > 0$ and concave *down* where $f'' < 0$.

(The fact gives no information if $f''(a) = 0$. In that case, as we'll see, f may be either concave up or concave down.)

■ **Example 1.** Interpret the concavity of the sine function using the second derivative.

Solution: If $f(x) = \sin x$, then $f'(x) = \cos x$ and $f''(x) = -\sin x$. (We'll "derive" both these formulas carefully later in this chapter. For the moment we'll assume that they hold.) Below are graphs of f and f'', on the same axes:

Graphs of f and f''

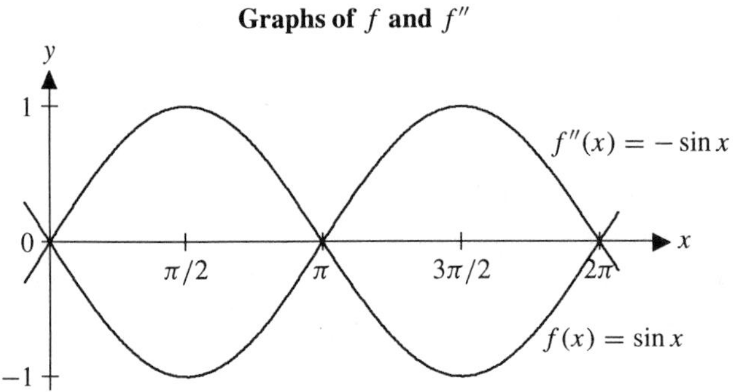

Do so!

It's easy to verify that the advertised relationship holds: f is concave up precisely where $f'' > 0$, and concave down where $f'' < 0$. □

Wave claims. We claimed above, on graphical evidence alone, that if $f(x) = \sin x$, then $f'(x) = \cos x$. Later we claimed that if $g(x) = \cos x$, then $g'(x) = -\sin x$. Both claims require careful proof.

Notice, though, that the two claims are essentially the same. Since the graphs of $f(x)$ and $g(x)$ differ only by a horizontal translation, so must the graphs of their derivatives.

Finding inflection points

A function f has an inflection point wherever the *sign* of f'' changes. It follows, therefore, that for nice functions

Every inflection point of f occurs at a root *of f''.*

On the sine graph, for instance, inflection points occur at every root of f''.

Derive carefully, again. The *converse* of the previous statement is false:

$f''(a)$ may *be zero even if no inflection occurs at $x = a$.*

The next example illustrates why: if $f''(a) = 0$ then a is a stationary point of f', but not necessarily a local maximum or local minimum.

■ **Example 2.** Graphs of a function f and its derivatives f' and f'' are shown below. Discuss concavity and inflection points of f.

The functions shown have simple formulas: $f(x) = x^4$, $f'(x) = 4x^3$, and $f''(x) = 12x^2$. We "hid" the formulas here in the margin because they're not really germane to this problem.

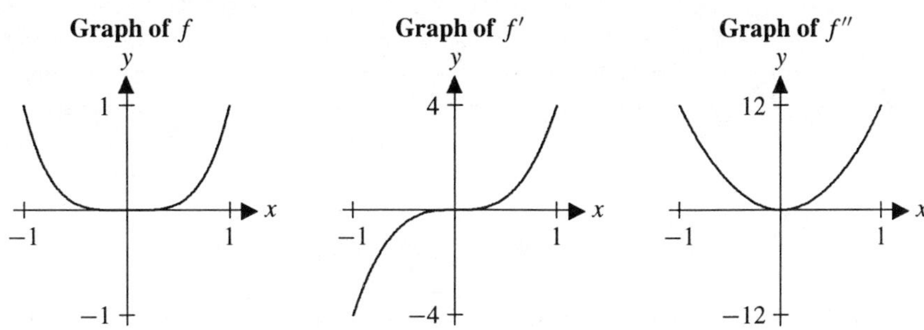

Solution: Although $f''(0) = 0$, $(0, 0)$ is *not* an inflection point. On the contrary, the graph of f is concave up *everywhere*, because f' is everywhere increasing.

Notice too how the shape of the f-graph reflects the fact that $f(0) = f'(0) = f''(0) = 0$. If *several* derivatives of a function are zero at a point $x = a$, the graph of f looks "flat" near $x = a$. □

The larger the number of derivatives that vanish at $x = a$, the "flatter" the graph.

All together now: maximum points, minimum points, concavity, and the second derivative

A stationary point on the graph of a function f may be a local maximum point, a local minimum point, or neither. If an accurate graph of f is available, it's usually obvious which case applies. If not, concavity often helps us distinguish among these alternatives. The idea is simple:

At a local minimum *point, the graph of f is concave* up.

At a local maximum *point, the graph of f is concave* down.

The following claims are all immediate consequences. Together they're known as the second derivative test:

> **Fact: (Second derivative test.)** Suppose that $f'(a) = 0$.
>
> If $f''(a) > 0$, then f has a local *minimum* at $x = a$.
>
> If $f''(a) < 0$, then f has a local *maximum* at $x = a$.
>
> If $f''(a) = 0$, anything can happen: f may have a local maximum, a local minimum, or neither at $x = a$, and the f-graph may be concave up, concave down, or have an inflection point.

If—but only if—appropriate care is taken, the second derivative test can be a convenient tool for finding maxima and minima of functions.

Stirring in the formulas

We return, finally, to the functions f, f', and f'' we first met at the beginning of the last section—this time with algebraic formulas added. Here are all three formulas:

$$f(x) = x^3 - x^2 - 6x; \qquad f'(x) = 3x^2 - 2x - 6; \qquad f''(x) = 6x - 2.$$

Here are all three graphs:

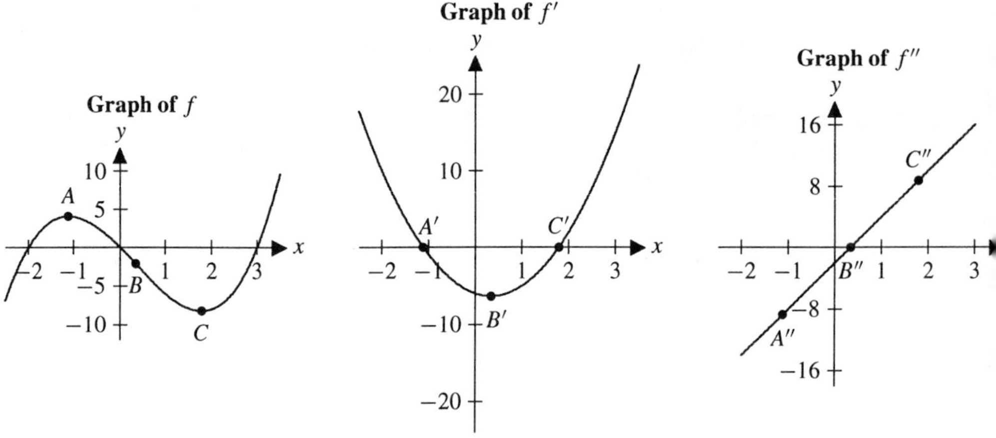

Combining graphs *and* formulas, we can sharpen and reinterpret our earlier observations:

What the derivative says. From either the graph or the algebraic definition of f' it's clear that as $x \to \infty$, $f'(x) \to \infty$. Therefore as $x \to \infty$ the *slope* of the f-graph is (a) positive and (b) increasing. Equivalently, the f-graph itself is (a) rising and (b) rising *faster and faster.*

Stationary points. The f-graph has horizontal tangent lines at the stationary points A and C. According to the derivative *formula*, stationary points occur at values of x for which

$$f'(x) = 3x^2 - 2x - 6 = 0$$

And, in some respects, atypical.

By great good luck, $f'(x)$ happens to be a quadratic polynomial. By the quadratic formula, the roots of f' fall at $x = (1 \pm \sqrt{19})/3$. In decimal form, the roots are $x_1 \approx -1.1196$ and $x_2 \approx 1.7863$.

How many stationary points? The calculation just above shows, too, that f' has *only* two roots. Hence A and C are the *only* stationary points of f.

Finding the inflection point. The inflection point B occurs where f' takes its minimum value, somewhere near $x = 0.3$. Where *exactly* is B?

The formula for f'' answers the question: A root of f'' occurs at $x = 1/3$, where

$$f''(x) = 6x - 2 = 0.$$

As its graph shows, f'' changes sign at $x = 1/3$, so f changes its direction of concavity there.

The formula for f'' shows a little more: f'' changes sign only at $x = 1/3$. Therefore f changes concavity only once.

Morals

We have mentioned a large, even bewildering, variety of connections among f, f', and f''. The reader may be tempted to *memorize* complicated lists of cases and subcases, particularly as applied to concavity, inflection points, and the second derivative. This would be a mistake. A better strategy is to learn—and understand—the single organizing principle behind this welter of information:

The derivative function f' tells whether, and how fast, the original function f increases or decreases.

A sample problem

The following multi-part example problem gives some idea of the variety of uses to which derivatives—and higher derivatives—can be put.

■ **Example 3.** The graph of f', the derivative of a certain function f, is shown below. (The f-graph is not shown!)

Graph of f'

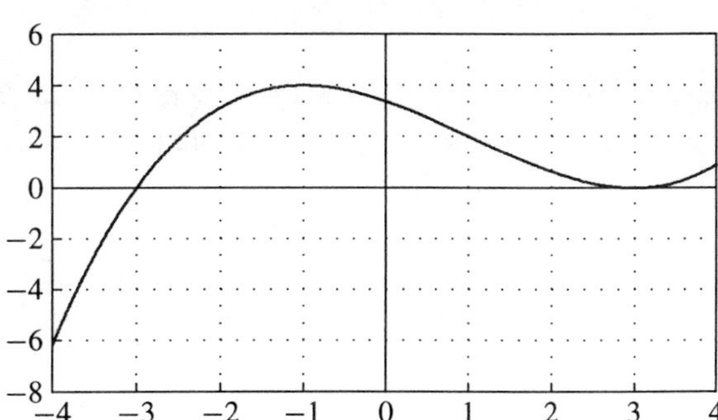

(a) Estimate $f''(-3)$.

(b) Where is f concave up? Concave down?

(c) Where does f have inflection points?

Solution: Looked at properly, the graph answers all our questions. It's crucial to remember—always—that the picture shows f', not f or f''.

(a) By definition, $f''(-3) = (f')'(-3)$, i.e., the slope of the graph above at $x = -3$. A careful look shows that this slope is about 5.

(b) Since $f''(-3) > 0$, f is concave *up* at $x = -3$. More generally, f is concave up wherever $f'' > 0$, i.e., where f' is increasing. The picture shows that this occurs for $-4 \le x \le -1$ and for $3 \le x \le 4$. For the same reason, f is concave down for $-1 \le x \le 3$.

(c) The function f has an inflection point wherever its direction of concavity changes. The previous part shows that this happens at $x = -1$ and at $x = 3$.

□

Exercises

1. The graph of a function f appears below.

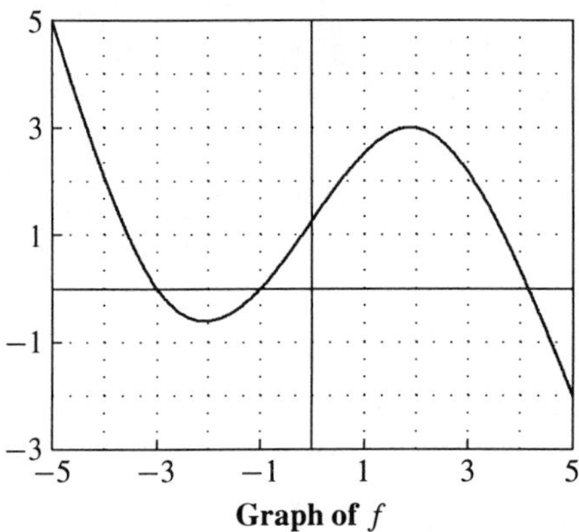

Graph of f

(a) For which values of x, if any, is $f''(x)$ negative? Positive? Zero?

(b) Rank the four numbers $f'(0)$, $f(2)$, $f'(2)$, and $f''(2)$ in increasing order.

2. The graph of a function f appears below. [NOTE: f has points of inflection near $x = 0.82$ and near $x = 1.93$; f has stationary points near $x = 0.52$, $x = 1.19$, and $x = 2.42$.]

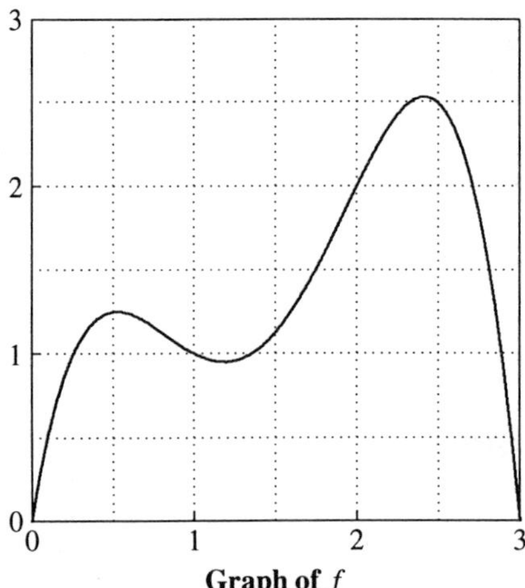

Graph of f

(a) Where is f'' positive? Negative? Zero?

(b) Rank the four values 0, $f''(0.5)$, $f''(1.2)$, and $f''(2.4)$ in increasing order.

3. The graph of the second derivative of a function g is shown below. Use this graph to answer the following questions about g and g'.

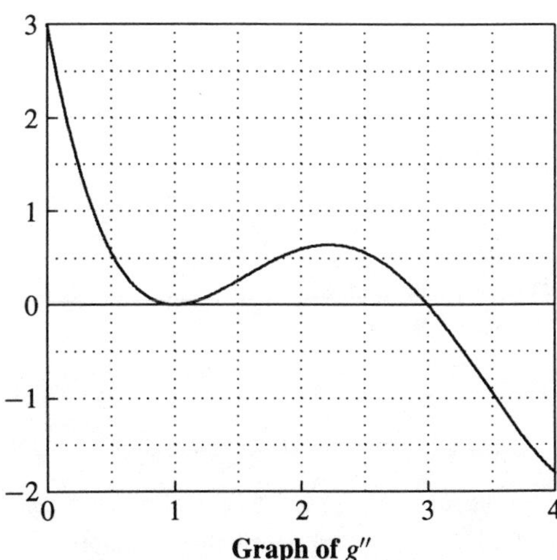

Graph of g''

(a) Where is g concave up?

(b) Where does g have points of inflection?

(c) Rank the four numbers $g'(0)$, $g'(1)$, $g'(2)$, and $g'(3)$ in increasing order.

(d) Suppose that $g'(0) = 0$. Is g increasing or decreasing at $x = 2$? Justify your answer.

(e) Suppose that $g'(0) = -4$. Is g increasing or decreasing at $x = 2$? Justify your answer.

(f) Suppose that $g'(1) = -1$. Is g increasing or decreasing at $x = 2$? Justify your answer.

4. Suppose that $g' = f$ where f is the function defined in problem 2 above.

(a) Estimate $g''(0)$, $g''(0.5)$, $g''(1)$, $g''(1.5)$, $g''(2)$, and $g''(3)$.

(b) Sketch a graph of g'' over the interval $[0, 3]$.

5. In the left-hand column below are graphs of several functions. In the right-hand column—in a different order—are graphs of the *second* derivatives of these functions. Match each function with its second derivative function. [NOTE: The scales on the graphs are not all the same.]

(a) 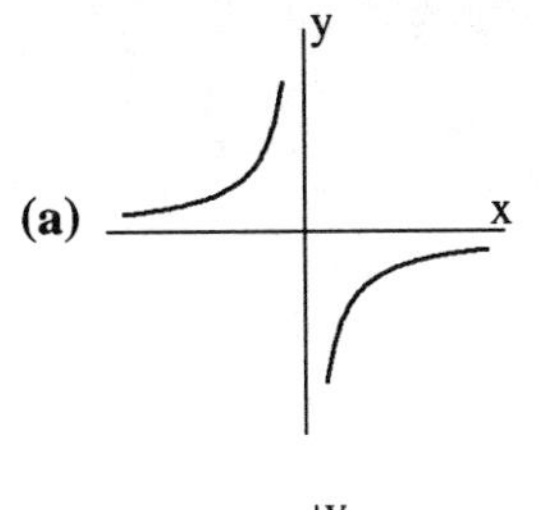

(i) 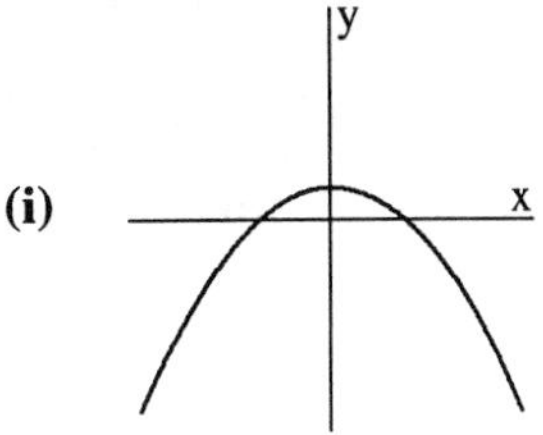

(b) 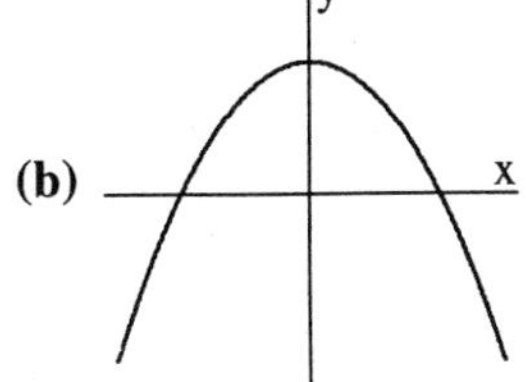

(ii) 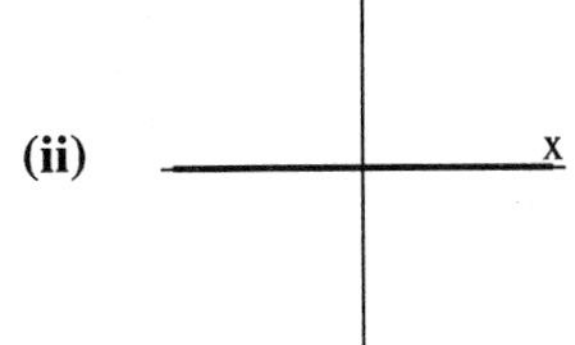

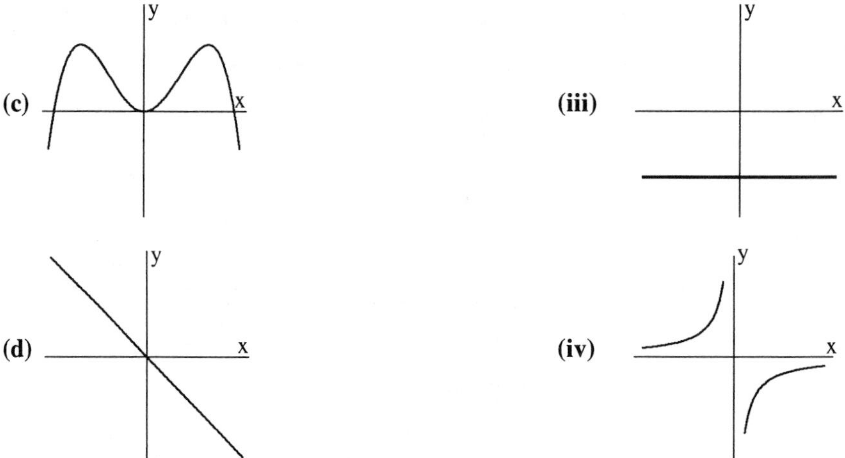

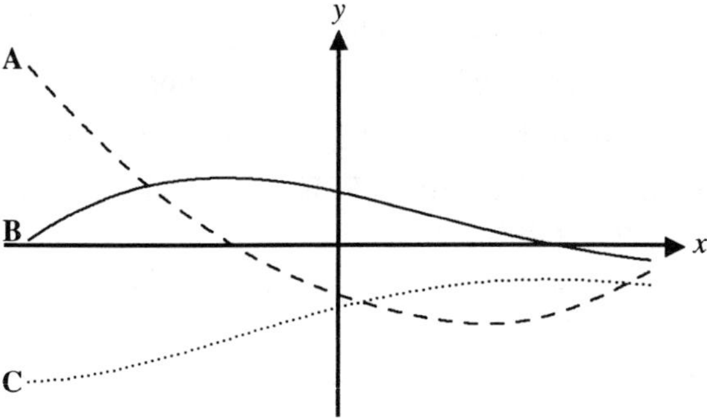

6. Graphs of f, f', and f'' appear below. Which is which? How can you tell?

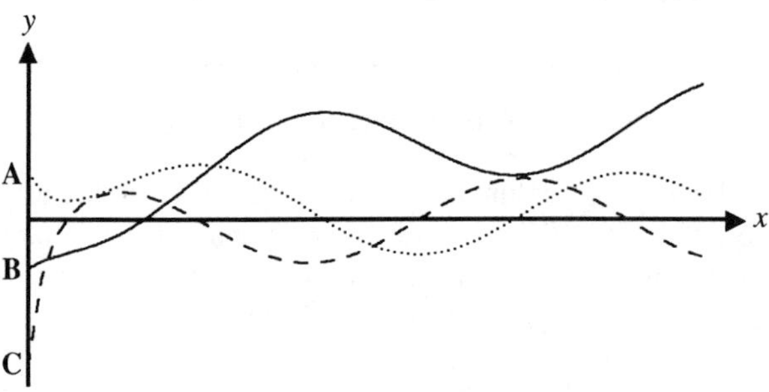

7. Graphs of f, f', and f'' appear below. Which is which? How can you tell?

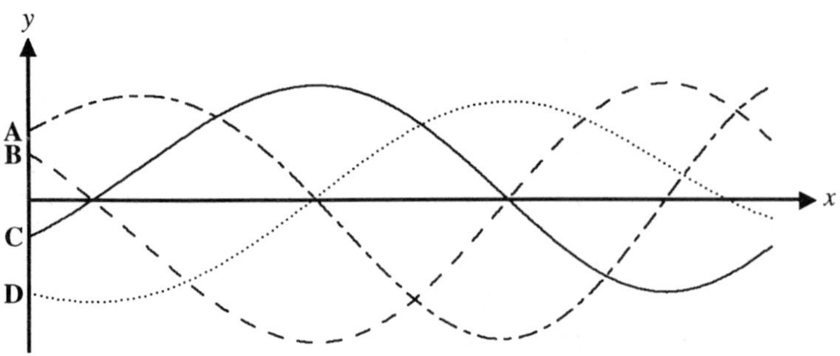

8. Graphs of f, f', f'', and g (not a derivative of f) are shown below. Which is which? How you can tell?

9. Suppose that the functions f, f', and f'' are continuous on $(-\infty, \infty)$ and that f has the following properties:

   (i) f is negative on $(-10, 1)$ and positive on $(3, 10)$.

   (ii) f is increasing on $(-\infty, 5)$ and decreasing on $(5, \infty)$.

   (iii) f is concave up on $(-\infty, 2)$ and concave down on $(2, \infty)$.

   Rank the five values $f'(0)$, $f'(1)$, $f'(2)$, $f''(2)$, and $f'(8)$ in increasing order.

10. Water flows at a constant rate into a large tank that is a cylinder with a circular base. Let $V(t)$ be the volume of water in the tank at time t and $H(t)$ be the height of the water in the tank at time t. Give a physical interpretation of each of the following expressions and indicate whether each is positive, negative or zero at the time t^* when the tank is one-quarter full:

    (a) $V'(t)$ (c) $V''(t)$

    (b) $H'(t)$ (d) $H''(t)$

11. Repeat problem #10 assuming that the tank is a sphere.

12. Repeat problem #10 assuming that the tank is an inverted cone (i.e., a cone with its vertex pointing down).

13. Interpret each sentence below as a statement about a function and its derivatives. In each case, indicate clearly what the function is and what each symbol means.

    (a) The child's temperature is still rising, but the penicillin seems to be taking effect.

    (b) The cost of a new car is increasing at an increasing rate.

    (c) Upper Midwest Industries profit growth slows.

14. Let $U(t)$ be the number of people unemployed in a country t months after the election of a economically conservative president. Translate each of the following facts about the graph of $U(t)$ into statements about the unemployment situation. (Don't forget to specify units in your answers.)

    (a) The y-intercept of $U(t)$ is 2,000,000.

    (b) $U(2) = 3{,}000{,}000$.

    (c) $U'(20) = 10{,}000$.

    (d) $U''(36) = 800$ and $U'(36) = 0$.

15. (a) Sketch the graph of a function f for which $f(x) > 0$, $f'(x) > 0$, and $f''(x) > 0$ for all x.

    (b) Sketch the graph of a function f for which $f(x) > 0$, $f'(x) < 0$, and $f''(x) > 0$ for all x.

16. (a) Sketch the graph of a function f for which $f(x) < 0$, $f'(x) < 0$, and $f''(x) < 0$ for all x.

    (b) Sketch the graph of a function f for which $f(x) < 0$, $f'(x) > 0$, and $f''(x) < 0$ for all x.

17. Is there a f for which $f(x) > 0$, $f'(x) < 0$, and $f''(x) < 0$ for all x? If so, sketch the graph of such a function. If not, explain why no such function exists.

18. Is there a function f for which $f(x) < 0$ and $f''(x) > 0$ for all x? If so, sketch the graph of such a function. If not, explain why a function with these properties can't be found.

19. Assume that f is a continuous function defined on the closed interval $[-3, 3]$ such that $f(-3) = 4$ and $f(3) = 1$. Furthermore, assume that f' and f'' are continuous on $(-3, 3)$ and that the following information is known about these functions:

x	$-3 \le x < -1$	-1	$-1 < x < 0$	0	$0 < x < 1$	1	$1 < x \le 3$
$f'(x)$	$+$	0	$-$	$-$	$-$	0	$-$
$f''(x)$	$-$	$-$	$-$	0	$+$	0	$-$

(a) Sketch the graph of a function that has the given properties.

(b) What are the x-coordinates of the points where f achieves its maximum and minimum values on the interval $[-3, 3]$? Justify your answer.

20. Sketch the graph of a continuous function g that has *all* of the following properties:

(i) The domain of g is the interval $[-3, 5]$.
(ii) $g''(x) < 0$ for all $x \in (-2, 1)$
(iii) $g''(x) > 0$ for all $x \in (1, 2)$
(iv) $g'(-2) < 0$
(v) $g'(4) > 0$
(vi) $g'(1) = 0$ but $g(1)$ is neither the maximum nor the minimum value of g over the interval $[-2, 4]$

21. Sketch the graph of a continuous function that satisfies the following conditions:

(i) $f'(x) < 0$ for all $x \neq 4$
(ii) $f'(4)$ does not exist
(iii) $f''(x) < 0$ for all $x < 4$
(iv) $f''(x) > 0$ for all $x > 4$

22. It can be shown that if f is an even function, then f' is an odd function, and that if f is an odd function, then f' is an even function. Use these facts to show that if f is an even function, then f'' is an even function.

23. Suppose that $1 \le f''(x) \le 3$ when $2 \le x \le 4$, that $f'(2) = 5$, and that $f(2) = -6$.

(a) Explain why $f'(3) \le 8$.

(b) Use part (a) to show that $f(3) \le 2$.

(c) Explain why $f'(3) \ge 6$.

(d) Find upper and lower bounds on $f'(4)$.

(e) Find upper and lower bounds on $f(4)$.

24. Suppose that the functions f, f', and f'' are continuous on $(-\infty, \infty)$, that $f'(2) = -1$, and that $0.1 < f''(x) < 0.5$ when $2 < x < 4$. Find upper and lower bounds on the value of $f'(3)$. [HINT: Apply the racetrack principle.]

25. Suppose that the line $y = 2x - 1$ is tangent to the graph of f at $x = 3$ and that $f''(x) > 0$ when $0 < x < 5$.

    (a) Find $f(3)$ and $f'(3)$.

    (b) Explain why $7 < f(4)$ must be true.

    (c) Find a lower bound on the value of $f(2)$.

26. Suppose that $f(2) = 5$, $f'(2) = 2$, and f is concave up everywhere.

    (a) How many roots could f have? What can you say about the location of these roots?

    (b) Find a lower bound on the value of $f(0)$.

    (c) Suppose that $f(-2) = -1$. Show that $f(0) < 3$.

27. Is the following statement true or false? Justify your answer.

    If $f(2) = 3$, $f'(2) = 1$, and $f''(2) = 0$, then the graph of $f(x)$ has an inflection point at $(2, 3)$.

28. Suppose that $f'(c) = f''(c) = 0$, but $f'''(c) > 0$. Does f have a local minimum, a local maximum, or an inflection point at c? Explain.

2.5 Average and instantaneous rates: defining the derivative

In previous sections we introduced and studied derivatives informally, interpreting them as rates or slopes. In this section we'll take a more formal point of view.

Given an original function f and an input $x = a$, what exactly do we mean, mathematically, by $f'(a)$? We've thought of $f'(a)$ as the slope of f at $x = a$, or as the instantaneous rate of change of y with respect to x at $x = a$, but important questions remain: What, exactly, is the *instantaneous* rate of change of a function at a point? How, precisely, is the tangent line to a graph at a point defined? Most important of all:

> *How can we use a formula for f to calculate—not just estimate—values of f'?*

The rate of change problem

Drivers calculate speed from odometer readings. This is a no-frills model.

Exactly at midnight, Professor X drives away in her brand-new "Göttingen" automobile. The odometer reads zero. There is no speedometer.

Consulting her odometer and wristwatch, Professor X can find for any time t (in hours) her total distance $D(t)$ (in miles) traveled since midnight. She might even plot her readings, as we did:

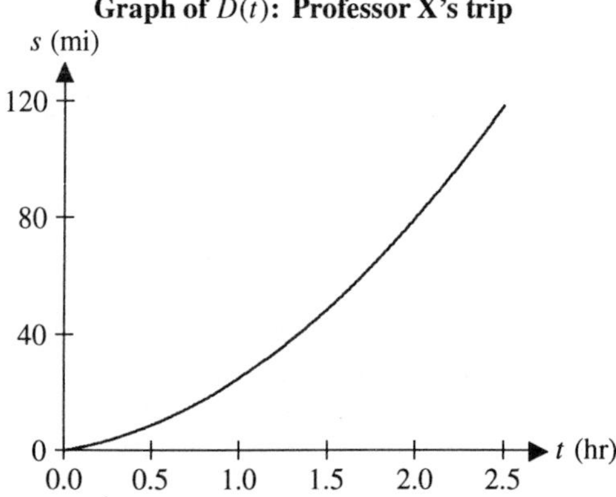

How can Professor X compute her speed at time $t = 2$, when she expects to reach a notorious speed trap? Reading the odometer at $t = 2$ won't help. It might say that she'd traveled, say, 80 miles in two hours, and hence that her *average* speed was 40 mph for the trip, but what about her speed at the *instant* $t = 2$?

She's right: the inexpensive Göttingen responds slowly both to throttle and to brake.

Professors say "hence," even to themselves.

Professor X reasons that her *average* speed over a short interval, say $t = 1.99$ to $t = 2.00$, should be about equal to her *instantaneous* speed at any time during the same interval. The odometer reports 0.6985 miles of travel during the interval. "Hence," thinks Professor X, "my average speed over the short period must have been

$$\frac{0.6985 \text{ miles}}{0.01 \text{ hours}} = 69.85 \text{ miles per hour}.$$

I'd better slow down."

The tangent line problem

The tangent line problem asks:

> *Given a curve C and a point P on C, describe the line tangent to C at P.*

■ **Example 1.** Which line is tangent to the graph of $f(x) = x^2 + x$ at $x = 2$?

Solution: Here's part of the graph, with a plausible tangent line at the point $P = (2, 6)$.

A tangent line to the graph of $y = x^2 + x$

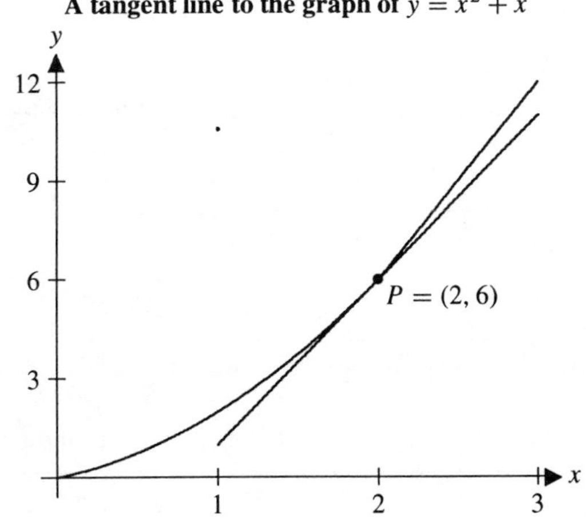

From the graph alone we can *estimate* that the tangent line L has slope 5. If we're right, then L has equation $y = 5(x - 2) + 6$.

Check this for yourself.

Finding the slope of L *exactly* is complicated by the fact that we know for certain only one point on L. To start, we might look at a line L' through *two* nearby points on the graph, such as those at $x = 2$ and $x = 2.01$. We expect that L and L' will have similar slopes. Knowing *two* points on L' means that its slope is easy to find:

$$\frac{\Delta f}{\Delta x} = \frac{f(2.01) - f(2)}{2.01 - 2} = \frac{6.0501 - 6}{0.01} = 5.01.$$

This numerical evidence further supports our guess that $f'(2) = 5$. □

Because of the shape of the graph near $x = 2$, the slope of L' slightly overestimates the slope of L.

Sharpening the tangent line problem

We stated the tangent line problem in intuitive but slightly vague terms. What does it mean for a curve to "be given," and how should we "describe" the line tangent to C at P?

Given by equations. Curves are often "given" as equations (e.g., $x^2 + y^2 = 4$) or as functions (e.g., $f(x) = x^2 + x$.) Some curves are given *only* graphically or numerically, without any algebraic formula attached. In that case tangent lines can be found only approximately. If a curve C *has* an exact formula, we'd like to use it to find an exact formula for the line tangent to C at P.

Wanted: slope. A line L is completely determined by its slope and a point P on it. In the tangent line problem, a point P is given from the start, so "finding" L means, in effect, finding the *slope* of L.

Estimating slope. If a curve C *has* a tangent line at P, we can estimate its slope either "by hand"—i.e., by drawing a line that "fits" C at P—or by "zooming in"—i.e., by viewing C near P in a plotting window small enough so that C appears straight.

No tangent line. Not every curve C *has* a tangent line at a given point P. For example, the graph of $y = |x|$ has a sharp corner at $P = (0, 0)$, so no single straight line can be said to "fit" the graph at P.

Draw a picture to convince yourself.

■ **Example 2.** We guessed above that the line L with equation $y = 5(x - 2) + 6$ is tangent to C, the graph of $f(x) = x^2 + x$, at $x = 2$. Does zooming support this guess? How?

Solution: Here are graphs of C and L at three scales:

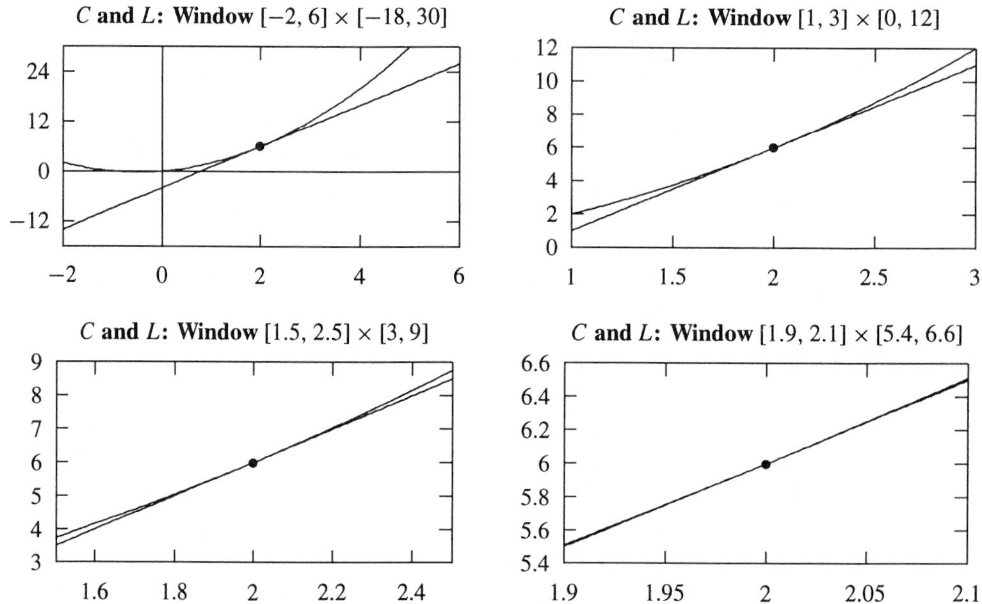

The graphs show that C, viewed close up, *does* resemble L, as claimed. In particular, because L has slope 5, so does the curve C at the point $(2, 6)$. □

The problems solved: secant lines and tangent lines, average rates and instantaneous rates

Graphical methods (zooming until straight, drawing tangent lines by hand, etc.) give simple and useful *estimates* of slopes and rates. For more precision—and to get deeper under the skin of the derivative—we need clear, concise definitions, in mathematical language, for instantaneous rates and for slopes of tangent lines. The concept of **limit** turns out to be just the tool we need.

We'll see more on limits in the next two sections.

We'll solve our two problems "in parallel." First we pose them explicitly:

The tangent line problem: Let $y = f(x)$ be a function. Find the slope of the line tangent to the graph of f at $x = 2$.

The instantaneous speed problem: Let the function $s = D(t)$ give the distance, in miles, traveled by a car up to time t, in hours. Find the instantaneous speed at time $t = 2$.

Secant lines, tangent lines, and limits

Given two points P and Q on a curve C, we can draw the *secant line* through P and Q. If P and Q are close together it's reasonable to expect the secant line they determine to resemble the line *tangent* to C at P.

Before reading on, draw some curves and secant lines to convince yourself of this easy but important idea.

Finding slopes of *tangent lines* poses a challenge, but finding slopes of *secant* lines is easy. If C is the graph of a function $y = f(x)$, and $P = (a, f(a))$ and

$Q = (b, f(b))$ are points on the graph, then, as the picture shows—

The secant line from $x = a$ to $x = b$

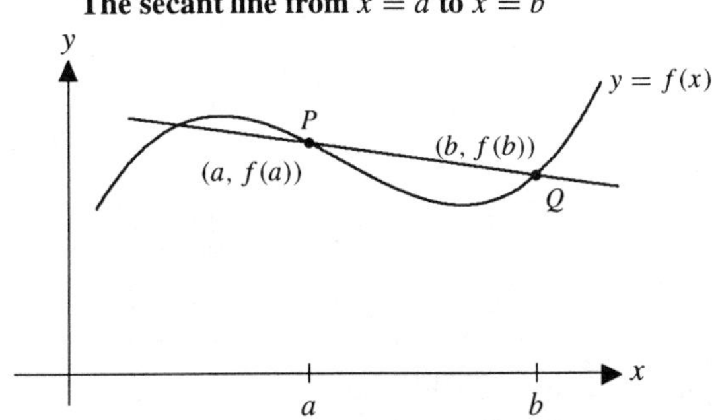

the slope of the secant line from P to Q (i.e., from $x = a$ to $x = b$) is

$$\frac{\Delta f}{\Delta x} = \frac{f(b) - f(a)}{b - a}.$$

Above we calculated that the secant line to $f(x) = x^2 + x$ from $x = 2$ to $x = 2.01$ has slope 5.01. This result suggests our strategy: We'll take the slope of the tangent line to be the **limit** of slopes of secant lines over smaller and smaller intervals.

What is a limit? The **limit** is a mathematical tool used to describe how a function $f(x)$ behaves for x *near* a specific value $x = a$. We'll discuss limits carefully in the next two sections. In this section we treat limits informally, in context.

■ **Example 3.** Compute slopes of secant lines to the graph of $f(x) = x^2 + x$ over small intervals near $x = 2$ and interpret the results in limit language. Draw (and defend) a conclusion about $f'(2)$.

Solution: Results for various small intervals appear below:

Slopes of secant lines over small intervals					
interval	[1.99, 2]	[1.999, 2]	[2, 2.001]	[2, 2.01]	[2, 2.1]
slope	4.99	4.999	5.001	5.01	5.1

Only a mathematician could doubt that these numbers approach 5.

To put things in limit language, consider the interval from $x = 2$ to $x = 2 + h$. Then the secant line from $x = 2$ to $x = 2 + h$ has slope

We think of h as a small (positive or negative) increment.

$$\frac{\Delta f}{\Delta x} = \frac{f(2+h) - f(2)}{(2+h) - 2} = \frac{f(2+h) - f(2)}{h}.$$

The slope of the *tangent* line at $x = 2$ is the limit as h tends to zero of the last expression above. In symbols:

$$f'(2) = \lim_{h \to 0} \frac{f(2+h) - f(2)}{h}.$$

At last we can put this problem out of its misery, by *calculating* the slope of the tangent line at $x = 2$:

$$\lim_{h\to 0} \frac{f(2+h)-f(2)}{h} = \lim_{h\to 0} \frac{(2+h)^2+(2+h)-6}{h}$$
$$= \lim_{h\to 0} \frac{5h+h^2}{h}$$
$$= \lim_{h\to 0} (5+h)$$
$$= 5.$$

□

(The limit calculation above should be intuitively reasonable. We'll study the algebra of limits carefully in the next two sections.)

Average speeds, instantaneous speeds, and limits

The rate-of-change problem, for Professor X, is to convert information about distance traveled into information about *instantaneous* speed. Its solution closely mimics the one above.

Average speed over an interval of time is easy to compute. As Professor X knows,

$$\text{average speed} = \frac{\text{distance traveled}}{\text{time elapsed}}.$$

The remaining problem is to connect *average* speeds (over intervals) with instantaneous speeds.

Again, limits provide the missing link: the *instantaneous* speed at time t_0 is the limit of *average* speeds over small time intervals that contain t_0. More succinctly put:

Again, h represents a small positive or negative increment.

Consider the interval from $t = 2$ to $t = 2 + h$ hours. The *average* speed from $t = 2$ to $t = 2 + h$ is

$$\frac{\Delta D}{\Delta t} = \frac{D(2+h)-D(2)}{(2+h)-2} = \frac{D(2+h)-D(2)}{h}.$$

The *instantaneous speed* at $t = 2$, therefore, is

$$\lim_{h\to 0} \frac{D(2+h)-D(2)}{h}.$$

We confess now that, all along, we've had the function $D(t) = 10t + 15t^2$ secretly in mind for Professor X's trip. Finding her speed at $t = 2$ hours is now a simple calculation:

But check each step!

$$\lim_{h\to 0} \frac{D(2+h)-D(2)}{h} = \lim_{h\to 0} \frac{10(2+h)+15(2+h)^2-80}{h}$$
$$= \lim_{h\to 0} \frac{70h+15h^2}{h}$$
$$= \lim_{h\to 0} (70+15h)$$
$$= 70.$$

At *exactly* 2:00 a.m., Professor X's Göttingen was doing *exactly* 70 mph.

Derivative: the formal definition

The tangent line and instantaneous speed problems turned out to be identical. Both problems—and many others—lead to limits of a common form. This form appears in the definition:

> **Definition:** Let f be a function defined near and at $x = a$. The **derivative of f at $x = a$**, denoted $f'(a)$, is defined by the limit
>
> $$f'(a) = \lim_{h \to 0} \frac{f(a+h) - f(a)}{h}.$$

This important definition deserves some amplification:

The most important in all of calculus.

Must $f'(a)$ exist? In a word, no. The limit in the definition may or may not exist. If it *does* exist, we say that f is **differentiable at $x = a$** or that f **has a derivative at $x = a$**. Most of the functions we treat in calculus are differentiable wherever they make sense.

The absolute value function $g(x) = |x|$ is one exception. The "kink" at $x = 0$ means that g has no tangent line—and hence no derivative—at $a = 0$. (We'll see in the next section why the limit that defines $g'(0)$ does not exist.)

Dividing by zero? The limit in the derivative definition *always* involves a denominator tending to zero; evaluating it always involves some trickery or other. In practice, things often work out as in the examples above—after some algebra in the numerator, the troublesome h in the denominator goes away.

But only if the algebra is done carefully.

Other forms. The limit in the derivative definition can be written in other equivalent forms. Here are several popular ones:

$$\lim_{h \to 0} \frac{f(a+h) - f(a)}{h} \qquad \lim_{\Delta x \to 0} \frac{f(a+\Delta x) - f(a)}{\Delta x}$$

$$\lim_{x \to a} \frac{f(x) - f(a)}{x - a} \qquad \lim_{\Delta x \to 0} \frac{\Delta f}{\Delta x}$$

Depending on f, one form may be simpler or easier to manipulate than another, but all convey the same information.

Difference quotients, average rates of change, and their limits

The quotients in the limits above are all instances of a general idea:

> **Fact:** For any function f, the ratio
>
> $$\frac{f(a+h) - f(a)}{h}$$
>
> is called a **difference quotient**. It measures the **average rate of change** of the function f from $x = a$ to $x = a + h$.

To understand what it tells, let's consider the difference quotient's various parts separately:

The denominator. The difference

$$h = (a + h) - a = \Delta x$$

represents a change, or increment, in the *input* variable, from $x = a$ to $x = a + h$. ("Change" may mean either "increase" or "decrease.")

The numerator. As x moves from $x = a$ to $x = a + h$, the output $f(x)$ changes too. The numerator

$$\Delta f = f(a + h) - f(a)$$

measures this change. Like Δx, Δf may have either sign.

The quotient. The difference quotient is the *ratio* of two changes Δf and Δx, so it represents a *rate* of change of $f(x)$ with respect to x. Because the changes occur over an *interval* in x, the quotient represents an *average* rate. The *sign* of $\Delta f/\Delta x$ tells whether x and $f(x)$ change in the same direction. If, say, $\Delta f/\Delta x < 0$, then an *increase* in x produces a *decrease* in $f(x)$.

From average to instantaneous. The difference quotient is an *average* rate of change over the interval $[a, a + h]$. Therefore the limit

$$\lim_{h \to 0} \frac{f(a + h) - f(a)}{h}$$

is the *instantaneous* rate of change at the "instant" $x = a$.

At any rate. In everyday speech, the words "rate" and "instantaneous" suggest quantities varying in *time*. "Rate of change" should be understood more generally in calculus. If f is *any* function—perhaps having nothing to do with time—the difference quotient $\Delta f/\Delta x$ and its limit are still thought of as rates; they measure how fast outputs from f change relative to inputs x.

A case could be made for replacing the customary phrase "rate of change"—which seems to apply equally well to increasing and decreasing quantities—with "rate of increase." "Rate of increase" makes the bookkeeping a little simpler: If $\Delta f/\Delta x > 0$, the rate of increase of $f(x)$ with respect to x is positive; this means that $f(x)$ increases as x does. If $\Delta f/\Delta x < 0$, the rate of increase is negative; $f(x)$ decreases as x increases.

Difference quotients and derivatives: what they mean in various settings

Any function f has many possible interpretations. Our old favorite $f(x) = x^2 + x$ could represent the weight in ounces of a kitten x days after birth, the area of a rectangle with variable sides, or almost anything else. Any particular interpretation of f leads to a corresponding interpretation of the difference quotient. We give several examples below. Notice that in every case, the difference quotient and derivative are rates of change. Notice too the various units of measurement: choices of units for x and y determine appropriate units for the difference quotient and the derivative.

Slopes. On any graph $y = f(x)$, the difference quotient represents the *slope of the secant line* from $x = a$ to $x = a + h$. The derivative $f'(a)$, as the limit of slopes of secant lines, represents the *slope of the tangent line* at $x = a$.

Speeds. If $y = f(x)$ represents the position of a moving object at time x, then the difference quotient $\Delta f / \Delta x$ represents *average speed* over the interval from $x = a$ to $x = a + h$. The derivative $f'(a)$, as a limit of average speeds, represents *instantaneous speed* at time a.

Gas mileage. Let y be the total distance (in miles) traveled by Professor X on x gallons of fuel. Then y is a function, say g, of x. (Even the Göttingen has a gas gauge.) The professor takes these readings:

x (gallons)	0	1.5	1.9	1.99	2
y (miles)	0	43.2725	55.4993	58.3969	58.7206

A difference quotient, such as

$$\frac{g(2) - g(0)}{2 - 0} = \frac{58.7206 \text{ miles}}{2 \text{ gallons}} = 29.3603 \text{ miles per gallon}$$

represents the *average* rate of gas consumption over the interval in which the first two gallons of gas were consumed. The *instantaneous* rate of gas consumption varies from moment to moment. To find the instantaneous rate at $x = 2$, we would need to find a limit. Without an explicit formula for g, we can only estimate. The table shows average rates for various intervals in x:

interval	$[0, 2]$	$[1.5, 2]$	$[1.9, 2]$	$[1.99, 2]$
average mpg	29.3603	30.8962	32.2127	32.3675

A sensible guess, then, is that at the moment when $x = 2$, gas mileage was about 32.4 mpg.

Units. What *units* make sense for difference quotients and derivatives? It depends on the units chosen for x and y. For Professor X's speed we had $s = D(t)$, with s in miles and t in hours; the natural rate unit, therefore, is *miles per hour.*

I.e., the quotient miles/hours.

For fuel consumption we used miles and gallons as units, so rates were measured in *miles per gallon*. Had Professor X chosen another vehicle and other units of distance and fuel (e.g., horse, leagues, and bales) the proper units for difference quotient and derivative would have been different (e.g., *leagues per bale*).

The tangent line problem in historical perspective

The problem of finding a straight line that "fits" a curve at a given point is very old. For the Greeks the problem had less to do with description—how to *define* the tangent line rigorously—than with construction—how, given a specific curve, to use ruler, compass, and other tools to *draw* tangent lines. For a *circle*, "constructing" the tangent line L in the Greek sense is easy: L is the line perpendicular to the radius at P. The Greeks could construct tangent lines for circles, parabolas, and a few other curves of classical geometry. In his treatise *On Spirals* (ca. 250 B.C.) Archimedes constructs tangent lines to certain spirals. The figure below illustrates the situation for circles and spirals:

A tangent to a circle

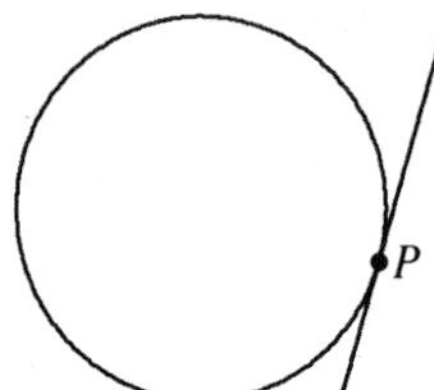

A tangent to a spiral

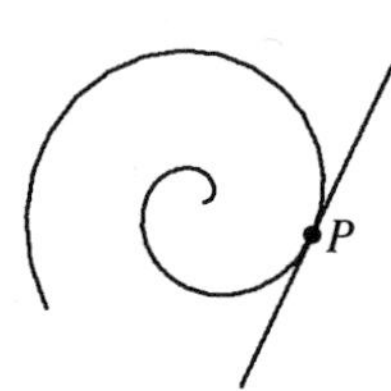

Tangere is Latin for "to touch."

If C is a circle, the tangent line L at P happens to be the only line through P that touches the circle only at P. This touches-only-at-P criterion works (i.e., identifies a line which deserves to be called "tangent") for some curves, but not for many others we meet in modern calculus courses. For the curve $y = \sin x$, for example, most tangent lines cross the curve at several points.

The Greeks seem to have taken the "touching" criterion as their *definition* of tangent line. That they should have done so is a bit surprising—even for the Archimedean spiral, the criterion fails: Every tangent line eventually crosses the spiral. Perhaps the Greeks accepted such an inadequate definition because they were less interested in *defining* tangent lines than in *constructing* them.

Finding the "right" definition of tangent line is slightly subtle. In one sense, the tangent line is anything we say it is; we can *define* it any way we like. We might, for example, foolishly define the line tangent to C at P to be the horizontal line through P. This definition is not so much logically incorrect as useless: tangent lines in this sense would tell us nothing about the direction of C near P. A *good* definition must be both simple enough to work with and precise enough to capture the essence of the idea in question.

A good mathematical definition starts with our general intuition, but makes it precise. For tangent lines we have plenty of geometric intuition to build on. Given a curve and a point on it, it is usually easy to *draw* a tangent line and agree that it's correct (allowing duly for imperfect pencils, rulers, eyesight, etc.). The challenge is to describe in *mathematical language* the line we'd draw anyway.

The "right" definition of tangent line involves a limit. In retrospect this conclusion seems obvious, but arriving at this definition was a long historical process. The question, as we've seen, goes back to ancient times, but not until the work of Cauchy in the 1820's—100 years after Newton's death—were limits in our sense known. This is not to say that nothing happened in the meantime. By 1630, Fermat had essentially the modern idea of tangent line. He used his idea to solve problems that (as the author George Simmons observes) would sound familiar in calculus courses today.

Exercises

1. Amy traveled from Chicago to Milwaukee. Due to road construction, she drove the first 10 miles at a constant 20 mph. For the next 30 miles she drove at a constant 60 mph. She stopped at a rest area for a 10-minute snack, then drove the last 45 miles at a constant 45 mph.

   (a) Plot Amy's distance along the road from her starting point as a function of time.

   (b) Plot Amy's velocity as a function of time.

(c) What was Amy's average speed for the trip (including the stop at the rest area)?

2. On a 50-minute trip, a car travels for 20 minutes with an average velocity of 30 mph, and then for 30 minutes with an average velocity of 50 mph. Find the total distance traveled and the average velocity over the entire trip.

3. (a) A car travels for 30 miles with an average velocity of 40 mph, and then for another 30 miles with an average velocity of 60 mph. What is the average velocity of the car for the entire trip?

   (b) Another car travels for 30 minutes at 40 mph and then for 30 minutes at 60 mph. Find the average velocity over the 1-hour time period.

   (c) A car is to travel two miles. It went the first mile at an average velocity of 30 mph. The driver wishes to average 60 mph for the entire two mile trip. Is this possible? Explain.

4. If $f(1) = 2$ and the average rate of change of f from $x = 1$ to $x = 5$ is 3, what's $f(5)$?

5. If $f(2) = 1$ and the average rate of change of f from $x = -3$ to $x = 2$ is 4, what's $f(-3)$?

6. True or False? Justify your answers.

   (a) Velocity is the rate of change of position with respect to time.

   (b) If the average rate of change of a function over an interval is zero, then the function must be constant.

   (c) If the average rate of change of a function over every interval is 17, then the graph of the function is a straight line.

7. The graph below shows how the price of a certain stock varied over a recent trading day.

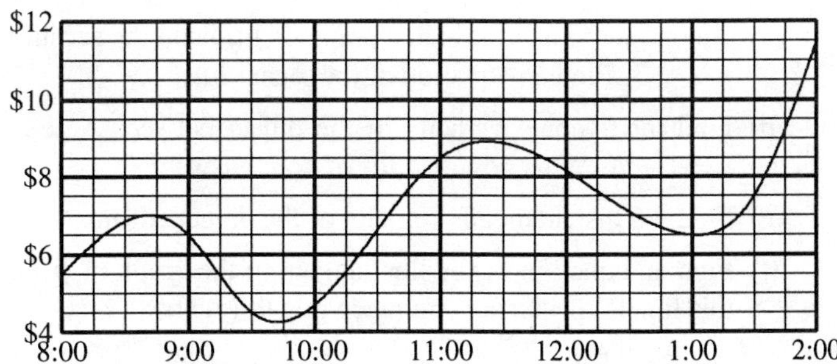

   (a) For each time interval below, find the total change in price and the average rate of change of price. (Be sure to indicate the units used to measure these quantities.)

      (i) 8:00 to 11:00

      (ii) 9:00 to 1:00

      (iii) 9:30 to 2:00

      (iv) 11:00 to 1:00

(b) Estimate the instantaneous rate of change of the stock's price at each of the following times. (Be sure to indicate units with your answers.)

(i) 9:15 a.m.
(ii) 10:30 a.m.
(iii) 12:15 p.m.
(iv) 1:45 p.m.

8. The number of deer in a forest at time t years after the beginning of a conservation study is shown on the graph below.

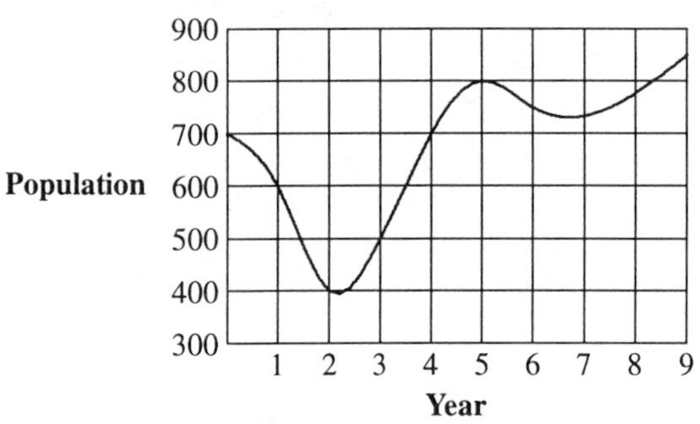

(a) Over which two of the following periods did the population of deer decline at an average rate of 50 deer per year?

(i) 1–2 (ii) 1–3 (iii) 1–4 (iv) 2–3 (v) 5–6

(b) Approximately how fast was the deer population increasing (or decreasing) at time $t = 1.5$? At time $t = 3$? (Include appropriate units.)

9. The position $p(t)$ of an object at time t (in seconds) along a line with units marked in meters is given by $p(t) = 3t^2 + 1$.

(a) Find the change in position of the object between time $t = 1$ and $t = 3$.

(b) Find the average velocity of the object between time $t = 1$ and $t = 3$.

(c) On one set of axes, sketch a graph of $p(t)$ and the secant line from $t = 1$ to $t = 3$. Find an equation of the secant line.

(d) Find the average velocity of the object between time $t = 1$ and time $t = 1 + h$. What are the *units* of your answer?

(e) Find the instantaneous velocity of the object at time $t = 1$.

(f) Find an equation of the line tangent to the graph of $p(t)$ at $t = 1$. Add this line to the sketch you made in part (c) above.

10. For each function f below, use a difference quotient with $h = 0.001$ to estimate the value of f' at the given point.

(a) $f(x) = x^2 - 3x$ at $x = 3$
(b) $f(x) = x^{1/3}$ at $x = 2$
(c) $f(x) = x^{-2}$ at $x = 1$
(d) $f(x) = \sin x$ at $x = 0$
(e) $f(x) = \cos x$ at $x = 0$
(f) $f(x) = \cos(3x)$ at $x = \pi/2$
(g) $f(x) = 2^x$ at $x = 0$
(h) $f(x) = \ln x$ at $x = 1$

11. For each of the following functions, use a graph of $g(\Delta x) = \dfrac{f(1+\Delta x) - f(1)}{\Delta x}$ over a small interval centered at $\Delta x = 0$ to estimate $f'(1)$.

(a) $f(x) = x^3$

(b) $f(x) = x + (1/x)$

(c) $f(x) = \sin(\pi x)$

(d) $f(x) = e^x$

12. Let $f(x) = \sqrt{x}$. Tabulate $f(x)$ at $x = 1.998, 1.999, 2.000, 2.001$, and 2.002 and use your results to answer the following questions. (Round numerical values of $f(x)$ to seven decimal places.)

(a) Explain how these tabulated values show that f is "locally linear" near $x = 2$.

(b) Estimate $f'(1.999)$, $f'(2)$, and $f'(2.001)$ using the tabulated values of f.

(c) Does $(f(2.001) - f(2))/0.001$ overestimate or underestimate the exact value of $f'(2)$? Why? [HINT: Look at a graph of $f(x)$ near $x = 2$.]

(d) Estimate $f''(2)$ using the results from part (b).

13. Repeat the previous problem for each of the following functions.

(a) $f(x) = x^2$

(b) $f(x) = \sin x$

(c) $f(x) = e^x$

(d) $f(x) = \ln x$

14. Suppose that f is a function for which $f'(2)$ exists. Use the values of f given below to estimate $f'(1.99)$, $f'(2)$, $f'(2.01)$, and $f'(2.1)$. Explain how you obtained your estimates.

x	1.9	1.99	1.999	2.0	2.001	2.01	2.1
$f(x)$	25.34	33.97	34.896	35	35.104	36.05	46.18

15. Suppose that f is a function for which $f'(2)$ exists. Use the values of f given below to estimate $f'(1.9)$, $f'(2)$, and $f'(2.02)$.

x	1.9	1.97	2.0	2.02	2.2
$f(x)$	6.6	6.905	7	7.059	7.5

16. Let $f(x) = |x|$.

(a) Sketch a graph of f over the interval $[-5, 5]$.

(b) Explain why $f'(x) = \begin{cases} -1, & \text{if } x < 0 \\ 1, & \text{if } x > 0. \end{cases}$

(c) Explain why $f'(0)$ doesn't exist.

17. Let $f(x) = 2^x$.

(a) Find the average rate of change of f between 0 and 0.01. Use this result to estimate $f'(0)$. Explain why this estimate is too large.

(b) Find the average rate of change of f between -0.01 and 0. Use this result to estimate $f'(0)$. Explain why this estimate is too small.

(c) Find the average rate of change of f between -0.01 and 0.01. Use this result to estimate $f'(0)$.

(d) Why is the estimate of $f'(0)$ found in part (c) more accurate than the estimates computed in parts (a) and (b)?

(e) Describe a method based on part (c) for estimating $f'(a)$ from tabulated data.

18. Each of the following limits is $f'(a)$ for some function f and some number a. In each case, identify f and a.

(a) $\displaystyle\lim_{x\to 4} \frac{\sqrt{x} - 2}{x - 4}$

(b) $\displaystyle\lim_{h\to 0} \frac{5^{2+h} - 25}{h}$

(c) $\displaystyle\lim_{u\to \pi/4} \frac{\cos u - \sqrt{2}/2}{u - \pi/4}$

(d) $\displaystyle\lim_{s\to 8} \frac{\log_2 s - 3}{s - 8}$

2.6 Limits and continuity

Limits arose in the previous section, in precisely defining the derivative. In this section we'll study limits in their own right. Then we'll use limits to define precisely another important concept: **continuity** of a function at a point of its domain.

The basic idea; simplest examples

The general idea of limit is simple. Suppose that f is a function defined near, but not necessarily *at*, $x = a$. To say that

$$\lim_{x \to a} f(x) = L$$

means, informally, that $f(x)$ "approaches" L as x "approaches" a. In other *symbols*,

$$f(x) \to L \quad \text{as} \quad x \to a.$$

In other *words*:

As inputs to f approach a, outputs from f approach L.

In still other words:

$$f(x) \approx L \textit{ whenever } x \approx a.$$

Intuitive ideas aren't formal definitions. We'll give one soon. First, some examples.

■ **Example 1.** What is $\lim_{x \to 3} x^2$? Why?

Solution: The answer is no surprise:

$$\lim_{x \to 3} x^2 = 9.$$

The squaring function $f(x) = x^2$ is well-behaved near $x = 3$. In particular, $f(x) \approx 9$ whenever $x \approx 3$. (In fact, $f(x)$ *equals* 9 when $x = 3$, but that's irrelevant to the limit.) □

■ **Example 2.** The statement

$$\lim_{x \to 3} \frac{x^2 - 9}{x - 3} = 6$$

is about the limit of a certain function at a certain point. Which function? Which point? What does the statement say? Is it true?

Solution: Our function➽ is defined by the rule $g(x) = (x^2 - 9)/(x - 3)$. The point in question is $x = 3$.

We'll call it g.

Notice that $g(x)$ is *not defined*➽ at the interesting point $x = 3$. (Everywhere else, the rule for g makes good sense.) The limit statement says that although g has no ordinary *value* at $x = 3$, it does the next best thing: $g(x)$ *approaches* 6 as x *approaches* 3. In symbols,

Why not?

$$g(x) \to 6 \quad \text{as} \quad x \to 3.$$

That's what the statement says. Is it true?

The *formula* for g isn't immediately helpful, precisely because $g(3)$ isn't defined. The *graph* of g helps:

Graph of $g(x) = (x^2 - 9)/(x - 3)$ near $x = 3$

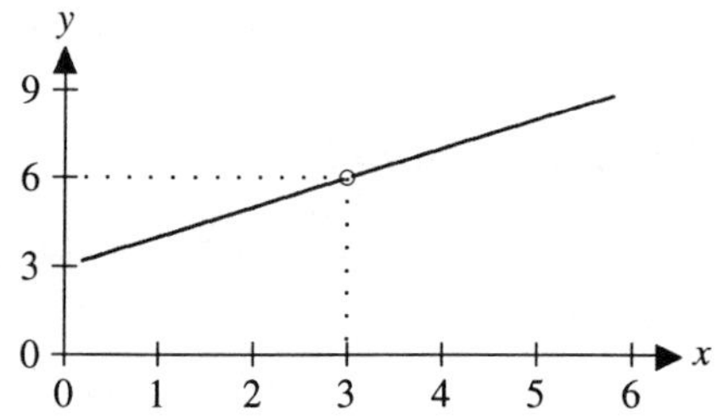

How does the gap appear on the graph?

It shows convincingly that the limit statement *is* true. Despite the "gap" at $x = 3$, $g(x)$ *does* approach 6 as x approaches 3, from either right or left.

Numerical evidence points to the same conclusion:

x	2.9	2.99	2.999	2.9999	...	3.0001	3.001	3.01	3.1
$g(x)$	5.9	5.99	5.999	5.9999	...	6.0001	6.001	6.01	6.1

Observe, finally, that the graph of g (except at $x = 3$) looks suspiciously like the line $y = x + 3$. A little algebra shows why: If $x \neq 3$,

$$g(x) = \frac{x^2 - 9}{x - 3} = \frac{(x - 3)(x + 3)}{x - 3} = x + 3.$$

(We repeat: The last equation holds *only* for $x \neq 3$—but that's good enough, because we're interested in $g(x)$ only for values *near* $x = 3$.) Now it's clear that

$$\lim_{x \to 3} g(x) = \lim_{x \to 3} (x + 3) = 6.$$

□

Why limits matter: functions with gaps

The simplest limit expressions (e.g., $\lim_{x \to 3} x^2 = 9$ and $\lim_{x \to 3} (x + 3) = 6$) illustrate what limits *are*, but not why they matter. Judging only from such examples, limits may seem to be much ado about little.

Like g above.

That impression is wrong. Limits *do* matter in calculus. One reason is that functions with "gaps" in their domains arise often in calculus. Finding derivatives is the most common—and most important—way such functions arise.

■ **Example 3.** Let $f(x) = x^2$. Use the limit definition to find the derivative $f'(3)$. What does the result mean graphically?

Difference quotients can be written in various forms. See page 143.

Solution: By definition, the derivative is a limit of difference quotients. We'll write ours like this:

$$f'(3) = \lim_{x \to 3} \frac{f(x) - f(3)}{x - 3} = \lim_{x \to 3} \frac{x^2 - 9}{x - 3}.$$

That's the limit we found just above, so $f'(3) = 6$. In graphical terms: *At $x = 3$ the curve $y = x^2$ has slope 6.* □

Limits in theory

Functions with gaps or other anomalies in their domains arise in connection with "instantaneous" phenomena: tangent lines, rates of change, etc. The previous example shows that the concept of limit permits us to handle such functions.

With a satisfactory theory of limits, based on precise definitions, mathematicians can make sense of—and calculate reliably with—mysterious-seeming concepts such as "infinitely small quantities." Without such a theory as footing, we would remain mired (as mathematicians did for hundreds of years) in the vague, metaphorical (sometimes even mystical) language of "fluxions," "fluents" and "indivisibles."

Seeing ghosts. A precise idea of limit is surprisingly subtle. Developing a rigorous but usable definition of limit was an important historical step in putting calculus on a sound logical footing.

The modern idea of limit stems from the work of the French mathematician Augustin Louis Cauchy, around 1820—over 150 years after Isaac Newton and Gottfried Leibniz developed calculus. Newton's and Leibniz's own understanding of limit could not have been, by modern standards, rigorous. Sensing this, Bishop Berkeley satirized the intellectual pretensions of mathematicians in his 1734 philosophical treatise *The Analyst: A Discourse Addressed to an Infidel Mathematician*, ridiculing Newton's limits as "ghosts of departed quantities."

Limits in practice

Most of the limits encountered in calculus are relatively simple and straightforward. Combining algebraic, graphical, and numerical tools makes them even more so. The rest of this section aims to support this claim.

■ **Example 4.** Let $f(x) = \sin x$. What limit defines $f'(0)$? What does the limit mean graphically? *Find* the limit.

Solution: The derivative $f'(0)$ is the slope of the *tangent* line to the curve $y = \sin x$ at $x = 0$. As we saw in the last section, this slope is the limit of slopes of *secant* lines over small intervals starting (or ending) at $x = 0$,

To investigate that limit we'll define a new function, g, by the rule

$$g(t) = \text{slope of the secant line joining } (0,0) \text{ and } (t, \sin t).$$

The rule makes sense for any $t \neq 0$, as the next picture shows:

Defining the function g

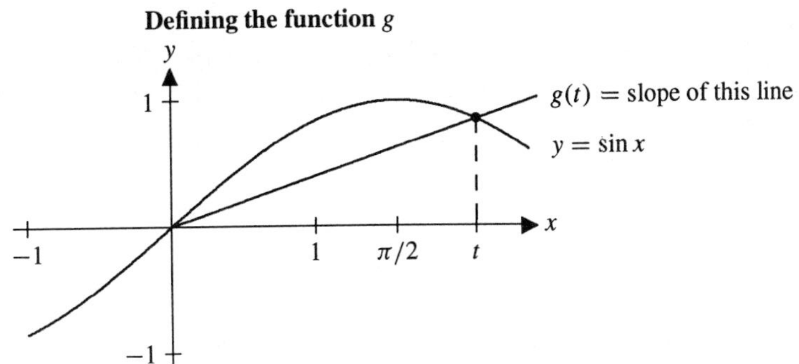

Even though $g(t)$ is not defined at $t = 0$, we'll find the limit $\lim_{t \to 0} g(t)$.

Though we defined g in words, finding an explicit formula isn't hard: For $t \neq 0$,

$$g(t) = \frac{\Delta y}{\Delta x} = \frac{\sin t}{t}.$$

We want to find

$$\lim_{t \to 0} g(t) = \lim_{t \to 0} \frac{\sin t}{t}.$$

Check some entries with a calculator—use radians!

Because $g(0)$ isn't defined, we'll examine values of $g(t)$ for t *near* 0. Here are some numerical results, rounded to 5 decimals:

t	-0.1	-0.01	-0.0001	...	0.0001	0.01	0.1
$g(t)$	0.99833	0.99998	1.00000	...	1.00000	0.99998	0.99833

For graphical evidence, plot $g(t)$ for t near 0.

The numbers suggest, rightly, that the limit is 1. An airtight proof takes more work. We won't give one here, but see Appendix I.

Draw this line on the previous graph to understand what tangency means.

The answer means that the line $y = x$, with slope 1, is *tangent* to the sine curve at $x = 0$. □

The importance of being algebraic. We calculated above that

$$\lim_{x \to 3} \frac{x^2 - 9}{x - 3} = \lim_{x \to 3} (x + 3) = 6.$$

Won't something similar work with $\lim_{x \to 0} \sin(x)/x$?

No. The difference is that $x^2 - 9$ is an *algebraic* expression, and so permits factoring, division, etc. The numerator $\sin x$, by contrast, isn't algebraic, so ordinary factoring and division aren't possible.

No limit. A function f may not *have* a derivative at a point of its domain. The absolute value function $f(x) = |x|$, for example, has a "kink" in its graph at $x = 0$. By rights, therefore, $f'(0)$ "shouldn't" exist. The next example shows exactly why it doesn't.

Again, here's our favorite "not-nice" function . . .

■ **Example 5.** Let $f(x) = |x|$. Show, using limits, that $f'(0)$ *doesn't* exist.

Solution: By definition,

$$f'(0) = \lim_{x \to 0} \frac{f(x) - f(0)}{x - 0} = \lim_{x \to 0} \frac{|x|}{x},$$

if the limit exists.

To see that the limit *doesn't* exist, consider the function h defined by $h(x) = |x|/x$. Does $\lim_{x \to 0} h(x)$ make sense? A moment's thought reveals that $h(x) = 1$ if $x > 0$, $h(x) = -1$ if $x < 0$, but $h(0)$ is undefined. The graph agrees:

Graph of $h(x) = |x|/x$

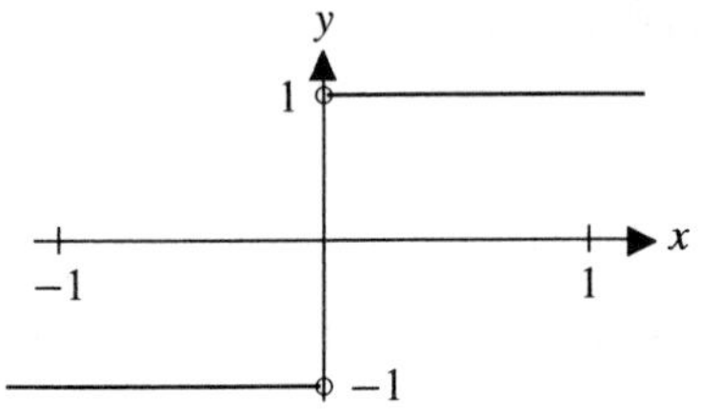

The limit $\lim_{x\to 0} h(x)$ does not exist—there is no *single* number to which $h(x)$ tends as x tends to 0. The problem is that as $x \to 0$ from the *left*, $h(x) \to -1$, but as $x \to 0$ from the *right*, $h(x) \to 1$. Because the limit doesn't exist, neither does $f'(0)$. □

Definitions of limit—informal and precise

Let L be any finite number. The limit expression

$$\lim_{x\to a} f(x) = L \tag{2.6.1}$$

means, informally, that $f(x)$ approaches L as x approaches a. To be precise, we'll say exactly what we mean by Equation 2.6.1, first informally and then rigorously.

Equation 2.6.1 has two types of ingredients:

- real numbers a and L;
- a function f defined for all x *near* $x = a$, but not necessarily *at* $x = a$.

Definition: (Limit, informally.) If $f(x)$ tends to a *single* number L as x approaches a, then $\lim_{x\to a} f(x) = L$.

Definition: (Limit, formally.)
Suppose that for every positive number ϵ, no matter how small, there is a positive number δ so that

$$|f(x) - L| < \epsilon \quad \text{whenever} \quad 0 < |x - a| < \delta .$$

Then

$$\lim_{x\to a} f(x) = L .$$

Note:

Estimating limits. If $\lim_{x\to a} f(x) = L$, then $f(x) \approx L$ if $x \approx a$. This means that we can investigate limits numerically (by *evaluating* $f(x)$ for x near a) and graphically (by *graphing* $f(x)$ for x near a).➻

We took both of these approaches above.

A gap at a? No problem. It's an important fact that $\lim_{x\to a} f(x)$ may exist *even if $f(a)$ is undefined.* Indeed, $f(a)$ is *usually* undefined in interesting cases, like these:

$$\lim_{x\to 4} \frac{\sqrt{x} - 2}{x - 4}; \qquad \lim_{x\to 4} \frac{x^2 - 16}{x - 4}; \qquad \lim_{x\to 0} \frac{\cos x - 1}{x}.$$

None of these functions is "defined at a." In a sense, the problem of limits is to *find* a suitable value for $f(a)$—if one exists.

No guarantees. Even if $f(a)$ *is* defined, there is no guarantee that $\lim_{x\to a} f(x) = f(a)$. The limit definition "doesn't see" $f(a)$. Whether or not $f(a)$ exists, the definition refers only to values of x for which $|x - a| > 0$—i.e., $x \neq a$. (See the next example.)

From Greek to English. In words, the formal definition of limit says:

We can assure that $f(x)$ differs from L by less than any prearranged amount ϵ by requiring that x be within δ of a.

The full idea is subtle, but the following "generic" picture gives some idea of how ϵ and δ are related:

Epsilon and delta: the generic picture

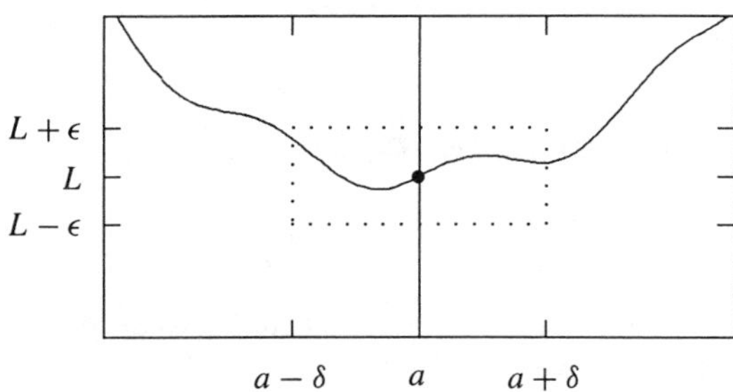

The formal definition means this, graphically:

> *For any $\epsilon > 0$ we can choose a viewing window centered at (a, L), of "width" 2δ and "height" 2ϵ, from which the f-graph never escapes out the top or bottom, except possibly at $x = a$.*

We'll be informal. In elementary calculus—and in this book—informal views of the limit are almost always adequate. In more advanced work (E.g., in "real analysis.") a rigorous understanding of limits is essential.

Airtight proofs. Careful proofs of limit statements are essential at higher levels of mathematical analysis; inevitably, such proofs involve careful balancing of ϵ's and δ's.

We are more interested in the *concept* of limit, and how to use it, than in formal proofs. We'll discuss some theoretical properties of limits, but mainly as aids to concrete computation.

Variations on a theme: one-sided limits

The most basic and most important limit idea is the one just studied: the (two-sided) limit of a function at a point. However, several variants on the same idea arise often enough to deserve mention: "one-sided" limits and limits that involve the ∞ symbol. (We'll see the latter in the next section.) Slightly different definitions apply to these variants; informal versions will be enough: (Notice the unusual use of "+" and "-" as superscripts.)

Definition: (Right-hand limit.) $\lim_{x\to a^+} f(x) = L$ means that $f(x) \to L$ as $x \to a$ from the *right*.

Definition: (Left-hand limit.) $\lim_{x\to a^-} f(x) = L$ means that $f(x) \to L$ as $x \to a$ from the *left*.

■ **Example 6.** In Example 5 we saw (E.g., from the graph.) that if $h(x) = |x|/x$, then $h(x)$ tends either to 1 or to -1 depending on whether x tends to 0 from the right or from the left. In one-sided limit notation:

$$\lim_{x\to 0^-} h(x) = -1 \quad \text{and} \quad \lim_{x\to 0^+} h(x) = 1. \qquad \square$$

Because the one-sided limits above aren't equal, we concluded that the *ordinary* limit $\lim_{x\to 0} h(x)$ does not exist. There's a useful principle lurking here:

> **Fact:** The ordinary limit $\lim_{x \to a} f(x)$ exists if and only if both corresponding one-sided limits exist, and are equal. In symbols:
>
> $$\lim_{x \to a} f(x) = L \iff \lim_{x \to a^+} f(x) = L = \lim_{x \to a^-} f(x).$$

Continuity

To say that f is **continuous** on an interval I means, roughly speaking, that the graph of f is "unbroken" for x in I. This intuitive idea, although not a formal definition, works reliably enough for most calculus functions.

■ **Example 7.** Each function below is continuous on the full set $(-\infty, \infty)$ of real numbers:

$$f(x) = x^2; \qquad g(x) = \sin x; \qquad h(x) = \frac{x^2}{x^2+1}; \qquad k(x) = |x|.$$

(The graph of k has a kink at $x = 0$, but that doesn't destroy continuity.)

By contrast, $\sqrt{x}$ is continuous on the interval $[0, \infty)$. The function $m(x) = 1/x$ is continuous on $(0, \infty)$ and on $(-\infty, 0)$, but not on any interval that contains 0. □

■ **Example 8.** A function n is shown graphically below. Where is n continuous?

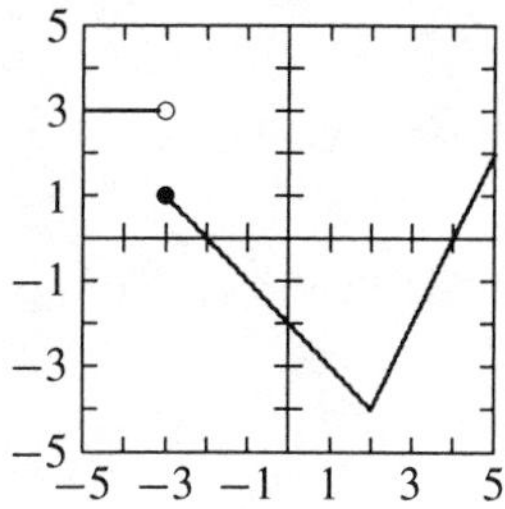

Solution: The only discontinuity occurs at $x = -3$. In particular, n is continuous on any interval that omits $x = -3$. □

Continuity defined: limits again

Graphical intuition is helpful, but a precise definition of continuity can't depend on pictures.➡ The idea of limit turns out to be the right one to express, in analytic terms, the geometric idea of "unbrokenness" at a point. Here's the formal definition:

One problem is that drawing accurate pictures is difficult. In higher dimensions, things are even worse.

> **Definition:** Let f be a function defined on an interval I containing $x = a$. If
>
> $$\lim_{x \to a} f(x) = f(a),$$
>
> then f is **continuous at** $x = a$. (If a is the left or right endpoint of I, then a right-hand limit or a left-hand limit replaces the two-sided limit above.) To say that f is continuous on I means that f is continuous at each point of I (including endpoints of I, if any).

The formal definition illustrates the important theoretical role limits play in calculus. In practice, however, the intuitive idea of continuity as "unbrokenness" is usually adequate. We'll content ourselves with several brief remarks:

Continuous where? A function f may be continuous on one set but discontinuous on another set. Thus the common phrase "f is continuous" is technically ambiguous—it doesn't say *where* f is continuous. Here's the rule of thumb:

> *Unless otherwise qualified, "continuous" means "continuous throughout the domain of f."*

No surprises. The definition says that f is continuous at a if whenever $x \to a$, $f(x) \to f(a)$. In other words, inputs near a produce outputs near $f(a)$. All this means, in effect, that f behaves "predictably" at $x = a$.

Continuity is the rule. As a rule, the elementary functions of calculus are continuous wherever they're defined. For example, $f(x) = \sqrt{x-1}$ is continuous for $x \geq 1$, i.e., on the natural domain of f. Similarly, every polynomial function $p(x)$ is continuous on the full set of real numbers. (Proofs of such facts are important in mathematical analysis; in this book we'll de-emphasize them.)

Easy limits. Finding limits of continuous functions is as easy as can be. If f is continuous at $x = a$, then—by the very definition of continuity,

$$x \to a \implies f(x) \to f(a).$$

In words: *The* limit *of f as x approaches a is the* value *of f at a.*

■ **Example 9.** Let $k(x) = x^2 + 3x + 5$. Find $\lim_{x \to 2} k(x)$.

Solution: The problem looks easy; neither the formula nor the graph of k suggests any surprises near $x = 2$:

Graph of $k(x) = x^2 + 3x + 5$

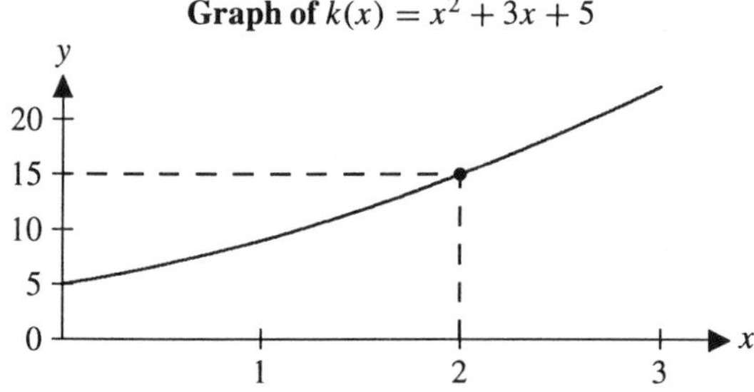

The obvious guess—

$$\lim_{x \to 2} k(x) = k(2) = 15$$

is correct, precisely because k is continuous at $x = 2$. □

As we said above, a polynomial function is continuous everywhere.

Discontinuity: three possible problems

A function f is *discontinuous* at $x = a$ if—for any reason—the limit condition in the definition doesn't hold. Three things can go wrong:

1. $f(a)$ may not be defined; this happens for $f(x) = 1/x$ at $x = 0$.

2. The limit $\lim_{x \to a} f(x)$ may not exist; this happens at $x = -3$ for the function n in Example 8.

3. The limit $\lim_{x \to a} f(x)$ may exist, but differ from $f(a)$.

The next example illustrates the last form of pathology.

■ **Example 10.** Consider the function f defined by

Plot this function by hand to understand the example.

$$f(x) = \begin{cases} x & \text{if } x \neq 0 \\ 1 & \text{if } x = 0. \end{cases}$$

What's $\lim_{x \to 0} f(x)$?

Solution: The fact that $f(0) = 1$ makes no difference to the limit. Because $f(x) = x$ for $x \neq 0$, we have

$$\lim_{x \to 0} f(x) = \lim_{x \to 0} x = 0.$$

In a sense, f has the "wrong" value at $x = 0$; for this reason f is called **discontinuous at** $x = 0$. □

Limits and computer graphics. Most plotting devices will successfully plot a function over an interval containing one suspicious point. Both *Maple* and the TI-85, for instance, draw reasonable pictures for $h(x) = |x|/x$ on $[-1, 1]$—even though h isn't defined at $x = 0$. If a device complains or produces nonsense, one can still use intervals that avoid the problem point. For $h(x) = |x|/x$ we might try graphs over $[-1, -0.01]$ and $[0.01, 1]$.

Sample problems

Here are two problems that combine ideas from this section.

■ **Example 11.** Let $f(x) = \begin{cases} bx^2 + 1, & x < -2 \\ x, & x \geq -2. \end{cases}$
What value of b makes f continuous at $x = -2$?

Solution: To make f continuous at $x = -2$ we need

$$\lim_{x \to -2} f(x) = f(-2) = -2.$$

Looking at the two lines of the definition separately shows that

$$f(x) \to 4b + 1 \quad \text{as} \quad x \to -2^-;$$
$$f(x) \to -2 \quad \text{as} \quad x \to -2^+.$$

For the two one-sided limits to be equal we need $4b + 1 = -2$, or $b = -3/4$. □

■ **Example 12.** Interpret $\lim_{h \to 0} \frac{e^h - 1}{h}$ as a derivative; estimate its value.

Solution: If $f(x) = e^x$, then

Check this equations.

$$\lim_{h \to 0} \frac{e^h - 1}{h} = \lim_{h \to 0} \frac{f(h) - f(0)}{h}.$$

Thus the given limit is (by the definition of derivative) the slope of the curve $y = e^x$ at $x = 0$. A close look at this curve suggests that this slope is 1. □

We took one in Section 2.2—look back or plot the curve yourself.

Exercises

1. Let $f(x) = \begin{cases} 1 & \text{if } x \text{ is an integer} \\ 2 & \text{if } x \text{ is not an integer.} \end{cases}$

   (a) Draw a graph of f over the interval $[0, 5]$.

   (b) Evaluate $\lim_{x \to 4} f(x)$.

   (c) Evaluate $\lim_{x \to 5/2} f(x)$.

   (d) For which values of a does $\lim_{x \to a} f(x)$ exist? Why?

Let f be the function whose graph is shown below. Using the graph, evaluate each of the following limits or explain why the limit does not exist. [NOTE: $f(1) = 2$.]

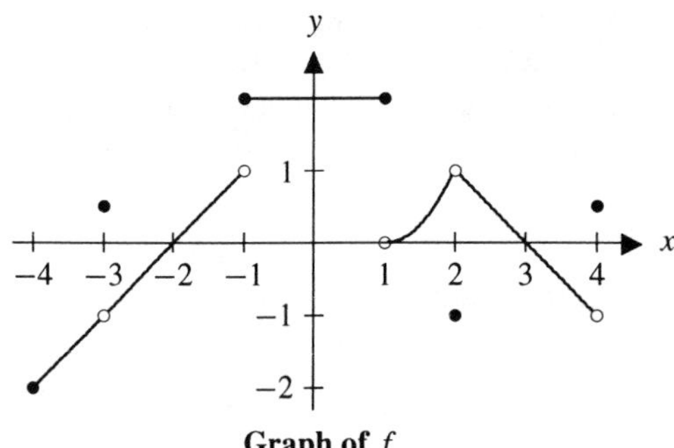

Graph of f

2. $\lim_{x \to 0} f(x)$
3. $\lim_{x \to -3} f(x)$
4. $\lim_{x \to -1} f(x)$
5. $\lim_{x \to 2^-} f(x)$
6. $\lim_{x \to 2^+} f(x)$
7. $\lim_{x \to 2} f(x)$
8. $\lim_{x \to -2^-} f(x)$
9. $\lim_{x \to 1^+} f(x)$
10. $\lim_{x \to -4^+} f(x)$
11. $\lim_{x \to 4^-} f(x)$
12. $\lim_{x \to 3} f'(x)$
13. $\lim_{x \to -1^+} f'(x)$
14. $\lim_{x \to -1^-} f'(x)$
15. $\lim_{x \to -3} f'(x)$

16. Over which intervals is f continuous?

Let g be the function whose graph is shown below. Using the graph, evaluate each of the following limits or explain why the limit does not exist.

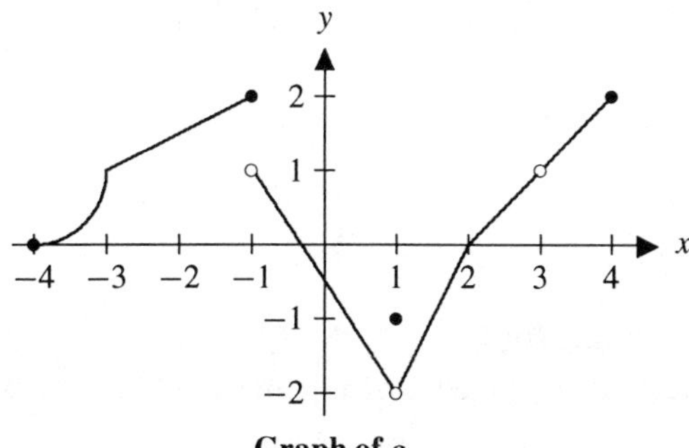

Graph of g

17. $\lim_{x \to -4^+} g(x)$

18. $\lim_{x \to -3} g(x)$

19. $\lim_{x \to -2} g(x)$

20. $\lim_{x \to -1^+} g(x)$

21. $\lim_{x \to -1} g(x)$

22. $\lim_{x \to 0^-} g(x)$

23. $\lim_{x \to 1} g(x)$

24. $\lim_{x \to 2} g(x)$

25. $\lim_{x \to 3} g(x)$

26. $\lim_{x \to 4^-} g(x)$

27. Over which intervals is g continuous?

28. Suppose that f is continuous at $x = 1$ and that $f(1) = -2$. Evaluate $\lim_{x \to 1} f(x)$.

29. Suppose that f is continuous at $x = 3$ and that $\lim_{x \to 3} f(x) = 17$. Indicate which of the following statements about f *must* be true, which *might* be true, and which *cannot* be true. Justify your answers.

   (a) 3 is in the domain of f.

   (b) $f(3) = 17$.

   (c) $\lim_{x \to 3^-} f(x) = 17$.

30. Let $f(x) = \begin{cases} \dfrac{\sin x}{x}, & x \neq 0 \\ 1 & x = 0. \end{cases}$

    Explain why f is continuous at $x = 0$.

31. Let $g(x) = \begin{cases} \dfrac{\sin x}{|x|}, & x \neq 0 \\ 1 & x = 0. \end{cases}$

    Is g continuous at $x = 0$? Justify your answer.

32. Let $h(x) = \begin{cases} \dfrac{\sin x}{\sqrt{1 - \cos^2 x}}, & x \neq 0 \\ 1 & x = 0. \end{cases}$

    Is h continuous at $x = 0$? Justify your answer.

33. Let $f(x) = \begin{cases} ax+1, & x < 2 \\ x^2, & x \geq 2. \end{cases}$

Find the value of a for which $\lim_{x \to 2} f(x)$ exists.

34. Suppose that the function f is continuous at $x = 2$ and that f is defined by the rule

$$f(x) = \begin{cases} ax^2+3, & x < 2 \\ 3x-5, & x \geq 2. \end{cases}$$

(a) Find the value of a.

Evaluate each of the following limits.

(b) $\lim_{x \to 3} f(x)$

(c) $\lim_{x \to 0} f(x)$

(d) $\lim_{x \to 2} f(x)$

(e) $\lim_{x \to 1} f(x)$

35. Let $g(x) = \begin{cases} x^2+a, & x < -1 \\ x+a^2, & x = -1 \\ a-x, & x > -1. \end{cases}$

(a) Find *all* values of a for which $\lim_{x \to -1} g(x)$ exists.

(b) Find *all* values of a for which g is continuous at $x = -1$.

36. Let $f(x) = \begin{cases} x^2-1, & x \leq b \\ x, & x > b. \end{cases}$

Find *all* values of b for which $\lim_{x \to b} f(x)$ exists.

Each of the following limits is $f'(a)$ for some function f and some number a. Identify f and a, then use a calculator or grapher to estimate the value of the limit.

37. $\lim_{h \to 0} \dfrac{\tan h}{h}$

38. $\lim_{h \to 0} \dfrac{\cos h - 1}{h}$

39. $\lim_{h \to 0} \dfrac{\sin(3h)}{h}$

40. $\lim_{x \to \pi} \dfrac{\sin x}{x - \pi}$

41. $\lim_{x \to \pi/2} \dfrac{\cos x}{x - \pi/2}$

42. $\lim_{x \to 16} \dfrac{\sqrt[4]{x} - 2}{x - 16}$

43. $\lim_{x \to 1} \dfrac{2^x - 2}{x - 1}$

44. $\lim_{h \to 0} \dfrac{\sqrt{9+h} - 3}{h}$

45. $\lim_{h \to 0} \dfrac{\sin(\pi/6 + h) - 1/2}{h}$

46. $\lim_{h \to 0} \dfrac{\ln(1+h)}{h}$

47. Let $s(t)$ be the slope of the secant line from $x = 3$ to $x = t$ on the graph of the function $f(x) = x^2 + x$.

(a) Find a formula for $s(t)$.

(b) Find $\lim_{t \to 3} s(t)$.

(c) What does your answer to part (b) imply about the graph of f? Draw graphs of f and the line tangent to f at $x = 3$ over the interval $[2, 4]$.

48. Suppose that $\lim_{x \to a} f(x) = L$. Explain why $\lim_{h \to 0} f(a+h) = L$.

49. Suppose that $\lim_{h \to 0} \frac{f(a+h) - f(a)}{h} = L$. Explain why $\lim_{x \to a} \frac{f(x) - f(a)}{x - a} = L$.

50. Suppose that g is the linear function $g(x) = mx + b$.

(a) Show that $g'(a) = \lim_{h \to 0} \frac{g(a+h) - g(a)}{h} = m$ for every value of a.

(b) Interpret the result in part (a) in terms of slopes and rates of change.

Use the graphs of the functions f and g shown on pages 160–161 to evaluate each of the following limits. If a limit does not exist, explain why.

51. $\lim_{x \to 0} \frac{f(x) - 2}{x}$

52. $\lim_{x \to 3} \frac{f(x)}{x - 3}$

53. $\lim_{x \to -1^+} \frac{f(x)}{x + 2}$

54. $\lim_{h \to 0} \frac{g(-2+h) - 3/2}{h}$

55. $\lim_{h \to 0^-} \frac{g(-1+h) - 2}{h}$

56. $\lim_{h \to 0} \frac{g(2+h)}{h}$

57. Let $f(x) = x^2$. Carefully explain each step in the following evaluation of $f'(1)$:

(a) $$f'(1) = \lim_{x \to 1} \frac{x^2 - 1}{x - 1}$$

(b) $$= \lim_{x \to 1} (x + 1)$$

(c) $$= 2.$$

58. Let $f(x) = x^2$. Carefully explain each step in the following evaluation of $f'(3)$:

(a) $$f'(3) = \lim_{h \to 0} \frac{(3+h)^2 - 9}{h}$$

(b) $$= \lim_{h \to 0} \frac{6h + h^2}{h}$$

(c) $$= \lim_{h \to 0} (6 + h)$$

(d) $$= 6.$$

Use the limit definition of the derivative to compute $f'(4)$ for each of the following functions.

59. $f(x) = 3$
60. $f(x) = 2x + 1$
61. $f(x) = x^2 - 3x$
62. $f(x) = \sqrt{x}$
63. $f(x) = x^{-1}$
64. $f(x) = 3x^{-2}$
65. $f(x) = x^{-1/2}$

66. Suppose that $f(x + y) = f(x) + f(y) + 3xy$ for all real numbers x, y, and that $\lim_{h\to 0} f(h)/h = 42$.
    (a) Explain why $f(0) = 0$. [HINT: Continuity of f *cannot* be assumed.]
    (b) Find a symbolic expression for $f'(x)$.

67. Suppose that $f'(2) = 3$. Find $\displaystyle\lim_{h\to 0} \frac{f(2-h) - f(2)}{h}$.

68. Each of the following limits has the form
$$\lim_{x\to a} f(x) = L\,.$$
For each, use a grapher to find a value of δ that guarantees that $|f(x) - L| < 0.001$ when $|x - a| < \delta$.
    (a) $\displaystyle\lim_{x\to 2} 3x = 6$
    (b) $\displaystyle\lim_{x\to 0} \frac{1 - \cos x}{x} = 0$
    (c) $\displaystyle\lim_{x\to 1} \frac{x+1}{x+3} = 0.5$
    (d) $\displaystyle\lim_{x\to 0} \frac{1 - \cos(2x)}{x^2} = 2$

In exercises 69–73, use the value of δ given to prove the limit. (Assume $\epsilon < 1$.)

69. $\displaystyle\lim_{x\to 5} x = 5;\quad \delta = \epsilon$
70. $\displaystyle\lim_{x\to 4} x^2 = 16;\quad \delta = \epsilon/10$
71. $\displaystyle\lim_{x\to 2} 6 = 6;\quad \delta = 0.2$
72. $\displaystyle\lim_{x\to 3} \frac{x^2 - 9}{x - 3} = 6;\quad \delta = \epsilon$
73. $\displaystyle\lim_{x\to 0} |x| = 0;\quad \delta = \epsilon$

74. Use the formal definition of limit to show that $\displaystyle\lim_{x\to 1} 0.99999x \neq 1$.

75. Let $f(x) = \begin{cases} x^2 + 1, & x \le 0 \\ -x, & x > 0\,. \end{cases}$
Use the formal definition of limit to show that f is not continuous at $x = 0$. [HINT: $f(0) - f(x) > 1$ when $x > 0$.]

76. Let f be the function defined in the previous problem.
    (a) Show that for every positive number δ, no matter how small, there is a positive number ϵ so that
$$|f(x) - 1| < \epsilon \quad \text{whenever} \quad 0 < |x| < \delta\,.$$
    (b) Why doesn't the result in part (a) show that f is continuous at $x = 0$? [HINT: Compare part (a) with the formal definition of limit.]

2.7 Limits involving infinity; new limits from old

In the previous section we defined limits, explored several examples and extensions of the idea, and then applied limits to define continuity. This section continues the limit theme. First we'll define another variant on the basic limit idea—limits that involve the ∞-symbol—and interpret results graphically in terms of asymptotes. Then we'll consider how to combine simple, "known" limits to obtain new, more challenging limits.

Limits at infinity, infinite limits, and asymptotes

Limits at infinity and infinite limits➽ describe the behavior of functions when either inputs or outputs increase or decrease "without bound." Informal definitions and examples will suffice to give the idea.

They're different!

Definition: (Limit at infinity.) $\lim_{x\to\infty} f(x) = L$ means that $f(x) \to L$ as $x \to \infty$ (i.e., as x increases without bound.)

Definition: (Infinite limit.) $\lim_{x\to a} f(x) = \infty$ means that $f(x) \to \infty$ (i.e., $f(x)$ blows up) as $x \to a$.

Additional variants➽ exist; defining them all separately would be tedious. What each means is usually clear from context.

E.g., limits as $x \to -\infty$, one-sided infinite limits.

■ **Example 1.** Discuss the meaning of each of the following limit statements:

- $\lim_{x\to\infty} \frac{1}{x} = 0$
- $\lim_{x\to 0} \frac{1}{x^2} = \infty$
- $\lim_{x\to 0^-} \frac{1}{x} = -\infty$
- $\lim_{x\to\infty} \sin x$ does not exist

Solution: The limit $\lim_{x\to\infty} \sin x$ does not exist because the sine function oscillates *forever*, never settling down near any single value. The graphs below should help the reader interpret the first three limits:➽

What other limit statements do the graphs suggest?

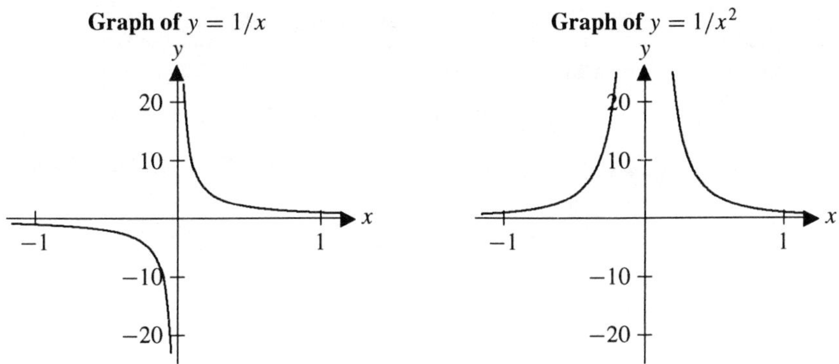

Notice especially the graphical meaning of each infinite limit and limit at infinity. Each one corresponds to an asymptote, either vertical or horizontal. We'll refine this observation below. □

Asymptotes and limits

The connection between asymptotes, limits at infinity, and infinite limits is easily summarized:

Horizontal asymptotes; limits at infinity: The horizontal line $y = L$ is an asymptote to the graph of f if (and only if) f approaches L as $x \to \pm\infty$—that is, if

$$\lim_{x\to\infty} f(x) = L \qquad \text{or} \qquad \lim_{x\to-\infty} f(x) = L.$$

Vertical asymptotes; infinite limits: The vertical line $x = a$ is an asymptote to the graph of f if (and only if) f "blows up" (or "blows down") at a—that is, if

$$\lim_{x\to a^-} f(x) = \pm\infty \qquad \text{or} \qquad \lim_{x\to a^+} f(x) = \pm\infty.$$

Limits and asymptotes of rational functions

Asymptote information is useful for any function. Horizontal asymptotes reflect "long-term" behavior; vertical asymptotes reveal sudden spikes and other anomalies. For polynomials and rational functions, the story is especially simple.

Quotients of polynomials.

Can polynomials have asymptotes? Polynomials can't have vertical asymptotes. A vertical asymptote occurs at a *finite* value of x, near which a function's value is unbounded. Since polynomials have the pleasant form

$$p(x) = a_0 + a_1x + \ldots + a_nx^n,$$

free of troublesome denominators, polynomials *can't* blow up (or down) except as x approaches $\pm\infty$.

Only a constant polynomial can have a *horizontal* asymptote. If, say, $p(x) = 3$, then the p-graph is itself horizontal—its own asymptote. Nonconstant polynomials *can't* have horizontal asymptotes. A bit more is true:

Draw the graph of $p(x) = 3$ to convince yourself.

> **Fact:** If $p(x)$ is a nonconstant polynomial, then
>
> $$\lim_{x\to\pm\infty} |p(x)| = \infty.$$

We won't prove this fact formally, but we'll illustrate why it holds.

■ **Example 2.** Let $p(x) = 2x^3 - 53x^2 - 123x$. How does p behave as $x \to \pm\infty$?

Solution: It's clear at a glance that as $x \to \infty$, $2x^3 \to \infty$, $-53x^2 \to -\infty$, and $-123x \to -\infty$. But what about the sum?

The trick is to *factor out the largest power of x*:

Convince yourself of each step. Is the last step in each operation plausible?

$$\begin{aligned}\lim_{x\to\infty}\left(2x^3 - 53x^2 - 123x\right) &= \lim_{x\to\infty} x^3\left(2 - \frac{53}{x} - \frac{123}{x^2}\right)\\ &= \lim_{x\to\infty} x^3 \cdot \lim_{x\to\infty}\left(2 - \frac{53}{x} - \frac{123}{x^2}\right)\\ &= \infty\cdot 2 = \infty.\end{aligned}$$

Similarly,

$$\begin{aligned}\lim_{x\to-\infty}\left(2x^3 - 53x^2 - 123x\right) &= \lim_{x\to-\infty} x^3 \cdot \lim_{x\to-\infty}(2 - \frac{53}{x} - \frac{123}{x^2})\\ &= -\infty\cdot 2 = -\infty.\end{aligned}$$

(In each calculation we used the fact that the limit of a product is the product of the limits.) □

More on this fact below.

Algebra with the infinity symbol. In the previous example we breezed past two possibly suspicious claims: $\infty \cdot 2 = \infty$ and $-\infty \cdot 2 = -\infty$. Do they really make sense? Since ∞ and $-\infty$ are *not numbers*, seeing them in equations should always raise flags of caution. Here, fortunately, we're OK—neither $\infty \cdot 2$ nor $-\infty \cdot 2$ is ambiguous. The following table collects some rules of etiquette with the infinity symbol.

Good and bad uses of ∞

Expression	What it means; remarks
$1/\infty = 0$	Usually OK, but if we really mean, say, $\lim_{x\to\infty} 1/x = 0$, why not say so?
$3 \cdot \infty = \infty$	OK as mathematical shorthand. It means: If any quantity increases without bound, so does three times that quantity.
$\infty + \infty = \infty$	OK again. It means: If two quantities increase without bound, so does their sum.
$1/0 = \infty$	Wrong. Division by 0 is not defined for real numbers. Worse, $1/x \to \infty$ as $x \to 0$ from the *right*, but $1/x \to -\infty$ as $x \to 0$ from the *left*.
$\infty - \infty = 0$	Wrong again. For example, as $x \to \infty$, $x^3 \to \infty$ and $x^2 \to \infty$, but $x^3 - x^2 \to \infty$.
$\infty/\infty = 1$	Wrong. For example, as $x \to \infty$, $x^3 \to \infty$ and $x^2 \to \infty$, but $x^3/x^2 = x \to \infty$.

Horizontal asymptotes of rational functions: appeal to higher powers. Finding horizontal asymptotes of rational functions means finding limits at infinity. A simple strategy applies:

To find limits at infinity of rational functions, factor out the highest powers of x from numerator and denominator.

Let's apply it:

■ **Example 3.** Consider the three rational functions

$$r(x) = \frac{2x^3 - x}{x^2 - 1}, \qquad s(x) = \frac{2x^3 - x}{x^3 - 1}, \qquad \text{and} \qquad t(x) = \frac{2x^3 - x}{x^4 - 1}.$$

Find all horizontal asymptotes.

Solution: The graphs are below, but we won't peek. Instead we'll use the factoring strategy above:

$$r(x) = \frac{2x^3 - x}{x^2 - 1} = \frac{x^3(2 - 1/x^2)}{x^2(1 - 1/x^2)} = x \cdot \frac{2 - 1/x^2}{1 - 1/x^2};$$

$$s(x) = \frac{2x^3 - x}{x^3 - 1} = \frac{x^3(2 - 1/x^2)}{x^3(1 - 1/x^3)} = \frac{2 - 1/x^2}{1 - 1/x^3};$$

$$t(x) = \frac{2x^3 - x}{x^4 - 1} = \frac{x^3(2 - 1/x^2)}{x^4(1 - 1/x^4)} = \frac{1}{x} \cdot \frac{2 - 1/x^2}{1 - 1/x^4}.$$

Convince yourself.

Now we can see that as $x \to \infty$,

$$r(x) \to \infty, \qquad s(x) \to 2, \qquad \text{and} \qquad t(x) \to 0.$$

As $x \to -\infty$,

$$r(x) \to -\infty, \qquad s(x) \to 2 \qquad \text{and} \qquad t(x) \to 0.$$

Thus s and t have *horizontal* asymptotes, at $y = 2$ and $y = 0$ respectively; r has none. □

Vertical asymptotes of rational functions: look for roots. Rational functions have vertical asymptotes, if at all, at roots of the denominator.

■ **Example 4.** Let r, s, and t be as above. Find all *vertical* asymptotes.

Solution: A rational function has a *vertical* asymptote anywhere the denominator is zero and the numerator isn't. (If *both* numerator and denominator are zero at the same place, they have a common factor; for present purposes, it can be cancelled.) To locate the asymptotes, factor the denominator. For r, s, and t:

Factoring polynomials of large degree can be hard or impossible. Authors usually choose polynomials to be easy to factor. So will we.

$$r(x) = \frac{2x^3 - x}{x^2 - 1} = \frac{2x^3 - x}{(x+1)(x-1)}$$

$$s(x) = \frac{2x^3 - x}{x^3 - 1} = \frac{2x^3 - x}{(x-1)(x^2+x+1)}$$

$$t(x) = \frac{2x^3 - x}{x^4 - 1} = \frac{2x^3 - x}{(x^2-1)(x^2+1)} = \frac{2x^3 - x}{(x-1)(x+1)(x^2+1)}$$

The factored denominators show that for each function, $x = \pm 1$ are the suspicious values, or singular points. Since the numerator $2x^3 - x$ is not zero at $x = \pm 1$, it follows that r and t have vertical asymptotes at $x = 1$ and at $x = -1$; s has a vertical asymptote at $x = 1$.

On either side of a vertical asymptote a function may tend either to ∞ or to $-\infty$. What happens at each asymptote above? Graphs make the answers obvious, but even *without* graphs, the question is easy to answer. We need only determine the *sign* of each function just to the right and left of each asymptote.

For $r(x)$, just to the left of $x = -1$, we see that

$$2x^3 - x < 0, \qquad x + 1 < 0, \qquad \text{and} \qquad x - 1 < 0.$$

r "blows down" to $-\infty$ as $x \to -1$ from the left.

Therefore $r(x) < 0$, so $\lim_{x \to -1^-} r(x) = -\infty$. A similar sign check reveals that r

blows *up* to ∞ as $x \to -1$ from the *right*.

We've waited long enough; here are the graphs:

Can you mimic this analysis for the functions s and t?

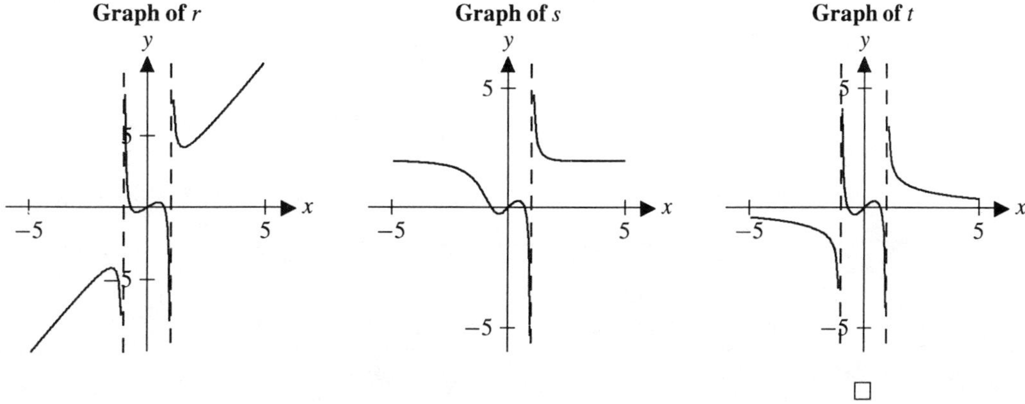

□

Asymptotes of other algebraic functions

Like rational functions, "other" algebraic functions may have asymptotes, with exactly the same conceptual connection to infinite limits and limits at infinity. *Calculating* these limits algebraically may take extra ingenuity.

■ **Example 5.** The algebraic function defined by $f(x) = \sqrt{x^2 + x} - x$ has a horizontal asymptote. Find it.

For $x > 0$.

Solution: How $f(x)$ behaves as $x \to \infty$ isn't obvious from the formula, but the following table of values argues persuasively for a limit of $1/2$:

Is it? Why or why not?

So would a graph; draw one.

As $x \to \infty$, $\sqrt{x^2+x} - x \to 1/2$									
x	1	2	4	8	16	32	64	128	256
$f(x)$	0.4142	0.4495	0.4721	0.4853	0.4924	0.4962	0.4981	0.4990	0.4995

With algebra we'll clinch our case; the first step is a trick:

Multiplying top and bottom by the "conjugate."

$$\begin{aligned}
\lim_{x\to\infty} (\sqrt{x^2+x} - x) &= \lim_{x\to\infty} \frac{(\sqrt{x^2+x} - x)(\sqrt{x^2+x} + x)}{\sqrt{x^2+x} + x} \\
&= \lim_{x\to\infty} \frac{x}{\sqrt{x^2+x} + x} \\
&= \lim_{x\to\infty} \frac{x}{x\left(\sqrt{1+1/x} + 1\right)} \\
&= \lim_{x\to\infty} \frac{1}{\sqrt{1+1/x} + 1} = \frac{1}{2}.
\end{aligned}$$

□

New limits from old: algebraic combinations

When calculating limits we often take a few basic limits to be "obvious" and try to reduce more complicated limits to algebraic combinations of these. The next example emphasizes this process.

■ **Example 6.** Find $\displaystyle\lim_{x\to\infty} \frac{x^2+3}{2x^2-5}$.

The key step is dividing numerator and denominator by x^2.

Solution: With a graph it would be easy to guess that the limit is 1/2. Algebra makes the case airtight:

$$\begin{aligned}\lim_{x\to\infty}\frac{x^2+3}{2x^2-5} &= \lim_{x\to\infty}\frac{x^2\cdot(1+3/x^2)}{x^2\cdot(2-5/x^2)}\\ &= \lim_{x\to\infty}\frac{1+3/x^2}{2-5/x^2}\\ &= \frac{\lim\limits_{x\to\infty}1+\lim\limits_{x\to\infty}3/x^2}{\lim\limits_{x\to\infty}2-\lim\limits_{x\to\infty}5/x^2}\\ &= \frac{1+0}{2-0}=1/2.\end{aligned}$$

□

We used several plausible facts in the calculations above: that $\lim\limits_{x\to\infty} 3/x^2 = \lim\limits_{x\to\infty} 5/x^2 = 0$, that the limit of a sum or quotient is the sum or quotient of the limits, etc.

The following theorem justifies "combining" old limits to find new ones. Each part tells how limits behave with respect to some algebraic operation on functions.

> **Theorem 1. (Algebra with limits.)** Suppose that
>
> $$\lim_{x\to a} f(x) = L \quad\text{and}\quad \lim_{x\to a} g(x) = M,$$
>
> where L and M are finite numbers. Let k be any constant. Then
>
> (i) $\lim\limits_{x\to a} kf(x) = kL$;
>
> (ii) $\lim\limits_{x\to a} [f(x)+g(x)] = L+M$;
>
> (iii) $\lim\limits_{x\to a} f(x)\cdot g(x) = L\cdot M$;
>
> (iv) $\lim\limits_{x\to a} \dfrac{f(x)}{g(x)} = \dfrac{L}{M}$ (if $M \neq 0$).

Remarks on the theorem.

Why they hold. Each rule is intuitively plausible, but rigorous proofs would require the epsilon-delta definition. We'll skip the proofs here, but a typical such proof can be found in Appendix I.

Limits that involve infinity. All the rules holds for limits at infinity (i.e., when a is $\pm\infty$). They also hold for infinite limits (i.e., when $L = \pm\infty$ and/or $M = \pm\infty$)—*but only if appropriate care is taken with with uses of the infinity symbol*, as described in the "usage" table above.

As we've already done implicitly in examples.

To be fully rigorous we'd have to prove even these limits.

"Obvious" limits. Using these rules we can find many new limits—provided that we know some old limits. To get such a foothold, we'll take as obvious limits like these:

"Obvious" Limits	
$\lim_{x\to 0} \lvert x\rvert = 0$	
$\lim_{x\to a} x = a$	for any real number a
$\lim_{x\to\infty} x^n = \infty$	for any $n > 0$
$\lim_{x\to\infty} \frac{1}{x^n} = 0$	for any $n > 0$

New continuous functions from old: algebraic combinations

If f and g are continuous functions, it sounds reasonable that such algebraic combinations as $f+g$, f/g, and $3f-2g$ should *also* define continuous functions. As a rule, they do. Because continuity is defined *via* limits, it's not surprising that properties of limits are reflected in properties of continuous functions. The next theorem gives the fine print:

See the previous section!

Theorem 2. (Algebra with continuous functions.) Suppose that both f and g are continuous at $x=a$. Then each of the functions

$$f+g, \quad f-g, \quad \text{and} \quad fg$$

is also continuous at $x=a$. If $g(a)\neq 0$, then f/g is continuous at $x=a$.

Proof. Each claimed property of continuous functions follows directly from the analogous property of limits. The first claim, for instance, goes like this:

$$\lim_{x\to a} f(x)+g(x) = \lim_{x\to a} f(x) + \lim_{x\to a} g(x) = f(a)+g(a).$$

The result is just what's needed to show that $f+g$ is continuous at $x=a$. □

Limits and inequalities: the squeeze principle

Algebraic limit rules don't help with limits like

$$\lim_{x\to 0} x\cdot\sin\left(\frac{1}{x}\right) \qquad \text{and} \qquad \lim_{x\to\infty} \frac{\sin x}{x}.$$

The product-of-limits rule doesn't apply to the first limit, for example, because the second factor, $\sin(1/x)$, *has* no limit as $x\to 0$. With graphs the limits are easy to guess, but let's try to compute them directly.

Squeezing inequalities. The idea is to use carefully-chosen inequalities to "squeeze' the function of interest between two simpler functions. For the first limit above, the key inequalities say that for any x,

$$-\lvert x\rvert \le x\sin\left(\frac{1}{x}\right) \le \lvert x\rvert.$$

A graph shows convincingly that the inequality is valid:

Finding a limit by squeezing

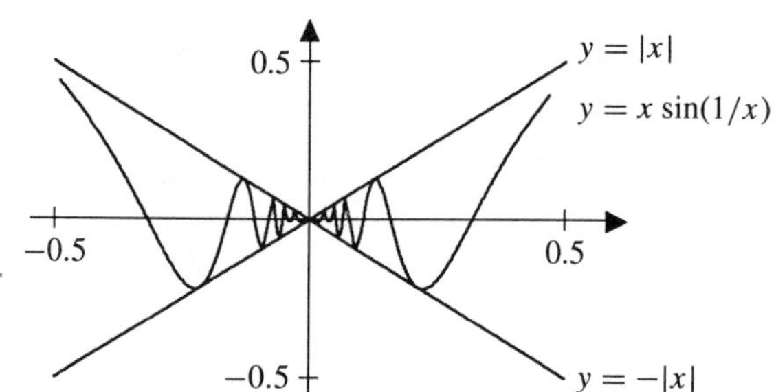

As $x \to 0$ both the *left* and *right* sides of this three-term inequality tend to 0. "Squeezed" between $-|x|$ and $|x|$, $x \sin(1/x)$ has only one place to go:

$$x \sin\left(\frac{1}{x}\right) \to 0 \quad \text{as} \quad x \to 0.$$

There's a general theorem here. The graph above makes it reasonable; we omit the formal proof.

> **Theorem 3. (The squeeze principle.)** Suppose that
>
> $$f(x) \le g(x) \le h(x)$$
>
> for all x near $x = a$. If $f(x) \to L$ and $h(x) \to L$ as $x \to a$, then $g(x) \to L$ as $x \to a$.

Note:

- The theorem is good for more than computation. It also guarantees that $\lim_{x \to a} g(x)$ *exists*—no matter how crazily g careens between f and h.
- The squeeze principle is conceptually easy; the hard part, in practice, is to choose the "bounding functions" f and h properly.

■ **Example 7.** Explain why $\lim_{x \to \infty} \frac{\sin x}{x} = 0$.

Solution: The inequality

$$-\frac{1}{x} \le \frac{\sin x}{x} \le \frac{1}{x}$$

Convince yourself; use graphics.

holds for all $x > 0$. Because the left and right sides tend to 0 as $x \to \infty$, so must the middle expression. □

Finding limits graphically and numerically

If $\lim_{x \to a} f(x) = L$, then $f(x) \approx L$ whenever $x \approx a$. Therefore, in order to guess or estimate L, it's natural to look at values of f near $x = a$. We can do this either numerically, by "plugging in numbers," or graphically, by plotting f near $x = a$. Each strategy has its advantages. Numerical outputs may be more accurate, but graphs show better how f varies. With technology, *both* approaches are almost painless.

■ **Example 8.** Let $f(x) = x \sin(1/x)$. Discuss $\lim_{x \to 0} f(x)$ and $\lim_{x \to \infty} f(x)$.

Can you guess these limits using only mental gymnastics?

Solution: We saw above, by "squeezing," that the first limit is 0. Numerical values of f near $x = 0$ (rounded to 4 decimal places) agree:

Check some with a calculator.

x	-0.1	-0.01	-0.001	...	0.001	0.01	0.1
$f(x)$	-0.0544	-0.0051	0.0008	...	0.0008	-0.0051	-0.0544

To investigate $\lim_{x \to \infty} f(x)$ we'll consider *large* values of x, first graphically—

Graph of $y = x \sin(1/x)$ for large x

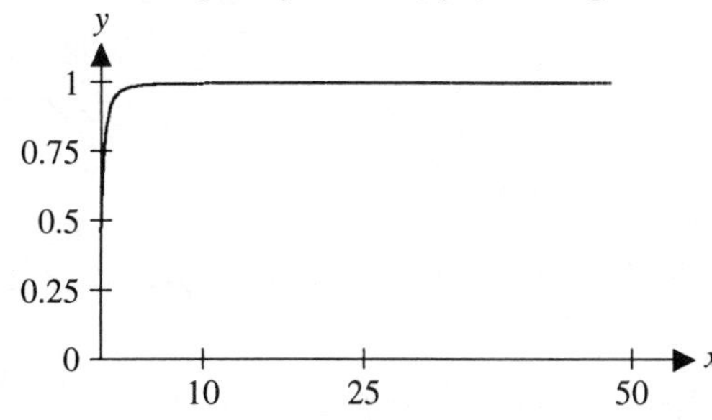

and now numerically, to 6 decimal places—

x	10	100	1000	10000
$f(x)$	0.998334	0.999983	1.000000	1.000000

Again the conclusion is irresistible: $\lim_{x \to \infty} f(x) = 1$. □

■ **Example 9.** Let $g(x) = \sin(1/x)$. Discuss $\lim_{x \to 0} g(x)$.

Solution: This time both graph and numbers look suspiciously chaotic:

The graph shown is of poor quality. What's wrong with it? Why is a good graph hard to find? Would a smaller window help?

A (poor quality) graph of $y = \sin(1/x)$

x	-0.1	-0.05	-0.025	...	0.001	0.0025	0.0075
$g(x)$	0.544	-0.913	-0.745	...	0.827	-0.851	0.983

In fact, *the limit doesn't exist.* As $x \to 0$ from the right, $1/x \to +\infty$, so $\sin(1/x)$ oscillates faster and faster between -1 and 1. □

Exercises

1. Let f and g be the functions whose graphs are shown below. Use the graphs to evaluate the following limits. If a limit doesn't exist, explain why. [NOTE: $f(1) = 2$.]

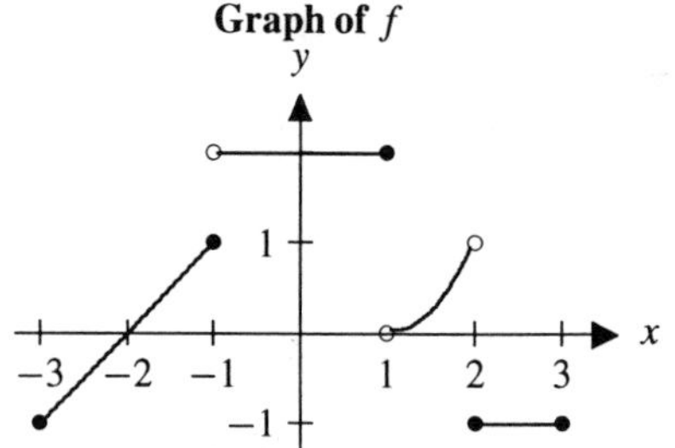

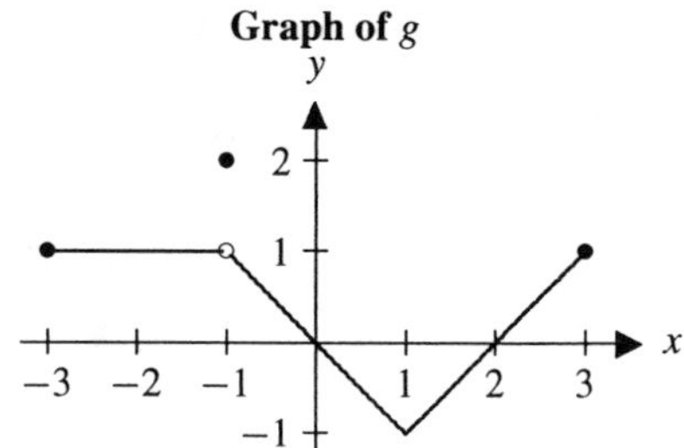

(a) $\lim_{x\to 0}\big(f(x)+g(x)\big)$

(b) $\lim_{x\to 2}\big(f(x)+g(x)\big)$

(c) $\lim_{x\to 1}\big(f(x)\cdot g(x)\big)$

(d) $\lim_{x\to 2}\big(f(x)\cdot g(x)\big)$

(e) $\lim_{x\to 0}\dfrac{f(x)}{g(x)}$

(f) $\lim_{x\to 0}\big(f(x)\cdot\cos x\big)$

(g) $\lim_{x\to -2} x^2 g(x)$

2. Let f and g be the functions whose graphs are shown below. Use the graphs to evaluate the following limits. If a limit doesn't exist, explain why.

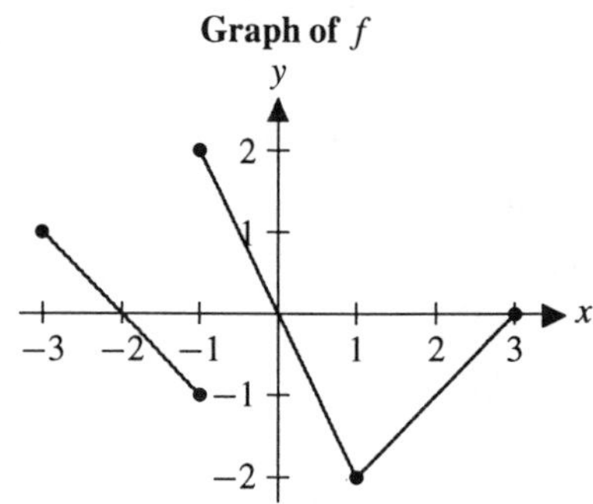

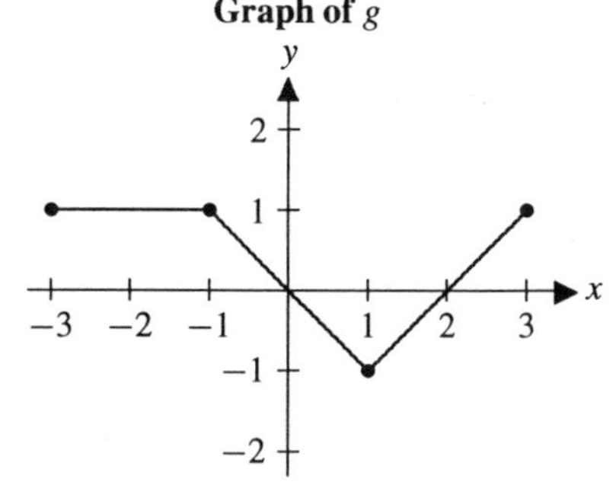

(a) $\lim_{x\to -2}\left(\dfrac{f(x)}{g(x)}\right)$

(b) $\lim_{x\to 2}\left(\dfrac{f(x)}{g(x)}\right)$

(c) $\lim_{x\to 0}\left(\dfrac{f(x)}{g(x)}\right)$

(d) $\lim_{x\to 1}\left(\dfrac{f(x)}{g(x)}\right)$

3. Use a calculator to estimate each of the following limits numerically.

(a) $\lim_{x\to\infty}\dfrac{3}{x^2}$

(b) $\lim_{x\to\infty}\dfrac{5}{\sqrt{x}}$

(c) $\lim_{x\to\infty}\dfrac{x^2+1}{x}$

(d) $\lim_{x\to 0^+}\dfrac{\sqrt{x}}{\sin x}$

(e) $\lim_{x\to 0^+} \left(x \log_{10} x\right)$

(f) $\lim_{x\to 0} \sin\left(\sin x\right)$

(g) $\lim_{x\to\infty} \dfrac{2^x}{x^2}$

(h) $\lim_{x\to\infty} \dfrac{x^2}{2^x}$

(i) $\lim_{x\to -\infty} \dfrac{2^x}{x^2}$

(j) $\lim_{x\to 0^+} x^x$

4. Use a grapher to guess whether each of the following limits exist. Estimate values of those that do exist.

(a) $\lim_{x\to\infty} \dfrac{2000x^2}{1000x^2 + \sin x}$

(b) $\lim_{x\to 0} \dfrac{1-\cos^2(3x)}{x^2}$

(c) $\lim_{x\to 0} \cos\left(\dfrac{1-\cos x}{x}\right)$

(d) $\lim_{x\to\infty} \dfrac{3^x - 3}{2^x - 2}$

(e) $\lim_{x\to -\infty} \dfrac{3^x - 3}{2^x - 2}$

5. (a) Evaluate $\lim_{x\to\infty} \sin\left(\dfrac{\pi}{x}\right)$.

(b) Evaluate $\lim_{x\to 0} \sin\left(\dfrac{\pi}{x}\right)$.

(c) Evaluate $\lim_{x\to\infty} \exp\left((3x^2 + x)/2x^3\right)$.

6. Let $f(x) = \sqrt[3]{x}$. Explain why $\lim_{x\to 0} f'(x) = \infty$.

7. Suppose that f is a (non-constant) periodic function. Explain why $\lim_{x\to\infty} f(x)$ does not exist.

8. Sketch the graph of a function f that has *all* of the following properties. (Be sure to label axes and indicate units on each axis.)

(i) f has domain $(-3, \infty)$

(ii) f has range $(-\infty, 2)$

(iii) $f(-1) = 0$; $f(0) = 0$; $f(5) = 0$

(iv) $\lim_{x\to -3^+} f(x) = -\infty$

(v) $\lim_{x\to 2} f(x) = -3$

(vi) $\lim_{x\to\infty} f(x) = 2$

9. Sketch the graph of a function f that has *all* of the following properties:

(i) f has domain $\mathbb{R}$

(ii) f has range $(-3, \infty)$

(iii) $\lim_{t\to 2} f(t) = -2$

(iv) $\lim_{t\to\infty} f(t) = -3$

(v) $\lim_{t\to -\infty} f(t) = 3$

10. Suppose that $\lim_{x\to 1} f(x) = 5$ and $\lim_{x\to 1} g(x) = -2$. Use this information to evaluate each of the following limits.

(a) $\lim_{x\to 1}\left(f(x) + g(x)\right)$

(b) $\lim_{x\to 1}\left(g(x) - f(x)\right)$

(c) $\lim_{x\to 1} \dfrac{f(x) + 2}{f(x)g(x)}$

11. Show that there is only one value of $k \geq 1$ for which $\lim_{x \to 0} \frac{\sin(2 \sin x)}{x^k}$ is a real number. Find this value of k and evaluate the limit.

12. Let $p(x) = (x+1)(2-x)$ and $q(x) = x^{17} - 3x^{14} + 39$. Evaluate each of the following:

(a) $\lim_{x \to \infty} p(x)$

(b) $\lim_{x \to -\infty} p(x)$

(c) $\lim_{x \to \infty} q(x)$

(d) $\lim_{x \to -\infty} q(x)$

14. Suppose that $r(x)$ is a polynomial of degree n such that $\lim_{x \to \infty} r(x) = -\infty$ and $\lim_{x \to -\infty} r(x) = -\infty$. Can you tell if n is even or odd? Explain.

15. Let h be a function that has a vertical asymptote at $x = 3$ and the properties $\lim_{x \to -\infty} h(x) = \infty$ and $\lim_{x \to \infty} h(x) = -1$.

(a) Must h have a horizontal asymptote? If so, what is it?

(b) Could h be a rational function? Why or why not?

16. Any rational function $r(x)$ behaves like ax^n for some real number a and some integer n in the sense that

$$\lim_{x \to \infty} \frac{r(x)}{ax^n} = 1 .$$

For example, $k(x) = 2x^3 / \left(x^2 + 1\right)$ behaves like $2x$ ($a = 2$ and $n = 1$) for large values of x because

$$\begin{aligned} \lim_{x \to \infty} k(x) &= \lim_{x \to \infty} \frac{2x^3}{x^2 + 1} \\ &= \lim_{x \to \infty} \left(2x \cdot \frac{x^2}{x^2 + 1}\right) \end{aligned}$$

and $\lim_{x \to \infty} x^2 / \left(x^2 + 1\right) = 1$.

Find the appropriate values of a and n for each of the following rational functions. Then graph the function and ax^n on the same axes for large values of x (e.g., on the interval [50, 100]).

(a) $f(x) = \dfrac{4x^2 + 3x}{3x^4 + 2x^2 - 1}$

(b) $g(x) = \dfrac{3x^4 - 2x^3 + 4x^2 - 5x + 7}{5x^4 - 12x^2 + 100}$

(c) $h(x) = \dfrac{2x^5 - 3x^2 + 15}{3x^2 + 4x - 5}$

17. Let $f(x) = \sqrt{x^2+1} - x$ and $g(x) = \sqrt{x^2+x} - x$.

(a) Use a calculator or a computer to complete the following table.

x	100	1000	10,000	100,000	1,000,000
$f(x)$					
$g(x)$					

(b) Use the results you recorded in the table above to estimate $\lim_{x\to\infty} f(x)$ and $\lim_{x\to\infty} g(x)$.

(c) What do your answers to part (b) imply about the graphs of f and g?

18. Give examples of polynomials $p(x)$ and $q(x)$ such that $\lim_{x\to\infty} p(x) = \infty$, $\lim_{x\to\infty} q(x) = \infty$, and

(a) $\lim_{x\to\infty} \dfrac{p(x)}{q(x)} = \infty$.

(b) $\lim_{x\to\infty} \dfrac{p(x)}{q(x)} = 2$.

(c) $\lim_{x\to\infty} \dfrac{p(x)}{q(x)} = 0$.

(d) $\lim_{x\to\infty} \dfrac{p(x)}{q(x)} = 1$ and $\lim_{x\to\infty} \big(p(x) - q(x)\big) = 3$.

19. For each part of the preceding problem, give a geometric explanation of how the graphs of p and q are related. [HINT: Graph your polynomials p and q on the same set of axes.]

20. Let $p(x) = ax^n + q(x)$ where $q(x)$ is a polynomial of degree $m < n$.

(a) What is $\lim_{x\to\infty} \dfrac{q(x)}{x^n}$?

(b) What is $\lim_{x\to-\infty} \dfrac{q(x)}{x^n}$?

(c) If $a > 0$ and n is *even*, what is $\lim_{x\to\infty} p(x)$?

(d) If $a > 0$ and n is *even*, what is $\lim_{x\to-\infty} p(x)$?

(e) How do your answers to parts (c) and (d) change if n is *odd*?

21. Suppose that the average rate of change of a function f over the interval from $x = 3$ to $x = 3 + h$ is $4e^h - 5\cos(2h)$. What is $f'(3)$?

22. Let $f(x) = \dfrac{2x^2 + x + a}{x^2 - 2x - 3}$.

(a) Can the number a be chosen so that $\lim_{x\to 3} f(x)$ exists? Explain your answer.

(b) Can the number a be chosen so that $\lim_{x\to\infty} f(x)$ exists? Explain your answer.

23. Explain why $\lim_{x\to\infty} \cos x$ does not exist.

24. Evaluate each of the following limits, if it exists. [HINT: Graphs may help.]

(a) $\lim_{x \to \infty} \frac{\sin x}{x}$ (b) $\lim_{x \to -\infty} \frac{x^3}{2 + \cos x}$

25. Suppose that neither $\lim_{x \to a} f(x)$ nor $\lim_{x \to a} g(x)$ exists. Find functions f and g so that the following limits exist or explain why it is impossible to do so.

(a) $\lim_{x \to a} \big(f(x) + g(x)\big)$

(b) $\lim_{x \to a} \big(f(x) \cdot g(x)\big)$

26. Let f be a function defined for all real numbers. Which of the following statements *must* be true about f? Which *might* be true? Which *must* be false? Justify your answers.

(a) $\lim_{x \to a} f(x) = f(a)$

(b) If $\lim_{x \to 0} \frac{f(x)}{x} = 2$, then $f(0) = 0$.

(c) If $\lim_{x \to 0} \frac{f(x)}{x} = 1$, then $\lim_{x \to 0} f(x) = 0$.

(d) If $\lim_{x \to 1^-} f(x) = 1$ and $\lim_{x \to 1^+} f(x) = 3$, then $\lim_{x \to 1} f(x) = 2$.

(e) If $\lim_{x \to 2} f(x) = 3$, then 3 is in the range of f.

(f) If $\lim_{x \to 0} \frac{f(x) - f(0)}{x} = 3$, then $f'(0) = 3$.

2.8 Power functions, polynomials, and their derivatives

Earlier in this chapter we introduced the idea of the derivative (*aka* rate) function and discussed geometric relationships between the functions f and f'. Next we looked closely at $f'(a)$, the value of the derivative function for a specific input $x = a$—how it's defined formally as a limit, how slopes of secant and tangent lines arise, and connections to average and instantaneous rates of change.

Now that we've seen what the derivative means and how it's defined, it's time to *calculate* some derivatives.

A well-behaved➧ function f has a well-behaved derivative function f'. If a function f has a simple algebraic formula, then it's reasonable to expect the derivative f' to have one, too. Finding a formula for f', given a formula for f, is the main subject of this section. For convenience we'll work mainly with **power functions**—just like polynomials except that *non-integer powers* are allowed.

Elementary functions are "well-behaved" in this sense. We'll see later that if f is elementary, so is f'.

At the end of this section we introduce the "inverse" problem (one we'll revisit often) of finding **antiderivatives**, i.e., functions with prescribed derivatives.

Other notations for the derivative

The "prime notation" f' for the derivative of f is convenient; it reminds us, too, of a derivative's ancestry: every f' comes from some "original" f.

Leibniz notation. Alternatives to the prime notation exist. Depending on context, one may be more convenient than the others. To illustrate what's available, let $y = f(x) = x^2$. The following notations all say the same thing:

$$f'(x) = 2x; \qquad \frac{dy}{dx} = 2x; \qquad \frac{d}{dx}\left(x^2\right) = 2x; \qquad \frac{df}{dx} = 2x.$$

So do these:

$$f'(3) = 6; \qquad \left.\frac{dy}{dx}\right|_{x=3} = 6; \qquad \left.\frac{d}{dx}\left(x^2\right)\right|_{x=3} = 6; \qquad \left.\frac{df}{dx}\right|_{x=3} = 6.$$

(We'll see just below *why* these statements are true. Here the point is notation.) The dy/dx form of the derivative is known as **Leibniz notation**, after Gottfried Wilhelm Leibniz (1646–1716), a contemporary of Newton. The "fractional" appearance of Leibniz notation recalls the definition of the derivative as a limit of difference *quotients*:

$$\frac{dy}{dx} = \lim_{\Delta x \to 0} \frac{\Delta y}{\Delta x}.$$

Notations for higher derivatives. Both "prime" and Leibniz notations exist for second, third, and higher derivatives, as well. The following notations all say the same thing about the function defined by $y = f(x) = x^2$:

$$f''(x) = 2; \qquad \frac{d^2y}{dx^2} = 2; \qquad \frac{d^2}{dx^2}\left(x^2\right) = 2; \qquad \frac{d^2f}{dx^2} = 2.$$

We'll use both prime and Leibniz notation in this book, as convenience dictates.

The derivative as a function: the definition revisited

In earlier work we formally defined $f'(a)$, the derivative of f at $x = a$. The definition below is essentially the same; using the "generic" x in place of the "specific" a emphasizes that f' is a *function*.

Definition: Let f be a function. The derivative of f, denoted f', is the function defined for an input x by

$$f'(x) = \lim_{h \to 0} \frac{f(x+h) - f(x)}{h}$$

Observe:

Domain. The domain of f' is the set of inputs x for which the limit exists. In the best cases (more often than not in calculus), the domain of f' is the full domain of f. For some functions f the domain of f' omits a few (usually obvious) points in the domain of f.

The domain of f' can't possibly be bigger than the domain of f, can it?

For $f(x) = |x|$, the domain of f' is smaller than the domain of f.

Finding the limit. The limit in the definition can almost *never* be found simply by plugging in $h = 0$; some trick or algebraic manipulation is almost always needed to eradicate the troublesome denominator.

Beyond algebra. If f is given by a graph, a table of values, in non-algebraic form, or even as a complicated algebraic formula, the limit above may be hard (or impossible) to find exactly. All is not lost: In such cases graphical or numerical estimates are usually possible.

The derivative of x^k

Our first order of business will be to find derivatives of functions of the form $f(x) = x^k$, for *any* constant k. We start with nonnegative integer powers.

Domains of these derivatives, as of the functions themselves, depend on k.

■ **Example 1.** Find derivative formulas for the linear, quadratic, and cubic power functions $l(x) = x$, $q(x) = x^2$, and $c(x) = x^3$. Interpret results graphically.

Solution: The function l is *linear*, with constant slope 1. Its derivative, therefore, is the constant function $l'(x) = 1$. Reassuringly, the limit definition says the same thing:

$$l'(x) = \lim_{h \to 0} \frac{l(x+h) - l(x)}{h} = \lim_{h \to 0} \frac{x + h - x}{h} = 1.$$

Higher powers of x require a little more algebraic work. For q:

Follow each step; watch for a crucial cancellation.

$$\begin{aligned} q'(x) &= \lim_{h \to 0} \frac{q(x+h) - q(x)}{h} \\ &= \lim_{h \to 0} \frac{(x+h)^2 - x^2}{h} \\ &= \lim_{h \to 0} \frac{x^2 + 2xh + h^2 - x^2}{h} \\ &= \lim_{h \to 0} (2x + h) \\ &= 2x. \end{aligned}$$

The cubic c requires more of the same:

$$\begin{aligned} c'(x) &= \lim_{h\to 0} \frac{c(x+h)-c(x)}{h} \\ &= \lim_{h\to 0} \frac{(x+h)^3 - x^3}{h} \\ &= \lim_{h\to 0} \frac{x^3 + 3x^2h + 3xh^2 + h^3 - x^3}{h} \\ &= \lim_{h\to 0} \left(3x^2 + 3xh + h^2\right) \\ &= 3x^2. \end{aligned}$$

In graphical form, our results look like this:

Do they look right? Do the derivative graphs plausibly represent slopes on the upper graphs?

Graph of $l(x) = x$

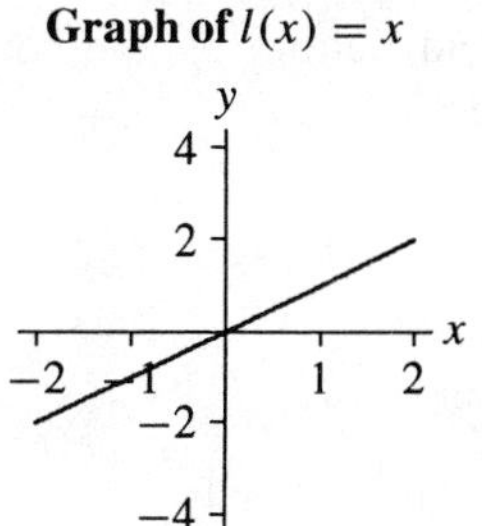

Graph of $q(x) = x^2$

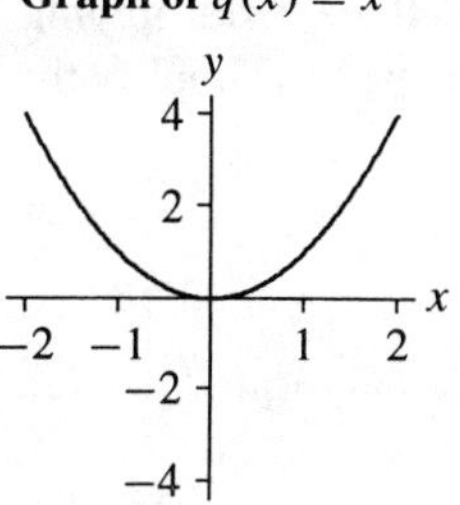

Graph of $c(x) = x^3$

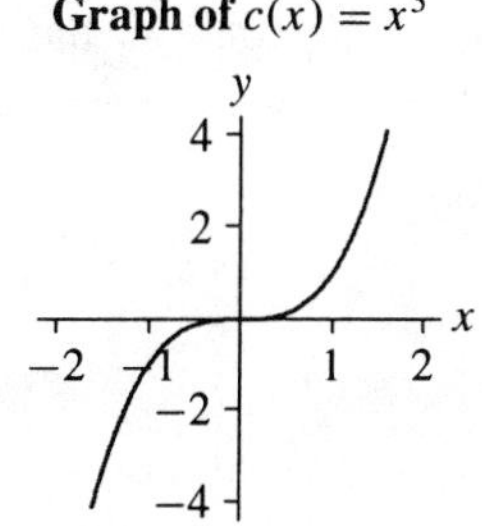

Graph of $l'(x) = 1$

Graph of $q'(x) = 2x$

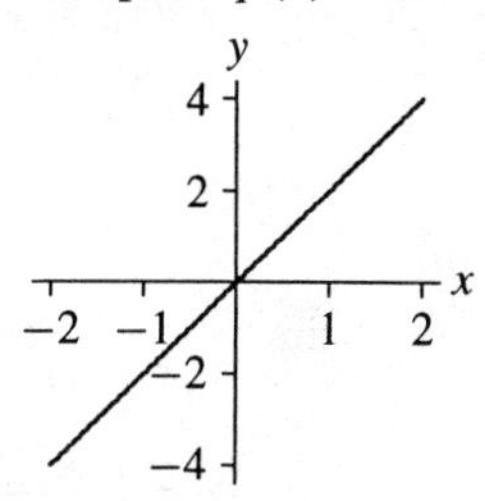

Graph of $c'(x) = 3x^2$

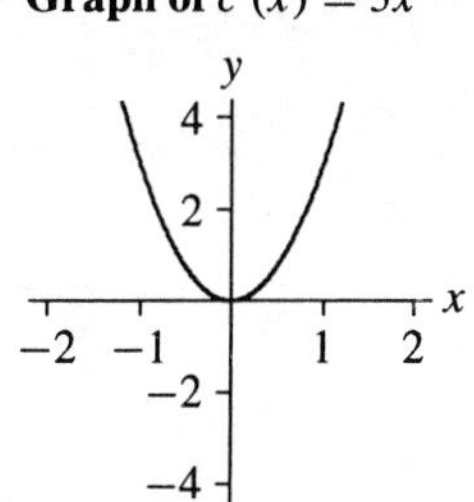

The answers aren't surprising; we've drawn such graphs before. The limit calculations assure us, for the first time, that our derivative formulas are *exact*. □

What can be said about power functions x^k for which k *isn't* a nonnegative integer?

■ **Example 2.** Find derivative formulas for the power functions $s(x) = \sqrt{x} = x^{1/2}$ and $n(x) = 1/x = x^{-1}$. What is the domain of each derivative function? Interpret results graphically.

Solution: This problem, like the last one, calls for limit computations. Here we'll need slightly more clever algebraic methods to eliminate the troublesome denominator h. For s:

$$
\begin{aligned}
s'(x) &= \lim_{h\to 0} \frac{s(x+h)-s(x)}{h} \\
&= \lim_{h\to 0} \frac{\sqrt{x+h}-\sqrt{x}}{h} \\
&= \lim_{h\to 0} \frac{\sqrt{x+h}-\sqrt{x}}{h} \cdot \frac{\sqrt{x+h}+\sqrt{x}}{\sqrt{x+h}+\sqrt{x}} \\
&= \lim_{h\to 0} \frac{1}{\sqrt{x+h}+\sqrt{x}} \\
&= \frac{1}{2\sqrt{x}} = \frac{1}{2}x^{-1/2}.
\end{aligned}
$$

(See the trick on the third line? Multiplying top and bottom by the conjugate expression $\sqrt{x+h}+\sqrt{x}$ helped us simplify the numerator.)

For n:

$$
\begin{aligned}
n'(x) &= \lim_{h\to 0} \frac{n(x+h)-n(x)}{h} \\
&= \lim_{h\to 0} \frac{\frac{1}{x+h}-\frac{1}{x}}{h} \\
&= \lim_{h\to 0} \frac{\frac{1}{x+h}-\frac{1}{x}}{h} \cdot \frac{(x+h)(x)}{(x+h)(x)} \\
&= \lim_{h\to 0} \frac{-h}{h\,x\,(x+h)} \\
&= \lim_{h\to 0} \frac{-1}{x(x+h)} \\
&= \frac{-1}{x^2} = -1x^{-2} = -x^{-2}.
\end{aligned}
$$

Here are all the graphs:

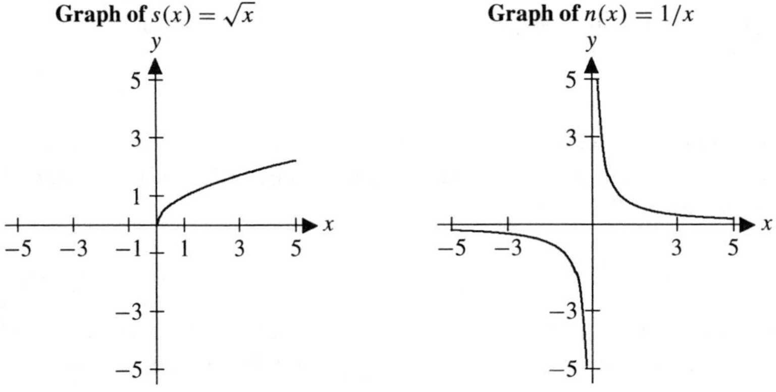

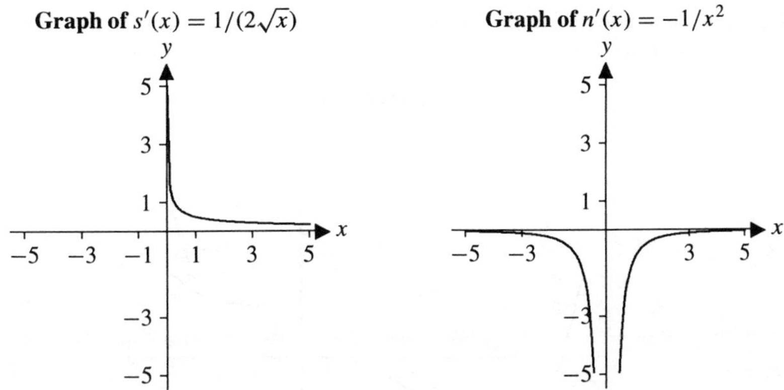

Observe the domains: the derivative s' is defined wherever s is defined—*except* at $x = 0$, where the graph of s has a vertical tangent line. The derivative n' has the same domain (all *nonzero* reals) as n itself. □

A general power rule

Each example above is an instance of a more general fact:➡

Do you see why? Convince yourself.

> **Theorem 4.** Let k be any real constant. If $f(x) = x^k$, then $f'(x) = kx^{k-1}$.

We won't prove this theorem rigorously; at the end of this section we'll relate it to the Binomial Theorem.

Combinations of power functions: the sum and constant rules

Knowing the derivatives of "pure" power functions, it's easy to find derivatives of *combinations* of power functions (like polynomials), "piece by piece."

■ **Example 3.** Let $p(x) = 3x^5 + 7x^4 - x^2/3 + 11$. Find $p'(x)$.

Solution: We'll break p apart, differentiate each piece separately, and then reassemble the results. In Leibniz notation:

$$\begin{aligned}
\frac{dy}{dx} &= \frac{d}{dx}\left(3x^5 + 7x^4 - \frac{1}{3}x^2 + 11\right) \\
&= 3\frac{d}{dx}\left(x^5\right) + 7\frac{d}{dx}\left(x^4\right) - \frac{1}{3}\frac{d}{dx}\left(x^2\right) + 11\frac{d}{dx}(1) \\
&= 3 \cdot 5x^4 + 7 \cdot 4x^3 - \frac{1}{3} \cdot 2x + 11 \cdot 0 \\
&= 15x^4 + 28x^3 - \frac{2}{3}x.
\end{aligned}$$

We made two leaps of faith, having to do with sums and constants. We'll justify them below. First, observe graphically that the result *looks* right:

Graphs of p and p'

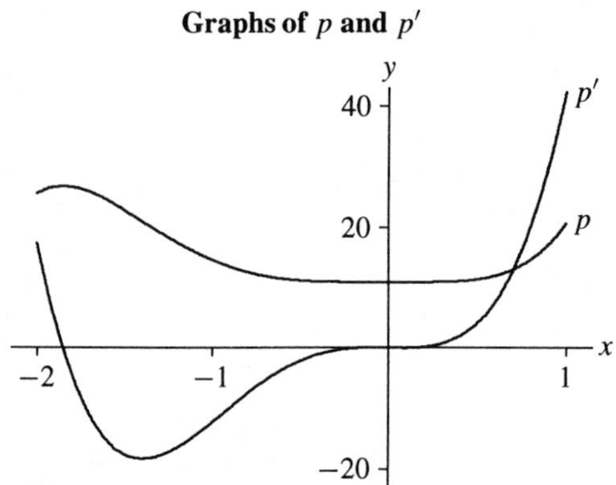

□

The sum and constant rules for derivatives

In the previous example we implicitly made two reasonable-seeming assumptions. Here they are explicitly, stated as theorems:

> **Theorem 5. (The sum rule for derivatives.)** Let f and g be differentiable functions and let $h = f + g$. Then
> $$h'(x) = (f+g)'(x) = f'(x) + g'(x).$$

> **Theorem 6. (The constant rule for derivatives.)** If k is any constant, f is any differentiable function, and $g(x) = kf(x)$, then
> $$g'(x) = (k \cdot f)'(x) = k \cdot f'(x).$$

Observe:

In words. In words, the theorems say:

The derivative of a sum of functions is the sum of their derivatives.
The derivative of a constant times a function is the constant times the derivative of the function.

Derivatives and limits. The sum and constant rules for *derivatives* can be proved using the analogous rules for *limits*. The argument for the sum rule runs like this:

$$\begin{aligned}\frac{d}{dx}\big(f(x)+g(x)\big) &= \lim_{h\to 0}\frac{\big(f(x+h)+g(x+h)\big)-\big(f(x)+g(x)\big)}{h}\\ &= \lim_{h\to 0}\frac{f(x+h)-f(x)}{h} + \lim_{h\to 0}\frac{g(x+h)-g(x)}{h}\\ &= f'(x)+g'(x).\end{aligned}$$

Geometric thinking. The constant rule can be interpreted geometrically. Recall that the graph of $kf(x)$ is obtained by stretching the graph of f vertically, with factor k. How does such a stretch affect a tangent line to the f-graph at $x = a$?

The constant rule gives the answer: A vertical k-stretch multiplies slopes of *everything*—the graph as well as the tangent line—by the same factor k.

Can you interpret the sum rule graphically?

Antiderivatives of polynomials and power functions

The relation between functions and derivatives runs both ways. If f is the derivative of F, then F is an **antiderivative** of f. For polynomials and power functions, finding antiderivatives is easy.

■ **Example 4.** Find antiderivative functions Q, R, and S for $q(x) = x^2$, $r(x) = 15x^4 + 28x^3 - 2x/3$, and $s(x) = \sqrt{x}$. How many answers are there?

Solution: Since $(x^3)' = 3x^2$, $Q(x) = x^3/3$ is a natural guess. It's easy to check this guess using the constant rule for derivatives:

$$Q'(x) = \left(\frac{1}{3}x^3\right)' = \frac{1}{3} \cdot 3x^2 = x^2.$$

Finding an antiderivative of r is even easier. As we showed in Example 3,

$$\frac{d}{dx}\left(3x^5 + 7x^4 - x^2/3 + 11\right) = 15x^4 + 28x^3 - 2x/3,$$

so $R(x) = 3x^5 + 7x^4 - x^2/3 + 11$ works.

Finding an antiderivative of s takes a bit more thought. The power rule for derivatives suggests we try a function of the form $S(x) = kx^{3/2}$, but for what constant k? Differentiating gives the answer: For the desired k,

$$S'(x) = k \cdot \frac{3}{2} \cdot x^{1/2} = x^{1/2}.$$

Therefore $k = 2/3$; the function $S(x) = 2x^{3/2}/3$ works.

These answers aren't (quite) unique. The functions

$$\frac{x^3}{3} + 1, \quad \frac{x^3}{3} - 5, \quad \text{and} \quad \frac{x^3}{3} - \pi^2 + e - \ln\left(15 + \sin^2(3)\right)$$

are all legitimate antiderivatives of q. ➻ □

So is any function of the form $x^3/3 + k$, for any constant k.

Antiderivatives aren't (quite) unique

The example just showed:

If F is an antiderivative for f, then so is $F + k$, for any constant k.

The reason is simple: Any two functions that differ by an additive constant have the same derivative. ➻

Interpret this graphically.

The converse is also true, but harder to prove: ➻

We'll prove it later.

If F and G have the same derivative, then they differ by a constant.

The antiderivative of x^k

The power rule for derivatives, read "backwards," gives a corresponding rule for *antiderivatives*.

> **Theorem 7.** For any constants C and k ($k \neq -1$), $\dfrac{x^{k+1}}{k+1} + C$ is an antiderivative of x^k.

Proof: With derivative rules, the proof is an easy computation:

$$\frac{d}{dx}\left(\frac{x^{k+1}}{k+1}+C\right)=\frac{(k+1)x^k}{k+1}+0=x^k,$$

just as we claimed. □

The exception: $k = -1$.

Notice that the theorem above can't possibly hold for $k = -1$, since division by zero isn't allowed. Nevertheless, the exceptional function $f(x) = 1/x$ *has* a well-behaved antiderivative, though not of the usual power form.

For $x > 0$, the natural log function $\ln(x)$ is an antiderivative of $1/x$

We'll revisit it soon.

The graphs below make this remarkable (but nontrivial) fact plausible:

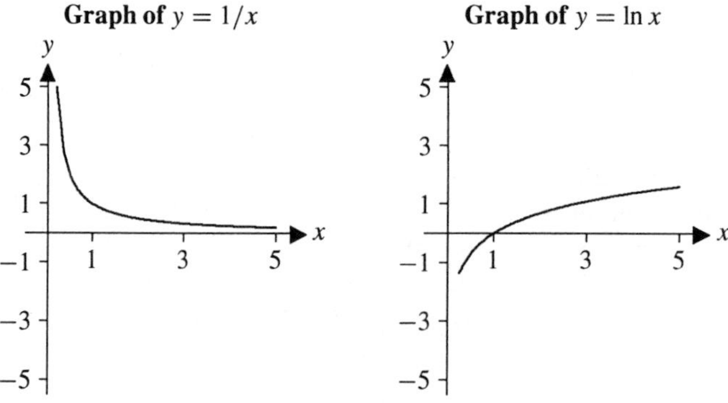

Antiderivatives of combinations

The constant and power rules for derivatives run in reverse: sums and constant multiples behave just as nicely for antiderivatives as for derivatives.

■ **Example 5.** Above we differentiated $p(x) = 3x^5 + 7x^4 - x^2/3 + 11$. Now let's antidifferentiate it.

Solution: Again we rend p asunder, antidifferentiate the fragments separately, and reassemble: An antiderivative of $3x^5$ is $x^6/2$; an antiderivative of $7x^4$ is $7x^5/5$; an antiderivative of $x^2/3$ is $x^3/9$; and an antiderivative of 11 is $11x$. Thus,

$$\frac{1}{2}x^6+\frac{7}{5}x^5-\frac{1}{9}x^3+11x+C$$

is an antiderivative of p for any constant C.

Do so!

Does all this make sense? Yes—it's easy to check by differentiating that the last expression is an antiderivative of p. □

Guess and check. The power rules make finding antiderivatives of polynomials and other power functions easy; checking answers is even easier. We'll see later that systematically finding antiderivatives of more complicated functions is often *much harder* than finding derivatives. There's a moral:

When finding antiderivatives, guess freely. Then check answers carefully.

Derivatives and antiderivatives in the real world

Calculating derivatives and antiderivatives is immensely useful in applying calculus to solve real problems. Here we give just two of many, many such applications.

Modeling motion: acceleration, velocity, and position

A falling object has, at any moment, an *acceleration* a, a *velocity* v, and a *height* h. All three quantities are natural functions of time: if t denotes time (measured in seconds after some reference time $t = 0$) and height is measured in feet above some reference point, then

$$h'(t) = v(t) \quad \text{and} \quad v'(t) = a(t).$$

Equivalently, h is an antiderivative of v and v is an antiderivative of a.

According to Newton's laws of motion, an object in free fall, i.e, affected *only* by gravity,➛ has a *constant* (downward) acceleration, of about -32 feet per second per second. In symbols: $a(t) = -32$.

See Section 2.1 for more on free fall.

Since v is an antiderivative of a,

$$v(t) = -32t + C,$$

for some constant C. *Which* constant? It depends on the setting—because $v(0) = C$,➛ C represents the **initial velocity** (i.e., the velocity at time 0). Therefore we'll write

Plug $t = 0$ into the formula for t.

$$v(t) = -32t + v_0.$$

Antidifferentiating again gives a formula for $h(t)$:

$$h(t) = -16t^2 + v_0 t + C.$$

Again $h(0) = C$, so we'll write

$$h(t) = -16t^2 + v_0 t + h_0,$$

where h_0 represents **initial height**.

■ **Example 6.** A cannon ball is shot upward from ground level, with initial velocity 288 feet per second.➛ Assuming free fall conditions, how high does the cannon ball rise? How long does it remain airborne?

Around 200 mph—possible for an old-fashioned cannon.

Solution: From the information above (with $v_0 = 288$ and $h_0 = 0$), the velocity and height functions must have these formulas:

$$v(t) = -32t + 288 \quad \text{and} \quad h(t) = -16t^2 + 288t + 0.$$

The ball is highest when $v(t) = 0$; solving this equation gives $t = 9$ seconds. Thus the cannonball rises to $h(9) = 1296$ feet;➛ it stays airborne until $h(t) = 0$. Solving *this* equation gives $t = 18$ seconds. □

About 1/4 mile.

Maximum-minimum problems and the derivative

Derivative formulas—if they're simple—make locating maxima and minima a routine matter. In "real-life" problems, the first step is translation into mathematical language.

■ **Example 7.** A gardener wants to enclose 1000 square feet of land using as little fencing as possible. The garden is to be rectangular; one side, unfenced, lies along a river. How much fencing is needed? (Note: This problem and others like it appear in more detail, with pictures, in Appendix H.)

Solution: Here's the setup:

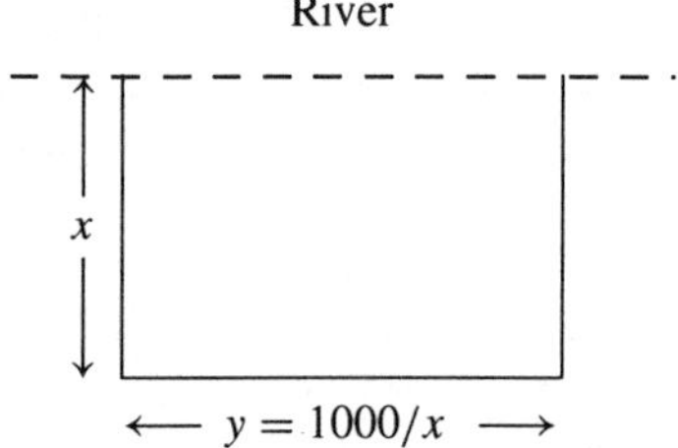

Let x and y denote the lengths shown. (By assumption, $xy = 1000$, so $y = 1000/x$.) If L denotes the total length of fence, then

$$L = 2x + y = 2x + \frac{1000}{x}.$$

We want to minimize L.

Draw your own.

A plot of L shows a minimum somewhere near $x = 20$. With the derivative we can locate this stationary point precisely:

$$L'(x) = 2 - \frac{1000}{x^2} = 0 \iff x = 10\sqrt{5} \approx 22.3607.$$

For this value of x, $y = 1000/x = 20\sqrt{5}$, and $L = 40\sqrt{5} \approx 89.44$. In agricultural terms: *The best garden's dimensions, in feet, are* $10\sqrt{5} \times 20\sqrt{5}$. *The garden needs* $40\sqrt{5}$ *feet of fence.* (Rounded more realistically: the garden is about $22.5' \times 45'$; it needs 90 feet of fence.) □

The power rule and the binomial theorem (optional)

See any college algebra book for a more complete treatment.

The binomial theorem of elementary algebra is an explicit formula for an expression of the form $(a + b)^n$, where n is any positive integer. It says, in brief:

$$(a+b)^n = a^n + na^{n-1}b + \frac{n(n-1)}{2}a^{n-2}b^2 + \cdots + nab^{n-1} + b^n.$$

What the ellipsis (...) stands for is, to an algebraist, the heart of the theorem; for us, only the first few terms matter. The example shows why and how.

■ **Example 8.** Let $y = x^n$, where n is any positive integer. Show that $dy/dx = nx^{n-1}$.

Solution: By definition,

$$\frac{dy}{dx} = \lim_{h \to 0} \frac{(x+h)^n - x^n}{h}.$$

Applying the binomial theorem in the numerator gives

$$\begin{aligned} \frac{dy}{dx} &= \lim_{h\to 0} \frac{\left(x^n + nx^{n-1}h + \frac{n(n-1)}{2}x^{n-2}h^2 + \ldots\right) - x^n}{h} \\ &= \lim_{h\to 0} \left(nx^{n-1} + h \cdot \text{stuff}\right) \\ &= nx^{n-1} \end{aligned}$$

as claimed. The key idea is that all terms after the first two involve at least *two* powers of h, and so vanish in the limit—even after dividing by the original denominator. □

An example problem

Here's a problem in the spirit of this section.

■ **Example 9.** The figure below shows a line segment and a piece of a parabola.

Bits of a line segment and a parabola

Find an equation for the parabola.

Solution: A parabola's equation has the form $p(x) = a + bx + cx^2$. We need to find numerical values for a, b, and c. The picture shows three things; we'll use them to find these values:

(i) The parabola passes through $(0, 0)$, so $p(0) = 0$. But $p(0) = a + b \cdot 0 + c \cdot 0^2 = a$, so $a = 0$. Thus $p(x) = bx + cx^2$, with b and c still to be found.

(ii) At $x = 0$ the parabola and the line segment have the *same slope.*➻ A look at the segment shows that this slope is -1. Therefore, $p'(0) = -1$.

Look closely to be sure you agree!

We'll use this information to find b. For any x, $p'(x) = b + 2cx$, so $p'(0) = b$. Therefore $b = -1$, and so $p(x) = -x + cx^2$. We still need to find c.

(ii) The parabola passes through $(1, 1)$, so $p(1) = 1$. But $p(x) = -x + cx^2$, so $p(1) = -1 + c$; for $p(1) = 1$ to hold we must have $c = 2$.

Thus $p(x) = -x + 2x^2$.➻ □

Try plotting both $p(x)$ and $y = -x$. Is the picture "right"?

Exercises

For each function f in exercises 1–10, find an algebraic expression for f', then sketch a graph of f and f' on the same axes.

1. $f(x) = 3x^2$
2. $f(x) = 7x^{-4}$
3. $f(x) = 4x^5 + 3x^2 - x$
4. $f(x) = 4\sqrt{x} + 1/x^3$
5. $f(x) = 3x^{-1/2} + 4x^{3/2}$
6. $f(x) = -7x^{1/4}$
7. $f(x) = x^3 + \sqrt[3]{x}$
8. $f(x) = 4\sqrt{x^3} - 5x^{-3/2}$
9. $f(x) = 1/\sqrt[3]{x^2} + 5$
10. $f(x) = 4\sqrt[5]{x^3} + 5/\sqrt[3]{x^4}$

11–20. Find the second derivative of each function in exercises 1–10, then sketch a graph of f and f'' on the same axes.

21–30. Find two antiderivatives of each function in exercises 1–10.

In exercises 31–35, let f be the function shown below, F be an antiderivative of f, and suppose that $F(0) = 10$. (The function f has a local maximum at $x = 1.14$, a point of inflection at $x = 4.67$, and a local minimum at $x = 8.19$.)

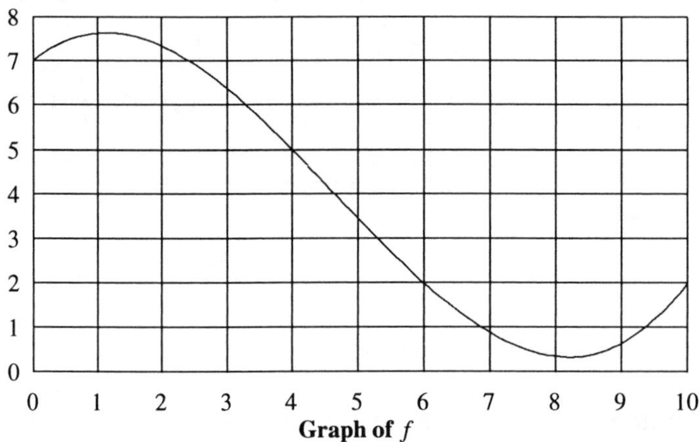

Graph of f

31. (a) What is the slope of F at $x = 4$? Justify your answer.
    (b) Where is F increasing? Justify your answer.
    (c) Where in the interval $[0, 5]$ does F achieve its largest value? Its smallest value? Justify your answers.

32. (a) Is it possible that $F(5) = 5$? Explain.
    (b) Is it possible that $F(5) = 15$? Explain.
    (c) Is $F(10) - F(5) < 0$? Explain.
    (d) Is $F(10) - F(7) > 6$? Explain.

33. (a) At which values of x, if any, does F have points of inflection? Explain.
    (b) Where is F concave down? Justify your answer.
    (c) Estimate the value of $F''(5)$.
    (d) Explain why F'' achieves its minimum value over the interval $[0, 10]$ at $x = 4.67$.
    (e) Where in the interval $[0, 10]$ does F'' achieve its largest value? Justify your answer.

34. Let L be the line tangent to F at $x = 0$.
    (a) Find an equation for L.
    (b) Does L lie above or below the curve $y = F(x)$ at $x = 1$? Justify your answer.

35. (a) Let g be the line through the points $(2, 7)$ and $(6, 2)$. This line lies below f on the interval $[2, 5]$, so $g(x) < f(x)$ on this interval. Use this fact to compute a lower bound on the value of $F(5) - F(3)$. [HINT: Use an antiderivative of g.]

(b) Let h be the line through the points $(2, 8)$ and $(6, 3)$. This line lies above f on the interval $[2, 6]$, so $h(x) > f(x)$ on this interval. Use this fact to compute an upper bound on the value of $F(5) - F(3)$.

36. The function F graphed below is an *antiderivative* of a function f. F has a root at $x = 8.8$ and stationary points at $x = 3.2$, $x = 6$, and $x = 13.3$; F has points of inflection at $x = 4.5$ and $x = 10.5$. [NOTE: Although the questions below ask about f and f', the graph of neither f nor f' is shown.]

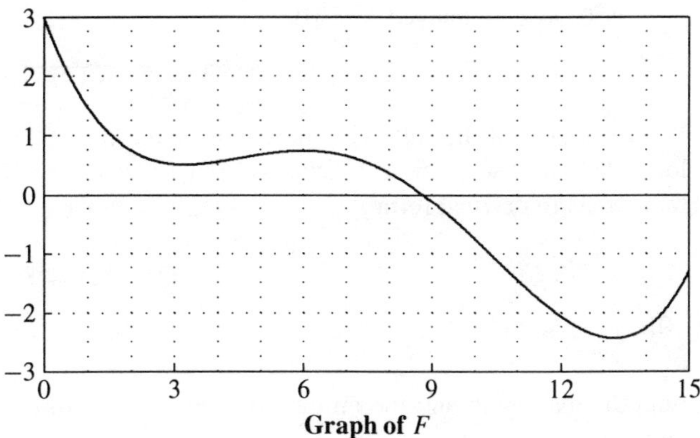

Graph of F

(a) Where is f positive? Justify your answer.

(b) How many roots does f have in the interval $[0, 15]$? Where are they located?

(c) Where is f increasing? Justify your answer.

(d) Rank the five values -1, $f(3)$, $f(6)$, $f(9)$, and $f(14)$ in increasing order.

(e) Where does f achieve its maximum value in the interval $[0, 15]$? Justify your answer.

(f) Rank the five values 0, $f'(3)$, $f'(6)$, $f'(10)$ and $f'(13)$ in increasing order.

37. Let f be a function such that $f(0) = 0$ and f' is the function shown below and let F be an antiderivative of f. [NOTE: The graph is of f', not f or F.]

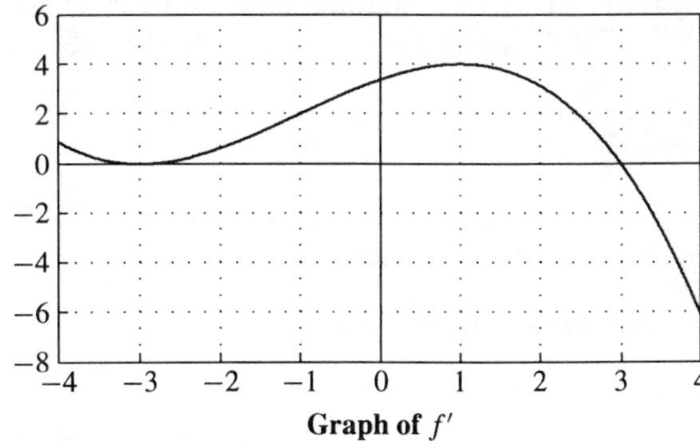

Graph of f'

(a) Is F concave up or concave down at $x = -3$? At $x = 0$? At $x = 1$? At $x = 3$. Justify your answers.

(b) Is F increasing, decreasing, or stationary at $x = -3$? At $x = 0$? At $x = 1$? At $x = 3$. Justify your answers.

(c) Where in the interval $[-4, 4]$ does F achieve its minimum value? Justify your answer.

(d) How many stationary points does F have in the interval $[-4, 4]$? Where are they located? Justify your answer.

(e) How many points of inflection does F have in the interval $[-4, 4]$? Where are they located? Justify your answer.

38. (a) How are your answers to the previous exercise affected if the condition $f(0) = 0$ is changed to $f(0) = 20$?

(b) How are your answers to the previous exercise affected if the condition $f(0) = 0$ is changed to $f(0) = -15$?

39. Suppose that $y(x)$ is proportional to x^3. Show that $y'(x)$ is proportional to x^2.

40. Where is each of the following functions increasing? Decreasing? Find *all* local maxima and minima. (Express your answers exactly—e.g., as $\sqrt{3}$—rather than in decimal form.)

(a) $f(x) = x^3 - 3x^2 + 5$

(b) $f(x) = 8x^9 - 9x^8 - 7$

(c) $g(x) = 7x^9 - 18x^7 + 63$

(d) $h(x) = 5x^6 + 6x^5 - 15x^4$

41. Find the maximum and the minimum value of each function over the given interval.

(a) $f(x) = x^3 - 3x + 5;\quad [0, 2]$

(b) $f(x) = 1 + 2x^3 - x^4;\quad [-1, 2]$

(c) $f(x) = \sqrt{x} - 3/x;\quad [0.25, 1]$

(d) $f(x) = x^3 - x^2;\quad [-2, 0]$

42. Find the maximum and the minimum value of $f(x) = x^4 - 3x^2 + 6$ over each interval below.

(a) $[-2, 2]$

(b) $[-4, -2]$

(c) $[-1, 2]$

(d) $[-1, 1]$

43. Find the maximum value of the derivative of $f(x) = 6x^2 - x^4$ on the interval $[-2, 2]$.

44. For which value(s) of x does the slope of the line tangent to the curve $y = -x^3 + 3x^2 + 1$ take on its largest value? Justify your answer.

45. Find an equation of the line tangent to the curve $y = x^3 - 6x^2$ at its point of inflection.

46. How many points of inflection does the graph of $y = 2x^6 + 9x^5 + 10x^4 - x + 2$ have? Where are they located?

47. Use graphs to show that $(e^x)' \neq xe^{x-1}$.

48. Suppose that $q(x)$ is a polynomial of degree $n \geq 2$. Explain why q has at most $n - 1$ local extrema. [HINT: $q'(x)$ is a polynomial of degree $n - 1$.]

49. Let $f(x) = ax^3 + bx^2 + cx + d$.

(a) Show that f has either no local extrema or a local maximum and a local minimum.

(b) Show that if they exist, the local extrema of f are located at $x = \dfrac{-b \pm \sqrt{b^2 - 3ac}}{3a}$.

50. Let $f(x) = 3x^2 - 8x^{-2}$. Evaluate $\lim_{h\to 0} \dfrac{f(2+h) - f(2)}{h}$.

51. Find a symbolic expression for the nth derivative of each of the following functions.

(a) $f(x) = 1/x$

(b) $f(x) = \sqrt{x}$

52. Suppose that g is an nth degree polynomial. Explain why $\dfrac{d^{n+1}}{dx^{n+1}} g(x) = 0$.

53. Let $p(x) = x^n + a_1 x^{n-1} + a_2 x^{n-2} + \cdots + a_{n-1}x + a_n$. Evaluate $\frac{d^n}{dx^n} p(x)$.

54. Is there a real number x such that $4x^3 - x^4 = 30$? Prove your answer.

55. Let $f(x) = x^n$ where $n \geq 2$ is an integer.

(a) Show that f is concave up on the interval $(0, \infty)$.

(b) What can be said about the concavity of f on the interval $(-\infty, 0)$. [HINT: Does it matter whether n is even?]

56. The function $f(x) = \dfrac{(x + 0.00001)^8 - x^8}{0.00001}$ is closely approximated by $g(x) = ax^b$ for appropriate values of a and b (i.e., for any x, $|f(x) - g(x)|$ is, in some sense, a "small" number). What are these values? Explain why g approximates f so well.

57. Use the limit definition of the derivative function to find f' for each function f below.

(a) $f(x) = (x+1)^2$

(b) $f(x) = 2x^3$

(c) $f(x) = \sqrt{x+3}$

(d) $f(x) = \dfrac{1}{x+5}$

58. Let p be the parabola defined by $p(x) = ax^2 + bx + c$ where a, b, and c are constants. Show that the vertex of the parabola is at $x = -b/2a$.

59. The figure below shows the graph of $f(x) = \sqrt{x}$ and its tangent line at $x = a$. Find the value of a.

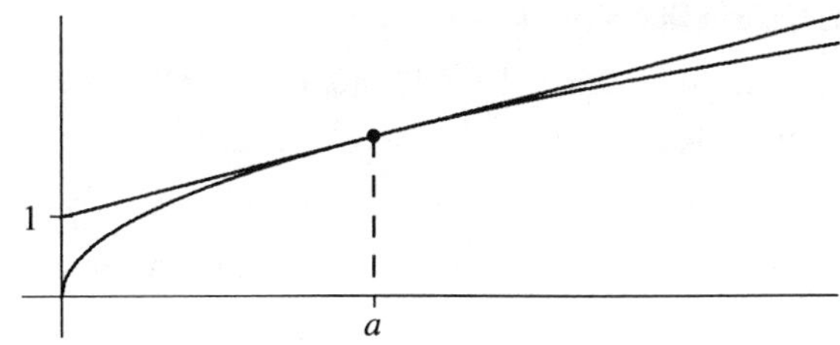

60. Find values of a and b so that the line $2x + 3y = a$ is tangent to the graph of $f(x) = bx^2$ at $x = 3$.

61. (a) Find constants a and b so that the polynomial $p(x) = x^3 + ax + b$ has a local minimum at $(2, -9)$.

(b) Draw a graph of p.

62. (a) Find the coefficients a, b, and c of a quadratic polynomial $p(x) = ax^2 + bx + c$ that is zero at $x = 1$, decreasing when $x < 2$, and increasing when $x > 2$.

    (b) Draw a graph of p.

63. (a) Find a cubic polynomial $q(x) = ax^3 + bx^2 + cx + d$ that has a local maximum at $(0, 2)$ and a local minimum at $(5, 0)$.

    (b) Draw a graph of q.

64. For which values of the constant k does the graph of $y = x^3 - 3x^2 + k$ have just one x-intercept? Two x-intercepts? Three x-intercepts? Justify your answers.

65. Find the value of k for which the graph of $f(x) = 2x^2 + k/x$ has a point of inflection at $x = -1$.

66. Let f be a function defined by $f(x) = Ax^2 + Bx + C$ with the following properties: (i) $f(0) = 2$; (ii) $f'(2) = 10$; (iii) $f''(10) = 4$. Find the value of $A + B + C$.

67. Find the value of b for which the function $y = x^4 + bx^2 + 8x + 1$ has both a horizontal tangent line and a point of inflection at the same value of x.

68. Find c so that the line $y = 4x + 3$ is tangent to the curve $y = x^2 + c$.

69. For what value of k will $(8x + k)/x^2$ have a local minimum at $x = 4$?

70. When an oil tank is drained for cleaning, there are $V(t) = 100000 - 4000t + 40t^2$ gallons of oil left in the tank t minutes after the drain valve is opened.

    (a) At what average rate does oil drain from the tank during the first twenty minutes?

    (b) At what rate does oil drain out of the tank twenty minutes after the drain valve is opened?

    (c) Explain what $V''(t)$ says about the rate at which oil is draining from the tank.

71. Under the influence of a rather complicated collection of forces, the altitude $h(t)$ of a rocket from its moment of launch until its fall to Earth is given by the formula $h(t) = -t^4 + 8t^3 + 375$. (Altitude is measured in feet above sea level; time from launch is measured in seconds.)

    (a) From what altitude is the rocket launched?

    (b) When does the rocket fall into the ocean?

    (c) What is the rocket's maximum altitude?

    (d) What is the rocket's maximum upward velocity?

    (e) What is the rocket's maximum downward velocity?

    (f) What is the rocket's maximum upward acceleration?

    (g) What is the rocket's maximum downward acceleration?

72. A particle moves on the x-axis in such a way that its position at time t is given by $x(t) = 3t^5 - 25t^3 + 60t$. For which values of t is the particle moving to the left?

73. A particle moves along a straight line so that its velocity is given by $v(t) = t^2$. How far does the particle travel between $t = 1$ and $t = 3$?

74. An object moves along a straight line in such a way that it is slowing down with an acceleration of -8 meters per second per second. The object has an initial velocity of 14 meters per second. Find the distance the object travels during the first 3 seconds.

75. Suppose that the brakes are applied on a car traveling 50 mph and that this gives the car a constant negative acceleration of 20 ft/sec^2. How long will it take the car to come to a stop? How far will the car travel before stopping?

76. A car traveling at a constant speed of 80 mph along straight highway fails to stop at a stop sign. Three seconds later, a highway patrol car starts from rest at the stop sign and maintains a constant acceleration of 8 ft/sec^2. How long will it take the patrol car to overtake the automobile? How far from the stop sign will this occur? What is the speed of the patrol car when it overtakes the automobile?

77. A fly is crawling from left to right along the edge of a curved barrier on the xy-plane whose shape is the graph of $y = 7 - x^2$. A spider waits at the point $(4, 0)$. Find the distance between the two creatures when they first see each other. [HINT: Draw a picture.]

78. Suppose that a rectangle has its base on the x-axis and its two upper corners on the curve $y = 2(1 - x^2)$.

    (a) What is the maximum perimeter of such a rectangle?

    (b) Show that there is no minimum perimeter rectangle. [HINT: The sides of a rectangle must have nonzero length.]

79. Find the shortest distance from the curve $xy = 4$ to the origin. [HINT: Minimize the *square* of the distance function.]

80. What is the area of the largest rectangle that has its base the x-axis and its upper corners on the curve $y = 12 - x^2$?

82. The cost of fuel for a luxury liner is proportional to the square of the speed v. At a speed of 10 km/hour, fuel costs \$3000/hour. Other fixed costs (e.g., labor) amount to \$12000/hour. Assuming that the ship is to make a trip of total distance D, find the speed which minimizes the cost of the trip. Does this speed depend on D?

83. An open box is made by cutting squares of side w inches from the four corners of a sheet of cardboard that is 24 inches by 32 inches and then folding up the sides. What should w be to maximize the volume of the box?

84. An open box with a capacity of 36,000 cubic inches is to be twice as long as it is wide. The material for the box costs \$0.10 per square foot. What are the dimensions of the least expensive box? How much does it cost?

85. Coffee mugs can be manufactured for sixty cents each. At a price of one dollar each, one thousand can be sold. For each penny the price is lowered, fifty more mugs can be sold. What price maximizes profit? How many mugs are sold at this price?

86. The arithmetic mean of n numbers $0 \leq a_1 \leq a_2 \leq \cdots \leq a_n$ is $A_n = (a_1 + a_2 + \cdots + a_n)/n$; their geometric mean is $G_n = (a_1 \cdot a_2 \cdots a_n)^{1/n}$.

   (a) Use algebra to show that $G_2 \leq A_2$.
   [HINT: $a_1 \cdot a_2 = \frac{1}{4}\left((a_1 + a_2)^2 - (a_1 - a_2)^2\right)$.]

   (b) Use the racetrack principle to show that $G_2 \leq A_2$.
   [HINT: Show that $f(a_2) = (a_1 + a_2)/2 - \sqrt{a_1 a_2} \geq 0$ when $a_2 \geq a_1$.]

   (c) Use the racetrack principle to show that $G_n \leq A_n$ when $n \geq 2$.
   [HINT: Show that $f(a_n) = A_n - G_n \geq 0$ when $x_n \geq x_{n-1}$.]

87. Let m, n be positive integers, and a, b be real numbers.

   (a) Show that $a^n - b^n = (a - b)\left(a^{n-1} + a^{n-2}b + a^{n-3}b^2 + \cdots + ab^{n-2} + b^{n-1}\right)$ by multiplying out the expression on the right.

   (b) Let $f(x) = x^n$. Use part (a) to show that $f'(a) = \lim_{x \to a} \dfrac{x^n - a^n}{x - a} = na^{n-1}$.

   (c) Let $g(x) = x^{-n}$. Use part (b) to show that $g'(a) = -na^{-n-1}$.
   [HINT: $\left(x^{-n} - a^{-n}\right)/(x - a) = (a^n - x^n)/\left(x^n a^n (x - a)\right)$.]

   (d) Let $h(x) = x^{m/n}$ where m is a positive integer. Use part (a) to show that $h'(a) = \frac{m}{n} a^{(m-n)/n}$. [HINT: $\frac{x^{m/n} - a^{m/n}}{x - a} = \frac{\left(x^{1/n}\right)^m - \left(a^{1/n}\right)^m}{\left(x^{1/n}\right)^n - \left(a^{1/n}\right)^n}$.]

   (e) Let $k(x) = x^{-m/n}$. Show that $k'(a) = -\frac{m}{n} a^{-(m+n)/n}$.

88. In the previous exercise you showed that if r is a rational number, then $\dfrac{d}{dx}\left(x^r\right) = rx^{r-1}$. In this exercise we extend this result to the case where r is a real number.

   Let r be a real number and p, q be rational numbers such that $0 < p < r < q$.

   (a) Assume that $x > 0$. Explain why $\dfrac{x^p - 1}{x - 1} < \dfrac{x^r - 1}{x - 1} < \dfrac{x^q - 1}{x - 1}$.
   [HINT: Consider the cases $0 < x < 1$ and $x > 1$ separately.]

   (b) Use part (a) to show that $p \leq \lim_{x \to 1} \dfrac{x^r - 1}{x - 1} \leq q$.

   (c) Explain why part (b) implies that $\lim_{x \to 1} \dfrac{x^r - 1}{x - 1} = r$.

   (d) Suppose that c is an arbitrary real number and $a \neq 0$. Show that

$$\frac{x^c - a^c}{x - a} = \left(\frac{w^c - 1}{w - 1}\right) a^{c-1} = -w^c \left(\frac{w^{-c} - 1}{w - 1}\right) a^{c-1}.$$

   (e) Use parts (c) and (d) to show that $(x^c)' = cx^{c-1}$ where c is any real number.

2.9 Derivatives of exponential and logarithm functions

Algebraic vs. transcendental functions

Using the limit definition to find the derivative of an **algebraic** function➻ can be messy, but it's usually routine.

Algebraic functions are those with algebraic formulas.

■ **Example 1.** If $f(x) = \sqrt{x+1}$, find $f'(x)$.

Solution: Here's the limit computation:

$$\begin{aligned} f'(x) &= \lim_{h\to 0} \frac{f(x+h)-f(x)}{h} \\ &= \lim_{h\to 0} \frac{\sqrt{x+1+h}-\sqrt{x+1}}{h} \\ &= \lim_{h\to 0} \frac{\sqrt{x+1+h}-\sqrt{x+1}}{h} \cdot \frac{\sqrt{x+1+h}+\sqrt{x+1}}{\sqrt{x+1+h}+\sqrt{x+1}} \\ &= \lim_{h\to 0} \frac{(x+1+h)-(x+1)}{h\cdot(\sqrt{x+1+h}+\sqrt{x+1})} \\ &= \lim_{h\to 0} \frac{1}{\sqrt{x+1+h}+\sqrt{x+1}} \\ &= \frac{1}{2\sqrt{x+1}}. \end{aligned}$$

We used an algebraic trick in the third line; otherwise the calculation was straightforward.➻ □

Was this painful computation really necessary? Could we have used, instead, the (known) derivative of $\sqrt{x}$?

Non-algebraic functions—those *without* algebraic formulas—are called **transcendental**. Exponential, logarithm, and trigonometric functions are all transcendental.

Finding derivatives of transcendental functions poses a special challenge. Without algebraic formulas, the limits that define derivatives usually don't succumb to the usual algebraic tricks. We'll need other methods. In another sense transcendental functions are like all others: given the graph of *any* function f, we can *graphically* estimate the behavior of f'. We'll begin with a graphical approach to each function we consider below.

Derivatives of exponential functions: graphical evidence

The natural exponential function

In Example 6, page 105, we conjectured, from direct graphical evidence, this remarkable property of the natural exponential function: *If* $f(x) = e^x$, *then* $f'(x) = e^x$.

Does something similar hold for exponential functions with other bases? Here are graphs of several:

Graphs of three exponentials

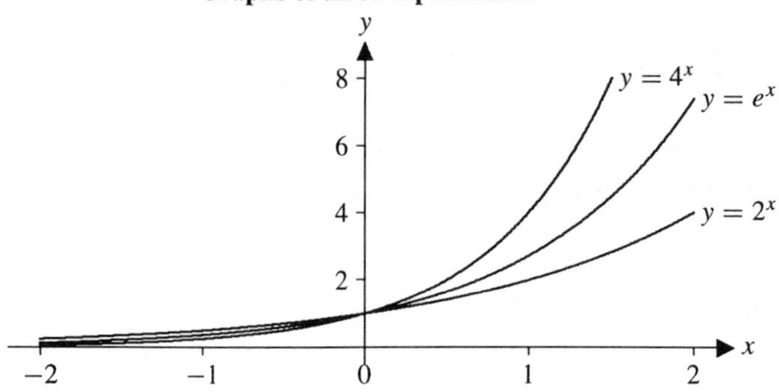

Observe:

Similar slope behavior. Slopes of all three graphs behave similarly. Moving from left to right on any graph, slopes start small (but positive) and increase through larger and larger positive values.

Common point, different slopes. The three graphs cross—but have different slopes—at $x = 0$. The e^x-graph has slope 1 at $x = 0$; hence the graphs of $y = 2^x$ and $y = 4^x$ have slopes respectively less than and greater than 1 at $x = 0$.

In particular, neither 2^x nor 4^x is *equal* to its own derivative expression.

Derivatives at $x = 0$: a closer look. All graphs of the form $y = b^x$ pass through the point (0, 1)—but with different slopes. Zooming in on this point shows how these slopes (i.e., the respective derivatives at $x = 0$) differ from each other:

Graphs of three exponentials: zooming in

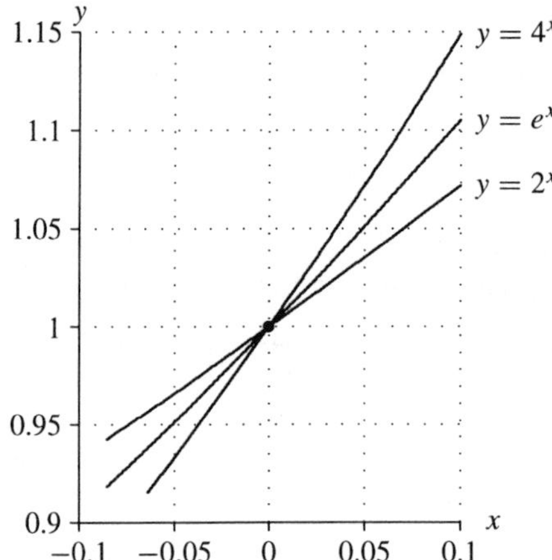

Notice:

- At this magnification, each exponential "curve" looks like a straight line—namely, its tangent line at $x = 0$.

Make them!

- Eyeball estimates for *slopes* of these lines say:

$$\left.\frac{d}{dx}2^x\right|_{x=0} \approx 0.7; \qquad \left.\frac{d}{dx}e^x\right|_{x=0} \approx 1; \qquad \left.\frac{d}{dx}4^x\right|_{x=0} \approx 1.4.$$

The middle "estimate" just above is crucial; it can be used to *define* the number e.

There are other ways to define e; we'll see one later.

Definition: The number e is the base for which the curve $y = b^x$ passes through $(0, 1)$ with slope 1.

Derivatives of exponentials: again, analytically

With graphical evidence as intuition, we're ready to sharpen our knowledge of derivatives of exponential functions, using the limit definition of derivative. We'll show:

Theorem 8. If $f(x) = e^x$, then $f'(x) = e^x$. If $g(x) = b^x$, then $g'(x) = b^x \ln b$.

Before plunging into calculations, let's observe:

- The first formula is a special case ($b = e$) of the second.
- The second formula says that for *any* positive base b, $g'(x) = kg(x)$, where $k = \ln b$ is a *constant.* Thus every exponential function g has this remarkable property:

  The instantaneous rate of change of g is proportional to the value of g.

  Many real-life varying quantities (populations, undisturbed bank balances, masses of radioactive minerals, comprehensive fees at St. Lena, etc.) exhibit this property. That's why exponential functions are essential tools in mathematical modeling.
- If $g(x) = 2^x$, then $g'(x) = 2^x \ln 2 \approx 0.693 \cdot 2^x$. If $h(x) = 4^x$, then $h'(x) = 4^x \ln 4 \approx 1.386 \cdot 4^x$. This result agrees with what we saw graphically above.

Calculating the derivative of b^x

Let $g(x) = b^x$. We'll show that $g'(x) = b^x \ln b$.

Step 1: Why $g'(x) = kg(x)$. The computation starts simply:

$$\begin{aligned} g'(x) &= \lim_{h\to 0} \frac{g(x+h) - g(x)}{h} \\ &= \lim_{h\to 0} \frac{b^{x+h} - b^x}{h} = \lim_{h\to 0} b^x \cdot \frac{b^h - 1}{h} \\ &= b^x \cdot \lim_{h\to 0} \frac{b^h - 1}{h} = b^x \cdot k. \end{aligned}$$

Two remarks:

- Pulling b^x outside the limit in the second last equality was legal because the limit depends on h, not on x.
- If the last limit—we called it k—exists, then we've shown what we claimed in Step 1: $(b^x)' = kb^x$.

Step 2: Why k exists. Does the limit k exist? What's k's numerical value?

The key is to interpret the limit k as the slope of the line tangent to the g-graph at $x = 0$. Since $g(x) = b^x$,

$$k = \lim_{h\to 0} \frac{b^h - 1}{h} = \lim_{h\to 0} \frac{b^h - b^0}{h} = \lim_{h\to 0} \frac{g(h) - g(0)}{h}.$$

The last form is by now familiar—it's the *definition* of the slope of the tangent line at $x = 0$. We saw graphically above that such tangent lines exist; their slopes depend on b.

Step 3: Why $k = \ln b$. We'll show in a moment that the numerical value of k (i.e., the slope of the line tangent to $y = b^x$ at $x = 0$) is $\ln b$. First, some numerical evidence for the case $b = 10$.

Our claim, numerically, is that

$$\lim_{h\to 0} \frac{b^h - 1}{h} = \ln 10 \approx 2.3026.$$

A machine did the work.

Let's tabulate values of the limit expression for small inputs h:

The slope at $x = 0$ of $y = 10^x$—numerical estimates						
h	-0.01	-0.001	-0.0001	0.0001	0.001	0.01
$(10^h - 1)/h$	2.2763	2.2999	2.3023	2.3029	2.3052	2.3293

See Appendix E for more details.

The numbers for $b = 10$ look convincing. To prove that $k = \ln b$ for *any* positive base b, we'll reduce things to the best understood case, $b = e$. A key relationship holds between $f(x) = e^x$ and $g(x) = b^x$:

$$g(x) = b^x = e^{x \ln b} = f\big((\ln b) \cdot x\big).$$

We studied horizontal squashing and stretching in Section 1.2.

How does horizontal compression affect a graph at $x = 0$?

In graphical language, g is obtained from f by a *horizontal compression*, with factor $\ln b$. By assumption, the f-graph has slope 1 at $x = 0$. The g-graph, therefore, has slope $\ln b$ at $x = 0$. We're done. □

Derivatives of logarithmic functions

To find the derivatives of the logarithm function $f(x) = \log_b x$, we'll use what we know about its inverse $f^{-1}(x) = b^x$. Here, in advance, are our conclusions—notice again the "naturality" of e:

> **Theorem 9.** For any positive base $b \neq 1$,
>
> $$\left(\log_b x\right)' = \frac{1}{x} \cdot \frac{1}{\ln b}.$$
>
> For the natural base $b = e$,
>
> $$(\ln x)' = \frac{1}{x}.$$

We'll show these facts geometrically; a formal proof would amount only to translating everything into symbolic form.

A picture "proof"

The key idea is that, for any base $b \neq 1$, the functions b^x and $\log_b x$ are *inverses.* Geometrically, this relationship means that either graph can be obtained from the other by reflection through the line $y = x$. The following figure—the case $b = e$ is shown—illustrates the crucial point for us: how such a reflection affects tangent lines.

As we saw, e.g., in Section 1.5.

Inverse functions and their derivatives

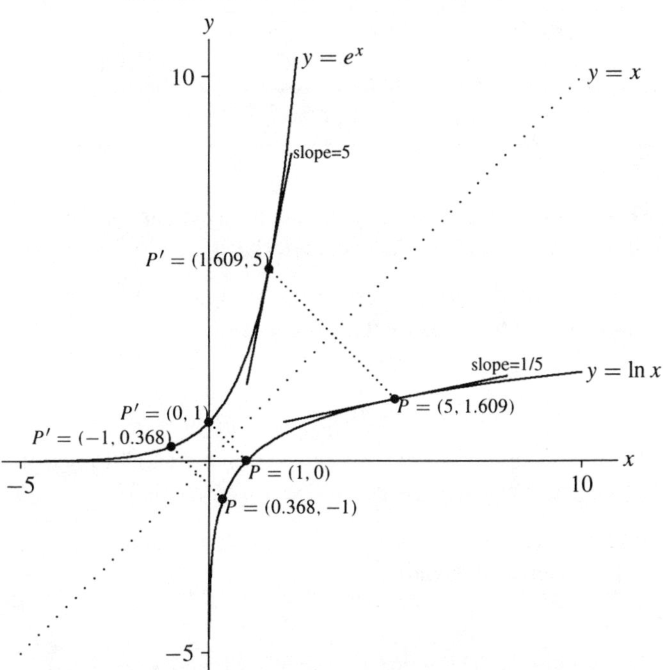

Notice:

Symmetric points. A point $P = (x, y)$ lies on one graph if and only if the point $P' = (y, x)$ lies on the other. Several such pairs are shown.

Symmetric tangent lines. Consider the lines tangent to the two graphs at corresponding points P and P'. (One such pair of tangent segments is shown.) Like the graphs themselves, these tangent lines are symmetric with respect to the line $y = x$. It follows that *the slopes of the tangent lines at P and P' are reciprocals.*

This is our key fact!

Reciprocal slopes. The slope of the tangent line at $P' = (\ln a, a)$ is the derivative of the function $y = e^x$ evaluated at $x = \ln a$. As we saw above, $(e^x)' = e^x$, so our particular tangent line has slope $e^{\ln a} = a$. It follows that the tangent line at $P = (a, \ln a)$ has slope $1/a$, just as the theorem predicts.

We've shown, so far, that the theorem holds in the case $b = e$. Since $\log_b x = \ln x / \ln b$, the general result follows easily. □

Antiderivatives of exponential and logarithm functions

Antidifferentiation is the inverse problem to differentiation: given a function f, we seek an *antiderivative* F, such that $F' = f$. As we've seen, antiderivatives aren't (quite) unique. If $F' = f$, then for *any* constant C, $(F(x) + C)' = f(x)$.

Derivatives are unique. For given f there's only one f'.

See page 185 to refresh memories on this subject.

On the other hand, different antiderivatives differ from each other only by additive constants, so finding one antiderivative is tantamount to finding all.

Very rare exceptions occur for functions with gaps in their domains. They won't trouble us.

Antiderivative formulas

Derivative rules for exponential functions run almost perfectly in reverse, so the following theorem closely resembles Theorem 8..

> **Theorem 10.** Let C be any constant and b any positive base. If $f(x) = e^x$, then $F(x) = e^x + C$ is an antiderivative of f. If $g(x) = b^x$, then $G(x) = \dfrac{b^x}{\ln b} + C$ is an antiderivative of g.

Notice:

Its own antiderivative, naturally. The natural exponential function e^x is not only its own derivative, but its own antiderivative, too.

For exactly the same reason!

Other bases. The second antiderivative formula is best checked by *differentiation*—notice how we use the constant rule:

$$\left(\frac{b^x}{\ln b} + C\right)' = \frac{1}{\ln b} \cdot \left(b^x\right)' = \frac{1}{\ln b} \cdot b^x \ln b = b^x.$$

Antiderivatives of logarithm functions—even the natural logarithm—are a little more complicated. For the moment we'll just *state* a formula.

> **Fact:** Let C be any constant. If $f(x) = \ln x$, then $F(x) = x \ln x - x + C$ is an antiderivative of f.

Notice:

Rabbit from a hat? The antiderivative formula above seems to have been plucked from thin air. Where did it come from? Why is it right? *Is* it right?

Tools we'll develop soon will let us show—by differentiation—that the formula is correct. Showing how one might *produce* such a formula will have to wait a little longer.

See the exercises, too.

Graphical evidence. Formal proofs will have to wait, but graphical evidence for the antiderivative formula is available right now. Here's some:

Antiderivatives of $y = \ln x$

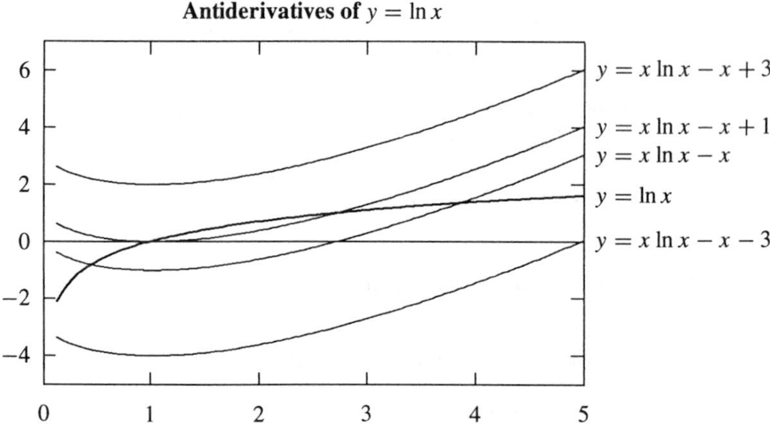

The picture shows graphs of $y = x \ln x - x + C$ for various values of C. As it should, each such graph looks plausibly like an antiderivative of $y = \ln x$ (shown in bolder style).

The antiderivatives differ from each other only by a vertical shift—all have the same derivative.

■ **Example 2.** Find an antiderivative of $f(x) = 3e^x - 2\ln x$. How many are there?

Solution: The theorems give antiderivatives of e^x and $\ln x$. Combining them appropriately➻ says that $3e^x - 2\cdot(x\ln x - x)$ is one suitable antiderivative. So, therefore, is any function of the form

We're using the sum and constant rules.

$$F(x) = 3e^x - 2\cdot(x\ln x - x) + C,$$

where C is any constant. □

A sample problem

Here's a problem that uses ingredients from this section.

■ **Example 3.** Let $f(x) = e^x = \exp(x)$. Let's consider how to find a linear function L and a quadratic function Q that "closely approximate" f near $x = 0$.

(a) Find constants a and b so that the linear function $L(x) = a + bx$ has the same value and first derivative as f at $x = 0$, i.e., such that $L(0) = f(0)$ and $L'(0) = f'(0)$.

(b) Find constants a, b, and c for which the quadratic function $Q(x) = a+bx+cx^2$ has the same value and first *two* derivatives as f at $x = 0$, i.e., such that $Q(0) = f(0)$, $Q'(0) = f'(0)$, and $Q''(0) = f''(0)$.

(c) Plot f, L, and Q on the same axes. How closely do L and Q approximate f on the interval $[-0.5, 0.5]$?

Solution: Observe for later reference that $f(x) = f'(x) = f''(x)$, so $f(0) = f'(0) = f''(0) = 1$.

(a) Let $L(x) = a + bx$; we need values for a and b. Note first that $L(0) = a$. To have $L(0) = f(0) = 1$, we must have $a = 1$. Similarly, $L'(x) = b$; to have $L'(0) = b = f'(0) = 1$, we must have $b = 1$. Thus $L(x) = 1 + x$.

(b) Let $Q(x) = a + bx + cx^2$. We need values for a, b, and c. As in the previous part,

$$Q(0) = f(0) = 1 \implies a = 1; \quad Q'(0) = f(0) = 1 \implies b = 1.$$

Thus $Q(x) = 1 + x + cx^2$, and we need only find c. Since $Q''(x) = 2c$,➻ we have

Check this!

$$Q''(0) = 2c = f''(0) = 1 \implies c = 1/2.$$

Thus $Q(x) = 1 + x + x^2/2$.

(c) Here are graphs of all three functions (the exponential function looks "bolder"):

Two approximations to $y = e^x$

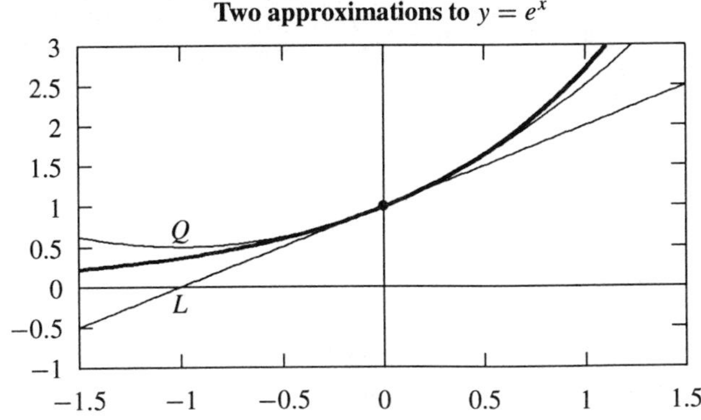

Use a calculator to check our numbers.

The picture shows that both L and Q approximate f well near $x = 0$, Q even better than L. A close look shows that for x in the interval $[-0.5, 0.5]$,

$$\begin{aligned} |f(x) - L(x)| &\le f(0.5) - L(0.5) \approx 0.149; \\ |f(x) - Q(x)| &\le f(0.5) - Q(0.5) \approx 0.024. \end{aligned}$$

□

Exercises

Find the derivative of each function in exercises 1–14.

1. $f(x) = 2e^x + \pi$
2. $f(x) = e^5 - 4e^x$
3. $f(x) = e^x + x^e + e$
4. $f(x) = 2e^{x+1}$
5. $f(x) = 2^x + x^2 + 2$
6. $f(x) = 3^x$
7. $f(x) = 2 \cdot 3^{x-1}$
8. $f(x) = e^\pi + \pi^x + x^\pi$
9. $f(x) = (\ln 5)\, e^x$
10. $f(x) = (\ln 5)^x$
11. $f(x) = (\ln 5)\, 5^x$
12. $f(x) = (\ln 5)\, x^5$
13. $f(x) = -2 \ln x$
14. $f(x) = 3 \log_2 x$

15–28. Find the second derivative of each function in exercises 1–14.

29–42. Find an antiderivative of each function in exercises 1–14.

43. (a) Find an expression for $\dfrac{d^n}{dx^n} e^x$.

    (b) Find an expression for $\dfrac{d^n}{dx^n} \ln x$.

44. Suppose that $b > 0$. Find an antiderivative of $\log_b x$. [HINT: Use Theorem .]

45. (a) Use Theorem to show that $\big(x \ln x\big)' = 1 + \ln x$.

    (b) Suppose that $b > 0$. Evaluate $\big(x \log_b x\big)'$.

46. Let $f(x) = \ln(kx)$ where k is a positive constant.

    (a) Show that $f'(x) = x^{-1}$. [HINT: $\ln(kx) = \ln k + \ln x$.]

    (b) Find an antiderivative of f.

47. Let $f(x) = b^x$.

    (a) Find all values of $b > 0$ such that $f'(0) > 0$.

    (b) Find all values of $b > 0$ such that $f'(1) > f(1)$.

48. Let $g(x) = \log_b x$.

    (a) Find all values of $b > 0$ such that $g'(1) > 1$.

    (b) Find all values of $b > 0$ such that $g'(1) > 0$.

49. Let $f(x) = e^{-x} = \exp(-x)$. Show that $f'(x) = -e^{-x}$.
[HINT: $e^{-x} = (1/e)^x$.]

50. Find the derivative of $f(x) = \ln(1/x)$. [HINT: $\ln(1/x) = -\ln x$.]

51. Let $f(x) = 2e^{x+3}$.

(a) Explain how a graph of f can be obtained from a graph of the natural exponential function using *only* vertical stretching.

(b) Use part (a) to find a symbolic expression for $f'(x)$.

52. Let $f(x) = 3e^{x+2}$.

(a) Explain how a graph of f can be obtained from a graph of the natural exponential function using *only* horizontal translation.

(b) Use part (a) to find a symbolic expression for $f'(x)$.

53. On January 1, 1950, the population of Boomtown was 50,000. Since then the size of the population has been accurately modeled by the function $P(t) = 50000(0.98)^t$, where t is the number of years since January 1, 1950.

(a) What was the population of Boomtown on January 1, 1990?

(b) At what rate was the population of Boomtown changing on January 1, 1990? Was it increasing or decreasing then?

54. The position of a particle on the x-axis at time $t > 0$ seconds, is $\ln t$ meters. Find the average velocity of the particle over the interval $1 \le t \le e$.

55. Find an equation of the line tangent to the curve $y = e^x$ at $x = 0$.

56. Find the x-intercept of the line tangent to the curve $y = 2^x$ at $x = 0$.
[HINT: Draw a picture.]

57. Does there exist a real number a such that the line tangent to the curve $y = e^x$ at $x = a$ passes through the origin? If so, find it. If not, explain why there is no number with this property.

58. Does there exist a real number a such that the line tangent to the curve $y = x - \ln x$ at $x = a$ passes through the origin? If so, find it. If not, explain why there is no number with this property.

59. Which of the following functions are solutions of the differential equation $f''(x) = f(x)$? Which are solutions of $f'''(x) = f'(x)$?

(i) $f(x) = \sqrt{3}$
(ii) $f(x) = x + 2$
(iii) $f(x) = e^x$
(iv) $f(x) = 2^x$
(v) $f(x) = \ln x$

60. Give an example of a function f with the property that $f''(x) = f'(x)$ but $f'(x) \neq f(x)$.

61. Let $f(x) = Ae^x$ and $g(x) = e^{x+k}$ where A and k are constants.

(a) Show (by differentiation) that $f'(x) = f(x)$.

(b) Show (by differentiation) that $g'(x) = g(x)$.

(c) Find the value of A that makes $f(0) = 3$.

(d) Find the value of k that makes $g(0) = 3$.

(e) Show that if $A > 0$, there is a value of k such that $f(x) = g(x)$ for all x.

(f) Show that if $A < 0$, there is a value of k such that $f(x) = -g(x)$ for all x.

(g) Find a function h such that $h'(x) = h(x)$ and $h(0) = -2$.

62. Let $f(x) = e^{kx} = \exp(kx)$ and $g(x) = Af(x)$ where A and k are constants.

(a) Explain why $f(x) = b^x$ for some positive number b. What is b?

(b) Use part (a) and Theorem 8. to show that $f'(x) = ke^{kx} = kf(x)$.

(c) Use part (b) to show that $g'(x) = kg(x)$.

(d) Find a function h such that $h'(x) = 3h(x)$ and $h(0) = 2$.

(e) Find a function h such that $h'(x) = -2h(x)$ and $h(0) = 3$.

63. (a) Let A be a constant. Show that $y(x) = 5 + Ae^x$ is a solution of the differential equation $y' = y - 5$.

(b) Find the solution of the differential equation $y' = y - 5$ with the property $y(0) = 6$.

(c) Find the solution of the differential equation $y' = y - 5$ that passes through the point $(1, 0)$.

64. Suppose that A is a constant. Verify that $x(t) = 1 + t + Ae^t$ is a solution of the differential equation $x' = x - t$.

65. Suppose that A is a constant. Verify that $y(x) = Ae^x - x - 1$ is a solution of the differential equation $yy' = y^2 + xy$.

66. Suppose that A and B are constants. Verify that $y(x) = A\ln x + B + x$ is a solution of the differential equation $xy'' + y' = 1$.

67. Suppose that A and B are constants. Verify that $y(x) = Ax^{-1} + B + \ln x$ is a solution of the differential equation $x^2y'' + 2xy' = 1$.

68. Let $f(x) = \sqrt{x} - \ln x$.

(a) Show that f achieves its (global) minimum value at $x = 4$.

(b) Show that f has an inflection point at $x = 16$.

69. Let $f(x) = \ln x - e^{x-1}$.

(a) Show that f achieves its (global) maximum value when $x = 1$. [HINT: $e^{x-1} = e^x/e$.]

(b) Show that f is concave down everywhere on its domain.

70. Let $f(x) = x - e\ln x$.

(a) Prove that $f(\pi) > 0$. [HINT: Show that f has a global minimum at $x = e$.]

(b) Use part (a) to show that $e^\pi > \pi^e$.

71. (a) Show that the distance between the point $(0, 0)$ and a point (a, b) on the curve $y = e^{x/2}$ is least when a is a solution of the equation $2a + e^a = 0$. [HINT: Minimize the square of the distance.]

(b) Estimate the distance in part (a).

72. Let $f(x) = 2^x$ and $g(x) = 7x/3 + 1$. What is the slope of the line tangent to the curve $y = f(x)$ at the point in $[0, 3]$ where the vertical distance between g and the curve is the greatest?

73. Find the area of the smallest rectangle that has sides on the coordinate axes, a corner at the origin, and a corner on the curve $y = \ln x$.

74. (a) Find the minimum value of $f(x) = e^x - 1 - x$.
   (b) Explain why part (a) shows that $e^x \geq 1 + x$ for all x.
   (c) Use the racetrack principle to show that $e^x \geq 1 + x$ for all x. [HINT: Consider the cases $x > 0$ and $x < 0$ separately.]
   (d) Show that $e^x \geq 1 + x + x^2/2$ for all $x \geq 0$.

75. (a) Show that $\left(1 + \frac{1}{n}\right)^n \leq e$ for any integer $n \geq 1$. [HINT: Let $x = 1/n$ and use part (b) of the previous exercise.]
   (b) Show that $e \leq \left(1 + \frac{1}{n}\right)^{n+1}$ for any integer $n \geq 1$. [HINT: Proceed as in part (a) but with $x = -1/(n+1)$.]
   (c) Let $a_n = \left(1 + \frac{1}{n}\right)^n$, $b_n = \left(1 + \frac{1}{n}\right)^{n+1}$. Show that $\lim_{n\to\infty} (b_n - a_n) = 0$.
   (d) Let $c_n = (a_n + b_n)/2$. Explain why c_n approximates e better than either a_n or b_n.

   [NOTE: It is a fact that $\lim_{n\to\infty} \left(1 + \frac{1}{n}\right)^n = e$, but we don't yet have the tools necessary to prove this fact.]

76. (a) Use the racetrack principle to show that $e^x > 2x$ for all $x \geq 1$.
   (b) Use part (a) to show that $e^x > x^2$ for all $x \geq 1$.

77. Show that $1 - \dfrac{1}{x} \leq \ln x \leq x - 1$ when $x > 0$. [HINT: Consider the cases $x \geq 1$ and $0 < x \leq 1$ separately.]

78. (a) Use the racetrack principle to show that $0 \leq \ln x \leq \sqrt{x} - 1/\sqrt{x}$ when $x \geq 1$.
   (b) Show that $\sqrt{x} - 1/\sqrt{x} \leq \ln x \leq 0$ when $0 < x \leq 1$.
   (c) Use part (b) to show that $\lim_{x\to 0^+} x \ln x = 0$.

79. (a) Prove that $\lim_{x\to\infty} \dfrac{\ln x}{x} = 0$. [HINT: Use the previous exercise.]
   (b) Prove that $\lim_{x\to\infty} \dfrac{\ln x}{\sqrt{x}} = 0$. [HINT: $\ln x/\sqrt{x} = 2\ln\left(\sqrt{x}\right)/\sqrt{x}$.]
   (c) Prove that if r is a positive real number, then $\lim_{x\to\infty} \dfrac{\ln x}{x^r} = 0$.

80. In this exercise we will prove that $\lim_{x\to\infty} \dfrac{x^r}{e^x} = 0$ for any real number r.
   (a) Prove that $2\ln x - x < 0$ for all $x > 0$.
   (b) Use part (a) to prove that $\lim_{x\to\infty} (r \ln x - x) = -\infty$ when $r \geq 1$. [HINT: If $r \geq 1$, then $r^2 \geq r$.]
   (c) Use part (b) to prove that $\lim_{x\to\infty} \dfrac{x^r}{e^x} = 0$ when $r \geq 1$. [HINT: $x^r = e^{r \ln x}$.]
   (d) Use part (c) to prove that $\lim_{x\to\infty} \dfrac{x^r}{e^x} = 0$ when $r < 1$.

81. (a) Assume that $x \geq 1$. Use the inequality $\ln x \leq x - 1$ to show that $x \ln x - x \leq x^2/2 - x - 1/2$.

    (b) Prove that $(x-1)/2 \leq \ln x$ when $1 \leq x \leq 3$. [HINT: Show that $f(x) = \ln x - (x-1)/2$ is decreasing on the interval $[1, 2]$ and increasing on $[2, 3]$.]

    (c) Use the inequality in part (b) to find a quadratic polynomial p with the property that $p(x) \leq x \ln x - x$ when $1 \leq x \leq 3$.

82. (a) Use the fact that $1/x \leq 1$ when $x \geq 1$ and the racetrack principle to show that $\ln x \leq x - 1$ when $x \geq 1$.

    (b) Use the fact that $1/x^2 \geq 1/x$ when $0 < x \leq 1$ and the racetrack principle to show that $1 - 1/x \leq \ln x$ when $0 < x \leq 1$.

83. (a) Assume that $x \geq 1$. Explain how the relation $\ln x \leq 2(\sqrt{x} - 1)$ can be derived from the relation $1/x \leq 1/\sqrt{x}$ using antiderivatives and the racetrack principle.

    (b) Assume that $0 < x \leq 1$. Explain how the relation $\ln x \geq 2(1 - 1/\sqrt{x})$ can be derived from the relation $1/x \leq 1/x^{3/2}$ using antiderivatives and the racetrack principle.

84. The derivative of a logarithmic function $f(x) = \log_b x$ is proportional to $1/x$. In fact, the constant of proportionality is $f'(1)$—the slope of the line tangent to the graph of f at $x = 1$. Justify each step in the following derivation of this result. [HINT: In line (iv), $w = h/x$.]

$$
\begin{aligned}
&\text{(i)} && \frac{d}{dx}\log_b x &&= \lim_{h\to 0} \frac{\log_b(x+h) - \log_b x}{h} \\
&\text{(ii)} && &&= \lim_{h\to 0} \frac{\log_b\left(\frac{x+h}{x}\right)}{h} \\
&\text{(iii)} && &&= \lim_{h\to 0} \frac{\log_b\left(1 + \frac{h}{x}\right)}{h} \\
&\text{(iv)} && &&= \lim_{w\to 0} \frac{\log_b(1+w)}{xw} \\
&\text{(v)} && &&= \frac{1}{x}\left(\lim_{w\to 0} \frac{\log_b(1+w)}{w}\right) \\
&\text{(vi)} && &&= \frac{f'(1)}{x}.
\end{aligned}
$$

85. The equation $a^x = 1 + x$ has at least one solution in the interval $[0, \infty)$ for every $a > 0$. For which values of $a > 0$ does this equation have a nonzero solution? For these values of a, how many nonzero solutions are there?

86. Find all the solutions of the equation $2^x = 2x$. Prove that you have found all the solutions. [HINT: Use the racetrack principle.]

87. The equation $b^x = bx$ has at least one solution in the interval $[0, \infty)$ for every $b > 0$. For which values of $b > 0$ does this equation have more than one solution?

88. Use mathematical induction to prove that $e^x \geq \sum_{k=0}^{n} x^n/n!$ for all $x \geq 0$. [HINT: See Exercise 74.]

Evaluate the limits in Exercises 89–92 by recognizing each as the definition of a derivative.

89. $\lim_{t\to 0} \dfrac{e^t - 1}{t}$

90. $\lim_{x\to 0} \dfrac{2^{3+x} - 2^3}{x}$

91. $\lim_{s\to 0} \dfrac{\log_5(25+s) - 2}{s}$

92. $\lim_{z\to e} \dfrac{\ln z - 1}{z - e}$

93. Evaluate $\lim_{x\to\pi} \dfrac{e^x - e^\pi}{x^e - \pi^e}$.

94. Let f, L, and Q be as in Example 3.

(a) Find the value of the constant d for which the cubic function $C(x) = Q(x) + dx^3$ has the properties $C(0) = f(0)$, $C'(0) = f'(0)$, $C''(0) = f''(0)$, and $C'''(0) = f'''(0)$.

(b) Graph f, L, Q, and C on the same axes over the interval $[-3, 3]$.

(c) Find an interval over which $|f(x) - L(x)| < 0.1$.

(d) Find an interval over which $|f(x) - Q(x)| < 0.1$.

(e) Find an interval over which $|f(x) - C(x)| < 0.1$.

95. Let $f(x) = \ln x$.

(a) Find values of the constants a and b so that the linear function $L(x) = a + b(x - 1)$ has the properties $L(1) = f(1)$ and $L'(1) = f'(1)$.

(b) Find the value of the constant c for which the quadratic function $Q(x) = L(x) + c(x - 1)^2$ has the properties $Q(1) = f(1)$, $Q'(1) = f'(1)$, and $Q''(1) = f''(1)$.

(c) Find the value of the constant d for which the cubic function $C(x) = Q(x) + d(x - 1)^3$ has the properties $C(1) = f(1)$, $C'(1) = f'(1)$, $C''(1) = f''(1)$, and $C'''(1) = f'''(1)$.

(d) Graph f, L, Q, and C on the same axes over the interval $[0.1, 3]$.

(e) Find an interval over which $|f(x) - L(x)| < 0.1$.

(f) Find an interval over which $|f(x) - Q(x)| < 0.1$.

(g) Find an interval over which $|f(x) - C(x)| < 0.1$.

2.10 Derivatives of trigonometric functions

We've already studied the trigonometric functions and some of their derivatives informally, by graphical techniques. In this section we take a more systematic point of view.

Derivatives of the sine and cosine functions—graphical evidence

We've already succumbed to the temptation, e.g., in Section 2.3.

Graphs suggest almost irresistibly that $(\sin x)' = \cos x$. Here are the graphs:

Graph of $f(x) = \sin x$

Graph of $f'(x) = \cos x$

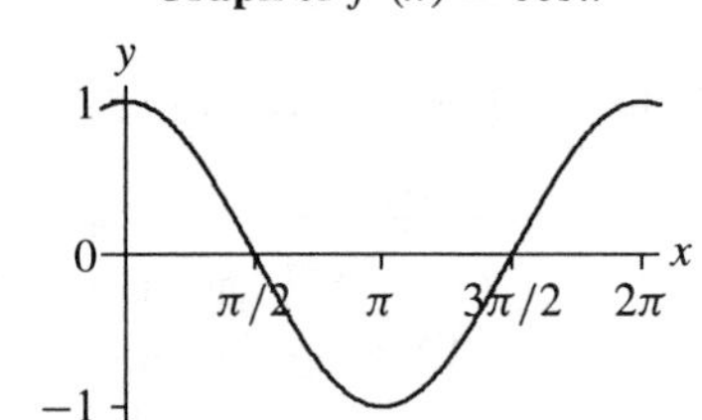

It's equally tempting to guess that $(\cos x)' = -\sin x$, as *these* graphs show:

Graph of $f(x) = \cos x$

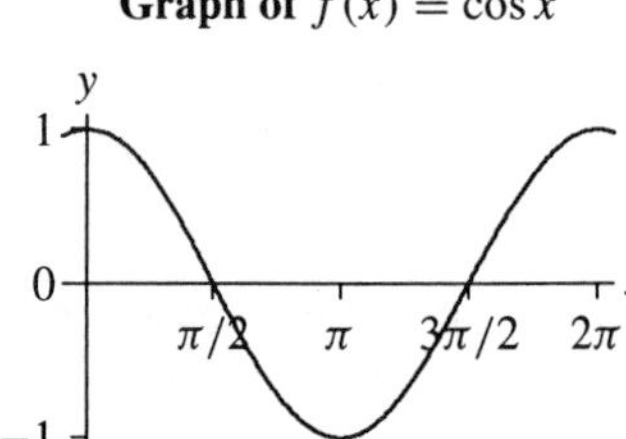

Graph of $f'(x) = -\sin x$

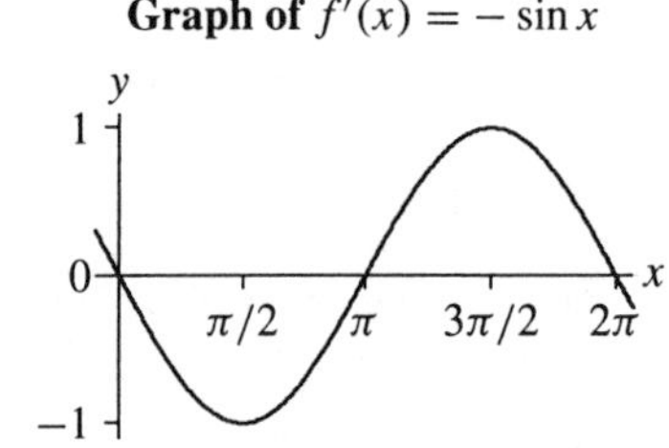

Convincing as they are, graphs aren't proofs. Rigor demands that we deal directly with the limit that defines the derivative.

Derivatives of the sine and cosine functions—analytic proofs

Differentiating the sine function. To show rigorously that $(\sin x)' = \cos x$, we need—somehow—to calculate the limit

$$\frac{dy}{dx} = \lim_{h\to 0} \frac{\sin(x+h) - \sin(x)}{h}.$$

cf. Appendix G.

Algebra isn't enough; we'll need the addition formula for sines:

$$\sin(x+h) = \sin(x)\cos(h) + \cos(x)\sin(h).$$

Check each step.

Now we can do algebra:

$$\begin{aligned}
\lim_{h\to 0} \frac{\sin(x+h) - \sin(x)}{h} &= \lim_{h\to 0} \frac{\big(\sin(x)\cos(h) + \cos(x)\sin(h)\big) - \sin(x)}{h} \\
&= \lim_{h\to 0} \left((\sin x) \cdot \frac{\cos h - 1}{h} + (\cos x) \cdot \frac{\sin h}{h} \right) \\
&= (\sin x) \cdot \lim_{h\to 0} \frac{\cos h - 1}{h} + (\cos x) \cdot \lim_{h\to 0} \frac{\sin h}{h}.
\end{aligned}$$

They depend on x, not h; that's why we could pull them outside the limits.

(As far as the limit is concerned, $\sin x$ and $\cos x$ are constants.)

To finish the computation, we need two non-trivial facts:

"Non-trivial" is the mathematician's euphemism for "hard."

$$\lim_{h\to 0}\frac{\cos h - 1}{h} = 0 \qquad \text{and} \qquad \lim_{h\to 0}\frac{\sin h}{h} = 1.$$

Assuming them for the moment, the conclusion follows easily:

$$\begin{aligned}\frac{d}{dx}\sin x &= (\sin x)\cdot\lim_{h\to 0}\frac{\cos h - 1}{h} + (\cos x)\cdot\lim_{h\to 0}\frac{\sin h}{h}\\ &= (\sin x)\cdot 0 + (\cos x)\cdot 1\\ &= \cos x.\end{aligned}$$

□

Two challenging limits. Each limit above can be interpreted as a certain derivative:

- The limit
$$\lim_{h\to 0}\frac{\cos h - 1}{h} = \lim_{h\to 0}\frac{\cos h - \cos 0}{h - 0}$$
defines the derivative of the cosine function at $x = 0$. The cosine graph is *horizontal* there, so the derivative and the limit are zero.

- A similar argument applies to
$$\lim_{h\to 0}\frac{\sin h}{h}.$$
The limit *defines* the derivative of the sine function at $x = 0$. In Example 4, page 153, we saw convincing graphical and numerical evidence that this derivative is 1.

- Graphs aren't proofs. For a more rigorous proof of the second limit above, see Appendix I.

Differentiating the cosine function. To show that $(\cos x)' = -\sin x$, we *could* mimic the argument just given for the sine function. Instead, we'll use facts we already know about the sine function.

As their graphs show, the sine and cosine functions differ only by a horizontal translation of $\pi/2$ units. In other words,

$$\cos x = \sin(x + \pi/2) \qquad \text{and} \qquad \cos(x + \pi/2) = -\sin x.$$

It follows that the cosine graph has the same slope at x as the sine graph has at $x + \pi/2$. Using the identities above and the fact that $(\sin x)' = \cos x$, we can express all this symbolically:

Think about this!

We just showed it.

$$\frac{d}{dx}\cos x = \frac{d}{dx}\sin(x + \pi/2) = \cos(x + \pi/2) = -\sin x,$$

just as desired. □

Derivatives of other trigonometric functions

Each of the functions tangent, secant, cotangent and cosecant is an algebraic combination of the sine and cosine functions. Not surprisingly, so is each derivative.

With ingenious algebra we could calculate from scratch the derivative of each of these "other" trigonometric functions. It's easier and more efficient, though, to wait until we develop explicit rules for derivatives of products and quotients. To

The wait will be short. In the meantime, see the exercises.

allay unbearable suspense, here's a graphical foretaste of what's to come:

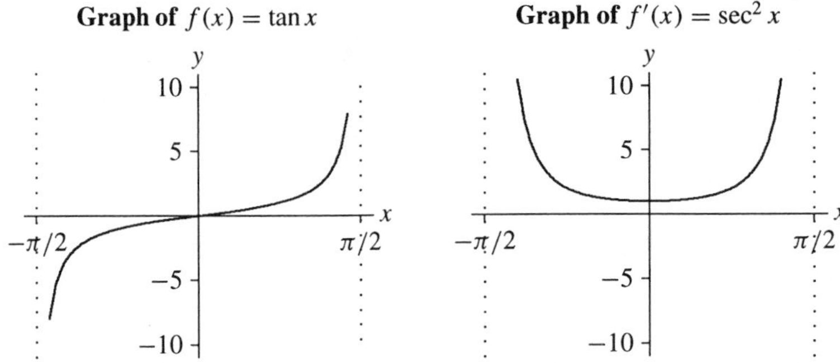

As it should, the second graph represents the slope behavior of the first. It amounts to circumstantial evidence—but only that—for the fact that $(\tan x)' = \sec^2 x$.

Antiderivatives of sines and cosines

That's signs, not sines.

With just a little care for signs, our derivative formulas can be "reversed" to give antiderivatives. Here are the details; they're easy to check by differentiation:

> **Theorem 11.** Let C be any constant. If $f(x) = \sin x$, then $F(x) = -\cos x + C$ is an antiderivative of f. If $g(x) = \cos x$, then $G(x) = \sin x + C$ is an antiderivative of f.

■ **Example 1.** Find an antiderivative of $f(x) = 3\sin x - 4\cos x$. How many antiderivatives are there?

We're using the sum and constant rules.

Solution: Theorem 11. gives antiderivatives of $\sin x$ and $\cos x$. Combining them appropriately says that $-3\cos x - 4\sin x$ is one suitable antiderivative. So, therefore, is *any* function of the form

$$F(x) = -3\cos x - 4\sin x + C,$$

Plot both f and F. Does the picture show what it should?

where C is any constant. □

Further transcendental meditations (optional)

Proving rigorously that a function is transcendental can be difficult. Consider, for example, the sine function. We *defined* the sine function using the unit circle—not by any algebraic formula. Nevertheless, the sine function might conceivably have some (probably complicated) algebraic formula.

In fact, the sine function has no algebraic formula; neither does any other trigonometric, logarithm, or exponential function. The following observations don't *prove* that the sine function is transcendental, but they give some idea of what's involved:

- Could $\sin x = p(x)$, for some *polynomial* $p(x)$?

  No. A polynomial of degree n has at most n roots; the sine function has infinitely many roots.

- Could the sine function be a rational function? That is, could $\sin x = p(x)/q(x)$, for some polynomials p and q?

  No again, for the same reason. A rational function has only finitely many roots.

- The sine function is 2π-periodic. None of the raw algebraic functions—powers, roots, etc.—is periodic. Creating a periodic function from non-periodic components seems difficult.

A sample problem

Here's a problem that uses ingredients developed in this section.

■ **Example 2.** Here's a graph of $f(x) = x + \cos x$; two interesting points are bulleted:

Graph of $y = x + \cos x$

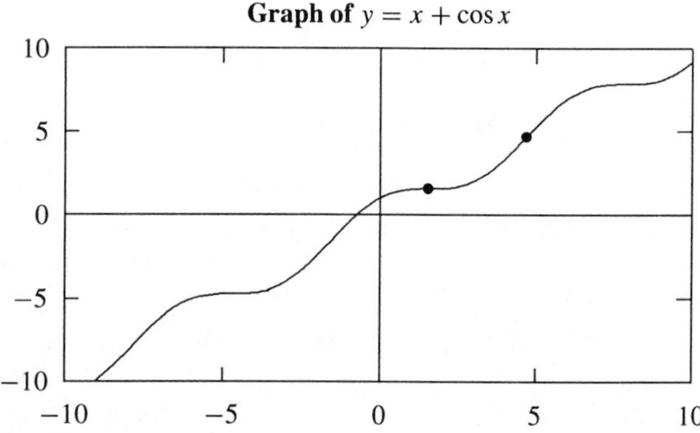

Are there local maxima or minima? Are there inflection points? If so, where?

Solution: The graph seems to have flat spots, such as at the left bullet, but are they local maxima, local minima, or just flat spots? The picture alone doesn't tell for sure.➻

Would zooming help? See for yourself if a plotting device is at hand.

With derivatives we can settle the question easily. Since $f(x) = x + \cos x$, $f'(x) = 1 - \sin x$ and $f''(x) = -\cos x$. Thus

$$f'(x) = 0 \iff \sin x = 1 \iff x = \frac{\pi}{2} + 2k\pi;$$
$$f''(x) = 0 \iff \cos x = 0 \iff x = \frac{\pi}{2} + k\pi.$$

In particular, the first bulleted point f is *both* a stationary point *and* an inflection point. In addition, f has *stationary points* at intervals of 2π, and *inflection points* at intervals of π. (The right bullet is another inflection point.)

Notice, finally, that $f'(x) = 1 - \sin x \geq 0$ for all x. Thus the stationary points are nothing but that—neither local maxima nor local minima. □

Exercises

Find the derivative of each function in exercises 1–4.

1. $f(x) = 2\sin x$
2. $f(x) = 3\cos x$
3. $f(x) = 3\sin x - 2\cos x$
4. $f(x) = 2\cos x - 3\sin x$

5–8. Find the second derivative of each function in exercises 1–4.

9–12. Find an antiderivative of each function in exercises 1–4.

13. Let $f(x) = \sin(x^2)$. Show that $f'(x) \neq \cos(x^2)$ in a way that your classmates would find convincing. [HINT: Compare graphs.]

14. Let $f(x) = x - \cos x$.

    (a) Does f have any stationary points in the interval $[0, 2\pi]$? If so, where?
    (b) Where in the interval $[0, 2\pi]$ is f increasing?
    (c) Find the maximum and minimum values of f over the interval $[0, \pi]$.
    (d) Where is f concave down?
    (e) Where is f increasing most rapidly? Evaluate f' there.

15. Repeat the previous exercise with $f(x) = x + \cos x$.

16. Draw a graph of each of the following functions over the interval $[0, 2\pi]$. On each graph, label local extrema, global extrema, and points of inflection with both coordinates. (Use exact values rather than decimal approximations for the coordinates.)

    (a) $f(x) = \frac{1}{2}x + \sin x$
    (b) $g(x) = x + \sin x$
    (c) $h(x) = \frac{3}{2}x + \sin x$
    (d) $f(x) = \sin x + \cos x$
    (e) $g(x) = 2\sin x - \sqrt{3}x$
    (f) $h(x) = \sqrt{3}\sin x + 3\cos x$

17. Let $f(x) = 2 - \sin x$ and $g(x) = 1 + \cos x$.

    (a) Find the maximum vertical distance between the curves $y = f(x)$ and $y = g(x)$ over the interval $[0, 2\pi]$.
    (b) Find the slopes of the lines tangent to f and g at the point in the interval $[0, 2\pi]$ where the the vertical distance between f and g is greatest.

18. Let $f(x) = \cos x$ and $g(x) = \sqrt{3}\sin x$.

    (a) Find the maximum vertical distance between the curves $y = f(x)$ and $y = g(x)$ over the interval $[0, \pi]$.
    (b) Find the slopes of the lines tangent to f and g at the point in the interval $[0, \pi]$ where the the vertical distance between f and g is greatest.

19. Suppose that two sides of a rectangle are on the coordinate axes and that a corner of the rectangle lies on the curve $y = 2\cos x$. Is it possible that the perimeter of the rectangle is $3\pi/2$? If so, find the coordinates of a rectangle with these properties. If not, find the coordinates of the rectangle with the greatest possible perimeter.

20. Suppose that one side of a rectangle is on the x-axis and that two corners of the rectangle lie on the curve $y = 2\sqrt{2}\sin x$. Among all such rectangles, find the perimeter of the one with maximum perimeter.

21. Suppose that two sides of a rectangle are on the coordinate axes and that a corner of the rectangle lies on the curve $y = k\cos x$, where $\pi/3 \le k \le \pi/2$. Show that k can be chosen so that the rectangle with maximum perimeter is a square.

22. Let $f(x) = A\cos x + B\sin x$ where A and B are constants.

    (a) Show that $f''(x) = -f(x)$.
    (b) Show that $f^{(4)}(x) = f(x)$.

(c) Find a function f such that $f''(x) = -f(x)$, $f'(\pi/3) = -1$, and $f(\pi/3) = \sqrt{3}$.

23. (a) What is the 50th derivative of $f(x) = \cos x$?

(b) What is the 51st derivative of $g(x) = \sin x$?

24. Show that $\frac{d^n}{dx^n} \sin x = \sin\left(x + n\frac{\pi}{2}\right)$ when $n \geq 1$.
[HINTS: $\sin(x + \pi/2) = \cos x$; $\sin(x + \pi) = -\sin x$.]

25. Find all values of $z \in [0, 2\pi)$ for which the line tangent to the function $f(x) = \cos x$ at z intersects the graph of the cosine function infinitely many times. Explain how you know that you have found all such values of z.

26. Suppose that the line tangent to the curve $y = \sin x$ at $x = z$ passes through the origin. Show that $\tan z = z$.

27. (a) Use the fact that $(\tan x)' = \sec^2 x$ to show that $x = 0$ is the only solution of the equation $x = \tan x$ in the interval $(-\pi/2, \pi/2)$.

(b) Suppose that $k \geq 1$ is an integer. Explain why the equation $x = \tan x$ has exactly one solution between $k\pi$ and $(2k + 1)\pi/2$.

(c) Let $k \geq 1$ be an integer, m be the x-intercept of the line tangent to the curve $y = \sin x$ at the point $w = (2k + 1)\pi/2 - 3/(\pi(2k + 1))$, and n be the x-intercept of the line tangent to the curve at the point $z = (2k + 1)\pi/2 - 2/(\pi(2k + 1))$. It can be shown that $n < 0 < m$. Use this fact to show that the function $f(x) = x - \tan x$ has a root in the interval (w, z).

28. Prove that $2 + \sin x - \cos x \leq e^x$ when $0 \leq x$.

29. Let $f(x) = 2x/\pi$.

(a) Prove that $f(x) \leq \sin x$ when $0 \leq x \leq \pi/2$.

(b) Show that the function $g(x) = \sin x - f(x)$ achieves its maximum value over the interval $[0, \pi/2]$ at the point where the slope of the line tangent to the sine function is $2/\pi$.

30. (a) Use the inequality $\cos x \leq 1$ to prove that $\sin x \leq x$ for all $x \geq 0$.

(b) Use part (a) to show that $1 - x^2/2 \leq \cos x$ for all $x \geq 0$.

(c) Explain why the inequality in part (b) is true for all x. [HINT: $\cos x$ is an even function.]

31. (a) Use the result in part (b) of the previous exercise to prove that $x - x^3/6 \leq \sin x$ when $x \geq 0$.

(b) Use part (a) to prove that $\cos x \leq 1 - x^2/2 + x^4/24$.

(c) Prove that $\sin x \leq x - x^3/6 + x^5/120$ when $x \geq 0$.

32. Let $f(x) = \sin x$.

(a) Find an equation of the line tangent to f at $x = 0$.

(b) Find an equation of the line tangent to f at $x = \pi/3$.

(c) Which of the tangent lines in parts (a) and (b) yields a better approximation of $\sin(\pi/6)$? How could you have used f'' to predict which tangent line would yield the better approximation?

33. Let $n \geq 0$ be an integer.

(a) Use mathematical induction to prove that

$$\sum_{k=0}^{2n-1}(-1)^k x^{2k}/(2k)! \leq \cos x \leq \sum_{k=0}^{2n}(-1)^k x^{2k}/(2k)!.$$

(b) Use mathematical induction to prove that

$$\sum_{k=0}^{2n-1}(-1)^k x^{2k+1}/(2k+1)! \leq \sin x \leq \sum_{k=0}^{2n}(-1)^k x^{2k+1}/(2k+1)!.$$

Evaluate the limits in exercises 34–37 by recognizing each as the definition of a derivative.

34. $\displaystyle\lim_{x\to\pi/2}\frac{\cos x}{x-\pi/2}$

35. $\displaystyle\lim_{x\to\pi}\frac{\sin x}{x-\pi}$

36. $\displaystyle\lim_{h\to 0}\frac{\sin(3\pi/2+h)+1}{h}$

37. $\displaystyle\lim_{h\to 0}\frac{2\cos(5\pi/4+h)+\sqrt{2}}{h}$

38. Evaluate $\displaystyle\lim_{h\to 0}\frac{\cos(x-h)-\cos(x+h)}{h}$.

39. Let $f(x)=\sin(x+k)$ where k is a constant.

(a) Use the limit definition of the derivative to show that $f'(x)=\cos(x+k)$.

(b) Interpret the result in part (a) graphically. [HINT: How is the graph of f related to the graph of the sine function?]

(c) Let $g(x)=\cos x$. Use the result in part (a) to show that $g'(x)=-\sin x$. [HINT: $\cos x=\sin(x+\pi/2)$.]

(d) Let $g(x)=\cos(x+k)$. Use the result in part (a) to show that $g'(x)=-\sin(x+k)$. [HINT: $\cos(x+k)=\sin(x+(k+\pi/2))$.]

(e) Let $h(x)=3\sin(x-2)$. Use the results in parts (a) and (d) to find $h'(x)$, $h''(x)$, and an antiderivative of h.

40. (a) Let $f(x)=\sin(kx)$ where k is a constant. Provide a justification for each step in the following proof that $f'(x)=k\cos(kx)$. [HINT: In line (iii), $w=kh$.]

$$\begin{aligned}
&\text{(i)} & \frac{d}{dx}\sin(kx) &= \lim_{h\to 0}\frac{\sin\big(k(x+h)\big)-\sin(kx)}{h}\\
&\text{(ii)} & &= \lim_{h\to 0}\frac{\sin(kx+kh)-\sin(kx)}{h}\\
&\text{(iii)} & &= \lim_{h\to 0} k\cdot\frac{\sin(kx+w)-\sin(kx)}{w}\\
&\text{(iv)} & &= \lim_{w\to 0} k\cdot\frac{\sin(kx+w)-\sin(kx)}{w}\\
&\text{(v)} & &= k\cdot\left(\lim_{w\to 0}\frac{\sin(kx+w)-\sin(kx)}{w}\right)\\
&\text{(vi)} & &= k\cos(kx).
\end{aligned}$$

(b) Use the result in part (a) to find the derivative of $g(x) = 3\sin(2x)$.

41. Let $f(x) = \cos(kx)$ where k is a constant.

(a) Use the limit definition of the derivative to prove that $f'(x) = -k\sin(kx)$.

(b) Use the result in part (a) to find the derivative of $g(x) = 2\cos(3x)$.

42. Let $f(x) = \sin x$.

(a) Find values of the constants a and b so that the linear function $L(x) = a + bx$ has the properties $L(0) = f(0)$ and $L'(0) = f'(0)$.

(b) Find the value of the constant c for which the quadratic function $Q(x) = L(x)+cx^2$ has the properties $Q(0) = f(0)$, $Q'(0) = f'(0)$, and $Q''(0) = f''(0)$.

(c) Find the value of the constant d for which the cubic function $C(x) = Q(x) + dx^3$ has the properties $C(0) = f(0)$, $C'(0) = f'(0)$, $C''(0) = f''(0)$, and $C'''(0) = f'''(0)$.

(d) Graph f, L, Q, and C on the same axes over the interval $[-4, 4]$.

(e) Find an interval over which $|f(x) - L(x)| < 0.1$.

(f) Find an interval over which $|f(x) - Q(x)| < 0.1$.

(g) Find an interval over which $|f(x) - C(x)| < 0.1$.

43. Repeat the previous problem with $f(x) = \cos x$.

44. Let $f(x) = \tan x$. Justify each step in the following proof that $f'(x) = \sec^2 x$.

$$\text{(i)} \quad \frac{d}{dx}\tan x = \lim_{h\to 0} \frac{\tan(x+h) - \tan x}{h}$$

$$\text{(ii)} \quad = \lim_{h\to 0} \frac{\frac{\sin(x+h)}{\cos(x+h)} - \frac{\sin x}{\cos x}}{h}$$

$$\text{(iii)} \quad = \lim_{h\to 0} \frac{\cos x \sin(x+h) - \sin x \cos(x+h)}{h\big(\cos x \cos(x+h)\big)}$$

$$\text{(iv)} \quad = \lim_{h\to 0} \frac{\cos(-x)\sin(x+h) + \sin(-x)\cos(x+h)}{h\big(\cos x \cos(x+h)\big)}$$

$$\text{(v)} \quad = \lim_{h\to 0} \frac{\sin h}{h\big(\cos x \cos(x+h)\big)}$$

$$\text{(vi)} \quad = \lim_{h\to 0} \left(\frac{\sin h}{h} \cdot \frac{1}{\cos x \cos(x+h)}\right)$$

$$\text{(vii)} \quad = \frac{1}{\cos^2 x}$$

$$\text{(viii)} \quad = \sec^2 x\,.$$

45. Let $f(x) = \cot x$. Use the limit definition of the derivative to show that $f'(x) = -\csc^2 x$.

46. Let $f(x) = \sec x$. Use the limit definition of the derivative to show that $f'(x) = \sec x \tan x$.

47. Let $f(x) = \csc x$. Use the limit definition of the derivative to show that $f'(x) = -\csc x \cot x$.

2.11 Chapter summary

Chapter 2 is the heart of Calculus I. Its main idea, the **derivative**, is the most important idea in calculus itself.

Amount functions, rate functions, slope functions. Section 2.1 approaches the derivative informally and intuitively, interpreting it either (depending on the situation) as the **rate function** or as the **slope function** derived from an "original function" or **amount function**. *Any* function can be thought of as "original"—to *any* function we can associate a rate function that describes how fast the original function varies.

For example, suppose that $s(t)$ describes the **position** of a moving object at time t, then its rate function $s'(t)$ (usually written $v(t)$) describes the object's **velocity**. If v is considered "original," then *its* rate function $v'(t)$ (usually written $a(t)$) describes the object's **acceleration**.

The **racetrack principle** relates the behavior of rate functions to that of amount functions. In its simplest form it says that if g grows *faster* than f over an interval, then g grows *more* than f over that interval—not a very surprising fact, but one that will prove useful later.

For a **linear function** the associated rate function (or slope function) is *constant*—its value is the slope itself. For a **non-linear function** the question of slope is stickier—what does it mean for a *curve* to have slope?

The answer—which we pursue in Section 2.2—is best understood graphically: The slope of a *curve* at a point is the slope of the **tangent line** at that point. Zooming helps us *find* this slope:

> *To find the slope of a* curve *at a point, zoom in until the curve "looks straight"—then find the slope.*

This trick really works—even for non-linear functions. It works because almost all calculus functions are "locally straight."

Derivatives, geometrically. Sections 2.3 and 2.4 are as important as any in this book. They describe—in great detail—how a function and its derivatives (first and second) are related graphically. The key idea is worth repeating:

> *The derivative f' of a function f tells whether and how fast the graph of f is rising.*

Almost everything in Sections 2.3 and 2.4 derives from this fact. Where a function increases or decreases, where it's concave up or concave down, how many and what types of stationary points it has—derivatives "carry" all such information.

The derivative as a limit. The formal definition of derivative involves this **limit of difference quotients**:

$$f'(x) = \lim_{h \to 0} \frac{f(x+h) - f(x)}{h}.$$

Section 2.5 explores this important limit and what it means in various settings. For a given function f the difference quotient has two main interpretations: it can be thought of either as the **slope of the secant line from x to $x + h$** or as the **average rate of change of f from x to $x + h$**. Taking these interpretations it follows that the derivative itself *also* has two main interpretations. The derivative $f'(x)$ can be thought of either as the **slope of the tangent line at x** or as the **instantaneous rate of change of f at x**. Both viewpoints are important—we'll use both throughout this book.

Limits. The derivative is defined as a **limit**; Sections 2.6 and 2.7 treat the idea of limit in its various forms. The basic idea is simple: $\lim_{x\to a} f(x) = L$ means that $f(x)$ *approaches* L as x *approaches* a. Section 2.6 explores this definition and some of its variants, in symbolic, graphical, and numerical forms.

Once understood, the limit is applied to define **continuity** of a function f at a point $x = a$ of its domain. In graphical terms, continuity of f means that the f-graph is "unbroken" at $x = a$; limits offer the right analytic language for describing this phenomenon.

Section 2.7 extends the idea of limits to **infinite limits** and **limits at infinity**—limits that involve the ∞ symbol. Such limits correspond graphically to **vertical and horizontal asymptotes**, respectively. Section 2.7 also tells how to combine old limits algebraically to form new ones, and, in the same spirit, how to combine old continuous functions to form new ones.

Derivatives of basic functions. Sections 2.8–2.10 return to derivatives, with emphasis on *calculating* derivatives—and understanding their meaning—for special classes of functions: algebraic, exponential, logarithmic, and trigonometric. Finding derivatives of **algebraic functions** is—no surprise here—usually a matter of algebra. For **transcendental functions** (the other families mentioned) finding derivatives takes a little more ingenuity.

Antiderivatives. Differentiation is a two-way street: if f is the derivative of g, then g is an **antiderivative** of f. Throughout the chapter we keep an eye on the "inverse" problem of finding antiderivatives for given functions. In general, the problem is harder than the "forward" problem of finding derivatives; we'll return—repeatedly—to finding antiderivatives in Calculus II.

A summary problem

Here's a problem that calls on ideas from various parts of this section. It's best read with a graphing calculator or other graphing technology at hand.

■ **Example 1.** In each case, decide whether a function with the given properties exists. If so, sketch the graph of such a function. If not, explain why there cannot be such a function.

(a) $\lim_{x\to\infty} f(x) = 5$ and $\lim_{x\to\infty} f'(x) = 1$.

(b) $f(x) < 0$ and $f'(x) > 0$ for all x.

(c) $f(x) < 0$ and $f'(x) < 0$ for all x.

(d) $f''(x) > 0$ and $f(x) < 0$ for all x.

(e) $f(x) > 0$, $f'(x) > 0$, and $f''(x) < 0$ for all x.

(f) $f(x) > 0$, $f'(x) > 0$, and $f''(x) < 0$ for all $x > 0$.

(g) $f(x)$ has a local maximum at $x = 3$ and $f''(3) = 0$.

Solution: (Note: Read these solutions with graphs at hand—use either some plotting technology or the graphs in Appendix J.)

(a) No function with these properties can exist. If $\lim_{x\to\infty} f'(x) = 1$, then, for large x, $f'(x) \approx 1$. This means that for large x, f increases at the rate of about one output unit for each input unit. Such a function can't have a horizontal asymptote as $x \to \infty$, as the statement $\lim_{x\to\infty} f(x) = 5$ implies.

Plot it!

(b) The conditions say that f should be *negative* and *increasing* for all x. The function $f(x) = -e^{-x}$ has these properties.

(c) The conditions say that f should be *negative* and *decreasing* for all x. The function $f(x) = -e^{x}$ has these properties.

(d) The conditions require that f be *concave up* and *negative* for all x. This is impossible. A graph that's concave up can't stay below the x-axis forever—think about it.

(e) The conditions require that f be *positive*, *increasing*, and *concave down* for all x. This is impossible, for the same reason as in (d): a graph that's concave down can't stay above the x-axis forever.

(f) The conditions mean that for positive x, f is *positive*, *increasing*, and *concave down*. The function $f(x) = \ln(x+1)$ has all these properties.

(g) The function $f(x) = -(x-3)^4$ has a local maximum at $x = 3$ and $f''(3) = 0$. (By contrast, $g(x) = -(x-3)^2$, but $g''(3) = -2$. It's interesting to plot both functions together to see the difference: f is "flatter" than g at $x = 3$.)

□

Exercises

1. Let f be the function whose graph is shown below. Rank the six values -2, 0, 2, $f'(1)$, $f'(3)$, $f'(4)$ in increasing order.

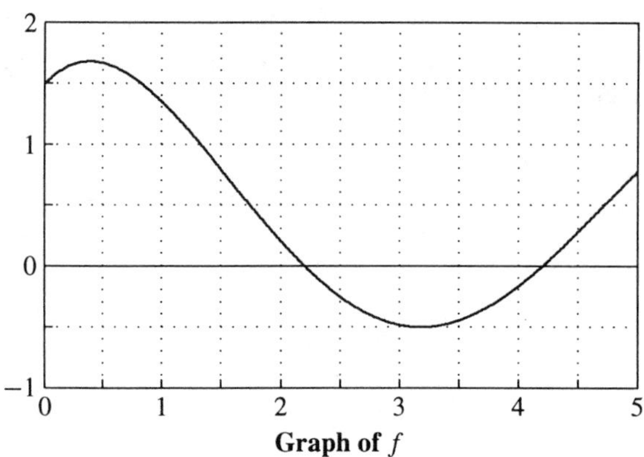

Graph of f

2. In each case, decide whether a function with the given properties exists. If so, sketch the graph of such a function. If not, explain why there cannot be such a function.

   (a) $\lim_{x\to\infty} f(x) = 5$ and $\lim_{x\to\infty} f'(x) = 1$.

   (b) $f(x) < 0$ and $f'(x) > 0$ for all x.

   (c) $f(x) < 0$ and $f'(x) < 0$ for all x.

   (d) $f''(x) > 0$ and $f(x) < 0$ for all x.

   (e) $f(x) > 0$, $f'(x) > 0$, and $f''(x) < 0$ for all x.

   (f) $f(x) > 0$, $f'(x) > 0$, and $f''(x) < 0$ for all $x > 0$.

   (g) $f(x)$ has a local maximum at $x = 3$ and $f''(3) = 0$.

3. A car travels on an east-west road. The function $D(t)$, plotted below, gives the car's distance (in miles) **east** of its starting point, at time t (in hours).

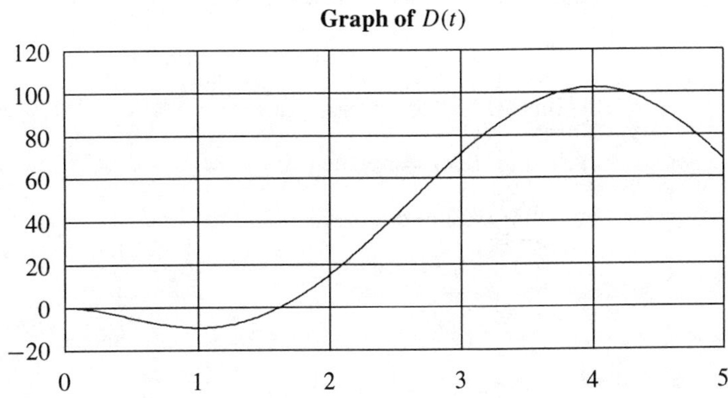

   (a) Estimate the car's velocity at $t = 2$. (Give units.) Which direction is the car traveling?

   (b) Find an inflection point on the graph. Carefully explain its significance in car talk.

   (c) At what time is the car moving fastest **westward**? How fast is this? How do you know?

4. A car travels on an east-west road. Let $D(t)$ represent the car's distance (in miles) east of a starting point at time t (in hours).

   (a) Interpret each of the following statements in car language; be careful with units.
   (i) $D(3) = -45$. (ii) $D'(3) = -45$. (iii) $D''(3) < 0$.

   (b) Interpret each of the following English statements in function notation, using D, D', and D'' as necessary.

      (i) The car decelerates over the interval from $t = 1$ to $t = 1.1$.

      (ii) At time $t = 2$ the car is 120 miles east of its starting point, traveling east at 42 mph and speeding up.

   (c) Draw a graph of $D(t)$ for $0 \le t \le 3$; the graph should incorporate all the information above.

5. Let g be the function

$$g(x) = \begin{cases} x^3 - 1, & \text{if } x \le -2 \\ \dfrac{2x-1}{x+2}, & \text{if } -2 < x \le 3 \\ \dfrac{-3x^4 + 2x - 65}{7x^5 - 6x^4 + 123}, & \text{if } x > 5 \end{cases}$$

(a) Evaluate $g(-2)$, $g(0)$, and $g(10)$.

(b) What is the domain of g?

(c) Evaluate $\lim_{x \to -\infty} g(x)$

(d) Evaluate $\lim_{x \to -2^-} g(x)$.

(e) Evaluate $\lim_{x \to -2^+} g(x)$.

(f) Does $\lim_{x \to -2} g(x)$ exist? Explain.

(g) Evaluate $\lim_{x \to \infty} g(x)$.

6. Indicate whether each of the following statements is true or false. If a statement is false, explain why it is false.

(a) $\lim_{x \to \infty} f(x) = -2$ implies that the graph of f has a vertical asymptote.

(b) $\lim_{x \to 3} g(x) = \infty$ implies that g has a vertical asymptote.

(c) If $\lim_{x \to 2^+} h(x) = \infty$, then $\lim_{x \to 2^-} h(x) = \infty$.

(d) If $\lim_{x \to 2} h(x) = \infty$, then $\lim_{x \to 2^+} h(x) = \infty$.

(e) $\lim_{x \to -1^+} \dfrac{x+3}{x^2 - 1} = \infty$.

(f) $\lim_{x \to \infty} \dfrac{4x^3 - 2x + 1}{2x^3 + 4x + 5} = 0$

7. The graph of the *derivative* of a certain function f appears below. *The graph of f itself is not shown!* Indicate clearly how you arrived at each answer below.

Graph of f'

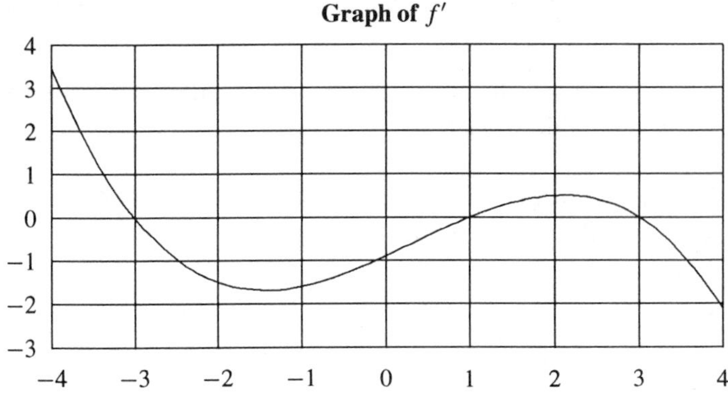

(a) Suppose that $f(1) = 5$. Find an equation of the **tangent line** to the f-graph at the point $(1, 5)$.

(b) Estimate $f''(-3)$. Show work.

(c) At which values of x does the f-graph have **inflection points**? Why?

(d) On what interval(s) within $[-4, 4]$ is f **increasing**? Why?

(e) Describe what happens on the f-graph at $x = -3$ and at $x = 1$.

(f) Among the graphs shown below, which could be f''? (Mark your answer clearly.)

Which is f''?

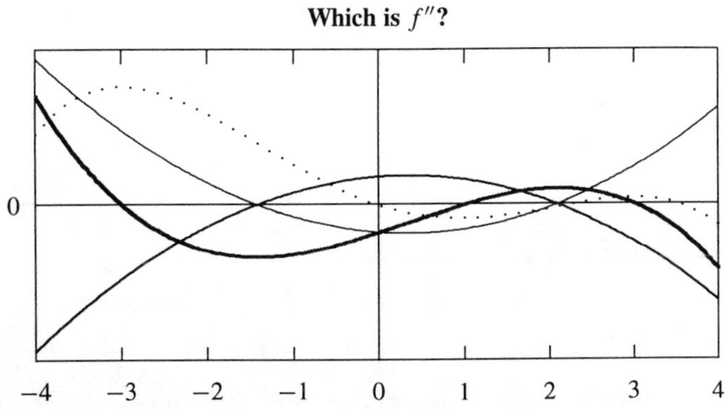

(g) Among the graphs above, which could be f? (Mark your answer clearly.)

8. Let f be any function and $x = 3$ a point of its domain. State carefully the **limit definition** of $f'(3)$. Then state in **one complete English sentence**—complete with appropriate capital letters, punctuation, spelling, etc.—exactly what $f'(3)$ tells us about the graph of f.

9. All parts of this problem refer to the function f defined by $f(x) = x^2 + 2$.

   (a) Use the limit definition to calculate $f'(3)$. (Show all algebraic work carefully. Don't forget to use "lim" wherever it's necessary.)

   (b) Find the slope of the **secant line** to the graph of f from $x = 3$ to $x = 3.01$.

10. Throughout this problem let $f(x) = \ln x$, $g(x) = x^2 + 2$, $h(x) = x + 2$.

    (a) On the same axes, draw graphs of f and $f \circ h$. (Very rough graphs are OK—the general shape is all that's needed.)

    (b) Write a formula for each of the following: (i) $f \circ g \circ h$; (ii) $g \circ f \circ h$; (iii) $f^{-1} \circ h$.

    (c) Choose any **one** of the functions from the previous part. Say which one and state its **domain**. (No explanation needed.)

    (d) Express each of the following functions as a composite of one or more of f, g, and h. (i) $l(x) = \ln(x) + 2$; (ii) $(\ln(x + 2))^2 + 3$.

11. Below is part of the graph of the rational function $r(x) = \dfrac{(3x^2+3)(x-3)}{4x(x+1)(x-2)} = \dfrac{3x^3-9x^2+3x-9}{4x^3-4x^2-8x}$. (The axes aren't marked with units, but you don't need them in this problem!)

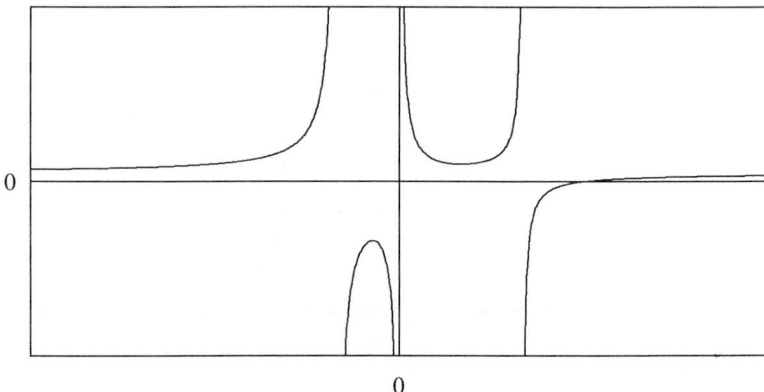

(a) Find *all* the **roots** of r. Label carefully any roots that appear on the graph. (If any roots lie outside the graph window, say so.)

(b) Find $\lim_{x\to\infty} r(x)$ and $\lim_{x\to-\infty} r(x)$. Show algebraic work carefully.

(c) Carefully draw all **horizontal asymptotes** (if there are any) on the graph. Label each one with its equation.

(d) Find and draw all **vertical asymptotes** (if there are any) on the graph. Label each one with its equation.

(e) For each vertical asymptote you found in the previous part, write down one **infinite limit** that corresponds to that asymptote. (No explanation needed.)

12. For some unaccountable reason, Eta wants to use 100 yards of fencing to build a rectangular pen with two vertical partitions. (Draw a picture first!) Advise Eta how to proceed.

13. Let f be the function whose graph is shown below.

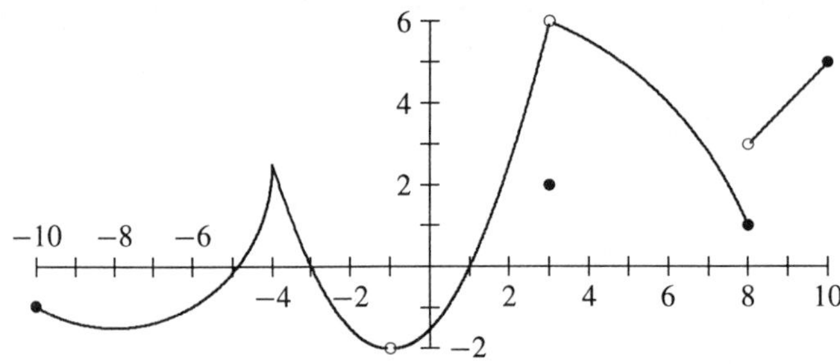

(a) Which of the values −4, 3, and 6 are in the domain of f?

(b) Which of the values −4, 3, and 6 are in the range of f?

(c) Where is f continuous? (Express your answer using interval notation.)

(d) For which values of a does $\lim_{x\to a} f(x)$ not exist?

(e) For which values of b does $\lim_{x\to b^-} f(x) \neq \lim_{x\to b^+} f(x)$?

(f) For which values of b does $\lim_{x \to b^-} f(x) \neq f(b)$?

(g) Estimate $\lim_{x \to -3} f(x)$.

(h) Is 5 an upper bound on the value of $|f(x)|$ when $x \in [-10, 2]$?

14. Let $f(x) = \begin{cases} x - 2 & \text{if } x < 0 \\ \sqrt{x+1} & \text{if } x \geq 0 \end{cases}$.

Evaluate each of the following limits.

(a) $\lim_{x \to 0^+} f(x)$

(b) $\lim_{x \to 0^-} f(x)$

(c) $\lim_{x \to 0} f(x^2)$

15. Let $g(x) = \dfrac{x^2 + 3x}{x^2 + x + 6}$.

(a) Explain why $x^2 + x + 6 > x^2$ when $x \in [3, \infty)$.

(b) Use part (a) to show that $g(x) < 1 + 3/x$ when $x \in [3, \infty)$.

(c) If $x \in (3, \infty)$, then $3x > x + 6$. Use this fact to show that $g(x) > 1$ when $x \in (3, \infty)$.

(d) It is a fact that $\lim_{x \to \infty} g(x) = 1$. Explain why this doesn't contradict the result in part (c).

16. Let f be the function shown below, F be an antiderivative of f, and suppose that $F(0) = 10$. (The function f has a local maximum at $x = 1.14$, a point of inflection at $x = 4.67$, and a local minimum at $x = 8.19$.)

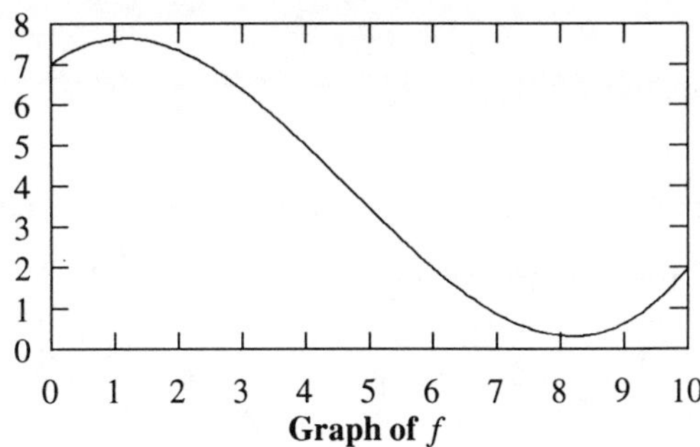

Graph of f

(a) Estimate $f'(5)$.

(b) Over which intervals, if any, is f' increasing?

(c) What is the slope of the F-graph at $x = 4$?

(d) Is F concave up at $x = 6$?

(e) At which values of x, if any, does F have points of inflection?

(f) Where in the interval $[0, 10]$ does F achieve its largest value? Its smallest value?

(g) Is it possible that $F(5) = 5$?

(h) Is it possible that $F(5) = 15$?

17. Suppose that a car is traveling on a straight east-west road. Let $D(t)$ represent the car's distance (in miles) east of a certain reference point at time t (in hours).

    (a) Translate each of the following statements about the function D into a sentence about the car. (Be sure to include units in your answers.)

    (i) $D(3) = 50$

    (ii) $D'(3) = 50$

    (iii) $D''(3) > 0$

    (b) Interpret the information contained in the following sentence in terms of the function D and its derivatives: *At time $t = 2$ the car is 30 miles east of the reference point, traveling west at 65 miles per hour, and slowing down.*

18. The graph of the derivative of a certain function f appears below.

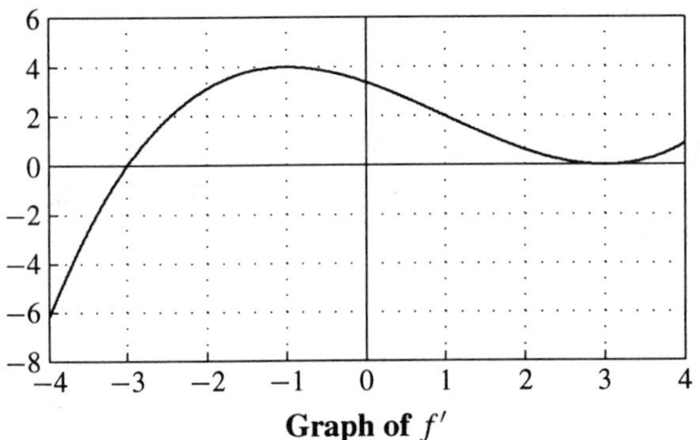

Graph of f'

    (a) Suppose $f(1) = 5$. Find an equation of the line tangent to the graph of f at $(1, 5)$.

    (b) Suppose $f(-1) = -2$. Could $f(3) = -6$?

    (c) Estimate $f''(-3)$.

    (d) At which values of x does $f(x)$ have points of inflection?

    (e) At which value of x in the interval $[-4, 4]$ does $f(x)$ achieve its largest value? Its smallest value?

    (f) Let F be an antiderivative of f. Where is F concave up? Concave down?

    (g) Suppose $f(-3) = 1$. Where is F increasing? Decreasing?

    (h) Suppose instead that $f(4) = -1$. Now, where is F increasing? Decreasing?

19. Let f be the function defined by

$$f(x) = \begin{cases} \pi, & \text{if } x \text{ is } \textit{not} \text{ an integer} \\ -6, & \text{if } x \text{ is an odd integer} \\ 3, & \text{if } x \text{ is an even integer.} \end{cases}$$

    Also, let $g(x) = f(3x/5)$, and $h(x) = \frac{4}{3}f(x)$.

    (a) Is f even, odd, or neither? Justify your answer.

    (b) Explain why f is a periodic function and find its period.

(c) Is g periodic? If so, explain why and find its period. If not, explain why it is not.

(d) Evaluate $g(5)$.

(e) Evaluate $\lim_{x \to 2} h(x)$.

20. Sketch the graph of a function f with *all* of the following properties

(i) $\lim_{x \to 4} f(x) = 0$

(ii) The range of f is $(-\infty, \infty)$.

(iii) $\lim_{x \to \infty} f(x) = 3$

(iv) $\lim_{x \to -\infty} f(x) = -3$

(v) The domain of f is $(-\infty, -2) \cup (-2, \infty)$.

(vi) $\lim_{x \to -2^+} f(x) = \infty$

(vii) $\lim_{x \to -2^-} f(x) = -\infty$

(viii) $f(4) = -5$

21. Using a calculator set in *degree* mode, estimate $\lim_{x \to 0} \dfrac{\sin x}{x}$. Have you seen this number before? [HINT: Express $\pi/180$ as a decimal number.]

22. (a) Using a calculator (set in *radian* mode!), estimate

$$\lim_{x \to 0} \frac{\sin(3x)}{x} .$$

(b) Let $u = ax$ where a is a nonzero real number. Show that

$$\lim_{u \to 0} \frac{\sin u}{u} = 1 \implies \lim_{x \to 0} \frac{\sin(ax)}{x} = a .$$

[HINT: $\lim_{u \to 0} (\sin u)/u = \lim_{x \to 0} \big(\sin(ax)\big)/(ax)$.]

23. Prove that $|\sin x| \le |x|$ for all x. [HINT: First prove that $\sin x \le x$ for all $x \ge 0$.]

Chapter 3

More on Functions and their Derivatives

3.1 New functions from old

Operations

Ordinary addition, as in $2+3=5$, is an **operation on numbers**: two "old" numbers are "operated on" to produce a "new" number. Subtraction, multiplication, division, and negation➻ are also operations on numbers. Each begins with one or more old numbers and—somehow or other—produces a new number.

Multiplication by negative 1.

Operations on functions are similar to operations on numbers. *Addition*, for instance, makes sense for functions: The function $h(x) = x + \cos x$ is, in a natural way, the *sum* of the functions $f(x) = \cos x$ and $g(x) = x$.

Every mathematical operation, whether on numbers or on functions, starts with one or more objects of some type and produces a new object *of the same type*. For functions the key idea is this:

> *An operation on functions accepts one or more* functions *as input, and produces a new* function *as output.*

Operations on functions: the machine view

Schematic diagrams like these—

$$x \longrightarrow \boxed{f} \longrightarrow f(x) \qquad\qquad x \longrightarrow \boxed{\text{sqr}} \longrightarrow x^2$$

represent functions as "input-output machines"—accepting inputs and producing outputs.➻ From this "mechanical" point of view, function operations hook simple machines together to produce fancier new ones.

The first function name is "generic"; the second refers to the squaring function.

A literal function machine. The boxes we use to represent functions in our machine diagrams resemble the function keys on a scientific calculator. This is a coincidence, but a happy one: calculator function keys, such as SIN, nicely illustrate the idea of a function machine. Pressing the SIN key takes an *input*—the displayed number—does something to it, and returns an *output*—the new display.

Adding machines

The picture below represents function *addition*: two function machines, f and g, are linked in "parallel" to form a new function machine, h:

Building a new function machine: addition

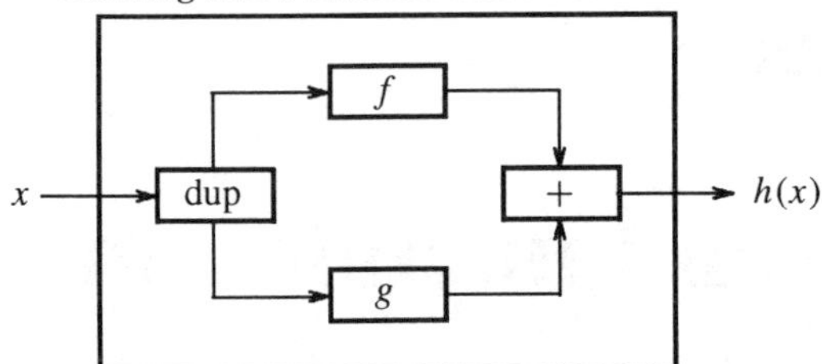

The first box *duplicates* an input x, because one copy is needed for each of f and g. The last box *adds* its two inputs. The large outer box represents the *new* function, h. Its presence emphasizes that the sum of two functions is another *function*.

The definition of function addition makes precise what the picture shows:

The other algebraic operations have similar definitions, and similar machine diagrams. We'll handle them less formally.

> **Definition:** Let f and g be two functions. Their sum, denoted $f+g$, is the new function defined by the rule
>
> $$(f+g)(x) = f(x) + g(x).$$

Algebraic operations on functions

Algebraic operations—addition, subtraction, multiplication, and division—on symbolically defined functions are simple and familiar. The following table illustrates various operations applied to the functions f and g defined by $f(x) = \cos x$ and $g(x) = x$.

Algebraic Operations on Functions

Operation	*Output*	*Rule*	*Domain*
addition	$f+g$	$\cos(x)+x$	$(-\infty, \infty)$
subtraction	$f-g$	$\cos(x)-x$	$(-\infty, \infty)$
multiplication	$f \cdot g$	$x\cos(x)$	$(-\infty, \infty)$
division	f/g	$\cos(x)/x$	$\{x \mid x \neq 0\}$

The table contains few surprises, but note:

- Each output is a new *function*; its rule appears in the third column.
- The domain of f/g is smaller than the domains of f and g: f and g accept *any* input x, but the quotient makes sense only if $g(x) \neq 0$.

Algebraic operations on "other" functions

As we've stressed before, not all functions *have* symbolic formulas. The next example shows that algebraic operations make sense for almost *any* real-valued functions.

■ **Example 1.** Let f be defined by the formula $f(x) = x^2 + 3/x$, and let g be defined by the table

x	-3	-2	-1	0	1	2	3	4
$g(x)$	-4	-9	-1	2	0	8	3	-2

Find the domains of $f + g$, $f \cdot g$, and f/g.

Solution: Consider $f + g$ first. The expression $f(x) + g(x)$ makes good sense if—but only if—both summands do. Thus,

$$(f + g)(1) = f(1) + g(1) = 4 + 0 = 4,$$

but $(f + g)(42) = f(42) + g(42)$ is undefined.

Because $g(x)$ is defined only for *integers* between -3 and 4, and $f(x)$ only for *nonzero* numbers, the sum $f(x)+g(x)$ is defined only for x in the set $\{-3, -2, -1, 1, 2, 3\}$—the intersection of the domains of f and g.

The domain of f/g is even smaller. Since $f(x)/g(x)$ is undefined whenever $g(x) = 0$, $x = 1$ is taboo as input.

The following table says all there is to know about $f + g$, $f \cdot g$, and f/g; gaps in the table reflect gaps in the functions' respective domains:➸

The domain of any algebraic combination of f and g is no larger than the intersection of the domains of f and g.

Algebraic Combinations of "Other" Functions

x	-3	-2	-1	0	1	2	3	4
$f(x)$	8	$5/2$	-2		4	$11/2$	10	$67/4$
$g(x)$	-4	-9	-1	2	0	8	3	-2
$(f+g)(x)$	4	$-13/2$	-3		4	$27/2$	13	$59/4$
$(f \cdot g)(x)$	-32	$-45/2$	2		0	44	30	$-67/2$
$(f/g)(x)$	-2	$-5/18$	2			$11/16$	$10/3$	$-67/8$

□

Composition

Let f and g be defined by $f(x) = x^2$ and $g(x) = \cos x$. The new functions

$$h(x) = \cos(x^2) \quad \text{and} \quad k(x) = (\cos x)^2$$

are constructed from f and g by **composition**, i.e., by following one with the other. More precisely:

> **Definition:** Let f and g be functions. The **composition** of f and g, denoted $f \circ g$, is the function defined by the rule
>
> $$(f \circ g)(x) = f(g(x)) .$$

For the functions f, g, h, and k given above:

$$(f \circ g)(x) = f(g(x)) = f(\cos x) = (\cos x)^2 = k(x);$$
$$(g \circ f)(x) = g(f(x)) = g\left(x^2\right) = \cos(x^2) = h(x).$$

Note:

Order of composition matters. If $f(x) = \sqrt{x}$ and $g(x) = x + 5$, then

$$\begin{aligned}(f \circ g)(x) &= f(x+5) = \sqrt{x+5}\,;\\ (g \circ f)(x) &= g\left(\sqrt{x}\right) = \sqrt{x} + 5\,.\end{aligned}$$

The two functions $f \circ g$ and $g \circ f$ are genuinely different. For instance, $(f \circ g)(4) = \sqrt{9} = 3$, but $(g \circ f)(4) = \sqrt{4} + 5 = 7$. The moral: *Order matters. For most functions f and g, $f \circ g \neq g \circ f$.*

The machine diagram below illustrates the idea: A legal input to $f \circ g$ mus pass successfully through the whole contraption.

Domains. A legal input x to $f \circ g$ must, first, be a legal input to g. To keep things moving, the output $g(x)$ must also be a legal input to f. Thus the domain of $f \circ g$ is a *subset* of the domain of g. For the functions above, the domains of $f \circ g$ and $g \circ f$ are, respectively, the intervals $[-5, \infty)$ and $[0, \infty)$.

Composition: function machines in series

The machine picture of composition is especially simple:

Mechanical composition

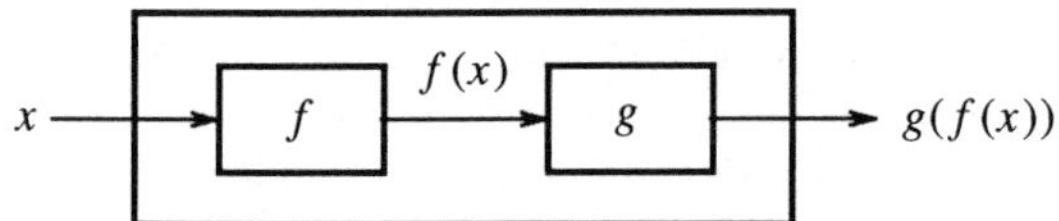

The machines f and g are linked "in series"—the output of f "piped" through g.

Pipes. Computer operating systems "compose" computer programs: the *output* of one program is often used as *input* to another. The ideas, and even the jargon, are similar to those mathematicians use. For example, the output from a word-processing program might be "piped" to a printing program to produce a paper copy. Such processes are so common that the UNIX computer operating system reserves the | symbol to indicate a "pipe."

Composing functions defined by formulas: substitution

Composing functions defined by explicit symbolic formulas, such as $f(x) = x + 2$ and $g(x) = \sin x$, is easy:

$$(f \circ g)(x) = \sin(x) + 2\,; \qquad (g \circ f)(x) = \sin(x+2)\,.$$

Like f and g themselves, the composite functions $f \circ g$ and $g \circ f$ have explicit formulas. Finding these formulas amounts to *substituting* one symbolic expression into another.

Composing "other" functions

Below we illustrate various ways of composing functions that are *not* given by formulas. The common thread among these disparate-seeming examples is the idea of composition itself.

■ **Example 2.** **(Composing with a tabular function.)** Let $f(x) = x + 2$; let g be defined by the table

x	-3	-2	-1	0	1	2	3	4
$g(x)$	-4	-9	-1	2	0	8	3	-2

Describe the functions $f \circ g$ and $g \circ f$.

Solution: Since $f(x) = x + 2$,

$$(f \circ g)(x) = g(x) + 2 \qquad \text{and} \qquad (g \circ f)(x) = g(x+2).$$

The formulas permit calculations like these:

$$\begin{aligned} (f \circ g)(2) &= g(2) + 2 = 8 + 2 = 10; \\ (g \circ f)(2) &= g(2+2) = g(4) = -2. \end{aligned}$$

But not just *any* input works:

$$(f \circ g)(10) = g(10) + 2$$

is undefined.

The problem is with *domains*. Although f accepts *any* real number as input, g has a tiny domain—the finite set $\{-3, -2, \ldots, 3, 4\}$. The effect is to restrict sharply the domains of both $f \circ g$ and $g \circ f$.

Which inputs pass safely through the composite functions $f \circ g$ and $g \circ f$? As we said above, only g presents an obstruction, so the domain of $f \circ g$ is the domain of g.

The domain of $g \circ f$ is different. Because $(g \circ f)(x) = g(x + 2)$, an input x survives the trip through f and g only if $x + 2$ is in the domain of g, i.e., only if $x \in \{-5, -4, \ldots, 2\}$.

The following table gives full details on both $g \circ f$ and $f \circ g$; gaps in the table reflect gaps in the respective domains:

Composition with a Tabular Function

x	-5	-4	-3	-2	-1	0	1	2	3	4
$g(x)$			-4	-9	-1	2	0	8	3	-2
$(f \circ g)(x)$			-2	-7	1	4	2	10	5	0
$(g \circ f)(x)$	-4	-9	-1	2	0	8	3	-2		

□

■ **Example 3.** **(Composing two graphical functions.)** Let f and g be the functions shown below:

Both f and g actually have fairly simple formulas. Try to guess them if you like, but here the graphs are the point.

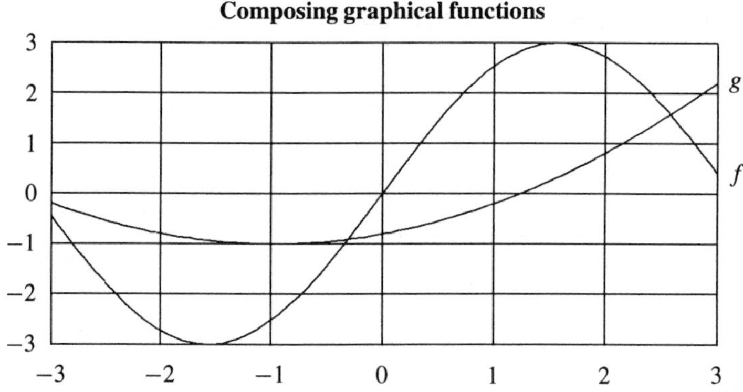

Find approximate values of the composite function $f \circ g$ for integer inputs in $[-3, 3]$; use them to sketch a graph. Is there an x for which $(f \circ g)(x) = 0$?

Verify these estimates for yourself.

Solution: By definition, $(f \circ g)(3) = f(g(3))$. Reading approximate values from the graphs gives

$$(f \circ g)(3) = f(g(3)) \approx f(2.1) \approx 2.6.$$

We chose f and g carefully. To permit computing values of $f \circ g$, all outputs of g must be legal inputs to f. What property of the graphs assured this?

Similar graphical estimates produced this table of values:

Composing Graphical Functions							
x	-3	-2	-1	0	1	2	3
$(f \circ g)(x)$	-0.6	-2.2	-2.5	-2.2	-0.6	2.2	2.6

It's shown in bold style.

With enough such data, we can plot $f \circ g$. We've done so below; the tabulated data points are "bulleted" for reference:

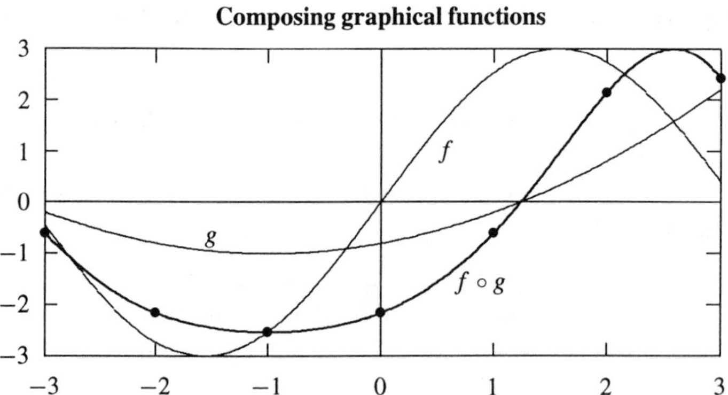

□

■ **Example 4. (Composing functions described in words.)** Motoring across Montana from Billings to Missoula, one's *altitude* (measured in feet above sea level) varies with *distance* traveled (in miles from Missoula). Distance, in turn, varies with *time* (in hours since departure), so altitude *also* varies with time. Interpret the situation in the language of functions and composition.

Solution: Let A, d, and t denote altitude, distance, and time. Altitude is a *function*, say f, of distance; distance is another *function*, say g, of time. In function notation,

$$A = f(d) \qquad \text{and} \qquad d = g(t).$$

The composite function

$$A(t) = (f \circ g)(t) = f(g(t))$$

represents altitude as a function of time. □

Composition, limits, and continuity

Limits often involve functions built up by composition, so it's helpful to know how the operations of composition and taking limits interact. First, some straightforward examples, chosen to illustrate the questions involved.

■ **Example 5.** Find and discuss each limit below:

Guess all three limits before reading on. With any luck you'll guess correctly.

$$L_1 = \lim_{x\to 0} \ln(\cos x); \qquad L_2 = \lim_{x\to 0} \ln\left(\frac{\sin x}{x}\right); \qquad L_3 = \lim_{x\to\infty} \exp\left(\frac{x+1}{x+2}\right).$$

Solution: The first limit is easiest:

$$\text{As } x \to 0,\ \cos x \to \cos 0, \text{ so } \ln(\cos x) \to \ln(\cos 0) = \ln 1 = 0.$$

Why did things work so well? Because both functions involved are *continuous* at the points that matter: As $x \to 0$, $\cos x \to \cos 0$ *because the cosine function is continuous at* $x = 0$; as $\cos x \to 1$, $\ln(\cos x) \to \ln 1$ *because the natural logarithm function is continuous at* $x = 1$.

To find L_2 we'll reason similarly. Recall, first, that as $x \to 0$, $(\sin x)/x \to 1$. Therefore:

We've used this fact repeatedly; see, e.g., Example 4, page 153, for graphical and numerical evidence.

$$\text{As } x \to 0,\ \frac{\sin x}{x} \to 1, \text{ so } \ln\left(\frac{\sin x}{x}\right) \to \ln 1 = 0.$$

Continuity helps again: Because ln is continuous at $x = 1$,

$$\frac{\sin x}{x} \to 1 \implies \ln\left(\frac{\sin x}{x}\right) \to \ln 1.$$

The limit L_3 is "at infinity," but the same sort of reasoning applies as for L_1 and L_2:

Convince yourself of the first implication.

$$x \to \infty \implies \frac{x+1}{x+2} \to 1 \implies \exp\left(\frac{x+1}{x+2}\right) \to \exp(1) = e.$$

Again, continuity is key: The second implication holds because the exponential function is continuous at $x = 1$. □

Limits of composite functions: a general principle. One basic principle applies to all three limits in the previous example. We'll state it below in general terms. (The formal proof, which we omit, appeals to the ϵ–δ definition of limit.)

In the Fact below, any of a, b, and c may be $\pm\infty$.

> **Fact: (Limit of a composite function.)** Let f and g be functions, such that $\lim_{x\to a} g(x) = b$ and $\lim_{x\to b} f(x) = c$. Then
>
> $$\lim_{x\to a} (f \circ g)(x) = c.$$

We used this fact repeatedly in Example 5.

The precise version says exactly where f and g must be continuous.

Composing continuous functions. Recall that, by definition, a function f is continuous at a point $x = a$ if and only if $\lim_{x \to a} f(x) = f(a)$. With this definition and the Fact above, it's easy to show that if f and g are continuous functions, then so is $f \circ g$. More precisely:

> **Theorem 1.** Suppose that g is continuous at $x = a$ and f is continuous at $g(a)$. Then $f \circ g$ is continuous at $x = a$.

Proof. If $x \to a$, $g(x) \to g(a)$, because g is continuous at a. As $g(x) \to g(a)$, $f(g(x)) \to f(g(a))$, because f is continuous at $g(a)$. Putting everything together,

$$x \to a \implies (f \circ g)(x) \to (f \circ g)(a).$$

That's exactly what we needed to show. □

The identity function

The numbers 0 and 1 are **identities** for (ordinary) addition and multiplication because

$$a + 0 = 0 + a = a \qquad \text{and} \qquad a \cdot 1 = 1 \cdot a = a$$

for any real number a.

A similar notion of identity applies for composition. Composition is an operation on *functions*, so an identity for composition must also be a *function*. We'll denote the **identity function** by I; I has a simple definition:

We'll assume that all functions here have sets of real numbers as their domain and range. This does no harm, and skirts distracting technicalities.

As a function machine I is just a hollow tube; inputs pass through unchanged.

> **Definition:** The **identity function** for composition is defined by the rule
> $$I(x) = x\,.$$

To deserve the name "identity function," I should satisfy the equations $f \circ I = I \circ f = f$. It does; for any input x,

$$(f \circ I)(x) = f(I(x)) = f(x) \qquad \text{and} \qquad (I \circ f)(x) = I(f(x)) = f(x)\,.$$

In words:

Composing any function f with I, in either order, leaves f unchanged.

Inverse functions

The word **inverse** has various meanings in mathematics. The numbers 3 and -3 are *additive* inverses because their *sum* is 0, the additive identity. Similarly, 3 and $1/3$ are *multiplicative* inverses because their *product* is 1, the multiplicative identity.

The term **inverse function** has yet another meaning. Two *functions* f and g are inverses if *composing* them—regardless of order—gives the identity function. Thus the inverse of a *function* f is another *function*, denoted f^{-1}, that "undoes" the effect of the original function f.

Beware: $f^{-1}(x) \neq 1/f(x)$.

The following examples illustrate the idea of inverse function in the best—and worst—possible cases.

f adds three; f^{-1} takes it away.

■ **Example 6.** If $f(x) = x + 3$, then $f^{-1}(x) = x - 3$. For any input x,

$$\begin{aligned}\left(f^{-1} \circ f\right)(x) &= f^{-1}(x+3) = (x+3) - 3 = x;\\ \left(f \circ f^{-1}\right)(x) &= f(x-3) = (x-3) + 3 = x.\end{aligned}$$

In other words, $f^{-1} \circ f = I = f \circ f^{-1}$—as required, both compositions give the identity function. □

■ **Example 7.** Let f be the *constant* function $f(x) = 3$. This f *has no inverse*. The problem is that for *any* function g, $f \circ g$ is *still* a constant function;➻ thus $f \circ g$ *can't* be the identity function $I(x)$. Specifically, if g is any function and x any input, then

$$(f \circ g)(x) = f(g(x)) = 3. \qquad \square$$

Composition with a constant function always produces a constant function. Do you see why?

Here is the scrupulously correct definition:

> **Definition:** Let f and g be functions. If the equations
>
> $$(f \circ g)(x) = x \quad \text{and} \quad (g \circ f)(x) = x$$
>
> hold for all x in the domains of f and g respectively, then f and g are **inverse functions**. In this case, we write $g = f^{-1}$ (and $f = g^{-1}$).

Notice:

Machine views. Viewing f and g as function machines, the definition says this:

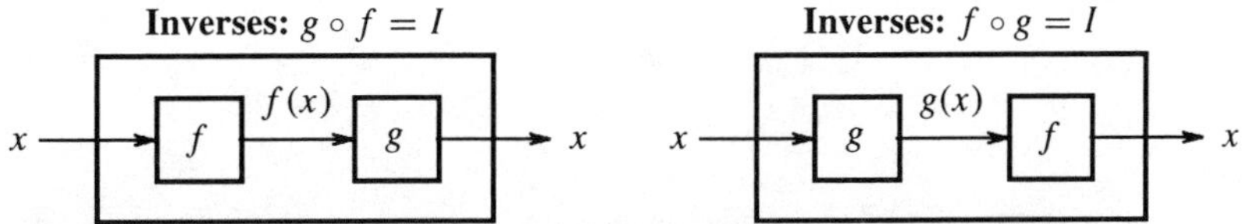

In effect the machine g is really the machine f running in reverse.

Famous inverses: logs and exponentials. Logarithm and exponential functions with the same base are the most important and useful examples of inverse functions.➻ Indeed, we've *defined* logarithms as inverses of exponentials.➻ In base e, for instance, the natural logarithm function is defined by the condition

$$y = \ln x \iff x = e^y.$$

Similarly, in base 10, $y = \log_{10} x \iff x = 10^y$.➻

We reviewed these functions in Section 1.5. See the graphs on page 4.

See Appendix F for more details.

Notice how log and exponential keys appear in "inverse" positions on a calculator keypad.

Equivalent conditions. If f and g are inverse functions, then

$$f(a) = b \iff g(b) = a,$$

for every a in the domain of f.

Domains and ranges. If f and g are inverses, then inputs to g are outputs from f and *vice versa*. Therefore the domain of f is the range of g, and the range of f is the domain of g.

Which functions have inverses?

We saw above that the constant function $f(x) = 3$ has no inverse function.➻ Which functions *do* have inverses?

Does every number have an additive inverse? A multiplicative inverse?

One-to-one functions. Every function f, invertible or not, sets up a correspondence between its domain and its range—to an input x from the domain, f assigns $f(x)$, one member of the range. An inverse function—if one exists—*reverses* this correspondence. To be invertible, therefore, f must be **one-to-one**, i.e., each output may correspond to *only one* input. A constant function fails this test—miserably: it sends *every* input to the same output.

Recognizing invertibility graphically

Graphically speaking, one-to-one functions are those that pass the **horizontal line test**:

No horizontal line crosses the graph more than once.

The test guarantees that every possible output y corresponds to no more that one input x.

Any function that's **strictly monotonic** (i.e., either strictly increasing or strictly decreasing, but not both) on its domain clearly passes this test, and so has an inverse.

Think about it graphically.

■ **Example 8.** Functions $f(x) = x^2$ and $h(x) = 2x + 3$ appear graphically below. Is either function invertible? If so, find its inverse.

$f(x) = x^2$: not one-to-one **$h(x) = 2x + 3$: one-to-one**

Solution: The function f is not one to one on the interval $[-3, 3]$, so it's not invertible on the domain $[-3, 3]$. The function h *is* one-to-one, and therefore invertible.

The graph of f fails the horizontal line test at $y = 4$, for example.

With algebra we can find an explicit formula for h^{-1}:

Check each step.

$$y = h^{-1}(x) \iff x = h(y) \iff x = 2y + 3 \iff y = h^{-1}(x) = \frac{x-3}{2}.$$

□

Inversion and symmetry

The definition of inverse function, interpreted graphically, says this:

A point (a, b) lies on the graph of f if and only if (b, a)—the reflection of (a, b) across the line $y = x$—lies on the graph of f^{-1}.

Graphs of h and h^{-1} from the previous example illustrate what this means:

Graphs of h and h^{-1}

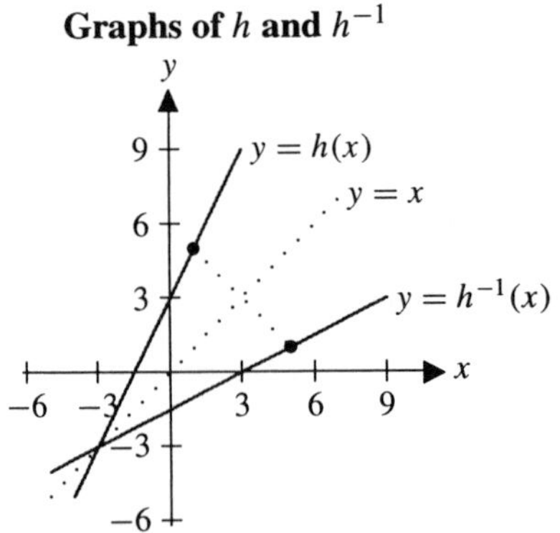

The two graphs are *symmetric* about the line $y = x$: every point on either graph is the "mirror image" of a point on the other. One symmetric pair of points—$(1, 5)$ and $(5, 1)$—is shown bulleted.

The graphs look symmetric because equal scales are used on the two axes.

The moral for people: To sketch graphs, exploit symmetry. To draw the graph of f^{-1}, a human with good geometric sense will exploit the symmetry property above and "reflect" the graph of f about the line $y = x$. With straight lines, this is easy; with other graphs, it can be hard.

The moral for computers: To sketch graphs, reverse coordinates. Most computers, being stupid but energetic, graph a function by plotting many, many points. An equally humble strategy draws *inverse* functions: For each original plot point (a, b), plot the "reflected" point (b, a). That strategy generated the pair of graphs above.

Restricting domains to make functions invertible

Is the function $f(x) = x^2$ invertible? Above we said no, judging from the graph over the interval $[-3, 3]$. But why isn't $g(x) = \sqrt{x}$ an inverse function?

Resolving this quandary requires a closer look at *domains*. We'll take one in the next example.

Ambiguous domains. Defining a function, we recall, means specifying both a rule *and* a domain. From this point of view, speaking of "the function $f(x) = x^2$" is technically ambiguous—it specifies a rule for f, but not a domain.

Such ambiguity about domains is usually harmless. The matter of inverses is an exception—*restricting* a function's domain suitably can make it one-to-one, and therefore invertible.

■ **Example 9.** Make careful sense of the functions $f(x) = x^2$ and $g(x) = \sqrt{x}$ as inverses. Compare the derivatives of f and g at the "symmetric points" $(2, 4)$ and $(4, 2)$.

Solution: The function $f(x) = x^2$ is *not* one-to-one➸ on its *natural* domain—the full set of real numbers. However, f *is* one-to-one if its domain is restricted to *nonnegative* inputs. With this restriction f *is* invertible, and has the expected inverse $g(x) = \sqrt{x}$, as the following graphs show:➸

Generally it's "two-to-one." Do you understand why?

Check algebraically, too, that $(f \circ g)(x) = x = (g \circ f)(x)$ for all appropriate values of x.

Inverses: $f(x) = x^2$, $g(x) = \sqrt{x}$, and two tangent lines

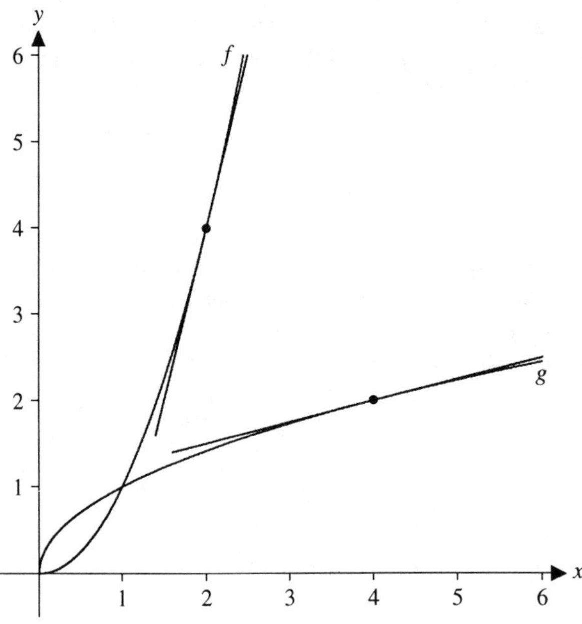

As expected, because f and g are inverses.

Convince yourself of this.

The bulleted points on the graphs show that $f(2) = 4$ and $g(4) = 2$. At these points, tangent line segments are shown; they appear to have *reciprocal slopes.* The formulas for f' and g' say the same thing:

$$f'(x) = 2x \implies f'(2) = 4; \qquad g'(x) = \frac{1}{2\sqrt{x}} \implies g'(4) = \frac{1}{4}. \qquad \square$$

The example illustrates a useful principle about functions, inverses, and their derivatives:

> **Fact:** Let f be continuous and strictly monotonic on a domain interval I. Then f has a continuous inverse function, g, defined on the interval $f(I)$. If a is in I, $f(a) = b$, and $f'(a) \neq 0$, then
>
> $$g'(b) = \frac{1}{f'(a)}.$$

Exercises

1. Let $f(x) = \sin x$, $g(x) = x^2$, and $h(x) = x + 3$. Write each of the following functions as a composition of the functions f, g, and h. [NOTE: Some answers will not involve all three functions.]

(a) $\sin(x + 3)$

(b) $(x + 3)^2$

(c) $\sin^2 x$

(d) $\sin\left(x^2\right)$

(e) $x^2 + 3$

(f) $3 + \sin x$

(g) $\sin^2(x + 3)$

(h) $\sin\left((x + 3)^2\right)$

(i) $\sin\left(x^2\right) + 3$

(j) $\left(\sin(x + 3)\right)^2$

(k) x^4

(l) $x + 6$

2. Write each of the following functions as the composition of two (or more) "simpler" functions. For example, the function $h(x) = (x+1)^2$ can be written $h(x) = (f \circ g)(x)$ where $f(u) = u^2$ and $g(v) = v + 1$.

   (a) $h(x) = \left(x^3 - 4x + 5\right)^6$

   (b) $h(x) = \sqrt{(x+1)^3}$

   (c) $h(x) = \ln(2 + \sin x)$

   (d) $h(x) = e^{x^2}$

   (e) $h(x) = \sqrt{1 + e^x}$

   (f) $h(x) = \left|x^2 - 4\right|$

   (g) $h(x) = \sin\left(x^2 - 4x + 4\right)$

   (h) $h(x) = \cos^2 x + 4\cos x + 4$

3. Let $h(x)$ be the density of oxygen (in atoms/cm^3) in the air x meters above sea level, and $g(x)$ be the number of breaths per minute an average person has to take when the density of oxygen in the air is x atoms/cm^3. Which of the following tells us something useful: $g \circ h$ or $h \circ g$? What does it tell us?

4. Suppose that f is an odd function, g is an even function, and h is a function that is neither even nor odd, all with domain $\mathbb{R}$.

   (a) Let $j(x) = (h \circ g)(x)$. Is j even, odd, or neither? Explain.

   (b) Let $k(x) = (g \circ f)(x)$. Is k even, odd, or neither? Explain.

   (c) Let $m(x) = f(f(x))$. Is m even, odd, or neither? Explain.

5. Let $f(x) = \begin{cases} 0 & \text{if } x \neq 0 \\ \pi & \text{if } x = 0. \end{cases}$

   Evaluate each of the following limits.

   (a) $\lim_{x \to 0} f(x)$

   (b) $\lim_{x \to 0} \cos(f(x))$

   (c) $\lim_{x \to 0} f(\sin x)$

   (d) $\lim_{x \to 0} (f \circ f)(x)$

6. Let f be the function shown graphically below.

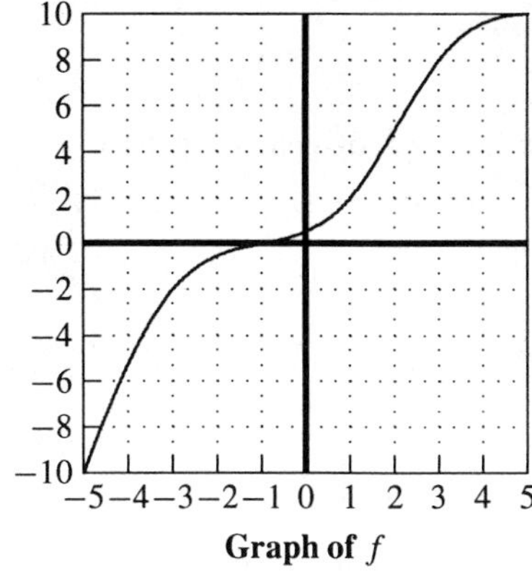

Graph of f

   (a) Explain why f is invertible.

   (b) What are the domain and range of f^{-1}?

   (c) Fill in the table below. (Because f is given graphically, your answers will be estimates.)

x	-3	0	2
$f^{-1}(x)$			
$f^{-1}(x+2)$			
$f^{-1}(x)+2$			
$2f^{-1}(x)$			
$f^{-1}(2x)$			

7. Find the domain, the range, and a symbolic expression for the inverse of each of the following functions. Also, sketch graphs of f and f^{-1} on the same axes. [HINT: In some cases you will need to restrict the domain of the given function to make it invertible.]

   (a) $f(x) = x^{1/3}$
   (b) $f(x) = -\sqrt{x}$
   (c) $f(x) = x^3 + 1$
   (d) $f(x) = 2 + 3x$
   (e) $f(x) = 1/x$
   (f) $f(x) = 2/(3+4x)$
   (g) $f(x) = \left(x^2+1\right)^2$
   (h) $f(x) = x/(x^2-4)$
   (i) $f(x) = x/(x-1)$
   (j) $f(x) = \sqrt{1-x^2}$
   (k) $f(x) = e^{x^2}$
   (l) $f(x) = \ln\bigl(x/(x+1)\bigr)$

8. For each of the following functions, find all values of the parameter k for which the function with domain $(-\infty, \infty)$ is invertible.

   (a) $f(x) = kx + \sin x$
   (b) $f(x) = kx + |x|$
   (c) $f(x) = kx^2 + e^x$

9. Let f be a continuous function with all of the following properties

   - The domain of f is $\mathbb{R}$
   - f is invertible
   - $f(1) = 2$
   - $\lim_{x\to\infty} f(x) = -\infty$
   - $\lim_{x\to-2} f(x) = 3$
   - $\lim_{x\to 7} f(x) = -5$

   (a) Sketch the graph of such a function.
   (b) Evaluate $f^{-1}(2)$.
   (c) Evaluate $\lim_{x\to 3} f^{-1}(x)$.
   (d) Let $g(x) = -4f(3x+1) + 5$. Evaluate $\lim_{x\to 2} g(x)$.

10. Suppose that f is a linear function that is one-to-one on an interval I. Show that f^{-1} is a linear function.

11. (a) Suppose that f is an invertible function and $g(x) = f(x+a)$. Show that $g^{-1}(x) = f^{-1}(x) - a$.
    (b) Use the result in part (a) to find an expression for f^{-1} if $f(x) = \ln(x+1)$.

12. (a) Suppose that f is an invertible function and $h(x) = f(ax)$. Show that $h^{-1}(x) = f^{-1}(x)/a$.

(b) Use the result in part (a) to find an expression for f^{-1} if $f(x) = e^{2x}$.

13. Suppose that f is a periodic function. Explain why f is not invertible on its natural domain.

14. Suppose that $h = f \circ g$ where f and g are invertible functions.

    (a) Show that $h^{-1} = g^{-1} \circ f^{-1}$.

    (b) Use the result in part (a) to obtain the result stated in Exercise 11.

    (c) Use the result in part (a) to obtain the result stated in Exercise 12.

15. Suppose that f is a continuous function that is one-to-one and concave up on an interval I. What additional condition on f allows you to conclude that f^{-1} is also concave up? [HINT: Consider $f(x) = e^x$ and $g(x) = e^{-x}$.]

16. Sketch the graph of a continuous function that is concave down but whose inverse is concave up.

17. Suppose that f is continuous and increasing on $(0, a)$, and that $\lim_{x \to a^-} f(x) = \infty$.

    (a) Explain why $\lim_{x \to \infty} f^{-1}(x) = a$.

    (b) Is $f^{-1}(1000)$ greater than, less than, or equal to a? Justify your answer.

18. Suppose that the line $y = a$ is a horizontal asymptote of the function f. What does this imply about f^{-1}?

19. Use the definition of the derivative to show that if f is differentiable at a, then f^{-1} is differentiable at b and $\left(f^{-1}\right)'(b) = 1/f'(a)$.

20. Suppose that f is differentiable and decreasing on an interval I. If $c \in I$, is $\left(f^{-1}\right)'(c)$ positive or negative? Justify your answer.

3.2 New derivatives from old: operations with constants

The theme of producing new functions from old runs throughout calculus. In Section 3.1 we discussed various operations—algebraic operations, composition, inversion, etc.—that produce new functions from old. In this section and the next we consider the problem of differentiating *any* function that is built from simpler functions using standard function operations.

The derivative of a "built-up" function f reflects—not surprisingly—both the *materials* from which f is built and the *operations* used to combine them. We've already seen this principle in action in simple cases.

■ **Example 1.** Let $f(x) = x^2 + 3\sin x$. What's $f'(x)$? Why?

We discussed them in Section 2.8.

Solution: According to the sum and constant rules,

$$f'(x) = \left(x^2 + 3 \cdot \sin x\right)' = \left(x^2\right)' + 3 \cdot (\sin x)' = 2x + 3\cos x.$$

If we let $g(x) = x^2$ and $h(x) = \sin x$, $f(x) = g(x) + 3 \cdot h(x)$, so the same result looks like this:

$$f'(x) = \left(g(x) + 3 \cdot h(x)\right)' = g'(x) + 3 \cdot h'(x).$$

In this (especially simple) case, f' is built from g' and h' *exactly* as f is built from g and h. □

Things aren't always so simple:

■ **Example 2.** Let $f(x) = x^2 \sin(x)$. What's $f'(x)$ now? Why?

Solution: It turns out that

$$f'(x) = 2x \cdot \sin x + x^2 \cdot \cos x.$$

To see that the method works in this case, plot f and f'.

We'll explain soon exactly how we computed f' and why the method works. At present the point is that the derivative of a product of two functions ($g(x) = x^2$ and $h(x) = \sin x$, here) is *not* just the product of their respective derivatives ($g'(x) = 2x$ and $h'(x) = \cos x$, here.)

On the contrary, the equation above suggests another pattern:

$$f'(x) = 2x \cdot \sin x + x^2 \cdot \cos x = g'(x) \cdot h(x) + g(x) \cdot h'(x).$$

The "product rule."

In the next section we'll state and defend this equation as a general rule. □

Derivatives and operations with constants

Given any function f and any constant a, we can form such new functions as

$$f(x+a), \quad f(x)+a, \quad f(a \cdot x), \quad \text{and} \quad a \cdot f(x).$$

In earlier sections we discussed the various effects on f and its graph—translation, stretching, squashing, etc. How do such operations with constants affect *derivatives*?

The following extended example illustrates the possibilities. This key insight may be helpful:

Suppose that a line L is tangent to a curve C at a point P. Stretching, squashing, horizontal translation, or vertical translation may alter L, C, and P, but the property of tangency remains: the new L remains tangent to the new C at the new P.

■ **Example 3.** A function f is defined by the first graph shown below. The tangent line at $x = 4$ also appears; it shows➻ that $f'(4) = -2$:

Convince yourself!

$f(x)$; $f'(4) = -2$

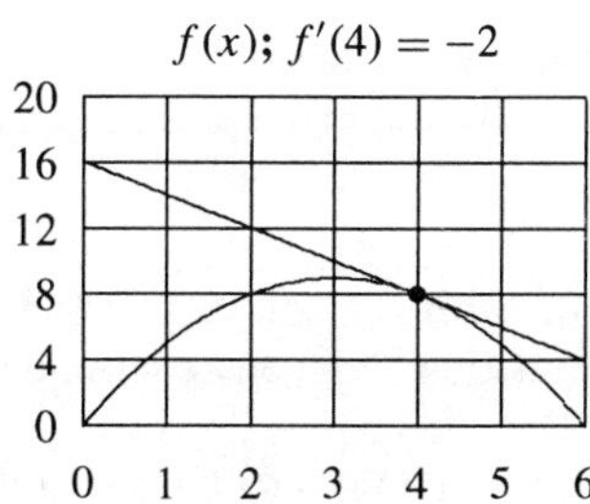

Using the constant $a = 2$, form the new functions

$$g(x) = f(x+2), \quad h(x) = f(x) + 2, \quad k(x) = f(2 \cdot x), \quad l(x) = 2 \cdot f(x).$$

What does the fact that $f'(4) = -2$ say about g', h', k', and l'? Interpret everything graphically.

Solution: Here are the graphs of g, h, k and l, each with a corresponding tangent line:

$g(x) = f(x+2)$; $g'(2) = f'(4) = -2$

$h(x) = f(x) + 2$; $h'(4) = f'(4) = -2$

$k(x) = f(2x)$; $k'(2) = 2f'(4) = -4$

$l(x) = 2f(x)$; $l'(4) = 2f'(4) = -4$

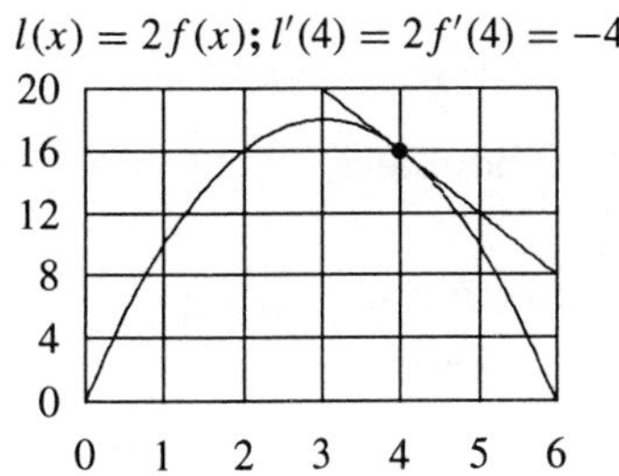

Consider each graph in turn:

The graph of g: The graph of $g(x) = f(x+2)$ is a horizontal translation of the f-graph. Like the graph itself, the tangent line moves two units *left*, but its *slope* remains unchanged. That's why $g'(2) = f'(4) = -2$.

The graph of h: The graph of $h(x) = f(x) + 2$ is a vertical translation of the f-graph. The tangent line, too, moves two units *up*, but its *slope* remains unchanged. That's why $h'(4) = f'(4) = -2$.➻

We knew this already from the sum rule.

The graph of k: The graph of $k(x) = f(2 \cdot x)$ is a horizontal compression of the f-graph, with factor 2. The tangent line at $x = 4$ is compressed in the same way: the new tangent line is at $x = 2$ and its slope is doubled. That's why $k'(2) = 2 \cdot f'(4) = -4$.

The graph of l: The graph of $l(x) = 2 \cdot f(x)$ is obtained by stretching the f-graph vertically with factor 2. The tangent line at $x = 4$ is stretched in the same way: stretching doubles its slope. That's why $l'(4) = 2 \cdot f'(4) = -4$.◀ □

We knew this already, too, from the constant rule.

The example concerned a specific function f, a specific constant $a = 2$, and a specific input $x = 4$, but the principles illustrated are much more general. We'll summarize them briefly in a theorem:

Theorem 2. (How constants affect derivatives.) Let f be a differentiable function and a any constant. Then

$$\begin{aligned} \big(f(x+a)\big)' &= f'(x+a) \\ \big(f(x)+a\big)' &= f'(x) \\ \big(f(a \cdot x)\big)' &= a \cdot f'(a \cdot x) \\ \big(a \cdot f(x)\big)' &= a \cdot f'(x) \end{aligned}$$

We won't prove this theorem—all its parts follow easily from the more general **chain rule**, which we'll see soon.

■ **Example 4.** Find derivatives of the functions defined by $\sin(x+3)$, $\sin(3x)$, and $3\sin(3x)$.

Remember?

Solution: All together, the theorem, the fact that $(\sin x)' = \cos x$,◀ and the constant rule say:

$$\begin{aligned} \big(\sin(x+3)\big)' &= \cos(x+3); \\ \big(\sin(3x)\big)' &= 3\cos(3x); \\ \big(3 \cdot \sin(3x)\big)' &= 3 \cdot \big(\sin(3x)\big)' = 3 \cdot 3\cos(3x) = 9\cos(3x). \end{aligned}$$ □

■ **Example 5.** Let k be any constant. If $f(x) = e^{kx} = \exp(kx)$, what's $f'(x)$?

Solution: Let $g(x) = e^x = \exp(x)$; from the previous section we know that g is its *own* derivative—that is, $g'(x) = e^x$. Therefore, from the theorem above,

$$f'(x) = \big(g(kx)\big)' = k \cdot g'(kx) = k \cdot e^{kx}.$$ □

■ **Example 6.** Let A and k be any constants. Show that the function $h(x) = Ae^{kx}$ satisfies these properties:

$$h(0) = A; \qquad h'(x) = k \cdot h(x).$$

Interpret the second property in the language of rates and proportionality.

Solution: Checking the first property is a simple calculation:

$$h(0) = A \cdot e^{k \cdot 0} = A \cdot 1 = A.$$

The second follows from the previous example and the constant rule:

$$h'(x) = \left(A \cdot e^{kx}\right)' = A \cdot \left(e^{kx}\right)' = A \cdot k \cdot e^{kx} = k \cdot A \cdot e^{kx} = kh(x).$$

The second property says that $h'(x)$ is *proportional*, with constant of proportionality k, to $h(x)$ itself. In other words, the growth rate of $h(x)$ is proportional to $h(x)$ itself. This is a property of many important real-life functions. □

Derivatives of algebraic combinations of functions

From given functions f and g we can form various algebraic combinations: $f + g$, $f - g$, $f \cdot g$, f/g, f^3/g, etc. How, exactly, are derivatives of such hybrids related to f, g, f', and g'?

We'll treat products and quotients in the next section. For the moment, the sum and constant multiple rules give the answers in the simplest situations. For instance:

$$(f - 2g + 3h)' = f' - 2g' + 3h'; \qquad \left(\frac{3f - g}{5}\right)' = \frac{3f' - g'}{5}.$$

A **linear combination** of functions is one that involves *only* addition and multiplication by constants. The built-up function $f - 2g + 3h = f - 2 \cdot g + 3 \cdot h$, for example, is a linear combination of the functions f, g, and h.

The sum and constant multiple rules make finding derivatives of linear combinations especially simple and convenient. Together, they say, for example, that

$$(f - 2g + 3h)' = f' - 2g' + 3h'.$$

In words:

> *The derivative of a linear combination is the* same *linear combination of derivatives.*

This property of derivatives is sometimes expressed by saying that the derivative is a **linear operator**. Linear combinations appear throughout mathematics.

A sample problem

Here's a problem that illustrates the interplay between constant parameters and derivatives.

■ **Example 7.** Let $f(x) = \cos(kx)$ and $g(x) = 1 - x^2$. Choose a value of k such that $f(0) = g(0)$, $f'(0) = g'(0)$, and $f''(0) = g''(0)$. Interpret the results graphically.

Solution: Notice first that $f(0) = 1 = g(0)$ regardless of k. We'll need these easily-checked facts for reference:

$$f'(x) = -k\sin(kx); \quad g'(x) = -2x; \quad f''(x) = -k^2\cos(kx); \quad g''(x) = -2.$$

From these facts it follows:

$$f'(0) = 0 = g'(0); \quad f''(0) = -k^2; \quad g''(0) = -2.$$

The only possibilities, therefore, are $k = \sqrt{2}$ and $k = -\sqrt{2}$. Plotting $f(x) = \cos(\sqrt{2}x)$ and $g(x) = 1 - x^2$ together shows what all this means:

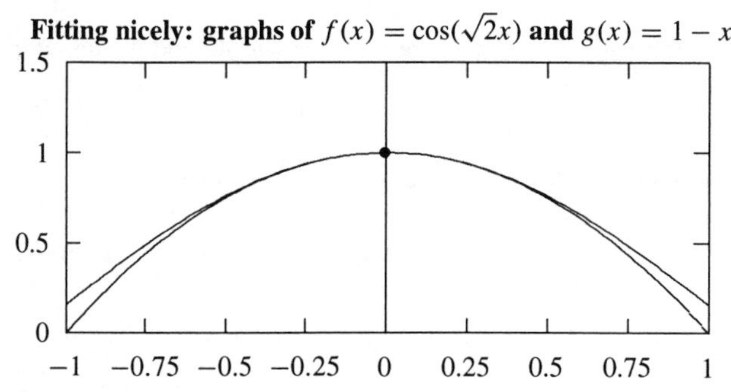

The two graphs fit nicely together at $x = 0$—they "agree" in value, first derivative, and second derivative there. ☐

What does the graph of $y = \cos(-\sqrt{2}x)$ look like?

Exercises

1. Evaluate the derivative of each of the following functions in two ways.

   (a) $f(x) = (x+1)^2 = x^2 + 2x + 1$
   (b) $g(x) = (2x)^3 = 8x^3$
   (c) $h(x) = e^{x+2} = e^x \cdot e^2$
   (d) $j(x) = \ln(3x) = \ln 3 + \ln x$

Find the derivative of each of the functions in exercises 2–15 below.

2. $f(x) = (x+2)^3$
3. $f(x) = 4(x-1)^5$
4. $f(x) = (x+4)^{-1}$
5. $f(x) = (x-2)^{100}$
6. $f(x) = 3(x+1)^{-2}$
7. $f(x) = \dfrac{1}{\sqrt{x+4}}$
8. $f(x) = 6\,(x+4)^{-5/3}$
9. $f(x) = \sqrt{x+3} + e^{2x}$
10. $f(x) = \cos(x+5)$
11. $f(x) = 2\sin(3x)$
12. $f(x) = 3\sin(x+2)$
13. $f(x) = 3e^{-2x} - 3\cos(4x)$
14. $f(x) = \ln(x+17)$
15. $f(x) = -\ln(4x)$

16–29. Find the second derivative of each of the functions in exercises 2–15 above.

30–43. Find an antiderivative of each of the functions in exercises 2–15 above.

44. Some values of the derivative of a function f are shown in the table below:

x	0	1	2	3	4	5	6
$f'(x)$	4	−3	2	0	−1	−6	1

[NOTE: No explicit formula for f is given!]

(a) Let $g(x) = f(x+3)$. For which values of x can you evaluate $g'(x)$? Evaluate $g'(x)$ for these values of x.

(b) Let $h(x) = 3f(x)$. For which values of x can you evaluate $h'(x)$? Evaluate $h'(x)$ for these values of x.

(c) Let $j(x) = f(3x)$. For which values of x can you evaluate $j'(x)$? Evaluate $j'(x)$ for these values of x.

(d) Let $k(x) = f(x) - 3$. For which values of x can you evaluate $k'(x)$? Evaluate $k'(x)$ for these values of x.

45. The range R of a projectile whose muzzle velocity is v meters per second and whose angle of elevation is x radians is given by

$$R = v^2 \sin(2x)/g$$

where g is the acceleration due to gravity.

(a) What angle of elevation gives the projectile maximum range? Justify your answer.

(b) What is the maximum range of the projectile?

46. Let f be an even function and g be an odd function.

(a) Show that f' is an odd function. [HINT: $f(-x) = f(-1 \cdot x)$.]

(b) Show that g' is an even function.

(c) Show that f'' is an even function. [HINT: Use part (b).]

(d) Is g'' even, odd, or neither? Justify your answer.

47. Suppose that f is a differentiable function. If f is periodic with period P, is f' also periodic? Explain.

48. Use the racetrack principle to show that $(1+x)^r \geq 1 + rx$ when $x \geq 0$ and $r \geq 1$.

49. Let k be a real number. Find a trigonometric identity for $\cos(x+k)$ by differentiating both sides of the identity $\sin(x+k) = \sin x \cos k + \cos x \sin k$.

50. (a) Over which intervals is $f(x) = (1000-x)^2 + x^2$ increasing? Decreasing? [HINT: $(1000-x)^2 = (x-1000)^2$.]

(b) Use part (a) to decide whether 1000^2 is bigger or smaller than $998^2 + 2^2$. Check your answer using a calculator.

(c) Generalize your result from part (a) to the function $f(x) = (c-x)^n + x^n$, where c is any positive number and n is an *even* positive integer. Use this result to decide whether 10000^{100} is bigger or smaller than $9000^{100} + 1000^{100}$

51. Let $f(x) = \cos x + \frac{1}{2}\cos(2x)$.

    (a) Determine where f has local maxima and minima over the interval $[0, 5]$.

    (b) Estimate where f has inflection points in the interval $[0, 5]$.

52. Repeat the previous problem using the function $f(x) = \sin x - \frac{1}{2}\cos(2x)$.

53. Use Theorem 1 to show that $\left(\ln|x|\right)' = x^{-1}$.
[HINT: $|x| = -x = -1 \cdot x$ when $x < 0$.]

54. Suppose that f is a function such that $f'(x) = x\cos x$.

    (a) Let $g(x) = f(x + \pi)$. Evaluate $g'(0)$.

    (b) Let $h(x) = f(2x)$. Evaluate $h'(\pi/2)$.

    (c) Let $j(x) = 2f(x) + 3$. Find an expression for $j'(x)$.

55. Suppose that F is an antiderivative of a function f.

    (a) Find an antiderivative of $g(x) = f(x) + 3$.

    (b) Find an antiderivative of $h(x) = f(x + 3)$.

    (c) Find an antiderivative of $j(x) = 3f(x)$.

    (d) Find an antiderivative of $k(x) = f(3x)$.

56. Find a function that satisfies each set of conditions below.

    (a) $f'(x) = 2x^3 + \sin(4x) - 3^x, \quad f(0) = 1$

    (b) $f'(z) = \cos(2z), \quad f\left(\frac{\pi}{2}\right) = 1$

    (c) $g'(w) = \sin(w + 2), \quad g(0) = 3$

    (d) $h'(t) = -2h(t), \quad h(1) = 1$

57. Let $f(x) = \ln|x|$, $g(x) = x^{-1}$, and $h(x) = \begin{cases} -2 + \ln x & \text{when } x > 0 \\ 3 + \ln(-x) & \text{when } x < 0. \end{cases}$

    (a) What is the domain of f? Of g?

    (b) Draw graphs of f, g, and h on the same set of axes.

    (c) Explain why f is an antiderivative of g. [HINT: f is an even function.]

    (d) Show that h is an antiderivative of g (i.e., show that $h'(x) = g(x)$ for all $x \neq 0$).

58. Let $f(x) = \cos(kx)$ and $g(x) = \sin(kx)$; k is a constant.

    (a) Show that $f''(x) = -k^2 f(x)$ and $g''(x) = -k^2 g(x)$.

    (b) Let $h(x) = Af(x) + Bg(x)$, where A and B are any real numbers. Show that $h''(x) = -k^2 h(x)$.

    (c) Let h be the function defined in part (b). Choose values of A and B so that $h''(x) = -4h(x)$, $h(0) = 2$, and $h'(0) = 8$.

59. Let $f(x) = e^{kx}$ and $g(x) = e^{-kx}$; k is a constant.

    (a) Show that $f''(x) = k^2 f(x)$ and $g''(x) = k^2 g(x)$.

(b) Let $h(x) = Af(x) + Bg(x)$ where A and B are any real numbers. Show that $h''(x) = k^2 h(x)$.

(c) Let h be the function defined in part (b). Choose values of A and B so that $h''(x) = 4h(x)$, $h(0) = 2$, and $h'(0) = 8$.

60. Using the results of the two previous problems, find functions that have the desired properties.

(a) $f''(x) = -f(x)$, $f(\pi/4) = 3$, and $f(\pi/2) = -2$.

(b) $g''(x) = -4g(x)$, $g'(0) = 4$, and $g(0) = 4$.

(c) $h''(x) = 4h(x)$, $h'(0) = 4$, and $h(0) = 4$.

61. Let k be a constant and f a differentiable function. If $g(x) = f(x+k)$, then $g'(x) = f'(x+k)$.

(a) Justify (with a short sentence) each step in the following proof of this result:

$$\begin{aligned}
&\text{(i)} & g'(x) &= \lim_{h\to 0} \frac{g(x+h) - g(x)}{h} \\
&\text{(ii)} & &= \lim_{h\to 0} \frac{f(x+k+h) - f(x+k)}{h} \\
&\text{(iii)} & &= \lim_{h\to 0} \frac{f(w+h) - f(w)}{h} \qquad \text{where } w = x+k \\
&\text{(iv)} & &= f'(w) \\
&\text{(v)} & &= f'(x+k).
\end{aligned}$$

(b) Explain this result geometrically.

62. Use the results of the previous problem to find the derivative of each of the following functions.

(a) $f(x) = (x+4)^5$

(b) $f(x) = (x-3)^{-2}$

(c) $f(x) = \sqrt{x-1}$

(d) $f(x) = \sqrt[3]{x+7}$

63. Let k be a constant and f a well-behaved function. If $g(x) = f(kx)$, then $g'(x) = kf'(kx)$. Justify (with a short sentence) each step in the following proof of this result: [HINT: In line (iv), $w = kh$.]

$$\begin{aligned}
&\text{(i)} & g'(x) &= \lim_{h\to 0} \frac{g(x+h) - g(x)}{h} \\
&\text{(ii)} & &= \lim_{h\to 0} \frac{f(kx+kh) - f(kx)}{h} \\
&\text{(iii)} & &= \lim_{w\to 0} k \cdot \frac{f(kx+w) - f(kx)}{w} \\
&\text{(iv)} & &= kf'(kx)
\end{aligned}$$

64. Evaluate the following limits by recognizing each as the definition of a derivative.

(a) $\lim_{t\to 0} \frac{e^{2t}-1}{t}$

(b) $\lim_{w\to 5} \frac{\log_2(w+11)-4}{w-5}$

(c) $\lim_{x\to 0} \frac{\sin(\pi x)}{x}$

65. Let $f(x) = \cos(2x)$ and $x_0 = 0$.

(a) Find values of the constants a and b so that the linear function $L(x) = ax + b$ has the properties $L(x_0) = f(x_0)$ and $L'(x_0) = f'(x_0)$.

(b) Find values of the constants c, d, and e so that the quadratic function $Q(x) = cx^2+dx+e$ has the properties $Q(x_0) = f(x_0)$, $Q'(x_0) = f'(x_0)$, and $Q''(x_0) = f''(x_0)$.

(c) Graph f, L, and Q on the same axes over the interval $[-3, 3]$.

(d) Find an interval over which $|f(x) - L(x)| < 0.1$.

(e) Find an interval over which $|f(x) - Q(x)| < 0.1$.

3.3 New derivatives from old: the product and quotient rules

Derivatives of products and quotients of functions need more care than sums and constant multiples. Sadly, the "naïve" rules for products and quotients—$(fg)' = f'g'$ and $(f/g)' = f'/g'$—are false.

■ **Example 1.** Show by examples that the "naïve" product and quotient rules fail.

Solution: Almost *any* functions f and g will do. If, say, $f(x) = x$ and $g(x) = 1$, then $f(x)g(x) = x$ and $f(x)/g(x) = x$. But

$$\big(f(x) \cdot g(x)\big)' = \big(x\big)' = 1 \neq f'(x) \cdot g'(x) = 1 \cdot 0 = 0.$$

The "false quotient rule" also produces nonsense:

$$\left(\frac{f(x)}{g(x)}\right)' = (x)' = 1 \neq \frac{f'(x)}{g'(x)} = \frac{1}{0}.$$

□

The (true) product and quotient rules

Below, stated as theorems, are the *true* product and quotient rules. Before considering *why* they hold, we'll illustrate how to use them.

In each theorem, u and v are differentiable functions.

For some reason, it's traditional in calculus to use u and v (not f and g) in this context. We won't buck tradition.

> **Theorem 3. (The product rule.)** If $p(x) = u(x) \cdot v(x)$, then
>
> $$p'(x) = \big(u(x) \cdot v(x)\big)' = u'(x) \cdot v(x) + u(x) \cdot v'(x).$$
>
> Equivalently, $(uv)' = u'v + uv'$.

> **Theorem 4. (The quotient rule.)** If $q(x) = u(x)/v(x)$, then
>
> $$q'(x) = \left(\frac{u(x)}{v(x)}\right)' = \frac{v(x)u'(x) - u(x)v'(x)}{v(x)^2}.$$
>
> Equivalently, $(u/v)' = \dfrac{vu' - uv'}{v^2}$.

■ **Example 2. (Antiderivatives of $\ln x$.)** In Section 2.9 we claimed, but didn't prove, that functions of the form $F(x) = x \ln x - x + C$ are antiderivatives of the natural logarithm function. Prove it now.

We did give graphical evidence. See page 202.

Solution: With the product rule, nothing could be easier. Watch:

$$(x \ln x - x + C)' = \ln x + x\,\frac{1}{x} - 1 = \ln x,$$

just as claimed. □

■ **Example 3.** Let $p(x) = x^2 \sin x$ and $q(x) = x^2/\sin x$. Find p' and q'.

Solution: In the notation above, $u(x) = x^2$ and $v(x) = \sin x$. Thus $u' = 2x$ and $v' = \cos x$. The rest is "pattern-matching":

$$\begin{aligned} p'(x) &= (uv)' = u'v + uv' = 2x \sin x + x^2 \cos x; \\ q'(x) &= (u/v)' = \frac{vu' - uv'}{v^2} = \frac{(\sin x)2x - x^2 \cos x}{(\sin x)^2}. \end{aligned}$$

(Some algebraic simplification of answers is possible, but since our main point concerns the derivatives themselves, we'll leave things as they are.) □

Recall: $\exp(x)$ *is another notation for* e^x.

■ **Example 4.** Find derivatives of $r(x) = 1/\exp(x)$ and $s(x) = \exp(-x)$.

We leave some algebraic details to you; recall that $(e^x)' = e^x$.

Solution: We can handle r with the quotient rule:

$$r'(x) = \left(\frac{1}{\exp(x)}\right)' = \frac{-e^x}{(e^x)^2} = -\frac{1}{e^x} = -e^{-x}.$$

Notice, next, that $s(x) = \exp(kx)$, where $k = -1$. Therefore, by the rules discussed at the beginning of this section,

$$s'(x) = k \cdot \exp(kx) = -1 \cdot \exp(-1x) = -e^{-x}.$$

Convince yourself!

Notice, finally, that $r' = s'$. That's no accident: despite first appearances, r and s are the same function. □

■ **Example 5.** Let f be a differentiable function; let $g = 1/f$. Find a formula for g' in terms of f and f'.

Use the product rule on the right.

Solution: We *could* apply the quotient rule to $1/f$, but we'll take another tack. Notice first that $1 = g(x)f(x)$ for all sensible inputs x. Differentiating both sides of this equation gives:

$$0 = g'f + gf' = g'f + \frac{f'}{f}.$$

Solving for g' gives our answer:

$$\left(\frac{1}{f}\right)' = g' = -\frac{f'}{f^2}.$$

□

Derivatives of the "other" trigonometric functions

In Section 2.10 we showed carefully that $(\sin x)' = \cos x$ and $(\cos x)' = -\sin x$. The quotient rule makes easy work of finding derivatives of the *remaining* trigonometric functions. We'll do one such computation, leaving the others as exercises.

■ **Example 6.** Find and simplify the derivative of $\tan x$.

Solution: Use the quotient rule:

$$(\tan x)' = \left(\frac{\sin x}{\cos x}\right)' = \frac{\cos^2 x + \sin^2 x}{\cos^2 x} = \frac{1}{\cos^2 x}.$$

To avoid fractions, the answer is usually written as $\sec^2 x$. □

The full story of trigonometric derivatives fits snugly in a table:

Derivatives of trigonometric functions						
Function	$\sin x$	$\cos x$	$\tan x$	$\cot x$	$\sec x$	$\csc x$
Derivative	$\cos x$	$-\sin x$	$\sec^2 x$	$-\csc^2 x$	$\sec x \tan x$	$-\csc x \cot x$

Evidence for the product rule

A formal proof➡ of the product rule involves difference quotients. Here we'll give two less formal "plausibility" arguments.

One appears in Appendix I.

Exhibit A: It works for linear functions. Suppose that $f(x) = ax + b$ and $g(x) = cx + d$. We'll differentiate $f \cdot g$ twice—with and without the product rule.

First, notice that

$$f(x) \cdot g(x) = (ax + b) \cdot (cx + d) = acx^2 + (ad + bc)x + bd.$$

The last expression is a polynomial in x; differentiating it directly gives

$$(fg)' = 2acx + (ad + bc).$$

Happily, the product rule agrees:

$$(fg)' = f'g + fg' = a \cdot (cx + d) + (ax + b) \cdot c = 2acx + ad + bc.$$

These computations show that the product rule gives the right answer for *linear* functions f and g. Most functions, of course, aren't linear. On the other hand, every differentiable function is "almost linear" in the sense that its graph looks straight if viewed at sufficiently small scale.➡

A rigorous proof of the product rule can be constructed from this idea.

Exhibit B: It works "in practice." Both U.S. population and U.S. per capita income vary with time; we'll denote them by $p(t)$ and $i(t)$ respectively. The *product* function $w(t) = p(t)i(t)$ describes the *total annual U.S. income*—another function of t. Let's ask:

How fast was total annual income growing at $t = 1990$?

In 1990, the population of the U.S. was about 250 million and increasing at the rate of about 3 million per year. Per capita income was about \$15,000 and growing at about \$1000 per year. In symbols:

$$p(1990) = 250 \text{ million}; \qquad p'(1990) = 3 \text{ million};$$
$$i(1990) = 15000; \qquad i'(1990) = 1000.$$

To answer the question, observe first that growth in w comes from *two sources*: rising population and rising per capita income. Over a year, rising population produces about 3 million new people, each earning about \$15,000, or a total of about

$$p'(1990) \cdot i(1990) = 3 \text{ million} \cdot 15000 = 45 \text{ billion}$$

dollars of new income. Similarly, rising personal income accounts for about

$$p(1990) \cdot i'(1990) = 250 \text{ million} \cdot 1000 = 250 \text{ billion}$$

dollars of new income. In all, therefore income rises at the rate of

$$\begin{aligned} p'(1990) \cdot i(1990) + p(1990) \cdot i'(1990) &= 45 \text{ billion} + 250 \text{ billion} \\ &= 295 \text{ billion} \end{aligned}$$

dollars per year—just as the product rule predicts.

Evidence for the quotient rule

Quotients are similar to products; in the same sense, the quotient rule follows directly from the product rule.

■ **Example 7.** Deduce the quotient rule from the product rule. (Assume that the derivative of the quotient exists.)

It does exist; showing that it does requires a proof similar to the one for the product rule in Appendix I.

Solution: Let u and v be differentiable functions, and let $q(x) = u(x)/v(x)$ be the quotient function. We want $q'(x)$.

The function q is defined wherever $v(x) \neq 0$.

By definition, $qv = u$. Differentiating both sides of this equation gives

Use the product rule.

$$(qv)' = q'v + v'q = q'v + v'\frac{u}{v} = u'.$$

Solving this last equation for q' gives the quotient rule:

$$q' = \frac{vu' - uv'}{v^2}.$$ □

Mixed examples

Functions built from *several* products and quotients need several applications of the rules.

■ **Example 8.** Let u, v, and w be differentiable functions. Find a formula for $(uvw)'$.

Solution: Used carefully, the product rule is enough:

$$\begin{aligned}(uvw)' &= ((uv)\cdot w)' && \text{[by grouping]}\\ &= (uv)'\cdot w + (uv)\cdot w' && \text{[product rule]}\\ &= (u'v + uv')\cdot w + uvw' && \text{[product rule]}\\ &= u'vw + uv'w + uvw'.\end{aligned}$$

Notice the pleasing symmetry of the result: each term involves *one* derivative. □

■ **Example 9.** Differentiate $x\,e^x \sin x$ and $x/(e^x \sin x)$.

Solution: By the rule just derived,

$$\left(x\,e^x \sin x\right)' = 1\cdot e^x \cdot \sin x + x\cdot e^x \cdot \sin x + x \cdot e^x \cdot \cos x.$$

The second expression requires the quotient and product rules:

$$\begin{aligned}\left(\frac{x}{e^x \sin x}\right)' &= \frac{(e^x \sin x)(x)' - x(e^x \sin x)'}{(e^x \sin x)^2}\\ &= \frac{(e^x \sin x) - x(e^x \sin x + e^x \cos x)}{(e^x \sin x)^2} && \text{[product rule]}\\ &= \frac{(\sin x)(1-x) + x\cos x}{e^x \sin^2 x} && \text{[simplified]}\end{aligned}$$ □

Sometimes other ingredients, such as constants, are involved.

Example 10. Differentiate $e^{2x}\sin(3x)$.

Solution: In the previous section we saw how to handle constants:

$$\left(e^{2x}\right)' = 2e^{2x}; \quad (\sin(3x))' = 3\cos(3x).$$

Now, by the product rule:

$$\left(e^{2x}\sin(3x)\right)' = 2e^{2x}\sin(3x) + 3\cos(3x)e^{2x}.$$ □

Guessing and checking antiderivatives: a sample problemm

Finding derivatives is relatively easy; with techniques from this section, we can handle a great many functions. Finding *antiderivatives* is often harder. Making a guess—and then checking it—is often an effective technique.

Example 11. Find antiderivatives for

$$f(x) = x^2\cos x + 2x\sin x \quad \text{and} \quad g(x) = \frac{x\cos x - \sin x}{x^2}.$$

Solution: The basic forms of f and g suggest, respectively, the *results* of applying the product and quotient rules. With this in mind, it's natural to guess

$$F(x) = x^2\sin x + C \quad \text{and} \quad G(x) = \frac{\sin x}{x} + C$$

as possible antiderivatives.➥ With the product and quotient rules it's easy to check our guesses. As desired,

In each, C stands for any constant.

$$\begin{aligned} F'(x) &= (x^2\sin x)' = x^2\cos x + 2x\sin x; \\ G'(x) &= \left(\frac{\sin x}{x}\right)' = \frac{x\cos x - \sin x}{x^2}, \end{aligned}$$

just as we'd hoped. □

Exercises

1. Find the derivative of each of the following functions two ways: (1) using the product rule, and (2) by multiplying out before differentiating.

   (a) $h(x) = x^3(x^2 - 4)$
   (b) $h(x) = (x+4)^2$
   (c) $h(x) = e^x \cdot e^{2x}$
   (d) $h(x) = \tan x \cdot \csc x$

2. Find the derivative of each of the following functions two ways: (1) using the quotient rule, and (2) algebraically simplifying, then differentiating.

(a) $h(x) = \dfrac{x^2}{x^3}$

(b) $h(x) = \dfrac{1-x^2}{1+x}$

(c) $h(x) = \dfrac{1}{e^t}$

(d) $h(x) = \dfrac{\cot x}{\csc x}$

3. Let $h(x) = f(x) \cdot g(x)$, and $j(x) = f(x)/g(x)$. Fill in the missing entries in the table below using the information about f and g given in the table and the definitions of h and j.

x	$f(x)$	$f'(x)$	$g(x)$	$g'(x)$	$h'(x)$	$j'(x)$
-2	1	-1	-3	4		$-1/9$
-1	0	-2	1	1	-2	
0	-1	2	-2	1		
1	2	-2	-1	2	6	
2	3	-1	2	-2		1

Find the derivative of each of the following functions.

4. $f(x) = x \sin x$
5. $f(x) = x^2 \cos x$
6. $f(x) = \sqrt{x} \ln x$
7. $f(x) = x^3 e^x$
8. $f(x) = \sin x \cos x$
9. $f(x) = (x^2+3)e^x$
10. $f(x) = x^{3/2} \sin x$
11. $f(x) = \dfrac{\sin x}{x^2}$
12. $f(x) = \dfrac{\cos x}{x^2 + e^{2x}}$
13. $f(x) = \dfrac{(x+1)^2}{x^2+1}$
14. $f(x) = \dfrac{\sin x}{\cos(2x)}$
15. $f(x) = \cot(3x)$
16. $f(x) = \sec(x+3)$
17. $f(x) = 3\csc(2x)$
18. $f(x) = 4\tan(x+5)$
19. $f(x) = x^3 e^{2x} \ln x$

Find an antiderivative of each of the following functions.

20. $g(x) = \sec^2 x$
21. $g(x) = 3 \sec x \tan x$
22. $g(x) = \sec^2(x+1)$
23. $g(x) = \csc^2(2x)$
24. $g(x) = 2x \cos x - x^2 \sin x$
25. $g(x) = (x+1)e^x$
26. $g(x) = e^{2x} \sin x - 2e^{2x} \cos x$
27. $g(x) = \dfrac{xe^x - e^x}{x^2}$
28. $f(x) = 2xe^x + x^2 e^x$
29. $f(x) = \frac{\sin x}{x} + \ln x \cos x$
30. $f(x) = e^x \sin x + e^x \cos x$
31. $f(x) = e^x \sin x - e^x \cos x$

32. Suppose that $f(0) = 3$ and f' is the function shown below. Let $g(x) = e^x f(x)$.

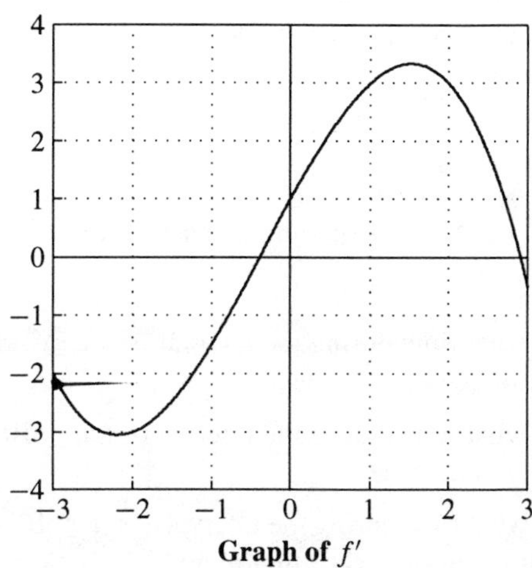

Graph of f'

(a) Evaluate $g'(0)$.

(b) Is g increasing at $x = 1$? At $x = 2$? At $x = -2$? Justify your answers.

(c) Estimate $g''(0)$.

(d) Is g concave up at $x = 1$? At $x = 2$? Justify your answers.

33. Let $f(x) = xe^x$. Find values of the parameters A and B so that $F(x) = (Ax + B)e^x$ is an antiderivative of f.

34. Let $g(x) = x^2e^x$. Find values of the parameters A, B, and C so that $G(x) = (Ax^2 + Bx + C)e^x$ is an antiderivative of g.

35. Let $h(x) = e^{2x} \sin x$. Find values of the parameters A and B, so that $H(x) = e^{2x}(A \cos x + B \sin x)$ is an antiderivative of h.

36. Consider the function $f(x) = \dfrac{\ln x}{x}$ on the interval $(1, \infty)$.

(a) Where does f achieve its maximum value? What is this value?

(b) Find all inflection points in the graph of f.

37. Let $f(x) = \dfrac{x + \sin x}{\cos x}$.

(a) Find $f'(x)$.

(b) Find an equation of the line tangent to the graph of f at $x = 0$.

38. Let $f(x) = e^x \cos x$.

(a) At which value of x in the interval $[0, \pi]$ does f achieve its maximum value? Its minimum value?

(b) At which value(s) of x in the interval $[0, \pi]$ does f have an inflection point?

39. Find the maximum and minimum values of $g(x) = e^{-x} \sin x$ over the interval $[0, \infty)$.

40. Let $f(x) = 2x + x\cos x + \sin x$.

 (a) Show that f has a local minimum at $x = (2k+1)\pi$, where $k = 0, 1, 2, \ldots$

 (b) Show that f has a local maximum at $x = -(2k+1)\pi$, where $k = 0, 1, 2, \ldots$

41. Suppose that $N(t)$, the number of bacteria in a culture at time t, is proportional to $25 + te^{-t/20}$.

 (a) At what time during the interval $0 \le t \le 100$ is the number of bacteria the smallest?

 (b) At what time during the interval $0 \le t \le 100$ is the number of bacteria the greatest?

 (c) At what time during the interval $0 \le t \le 100$ is the rate of change of the number of bacteria a minimum?

42. What is the area of the largest triangle that can be formed in the first quadrant by the x-axis, the y-axis, and a line tangent to the graph of $y = e^{-x}$?

43. (a) Show that $x + x^{-2} \ge 2$ if $0 < x \le 1$. [HINT: Use the racetrack principle.]

 (b) Use part (a) to show that $\sin x + \tan x \ge 2x$ when $0 \le x < \pi/2$.

44. Show that $\dfrac{x}{1+x} \le \ln(1+x) \le x$ for all real numbers $x \ge 0$.
[HINT: Use the "racetrack principle."]

45. Suppose that f is a differentiable function, $g(x) = \big(f(x)\big)^2$, and $h(x) = \big(f(x)\big)^3$.

 (a) Use the product rule to show that $\big(g(x)\big)' = 2f(x)f'(x)$.
 [HINT: $\big(f(x)\big)^2 = f(x) \cdot f(x)$.]

 (b) Use part (a) and the product rule to find an expression for $\big(h(x)\big)'$.

46. Suppose that f is a differentiable function and $g(x) = \big(f(x)\big)^2$.

 (a) Show that every stationary point of f is a stationary point of g.

 (b) If x_0 is a local maximum point of f, is x_0 also a local maximum point of g? Explain.

47. (a) Show that $F(x) = x(\ln x - 1)$ is an antiderivative of $f(x) = \ln x$.

 (b) Find an antiderivative of $g(x) = \log_b x$. [HINT: Use part (a).]

48. Let $f(x) = \dfrac{\ln x}{k} - \dfrac{kx}{x+1}$ where k is a positive constant.

 (a) Show that if $0 < k \le 2$, f has no local extrema.

 (b) Show that f has local extrema if $k > 2$. Determine how many and where they are located.

49. Evaluate the following limits by recognizing each as the definition of a derivative.

(a) $\displaystyle\lim_{x\to\pi} \frac{x\cos x + \pi}{x - \pi}$

(b) $\displaystyle\lim_{t\to 0} \frac{1}{t}\cdot\left(\frac{t^2 - 3t + 4}{5t + 2} - 2\right)$

50. Let $f(x) = xe^x$.

(a) Find values of the constants a and b so that the linear function $L(x) = ax + b$ has the properties $L(0) = f(0)$ and $L'(0) = f'(0)$.

(b) Find the value of the constant c for which the quadratic function $Q(x) = L(x) + cx^2$ has the properties $Q(0) = f(0)$, $Q'(0) = f'(0)$, and $Q''(0) = f''(0)$.

(c) Graph f, L, and Q on the same axes over the interval $[-3, 3]$.

(d) Find an interval over which $|f(x) - L(x)| < 0.1$.

(e) Find an interval over which $|f(x) - Q(x)| < 0.1$.

51. Let $f(x) = \dfrac{x}{3 + x^2}$.

(a) Find values of the constants a and b so that the linear function $L(x) = a(x - 1) + b$ has the properties $L(1) = f(1)$ and $L'(1) = f'(1)$.

(b) Find the value of the constant c for which the quadratic function $Q(x) = L(x) + c(x - 1)^2$ has the properties $Q(1) = f(1)$, $Q'(1) = f'(1)$, and $Q''(1) = f''(1)$.

(c) Graph f, L, and Q on the same axes over the interval $[-3, 3]$.

(d) Find an interval over which $|f(x) - L(x)| < 0.1$.

(e) Find an interval over which $|f(x) - Q(x)| < 0.1$.

52. Suppose that f, g, and h are differentiable functions and that $h(x) = f(x)g(x)$. Show that if $h'(1) \neq 0$, then $\big(f(1)\big)^2 + \big(g(1)\big)^2 > 0$.

53. Suppose that the functions f and g both have the following properties:

(i) $f(x + y) = f(x)f(y)$

(ii) $f(0) \neq 0$

(iii) $f'(0) = 1$

(a) Show that $f(0) = 1$. [HINT: Let $x = y = 0$ in (i).]

(b) Show that $f(x) \neq 0$ for all x. [HINT: Let $y = -x$ in (i).]

(c) Show that $f'(x) = f(x)$ for all x. [HINT: Use the definition of the derivative.]

(d) Let $k(x) = f(x)/g(x)$. Show that k is defined for all real inputs and find an expression for $k'(x)$.

(e) Use part (d) to show that $f(x) = g(x) = e^x$.

54. Suppose that f and g are differentiable functions and that $h(x) = f(x)g(x)$. Find symbolic expressions involving only numerical constants and derivatives of f and g for each of the following.

(a) $h''(x)$ (b) $h'''(x)$

(c) $h^{(n)}(x)$ [HINT: Express your answer in terms of the binomial coefficients $\binom{n}{k} = n!/\big(k!(n-k)!\big)$.]

55. This problem presents an alternative proof of the product rule.

Suppose that f and g are differentiable functions and that $h(x) = f(x)g(x)$.

(a) Use the definition of the derivative to show that $\left(\left(f(x)\right)^2\right)' = 2f(x)f'(x)$.
[HINT: Use the algebraic identity $a^2 - b^2 = (a-b)(a+b)$.]

(b) Show that $h(x) = \frac{1}{2}\left(\left(f(x)+g(x)\right)^2 - \left(f(x)\right)^2 - \left(g(x)\right)^2\right)$.

(c) Use parts (a) and (b) to show that $h'(x) = f(x)g'(x) + f'(x)g(x)$.

56. Suppose that f and g are differentiable at $x = a$, that $g(a) \neq 0$, and that $h(x) = f(x)/g(x)$. If we *assume* that h is differentiable at $x = a$, the quotient rule can be deduced from the product rule. Do so by differentiating both sides of the equation $f(x) = g(x)h(x)$ and then solving for $h'(x)$.

3.4 New derivatives from old: the chain rule

The last two sections were about differentiating new functions constructed by *algebraic* operations on simpler functions. In this section we continue the same theme, but with respect to the operation of *composition*.

Derivatives of compositions

With the sum, constant multiple, product, and quotient rules we can differentiate any *algebraic* combination of elementary functions—even monsters like

If we want.

$$\frac{x^2 \sin x}{\tan x} - \frac{\sin x \ln x + \cos x}{x^5 + 1} \cdot \left(2^x + \frac{3^x}{\ln x}\right).$$

The question

All that remains before we can differentiate "any" elementary function is to handle functions like

$$\sin\left(x^2\right), \qquad (\sin x)^2, \qquad \text{and} \qquad \sin^3\left(x^2\right)$$

constructed by *composing* simpler functions.

The "simpler" functions involved here are

The "neutral" variable name u avoids conflict with x, which is used a bit differently above.

$$f(u) = \sin u, \qquad g(u) = u^2, \qquad \text{and} \qquad h(u) = u^3.$$

Finding f', g', and h' is (by now) no problem; the real question is how to combine everything to find derivatives of composite functions. In simplest form, our question is:

How do we combine f, g, f', *and* g' *to find* $(f \circ g)'$?

The answer

The **chain rule** is the missing link. In stating it, we assume as usual that f and g are "nice enough" (i.e., that f, g, f' and g' have large enough domains to permit the desired operations).

The name is apt: composed functions are "chained" together in series.

Sorry.

More fine print after the theorem.

Theorem 5. (The chain rule.) Let f and g be well-behaved functions. Then
$$(f \circ g)'(a) = f'(g(a)) \cdot g'(a).$$

This important theorem deserves several closer looks:

The derivative exists. The theorem guarantees (among other things) that the derivative $(f \circ g)'(a)$ *exists*, provided that both $f'(g(a))$ and $g'(a)$ exist.

Why a product? The theorem says that the derivative of the *composition* $f \circ g$ is a certain *product* of the derivatives f' and g'. Why is a *product* appropriate?

Interpreting derivatives as rates of change gives some clue. Suppose, say, that $y = f(u)$, $u = g(x)$, $f'(u) = 3$, and $g'(x) = 2$. This means, in rate language, that y changes *three* times as fast as u, and u changes *twice* as fast as x. It sounds reasonable, then, that y should change *six* times as fast as x. (Additional evidence for the chain rule appears later in this section.)

In other words, the "naïve" chain rule $(f \circ g)' = f'g'$ is false!

Which product? The chain rule involves a certain *product* of derivatives of f and g. But care is needed: The factors $f'(g(a))$ and $g'(a)$ show that f' and g' are evaluated for *different inputs.*

Other notations. In the theorem, we used a specific input, $x = a$, to emphasize the point made just above. Since the theorem holds for *any* sensible input a, we can also think of it as a relation among *functions.* From this point of view, we might prefer to state the chain rule as

$$(f \circ g)'(x) = f'(g(x)) \cdot g'(x),$$

or, equivalently, as

$$(f \circ g)' = (f' \circ g) \cdot g'.$$

A fully rigorous proof of the chain rule runs quickly into delicate technical problems. We'll settle for plausible evidence. First, however, some examples.

■ **Example 1.** Differentiate $\sin(x^2)$ and $\sin^2 x$. Are the answers the same? Should they be?

Solution: No and no.

The trick is to keep clear exactly what's meant, in context, by f, g, f', and g'. If we let $f(u) = \sin u$ and $g(u) = u^2$, then

$$\sin x^2 = (f \circ g)(x) \qquad \text{and} \qquad \sin^2 x = (g \circ f)(x).$$

From the chain rule and the derivatives of f and g:

$$\left(\sin x^2\right)' = (f \circ g)'(x) = f'(g(x)) \cdot g'(x) = \cos\left(x^2\right) \cdot 2x.$$

Similarly,

$$\left(\sin^2 x\right)' = (g \circ f)'(x) = g'(f(x)) \cdot f'(x) = 2\sin x \cdot \cos x.$$

The two answers are different—as they should be. Composition, after all, isn't commutative. □

■ **Example 2.** Differentiate $\sin(3x)$ and $\sin(x+3)$ using the chain rule. How could we have found these derivatives earlier?

Solution: Let $f(u) = \sin u$, $g(x) = 3x$, and $h(x) = x + 3$. Then

$$(\sin(3x))' = (f \circ g)'(x) = f'(g(x)) \cdot g'(x) = \cos(3x) \cdot 3.$$

Similarly,

$$(\sin(x+3))' = (f \circ h)'(x) = f'(h(x)) \cdot h'(x) = \cos(x+3) \cdot 1.$$

We *could* have done these problems earlier, using the derivative rules—see Theorem 2., page 246—for functions that involve *constant* parameters. □

■ **Example 3.** Differentiate $\sin^3(x^2)$.

Solution: We'll need to keep our wits about us here. Let $f(u) = \sin u$, $g(u) = u^2$, and $h(u) = u^3$; then

$$(h \circ f \circ g)(x) = \left(\sin(x^2)\right)^3 = \sin^3(x^2).$$

To handle the "three-deep" composition $h \circ f \circ g$, we'll group it in the form $h \circ (f \circ g)$ and use the chain rule *twice*:

$$(\, h \circ (f \circ g)\,)' = (h' \circ (f \circ g)) \cdot (f \circ g)' = (h' \circ (f \circ g)) \cdot \left(f' \circ g \cdot g'\right).$$

For our particular f, g, and h we get

$$\begin{aligned} \left(\, (\sin x^2)^3\, \right)' &= 3\left(\sin x^2\right)^2 \cdot \left(\sin x^2\right)' \\ &= 3\left(\sin x^2\right)^2 \cdot \left(\cos x^2 \cdot 2x\right) \\ &= 6x\left(\sin x^2\right)^2 \cos x^2. \end{aligned}$$

□

Working from outside in: how to use the chain rule. Composing two functions can be thought of as *nesting* one within the other. Using nested parentheses, as in $f(g(x))$, reflects this point of view: here f is the "outer" function and g the "inner." In this language the chain rule says, in effect, to *work from outside in*, one level at a time. More precisely:

> *To differentiate $f(g(x))$, first differentiate the outer function, leaving the inner function alone. Then multiply by the derivative of the inner function.*

This rule works nicely for *any* level of nesting, as the next example shows:

■ **Example 4.** Differentiate $\sin(\sin(\sin x))$.

Solution: Watch➻ the de-nesting, step by step:

Carefully!

$$\begin{aligned} (\, \sin(\sin(\sin x))\,)' &= \cos(\sin(\sin x)) \cdot (\, \sin(\sin x)\,)' \\ &= \cos(\sin(\sin x)) \cdot \cos(\sin x) \cdot (\, \sin x\,)' \\ &= \cos(\sin(\sin x)) \cdot \cos(\sin x) \cdot \cos x. \end{aligned}$$

□

■ **Example 5.** Let n be any real number. Differentiate $\sin^n x$; then differentiate $f(x)^n$, where f is *any* differentiable function.

Solution: From the chain rule,➻

Here the "outer" function is u^n.

$$\left(\, (\sin x)^n\, \right)' = n\,(\sin x)^{n-1} \cdot \cos x.$$

The same idea works for *any* "inner" function f:

$$\left(\, f(x)^n\, \right)' = n\, f(x)^{n-1} \cdot f'(x).$$

(This last formula is sometimes called the **general power rule**.) □

Evidence for the chain rule

As for the other rules, we'll argue informally.

Exhibit A: It works for linear functions. Let $f(x) = ax + b$ and $g(x) = cx + d$. We'll differentiate $f \circ g$ twice—with and without the chain rule. Notice first that

$$(f \circ g)(x) = a(cx + d) + b = acx + ad + b.$$

The last form shows that $f \circ g$ is *another* linear function; its derivative is the constant ac.

The chain rule gives the same result. Because $f'(x) = a$ and $g'(x) = c$, it's easy to calculate that $f'(g(x)) \cdot g'(x) = ac$, just as claimed.

As we've remarked before, and seen graphically.

Exhibit B: Differentiable functions are "almost linear." Let f and g be any differentiable functions. Because f and g are differentiable, they're "almost linear": near the point of tangency, they're well approximated by their tangent lines. Since the slope of the g-graph at $x = a$ is $g'(a)$, "locally straight" means that near $x = a$, $g(x)$ is well approximated by a *linear* function l with slope $g'(a)$ (i.e., $g(x) \approx l(x) = g'(a)x + k$, for some constant k; the value of k doesn't matter here).

For convenience, let's write $g(a) = b$. For reasons like those above, $f(x)$ is well approximated near $x = b$ by *another* linear function m, this time with slope $f'(b)$. In other words, $f(x) \approx m(x) = f'(b)x + K$, for some other constant K.

From all the foregoing, $(f \circ g)(x) \approx (m \circ l)(x)$. Because l and m are linear, Exhibit A says that

$$(m \circ l)' = f'(b) \cdot g'(a) = f'(g(a)) \cdot g'(a),$$

just as the chain rule predicts.

The chain rule in Leibniz notation

When we don't want to name functions, for example.

The chain rule is easy to remember, and sometimes convenient to state, in Leibniz form. Here's what it says, informally:

> *Let y be a nice function of u, and u a nice function of x. Then y is a (composite) function of x; the derivative of y with respect to x is*
>
> $$\frac{dy}{dx} = \frac{dy}{du} \cdot \frac{du}{dx}.$$

■ **Example 6.** Differentiate $y = \sin\left(x^2\right)$ yet again.

Solution: We have $y = \sin u$ and $u = x^2$, so

$$\frac{dy}{dx} = \frac{dy}{du} \cdot \frac{du}{dx} = \cos u \cdot 2x = 2x \cdot \cos x^2.$$

(At the last step we *replaced* u with x^2.) □

Derivatives of inverses and the chain rule

The chain rule can be used to relate the (known) derivative of a function to the (unknown) derivative of its *inverse*.

Recall: If f and g are inverse functions, then the equation

$$(f \circ g)(x) = f(g(x)) = x$$

must hold for all x in the domain of g. Differentiating both sides—the left side needs the chain rule—gives

$$(f \circ g)'(x) = f'(g(x)) \cdot g'(x) = 1.$$

With a little algebra, our desired formula now follows:

Fact: Let f and g be inverse functions. Then

$$g'(x) = \frac{1}{f'(g(x))}$$

for all x for which the right side is defined.

In the next section we'll use this formula to find derivatives of *inverse trigonometric functions*. For the moment we'll content ourselves with a simpler example.

■ **Example 7.** Use the fact that e^x and $\ln x$ are inverses and the fact that $(e^x)' = e^x$ to find (again!) the derivative of $\ln x$.

Solution: Let $f(x) = e^x$ (so that $f'(x) = e^x$) and $g(x) = \ln x$. Then by the formula above,

$$g'(x) = (\ \ln x\ )' = \frac{1}{f'(g(x))} = \frac{1}{e^{\ln x}} = \frac{1}{x}.$$ □

Guessing and checking antiderivatives: a sample problem

With the chain rule in our toolkit, we can easily differentiate almost any elementary function. Finding *antiderivatives*, however, is another matter. Making a guess—and then checking it—is often the best strategy.

■ **Example 8.** Find antiderivatives for

$$f(x) = x\cos(x^2) \quad \text{and} \quad g(x) = \frac{\cos x}{\sin x}.$$

Solution: The basic form of f suggests the result of applying the chain rule, perhaps to the expression $\sin(x^2)$. A check shows that our guess is *almost* correct:

$$\left(\sin(x^2)\right)' = \cos(x^2) \cdot 2x = 2x\cos(x^2).$$

To dispose of that extra factor of 2, we simply divide it out. It follows➽ that for any constant C,

Check for yourself.

$$F(x) = \frac{\sin(x^2)}{2} + C$$

is an antiderivative.

It's a little harder to recognize g as a derivative, but if we notice that the numerator is the derivative of the denominator, we might suspect that a logarithm function is involved. So it is; the guess $G(x) = \ln(\sin x) + C$ turns out to be correct:

$$G'(x) = (\ln(\sin x) + C)' = \frac{\cos x}{\sin x},$$

as desired. □

Exercises

1. Let $h(x) = f(g(x))$. Use the information about f and g given in the table below to fill in the missing information about h and h'.

x	$f(x)$	$f'(x)$	$g(x)$	$g'(x)$	$h(x)$	$h'(x)$
1	1	2	4	3		
2	2	1	3	4		
3	4	3	1	2		
4	3	4	2	1		

2. Let $h(x) = (f \circ g)(x)$ and $j(x) = f(x) \cdot g(x)$. Fill in the missing entries in the table below.

x	$f(x)$	$f'(x)$	$g(x)$	$g'(x)$	$h(x)$	$h'(x)$	$j(x)$	$j'(x)$
-1	3	2	1		0	$-1/2$	3	
0	0	$1/2$	-1	1			0	$-1/2$
1		-5	0			2	0	

3. Assume that g is an unknown function such that $g'(x)$ exists for all x. Find the derivative of each of the following functions. (Answers will involve g and g'.)

   (a) $f(x) = \big(g(x)\big)^n$

   (b) $f(x) = e^{g(x)}$

   (c) $f(x) = \ln\big(g(x)\big)$

   (d) $f(x) = \sin\big(g(x)\big)$

   (e) $f(x) = \tan\big(g(x)\big)$

   (f) $f(x) = g(x^n)$

   (g) $f(x) = g(e^x)$

   (h) $f(x) = g(\ln x)$

   (i) $f(x) = g(\sin x)$

   (j) $f(x) = g(\tan x)$

Find the derivative of each of the following functions.

4. $f(x) = \left(x^2 + 3\right)^{29}$

5. $f(x) = \left(1 + e^x\right)^{33}$

6. $f(x) = \sqrt{2 + \sin x}$

7. $f(x) = \sin\left(e^{3x}\right)$

8. $f(x) = \cos\left(x^2\right)$
9. $f(x) = \tan\left(\sqrt[3]{x}\right)$
10. $f(x) = \ln\left(4x^2 + 3\right)$
11. $f(x) = \sqrt{x^2 + e^{-3x}}$
12. $f(x) = \cos\left(\sqrt{x} + e^{-x}\right)$
13. $f(x) = \left(2x^{3/4} + 5x^{-1/6}\right)^{12}$
14. $f(x) = \left(x^{3/2} - 4x^{2/3} + 17\right)^{421}$
15. $f(x) = (x + \ln x)^{14}$
16. $f(x) = \ln\left(x^2 + 3\sin x\right)$
17. $f(x) = \sin\left(e^{2x} + \tan(3x)\right)$
18. $f(x) = \cos^3(x^4)$
19. $f(x) = \ln\left(e^{3x} + \cos^2 x\right)$
20. $f(x) = \tan\left(e^{x^2}\right)$
21. $f(x) = \sin^5\left(3x^4\right)$
22. $f(x) = \sqrt{4 + \cos^2(3x)}$
23. $f(x) = \sqrt[3]{\cos\left(4x^2\right)}$
24. $f(x) = \cos^2\left(e^{3x}\right)$
25. $f(x) = x^2\left(4x^3 + 5\right)^6$
26. $f(x) = x\ln(2 + \sin(3x))$
27. $f(x) = e^{x^3}\cos\left(4x^5 + 2\right)$
28. $f(x) = \sin^2(x\cos x)$
29. $f(x) = \sqrt{3 + x\cos x}$
30. $f(x) = e^{x\sin x}$
31. $f(x) = \tan\left(x^2\ln x\right)$
32. $f(x) = \cos\left(xe^{2x}\right)$
33. $f(x) = x^2\sin\left(e^x\ln x\right)$

34. Let $h(x) = f\left(\dfrac{g(x)}{x^2+1}\right)$. If $f(1) = 3$, $f(2) = 5$, $f'(1) = 7$, $f'(2) = 11$, $g(1) = 2$, and $g'(1) = 4$, what is $h'(1)$?

In exercises 35–37, f and g are the functions defined by the graphs below.

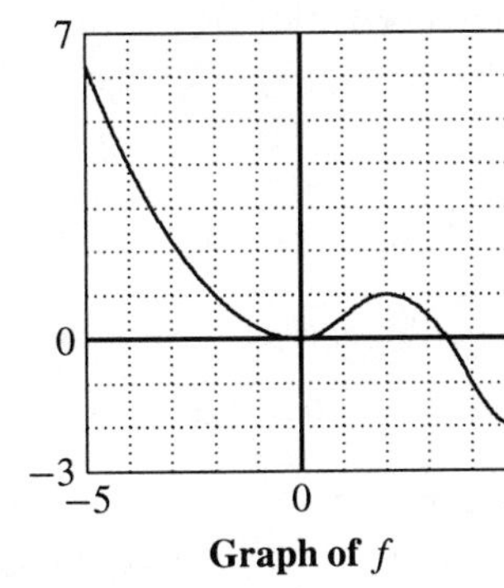

Graph of f

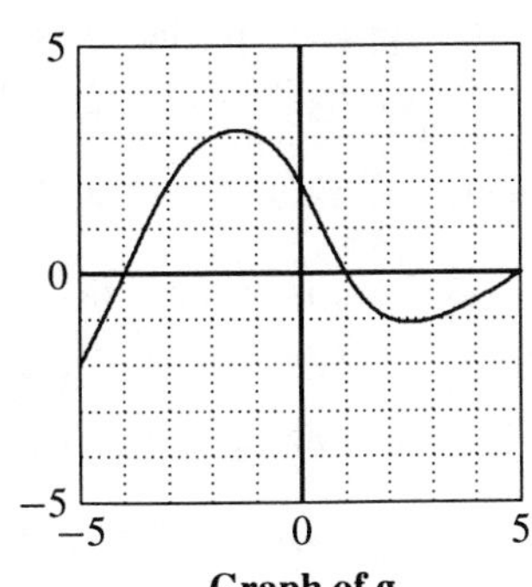

Graph of g

35. Let $h(x) = (f \circ g)(x)$.
   (a) Evaluate $h(-2)$, $h(1)$, and $h(3)$.
   (b) Is $h'(-1)$ positive, negative, or equal to zero? Justify your answer.
   (c) Estimate $h'(-2)$, $h'(1)$, and $h'(3)$.
   (d) What values of x correspond to stationary points of $h(x)$?

36. Let $j(x) = f(x^4)$. Is j increasing or decreasing at $x = -1$? Justify your answer.

37. Let $k(x) = f(e^{-x})$.

    (a) Determine whether k is increasing, decreasing, or stationary at $x = -1$, $x = 0$, and $x = 1$. Justify your answers.

    (b) Show that $x = -\ln 2$ is a stationary point of k and determine whether it corresponds to a local maxima or a local minima. Justify your answer.

Find an antiderivative of each of the following functions. [HINT: See part (c) of problem 3.]

38. $f(x) = xe^{x^2}$

39. $f(x) = 2x\cos\left(x^2\right)$

40. $f(x) = x^2\sin\left(2x^3\right)$

41. $f(x) = x\left(x^2+3\right)^4$

42. $f(x) = x^3\left(2x^4+6\right)^5$

43. $f(x) = \dfrac{3x}{4+x^2}$

44. $f(x) = \dfrac{x}{\sqrt{1+x^2}}$

45. $f(x) = x\sin\left(1-x^2\right)$

46. $f(x) = \dfrac{e^{\sqrt{x}}}{\sqrt{x}}$

47. $f(x) = e^{3x}\sec^2\left(e^{3x}\right)$

48. $f(x) = e^{\cos x}\sin x$

49. $f(x) = e^x\cos\left(e^x\right)\sin\left(e^x\right)$

50. $f(x) = \dfrac{3x^2-5}{x^3-5x}$

51. $f(x) = \dfrac{2x+3}{x^2+3x+5}$

52. $f(x) = \dfrac{e^x}{1+e^x}$

53. $f(x) = \dfrac{\cos x}{2+\sin x}$

54. Suppose that f is a function such that $f(\pi/2) = 17$ and $f'(x) = 2e^{x\cos x}$.

    (a) Find an equation of the line tangent to the graph of f at $x = \pi/2$.

    (b) Let $L(x)$ be the line tangent to the graph of f at $x = \pi/2$. Is $L(2) < f(2)$? Justify your answer.

55. Let $f(x) = \ln(2+\cos x)$.

    (a) What is the domain of f?

    (b) At which values of x does f have local maxima? Local minima?

    (c) At which values of x does f have inflection points?

56. (a) Suppose that f is a function such that $f'(x) > 0$ for all x. If $g(x) = f(f(x))$, must g be increasing for all x? Explain your answer.

    (b) Suppose that f is a function such that $f'(x) < 0$ for all x. If $g(x) = f(f(x))$, must g be decreasing for all x? Explain your answer.

57. Use the identity $\dfrac{f(x)}{g(x)} = f(x)\cdot\left(g(x)\right)^{-1}$ together with the product and chain rules to derive the quotient rule.

58. Let $h = f\circ g$. Show that $h''(a) = f''\big(g(a)\big)\big(g'(a)\big)^2 + f'\big(g(a)\big)g''(a)$.

59. Let $f(x) = (1 + e^x)^{-1}$.

    (a) Evaluate $\lim_{x \to \infty} f(x)$.

    (b) Evaluate $\lim_{x \to -\infty} f(x)$.

    (c) Explain why f is invertible.

    (d) What are the domain and range of f^{-1}?

60. Let $f(x) = \sin(|x|)$.

    (a) What is the domain of f? Of f'?

    (b) Find an expression for $f'(x)$.

61. Suppose that $f'(x) = g(x)$ and that $h(x) = x^2$. Express $\big(f(h(x))\big)'$ in terms of g and x.

62. Suppose that f and g are functions such that

    (i) $f(0) = 0$
    (ii) $g(0) = 1$
    (iii) $f'(x) = g(x)$ for all x
    (iv) $g'(x) = -f(x)$ for all x

    (a) Show that $h(x) = \big(f(x)\big)^2 + \big(g(x)\big)^2 = 1$ for all x. [HINT: Show that $h(0) = 1$ and $h'(x) = 0$ for all x.]

    (b) Let $k(x) = \big(F(x) - f(x)\big)^2 + \big(G(x) - g(x)\big)^2$ where F and G are another pair of functions that satisfy the properties (i)–(iv). Show that $k'(x) = 0$ for all x.

    (c) Use part (b) to show that $F(x) = f(x) = \sin x$ and that $G(x) = g(x) = \cos x$ for all x.

63. Let $f(x) = \sin x + \cos x$ on the interval $[-3\pi/4, \pi/4]$.

    (a) Show that f has an inverse.

    (b) Find an expression for $\big(f^{-1}\big)'(x)$. [HINT: $(\sin x - \cos x)^2 = 2 - (\sin x + \cos x)^2$.]

64. Let $g(x) = f(x^2)$ where f is a function with the following properties:

    (i) f, f', and f'' have domain $\mathbb{R}$
    (ii) $f(0) = 1$
    (iii) $f'(x) > 0$ for all $x \neq 0$
    (iv) f is concave down on $(-\infty, 0)$
    (v) f is concave up on $(0, \infty)$

    (a) Where does g have local minima?

    (b) Where is g concave up?

    (c) Sketch the graph of a suitable function g.

65. Dan R. Steele is staff mathematician at St. Olav's Hospital. Dan's job is to describe everything he can using functions and formulas. During his first few days on the job, he decides to focus on the hospital's expenditures. Dan figures that the hospital's daily expenditures, which he calls E, are a function of how many of the hospital's beds are in use. Our hero decides that

$$E(B) = 15000 + \ln(B + 1),$$

where B denotes the number of beds in use. Of course, B is not constant; B varies with time. Dan estimates that

$$B(t) = 20\sin\left(\frac{t}{10}\right) + 55,$$

where t denotes time measured in days.

(a) Does Dan use an increasing or a decreasing function to describe $E(B)$? Does his choice make sense?

(b) Is the function $E(B)$ concave up or concave down? Does this seem appropriate?

(c) What is the function that describes E as a function of time?

(d) When $B(t)$ is decreasing, what happens to $E(B)$? Does this make sense? Is this consistent with the chain rule?

66. Evaluate $\lim_{x\to\pi} \dfrac{5^{\sin x} - 1}{x - \pi}$ exactly (i.e., as a value of an elementary function).

3.5 Implicit differentiation

Implicitly vs. explicitly defined functions

The equation $y = -3x + 5$ defines y **explicitly** as a function (we'll call it f) of x—for an input x, the output is given by the explicit rule $f(x) = -3x + 5$.

Consider, by contrast, the equivalent equation $6x + 2y = 10$. Although it doesn't display y explicitly as a function of x, the new equation defines y **implicitly** as a function of x. *Solving* for y gives the same explicit formula we had before:

$$6x + 2y = 10 \iff 2y = -6x + 10 \iff y = -3x + 5.$$

For the linear equation $6x + 2y = 10$ it was easy to find an explicit formula for y. Things aren't always so simple. More complicated equations are much harder—or even impossible—to solve explicitly for y. Even simple equations, moreover, may not define y uniquely as a function of x, because the graph of an *equation* need not be the graph of a *function*.

■ **Example 1.** Does the equation $x - y^2 = 0$ define y as a function of x?

Solution: No. Solving algebraically for y shows why:

$$x - y^2 = 0 \implies y^2 = x \implies y = \pm\sqrt{x}.$$

In effect, the equation defines *two* functions of x: $f_1(x) = \sqrt{x}$ and $f_2(x) = -\sqrt{x}$, each defined for nonnegative inputs x. The picture agrees:

Graph of $x - y^2 = 0$

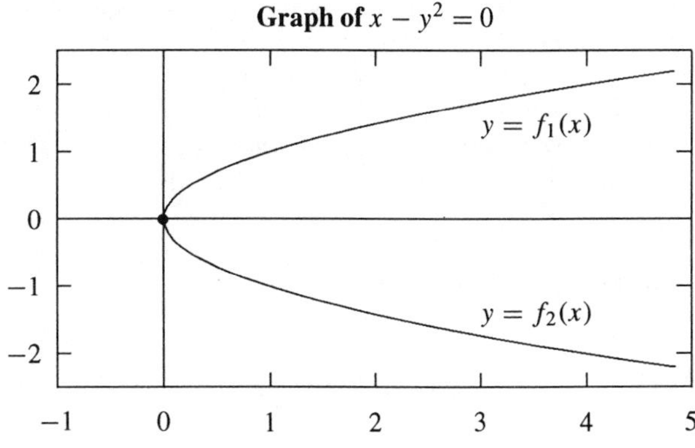

The "sideways" parabola is not the graph of a function because each value of x corresponds to *two* values of y. The upper and lower halves of the graph *do* define functions of x—the same two functions we wrote explicitly above. □

It fails the vertical line test.

f_1 and f_2

■ **Example 2.** Does the equation $5x^2 - 6xy + 5y^2 = 16$ implicitly define y as *one* function of x? As several functions of x?

Solution: Here's the graph, an ellipse; the points $(2, 2)$ and $(1, -1)$ are bulleted.

Graph of $5x^2 - 6xy + 5y^2 = 16$

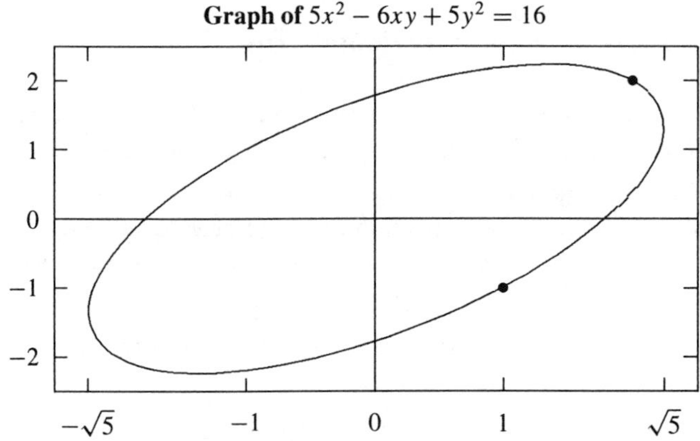

Like the previous graph, this one defines *two* different functions y of x, corresponding to the "upper" and "lower" halves of the ellipse. (The upper half, passing through $(2, 2)$, defines a function g_1 for which $g_1(2) = 2$. The lower half defines *another* function g_2, for which $g_2(1) = -1$. Below we'll find derivatives at these points.) The domain of each function is the interval $[-\sqrt{5}, \sqrt{5}]$. Solving for y is harder this time; we won't bother. □

Implicit functions, implicit derivatives

All three of the equations $6x+2y = 10$, $x = y^2$, and $5x^2-6xy+5y^2 = 16$ implicitly define one or more functions of x. How might we *differentiate* such functions?

If we can solve *explicitly* for y, there's no problem. For $x = y^2$, for instance,

$$f_1(x) = \sqrt{x} \implies f_1'(x) = \frac{1}{2\sqrt{x}}; \quad f_2(x) = -\sqrt{x} \implies f_2'(x) = -\frac{1}{2\sqrt{x}}.$$

What if we *can't* (or don't want to) solve explicitly for y? In that case, we use **implicit differentiation**, a technique for differentiating an *equation*—without first solving it for one of the variables. Here's the idea for an equation in x and y:

> **Implicit differentiation:** *Differentiate both sides of the equation, treating y as an (implicitly defined) function of x; use the chain rule. The resulting equation involves x, y, and dy/dx; it can be solved, if necessary, for dy/dx.*

We'll illustrate with examples.

■ **Example 3.** Let $x = y^2$; find dy/dx by implicit differentiation.

Solution: We differentiate both sides of the equation, treating y as a function of x:

$$x = y^2 \implies \frac{d}{dx}(x) = \frac{d}{dx}\left(y^2\right) \implies 1 = 2y\frac{dy}{dx}.$$

Note the use of the chain rule: Since y is a function of x, $(y^2)' = 2yy'$. Solving for dy/dx is easy:

$$1 = 2y\frac{dy}{dx} \implies \frac{dy}{dx} = \frac{1}{2y}.$$

This agrees—as it should—with *both* of our earlier answers:

$$y = \sqrt{x} \implies y' = \frac{1}{2\sqrt{x}} = \frac{1}{2y};$$
$$y = -\sqrt{x} \implies y' = -\frac{1}{2\sqrt{x}} = \frac{1}{2y}.$$ □

■ **Example 4.** As the graph in Example 2 shows, the equation $5x^2 - 6xy + 5y^2 = 16$ defines y implicitly as a function of x near the point $(2, 2)$. Find dy/dx in terms of x and y. What is its value at the point $(2, 2)$? At $(1, -1)$? What do these values *mean*?

Solution: First, we differentiate our equation with respect to x:➸

Don't forget: y is a function of x, so the chain rule applies.

$$5x^2 - 6xy + 5y^2 = 16 \implies 10x - 6y - 6x\frac{dy}{dx} + 10y\frac{dy}{dx} = 0.$$

(The middle term $-6xy = -6x \cdot y$ is a *product*, so we used the product rule.)
Now we solve for dy/dx:

$$10x - 6y - 6x\frac{dy}{dx} + 10y\frac{dy}{dx} = 0 \implies \frac{dy}{dx}(-6x + 10y) = 6y - 10x$$
$$\implies \frac{dy}{dx} = \frac{6y - 10x}{10y - 6x}.$$

At $(2, 2)$, therefore, $dy/dx = -1$; at $(1, -1)$, $dy/dx = 1$.➸ Geometrically, these results mean that the curve shown has slopes -1 and 1, respectively, at the bulleted points $(2, 2)$ and $(1, -1)$.➸ □

Check these simple calculations.

Convince yourself that these results are graphically plausible.

Implicit differentiation: pros and cons. Implicit differentiation neatly avoids the hard problem of solving complicated equations explicitly for y. As usual in life and work, there's a price to pay for such convenience: derivative formulas obtained via implicit differentiation usually involve both x and y.

A sample problem

Here's a problem that applies ideas of this section.

■ **Example 5.** Use implicit differentiation to find points on the unit circle $x^2+y^2 = 1$ at which the tangent line has slope 1.

Solution: Implicit differentiation with respect to x gives➸

Check the easy steps.

$$x^2 + y^2 = 1 \implies 2x + 2y\frac{dy}{dx} = 0 \implies \frac{dy}{dx} = \frac{-x}{y}.$$

Thus $dy/dx = 1$ if and only if $y = -x$, i.e., where the line $y = -x$ intersects the unit circle. From a picture➸ it's easy to see that these intersections occur at the points $(-\sqrt{2}/2, \sqrt{2}/2)$ and $(\sqrt{2}/2, -\sqrt{2}/2)$. □

Draw your own!

Exercises

1. The equation $2x + 3y = 6$ implicitly defines y as a function of x.

   (a) By solving for y, find an *explicit* formula for y as a function of x. Use the result to find dy/dx.

   (b) Find dy/dx by implicit differentiation; compare results with the previous part.

2. The equation $4x^2y - 3y = x^3$ implicitly defines y as a function of x.

   (a) Use implicit differentiation to find dy/dx.

   (b) Write y as an explicit function of x and compute dy/dx directly.

3. The equation $x^2 + y^2 = 1$ defines *two* different functions of x:

$$x^2 + y^2 = 1 \implies y = \pm\sqrt{1 - x^2}.$$

   (a) Find dy/dx by implicit differentiation.

   (b) Find dy/dx (directly) for each of the functions $y = \pm\sqrt{1 - x^2}$. Compare your results with those found in part (a).

4. Each of the following equations defines a curve in the xy-plane. Use implicit differentiation to find dy/dx for each curve.

   (a) $x^2 + 2y^2 = 4$

   (b) $4x^2 - 9y^2 = 36$

   (c) $y^2 - x^2 = x^2y^2$

   (d) $y^2(2 - x) = x^3$

   (e) $x^3 + y^3 = 3xy$

   (f) $y^4 = y^2 - x^2$

   (g) $x^{2/3} + y^{2/3} = 1$

   (h) $\left(x^2 + y^2 - 2y\right)^2 = x^2 + y^2$

   (i) $\left(x^2 + y^2\right)^2 = x^2 - y^2$

   (j) $\left(x^2 + y^2\right)^2 = 2xy$

5. Sketch a graph of the curve defined by the equation $y^2 = x^3$ and find equations of the *two* lines tangent to the curve at $x = 1$.

6. Sketch a graph of the curve defined by the equation $y^4 = 4y^2 - x^2$ and find equations of the *four* lines tangent to the curve at $x = 1$.

3.6 Inverse trigonometric functions and their derivatives

The natural logarithm and exponential functions are *inverses*; each "undoes" the other. In symbols:

The first equation holds for all x, the second only for $x > 0$.

$$\ln\left(e^x\right) = x \qquad \text{and} \qquad e^{\ln x} = x.$$

In this section we find and discuss inverses for several *trigonometric* functions.

Nomenclature: "arc" or "inverse"?

Two common forms are used to denote inverse trigonometric functions:

> $\arcsin x$, $\arccos x$, *and* $\arctan x$ *are synonyms for* $\sin^{-1} x$, $\cos^{-1} x$, *and* $\tan^{-1} x$.

Each form has its advantages. The first makes explicit the connection with arcs on the unit circle; the second reminds us that function inversion is involved. We'll use both.

Don't confuse $\sin^{-1} x$ with $1/\sin x$. They're entirely different.

A technical problem and its solution: restricting domains

To be invertible, a function must be one-to-one; graphically speaking, it must pass the "horizontal line test." Alas, *no* trigonometric function has this property. Far from it—trigonometric functions, being 2π-periodic, repeat themselves on intervals of length 2π, "hitting" each output value *infinitely often*. The next example illustrates the problem.

■ **Example 1.** By any sensible definition, $\arcsin(0.5)$ should be a number whose sine is 0.5. Find such a number. How many are there?

We'll give a formal definition below.

Solution: The picture below shows *four* inputs x for which $\sin x = 0.5$.

Values of x for which $\sin x = 0.5$

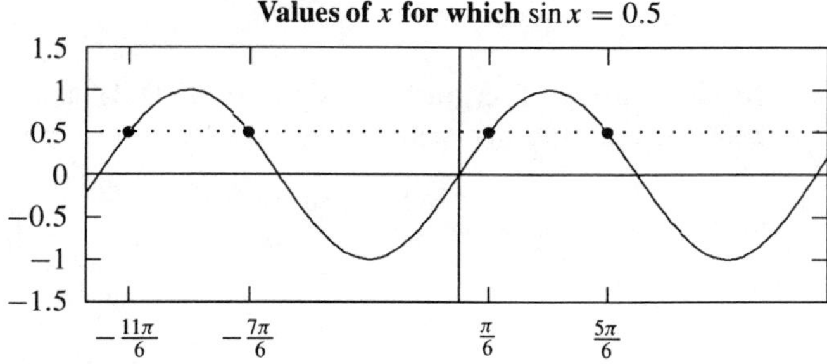

The bulleted points show that

$$0.5 = \sin\left(-\tfrac{11\pi}{6}\right) = \sin\left(-\tfrac{7\pi}{6}\right) = \sin\left(\tfrac{\pi}{6}\right) = \sin\left(\tfrac{5\pi}{6}\right).$$

Moreover, this list is far from exhaustive—infinitely many more solutions of the equation $\sin x = 0.5$ exist outside our viewing window.

Which of these numbers deserves to be called $\arcsin(0.5)$? None especially, but if *forced* to choose, we might reasonably select $\pi/6$, the solution nearest to zero. Any scientific calculator agrees. According to an HP-28S, for instance,

aka $\sin^{-1}(0.5)$

$$\sin^{-1}(0.5) = 0.523598775598 \approx \frac{\pi}{6}. \qquad \square$$

Surgery on domains

The problem just seen—choosing from among reasonable candidates—arises because the trigonometric functions aren't one-to-one. Our solution is crude but effective: amputate the offending part of each function's domain, and thus *make* it one-to-one. Graphs will show us where to cut.

Inverting the sine function

The sine function is *increasing*, and therefore one-to-one, on the interval $[-\pi/2, \pi/2]$. (There are, of course, many other intervals on which the sine function is one-to-one. Among all such intervals, this one, centered at 0, seems most natural.) The picture below shows both the ordinary sine curve (drawn dotted), and the special piece (drawn solid) in question here:

Restricting the sine function

Restricted to this domain, the sine function *is* invertible; its inverse is defined formally as follows:

> **Definition:** For x in $[-1, 1]$, $\sin^{-1} x$ (or $\arcsin x$) is defined by the conditions
> $$x = \sin y \quad \text{and} \quad -\frac{\pi}{2} \le y \le \frac{\pi}{2}.$$
> In words: $\arcsin x$ is the (unique) angle between $-\pi/2$ and $\pi/2$ whose sine is x.

Note:

Graphical symmetry. The graphs of $\sin x$ (restricted!) and $\sin^{-1} x$ show the expected reflective symmetry:

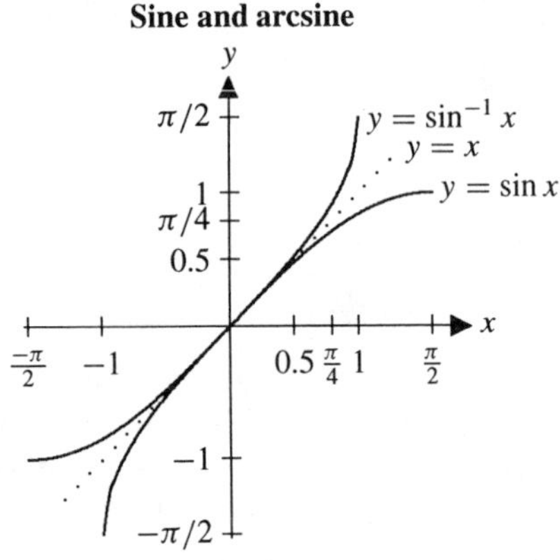

Sine and arcsine

Domain and range. The sine function (as we've restricted it) has domain $[-\pi/2, \pi/2]$ and range $[-1, 1]$. The *inverse* sine function has it the other way around—its domain is $[-1, 1]$ and its range $[-\pi/2, \pi/2]$.

Collapsing equations By the definition of inverse function, these equations hold:

$$\sin\left(\sin^{-1} x\right) = x \qquad \text{if } -1 \leq x \leq 1;$$

$$\sin^{-1}(\sin x) = x \qquad \text{if } -\pi/2 \leq x \leq \pi/2$$

Inverting the cosine function

The cosine function➡ becomes one-to-one, and therefore invertible, when restricted to the interval➡ $[0, \pi]$. This understood, the graphs and formal definition follow naturally:

The situation for $\cos x$ differs only in details from that for $\sin x$.

Restricting $\cos x$ to $[-\pi/2, \pi/2]$ doesn't work. Do you see why not?

Restricting the cosine function

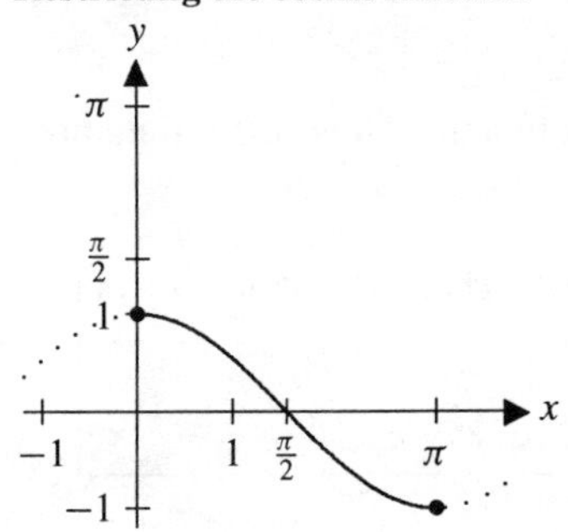

Graphs of cosine and arccosine

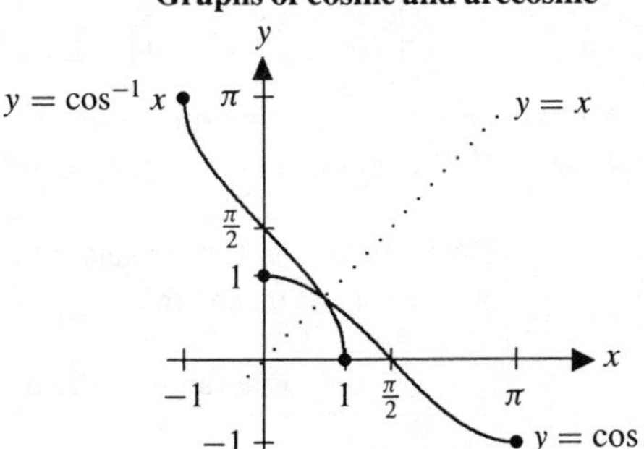

> **Definition:** For x in $[-1, 1]$, $\cos^{-1} x$ (or $\arccos x$) is defined by the conditions
>
> $$x = \cos y \quad \text{and} \quad 0 \leq y \leq \pi.$$
>
> In words: $\arccos x$ is the (unique) angle between 0 and π whose cosine is x.

Note:

Graphical symmetry. The graphs of cos and $\cos^{-1}$ show the usual symmetry for inverse functions—they're symmetric with respect to the line $y = x$.

Domain and range. We restricted the cosine function to have domain $[0, \pi]$ and range $[-1, 1]$. The *inverse* cosine function, therefore, has domain $[-1, 1]$ and range $[0, \pi]$.

Collapsing equations. As with the arcsine, two equations express the inverse relationship between cos and arccos:

$$\cos\left(\cos^{-1} x\right) = x \qquad \text{if } -1 \leq x \leq 1;$$

$$\cos^{-1}(\cos x) = x \qquad \text{if } 0 \leq x \leq \pi.$$

Inverting the tangent function

The tangent function is one-to-one if restricted to any of its "branches." We'll use the "middle" branch, through the origin:

The tangent function: one-to-one on the middle branch

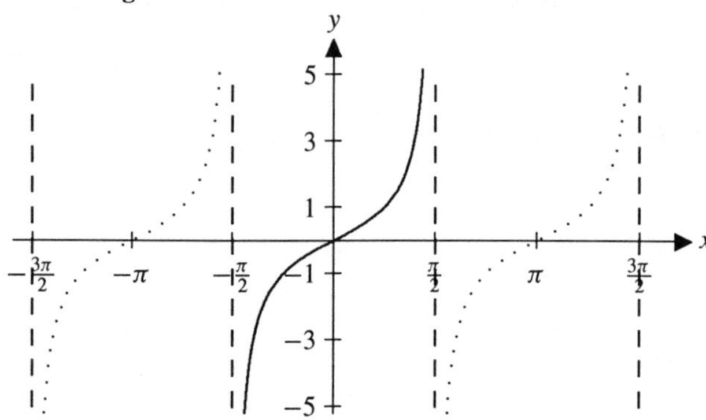

The graph shows this. Do you agree?

Unlike the sine and cosine functions, the tangent function "hits" *all* real numbers as outputs. The arctangent function, therefore, accepts *all* real inputs.

> **Definition:** Let x be any real number. Then $y = \tan^{-1} x$ (or $y = \arctan x$) means that
>
> $$x = \tan y \quad \text{and} \quad -\pi/2 < y < \pi/2.$$

Note:

Symmetry. The domain of $\arctan x$ (i.e., the range of $\tan x$) is infinite, so any picture of its graph is incomplete. The figure below gives the idea; notice the usual symmetry between a function and its inverse:

The tangent function and its inverse

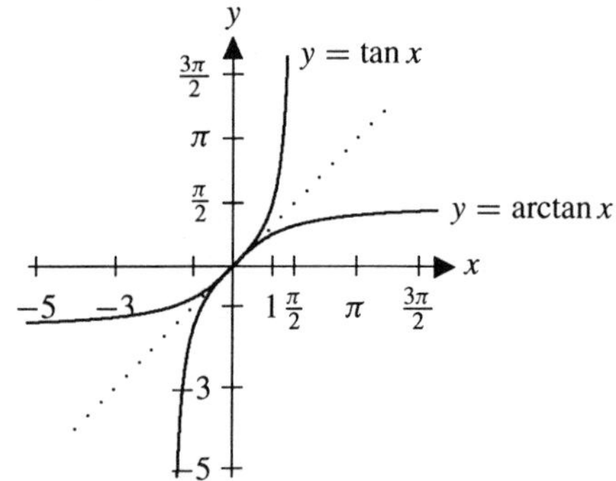

Infinite domain. The tangent function (as restricted) has *domain* $(-\pi/2, \pi, 2)$ and *range* $(-\infty, \infty)$. The arctangent function turns things around: it has *range* $(-\pi/2, \pi, 2)$ and *domain* $(-\infty, \infty)$.

Other inverse trigonometric functions

As your calculator knows.

All six trigonometric functions have inverses. As for $\arcsin x$, $\arccos x$, and $\arctan x$, defining $\operatorname{arcsec} x$, $\operatorname{arccsc} x$, and $\operatorname{arccot} x$ requires care with domains and ranges. Among these "other" functions, the arcsecant is most useful; it appears occasionally in antiderivatives.

There's trouble if $\cos t = 0$.

For any legal input t, $\sec t = 1/\cos t$. The simplest definition of $\operatorname{arcsec} x$—based on $\arccos x$—reflects this fact:

Definition: For any x with $|x| \geq 1$,

$$\operatorname{arcsec}(x) = \sec^{-1}(x) = \cos^{-1}(1/x).$$

In particular,

$$y = \operatorname{arcsec}(x) = \arccos\left(\frac{1}{x}\right) \implies \cos y = \frac{1}{x} \implies \sec y = x,$$

as we'd expect.

Plot your own copy of the arcsecant function; experiment with various domains. See the exercises for more on the arcsecant function.

Inverse trigonometric functions and the unit circle

We defined the sine, cosine, and tangent functions in terms of the unit circle. Their *inverses*, too, can be interpreted in the same way. Examples show how.

■ **Example 2.** A unit circle appears below; arclengths appear in radians. Use the picture to estimate arcsin(0.5) and arctan 2.

Starting from the point $(1, 0)$.

Arctangent, arcsine, and the unit circle

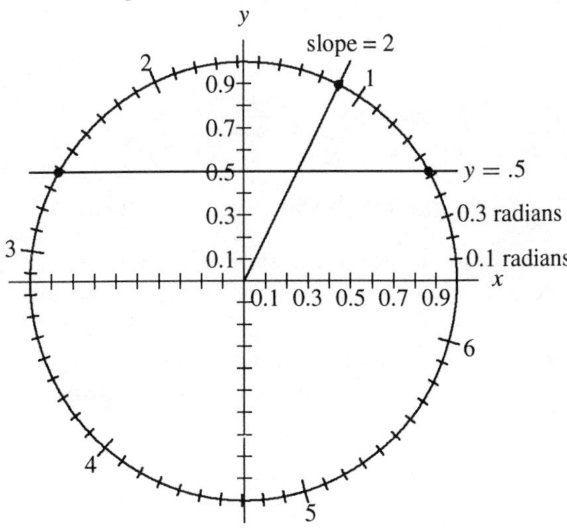

Solution: By definition, arctan 2 is an angle whose tangent is 2. Recall that the tangent of *any* angle is the *slope* of the line that angle determines. Therefore, we want an angle—the one between $-\pi/2$ and $\pi/2$—that corresponds to a slope of 2. To find this angle, we draw a line from the origin, with slope 2, and observe the radian measure of the angle it determines. The picture shows that the line determines an arc of radian measure about 1.1; this is our estimate for arctan 2.

Or "arc."

Don't recall? See Appendix G.

According to an HP-28S calculator, arctan 2 ≈ 1.10714871779.

Reading $\sin^{-1}(0.5)$ from the unit circle is similar. By definition, $\sin t$ is the y-coordinate of the point determined by an arc of length t on the unit circle. Therefore arcsin(0.5) is the (one and only) angle between $-\pi/2$ and $\pi/2$ (i.e., to the right of the y-axis) whose corresponding y-coordinate is 0.5. To find this angle, we draw the line $y = 0.5$ (as shown in the picture above). It crosses the circle at the bulleted point, the end of an arc with radian measure about 0.52; therefore, $\arcsin(0.5) \approx 0.52$. □

This estimate is surprisingly good: The "right" answer is about 0.523598775598.

Combining ordinary and inverse trigonometric functions

In practice, inverse trigonometric functions are often combined with ordinary trigonometric functions. Diagrams like the one below can be helpful in seeing how the process works.

Relating inverse trigonometric functions: pictorial aids

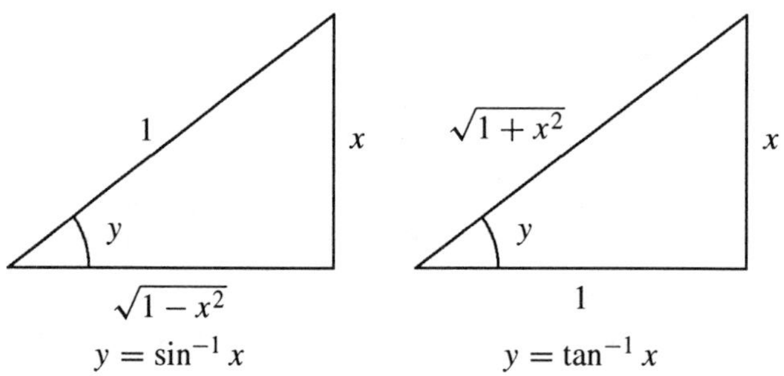

$y = \sin^{-1} x$ $\qquad$ $y = \tan^{-1} x$

The first figure shows (among other things):

$$\cos(\sin^{-1} x) = \frac{\text{adjacent}}{\text{hypotenuse}} = \sqrt{1-x^2}.$$

From the second figure, similarly:

$$\sin(\tan^{-1} x) = \frac{\text{opposite}}{\text{hypotenuse}} = \frac{x}{\sqrt{1-x^2}}.$$

Derivatives of inverse trigonometric functions

We know derivatives of the ordinary trigonometric functions; with the chain rule, we can find derivatives of their inverses. After tabulating the derivatives, we'll derive them.

Derivatives of ordinary trigonometric functions are other trigonometric functions. Surprisingly, *inverse* trigonometric functions have *algebraic* derivatives:

Derivatives of inverse trigonometric functions

Function	$\arcsin x$	$\arccos x$	$\arctan x$	$\operatorname{arcsec} x$
Derivative	$\dfrac{1}{\sqrt{1-x^2}}$	$\dfrac{-1}{\sqrt{1-x^2}}$	$\dfrac{1}{1+x^2}$	$\dfrac{1}{\lvert x\rvert\sqrt{x^2-1}}$

Notice:

See the exercises for more detail.

Restricted domains. The functions $\arcsin x$, $\arccos x$, and $\operatorname{arcsec} x$ have restricted domains. So, therefore, must their derivatives.

Not much difference. The derivatives of $\arcsin x$ and $\arccos x$ differ only in *sign*. Therefore $(\arcsin x + \arccos x)' = 0$, for all legal inputs x. This is no accident, of course. For all x in $[-1, 1]$,

$$\arcsin x + \arccos x = \frac{\pi}{2}.$$

Graph both on the same axes to see why.

(The graphs of $\arcsin x$ and $\arccos x$ say the same thing.)

Graphical evidence. We'll see below, by calculation, *why* these formulas hold. Graphs show convincingly *that* they hold. Here, for instance, are graphs of the arctangent function and its claimed derivative:

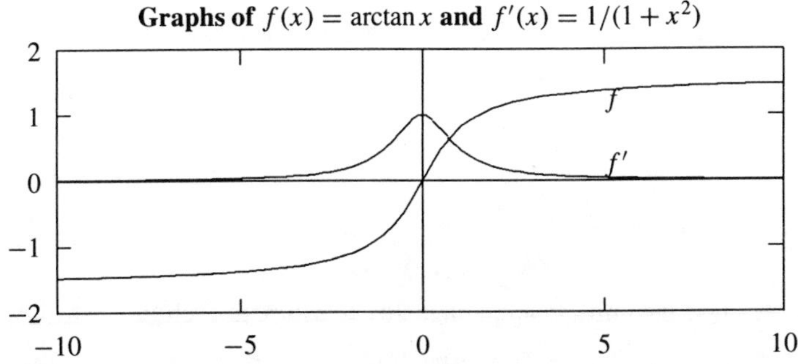

■ **Example 3.** Explain why $(\arctan x)' = \dfrac{1}{1+x^2}$.

Solution: If $f(x) = \tan x$ and $g(x) = \arctan x$, then f and g are inverses, and $f'(x) = \sec^2 x$. Unraveling the derivative formula above gives

$$(\arctan x)' = \frac{1}{f'(g(x))} = \frac{1}{\sec^2(\arctan x)}.$$

Despite first appearances, the result is correct. We can simplify the last quantity using the trigonometric identity $\sec^2 t = 1 + \tan^2 t$:

$$\frac{1}{\sec^2(\arctan x)} = \frac{1}{1+\tan^2(\arctan x)} = \frac{1}{1+x^2}. \qquad \square$$

■ **Example 4.** Explain why $(\arcsin x)' = \dfrac{1}{\sqrt{1-x^2}}$.

Solution: We play the same game as before, with slightly different twists. If $f(x) = \sin x$ and $g(x) = \arcsin x$, then $f'(x) = \cos x$, so➸

Watch for the combination of the cosine and arcsine functions below.

$$\begin{aligned}(\arcsin x)' &= \frac{1}{f'(g(x))}\\ &= \frac{1}{\cos(\arcsin x)}\\ &= \frac{1}{\sqrt{1-\sin^2(\arcsin x)}}\\ &= \frac{1}{\sqrt{1-x^2}}.\end{aligned} \qquad \square$$

The remaining derivative formulas can be found similarly.

Exercises

1. Find each of the following numbers exactly (in radians).

   (a) $\sin^{-1}(1)$
   (b) $\sin^{-1}\left(\sqrt{3}/2\right)$
   (c) $\cos^{-1}(-1)$
   (d) $\cos^{-1}\left(-\sqrt{2}/2\right)$
   (e) $\tan^{-1}(1)$
   (f) $\tan^{-1}\left(\sqrt{3}\right)$

2. Use the unit circle on page 281 to estimate each of the following numbers.

   (a) $\sin^{-1}(0.8)$
   (b) $\cos^{-1}(0.6)$
   (c) $\tan^{-1}(0.4)$
   (d) $\tan^{-1}(3)$

3. The table gives samples of what one calculator knows (and doesn't know) about inverse trigonometric functions:

Inverse Trigonometric Function Values

x	-2	-1	-0.5	-0.25	0	0.25	0.5	1	2	5	100
$\sin^{-1} x$		-1.57	-0.52	-0.25	0.00	0.25	0.52	1.57			
$\cos^{-1} x$		3.14	2.09	1.82	1.57	1.31	1.04	0.00			
$\tan^{-1} x$	-1.11	-0.79	-0.46	-0.24	0.00	0.24	0.46	0.79	1.11	1.37	1.56

   (a) Can the gaps in the table above be filled in? Why or why not? Answer using the word "domain."
   (b) In each column, the entries for $\sin^{-1} x$ and $\cos^{-1} x$ add to 1.57. Surely this can't be coincidence! What's going on?

4. Use a calculator to find 4 values of x for which $\cos x = 0.5$

5. Use a calculator to find 4 values of x (2 positive, 2 negative) for which $\tan x = 2$.

6. The graph of the tangent function has *vertical* asymptotes. Where are they? Does the graph of the *arctangent* function have asymptotes? If so, where? Why? [HINT: Look carefully at the graphs of the tangent function and its inverse. Explain what you see in terms of reflection across the line $y = x$.]

7. The equation $\sin^{-1}(\sin x) = x$ suggests that the graph of $y = \sin^{-1}(\sin x)$, over any interval, might be the straight line $y = x$. It isn't (see below).

Graphs of $y = \arcsin(\sin x)$ and $y = x$

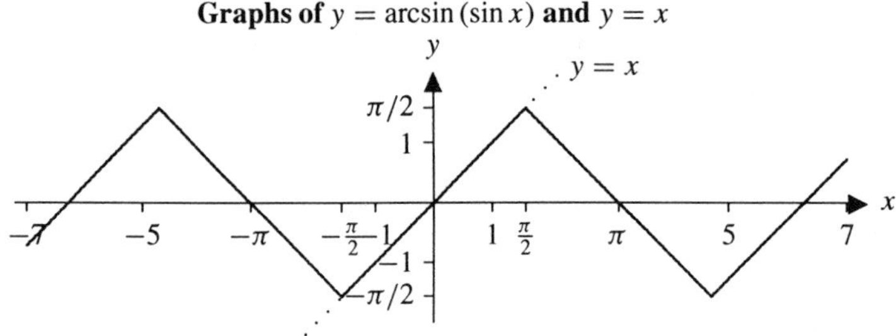

   (a) Explain why $\arcsin(\sin 5) \neq 5$.

(b) For which values of x *does* the equation $\arcsin(\sin x) = x$ hold?

(c) Let $f(x) = \arcsin(\sin x)$. Show that $f'(x) = \dfrac{\cos x}{|\cos x|}$.

(d) How is the result in part (b) related to the graph shown above?

8. (a) The function $\operatorname{arcsec} x$ accepts as inputs only values of x for which $|x| \geq 1$. Why is this restriction necessary? [HINT: What's the domain of $\arccos x$?]

   (b) What's the *range* of $\operatorname{arcsec} x$? [HINT: What's the range of $\arccos x$?]

9. Write each of the following as an algebraic expression. For example, $\cos(\arcsin x) = \sqrt{1 - x^2}$.

   (a) $\sin(\arccos x)$

   (b) $\tan(\arcsin x)$

   (c) $\sin(\arctan x)$

   (d) $\cos(\arctan x)$

10. (a) What is the domain of the derivative of the arcsine function? Give a geometric explanation for why it is not the same as the domain of the arcsine function.

    (b) What is the domain of the derivative of the arctangent function? Is it the same as the domain of the arctangent function?

    (c) What is the domain of the derivative of the arcsecant function? Is it the same as the domain of the arcsecant function?

11. Let $f(x) = \arctan x$

    (a) Plot graphs of f and f' on the same axes.

    (b) Evaluate $\lim_{x\to\infty} f(x)$, $\lim_{x\to-\infty} f(x)$, $\lim_{x\to\infty} f'(x)$, and $\lim_{x\to-\infty} f'(x)$. What do these results imply about the graph of the arctangent function?

    (c) Is f even, odd or neither?

    (d) Show that f is increasing on $(-\infty, \infty)$. How does the graph of f' reflect this fact?

    (e) Where is f concave up? Concave down? Does f have any inflection points? If so, where?

12. Let $f(x) = \arcsin x$.

    (a) Plot graphs of f and f' on the same axes.

    (b) Evaluate $\lim_{x\to 1^-} f(x)$, $\lim_{x\to -1^+} f(x)$, $\lim_{x\to 1^-} f'(x)$, and $\lim_{x\to -1^+} f'(x)$. What do these results imply about the graph of the arcsine function?

    (c) Is f even, odd or neither?

    (d) Show that f is increasing on $(-1, 1)$. How does the graph of f' reflect this fact?

    (e) Where is f concave up? Concave down? Does f have any inflection points? If so, where?

    (f) How does the graph of f' reflect the information found in part (e)?

13. Let $f(x) = \arccos x$.

    (a) Plot graphs of f and f' on the same axes.

(b) Evaluate $\lim_{x\to 1^-} f(x)$, $\lim_{x\to -1^+} f(x)$, $\lim_{x\to 1^-} f'(x)$, and $\lim_{x\to -1^+} f'(x)$. What do these results imply about the arccosine function?

(c) Is f even, odd or neither?

(d) Show that f is decreasing on $(-1, 1)$. How does the graph of f' reflect this fact?

(e) Where is f concave up? Concave down? Does f have any inflection points? If so, where are they located?

(f) How does the graph of f' reflect the information found in part (e)?

14. Let $f(x) = \operatorname{arcsec} x$.

(a) Plot graphs of f and f' using the plotting window $[-5, 5] \times [0, 5]$. [NOTE: If your calculator or computer doesn't recognize the arcsecant function, trick it by plotting $\arccos(1/x)$ instead.]

(b) Evaluate $\lim_{x\to 1^+} f(x)$, $\lim_{x\to -1^-} f(x)$, $\lim_{x\to 1^+} f'(x)$, and $\lim_{x\to -1^-} f'(x)$. What do these results imply about the graph of the arcsecant function?

(c) Evaluate $\lim_{x\to \infty} f(x)$, $\lim_{x\to -\infty} f(x)$, $\lim_{x\to \infty} f'(x)$, and $\lim_{x\to -\infty} f'(x)$. What do these results imply about the graph of the arcsecant function?

(d) Is f even, odd or neither?

(e) Show that f is increasing everywhere in the interior of its domain. How does the graph of f' reflect this fact?

(f) Where is f concave up? Concave down? Does f have any inflection points? If so, where are they located?

(g) How does the graph of f' reflect the information found in part (f)?

15. Find the derivative of each function below.

(a) $f(x) = \arctan(2x)$

(b) $f(x) = \arctan\left(x^2\right)$

(c) $f(x) = \sqrt{\arcsin x}$

(d) $f(x) = \arcsin(\sqrt{x})$

(e) $f(x) = \arcsin\left(e^x\right)$

(f) $f(x) = e^{\arctan x}$

(g) $f(x) = \arctan(\ln x)$

(h) $f(x) = \arccos(2x + 3)$

(i) $f(x) = \operatorname{arcsec}(x/2)$

(j) $f(x) = \arcsin x / \arccos x$

(k) $f(x) = x^2 \arctan\left(\sqrt{x}\right)$

(l) $f(x) = \ln\left(2 + \arcsin x\right)$

16. Find an antiderivative of each of the following function.

(a) $f(x) = 1/\left(1 + x^2\right)$

(b) $f(x) = 1/\sqrt{1 - x^2}$

(c) $f(x) = 2/\left(1 + 4x^2\right)$

(d) $f(x) = 3/\left(9 + x^2\right)$

(e) $f(x) = 1/\sqrt{9 - x^2}$

(f) $f(x) = 1/\sqrt{1 - 4x^2}$

(g) $f(x) = e^x/\left(1 + e^{2x}\right)$

(h) $f(x) = x/\sqrt{1 - x^4}$

(i) $f(x) = (2\arctan x)/(1 + x^2)$

(j) $f(x) = (\cos x)/\left(1 + \sin^2 x\right)$

(k) $f(x) = e^{\arcsin x}/\sqrt{1 - x^2}$

(l) $f(x) = 1/\left(x\left(1 + (\ln x)^2\right)\right)$

(m) $f(x) = 1/\left(\left(1 + x^2\right)\arctan x\right)$

17. (a) Show that $\arctan x + \arctan(1/x) = \pi/2$ for all $x > 0$. [HINT: Start by differentiating both sides of the equation.]

(b) Find an equation similar to the one in part (a) that is valid when $x < 0$.

18. Use calculus to prove each of the following identities. [HINT: See part (a) of the previous exercise.]

(a) $\arcsin(-x) = -\arcsin(x)$

(b) $\arccos(-x) = \pi - \arccos(x)$

(c) $\arccos x = \frac{\pi}{2} - \arcsin x$

(d) $\arctan\left(\dfrac{x}{\sqrt{1-x^2}}\right) = \arcsin x$

(e) $\arcsin\left(\dfrac{x-1}{x+1}\right) = 2\arctan(\sqrt{x}) - \pi/2$

19. (a) Show that $2\arcsin x = \arccos(1-2x^2)$ when $0 \le x \le 1$.

(b) Find an identity similar to the one in part (a) that is valid when $-1 \le x \le 0$.

20. Let $f(x) = \arctan\left(\frac{1+x}{1-x}\right)$.

(a) Assume that $x < 1$. Show that there is a constant C such that $f(x) = C + \arctan x$.

(b) Use the result in part (a) to evaluate $\lim\limits_{x\to 1^-} f(x)$.

(c) Evaluate $\lim\limits_{x\to 1^+} f(x)$.

21. (a) Show that $\tan(\operatorname{arcsec} x) = \sqrt{x^2-1}$ when $x \ge 1$.

(b) Find an algebraic expression for $\tan(\operatorname{arcsec} x)$ when $x \le -1$.

22. (a) Derive the identity $\arctan x + \arctan y = \arctan\left(\frac{x+y}{1-xy}\right)$ from the identity $\tan(x+y) = \frac{\tan x + \tan y}{1 - \tan x \tan y}$.

(b) What conditions must be satisfied by x and y for the identity derived in part (a) to hold?

23. (a) Use the identity in part (a) of the previous problem to show that $\pi/4 = \arctan(1/2) + \arctan(1/3)$.

(b) Show that $\pi/4 = 2\arctan(1/4) + \arctan(7/23)$. [HINT: Use the identity in part (a) of the previous problem twice.]

3.7 Why continuity matters

In Section 2.5 we defined continuity in terms of limits: f is **continuous** at $x = a$ if

$$f(x) \to f(a) \quad \text{as} \quad x \to a.$$

The standard elementary functions—algebraic, exponential, logarithm, and trigonometric functions—are continuous wherever they're defined. Combinations—sums, products, quotients, compositions, etc.—of elementary functions are *also* continuous wherever they're defined, thanks to the analogous properties of limits. (See, e.g., Theorem 2., page 171.)

Indeed, continuity is so much the rule in calculus that its importance may be hard to appreciate. This section aims to remedy that oversight.

The importance of being continuous: the intermediate value theorem and the extreme value theorem

Continuity is clearly a desirable property for a function to have. The intermediate value theorem (IVT) and the extreme value theorem (EVT) give two good reasons why. We won't prove either, but we'll indicate why the property each guarantees is practically useful.

Each theorem pertains to a continuous function f on a *closed and bounded* interval.

See the exercises for more on why $[a, b]$ must be closed.

Theorem 6. (The intermediate value theorem.) Let f be continuous on the closed and bounded interval $[a, b]$, and let y be any number between $f(a)$ and $f(b)$. Then for some input c between a and b, $f(c) = y$.

Theorem 7. (The extreme value theorem.) Let f be continuous on the closed, bounded interval $[a, b]$. Then f assumes both a maximum value and a minimum value somewhere on $[a, b]$.

Existential philosophy

The EVT and the IVT are **existence theorems**. Each guarantees the existence of (at least) one point in the domain with some desirable property. Neither theorem says *where* in $[a, b]$ these points may fall, or *how many* there may be. Such high-toned philosophy might suggest that these theorems, whatever their theoretical importance, have little practical use. That's wrong, as we'll see.

The IVT, pictorially

The IVT says that if f is continuous on $[a, b]$, then the range of f contains not just $f(a)$ and $f(b)$ but *everything in between*. This means that the graph of a continuous function f is "unbroken" in the following sense:

> *Enroute from $(a, f(a))$ to $(b, f(b))$, the graph of f crosses every horizontal line between $y = f(a)$ and $y = f(b)$.*

Here's the picture:

The IVT: f "hits" every intermediate value

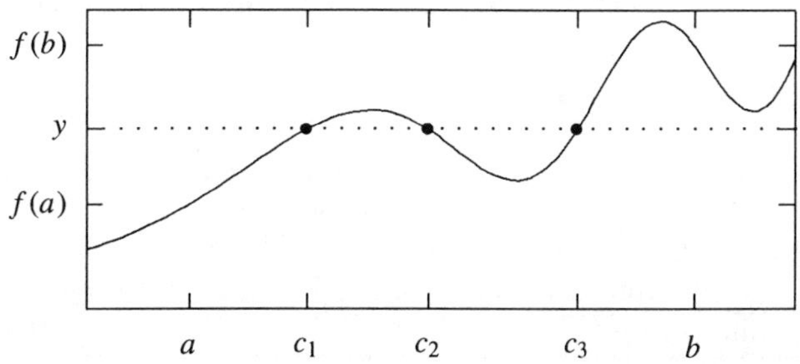

The EVT, pictorially

The EVT guarantees that if f is continuous on the *closed* interval $[a, b]$, then f attains both a maximum and a minimum somewhere therein. In the case pictured below these extreme values are attained at $x = x_{max}$ and $x = x_{min}$, respectively:

The EVT: on $[a, b]$, f assumes extreme values

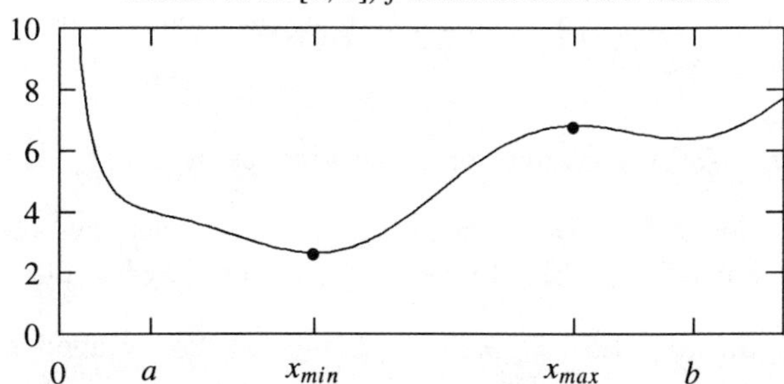

Both hypotheses of the EVT—that f be *continuous* and that the interval be closed—are necessary. If either fails, f need *not* assume a maximum or a minimum. In the case pictured above, for instance, f does not achieve a maximum on the *open* interval $(0, b)$, even though f is continuous there.

From abstract theory, a concrete payoff

The IVT is a theoretical result, but it has useful, concrete consequences. One of them, called the **bisection method,** is a simple but effective technique for solving equations. First, some preliminaries.

aka **interval-halving method**

A number r is a **root** (or **zero**) of a function f if $f(r) = 0$.

■ **Example 1.** The function $f(x) = x^2 - 1 = (x - 1)(x + 1)$ has *two* roots, at $x = \pm 1$. The function $g(x) = x^2$ has *one* root, at $x = 0$. Since $h(x) = x^2 + 1 \geq 1$ for all x, h has *no* roots. How many roots can any quadratic polynomial have?

Solution: The **quadratic formula**

$$r = \frac{-b \pm \sqrt{b^2 - 4ac}}{2a}$$

finds all roots—there may be 0, 1, or 2—of any quadratic polynomial $p(x) = ax^2 + bx + c$. □

Digging systematically for roots

Such as the quadratic formula.

Finding roots by algebraic solution techniques is often difficult or impossible. Even when algebraic methods do succeed, finding *decimal* equivalents may remain a problem. It's clear, for example, that $x = \sqrt{2}$ is a root of $x^2 - 2$, but how can we find an accurate *decimal* value?

The bisection method will help; it's based on this key fact:

> **Fact:** If f is continuous on $[a, b]$, and $f(a)$ and $f(b)$ have opposite signs, then $[a, b]$ contains a root of f. Hence the *midpoint* $(a+b)/2$ of $[a, b]$ differs from a root of f by no more than $(b-a)/2$—the "radius" of $[a, b]$.

This fact follows directly from the IVT. Because f is negative at one end of $[a, b]$ and positive at the other, the IVT guarantees that $f(r) = 0$ somewhere in between—i.e., that a root r lies *somewhere* in $[a, b]$. Lacking further information, the *midpoint* of $[a, b]$ is as good an estimate of r as any. By applying this fact *repeatedly*, we can approximate a root as closely as we wish.

■ **Example 2.** We'll use the bisection algorithm to estimate $\sqrt{2}$ accurately. Since $\sqrt{2}$ is a root of $f(x) = x^2 - 2$, and certainly lies somewhere in $[1, 2]$, we have all we need to get started.

Solution: We'll "converge" on an answer, step by step:

Step 1. Since $f(1) = -1$ and $f(2) = 2$, our fact says that $m_1 = 1.5$—the midpoint of $[1, 2]$—differs from a root of f by less than 0.5.

Step 2. Since $f(1.5) = 0.25 > 0$, the fact above applies to the new—and shorter—interval $[1, 1.5]$. Conclusion: $m_2 = 1.25$, the new midpoint, differs from a root by less than 0.25.

Step 3. Since $f(1.25) = -0.4375 < 0$, our *latest* interval is $[1.25, 1.50]$. Conclusion: $m_3 = 1.375$ differs from a root by less than 0.125.

We can continue this as long as we like—in practice, until we're sure of some pre-determined accuracy. (The next few estimates are 1.4375, 1.40625, 1.421875, 1.4140625, 1.41796875, and 1.416015625, not far from $\sqrt{2} \approx 1.41421356237$.) □

Satisfaction guaranteed—up to a point

Each step *doubles* the guaranteed precision of our estimate. In other words, the n-th midpoint m_n can't possibly miss a root c by more than the radius of the n-th interval. More precisely,

$$|m_n - c| < \frac{b-a}{2^n}.$$

On the other hand, there's no guarantee of *ever* finding a root exactly. In real life, excellent approximations are almost always good enough.

If a and b are rational numbers, then so is each midpoint m_n. Thus if a root c is irrational, the method can't ever locate c exactly.

A bisection algorithm

The bisection method is an **algorithm**—a finite sequence of explicit instructions which, starting from appropriate inputs, reliably produces a desired output. ("Explicit" means, roughly, "executable by a machine." Computer programs are prime examples of algorithms.)

To emphasize the algorithmic nature of the bisection method, we've stated it explicitly below in **pseudocode**—a sort of generic computer language. (Computerese appears in the "typewriter" typeface.) Notice that the error tolerance is stated up front, as an input to the "program." Once a root is found to within that tolerance, the procedure stops. (Without a "stopping rule," a program might run forever.)

Input: A continuous function f, an interval $[a, b]$, and a tolerance $t > 0$. (For simplicity, we'll assume that $f(a) < 0$ and $f(b) > 0$.)

Output: An approximate root of f, i.e., a number m which differs from a root by less than the tolerance t.

Step 1:	(Find midpoint)	`m:=(b+a)/2`
Step 2:	(Done?)	`if b-a<2t then output m; QUIT`
Step 3.	(New interval)	`if f(m)<0 then a:=m else b:=m`
Step 4.	(Start again)	`return to step 1`

A sample problem

Here's a problem that exploits ideas of this section.

■ **Example 3.** Let $f(x) = \sqrt{x}$.

(a) What does the EVT say about f on the interval $[0, 1]$?

(b) Although f is continuous on $[0, \infty)$, it has no maximum value on this interval. Doesn't this contradict the EVT?

(c) Although f is continuous on $(0, 1]$, it assumes no maximum value on this interval. Doesn't *this* contradict the EVT?

(d) Show that the IVT holds for f on $[0, 4]$ and $y = 1$.

Solution:

(a) The EVT says that f must achieve a maximum and a minimum somewhere on $[0, 1]$. It does—$f(0) = 0$ is the minimum value and $f(1) = 1$ is the maximum value.

(b) and (c) There's no contradiction in either part. The EVT applies only for closed and bounded intervals—neither $[1, \infty)$ nor $(0, 1]$ is closed and bounded.

(d) The IVT says that f must assume all values between $f(0) = 0$ and $f(4) = 2$. In particular, $y = 1$ is one such value. Sure enough, $f(1) = 1$, as the IVT requires. □

Exercises

1. Let f and g be the functions shown graphically below. Use the graphs to answer the following questions; no formulas are given (or needed). Notice that f is continuous *except* at $x = -1$, $x = 1$, and $x = 2$.

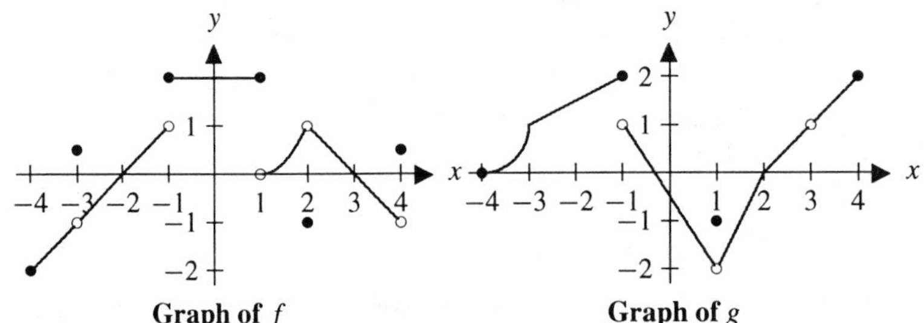

   (a) Over what intervals is g continuous?

   (b) Which of the following functions are continuous at $x = 2$? (Justify your answers.)

$$f(x) + g(x) \qquad f(x) \cdot g(x) \qquad \frac{f(x)}{g(x)} \qquad \frac{g(x)}{f(x)}$$

2. Let f and g be the functions defined in the previous problem. Neither f nor g is continuous on the entire interval $[-4, 4]$, so neither satisfies the hypothesis of the EVT or the IVT. Still, it's possible that either theorem's *conclusion* might hold.

   (a) Does the conclusion of the IVT hold for f on $[-4, 4]$? Explain.

   (b) Does the conclusion of the IVT hold for g on $[-4, 4]$? Explain.

   (c) Does the conclusion of the EVT hold for f on $[-4, 4]$? Explain.

   (d) Does the conclusion of the EVT hold for g on $[-4, 4]$? Explain.

   (e) The function g *is* continuous on $[-4, -1]$, so the EVT holds. What are the maximum and minimum values of g on $[-4, -1]$? Where are they attained?

3. Suppose that $f(x)$ is a continuous function defined for all real numbers and that f achieves a maximum value of 5 and a minimum value of -7. Determine which of the following statements **must** be true, which **might** be true, and which **cannot** be true.

   (a) The maximum value of $f(|x|)$ is 7.

   (b) The minimum value of $f(|x|)$ is 0.

   (c) The maximum value of $|f(x)|$ is 7.

   (d) The minimum value of $|f(x)|$ is 5.

4. Let $f(x) = 1/x$.

   (a) What does the EVT say about f on the interval $[0.1, 1]$?

   (b) Although f is continuous on $[1, \infty)$, it has no minimum value on this interval. Why doesn't this contradict the EVT?

(c) Although f is continuous on $(0, 1]$, it assumes no maximum value on this interval. Why doesn't this contradict the EVT?

(d) What does the EVT say about f on the interval $[0, 1]$?

(e) Although $f(-1) = -1$ and $f(1) = 1$, there is no value of c for which $f(c) = 0$. Why doesn't this contradict the IVT?

(f) Show that the IVT holds for f on $[0.1, 1]$ and $y = 5$.

5. Suppose that f is a continuous function and $f(3) = -1$. Evaluate $\lim_{x\to 3} f(x)$.

6. Determine which of the following statements **must** be true, which **might** be true, and which **cannot** be true.

(a) If $f(1) < 0$ and $f(5) > 0$, then there must be a number c in $(1, 5)$ such that $f(c) = 0$.

(b) If f is continuous on $[1, 5]$, $f(1) > 0$, and $f(5) < 0$, then there must be a number c in $(1, 5)$ such that $f(c) = 0$.

(c) If f is continuous on $[1, 5]$ and there is a number c in $[1, 5]$ such that $f(c) = 0$, then $f(1) \cdot f(5) \le 0$.

(d) If f is continuous and has no roots in $[1, 5]$, then $f(1) \cdot f(5) > 0$.

7. Use the IVT to show that $f(x) = x^5 + x^3 - 5x + 2$ has a root in $[0, 1]$.

8. Use the IVT to find an interval in which $f(x) = x^5 + x^3 + 5x + 2$ has a root.

9. Use paper and pencil alone to find the first four midpoint approximations to $\sqrt{3}$, starting with the interval $[1, 2]$. Express your answers as rational numbers.

10. Use a calculator to find the first six midpoint approximations to a root of $\cos x - x$, starting on $[0, 1]$. Then use graphics or any other method to find the root to within 0.001.

11. Let

$$f(x) = \begin{cases} ax^2 + 3, & x < 2 \\ 3x - 5, & x \ge 2. \end{cases}$$

Find the value of a that makes f continuous at $x = 2$.

12. Suppose that f is defined on $[-5, 5]$, that $f(-5) = 2$ and $f(5) = -2$. If f assumes every value in $[-2, 2]$, must f be continuous? Explain. [HINT: The answer is *no*. Draw a graphical example that illustrates this.]

13. Use the IVT to prove this **fixed point theorem**: If f is continuous on $[0, 1]$, and has range contained in $[0, 1]$, then f has a **fixed point**—i.e., an input x for which $f(x) = x$. [HINT: Consider $g(x) = f(x) - x$.]

14. Let

$$f(x) = \begin{cases} x, & \text{if } x \text{ is rational} \\ 0, & \text{otherwise.} \end{cases}$$

Show that f is continuous at 0.

15. **(This problem works only with Maple.)** Below is a *Maple* version of the bisection algorithm.

```
bisect := proc(f,a,b,acc)
          if b-a < acc then  evalf((a+b)/2); RETURN(); fi;
          m := (b+a)/2 ; print( evalf(m) );
          if f(m)*f(a)>0 then bisect(f,m,b,acc)  else
          bisect(f,a,m,acc)  fi;
          end;

f := x -> x^2-2;
```

The inputs are, in order:

f A function, described in *Maple* syntax. (An example is given below the algorithm.)

a The left endpoint of an interval on which f changes sign.

b The right endpoint of an interval on which f changes sign.

acc The desired accuracy.

Use this bisection algorithm to estimate $\sqrt{2}$ with accuracy 0.0001. Notice that $\sqrt{2}$ is a root of $f(x) = x^2 - 2$, and clearly lies somewhere in $[1, 2]$. Therefore, we can use the *Maple* command `bisect(f,1,2,0.0001);`.

(a) How many steps were needed? Could this have been predicted in advance?

(b) Try `bisect(f,1.1,2,0.0001);`. Is the result the same as above? Explain your answer.

3.8 Why differentiability matters; the mean value theorem

Recall the limit definition of derivative, from Section 2.4:

> **Definition:** Let f be a function defined near and at $x = a$. Then
> $$f'(a) = \lim_{h \to 0} \frac{f(a+h) - f(a)}{h}.$$

For a given function f and $x = a$, the limit in the definition may or may not exist. If it *does* exist, we say that f is **differentiable** at $x = a$.

The standard elementary functions—algebraic, exponential, logarithm, and trigonometric functions—are differentiable wherever they're defined. Combinations—sums, products, quotients, compositions, etc.—of elementary functions are *also* differentiable where they're defined, thanks to the constant, sum, product, quotient, and chain rules.

Like continuity, differentiability is the rule in calculus—so much so, perhaps, that its importance might be overlooked. This section aims to remedy that oversight.

Differentiable functions are continuous

The absolute value function $g(x) = |x|$ is *continuous* at $x = 0$, but not *differentiable* at $x = 0$. On the other hand, a differentiable function *must* be continuous.

> **Theorem 8.** If f is differentiable at $x = a$, then f is also continuous at $x = a$.

Proof. The theorem is both graphically plausible—it's hard to imagine a *discontinuous* graph having a tangent line—and easy to prove. To prove the theorem we need only show that

$$f(x) \to f(a) \quad \text{as} \quad x \to a.$$

(This is the formal definition of continuity of f at $x = a$.) The definition of differentiability at $x = a$ means that as $x \to a$,

$$\frac{f(x) - f(a)}{x - a} \to f'(a).$$

From this fact it follows easily that as $x \to a$,

$$f(x) - f(a) = \frac{f(x) - f(a)}{x - a} \cdot (x - a) \to f'(a) \cdot 0 = 0,$$

as desired. □

Theory and practice: a case study

Calculus is more than a set of powerful methods for solving important problems. It is also a mathematical *theory*—a coherent, rigorously developed body of definitions and theorems. We don't aim here (or elsewhere) to present the theory of calculus in full detail, or with full rigor.➛ This section, instead, is a sort of case study—a close look at one important theorem in its mathematical context.

In later mathematics courses, such as elementary real analysis, the theory of calculus is the main subject.

The guts (and the beauty) of the machine. Using calculus, like driving a car, can be done effectively without perfect or constant attention to the machine's inner workings. Why bother with theory?

One good reason is that ignorance of underlying principles leaves one vulnerable in unexpected situations—no owner's manual can cover everything. A better reason concerns the difference between driver's education and calculus. Driving is a useful skill, but mathematics is a *science*.

Another good reason is that the theory of calculus is a human creation of unparalleled power and beauty—putting even the internal combustion engine to shame.

The mean value theorem in context

See Section 3.6

The **intermediate value theorem** and the **extreme value theorem** guarantee that a *continuous* function assumes certain desirable values on a closed interval. The **mean value theorem**, similar in spirit, guarantees that the *derivative* of a well-behaved function assumes a certain desirable "mean" value.

Theorem 9. (The mean value theorem.) Suppose that f is continuous on the closed interval $[a, b]$ and differentiable on the open interval (a, b). Then for *some* c between a and b,

$$f'(c) = \frac{f(b) - f(a)}{b - a}.$$

Few statements of any kind make much sense out of context. Ask a politician.

Taken out of context the mean value theorem (hereafter, MVT) is difficult to understand, let alone appreciate for what it is: one of the two or three "big" theorems of calculus.

Most of what follows aims to put the theorem in context. What do its words mean? Why is the name appropriate? What does it say? Are the hypotheses really necessary? What questions does the theorem answer? Why do the answers matter? What makes the MVT a "big" theorem?

What the MVT says

The MVT says that under appropriate hypotheses on f, the derivative f' must assume a certain "mean" value. Interpreting f' either as an instantaneous rate or as a slope makes everything plausible.

The MVT—a motorist's view

If a car *averages* 60 mph over an interval of time, then, at some instant, the speedometer must have read exactly 60.

The MVT says the same thing, a little more generally. If $f(t)$ represents a car's position, in miles, at time t, in hours, then $f'(t)$ represents *instantaneous velocity* at time t, and $(f(b) - f(a))/(b - a)$ represents *average velocity* over the interval $a \le t \le b$. In this language, the MVT equation

As we saw in Section 2.1.

$$f'(c) = \frac{f(b) - f(a)}{b - a}$$

reads like this:

> *At some time c between a and b, the instantaneous velocity is equal to the average (i.e., mean) velocity over the entire interval.*

The MVT—a graphical view

On the graph of f, each side of the MVT equation represents a *slope*—of the *tangent* line at $x = c$ and of the *secant line* from a to b, respectively. The theorem asserts that for at least one value of c between a and b, these two slopes are equal. In the case shown graphically below, *two* such c's exist:

The mean value theorem

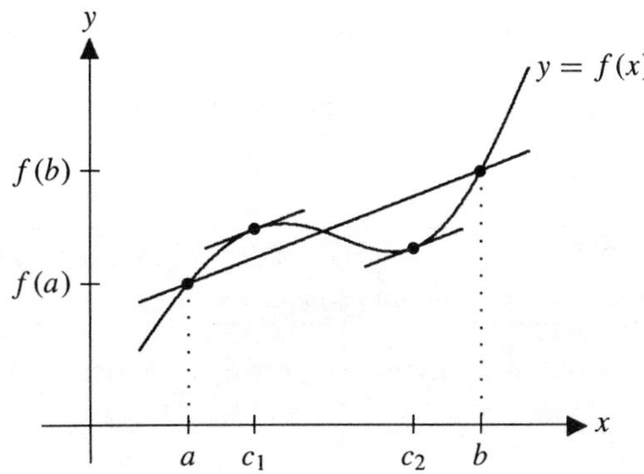

The hypothesis of differentiability; why it matters

The MVT requires that $f'(x)$ should exist for *every* x in (a, b). (Most often, $f'(x)$ exists at the endpoints, too, but that isn't strictly necessary.)

Mathematicians like to state theorems as generally as possible.

This differentiability hypothesis can't be diluted. If f isn't differentiable at even *one* point in (a, b), the MVT can fail. The function $f(x) = |x|$ on the interval $[-1, 1]$ illustrates this problem.

Two natural questions, their answers, and how the MVT helps

The MVT has important theoretical uses; many amount to putting intuitively reasonable results on a sound logical footing. Here we illustrate two such uses; we'll see others later.

Question 1: When is a function constant?

It's clear either from the definition of derivative or from graphical arguments that the derivative of a constant function is the zero function. In other words:

If $f(x) = k$ for all inputs x, then $f'(x) = 0$.

Is the **converse** true? In other words, does our supposed "theorem" really hold?

> **Theorem 10.** If $f'(x) = 0$ for all x in an interval I, then f is *constant* on I.

Geometric intuition supports the theorem—if the graph of f has a horizontal tangent line everywhere, then it's natural to expect the graph *itself* to be horizontal. Not surprisingly, the theorem *is* true. What *is* surprising is that proving this "obvious" fact requires a gun of the MVT's caliber.

Proof: To show that f is constant it's enough to show that for any two inputs $x = a$ and $x = b$, $f(a) = f(b)$. According to the MVT, there's *some* input c between a and b for which

We don't care which constant.

$$f'(c) = \frac{f(b) - f(a)}{b - a}.$$

We don't know *which* c works, but here it doesn't matter. By hypothesis, $f'(c) = 0$ for *any* input c. Thus

$$0 = f'(c) = \frac{f(b) - f(a)}{b - a} \implies f(b) - f(a) = 0 \implies f(b) = f(a). \quad \square$$

A simple but important consequence follows:

Any two antiderivatives of the same function differ by a constant.

More succinctly stated:

> **Theorem 11.** If $F'(x) = G'(x)$ for all x in an interval I, then $F(x) = G(x) + C$ for some constant C.

The theorem is proved by applying the previous theorem to the *difference* function $F(x) - G(x)$. $\square$

Question 2: When is a function increasing?

Up to now we've often stressed—but never proved—the general principle that the *sign* of f' determines whether f increases or decreases over an interval. The MVT offers a simple but rigorous proof. First, a concise statement:

> **Theorem 12.** Suppose that $f'(x) > 0$ for all x in an interval I. Then f is increasing on I.

Proof: It's enough to show that for any a and b in I, and $a < b$, $f(a) < f(b)$. By the MVT, there's a c in (a, b) for which

As above, the location of c doesn't matter.

$$f(b) - f(a) = (b - a) \cdot f'(c).$$

Since both factors on the right must be *positive*, so must $f(b) - f(a)$, so $f(b) > f(a)$. $\square$

Why?

The MVT and the racetrack principle

One version of the **racetrack principle** says, in functional language:

We introduced it in Section 2.1, using canine language.

If $f(a) = g(a)$ and $f'(x) \le g'(x)$ for $x \ge a$, then $f(x) \le g(x)$ for $x \ge a$.

The racetrack principle (like so much else) can be proved by applying the MVT to the "right" function—in this case, to the function $h(x) = g(x) - f(x)$. Let's do so.

The hypotheses say that $h(a) = 0$ and $h'(x) \ge 0$ if $x \ge a$. The MVT assures that for any $x \ge a$, there's a number $c \ge a$ such that

$$h'(c) = \frac{h(x) - h(a)}{x - a} = \frac{h(x)}{x - a}.$$

By hypothesis, moreover, $h'(c) \ge 0$. The rest is easy. If $x \ge a$, then

But check each step.

$$g(x) - f(x) = h(x) = h(x) - h(a) = h'(c) \cdot (x - a) \ge 0 \cdot (x - a) = 0. \quad \square$$

Proving the MVT, step by step (optional)

Understood graphically, the MVT may seem so natural as to require no proof at all. That impression, although understandable, is wrong. A rigorous proof of the MVT involves several steps and appeals to several other results.

The same holds, for excellent reasons, for other powerful, important theorems of mathematics.

Two lemmas

We'll sketch the outline of a proof, based on two preliminary lemmas.

The term **lemma** *denotes an auxiliary result, used to help prove another.*

> **Lemma:** Suppose that f assumes either its maximum or its minimum on $[a, b]$ at a point c between a and b. If $f'(c)$ exists, then $f'(c) = 0$.

Proof: We'll show what happens if $f(c)$ is a maximum—the minimum case is similar. By the definition of derivative,

$$f'(c) = \lim_{h\to 0} \frac{f(c+h) - f(c)}{h} = \lim_{h\to 0^-} \frac{f(c+h) - f(c)}{h} = \lim_{h\to 0^+} \frac{f(c+h) - f(c)}{h}.$$

(Because the ordinary limit exists, so must the left-hand and right-hand limits, and all three are equal.) Notice first that since f assumes a maximum at c, the *numerator* $f(c+h) - f(c)$ in all three limit expressions must be negative. The *denominator* h, on the other hand, is negative if $h \to 0^-$ and positive if $h \to 0^+$. Therefore

$$f'(c) = \lim_{h\to 0^-} \frac{f(c+h) - f(c)}{h} = \lim_{h\to 0^-} [\text{positive stuff}] \geq 0.$$

Similarly,

$$f'(c) = \lim_{h\to 0^+} \frac{f(c+h) - f(c)}{h} = \lim_{h\to 0^+} [\text{negative stuff}] \leq 0.$$

The only possible conclusion is that $f'(c) = 0$, as desired. □

> **Lemma: (Rolle's theorem.)** Suppose that f is continuous on $[a, b]$, differentiable on (a, b), and $f(a) = f(b)$. Then for *some* c between a and b, $f'(c) = 0$.

Remark: This lemma, known as **Rolle's theorem**, is nothing more (or less) than the MVT in the special case that $f(a) = f(b)$. The picture, too, is similar:

Rolle's theorem

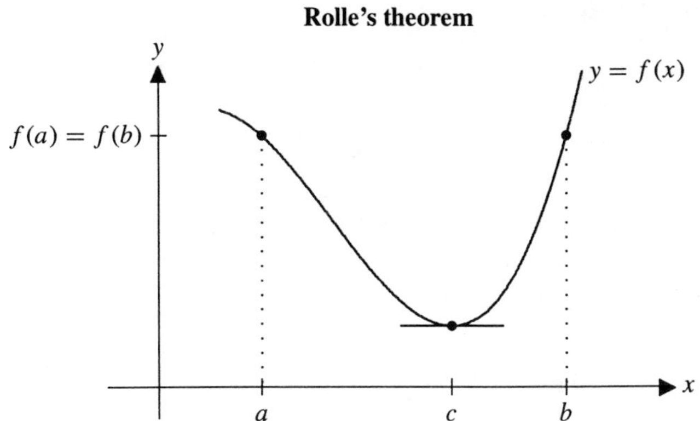

Proof of Rolle's theorem: Because f is continuous on $[a, b]$, the **extreme value theorem** guarantees that f assumes both a maximum and a minimum somewhere in $[a, b]$. If both maximum and minimum occur at the endpoints a and b, then, since $f(a) = f(b)$, f must be a *constant function*. In this case, there's nothing more to do—*any* c works.

The alternative is that at least one of the maximum and the minimum lies at some c, *between* a and b. But by Lemma 1, $f'(c) = 0$. □

All together now: proving the MVT

Using Rolle's theorem to prove the MVT requires a technical step—using f, a, and b, we create a new function to which Rolle's theorem applies.

Proof of the mean value theorem: Given f as in the mean value theorem, consider the *linear* function l whose graph is the secant line to f from a to b, as shown:

Proving the mean value theorem: f and l

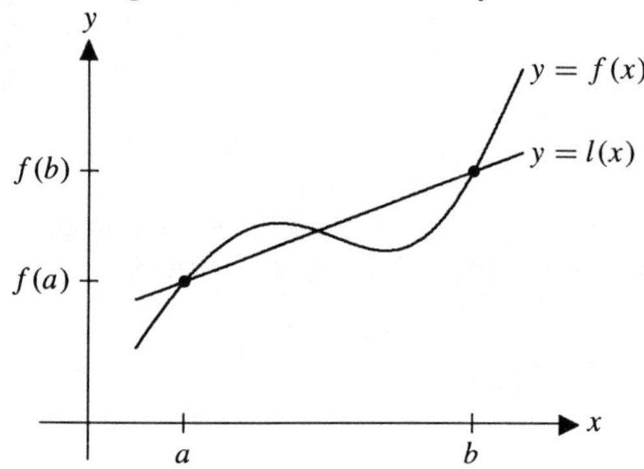

The precise formula for l doesn't matter—what does matter is that

$$l(a) = f(a); \quad l(b) = f(b); \quad \text{and} \quad l'(x) = \frac{f(b) - f(a)}{b - a}.$$

Finally, we consider the difference function $g(x) = f(x) - l(x)$. By design, $g(a) = 0 = g(b)$, so Rolle's theorem applies to g. The rest is bookkeeping: For some c in (a, b),

$$0 = g'(c) = f'(c) - l'(c) = f'(c) - \frac{f(b) - f(a)}{b - a}.$$

We're done. □

Sample problems

Here are two sample problems that show the mean value theorem in action.

■ **Example 1.** Show, using derivatives, that if $x > 0$, then $\sin x \le x$.

Solution: One approach uses the racetrack principle. If $f(x) = \sin x$ and $g(x) = x$, then $f'(x) = \cos x$ and $g'(x) = 1$, so $f'(x) \le g'(x)$ for all x. By the racetrack principle, $f(x) \le g(x)$, as desired. □

■ **Example 2.** Suppose that the function f is differentiable for all x, and that f has n roots. Show that f has *at least* $n - 1$ stationary points.

Solution: We'll show that *between* any two roots, there's at least one stationary point. Suppose, then, that x_0 and x_1 are roots, so $f(x_0) = 0 = f(x_1)$. By the mean value theorem, there's a c between x_0 and x_1 such that

$$\frac{f(x_1) - f(x_0)}{x_1 - x_0} = f'(c).$$

But since x_0 and x_1 are roots, the left side is zero, so c is a stationary point. □

Exercises

1. Throughout this problem, $f(x) = |x|$.
   (a) Does f satisfy all hypotheses of the MVT on $[a, b] = [-1, 1]$? Explain.
   (b) Does f satisfy the conclusion of the MVT on $[a, b] = [-1, 1]$? Explain.
   (c) Does f satisfy all hypotheses of the MVT on $[a, b] = [1, 2]$? Explain.
   (d) Does f satisfy the conclusion of the MVT on $[a, b] = [1, 2]$? If so, find at least one suitable value of c. How many such c's exist?

2. Throughout this problem, $f(x) = x^2$. Because f is differentiable everywhere, it satisfies all hypotheses of the MVT on any interval $[a, b]$.
   (a) What does the MVT say about f on $[a, b] = [-1, 1]$? Find all suitable values of c. How many are there?
   (b) What does the MVT say about f on $[a, b] = [1, 2]$? Find all suitable values of c. How many are there?
   (c) (A little harder) Show that for $f(x) = x^2$ and *any* interval $[a, b]$, the MVT's number c is the *midpoint* of $[a, b]$.

3. Let $f(x) = x^7 - x^5 - x^4 + 2x + 1$. Explain why there must exist a point c in the interval $(-1, 1)$ such that the line tangent to the graph of f at the point $(c, f(c))$ has slope 2.

4. Let $g(x) = x^{2/3} - 1$. Notice that although $g(-1) = g(1) = 0$ there is no point c in the interval $(-1, 1)$ where $g'(c) = 0$. Why doesn't this contradict Rolle's Theorem?

5. The sketch below shows portions of the graph of a continuous function f.

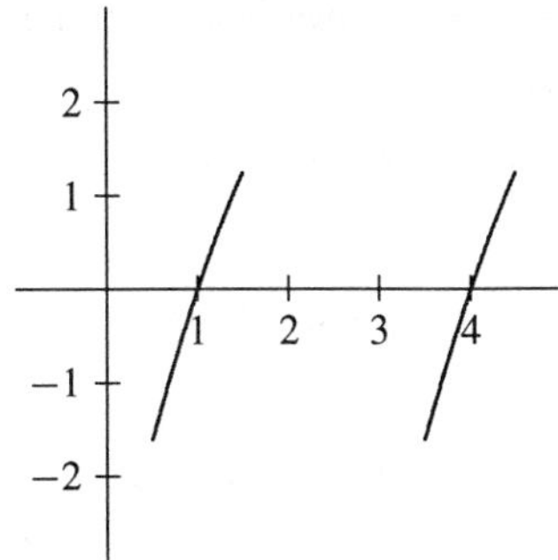

Graph of f

   (a) Explain why f must have a root in the interval $(1, 4)$.

(b) Assume that f' is a continuous function. Explain why f' must have a root in the interval $(1, 4)$.

(c) Assume that f' is a continuous function. Explain why the graph of f must have a horizontal tangent line somewhere between $x = 1$ and $x = 4$.

(d) Why is it necessary to assume that f' is continuous in parts (b) and (c)? Sketch a function f that is continuous on the interval $(1, 4)$ for which $f'(x) \neq 0$ anywhere in this interval.

6. Let f be a continuous function that is positive on the interval $[0, 4]$ and differentiable on $(0, 4)$. Answer "yes" or "no" to each of the following questions about f. If you answer "yes" explain how you know that the statement is true. (Your answer should include references to appropriate theorems.) If you answer "no" give an example of a function that shows that the statement is not always true.

   (a) Is it *always* possible to find a $c \in [0, 4]$ such that $f(x) \leq f(c)$ for all $x \in [0, 4]$?

   (b) Is it *always* possible to find a $c \in [0, 4]$ such that the instantaneous rate of change of f at c equals the average rate of change of f over the interval $[0, 4]$?

   (c) Is it *always* possible to find a $c \in [0, 4]$ such that the line tangent to the graph of f at $(c, f(c))$ is horizontal?

7. Let f be a function such that $f(0) = 0$ and $\frac{1}{2} \leq f'(x) \leq 1$ for all values of x.

   (a) Use the Mean Value Theorem to explain why $f(2)$ cannot be equal to 3.

   (b) Find upper and lower bounds for the value of $f(3)$.

   (c) Find upper and lower bounds for the value of $f(-1)$.

8. Use the Mean Value Theorem to show that $|\sin b - \sin a| \leq |b - a|$. [HINT: $|\cos x| \leq 1$ for all x.]

9. Let f be a function that is differentiable everywhere. Furthermore, assume that the line $y = 3x - 1$ is tangent to f at $x = 1$ and that the line tangent to f at $x = 3$ passes through the points $(0, 5)$ and $(4, 1)$.

   (a) Evaluate $f'(1)$ and $f'(3)$.

   (b) Evaluate $f(1)$ and $f(3)$.

   (c) Explain why there must exist a number c in the interval $[1, 3]$ such that $f'(c) = 0$.

   (d) Suppose that it is known that $f''(x) < 0$ for all $x \in [1, 3]$. Explain why this implies that f has a *unique* maximum value in the interval $[1, 3]$.

10. Suppose that f is differentiable for all values of x, $f(-3) = -3$, $f(3) = 3$, and $|f'(x)| \leq 1$ for all x in the interval $[-3, 3]$. Show that $f(0) = 0$.

11. At 1:00 p.m. a truck driver picked up a fare card at the entrance of a tollway. At 2:15 p.m., the trucker pulled up to a toll booth 100 miles down the road. After computing the trucker's fare, the toll booth operator summoned a highway patrol officer who issued a speeding ticket to the trucker. (The speed limit on the tollway is 65 mph.)

(a) The trucker claimed that he hadn't been speeding. Is this possible? Explain.

(b) The fine for speeding is $35 plus $2 for each mph by which the speed limit is exceeded. What is the trucker's minimum fine?

3.9 Optimization

Optimization and the derivative

Optimization is a two-dollar word for the general problem of finding maximum or minimum values of functions. By now it should be clear that the derivative is a useful optimization tool: anywhere f' is zero is a natural candidate for a maximum or minimum of f. Several subtleties can arise, however. A root of f' might, for instance, correspond to a local maximum, to a local minimum, or to neither. A maximum, in turn, may be global or merely local.

To help sort things out, we'll collect and summarize the language, the techniques, and a few of the subtleties involved in optimization problems.

Stationary points and critical points. Let f be a function and f' its derivative. As we've seen, f increases where $f' > 0$ and decreases where $f' < 0$. Any point x_0 at which f' *changes sign* is therefore naturally of interest.

We do bar them.

Barring bizarre circumstances, f' can change sign at x_0 in *only two ways*:

Either $f'(x_0) = 0$ *or* $f'(x_0)$ *doesn't exist.*

If the first condition holds, x_0 is a **stationary point** of f. If *either* condition holds, or if x_0 is an *endpoint* of the domain of f, then x_0 is a **critical point** of f.

Draw—or imagine—the graph of f.

■ **Example 1.** The function $f(x) = |x|$ has *no* stationary points, because $f'(x)$ is never zero. The critical point $x_0 = 0$ (where the derivative fails to exist) is a local minimum point of f. □

Local vs. global extreme values. Local maximum and minimum values of a function may or may not be *global.* The function $f(x) = x/2 + \sin(x)$, for example, has *many* local maxima and minima on $(-\infty, \infty)$, but *none* is global—this f is unbounded above *and* below on $(-\infty, \infty)$. The graph agrees:

Formal definitions of these words appear in Section 2.3.

Local but not global maxima and minima: $f(x) = x/2 + \sin x$

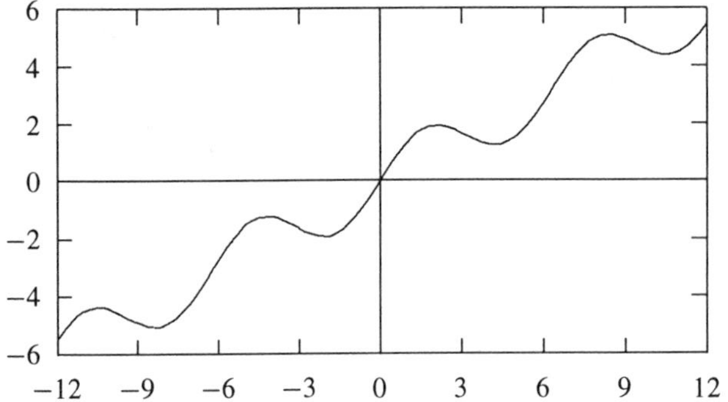

Which functions *have* global maxima and minima? Continuous functions on closed intervals. As we just saw for $f(x) = x/2+\sin(x)$ on $(-\infty, \infty)$, a function may have neither a maximum nor a minimum on a given interval. All is not lost. The **extreme value theorem** guarantees that a *continuous* function f on a *closed* interval $[a, b]$ must assume both a global maximum and a global minimum.

See Section 3.6.

Another look at the previous graph shows that this property holds for $f(x) = x/2 + \sin(x)$ on the closed interval $[-12, 12]$. In this case f takes its largest and smallest values (± 5.5, approximately) at the interval's endpoints, $x = \pm 12$.

Evidently a continuous function.

Finding maxima and minima of f on $[a, b]$. If f is continuous on a *closed* interval $[a, b]$, then global maxima and minima of f on $[a, b]$ must exist. The following fact is key to finding them:

The extreme value theorem guarantees that they exist.

Fact: A continuous function f on a closed interval $[a, b]$ can assume its maximum and minimum values *only* at critical points.

(We stated and proved an equivalent fact in the first Lemma on page 299.) The Fact says that the only possible candidates for maximum and minimum points of f are (1) the endpoints a and b; (2) roots of f'; (3) points at which f' doesn't exist. In practice this slate of candidates is usually short. Choosing among them is usually easy, with or without computer graphics.

■ **Example 2.** Find the maximum and minimum values of $f(x) = x/2 + \sin(x)$ on $[0, 3]$.

Solution: First we find critical points; since f' exists everywhere, it's enough to find roots of f'. An easy computation does the trick:

$$f'(x) = \frac{1}{2} + \cos x = 0 \iff \cos x = -1/2.$$

The only such x in $[0, 3]$ is $x = 2\pi/3 \approx 2.094$.

Right? See for yourself.

According to the fact above, both the maximum and minimum of f on $[0, 3]$ can occur only at 0, 3, or $2\pi/3$. Checking f at these values is all that remains:

$$f(0) = 0; \quad f\left(\frac{2\pi}{3}\right) = \frac{\pi}{3} + \frac{\sqrt{3}}{2} \approx 1.91; \quad f(3) = \frac{3}{2} + \sin 3 \approx 1.64.$$

The conclusion for f on $[0, 3]$ is now clear: f assumes its minimum value, 0, at $x = 0$, and its maximum value, 1.91, at $x = 2\pi/3$. □

Finding maxima and minima on *any* interval. The fact above applies only for *closed* intervals. On an arbitrary interval, f may or may not assume global maximum and minimum values. In practice, however, it's usually clear either from context or from graphics whether extreme values exist, and how to find them. Critical points are still key.

■ **Example 3.** Which point on the line $y = -2x + 2$ is closest to the origin?

Solution: Theory temporarily aside, it's intuitively clear that *some* point on the line minimizes the distance in question. To find it, let's define the function

$$f(x) = \text{distance from } (0, 0) \text{ to } (x, -2x + 2),$$

as shown below; $f(x)$ is the dotted distance.

Which point on $y = -2x + 2$ is closest to $(0, 0)$?

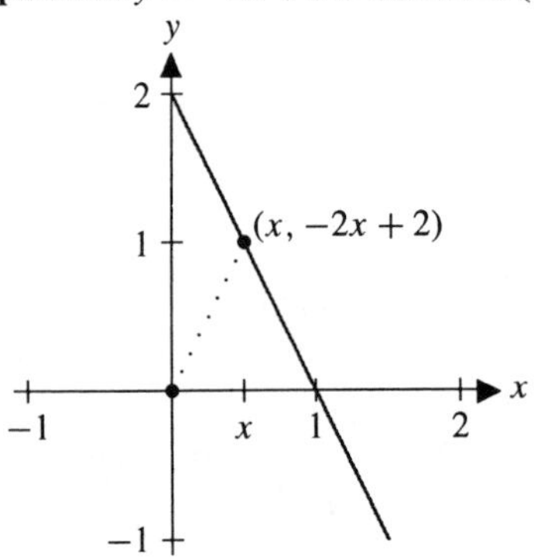

Use the distance formula in the plane.

An explicit formula for f is easy to find:

$$f(x) = \sqrt{x^2 + (-2x+2)^2} = \sqrt{5x^2 - 8x + 4}.$$

Use the chain rule.

Intuition (or a graph) says that f has just one local (and therefore global) minimum; theory tells us to look for a stationary point. Finding one involves symbolic calculus and algebra:

$$f'(x) = \frac{10x - 8}{2\sqrt{5x^2 - 8x + 4}} = 0 \iff 10x - 8 = 0 \iff x = \frac{4}{5}.$$

Convince yourself that the answer is reasonable.

Thus the minimum distance occurs at the point $(4/5, 2/5)$; the distance itself is $\sqrt{(4/5)^2 + (2/5)^2} \approx 0.8944$. (A slightly different approach is to minimize the *square* of the distance. This eliminates square roots, and so makes the algebra simpler.) □

The best pop cans: an extended example

Real-world calculus optimization problems usually involve translating English prose into—and out of—mathematical language. Once translated into mathematical terms, more than one solution avenue may be open. Mathematical solutions, once found, require interpretation in the original context.

The next example, chosen to illustrate the points above, has to do with the design of ordinary 12-ounce (355 ml) aluminum soft drink containers. Do such cans have the "right" dimensions? What does "right" mean? Why do other products come packed in cans of other shapes?

■ **Example 4.** An ordinary pop can has a volume of 355 cm^3. Find the dimensions (radius r and height h) that minimize the surface area of such a can.

Solution: We'll offer two solutions, the first using ordinary derivatives and the second *implicit* derivatives.

Solution 1: The can's volume V and surface area A are given by

$$V = 355 = \pi r^2 h; \qquad A = 2\pi r h + 2\pi r^2.$$

From the first equation, $h = 355/(\pi r^2)$, so

$$A = 2\pi r h + 2\pi r^2 = 2\pi r \cdot 355/\left(\pi r^2\right) + 2\pi r^2 = 710/r + 2\pi r^2.$$

Therefore

$$\frac{dA}{dr} = -710/r^2 + 4\pi r = 0 \implies 710 = 4\pi r^3$$
$$\implies r = (710/(4\pi))^{1/3} \approx 3.837.$$

It's easy to check (either graphically or by taking another derivative) that A has a local *minimum* here. Thus the can's optimal dimensions are $r \approx 3.84$ cm and $h = 355/\left(\pi r^2\right) \approx 7.67\,\text{cm} = 2r$. In particular, the optimal can has a *square* profile!

Not a local maximum or just a flat spot.

Solution 2: We start with the same equations: $A = 2\pi rh + 2\pi r^2$ and $V = \pi r^2 h = 355$. Differentiating both equations implicitly with respect to r gives

$$\frac{dA}{dr} = 2\pi h + 2\pi r\frac{dh}{dr} + 4\pi r; \quad \frac{dV}{dr} = 0 = 2\pi rh + \pi r^2\frac{dh}{dr} \implies \frac{dh}{dr} = -\frac{2h}{r}.$$

Now we substitute the last result into the expression for dA/dr and simplify:

$$\frac{dA}{dr} = 2\pi h + 2\pi r\left(-\frac{2h}{r}\right) + 4\pi r = 0 \implies h = 2r.$$

Thus the optimal can has a square profile. □

■ **Example 5.** Example 4 showed that to minimize surface area, a pop can should have a square profile. Why don't real pop cans have this shape?

Solution: Minimizing surface area does not necessarily minimize the *cost* of a can. Surface area ignores, for instance, the extra cost of the can's top, which is thicker than the sides. □

Look carefully at an aluminum pop can. Is the top obviously thicker?

■ **Example 6.** It's reasonable to suppose that the top of a can is three times as thick as its sides. Choose h and r to minimize the amount of aluminum in the can.

Solution: For simplicity let's pretend that the top is made of *three layers* of aluminum, and still minimize total "area" A. The argument runs as above, except that now

$$A = \text{sides} + \text{bottom} + \text{top} = 2\pi rh + \pi r^2 + 3\pi r^2 \implies A = 710/r + 4\pi r^2.$$

Now

$$\frac{dA}{dr} = \frac{-710}{r^2} + 8\pi r = 0 \implies r = (710/(8\pi))^{1/3} \approx 3.046.$$

Therefore the optimal dimensions are now $r \approx 3.046$ cm and $h = 12.182$ cm. □

■ **Example 7.** What are the dimensions of a real pop can? Are they "right"?

Solution: Measuring a real can gives $h \approx 12.5$ cm; $r \approx 3.1$ cm. These correspond well to the numbers computed above—they're a bit too big, since pop cans have some room to spare. Moreover, the tops of pop cans *do* seem to be about three times as thick as the sides. □

On beyond soda pop

Derivatives are good for more than designing aluminum cans for carbonated beverages. They work with non-carbonated beverages, too.

■ **Example 8.** Fruit juice is often sold in 6-ounce ($\approx 168\ \text{cm}^3$) *steel* cans. Assuming that the top of such a can is no thicker than the sides, find the dimensions that minimize surface area. Are the results realistic?

Solution: Mimicking the work done above shows, as in Example 4, that $h = 2r$ for the optimal can. From this it follows that $r \approx 2.99$ cm and $h \approx 5.98$ cm.

Actual juice cans have a "taller" profile than these numbers suggest, perhaps in order to fit the hand. □

Exercises

1. Show that if a rectangle has its base on the x-axis and two of its vertices on the curve $y = \exp(-x^2)$, then the rectangle will have the largest possible area if the two vertices on the curve are at the points of inflection of the curve.

2. The profit earned from manufacturing x widgets is $0.0001x^3 - 0.21x^2 + 135x - 20{,}000$ dollars. Other constraints dictate that at least 600 widgets, but no more than 1000 widgets be manufactured. How many widgets should be produced to earn the maximum profit?

3. What are the dimensions of a rectangle with area 32 in^2 if the distance from one corner to the midpoint of a nonadjacent side is as small as possible.

4. A Norman window is a rectangle surmounted by a semicircle. The rectangle is of clear glass while the semicircle is of rose-colored glass (the better for seeing the world) that transmits only half as much light per square foot as clear glass does. The total perimeter is fixed. Find the proportions of the window that will admit the most light.

5. Soup cans are to be manufactured to contain a given volume V. No waste is involved in cutting the material for the vertical sides, but the top and bottom (circles of radius r) are cut from squares that measure $2r$ units on a side. Thus the area A of material consumed for a can of height h is $A = 2\pi rh + 8r^2$. Find the ratio of height to diameter for the most economical can (i.e., the can requiring the least material). [HINT: Use the fact that $V = \pi r^2 h$ to express A as a function of r.]

6. A plot of ground in the shape of a circular sector (a wedge of pie) is to have a border of roses along the straight lines and tulips along the circular arc. Roses cost \$20/meter; tulips cost \$15/meter. If the area of the plot is to be 100 square meters, what is the least the flowers can cost?

7. A piece of wire 100 cm long is going to be cut into several pieces and used to construct the skeleton of a rectangular box with a square base.

   (a) How much volume can such a box contain?

   (b) What is the largest possible surface area?

8. A lightning rod manufacturer has monthly overhead costs of \$6000. Materials cost \$1.00 per unit. If no more than 4500 lightning rods are made in a month, labor cost is \$0.40 per unit; for each unit over 4500, the manufacturer must pay time-and-a-half for labor. The manufacturer can sell 4000 units per month at \$7.00 per unit. Monthly sales are expected to rise by 100 for each \$0.10

reduction in price. How many lightning rods should be manufactured each month to maximize profit?

9. A successful retail store must control its inventory. Too much inventory results in excessive interest costs, extra warehouse fees, and the danger of obsolescence. Too small an inventory requires more paperwork for reordering, extra delivery charges, and increases the likelihood of shortages.

   If microwave ovens are ordered in batches of size n, on average $n/2$ ovens will be in stock at any time. An appliance store estimates that it costs \$25 to hold an oven in stock for a year.

   The cost of ordering n ovens is \$250 plus \$2.50 for each oven.

   Assume that the store sells 1000 microwave ovens each year and that it always orders the ovens in "lots" of size n. What lot size will result in the smallest total yearly cost? Is your answer reasonable? Why or why not?

10. Financial reversals forced the owner to convert a hotel into rental units. At \$300 per month, all the units could be rented. For each \$10 that the monthly rent is raised, one of the units becomes vacant. Each occupied unit requires \$30 in service each month (usually performed by the little people who pay taxes). How much rent should be charged to maximize the owner's profit? Show that the answer depends on whether there are an odd or an even number of apartments in the building.

11. Most U.S. post offices limit the size of a mailable parcel: the length of the longest side plus the girth (the perimeter of a cross-section perpendicular to the longest side) may not exceed 108 inches.

    (a) Which mailable cube has largest volume?

    (b) Find the dimensions of the mailable rectangular parcel with a square base that has the largest volume. [HINT: Consider two cases, depending on which side is longest.]

    (c) Among mailable right circular cylinders, which has the largest volume? [HINT: Again, consider two cases.]

    (d) Give an example of a mailable parcel with larger volume than a non-mailable parcel.

12. It's 9:30 p.m. Your snowmobile is out of gas and you are 3 miles due south of a major highway. The nearest service station on the highway is 6 miles east of your position; it closes at midnight. You can walk 4 miles per hour on roads, but only 3 miles per hour through snowy fields. Can you make it to the service station? What route is best?

13. The water depth in Moon River x miles downstream from Hard Rock is $D(x) = 20x + 10$ feet; the width of the river is $W(x) = 10(x^2 - 8x + 22)$ feet. To create Moon Lake, a dam is to be built downstream from Hard Rock. For engineering reasons, the dam cannot be more than 130 feet high or 310 feet wide.

    (a) For which values of x is $D(x) \leq 130$ and $W(x) \leq 310$?

    (b) How far downstream can the dam be built? If the dam were constructed at this point, how wide would it be? How high?

    (c) What are the dimensions of the *widest* dam that could be constructed?

    (d) What are the dimensions of the *narrowest* dam that could be constructed?

(e) If the cost of building the dam is proportional to the product of the length and the depth of the dam, where should the cheapest dam be located?

14. A truck driving over a flat interstate at a constant speed of 50 mph gets 4 miles to the gallon. Fuel costs $1.19 per gallon. The truck loses a tenth of a mile per gallon in fuel efficiency for each mile per hour increase in speed. Drivers are paid $27.50 per hour in wages and benefits. Fixed costs for running the truck are $11.33 per hour. A trip of 300 miles is planned. What speed minimizes operating expenses?

15. Of all triangles that pass through the point (2, 1) and have two sides lying on the coordinate axes, one has the smallest area. How long are its sides?

3.10 Chapter summary

Chapter 3 continues our study of derivatives—how to calculate and combine them, how to use them, and why they matter.

New functions from old. Section 3.1 concerns various ways to combine old function to form new functions. Algebraic combinations—sums, differences, products, and quotients—are simplest; **composition** and **inversion**, perhaps less familiar, are equally important in calculus.

New derivatives from old. In Chapter 2 we found derivatives of (almost) all the basic elementary functions. In Chapter 3 we combine them—in the appropriate ways—to find derivatives of functions built from these basic elements.

Calculating derivatives and antiderivatives. For the simplest functions—but only for those—the limit definition itself can be used to calculate derivatives. For almost all other functions, it's far easier to combine known derivatives to find unknown derivatives.

Sections 3.2–3.5 are about calculating derivatives (and, sometimes, antiderivatives). The main problem has to do with combinations: how, given derivatives for f and g, can we find derivatives of such combinations as fg, f/g, and $f \circ g$? Answers come from the **product rule**, the **quotient rule**, and the **chain rule**, respectively. Sometimes, functions are given implicitly, by equations, rather than explicitly, by formulas. In such cases the method of **implicit differentiation** applies.

Inverse trigonometric functions. Inverse trigonometric functions (aka "arc" functions) are defined as inverses—in the sense that the natural log and exponential functions are inverses—of the trigonometric functions. In Section 3.6 we explore these functions and their derivatives, using tools (such as implicit differentiation) developed in earlier sections.

Continuity and differentiability. Sections 3.7 and 3.8 are brief excursions into the theory of calculus, exploring, respectively, the mathematical significance of continuity and differentiability. The most important results are three "value theorems": the **intermediate value theorem**, the **extreme value theorem**, and, most important of all, the **mean value theorem**. All three results are implicit in much of the machinery of calculus; in these sections we pay these fundamental results explicit, if brief, attention.

Exercises

1. Let $f(x) = |x|$ and $g(x) = x + 3$. Draw (by hand) a graph for each of the following functions. In (b)–(d), explain your answers briefly in terms of translation, compressions, or reflections.

   (a) f (b) $g \circ f$ (c) $f \circ g$ (d) $f(2x) + 1$ (e) $f + g$ (f) $f \circ g^{-1}$

2. Suppose that F is a differentiable function and that $F'(x) = f(x)$ for all $x \in \mathbb{R}$.

   (a) Let $G(x) = e^x F(x)$. Find an expression for $G'(x)$.

(b) Let $H(x) = F(\sin x)$. Find an expression for $H'(x)$.

(c) Let $J(x) = F(x)/x$. Find an expression for $J'(x)$.

(d) Let $k(x) = 2f(x-3)$. Find an antiderivative of k.

(e) Let $m(x) = x^2 f(x^3)$. Find a function M such that $M'(x) = m(x)$.

3. Some values of a function f and its derivative f' are tabulated below:

x	-3	-2	-1	0	1	2	3
$f(x)$	4	-1	1	3	-2	2	5
$f'(x)$	0	1	2	-1	3	-2	-3

(a) Let $g(x) = 2f(x+3)$. Evaluate $g'(-2)$.

(b) Let $h(x) = \dfrac{\ln x}{f(x)}$. Is $x = 1$ a stationary point of h? Justify your answer.

(c) Let $j(x) = f(x^3)$. Is j increasing or decreasing at $x = -1$? Justify your answer.

(d) Suppose that F is an antiderivative of f and that $F(0) = 3$. If $k(x) = \left(F(x)\right)^2$ is k concave up or concave down at $x = 0$? Justify your answer.

4. The equation $y^3 + 1 = xy^2$ defines two curves in the xy-plane. One of these curves passes through the point $(0, -1)$. Use implicit differentiation to find the slope of this curve at that point.

5. (a) Show that the equation $\cos x = x$ has a solution in $[0, 1]$. Estimate it to two decimal place accuracy.

(b) Show that the equation $\cos x = x$ does *not* have a solution in $[1, 2]$.

6. Suppose that f is a function with the following properties:

(i) f is continuous on $[-5, 5]$.
(ii) The range of f is $[-12, 17]$.
(iii) f is an even function.
(iv) $f(28) = -11$
(v) f assumes the values tabulated below:

x	-9	-4	-2	0	3	6
$f(x)$	5	14	9	-1	4	-3

Indicate whether each of the following statements ***must*** be true, ***might*** be true, or ***cannot*** be true.

(a) 1 is in the domain of f.

(b) -6 is in the domain of f.

(c) 8 is in the domain of f.

(d) $f(-3) = 5$

(e) $f(-1) > -100$

(f) 17 is an upper bound for f over the interval $[0, 3]$.

(g) f has a root in the interval $[-3, 4]$.

(h) $\lim_{x \to -4} f(x) = 6$

(i) $\lim_{x \to 28} f(x) = -11$

(j) There is a number $c \in [-4, 3]$ such that $f(c) = 12$.

Chapter 4

Applications of the Derivative

4.1 Differential equations and their solutions

Such as Pythagoras's formula, $a^2 + b^2 = c^2$.

Equations that involve derivatives.

Algebraic equations↞ describe relations among varying quantities. *Differential equations*↞ go one step—a giant step—further: they describe relations among changing quantities and the *rates* at which they change. Only by solving differential equations can many real-life phenomena be usefully described. As someone put it:

> *Nature's voice is mathematics; its language is differential equations.*

The idea of a differential equation first appeared, informally, in Section 2.1. Here and in the next section we take a closer look.

Differential equations and initial value problems: basic ideas

Observe the various derivative notations; all are used in practice.

A **differential equation** (**DE**, for short) is any equation that contains one or more derivatives. Each of the following is a DE:↞

$$f'(x) = 6x + 5; \qquad y' = y; \qquad \frac{dy}{dx} = 5; \qquad g'(x) = kg(x).$$

Or more than one.

To **solve** a differential equation means to find a *function*↞ that satisfies the DE. Any such function is called a **solution** to the DE. This definition bears repeating:

> *A solution to a DE is a* function *that satisfies the DE. A solution is* not *a number.*

You'll get no arguments here. DE's are often stated "without arguments." For example, all of the DE's

$$y' = y, \quad y'(x) = y(x), \quad \text{and} \quad y'(t) = y(t)$$

say the same thing: *the desired function y is its own derivative.* The input variable name, or **argument**—either x or t in the examples above—can safely be "understood," so it's often omitted. Once gotten used to, omitting arguments causes little confusion.

Omitting inessential function arguments sometimes unclutters and simplifies a DE's appearance. For example, both

$$\frac{d^2y}{dt^2} + 2t\frac{dy}{dt} + t = y(t) \quad \text{and} \quad y'' + 2ty' + t = y$$

say the same thing, but the latter form is more economical and (depending on the method) easier to handle.

Finding solutions vs. checking solutions. Finding solutions to DE's, starting from scratch, can be very difficult. Many thick books treat the subject. *Checking* whether a given function satisfies a DE, by contrast, is usually much easier.➻

Solving DE's is, in this sense, similar to antidifferentiation: finding antiderivatives can be hard, but checking answers is easy.

The next examples show what it means to solve a DE, and that a single DE has many solutions.

■ **Example 1.** Solve the DE $f'(x) = 6x + 5$. How many solutions are there? How are they related?

Solution: The DE asks for an *antiderivative* f of the function $6x + 5$. It's easy to check➻ that for any constant C, the function $f(x) = 3x^2 + 5x + C$ does the job. Thus this DE has infinitely many solutions; they differ by *additive* constants. □

But do so now!

■ **Example 2.** Solve the DE $y' = y$. How many solutions are there? How are they related?

Solution: The function $y(t) = e^t$ solves the DE.➻ Why we chose *this* function might seem mysterious, but it's easy to check that our guess works:

We wrote y as a function of t, but any other input variable name (x, z, u, etc.) would have done as well.

$$y(t) = e^t \implies y'(t) = e^t = y(t).$$

Thus $y' = y$, so $y(t) = e^t$ is indeed a solution of the DE.

How *did* we guess that $y(t) = e^t$? The DE itself tipped us off—the equation $y' = y$ says, in words:

The function y is its own derivative.

As we know, the natural exponential function e^t has that property.

Are there other solutions? Given previous work, we might try $y(t) = e^t + C$ for a nonzero constant C. Good guess, but no cigar:

$$y(t) = e^t + C \implies y'(t) = e^t \neq y(t).$$

Other solutions *do* exist. For any real constant C, $y(t) = Ce^t$ works:➻

Is $C = 0$ OK? Why or why not?

$$y(t) = Ce^t \implies y'(t) = Ce^t = y(t).$$

Again we have infinitely many solutions; this time they differ from each other by *multiplicative* constants. □

Initial value problems

The examples above are typical. DE's often have *families* of solutions; family members differ from each other by additive or multiplicative constants. If we specify the value of a solution for some particular input—often called an **initial value condition**, we expect *only one solution*.➻ Such a combination of differential equation and initial value condition is called an **initial value problem—IVP** for short.

A "unique" solution, in math-talk.

■ **Example 3.** Solve the IVP

$$f'(x) = 6x + 5; \quad f(0) = 42.$$

Solution: Any function➻ of the form $f(x) = 3x^2 + 5x + C$ is a solution of the DE. With the initial value condition we can find C:

As we saw above.

$$f(0) = 3 \cdot 0^2 + 5 \cdot 0 + C = 42 \implies C = 42.$$

Thus $f(x) = 3x^2 + 5x + 42$ is the *unique* solution to the IVP. □

■ **Example 4.** Solve the initial value problem

$$y' = y; \quad y(0) = 42.$$

As we saw above.

Solution: Any function of the form $y(t) = Ce^t$ solves *this* DE. Here, again, the initial value requirement forces C to be 42; $y(t) = 42e^t$ is the *unique* solution to the IVP. □

Solving DE's and IVP's: guessing, checking, and parameters

Checking a guess

Given a DE and a *guess* at a solution, it's straightforward to *check* whether the guess works. The next example shows what we mean.

■ **Example 5.** Consider the DE $y' = k(y - T)$, where k and T are constants. Is $y(t) = T + Ae^{kt}$ a solution? Does the value of A matter?

Solution: Deciding whether $y(t) = T + Ae^{kt}$ solves the DE is a straightforward calculation—we'll calculate both sides (LHS and RHS) of the DE using this y and compare:

$$\text{LHS} = y'(t) = k \cdot Ae^{kt}; \quad \text{RHS} = k(y - T) = k(T + Ae^{kt} - T) = k \cdot Ae^{kt}.$$

The two sides *are* equal, so y *is* a solution.

So far the value of A hasn't mattered—y solves the DE for *any* constant A. Had we specified an initial condition, a specific value of A would have been needed. □

See the next example.

From one solution, many: choosing values of parameters

The DE $y' = k(y - T)$ involves two constant parameters, k and T. The general solution, $y(t) = T + Ae^{kt}$, involves still another parameter, A.

Such parameters offer an important "leverage" advantage. Assigning them specific values as needed permits us, in effect, to solve infinitely many differential equations for the price of one. We illustrate by example.

■ **Example 6.** Freshly-poured coffee has temperature 190° F. As it cools, the coffee obeys **Newton's law of cooling:**

Cooling is, in reality, more complicated than this simple model suggests.

> *The rate at which an object cools is proportional to the temperature* difference *between the object and its environment.*

Assume that room temperature is a constant 65° F, and that after 2 minutes, the coffee has cooled to 160° F. Find a formula for temperature at time t.

Solution: Under the verbiage lies the DE of the previous example. If $y(t)$ represents temperature at time t, then Newton's law says in this situation that for some constant k,

We'll evaluate k below.

$$y' = k(y - 65), \qquad y(0) = 190, \qquad \text{and} \qquad y(2) = 160.$$

As we saw in Example 5, a solution of this DE has the general form

$$y(t) = 65 + Ae^{kt},$$

for some constants A and k. All that remains is to give them numerical values.

From the initial condition $y(0) = 190$ it follows immediately that

$$190 = y(0) = 65 + Ae^{k \cdot 0} = 65 + A \implies A = 125.$$

Similarly, $y(2) = 160$ means➻ that

Check the steps.

$$160 = y(2) = 65 + 125e^{2k} \implies e^{2k} = \frac{95}{125}.$$

Solving the last equation➻ gives $k = (\ln 95 - \ln 125)/2 \approx -0.13722$. Putting it all together gives (approximately)

Take logs of both sides.

$$y(t) = 65 + 125e^{-0.13722t}.$$

Is the answer plausible? A graph of y over a 50-minute period suggests so:

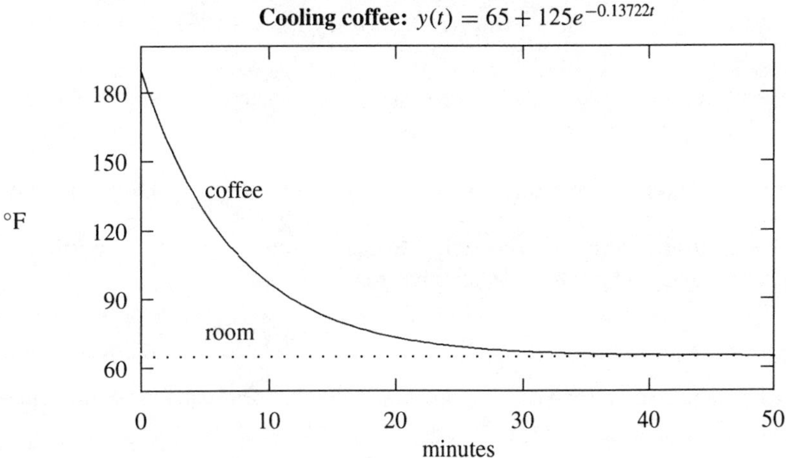

The moral: For best results, drink the coffee quickly. □

Finding solutions: antiderivatives and the chain rule

Checking candidate solutions to DE's is easy enough, but how can we *find* them?

There's no single (or simple) answer. Solving DE's in general is a nontrivial problem; techniques depend strongly on the algebraic form of the DE itself.➻

We'll see several such techniques later.

In the best possible circumstances, solving a DE boils down to finding an antiderivative, and then interpreting it properly. Below we illustrate the process in several relatively simple cases. Notice carefully how antiderivatives and the chain rule are involved.

■ **Example 7.** Solve the DE $g'(x) = 2x \cos\left(x^2\right)$.

Solution: A solution to this DE is a function g for which $g'(x) = 2x \cdot \cos\left(x^2\right)$. The general form of g suggests the result of applying the *chain rule* to some composite function. So it is: if $g(u) = \sin u$ and $u(x) = x^2$, then $g(x) = \sin\left(x^2\right)$, so by the chain rule, $g'(x) = \cos\left(x^2\right) \cdot 2x$, just as we wanted. Thus $y = \sin\left(x^2\right)$ is one solution. So is *any* function of the form

$$g(x) = \sin\left(x^2\right) + C,$$

with C any constant. □

■ **Example 8.** Solve the IVP

$$y' = 0.05y; \quad y(0) = 29.$$

Solution: A solution function $y(t)$ must satisfy both requirements above. We'll *find* such a function y by manipulating the DE.

First we rewrite the DE in the form

$$\frac{y'(t)}{y(t)} = 0.05.$$

The next step is to *antidifferentiate* both sides of the new equation. The right side is easy: For any constant C_1, $0.05t + C_1$ is an antiderivative. For the left side, the chain rule is again the key. It says that

$$\frac{d}{dt}\big(\ln(y(t))\big) = \frac{1}{y(t)}y'(t) = \frac{y'(t)}{y(t)}.$$

Therefore, for any constant C_2, $\ln(y(t)) + C_2$ is an antiderivative of the left side.

Putting these pieces together gives

$$\ln(y(t)) + C_2 = 0.05t + C_1 \quad \Longrightarrow \quad \ln(y(t)) = 0.05t + C_1 - C_2.$$

One arbitrary constant is enough. Because both C_1 and C_2 are arbitrary, so is $C = C_1 - C_2$. Thus we have, simply,

$$\ln(y(t)) = 0.05t + C.$$

Now we can solve for $y(t)$: exponentiating both sides strips away the logarithm, to give

$$y(t) = e^{0.05t+C} = e^{0.05t} \cdot e^C = A \cdot e^{0.05t},$$

where $A = e^C$ is *still* an undetermined constant.

Do check it.

And easy to check!

We're almost done. We've found the formula $y(t) = Ae^{0.05t}$; it's easy to check that this y does indeed solve our DE. The initial condition $y(0) = 29$, finally, imposes a specific value for A. Because $y(0) = Ae^0 = A$, it's clear at last that

$$y(t) = 29e^{0.05t}$$

solves our original IVP. □

■ **Example 9.** We saw above, by a direct check, that for any constants T, A, and k, $y = T + Ae^{kt}$ solves the DE $y' = k(y - T)$. How did we find this y?

Solution: We found it from the chain rule. Here's how.

First we rewrote the DE, bringing all y's to the left:

$$y'(t) = k\,(y(t) - T) \Longrightarrow \frac{y'(t)}{y(t) - T} = k.$$

Check this—differentiate $\ln(y(t) - T)$ for yourself.

Then we recognized the left side as the *derivative*—via the chain rule—of $\ln(y(t) - T)$. Therefore, reasoning as in the previous example, we have

$$\ln(y(t) - T) = kt + C \Longrightarrow y(t) - T = e^{kt+C} \Longrightarrow y(t) = T + Ae^{kt},$$

where (as before) $A = e^C$, and C is an arbitrary constant. □

Hard work, but worth doing. Solving DE's can be much more complicated than our simple examples suggest. A gigantic literature exists on the theory and methods of solving many sorts of differential equations. This fact attests to the depth and subtlety of the subject—but even more to its practical importance.

Exercises

1. Decide whether each of the following functions is a solution of the differential equation given with it.

   (a) $y(t) = t^2/2$; $y' = t$

   (b) $y(t) = t^2/2$; $y' = y$

   (c) $y(t) = e^t$; $y' = y$

   (d) $y(t) = 42e^t$; $y' = y$

   (e) $y(t) = -e^t$; $y' = -y$

   (f) $y(t) = e^{-t}$; $y' = -y$

   (g) $y(t) = 42e^{-t}$; $y' = -y$

   (h) $y(t) = Ce^{kt} + A$; $y' = k(y - A)$

   (i) $y(t) = e^t + \frac{1}{2}t^2$; $y' = y + t$

   (j) $y(t) = \frac{1}{2}e^{t^2}$; $y' = ty$

   (k) $y(t) = e^{t^2/2}$; $y' = ty$

2. Show that $y(x) = x^{-1} - 1$ is a solution of the differential equation $x^3y'' + x^2y' - xy = x$.

3. Is $y(t) = \frac{1}{2}t^4 + \frac{3}{2}t^2 + \frac{1}{4}$ a solution of the differential equation $y' - 2y/t = t^3$? Justify your answer.

4. (a) Show that $y(t) = 65 + 125\left(\sqrt{95/125}\right)^t = 65 + 125\,(95/125)^{t/2}$.

   (b) How long does the coffee in Example 6 remain above 100° F?

   (c) In a foam cup, coffee cools only to 180° F in two minutes. Let $z(t)$ be the temperature of the coffee in such a cup. Find a formula for $z(t)$. How long does coffee in a foam cup stay above 100° F?

   (d) Plot $y(t)$ and $z(t)$ on the same axes.

5. Verify by direct calculation that the function

$$P(t) = \frac{C}{1 + d\,e^{-k \cdot C \cdot t}}$$

   is a solution of the **logistic DE** $P' = kP(C - P)$ for any constants k, C, and d. (We'll see the logistic DE in later applications.)

6. Find real numbers a and b so that $y = e^x$ and $y = e^{2x}$ are both solutions of the differential equation $ay'' + by' + y = 0$.

7. Find functions $f(x)$ and $g(x)$ so that $y = x$ and $y = x^2$ are both solutions of the differential equation $f(x)y'' + g(x)y' + y = 0$.

8. Consider the function f shown below.

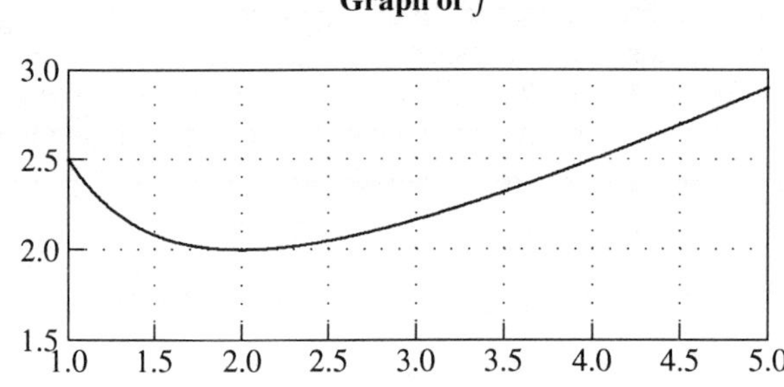

$y = f(x)$ is a solution of one of the following differential equations. Decide which one. Then explain why each of the others is not a solution.

(a) $y' = \dfrac{y - x}{x}$ (b) $y' = \dfrac{x - y}{x}$ (c) $y' = \dfrac{x^2 - y}{x}$

9. When the valve at the bottom of a cylindrical tank is opened, the rate at which the level of the liquid in the tank drops is proportional to the square root of the depth of the liquid. Thus, if $y(t)$ is the liquid's depth at time t minutes after the valve is opened, $y' = -k\sqrt{y}$ for some positive constant k.

   (a) Does the water level drop faster when the tank is full or when it is half full? Justify your answer.

   (b) Verify that the function $y(t) = (C - kt)^2/4$ is a solution of the differential equation $y' = -k\sqrt{y}$ for any values of the constants C and k.

   (c) Suppose that $y(0) = 9$ feet and $y(20) = 4$ feet. Find an equation for $y(t)$.

   (d) At what time is the water level dropping at a rate of 0.1 feet per minute?

10. Consider the following model for the growth of a city: The shape of the city always remains roughly circular so that the maximum travel time between two locations in the city is proportional to the diameter of the city. The population of the city is proportional to the area of the city. The rate of increase of the city's population is inversely proportional to the maximum travel time.

   (a) This model predicts that the population of the city $P(t)$ satisfies the differential equation
   $$\frac{dP}{dt} = \frac{K}{\sqrt{P(t)}}$$
   where K is a constant. Explain why.

   (b) Verify (by differentiation) that $P(t) = \left(\frac{3}{2}Kt + C\right)^{2/3}$ is a solution of the differential equation given in part (a).

   (c) If the population of the city was 5000 in 1900 and 20,000 in 1950, what is the predicted population of the city in the year 2000?

11. Psychologists in learning theory study learning curves, graphs of "performance functions." A performance function $P(t)$ describes someone's skill at a task as a function of the training time t. It has been noted that learning is at first rapid, then tapers off (the rate of learning decreases) as the value of $P(t)$ approaches M, the maximal level of performance.

(a) Explain how the differential equation $P' = k(M - P)$, where k is a positive constant, describes this situation.

(b) Suppose that for a certain learning activity it is known that $P(0) = 0.1M$ and $k = 0.05$ when t is measured in hours. How long does it take to reach 90% of the maximum level of performance?

12. Assume that influenza spreads through a university community at a rate proportional to the product of the number of those already infected and the number of those not yet infected. If the total number of students at the institution is 3000 and $P(t)$ represents the number of students infected after t days, express the preceding statement as a differential equation.

13. It's a winter day in Northfield, Minnesota—10 degrees below zero Celsius. Ole and Lena stop at a convenience store for hot (initially, 90° C) coffee to warm them on the cold, windy walk back to Manitou Heights. Two types of cups are available: environmentally destructive foam and politically correct cardboard.

    Ole wants foam. "What do I care about the greenhouse effect?" he asks. "Everything in Edina is air-conditioned anyway. Besides, remember the proportionality constant k in Newton's Law of Cooling:

    $$T'(t) = -k \cdot (T(t) - C),$$

    where C is the environmental temperature, $T(t)$ is the Celsius temperature of the coffee at time t, and t is measured in minutes? Well, for foam, $k = 0.05$. For cardboard, k is a pathetic 0.08."

    "Do what you want, Attila," says Lena. "I'd rather save the world. I'm having cardboard. And make mine Nicaraguan decaf."

    (a) How long does Ole's coffee stay above 70 degrees? How about Lena's? How hot is each cup after 5 minutes?

    (b) Answer the questions posed in part (a) assuming that Ole and Lena drink their coffee in the overheated (25° C) convenience store.

    (c) What value of k is needed to assure that coffee, starting at 90 degrees, is still at least 70 degrees after 5 minutes, outdoors. How about indoors? [HINT: Use the solution function to set up an appropriate equation; then solve for k.]

14. A crucible is removed from an oven whose temperature is $500°C$ and placed in a room in which the air temperature is kept at $20°C$. If the temperature of the crucible has fallen to $260°C$ after one-half hour, how long will it take before the temperature of the crucible reaches $80°C$? (Assume that Newton's Law applies.)

15. By Newton's Law, the rate of cooling of an object in air is proportional to the difference between the object and the temperature of the air. If the temperature of the air is $20°C$ and boiling water cools in 20 minutes to $60°C$, how long will it take for the water to drop in temperature to $30°C$?

16. An indoor thermometer, reading 60°, is placed outdoors. Ten minutes later it reads 70°. After another ten minutes it reads 76°. What is the outdoor temperature?

17. Experience suggests that the rate at which people contribute in a charity drive is proportional to the difference between the current total and the announced goal. A fund drive is announced with a goal of \$90,000 and an initial contribution of \$10,000. One month later, \$30,000 has been contributed. What does the model predict at the end of two months?

18. A certain classroom has volume 6000 cubic feet. When the concentration of carbon dioxide in the air reaches 0.16%, the ventilation system is activated. The ventilation system brings in air containing 0.04% carbon dioxide at a rate of 1000 cubic feet per minute and drives out the mixture of stale air and fresh air at the same rate. Assuming complete and instantaneous mixing, what is the percentage of carbon dioxide in the air in the room after 5 minutes of ventilation?

19. A man eats a diet of 2500 cal/day; 1200 of them go to basal metabolism (i.e., get used up automatically). He spends approximately 16 cal/kg times his body weight in weight-proportional exercise each day.

    (a) Determine how the man's weight varies with time.

    (b) Does the man reach an equilibrium weight?

    (Assume that the storage of calories as fat is 100% efficient and that 1 kg fat contains 10,000 cal.)

4.2 More differential equations: modeling growth

Exponential growth

Exponential functions have an important property, best expressed in terms of rates:

> *Exponential functions grow at a rate proportional to their size, i.e., "with interest."*

Thanks to this property,➻ exponential functions model many real phenomena which, too, grow "with interest."

We discussed this property in Section 2.9.

Let's interpret this property in the language of DE's and IVP's. For any constants A and k, let $y(t) = Ae^{kt}$. Two key properties➻ of y matter here:

Check these claims carefully!

$$y'(t) = Ake^{kt} = ky(t) \quad \text{and} \quad f(0) = Ae^0 = A.$$

In other words:

> **Theorem 1.** For any constants A and k, the exponential function $y = Ae^{kt}$ solves the initial value problem
>
> $$y' = ky; \quad y(0) = A.$$

This theorem offers considerable practical horsepower. Just by choosing k and A judiciously, we can solve a surprising number of useful and important DE's.

Modeling things that grow "with interest"

Many real-world quantities grow or "decay" like exponential functions, at rates proportional to their size. The Consumer Price Index, the value of a financial deposit, college fees,➻ radioactive decay, biological populations—all can be modeled, more or less accurately, by the IVP of Theorem 1..

Recall Uncle Eric, in Section 1.6.

The federal deficit: keeping rates straight

Differential equations relate varying quantities to their derivatives, i.e., their *instantaneous rates* of change. Practical problems, on the other hand, often mention other sorts of rates: average rates, interest rates, percentages, etc. Teasing out the derivatives from all this loose talk may take some care.

■ **Example 1.** At time $t = 0$ years, the federal deficit was \$300 billion and growing fast. "*How* fast?" worries Senator Smith. "What will the deficit be 6 years hence,➻ when I face re-election?" In Senate hearings Economist A predicts:

Politicians say "hence."

> *The federal deficit will grow at an instantaneous rate of 15% per year.*

"Balderdash," says Economist B,

> *The federal deficit will grow 15% each year.*

Do Economists A and B disagree? How seriously? Whom would Senator Smith rather believe?

Solution: Economists A and B agree on one thing: that the deficit grows at a rate proportional to itself. In DE terms, if $y(t)$ represents the deficit in billions, t years out, A and B agree that for some constant k,

$$y'(t) = ky(t).$$

They *disagree* on the value of k.

Economist B's statement refers to an *average* rate: over a one-year *interval*, the deficit rises 15%. Economist A's statement means something else: at any *instant*, the deficit's rate of increase, if it remained unchanged for a year, would raise the deficit by 15%.

To understand the difference, and see its effects, we'll recast the predictions as IVP's. Combined with the initial value ($300 billion) of the deficit, A's claim comes to this:

$$y'(t) = 0.15 \cdot y(t); \qquad y(0) = 300.$$

B says something else:

$$y'(t) = k \cdot y(t); \qquad y(t+1) = 1.15 \cdot y(t); \qquad y(0) = 300.$$

We'll solve both IVP's and compare the results. A's claim fits perfectly into Theorem 1.'s template:

$$\text{Since } y'(t) = 0.15 \cdot y(t) \text{ and } y(0) = 300,\ y(t) = 300e^{0.15t}.$$

Again.

Solving B's IVP takes one more step. By Theorem 1.,

$$\text{Since } y'(t) = k \cdot y(t) \text{ and } y(0) = 300,\ y(t) = 300e^{kt}.$$

Check the algebra carefully.

Now we'll find a value for k. Our new formula $y(t) = 300e^{kt}$ gives $y(t+1) = 300e^{k(t+1)}$. Therefore

$$\begin{aligned} y(t+1) = 1.15 \cdot y(t) \quad &\Longrightarrow \quad 300e^{k(t+1)} = 1.15 \cdot 300e^{kt} \\ &\Longrightarrow \quad e^k = 1.15 \\ &\Longrightarrow \quad k = \ln 1.15 \approx 0.13976. \end{aligned}$$

Economist B models the deficit with the function $y(t) = 300e^{0.13976t}$.

What does each scenario predict over the next 6 years? Graphs answer best:

A's and B's predictions diverge as time goes on. At $t = 6$, the difference is

$$300e^{0.15\times 6} - 300e^{0.13976\times 6} \approx 43.97 \text{ billion dollars.}$$

Which view will Senator Smith prefer? It depends, perhaps, on Senator Smith. A Washington insider might prefer B's "rosier" view; an outsider, A's "gloomy" view.□

Money in the bank

Bank interest offers the most familiar example of "growth with interest." Its crucial feature—shared by exponential growth in *all* forms—is that *the rate at which the account's value grows is proportional to the value itself.* The rich don't only get richer—they also get richer *faster.*

Bank interest may even be *too* familiar: some care is needed in translating banking language into mathematical terms. The next example illustrates this.

■ **Example 2.** A savings account pays a **nominal annual interest rate** of 6%, compounded daily. Model the situation in DE language. How much does the account increase over one year?

Solution: If $b(t)$ represents the balance (in dollars) at time t (in years), the terms above mean➻ that each day, the balance is multiplied by the same small factor:

In a 365-day year.

$$b\left(t+\frac{1}{365}\right)=b(t)\cdot\left(1+\frac{0.06}{365}\right). \tag{4.2.1}$$

With initial balance $b(0)$, for instance, here's what happens for the first two days:

$$b\left(\frac{1}{365}\right)=b(0)\cdot\left(1+\frac{0.06}{365}\right);\qquad b\left(\frac{2}{365}\right)=b(0)\cdot\left(1+\frac{0.06}{365}\right)^2.$$

Over a full year, therefore, the balance increases by the factor

$$\left(1+\frac{0.06}{365}\right)^{365}\approx 1.0618.$$

The **effective annual interest rate**, therefore, is 6.18%—over a one-year interval, the balance rises by this percentage.

How do interest rates, nominal or effective, translate into DE language?

- In reality, the balance $b(t)$ varies **discretely,**➻ at regular intervals and in jumps of at least one cent. Any DE model, being continuous, must commit *some* error. In practice such errors are usually small enough to ignore.

Not continuously.

- On a time-scale measured in years, a single day is effectively an "instant." The *nominal* interest rate, therefore, can serve as "k" in the DE of Theorem 1.. In other words, the balance $b(t)$ can be taken➻ to satisfy the DE

With very little error.

$$b'(t)=0.06\cdot b(t).$$

Theorem 1. *solves* the DE above. If the initial balance is b_0, then

$$b'(t)=0.06\cdot b(t)\quad\text{and}\quad b(0)=b_0 \implies b(t)=b_0\cdot e^{0.06t}.$$

After one year the balance is

$$b(1)=b_0\cdot e^{0.06}\approx b_0\cdot 1.0618.$$

As it should, the balance rises by 6.18%, the *effective* interest rate. □

Interest rates and derivatives: continuous compounding. The DE $b'(t) = 0.06 \cdot b(t)$ does a good—but not perfect—job of modeling 6% annual interest, compounded *daily*. The model would do better if interest were compounded *hourly*, or even every *minute*. The DE represents **continuous compounding**, i.e., the limiting case as the number of compounding periods tends to infinity.

Why does the DE $b'(t) = 0.06 \cdot b(t)$ approximate daily compounding as well as it does? Equation 4.2.1 and the following computation (for those who wish to follow it) explains. The result shows, too, how the frequency of compounding affects the "goodness" of approximation.

$$\begin{aligned} b'(t) &\approx \frac{b(t+1/365) - b(t)}{1/365} \\ &= \left(b(t)\cdot\left(1+\frac{0.06}{365}\right) - b(t)\right)\cdot 365 \\ &= b(t)\cdot\left(1+\frac{0.06}{365} - 1\right)\cdot 365 \\ &= 0.06\cdot b(t). \end{aligned}$$

Radioactive decay

A sample of carbon-14 (a radioactive isotope of ordinary carbon) decays at time t (in years) at a rate proportional (with $k = -0.000121$) to its weight. In DE language,

$$W'(t) = -0.000121\, W(t).$$

(The constant k is *negative* because W *shrinks*. In banking terms, carbon-14 pays negative interest.)

■ **Example 3.** If a sample of carbon-14 weighed W_0 pounds in 1991, how much will it weigh in 2991? What did it weigh in 991? How long does it take the sample to lose *half* its weight? (This period is called the sample's **half-life**.)

So $t = 0$ in 1991.

Solution: If $W(t)$ represents the sample's weight t years after 1991, then $W(t)$ solves the IVP

$$W'(t) = -0.000121\, W(t); \qquad W(0) = W_0.$$

According to Theorem 1., $W(t) = W_0 e^{-0.000121t}$. Therefore

$$\begin{aligned} \text{weight in 2991} &= W(1000) = W_0 e^{-0.121} \approx 0.88603\, W_0; \\ \text{weight in 991} &= W(-1000) = W_0 e^{0.121} \approx 1.12862\, W_0. \end{aligned}$$

The sample loses a bit more than 12% of its weight over 1000 years.

The sample's half-life is the value of t for which $W(t) = W_0/2$. To find it, we solve for t:

$$\begin{aligned} W(t) = \frac{W_0}{2} &\iff W_0 e^{-0.000121t} = 0.5 W_0 \iff -0.000121t = \ln(0.5) \\ &\iff t \approx 5728 \text{ years.} \end{aligned}$$

□

Some biological populations grow exponentially

Certain biological populations grow exponentially—at least for a while.➽ A fruit fly population in laboratory conditions, for example, might reasonably grow at an *instantaneous* rate of 5% per day, i.e., at a rate proportional (with $k = 0.05$) to the population itself. In DE language, if the population $P(t)$ starts at P_0, then P satisfies the IVP

$$P'(t) = 0.05P(t); \quad P(0) = P_0.$$

We'll see below why such growth can't last forever.

Notice the analogy with ordinary interest: each day's crop of new fruit flies can safely (if unpalatably) be thought of as "interest" added to the previous day's "balance."

■ **Example 4.** A population of fruit flies grows at an instantaneous rate of 5% per day. How long does it take for the population to double?

Solution: Given an initial population➽ of P_0 flies, Theorem 1., page 313, gives the formula

$$P(t) = P_0\, e^{0.05t}.$$

I.e., at $t = 0$.

A little algebra shows that the population doubles in less than 14 days:

$$P(t) = P_0\, e^{0.05t} = 2\, P_0 \iff 0.05t = \ln 2 \iff t \approx 13.8629. \qquad \square$$

Not all populations grow exponentially: logistic growth

Real biological populations can't grow exponentially forever. An "initial deposit" of 100 fruit flies, growing as above, would number over 8 billion in a year. In a decade, the flies would outnumber Earth's molecules.➽

A logical—not just biological—impossibility.

Any exponentially-growing population sooner or later exceeds the limits (physical or biological) of its environment. Just this possibility, applied to human population, worried the 19th century clergyman Thomas Malthus, who predicted an early and unpleasant end to the human race.➽

Was Malthus right? It's too early to tell. Some evidence may even suggest that Malthus was too optimistic.

Whether Malthus himself was right or wrong, exponentially-growing biological populations *do* eventually outgrow their environments. How real populations cope with this mathematical certainty➽ varies: some (e.g., lemmings and Dungeness crabs) have boom-bust cycles; others eat up their environments and die off completely.

And with other vagaries of real life.

A third (happier) possibility is **logistic growth**. As a population approaches an upper limit C (the environment's **carrying capacity**), growth slows. For our flies, logistic growth might lead to the lower graph shown below:

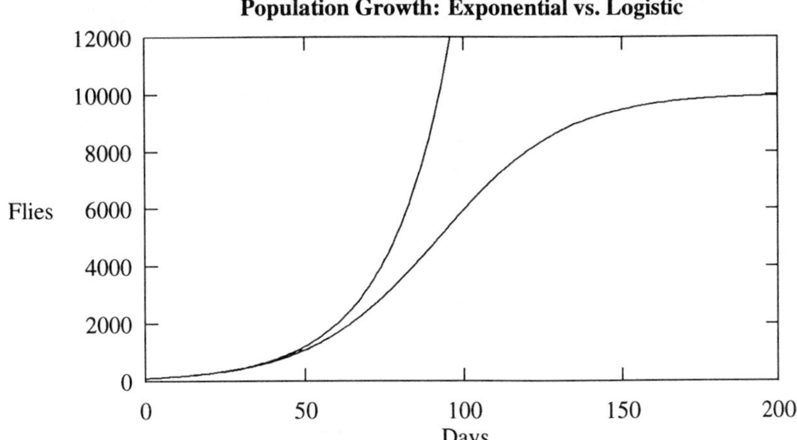

Notice that the two graphs are, toward the beginning, almost identical. This reflects the fact that when populations are small, the effects of "crowding" are scarcely felt, so logistic growth is essentially exponential.

Like exponential growth.

Logistic growth is characterized by a rate property, and therefore by a DE (called the **logistic DE**):

The population's growth rate is proportional both to the population itself and to the difference between the carrying capacity and the population.

In symbols:

$$P' = kP(C - P),$$

where P represents the population, P' the population's growth rate, C the carrying capacity of the environment, and k a constant of proportionality.

P and P' vary with time; k and C are parameters.

Wise flies: a case study in logistic growth

A population of prudent fruit flies, eager to avoid crowding, choose to reproduce logistically. This is their story.

Fly specs

On a certain day, the fly population is 1000, and growing at the (net) instantaneous rate of 50 flies per day. The environment can support 10,000 flies.

Questions. Given what we know of growth *rates*, it's natural to wonder about population *amounts*:

- What will the population be in 10 days? 100 days? 200 days?
- When is the population 5000? 9000? 9900?
- When does the population grow fastest? What's the population then?

Solving the logistic DE

Modeling logistic population growth boils down to solving an IVP. If a population has P_0 members at $t = 0$ and grows logistically, then the population function $P(t)$ is a solution of the IVP

$$P' = kP(C - P); \qquad P(0) = P_0.$$

Searching systematically for a solution, given our present tools, is a slightly messy process. It turns out, suffice it to say, that for any constants k, C, and d, the function

It will get easier with techniques we'll study later.

$$P(t) = \frac{C}{1 + d\,e^{-k \cdot C \cdot t}}$$

solves the logistic DE $P' = kP(C - P)$. (The constants k and C in the solution are the same as those in the DE; d depends, as we'll see, on the initial population.)

Try checking this: it's messy but not really hard.

What solutions mean for our flies

To put things in context, let's define:

Measuring population in thousands removes pesky zeros from later computations.

$$\begin{aligned} t &= \text{time, in days, since the original measurement;} \\ P(t) &= \text{population of flies, in thousands, at time } t; \\ P'(t) &= \text{growth rate, in thousands of flies per day, at time } t. \end{aligned}$$

Evaluating the parameters. We know three things: $P(0) = 1$, $P'(0) = 0.05$, and $C = 10$. We'll use what we know to evaluate k and d. Since

$P'(0) = 0.05$ corresponds to 50 flies/day.

$$P'(0) = 0.05 = k \cdot P(0) \cdot (10 - P(0)) = k \cdot 1 \cdot 9,$$

it follows that $k = 1/180 \approx 0.00556$.

Now we can evaluate d. By assumption,

$$P(0) = 1 = \frac{10}{1 + d\, e^{-k \cdot C \cdot 0}} = \frac{10}{1+d},$$

so $d = 9$. Putting everything together gives, at last, an explicit formula for $P(t)$:

$$P(t) = \frac{C}{1 + d\, e^{-k \cdot C \cdot t}} = \frac{10}{1 + 9\, e^{-0.0556t}}.$$

Here's a graph of P:

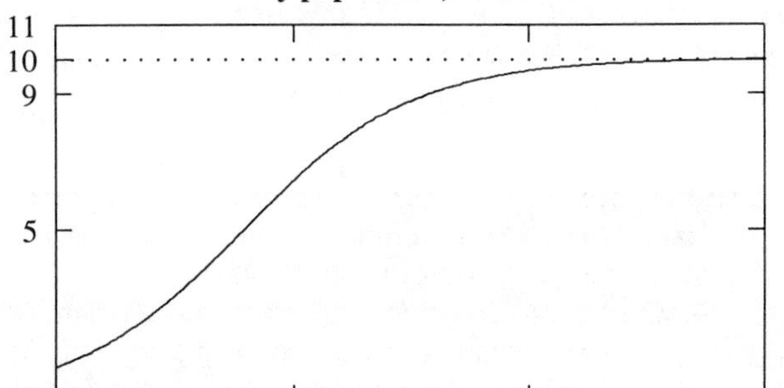

Our questions answered: What the graph and formula say. With the formula and the graph we can answer all the questions posed above.

Approximately, at least.

- The graph shows that on day 100, the population was about 9700; room is quickly running out. Day 200 isn't shown, but the graph's asymptotic behavior shows that at $t = 200$, the population should *still* be just short of 10,000. The formula agrees:

$$P(200) = \frac{10}{1 + 9\, e^{-0.0556 \cdot 200}} \approx 9.99867.$$

  Thus the population is *at* full capacity—rounding to the nearest whole fly.

The only reasonable way to round flies.

- Both graph and formula show that the population reaches 5000 (half the upper limit) in about 40 days. Around day 80, the population reaches 9000—90% capacity. Around day 130, 99% capacity is reached.

All of these numbers can be checked with the formula.

- Intuition says that under logistic conditions a population increases slowly at first (when there are few breeding members), faster as the population rises, and then slowly again as the upper limit nears.

  The graph agrees. Population grows fastest when our graph points most steeply upward, i.e., around day 40. At this time the population is about 5000—exactly *half* the carrying capacity. This isn't a coincidence. Under logistic conditions, it's a disadvantage for a population to be either too large *or* too small. Thus, intuitively, we'd expect growth conditions to be optimal at the *halfway* point.

Take a close look; do you agree?

Afterword: discrete vs. continuous growth

All mathematical models simplify, more or less, the phenomena they describe. Using DE's and IVP's to model phenomena of growth is no exception to this rule.

One sense in which DE's and IVP's may describe reality imperfectly concerns the difference between **discrete** and **continuous** phenomena of change. Human population, for instance, grows "discretely"—in jumps of at least one unit. Hot coffee in a cool room, by contrast, cools "continuously"—its temperature takes *all* intermediate values on the way down.

DE's and IVP's are *continuous* models of growth. Solutions to DE's and IVP's are *continuous* functions, so they can't, by definition, describe *discrete* phenomena exactly. (Neither, for the same reason, can discrete models perfectly describe continuous phenomena.)

Such philosophical problems, though undeniable, need not be fatal. In practice, differences between discrete and continuous growth models are often unimportant—especially when "jumps" are small. It matters little, for instance, whether coffee temperature falls continuously or in tiny increments of 0.0001 degrees. Perfection is impossible, but DE's and IVP's *can* be used to model growth—even discrete growth—easily, effectively, and accurately.

And are.

Discrete models of continuous phenomena. DE's and IVP are *continuous* entities; they're often used to describe phenomena that vary *discretely*. Sometimes things go the other way: continuously-changing phenomena can be modeled discretely. Movies, digital watches, and electronic computing all depend, in various ways, on discrete approximations to continuous reality.

Exercises

1. Use Theorem 1., page 313, to solve each of the following IVP's. Check answers by differentiation.

   (a) $y' = 0.1y; \quad y(0) = 100$

   (b) $y' = -0.0001y; \quad y(0) = 1$

   (c) $y' = (\ln 2) \cdot y; \quad y(2) = 4$

   (d) $y' = ky; \quad y(10) = 2y(0)$
   [HINT: Solve for k using the initial condition.]

2. Suppose that the "wise flies" described in this section had begun by breeding at the net rate of 100 (rather than 50) flies per day. How would things be different? More specifically, answer these questions, and compare the results with those given on page 319.

   (a) What will the population be in 10 days? 100 days?

   (b) When is the population 5000? 9000? 9900?

   (c) When does the population grow fastest? What's the population then?

3. A certain menacing biological culture (aka The Blob) grows at a rate proportional to its size. When it arrived unnoticed one Wednesday noon in Chicago's Loop, it weighed just 1 gram. By the 4:00 p.m. rush hour it weighed 4 grams.

   The Blob has its "eye" on the Sears Tower, a tasty morsel weighing around 3000000000000 (i.e., 3×10^{12}) grams. The Blob intends to *eat* the Sears Tower as soon as it weighs 1000 times as much (i.e., 3×10^{15} grams). By what time must the Blob be stopped? Will Friday's rush-hour commuters be delayed?

4. A mold grows at a rate that is proportional to the amount present. Initially, its weight is 2 grams; after two days, it weighs 5 grams. How much does it weigh after eight days?

5. A bacterial culture is placed in a large glass bottle. Suppose that the volume of the culture doubles every hour, and the bottle is full after one day.

   (a) If the culture was placed in the bottle at time $t = 0$ hours, when was the bottle half full?

   (b) Assume that the bottle is "almost empty" when the culture occupies less than 1% of its volume. How long is the bottle "almost empty"?

6. The police guard gave Sara a cold look, but his voice was polite as he directed her to the room she sought. "Don't touch anything, please, Ms. Abrams. The Chief said I had to let you in, but he said to tell you to mind your fingers." "Thank you," Sara replied cooly. "The Chief knows he can trust me." The guard opened his mouth as if to speak, but he merely shook his head and withdrew.

   Sara was standing in what appeared to be a combination bedroom and laboratory. A relative had found Dr. Howell's body on the floor of this room that morning. By 9:00 a.m., the coroner had completed his examination; he stated that death was due to a severe blow to the head, and that Dr. Howell had been dead between 36 and 40 hours. It seemed critical to Sara to know exactly when Dr. Howell had died so that she could eliminate certain suspects. But how could she possibly discover exactly when he was killed? Puzzled, she wandered around the small, cluttered room, being careful not to touch anything. The old doctor apparently was conducting an experiment when he was killed. Sara absent-mindedly read from the notebook which was lying open on the bench.

   > *The fungus grows at a rate proportional to its current weight.*

   "Great," she thought, "I'm here to investigate a murder and instead I'm getting a biology lesson." At a loss for what else to do, she continued reading.

   > *To exemplify this biological truth, I place the fungus on a scale and record its weight at various times:*

10 *g*	5:30 p.m.
12 *g*	6:15 p.m.
13	

   "Hmm," Sara mused, "the poor guy didn't even get to finish the last entry." Sara suddenly frowned in concentration. She searched her pockets until she found a pencil stub and an old receipt. When the guard entered the room a few minutes later, Sara had just finished scribbling on the receipt. She smiled as she shoved the receipt and the pencil stub back into her pocket.

"Don't worry," Sara said cheerfully, "I'm leaving. I now know exactly when Dr. Howell was killed." The guard looked sourly at Sara's back as she left the room.

When was Dr. Howell killed? How did Sara know?

7. Oil is pumped continuously from a well at a rate proportional to the amount of oil left in the well. Initially there were 1,000,000 barrels of oil in the well; 6 years later 500,000 barrels remain.

   (a) At what rate was the amount of oil in the well decreasing when there were 600,000 barrels of oil remaining?

   (b) It will no longer be profitable to pump oil from the well when there are fewer than 50,000 barrels remaining. When should pumping stop?

8. Human skeletal fragments showing ancient Neanderthal characteristics were found in a Palestinian cave and brought to a laboratory for carbon dating. Analysis showed that the proportion of C^{14} to C^{12} is only 6.25% of the value in living tissue. How long ago did this person die?

9. A tank initially contains 100 gallons of water and 10 pounds of salt, thoroughly mixed. Pure water is added at the rate of 5 gallons per minute, and the mixture is drained off at the same rate. (Assume complete and instantaneous mixing.)

   (a) Explain why $S(t)$, the amount of salt in the tank at time t, is the solution of the IVP
   $$S' = -\tfrac{5}{100}S; \quad S(0) = 10.$$

   (b) Using Theorem 1., page 313, find a solution of this IVP.

   (c) How much salt is left in the tank after 1 hour?

4.3 Linear and quadratic approximation; Taylor polynomials

In this section we consider how to find and use polynomial functions that approximate other (non-polynomial) functions. What does it *mean* for a function f to approximate another function g? How can "good" polynomial approximations be chosen? How are derivatives involved?

We'll start with the simplest cases: linear and quadratic polynomials. Then we'll describe how to find polynomials of *any* degree, called **Taylor polynomials**, that approximate a given function.

Why bother? Often in mathematics and applied mathematics one wants to approximate one function, say f, with another, say g. Why bother? For several possible reasons: if f is complicated, imperfectly understood, or otherwise inconvenient, it's useful to replace f with a simpler, better behaved, more tractable, or better understood g.

Polynomial functions are simple, convenient, well understood, and easy to use, so it's natural to use them to approximate more complicated functions.

Tangent lines and linear approximation

The line tangent to the graph of a function f at $x = x_0$ can be thought of in several ways. Geometrically, the tangent line is the straight line that best "fits" the graph of f at $x = x_0$. Analytically, the tangent line represents the linear *function* that best "approximates" f near $x = x_0$.

■ **Example 1.** If $f(x) = \sqrt{x}$, then $f(64) = 8$. How closely does the tangent line function approximate values of $f(x)$ for x *near* 64?

Solution: Since $f'(x) = 1/(2\sqrt{x})$, $f'(64) = 1/16$. Therefore the line tangent to the f-graph at $(64, 8)$ has equation➸ *Verify this.*

$$\ell(x) = f(64) + f'(64)(x - 64) = 8 + \frac{x - 64}{16} = 4 + \frac{x}{16}.$$

Here are graphs of both f and ℓ:

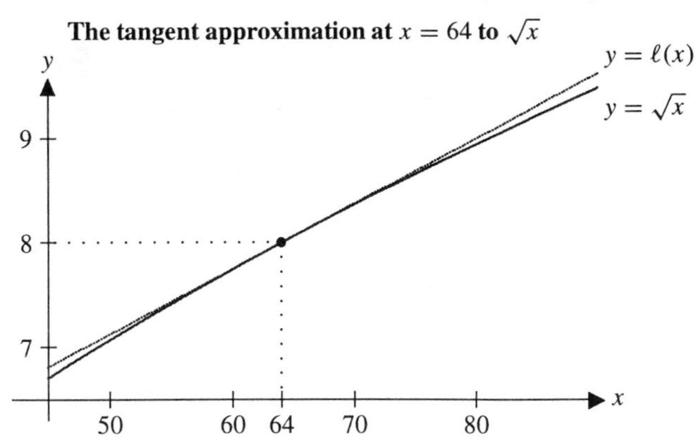

Observe:

- The tangent line hugs the graph of f closely; ℓ should therefore approximate f well for x near $x = 64$—the nearer the better.
- The graph of f is concave *down*, so it lies *below* its tangent line. Therefore, the tangent line function ℓ *overestimates* f for each $x \neq 64$.

But only slightly!

Constant, linear, and quadratic approximations

How might we approximate *any* function f near *any* convenient "base point" $x = x_0$? The previous example showed that the tangent line at $x = x_0$ defines a good **linear approximation** to f at x_0. **Constant** and **quadratic approximations** are also possible.

■ **Example 2.** Which *constant* function best approximates $f(x) = \sqrt{x}$ near $x = 64$? Which *quadratic* function?

Solution: Since $f(64) = 8$, the constant function $c(x) = 8$ is the only sensible choice; c has the "right" value at $x = 64$.

How should we choose a good *quadratic* approximation q? For the *linear* approximation ℓ we required that

$$\ell(64) = f(64) = 8 \quad \text{and} \quad \ell'(64) = f'(64) = \frac{1}{16}.$$

It's reasonable, then, to ask that a good *quadratic* approximation q go one step further:

Why is $f''(64) = -1/2048$? Check for yourself.

$$q(64) = 8; \quad q'(64) = \frac{1}{16}; \quad q''(64) = f''(64) = -\frac{1}{2048}. \tag{4.3.1}$$

In other words, our desired quadratic function q should "agree" with f at $x = 64$, both in its value and in its first *two* derivatives.

The easiest way to construct such a q is to write it in the form

Writing q in powers of $(x - 64)$, not x, greatly simplifies some of the algebra.

$$q(x) = a + b(x - 64) + c(x - 64)^2,$$

and then choose the coefficients a, b, and c appropriately. Since we'll need them below, we'll first calculate several values and derivatives of q:

Watch carefully—here's where the form of q pays off.

$$\begin{aligned} q(x) &= a + b(x - 64) + c(x - 64)^2 \implies q(64) = a; \\ q'(x) &= b + 2c(x - 64) \implies q'(64) = b; \\ q''(x) &= 2c \implies q''(64) = 2c. \end{aligned}$$

Choosing a, b, and c is now easy:

Choosing a. Equation 4.3.1 requires that $q(64) = 8$. But $q(64) = a$, so $a = 8$.

Choosing b. Equation 4.3.1 requires that $q'(64) = 1/16$. But $q'(64) = b$, so $b = 1/16$.

Choosing c. Equation 4.3.1 requires that $q''(64) = -1/2048$. But $q''(64) = 2c$, so $c = -1/4096$.

Where did the factor of 2 come from?

Putting everything together gives

$$q(x) = 8 + \frac{x-64}{16} - \frac{(x-64)^2}{4096}$$

as the "best" quadratic approximation to f at $x = 64$.

Graphs of c, ℓ, q, and f show what's happening:

Constant, linear, and quadratic approximations to $f(x) = \sqrt{x}$

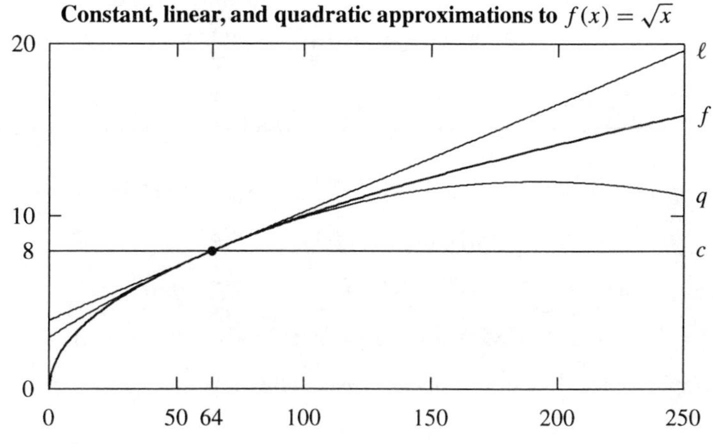

Observe:

- All three approximating functions (c, ℓ, and q) have the "right" value *at* $x = 64$.
- The graphs of ℓ and q (but not of c!) are *tangent* to the f-graph at $x = 64$. *I.e., have the same slope.*
- The function q "fits" f *better* than ℓ near $x = 64$. The fact that $q''(64) = f''(64)$ means that q and f have the same *concavity* at $x = 64$. *And much better than c.*

How well, numerically, do c, ℓ, and q approximate f? A table gives some idea:

Three approximations to $f(x) = \sqrt{x}$

x	50	63	63.9	64	64.1	65	80
$c(x)$	8.00000	8.00000	8.00000	8	8.00000	8.00000	8.00000
$\ell(x)$	7.12500	7.93750	7.99375	8	8.00625	8.06250	9.00000
$q(x)$	7.07715	7.93726	7.99375	8	8.00625	8.06226	8.93750
$f(x)$	7.07107	7.93725	7.99375	8	8.00625	8.06226	8.94427

The numbers agree with the graphs: q approximates f best, especially near $x = 64$.□

Definitions

Linear and quadratic approximations can be chosen for *any* well-behaved function f, at *any* base point x_0. The formal definition summarizes, in general language, what we did above for $f(x) = \sqrt{x}$ and $x_0 = 64$.

Definition: Let f be any function for which $f'(x_0)$ and $f''(x_0)$ exist. The **linear approximation to f, based at** x_0, is the linear function

$$\ell(x) = f(x_0) + f'(x_0)(x - x_0).$$

The **quadratic approximation to f, based at** x_0, is the quadratic function

$$q(x) = f(x_0) + f'(x_0)(x - x_0) + \frac{f''(x_0)}{2}(x - x_0)^2.$$

■ **Example 3.** Let $f(x) = 10^x$. Find ℓ and q, the linear and quadratic approximations to f, based at $x = 3$. Use each to estimate $f(3.1)$.

Check our work.

Solution: We'll need two derivatives and a value for f, all at $x = 3$. Calculation gives $f(x) = 10^x$, $f'(x) = 10^x \ln 10$, and $f''(x) = 10^x (\ln 10)^2$, so

$$f(3) = 10^3 = 1000; \quad f'(3) = 1000 \ln 10 \approx 2302.5851;$$
$$f''(3) = 1000(\ln 10)^2 \approx 5309.8981.$$

The definitions say:

$$\begin{aligned} \ell(x) &= f(3) + f'(3) \cdot (x-3) \approx 1000 + 2302.5851(x-3); \\ q(x) &= \ell(x) + \frac{f''(3)}{2} \cdot (x-3)^2 \approx 1000 + 2302.5851(x-3) + \\ &\quad 2650.9491(x-3)^2. \end{aligned}$$

By calculator!

Numerical calculation shows:

$$\ell(3.1) \approx 1230.2585; \quad q(3.1) \approx 1256.7680; \quad f(3.1) \approx 1258.9254.$$

The graphs below, like the numbers above, show how much better q does than ℓ in "fitting" f:

Linear and quadratic approximations to $f(x) = 10^x$

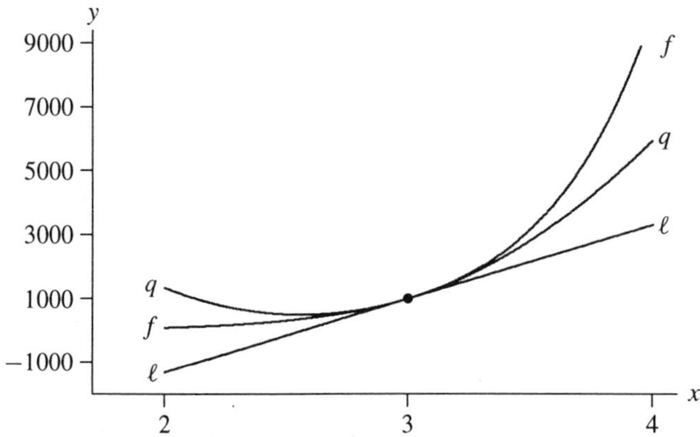

The picture shows why ℓ fits f so poorly: f bends sharply away from ℓ, even quite near $x = 3$. The second derivative, f'', explains why. Any *linear* function ℓ has *zero* second derivative. Our target function f, by contrast, has a *huge* second derivative: $f''(3) \approx 5000$. Because f is so drastically non-linear, it is badly approximated by any straight line—even the best-fitting one. □

Taylor polynomials

Linear and quadratic approximations ℓ and q are built to "match" f as well as possible at x_0: more precisely, ℓ and f have the same value and *first* derivative at x_0; q and f have the same value and first *two* derivatives at x_0.

An important example.

Still better "agreement" is possible if polynomials of degree 3, 4, and higher are used to approximate f. An example will illustrate the idea.

Made to order. The constant, linear, and quadratic approximations are sometimes called **zeroth-order**, **first-order**, and **second-order** approximations to f near x_0. In each case **order** refers to the number of derivatives of f that a particular approximation "agrees" with at x_0.

■ **Example 4.** Find a fifth-degree polynomial p_5 that agrees with $f(x) = e^x$ to order 5 at $x_0 = 0$, i.e., such that

A "quintic."

$$\begin{array}{lll} p_5(0) = f(0) & p_5'(0) = f'(0) & p_5''(0) = f''(0) \\ p_5^{(3)}(0) = f^{(3)}(0) & p_5^{(4)}(0) = f^{(4)}(0) & p_5^{(5)}(0) = f^{(5)}(0) \end{array}$$

Solution: We'll need values for several derivatives of f, all at $x = 0$. That $f(x) = e^x$ makes calculating derivatives very, very easy:

That's why we chose this f!

$$f(x) = e^x \implies f(0) = f'(0) = f''(0) = f^{(3)}(0) = f^{(4)}(0) = f^{(5)}(0) = 1.$$

We want a polynomial p_5 with the *same* derivatives at $x = 0$. To begin, we write $p_5(x)$ in standard form:

Recall that e^x itself is not a polynomial.

$$p_5(x) = a_0 + a_1x + a_2x^2 + a_3x^3 + a_4x^4 + a_5x^5;$$

the coefficients a_i are still to be found.

For each i, a_i is the coefficient of the ith power x^i.

Finding a_0 through a_5 is surprisingly easy. The key idea is that the a_i are closely related to *derivatives* of p_5 at $x = 0$. Specifically:

Check these easy but important calculations.

$$\begin{array}{lclcl} p_5(x) & = & a_0 + a_1x + a_2x^2 + a_3x^3 + a_4x^4 + a_5x^5 & \implies & p_5(0) = a_0 \\ p_5'(x) & = & a_1 + 2a_2x + 3a_3x^2 + 4a_4x^3 + 5a_5x^4 & \implies & p_5'(0) = a_1 \\ p_5''(x) & = & 2a_2 + 3 \cdot 2a_3x + 4 \cdot 3a_4x^2 + 5 \cdot 4a_5x^3 & \implies & p_5''(0) = 2a_2 \\ p_5'''(x) & = & 3 \cdot 2a_3 + 4 \cdot 3 \cdot 2a_4x + 5 \cdot 4 \cdot 3a_5x^2 & \implies & p_5'''(0) = 6a_3 \\ p_5^{(4)}(x) & = & 4 \cdot 3 \cdot 2a_4 + 5 \cdot 4 \cdot 3 \cdot 2a_5x & \implies & p_5^{(4)}(0) = 24a_4 \\ p_5^{(5)}(x) & = & 5 \cdot 4 \cdot 3 \cdot 2a_5 & \implies & p_5^{(5)}(0) = 120a_5. \end{array}$$

The pattern of coefficients should now be clear: *For each i, $p_5^{(i)}(0) = i!\,a_i$.* In other words:

*$i!$ denotes the **factorial** of i. See below for more on factorials.*

$$a_0 = p_5(0); \quad a_1 = p_5'(0); \quad a_2 = \frac{p_5''(0)}{2!}; \quad a_3 = \frac{p_5'''(0)}{3!}; \quad \ldots \quad a_5 = \frac{p_5^{(5)}(0)}{5!}.$$

Now we can find p_5. By design,

$$p_5(0) = f(0) = 1; \quad p_5'(0) = f'(0) = 1; \quad p_5''(0) = f''(0) = 1; \quad \ldots \quad p_5^{(5)}(0) = f^{(5)}(0) = 1.$$

Thus

$$a_0 = 1; \quad a_1 = 1; \quad a_2 = \frac{1}{2!}; \quad a_3 = \frac{1}{3!}; \quad a_4 = \frac{1}{4!}; \quad a_5 = \frac{1}{5!}.$$

Our search is over:

$$p_5(x) = \frac{1}{0!} + \frac{x}{1!} + \frac{x^2}{2!} + \frac{x^3}{3!} + \frac{x^4}{4!} + \frac{x^5}{5!} = 1 + x + \frac{x^2}{2} + \frac{x^3}{6} + \frac{x^4}{24} + \frac{x^5}{120}.$$

How well does p_5 approximate f near $x = 0$? Very well indeed:

A fifth-order polynomial approximation to $f(x) = e^x$

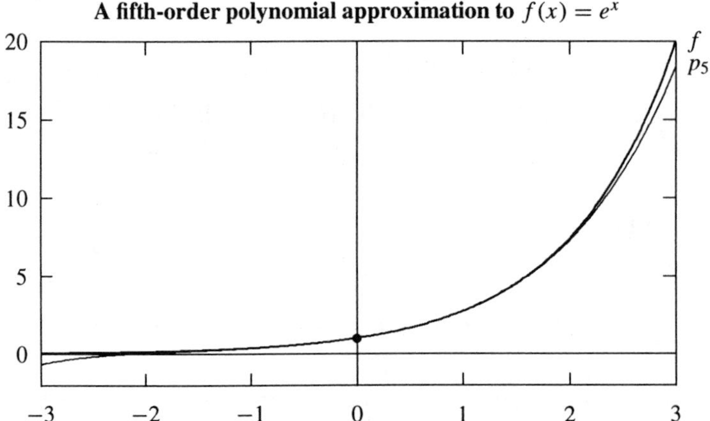

The graphs of f and p_5 are almost identical near $x = 0$. Compare, for instance, $f(1)$ and $p_5(1)$. Easy calculations show that

A calculator helps.

$$p_5(1) = 1 + 1 + \frac{1}{2} + \frac{1}{6} + \frac{1}{24} + \frac{1}{120} = \frac{163}{60} \approx 2.717; \quad f(1) = e \approx 2.718. \quad \square$$

Factorials

The repeated product $i \cdot (i-1) \cdot (i-2) \cdots 2 \cdot 1$, denoted $i!$, is called the **factorial** of i. (By convention, $0! = 1$.) Factorials appear often in mathematics, especially when (as above) an operation is performed repeatedly. Factorials are important enough in practice that many calculators have a factorial key.

Does yours? If so, try it. If not, calculate some factorials "from scratch."

Definitions

The polynomial p_5 constructed above is the **fifth-order Taylor polynomial for $f(x) = e^x$ based at $x = 0$**. Here is the general definition:

> **Definition: (Taylor polynomials.)** Let f be any function whose first n derivatives exist at $x = x_0$. The **Taylor polynomial of order n, based at x_0,** is defined by
>
> $$p_n(x) = f(x_0) + f'(x_0)(x - x_0) + \frac{f''(x_0)}{2!}(x - x_0)^2 + \frac{f^{(3)}(x_0)}{3!}(x - x_0)^3 + \cdots + \frac{f^{(n)}(x_0)}{n!}(x - x_0)^n.$$

Taylor's idea? The idea of Taylor polynomials predates Brook Taylor (1685–1731), a contemporary of Isaac Newton, for whom they are named. According to the author George Simmons, the underlying idea of Taylor polynomials appears in work of John Bernoulli, published in 1694, when Taylor was only 9. The same versatile Bernoulli is also credited with having discovered—behind the scenes—the famous technical lemma known as l'Hôpital's Rule. (We'll see it later in this book.)

■ **Example 5.** Let $f(x) = \sqrt{x}$. Find the first three Taylor polynomials p_1, p_2, and p_3, all based at $x_0 = 64$.

Solution: We'll need the value and first three derivatives of f at $x = 64$:

Check the last one; we found the others above.

$$f(64) = 8; \quad f'(64) = \frac{1}{16}; \quad f''(64) = -\frac{1}{2048}; \quad f'''(64) = \frac{3}{262144}.$$

Plugging these values into the definition gives our results:

The first two are familiar.

$$\begin{aligned} p_1(x) &= 8 + \frac{x-64}{16}; \\ p_2(x) &= 8 + \frac{x-64}{16} - \frac{(x-64)^2}{2! \cdot 2048} = 8 + \frac{x-64}{16} - \frac{(x-64)^2}{4096}; \\ p_3(x) &= 8 + \frac{x-64}{16} - \frac{(x-64)^2}{4096} + \frac{3}{3! \cdot 262144}(x-64)^3 \\ &= 8 + \frac{x-64}{16} - \frac{(x-64)^2}{4096} + \frac{(x-64)^3}{524288}. \end{aligned}$$

□

More on the definition

The Taylor polynomial definition deserves a closer look:

Why powers of $(x - x_0)$? Polynomials usually involve powers of x. Here, though, powers of $(x - x_0)$ are more convenient. Above, for instance, using powers of $(x-64)$ simplified our calculations, most of which involved $x = 64$.

x, x^2, x^3, etc.

$(x - x_0), (x - x_0)^2, (x - x_0)^3$, etc.

Maclaurin polynomials. Taylor polynomials that happen to based at $x = 0$ are known as **Maclaurin polynomials**. Maclaurin polynomials look a little simpler:

They're simpler only in appearance.

$$P_n(x) = f(0) + f'(0)x + \frac{f''(0)}{2}x^2 + \cdots + \frac{f^{(n)}(0)}{n!}x^n.$$

In Example 4 we found the **fifth-order Maclaurin polynomial for** $f(x) = e^x$.

Order, degree. A Taylor polynomial P_n of **order** n is chosen so that its value and first n derivatives at $x = x_0$ agree with those of f. The definition shows that P_n also has **degree** n, i.e., it involves powers of $(x - x_0)$ up through the nth. (If, by chance, $a_n = 0$, then P_n has smaller degree.)

Many symbols, just one variable. The definition involves many symbols: a, x, i, x_0, f, and n. It helps to remember, while in this thicket, that x *is the only variable*. In specific cases all the other symbols take *numerical* values.

As in Example 5.

From P_n to P_{n+1}. Let f be a function and P_n the Taylor polynomial of order n based at x_0. The *next* Taylor polynomial, P_{n+1}, has just one more term:

$$P_{n+1}(x) = P_n(x) + \frac{f^{(n+1)}(x_0)}{(n+1)!}(x - x_0)^{n+1}.$$

Approximating functions with Taylor polynomials

An important use of Taylor polynomials is in approximating other, more complicated functions. For example, the sine function—which has no algebraic formula—is a good candidate for approximation by polynomials.

■ **Example 6.** Find P_1, P_3, P_5, and P_7, the Taylor (aka Maclaurin) polynomials for $f(x) = \sin x$ based at $x = 0$. Plot everything on one set of axes. How closely does each polynomial approximate $\sin 1$?

Check this easy calculation.

Solution: To find P_7 we'll need the value and the first through seventh derivatives of $f(x) = \sin x$ at $x = 0$. Here they are, in order: 0, 1, 0, −1, 0, 1, 0, −1. It follows, therefore, that

$$P_7(x) = 0 + 1x + 0x^2 - \frac{1}{3!}x^3 + 0x^4 + \frac{1}{5!}x^5 + 0x^6 - \frac{1}{7!}x^7,$$

and hence that

$$P_1(x) = x; \quad P_3(x) = x - \frac{x^3}{6}; \quad P_5(x) = x - \frac{x^3}{6} + \frac{x^5}{120};$$
$$P_7(x) = x - \frac{x^3}{6} + \frac{x^5}{120} - \frac{x^7}{5040}.$$

Here are all five graphs:

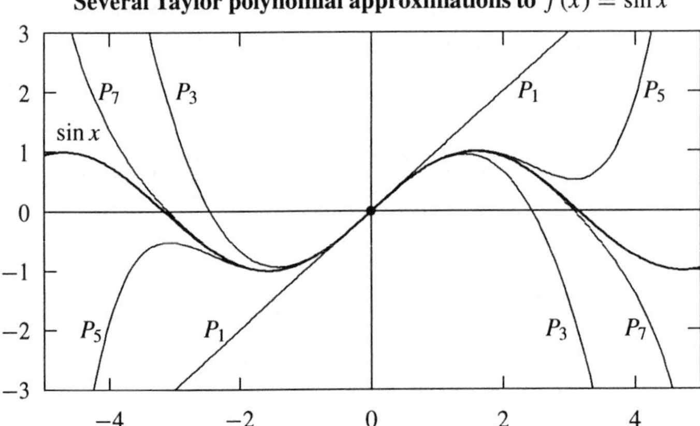

The picture shows:

In either direction.

Snug fits near $x = 0$. All four Taylor polynomials "fit" the sine curve well *near* the base point $x = 0$. Differences appear as we move *away* from $x = 0$.

Better and better. Higher-order Taylor polynomials approximate the sine function *better* than lower-order ones. P_7, for instance, "follows" the sine curve much farther than P_1 or P_3. than

Trace P_3 carefully to see this.

Wiggly is good when approximating a sine curve!

Standard shapes. The graphs of P_1 and P_3 have "standard" shapes for linear and cubic functions. The wigglier appearance of P_5 and P_7 reflects their higher degree.

Intuition suggests that P_1, P_3, P_5, and P_7 should give successively closer and closer estimates for $\sin 1 \approx 0.84147$. So they do:

$$P_1(1) = 1; \quad P_3(1) = \frac{5}{6} \approx 0.83333;$$
$$P_5(1) = \frac{101}{120} \approx 0.84167; \quad P_7(1) = \frac{4241}{5040} \approx 0.84147.$$

□

Bounding the error of linear approximation *(optional)*

An error bound formula

How large, numerically, are the errors committed when Taylor polynomials approximate a function f? We'll address the question only for *linear* approximations; for higher-order approximations the ideas are similar but the calculations are more complicated.

Comparing results from Example 2 and Example 3 shows that the error of a linear approximations depends on two factors:

1. the distance from x to x_0;
2. the size of the second derivative f'' near x_0. (Large values of $|f''|$ means that the f-graph bends *sharply* away from its tangent line; small➻ values of $|f''|$ mean that the f-graph is nearly straight near x_0, and therefore closely approximated by its tangent line.)

I.e., near 0.

The following theorem restates these ideas quantitatively. Throughout, f is a differentiable function, ℓ is the linear approximation based at $x = x_0$, and I is an interval containing x_0:

Theorem 2. (An error bound for linear approximation.) Suppose that the inequality

$$|f''(x)| \le K$$

holds for all x in I. Then for all x in I,

$$|f(x) - \ell(x)| \le \frac{K}{2}(x - x_0)^2.$$

Note:

The error function. The function $f(x) - \ell(x)$ on the left above is called an **error function**: we'll call it $e(x)$. For a given x, $e(x)$ is the **error** committed by ℓ in approximating f. Ideally, $e(x) \approx 0$.

An error bound formula. The inequality

$$|f(x) - \ell(x)| \le \frac{K}{2}(x - x_0)^2.$$

is (appropriately) called an **error bound formula**; it guarantees that the error function is no larger than the *computable* quantity on the right.

It's OK to overestimate K. *Any* upper bound for $|f''(x)|$ on I can serve as K in the inequality. Choosing K as small as possible "improves" the error bound, but the inequality holds even for larger values of K.➻

It's safe to overestimate K, but not to underestimate.

Worst-case scenario. The function $f(x) = K(x - x_0)^2/2$ represents the "worst case" that the hypothesis allows. For this f,

$$f(x_0) = 0, \quad f'(x_0) = 0; \quad \text{and} \quad f''(x) = K.$$

In this case the linear approximation is simply $\ell(x) = 0$, and error ℓ commits is as large as the theorem permits:

$$|f(x) - \ell(x)| = f(x) = \frac{K}{2}(x - x_0)^2.$$

Before proving the error bound theorem, we'll show it in action.

Satisfaction guaranteed

The practical value of an error bound formula is in *guaranteeing* the accuracy of an approximation.

■ **Example 7.** We showed above that $\ell(x) = 4 + x/16$ is the linear approximation to $f(x) = \sqrt{x}$ at $x = 64$. What accuracy does the error bound formula guarantee if ℓ approximates f on the interval $[50, 80]$? What does the formula guarantee for the interval $[63, 65]$?

Check ours.

Solution: First we'll need a suitable K. Calculation shows that

$$f''(x) = \frac{d^2}{dx^2}\left(\sqrt{x}\right) = -\frac{1}{4x^{3/2}} \implies |f''(x)| = \frac{1}{4x^{3/2}}.$$

Or a look at the graph of $|f''|$.

$|f''(x)|$ is largest at the left endpoint.

Watch all inequalities carefully.

A moment's thought shows that $|f''(x)|$ *decreases* as x increases. For the interval $[50, 80]$, therefore, we may use $K = |f''(50)| \leq 0.00071$. On $[63, 65]$, $K = |f''(63)| \approx 0.0005$ works.

All ingredients are ready. The theorem says:

- For x in $[50, 80]$ the largest possible error is no more than

$$|\sqrt{x} - \ell(x)| \leq \frac{0.0007}{2}(x-64)^2 \leq \frac{0.0007}{2}(80-64)^2 \approx 0.09.$$

(We used $x = 80$, not $x = 50$, to make $(x-64)^2$ as large as possible.) In other words: On $[50, 80]$, ℓ approximates f to about *one decimal place accuracy.*

- For x in $[63, 65]$ the largest possible error is even less:

$$|\sqrt{x} - \ell(x)| \leq \frac{0.0005}{2}(x-64)^2 \leq \frac{0.0005}{2}(65-64)^2 \approx 0.00025.$$

In other words: On $[63, 65]$, ℓ approximates f to about *three decimal place accuracy.*

The table on page 325 shows that these error estimates are conservative: ℓ and q behave a little "better" than the theorem predicts. □

A proof of the error bound formula

We'll take f, ℓ, and K to be as in the theorem. From these data we'll construct two new functions—an **error function** e and and a **bounding function** b, defined as follows:

$$e(x) = f(x) - \ell(x); \qquad b(x) = K\frac{(x-x_0)^2}{2}.$$

The same proof, with minor variations, shows that the inequality holds for $x < x_0$ and in absolute value.

The theorem claims—and we need to show—that for x in I, $|e(x)| \leq b(x)$. To simplify things slightly we'll show only that $e(x) \leq b(x)$ for $x \geq x_0$.

To our aid come three key properties of e and b:

(4.3.2) $e(x_0) = 0 = b(x_0)$; $\quad e'(x_0) = 0 = b'(x_0)$; $\quad |e''(x)| \leq K = b''(x)$.

Make them!

We met it first in Section 2.1.

(All three properties of e follow from the "construction" of ℓ: by design, $\ell(x_0) = f(x_0)$, $\ell'(x_0) = f'(x_0)$, and $e''(x) = f''(x) - l''(x) = f''(x)$. All three properties of b come from direct calculations.)

To finish the proof we'll use the "racetrack principle." Recall what it says about *any* functions g and h:

If $g(x_0) = h(x_0)$ and $g'(x) \le h'(x)$ for $x \ge x_0$, then $g(x) \le h(x)$ for $x \ge x_0$.

Let's apply the racetrack principle to e and b. As we saw above, $e(x_0) = 0 = b(x_0)$. We'll be done, says the racetrack principle, if we can somehow show that $e'(x) \le b'(x)$ for $x \ge x_0$.

To do so we apply the racetrack principle *again*, but this time to e' and b', and *their* derivatives e'' and b''. Equations 4.3.2 contain everything we need: $e'(0) = b'(0)$ and $e''(x) \le b''(x)$. Thus the racetrack principle says that $e'(x) \le b'(x)$ for $x \ge x_0$—exactly what we need to finish the proof. □

Exercises

1. In each part below, first find the indicated Taylor polynomial P_n of order n for the function f with base point x_0. Then plot both f and P_n on the same axes. Choose your plotting window appropriately to show clearly the relationship between f and P_n.

   (a) $f(x) = \dfrac{1}{1-x}$, $n = 3$, $x_0 = 0$.

   (b) $\sin x + \cos x$, $n = 4$, $x_0 = 0$.

   (c) $f(x) = \ln x$, $n = 3$, $x_0 = 1$,

   (d) $f(x) = \tan x$, $n = 2$, $x_0 = 0$,

   (e) $\sqrt{x}$, $n = 3$, $x_0 = 4$.

2. This problem refers to Example 6, p. 330—especially the graphs. Throughout this problem, $f(x) = \sin x$, and $P_n(x)$ is the Taylor (Maclaurin) polynomial of order n based at $x = 0$.

   (a) Every function mentioned in Example 6—f, P_1, P_3, P_5, and P_7—is odd. How is this fact "reflected" in their graphs?

   (b) Find the *even-order* Maclaurin polynomials P_2, P_4, P_6, and P_8 for $f(x) = \sin x$. How are they related to P_1, P_3, P_5, and P_7?

3. Throughout this problem, $g(x) = \cos x$ and $P_n(x)$ is the Taylor (Maclaurin) polynomial of order n based at $x = 0$. For use below, here are graphs of g, P_0, P_2, P_4, and P_6.

Several Taylor polynomial approximations to $f(x) = \cos x$

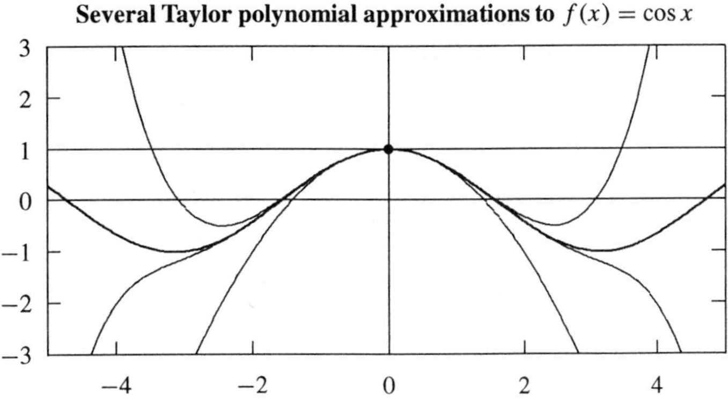

(a) Find formulas for P_0 through P_6, the Maclaurin polynomials through order 6 for g based at $x = 0$. Use your results to label the graphs shown above.

(b) Is g odd, even, or neither? What about the Maclaurin polynomials for g found in part (a)? How do the graphs "reflect" the situation?

(c) In Example 6 we found the Maclaurin polynomials P_1, P_3, P_5, and P_7 for $f(x) = \sin x$. Find the *derivatives* $P_1'(x)$, $P_3'(x)$, $P_5'(x)$, $P_7'(x)$, and $f'(x)$ of these functions. How are the results related to the rest of this problem?

4. In Example 2 we worked with the quadratic function $q(x) = a + b(x - 64) + c(x - 64)^2$. Here are more details:

(a) We claimed that $q'(x) = b + 2c(x - 64)$ and that $q''(x) = 2c$. Verify these claims by differentiation.

(b) Rewrite q in powers of x, i.e., in the form $q(x) = A + Bx + Cx^2$.

(c) Rewrite $q'(x) = b + 2c(x - 64)$ in powers of x. Does your answer agree as it should with the previous part?

5. Estimate the value of each of the following expressions using a linear approximation. Then compute the difference between your estimate and the value given by a scientific calculator.

(a) $\sqrt{103}$

(b) $\sqrt[3]{29}$

(c) $\tan 31^\circ$

(d) 0.8^{10}

6. For each part of the previous exercise, compare the "actual" approximation error with the theoretical error bound.

7. Repeat the previous exercise using a quadratic approximation.

8. The line tangent to the curve $y = g(x)$ at the point $(3, 5)$ intersects the y-axis at the point $(0, 10)$.

(a) What is $g'(3)$?

(b) Estimate $g(2.95)$ using a linear approximation.

9. Suppose that f is a function such that $f'(x) = \sin\left(x^2\right)$ and $f(1) = 0$. [NOTE: No explicit formula for f is given.]

(a) Estimate the value of $f(0.5)$ using a linear approximation.

(b) Is the estimate you computed in part (a) greater than or less than the exact value of $f(0.5)$? Explain.

(c) Estimate the value of $f(0.5)$ using a quadratic approximation.

10. The linear approximation $(1 + x)^k \approx 1 + kx$ is often useful for "back of the envelope" computations. Find the error made in using this expression to approximate each of the following expressions.

(a) $(1.03)^2$

(b) $\sqrt{1.0404}$

(c) 1.001^{-1}

11. Find the linear and quadratic approximations of each of the following functions at $x_0 = 0$.

    (a) $f(x) = \sin x$
    (b) $f(x) = \cos x$
    (c) $f(x) = \tan x$
    (d) $f(x) = e^x$
    (e) $f(x) = \tan^{-1} x$
    (f) $f(x) = \sin^{-1} x$

12. (a) For each function in the previous problem, find an interval over which the linear approximation makes an error no greater than 0.01.

    (b) For each function in the previous problem, find an interval over which the quadratic approximation makes an error no greater than 0.01.

13. Let g be a well-behaved function defined on the interval $[0, 10]$ such that the graph of g passes through the point $(5, 2)$ and the derivative of g is the function sketched below.

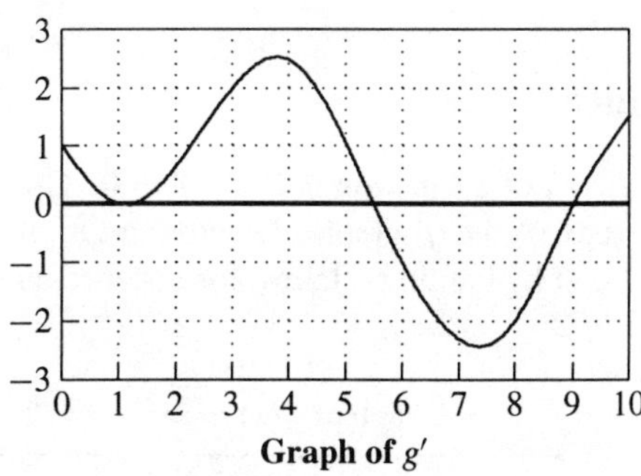

Graph of g'

    (a) Estimate $g(0)$ using a linear approximation.

    (b) Estimate $g(8)$ using a quadratic approximation.

14. Suppose that h is a well-behaved function such that $h(2) = 3$, $h'(2) = -2$, and $-2 \leq h''(x) \leq 1$ for all $x \in (0, 4)$. Show that $0 \leq h(3) \leq 2$.

4.4 Newton's method: finding roots

Consider these problems:

- Let $f(x) = 2x^3 - x - 2$. Find a number r for which $f(r) = 0$.
- Estimate $\sqrt{2}$ with high numerical accuracy.
- Find a number r such that

$$150r = (1 + r)^{31} - 1.$$

Each problem above involves finding a **root** of some function f, i.e., a number r such that $f(r) = 0$. None can be solved easily or directly by algebraic methods. Newton's method offers a simple and efficient alternative to finding roots algebraically. We'll use it to solve all three problems above.

Roots, graphically

A number r is a root of a function f if $f(r) = 0$. Graphically speaking, a root of f is an x-**intercept** of the f-graph. Given a graph of f it's easy to find roots—approximately—just by looking. Below, for instance, are two views of the graph of $f(x) = 2x^3 - x - 2$:

Graph of $f(x) = 2x^3 - x - 2$

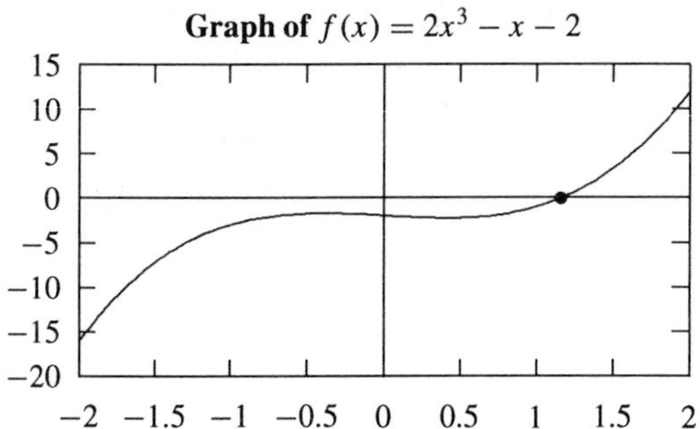

A closer view: $f(x) = 2x^3 - x - 2$

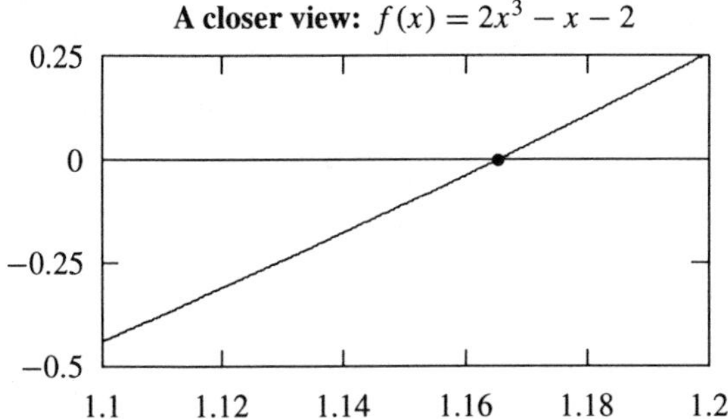

The first graph shows a root somewhere near $x = 1$; the second locates it more precisely, near $x = 1.17$. Further zooming might reveal additional digits. Newton's method offers a more efficient strategy, so we won't bother.

■ **Example 1.** Graphically estimate a root of $f(r) = (1 + r)^{31} - 1 - 150r$. (Such a root solves the equation $150r = (1 + r)^{31} - 1$, mentioned above.)

Solution: The graph—

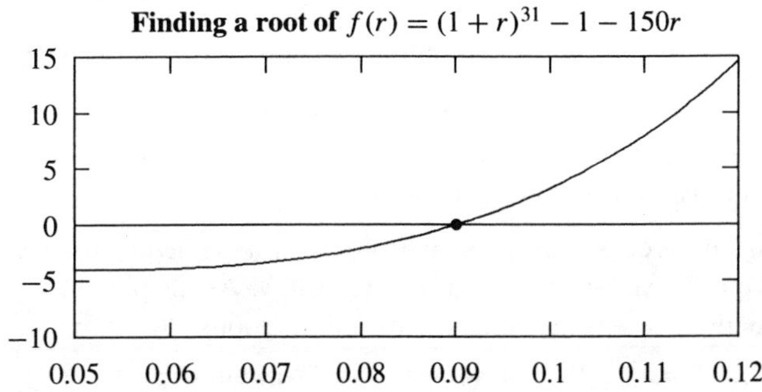

shows a root *near* $r = 0.09$. A numerical check shows that $f(0.09) \approx -0.0382$, so our guess isn't exact. We'll refine it below with Newton's method. □

Roots, algebraically

Roots can sometimes be found algebraically, by solving equations. Unfortunately, such methods often fail: unless a function has an algebraic formula—a simple one—solving algebraically for roots may be hard or impossible. For *linear functions*, roots are easy to find.

Don't skip this example; we'll refer to it below.

■ **Example 2.** A line passes through the point (x_0, y_0), with slope m. Find its x-intercept.

Solution: The line has point-slope equation $y - y_0 = m(x - x_0)$. To find the x-intercept, we set $y = 0$ and solve for x:

$$-y_0 = m(x - x_0) \iff x = x_0 - \frac{y_0}{m}. \tag{4.4.1}$$

(This formula fails, of course, if $m = 0$. The line is horizontal and so has no x-intercept.) □

Unless $y_0 = 0$, in which case the line is the x-axis itself.

Newton's idea: ride the tangent line

Most functions aren't linear, and so don't lend themselves easily to algebraic root-finding. When algebra fails, Newton's method often succeeds.

Newton's method starts with one approximation to a root and produces another, better approximation. The following picture illustrates one **Newton step**:

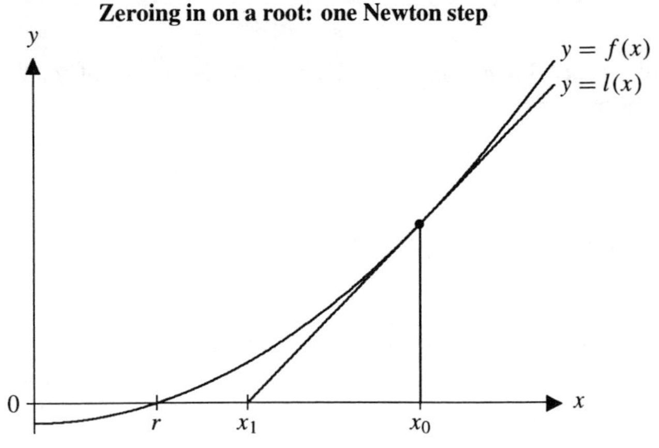

Observe:

- In the picture above, r is the sought-after root, x_0 is an **initial guess** for r, and x_1 is an *improved* approximation to r—the result of one Newton step.
- If f happens to be linear, then for *any* initial guess x_0, the next estimate x_1 is an *exact* root of f. In other words, for a linear function Newton's method succeeds *exactly* in only one step.

Repeating the process shown above produces a *sequence* $x_0, x_1, x_2, x_3, \ldots$ of successive approximations to r, as shown below. As the picture suggest, successive approximations "converge" quickly toward the root, r.

Finding a root: several Newton steps

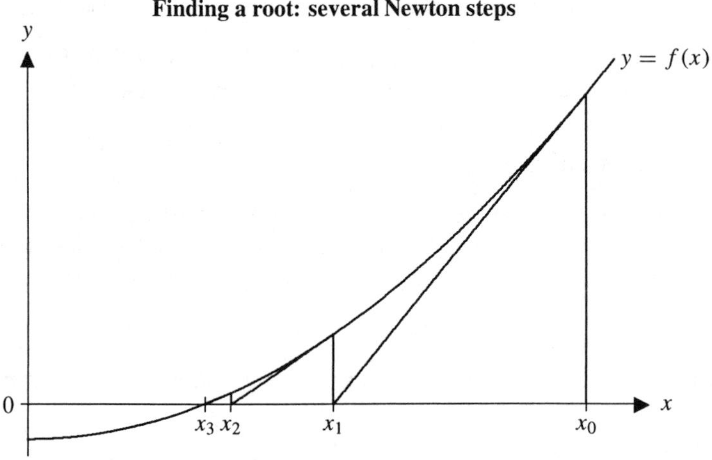

Each approximation is obtained from its predecessor in the same way:

x_{n+1} *is the x-intercept of the tangent line at* $x = x_n$.

Using Equation 4.4.1, with $m = f'(x_0)$, gives an explicit **iteration rule**, i.e., an explicit recipe for moving from one estimate to the next:

> **Fact:** **(Newton's iteration formula.)** Let f be a function and x_0 an initial guess at a root. For $n \geq 0$,
>
> (4.4.2) $$x_{n+1} = x_n - \frac{f(x_n)}{f'(x_n)}.$$

Notice:

Iteration. The Fact defines $x_1, x_2, x_2, x_3, \ldots$ **iteratively**—each term is defined by its predecessor. Each successive use of the formula is called an **iteration**.

Found a root? Then stop. If x_n happens to *be* a root of f, then $x_{n+1} = x_n$. Here's why:

$$x_{n+1} = x_n - \frac{f(x_n)}{f'(x_n)} = x_n - \frac{0}{f'(x_n)} = x_n.$$

A new function. Consider the new function $g(x) = x - f(x)/f'(x)$; then

$$x_1 = g(x_0),\ x_2 = g(x_1),\ x_3 = g(x_2),\ \ldots,\ x_{n+1} = g(x_n).$$

Newton's method, then, amounts to applying g *repeatedly* to x_0; r is a root of f if and only if $g(r) = r$. Such an r is called a **fixed point** of g. (The modern theory of **dynamical systems** studies how inputs behave under repeated applications of a function.)

Aren't graphs enough? Isaac Newton didn't have computer graphics. We do, so why should we bother with Newton's method? Why not just zoom in, again and again if necessary, to find roots to any desired accuracy?

One reason is that the process can be tedious, especially if many decimal places of accuracy are required. Some graphics hardware and software, moreover, don't display more than 8 or 10 digits.

A better reason concerns efficiency of effort. Whether done by human or machine, plotting any function typically requires dozens, if not hundreds, of function evaluations—an "expensive" proposition. Newton's method is much more efficient. For most functions, successive Newton estimates converge to a root with remarkable speed: each estimate has about *twice as many correct digits* as its predecessor.

■ **Example 3.** We estimated graphically that $f(x) = 2x^3 - x - 2$ has a root near $x = 1.17$. Use Newton's method to do better.

Solution: Since $f(x) = 2x^3 - x - 2$, $f'(x) = 6x^2 - 1$. By the previous Fact,

$$x_{n+1} = x_n - \frac{f(x_n)}{f'(x_n)} = x_n - \frac{2x_n^3 - x_n - 2}{6x_n^2 - 1}.$$

If, say, $x_0 = 1$, then➻ *Check some of these numbers.*

$$x_1 = 1.2, \quad x_2 \approx 1.16649, \quad x_3 \approx 1.16537, \quad \text{and} \quad x_4 \approx 1.16537.$$

Our guess, then, is $r \approx 1.16537$. It checks out numerically:➻ $f(1.16537) \approx -0.00002$.□ *Graphically, too.*

Newton's method in action

Applying calculus ideas successfully to solve real problems often depends, sooner or later, on finding roots. Newton's method often simplifies the process.

■ **Example 4.** Which point P on the parabola $y = x^2$ is closest to $(2, 1)$?

Solution: Here's the picture:

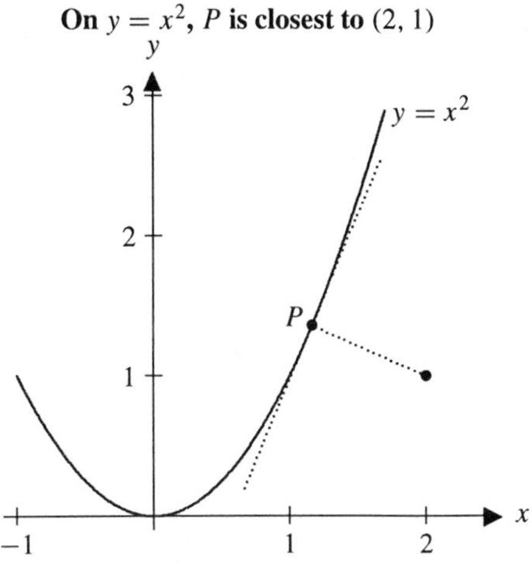

Do so now.

From the picture alone we can only estimate P. However, the picture suggests the crucial idea:

> *The line segment from* (2, 1) *to* P *is* perpendicular *to the tangent line at* P.

We'll translate this condition into an equation, then solve it to find P.

Because $y = x^2 \implies dy/dx = 2x$.

Perpendicular lines have negative reciprocal *slopes.*

Since P lies on the parabola, its coordinates have the form (r, r^2). Thus the line tangent to $y = x^2$ at P has slope $2r$, and the line segment from (2, 1) to P has slope $(r^2 - 1)/(r - 2)$. The perpendicularity condition, therefore, reads symbolically like this:

$$\frac{r^2 - 1}{r - 2} = -\frac{1}{2r}.$$

Convince yourself of the equivalence.

Equivalently, $2r^3 - r - 2 = 0$.

This last equation should look familiar—we solved it earlier, with Newton's method; we got $r \approx 1.16537$. (The result looks graphically plausible, too.) □

■ **Example 5.** Calculators "know" that $\sqrt{2} \approx 1.4142136$. Use Newton's method to derive such an estimate.

Check the last algebraic step.

Solution: Our target, $\sqrt{2}$, is a root of $f(x) = x^2 - 2$. Applied to f, Newton's formula is especially simple:

$$x_{n+1} = x_n - \frac{f(x_n)}{f'(x_n)} = x_n - \frac{x_n^2 - 2}{2x_n} = \frac{x_n}{2} + \frac{1}{x_n}.$$

Check some with a calculator.

Starting with $x_0 = 1$, successive estimates zero quickly in on $\sqrt{2}$:

$$x_1 = 1.5, \quad x_2 \approx 1.4166667, \quad x_3 \approx 1.4142157, \quad x_4 \approx 1.4142136.$$ □

Root-grubbing for money: IRA's and Newton's method

By U.S. law taxpayers may deposit \$2000 per year in tax-sheltered Individual Retirement Accounts (IRA's). Doing so raises interesting questions, like these: How much will such an account be worth after 30 years of faithful contributions? What interest rate will produce \$300,000 after 30 years?

Expressed as a decimal number, not a fraction.

The **compound amount formula** helps answer such questions. If p dollars are deposited yearly, at effective annual interest rate r, then after n years the total value $V(n)$ is given by

$$V(n) = \frac{p}{r}\left((1 + r)^{n+1} - 1\right).$$

How nice? It depends, e.g., on inflation and tax rates 30 years hence.

For an IRA paying 6% over 30 years, we'd use $p = 2000$, $r = 0.06$, and $n = 30$. The result is a nice little nest egg:

$$V(30) = \frac{2000}{0.06}\left((1.06)^{31} - 1\right) \approx \$169{,}603.32.$$ □

■ **Example 6.** Riskier investments might yield higher interest rates for one's IRA. What interest rate would assure a value of \$300,000 after 30 years of \$2000 contributions?

Solution: We need a value of r for which

$$V(30) = \frac{2000}{r}\left((1+r)^{31} - 1\right) = 300000.$$

Solving this equation *algebraically* for r is hard, so we'll resort to Newton's method. A little preliminary algebra simplifies things:

$$\frac{2000}{r}\left((1+r)^{31} - 1\right) = 300000 \iff \left((1+r)^{31} - 1\right) - 150r = 0.$$

In Example 1, page 336, we estimated $r \approx 0.09$ as a root of the last equation. With

$$f(r) = \left((1+r)^{31} - 1\right) - 150r, \quad f'(r) = 31(1+r)^{30} - 150,$$

and initial guess $x_0 = 0.09$, Newton's method gives➺

By hand the computations are messy. With a calculator they're easy.

$$x_1 \approx 0.09014631, \quad x_2 \approx 0.09014585, \quad x_3 \approx 0.09014585.$$

After just three Newton steps the answer is clear; an annual interest rate of 9.015% will suffice. □

When things go wrong

Newton's method, though impressive when it works, sometimes fails. Several problems can arise.

Horizontal tangent lines. If $f'(x_n) = 0$, then the recursion formula

$$x_{n+1} = x_n - \frac{f(x_n)}{f'(x_n)}$$

makes no sense, and the process fails. In graphical terms the problem is that the tangent line at x_n is horizontal, and so *never* meets the x-axis.

Near-horizontal tangent lines. The previous problem occurs only rarely in practice—"hitting" a point of horizontal tangency *exactly* is unlikely. Trouble may still occur, however, if x_n lands too *near* a root of f'. The next example shows how.

■ **Example 7.** Let $f(x) = \sin x$ and $x_0 = 1.3$. Among the roots of f, $r = 0$ lies closest to x_0. What does Newton's method say?

Solution: Applied to f, with initial guess $x_0 = 1.3$, Newton's method gives

$$x_1 \approx -2.3021; \quad x_2 \approx -3.4166; \quad x_3 \approx -3.1344; \quad x_4 \approx -3.1416.$$

We found a root,➺ but the "wrong" one. The picture shows what happened:

The one at $x = -\pi$.

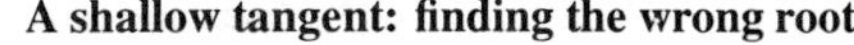

A shallow tangent: finding the wrong root

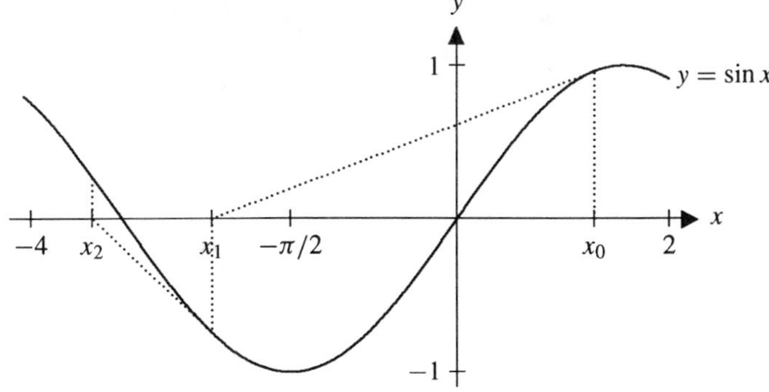

At x_0 the tangent line was too nearly horizontal—riding it to the x-axis took us far away from the expected root. □

But interesting!

Cycling. In rare circumstances successive Newton's approximations "cycle," repeating endlessly without converging to a root.

■ **Example 8.** What happens if Newton's method is applied to $f(x) = x^3 - 6x^2 + 7x + 2$, with initial guess $x_0 = 1$. Why does it happen?

Solution: Successive estimates $x_0, x_1, x_2, x_3, \ldots$ follow this repeating pattern $1, 3, 1, 3, \ldots$. The picture shows why:

Cycling around with Newton's method

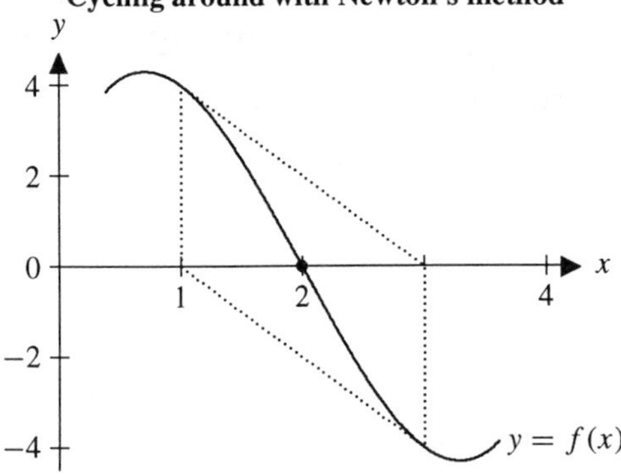

By careful planning we chose the *worst* possible initial guess x_0. Almost any other initial estimate will lead to a root. So, for that matter, will algebra—it's easy to check that $x = 2$ is a root. □

One that won't, however, is $x_0 = 3$. Do you see why not?

Other root-finding methods. Newton's method is only one of several common root-finding techniques; the **bisection method** and the **secant method** are two others. The bisection, or **interval-halving**, method (discussed earlier in this book; see the index) works by isolating a root in smaller and smaller *intervals*. The secant method resembles Newton's "tangent" method, except that secant lines replace the tangent lines of Newton's method.

Exercises

1. For the sample problems on the first page of this section , try to find roots by solving algebraically; the point is to see that this can't always be done.

2. Showing your work, derive Equation 4.4.1, page 337. Use the result to find the x-intercepts of each of the following lines:

   (a) Through $(1, 1)$, with slope 1.

   (b) Through $(1, 2)$, with slope 3.

   (c) The line with equation $y = mx + b$.

   (d) The tangent line at $x = 1$ to the graph of $y = x^2$.

(e) The tangent line at $x = 1$ to the graph of $y = x^2 - 3$.

3. Use Equation 4.4.1 to derive Equation 4.4.2. Show all work.

4. Here's another way to find the point P on the parabola $y = x^2$ that's closest to $(2, 1)$:

   (a) Let $d(r)$ be the distance from $(2, 1)$ to $P = (r, r^2)$. Write a formula for $d(r)$.

   (b) At the desired value of r, d has a local minimum, so $d'(r) = 0$. Write out and simplify the equation $d'(r) = 0$. Does the result look familiar?

5. By hand, find the first three Newton estimates for $\sqrt{5}$, starting with $x_0 = 2$. Write answers as fractions. [HINT: First use the Fact on page 338 to write a simple formula for x_{n+1} in terms of x_n.]

6. Let $f(x) = x^2 - a$.

   (a) Explain why the two numbers x and a/x bracket $\sqrt{a}$.

   (b) Show that Newton's method applied to f gives the iteration function $n(x) = (x + a/x)/2$—i.e., the average of x and a/x.

   (c) What happens if $x_n = \sqrt{a}$?

7. Using the value of x_0 indicated, use Newton's method to compute approximate values of each of the following expressions. (Iterate until successive approximations agree to three decimal places.)

   (a) $\sqrt[3]{100}$; $x_0 = 4.5$ (b) $(13)^{-2}$; $x_0 = 0.01$

8. (a) Show that the equation $x^5+4x-3 = 0$ has a solution in the interval $[0, 1]$.

   (b) Use Newton's method to find the solution of the equation in part (a) to three decimal place accuracy.

   (c) Does the equation in part (a) have any other solutions? Explain.

9. Find a solution of the equation $x \tan x = 1$ in the interval $[0, \pi/2]$ to three decimal accuracy.

10. Let $f(x) = x^3 - 2x^2 - 5x + 7 = (x - 3)(x - 1)(x + 2) + 1$.

    (a) Explain why it is natural to guess that f has roots near $x = 3$, $x = 1$, and $x = -2$.

    (b) Use Newton's method to estimate the actual values of the roots of f to four decimal places.

11. Let $f(x) = x^3 - 10x^2 + 22x + 6$.

    (a) Find each of the three roots of f to three decimal places.

    (b) What happens when Newton's method is used with $x_0 = 2$? Explain why this happens.

    (c) Newton's method behaves oddly if $x_0 = 1.39$. How? Why?

12. Let $h(x) = 179.5x^6 - 436.8x^4 + 257.3x^2 - 1$.

    (a) $h(x)$ has three positive roots. Use Newton's method to find each one to three decimal places.

(b) $h(x)$ has three negative roots. How are they related to the three positive roots you found in part (a)?

13. Find (approximately) the minimum value of $g(x) = 10x^{-2} + 3x^2 + x - 4$ when $1 \le x \le 10$.

14. Let $f(x) = x^2 \sin x^2$ on the interval $[0, 3]$.

(a) Find (approximately) each of the following numbers to two decimal places using Newton's method:

(i) The minimum value of f.

(ii) The maximum value of f.

(iii) The inflection points of f.

(b) Sketch a graph of f and label both coordinates of each of the points you found above.

15. Apply Newton's method to $f(x) = x^{1/3}$, starting from $x_0 = 1$. Explain what happens.

16. Apply Newton's method to $f(x) = e^{-x}$, starting from $x_0 = 0$. Explain what happens.

4.5 Splines: connecting the dots

How does one draw a "curve" through several—perhaps many—points in a plane? (Note: In this section **curve** means *any* unbroken line, with or without "corners.")

The answer depends partly on *who* does the drawing. For a human "artist" it's easy to draw freehand "curves" that pass through, say, five given points. Indeed, there are *many* ways to do so. Here are four possibilities:

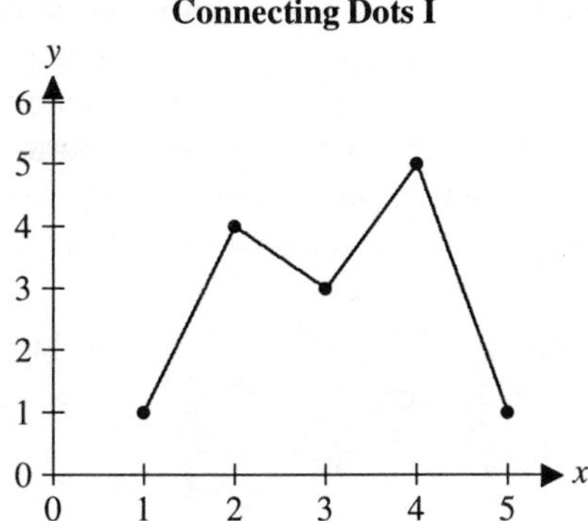

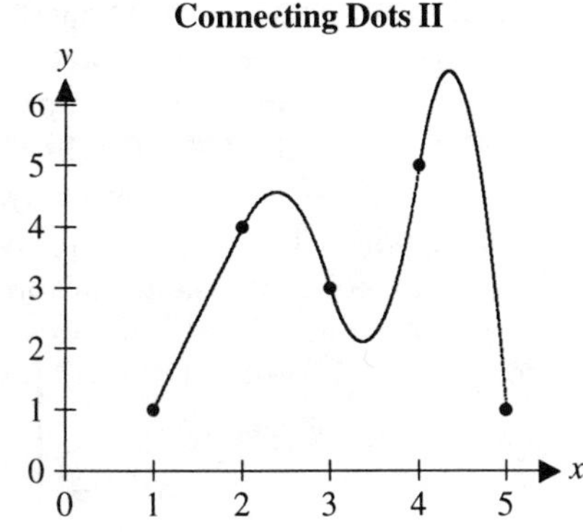

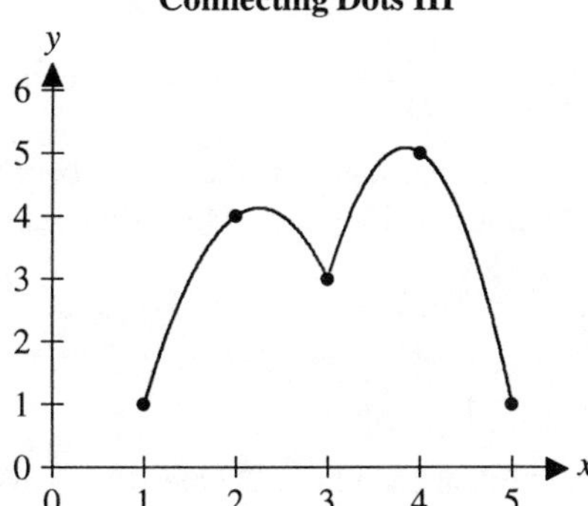

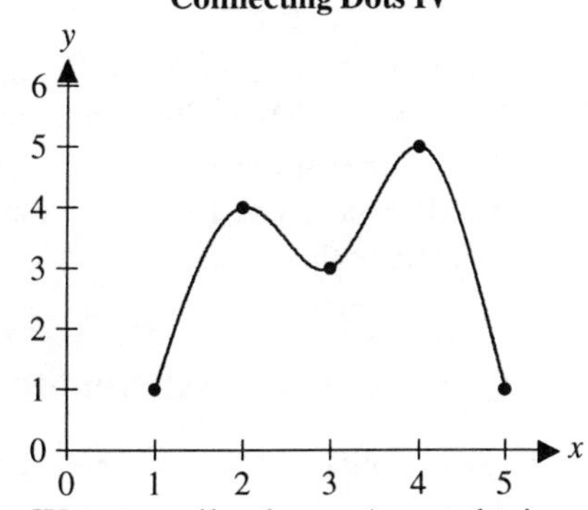

For humans such ambiguity is no problem. We can easily choose (on aesthetic, physical, or other grounds) *one* curve through the given points that meets our purposes.

Computers, on the other hand, need *precise* instructions, in their own language—mathematics. Calculus provides the tools both to *find* curves that "fit" data points and to *describe* these curves in terms computers can "understand."

Splines: basic ideas and key words

The idea behind splines is to "tie" small curve segments, called **elements**, together to form a single larger curve, called a **spline**. The points at which elements are tied together➻ are called **knots**.

The "dots" pictured above.

Our connect-the-dots pictures illustrate these ideas. Picture I, formed from *line* segments, shows a **linear spline**. Picture II shows a **quadratic spline**, formed by joining pieces of four *parabolas*. Picture III shows another➻ possible way of joining parabolic arcs. Picture IV shows a **cubic spline**, formed by joining pieces of four *cubic* arcs. (A cubic arc is defined by a *cubic* polynomial $a + bx + cx^2 + dx^3$.)

Perhaps less pleasing.

Linear, quadratic, and cubic splines are formed by joining, end to end, pieces of lines, parabolas, or cubic curves. Individual lines, parabolas, and cubic arcs are smooth and unbroken, so any new curve built from such pieces is *also* smooth and unbroken, *except perhaps at the knots*. With help from derivatives we'll fit such elements together properly *even at the knots*.

Linear splines: continuous but crooked

The simplest splines are formed from straight lines.

■ **Example 1.** Write a formula for the linear spline in Picture I.

Solution: The curve in question is **piecewise-linear**, i.e., built from several straight-line pieces. The "formula" for a piecewise-linear function has several parts, one for each "piece." The first piece above, for instance, is part of the line joining the points $(1, 1)$ and $(2, 4)$. This line has slope 3, so its equation in point-slope form is $y - 1 = 3(x - 1)$, or, equivalently, $y = 3x - 2$. This equation describes *only* the first piece, where $1 \le x \le 2$. Applying similar reasoning to the other spline elements gives the following multi-line formula for the spline function S:

Convince yourself of this.

$$S(x) = \begin{cases} 3x - 2 & \text{if } 1 \le x \le 2; \\ -x + 6 & \text{if } 2 \le x \le 3; \\ 2x - 3 & \text{if } 3 \le x \le 4; \\ -4x + 21 & \text{if } 4 \le x \le 5. \end{cases}$$

The formula, like the graph, is "piecewise-linear": on each *piece* of its domain the function S is defined by a *linear* polynomial. □

A **linear spline**, by definition, is a piecewise-linear function that's also *continuous*. For piecewise-linear functions continuity holds as long as the linear pieces join properly at their ends.

Quadratic splines: smoother

Linear splines, although simple, have an ugly kink at each knot. One way to avoid such kinks is to use a **quadratic spline**, formed by linking *parabolic* pieces.

Unless, by pure chance, successive slopes match up.

Each piece is defined by a quadratic equation.

When is a parabola degenerate? A quadratic polynomial q has the form $q(x) = a + bx + cx^2$, where a, b, and c are constants. The graph of a quadratic polynomial is—almost always—a parabola. There's *one* exception: if, by chance, $c = 0$, then $q(x) = a + bx + 0x^2 = a + bx$. In this case, q is actually a *linear* polynomial; its graph is a straight line.

To allow for this possibility it's often best to interpret "quadratic" as "having powers *no greater than two.*" Similarly, cubic polynomials involve powers *no greater than three.* A polynomial that happens to have less than its "advertised" power is sometimes called **degenerate**. (Mathematicians attach no stigma to degeneracy.) From this point of view a line can be thought of as a "degenerate" parabola.

Linear splines are crooked because *only one possible line segment* can join one knot to the next. *Quadratic* segments are more flexible. Given any two successive knots, we can find a parabola joining them *with any desired slope at the left knot.* Here, for instance, are several parabolas joining $(0, 0)$, and $(1, 1)$, each labeled with its slope at $(0, 0)$:

Literally!

See the exercises for more on these parabolas.

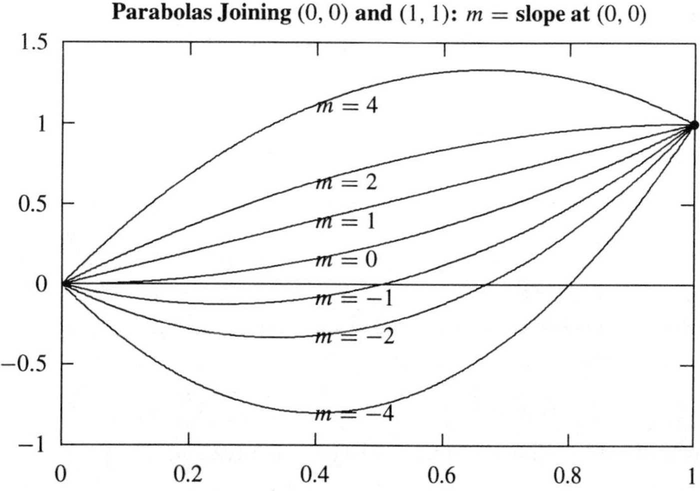

(One "parabola" is actually a *line*—which one?) By choosing slopes judiciously at each knot we can iron out the kinks. The next example shows exactly how.

■ **Example 2.** Use quadratic pieces to form a *smooth* spline through the same knots as in the previous example:

x	1	2	3	4	5
y	1	4	3	5	1

Solution: To join each knot to the next we'll choose a parabolic curve. We'll produce, in other words, a **piecewise-quadratic function.** To avoid kinks we'll assure that the *slopes* of "incoming" and "outgoing" elements match at each knot. The first spline element S_1 (from $x = 1$ to $x = 2$) is simplest. Smoothness is no problem at the *first* knot so *any* quadratic curve joining $(1, 1)$ to $(2, 4)$ will do. The simplest choice, perhaps, is a straight line; we'll start with that. We saw in the previous example that the linear function $S_1(x) = 3x - 2$ "works." In particular, $S_1'(2) = 3$.

From among the infinitely many possibilities.

I.e., a function defined by a quadratic expression on each piece of its domain.

Smoothness is an issue only where two curves join.

A straight line is a "degenerate" parabola.

The second spline element (from $x = 2$ to $x = 3$) is more interesting. We need a quadratic polynomial $S_2(x)$ which joins the second and third knots, and *also* "agrees" in slope with S_1 at $x = 2$. In other words, our quadratic polynomial S_2 should satisfy three conditions:

We saw above that $S_1'(2) = 3$.

$$S_2(2) = 4; \qquad S_2'(2) = 3; \qquad S_2(3) = 3.$$

How can we *find* such a polynomial? The following strategy simplifies the algebra considerably. *Write S_2 in powers of* $(x - 2)$, like this:

$$S_2(x) = a + b(x - 2) + c(x - 2)^2.$$

(Using powers of $(x - 2)$ (not powers of x or powers of $(x - 3)$) conveniently "fixes" things at the current "starting point.") Now we'll choose the constants a, b, and c properly; having written S_2 as we did makes doing so quite easy.

Setting $x = 2$ in the expression above gives $S_2(2) = a$. Thus, to arrange that $S_2(2) = 4$, we need $a = 4$. Choosing b is similar, but starts with a derivative:

$$S_2(x) = a + b(x-2) + c(x-2)^2 \implies S_2'(x) = b + 2c(x-2) \implies S_2'(2) = b = 3.$$

Now we know that $S_2(x) = 4 + 3(x-2) + c(x-2)^2$; only c is still to be found. To find c we use the remaining condition $S_2(3) = 3$, as follows:

We've already used the other two conditions: $S_2(2) = 4$ and $S_2'(2) = 3$.

$$3 = S_2(3) = 4 + 3(3-2) + c(3-2)^2 = 7 + c \implies c = -4.$$

Everything is now in place:

Check for yourself that S_2 does indeed satisfy all three requirements above.

$$S_2(x) = a + b(x-2) + c(x-2)^2 = 4 + 3(x-2) - 4(x-2)^2 = -18 + 19x - 4x^2.$$

(The last expression above can be found by expanding the previous expression. Although shorter typographically, the last version is not necessarily "simpler"—the previous version shows better how the coefficients were found.)

I.e., multiplying out.

The remaining spline elements are found in just the same way. The next one, S_3, must pass through the third and fourth knots, and—to assure smoothness—must "agree" in slope with S_2 at $x = 3$. The formula above shows that $S_2'(x) = 19 - 8x$, so $S_2'(3) = -5$. Thus S_3 must satisfy these three conditions:

$$S_3(3) = 3; \qquad S_3'(3) = -5; \qquad S_3(4) = 5.$$

It follows, as above, that

Convince yourself; only the last coefficient takes much effort.

$$S_3(x) = a + b(x-3) + c(x-3)^2 = 3 - 5(x-3) + 7(x-3)^2 = 81 - 47x + 7x^2.$$

Similarly, S_4 is chosen to satisfy

Verify that $S_3'(4) = 3$.

$$S_4(4) = 5; \qquad S_4'(4) = S_3'(4) = 9; \qquad S_4(5) = 1.$$

The result is

Details left to you; see the exercises.

$$S_4(x) = a + b(x-4) + c(x-4)^2 = 5 + 9(x-4) - 13(x-4)^2 = -239 + 113x - 13x^2.$$

Joining the elements produces this quadratic spline:

$$S(x) = \begin{cases} S_1(x) = 1 + 3(x-1) & \text{if } 1 \le x \le 2; \\ S_2(x) = 4 + 3(x-2) - 4(x-2)^2 & \text{if } 2 \le x \le 3; \\ S_3(x) = 3 - 5(x-3) + 7(x-3)^2 & \text{if } 3 \le x \le 4; \\ S_4(x) = 5 + 9(x-4) - 13(x-4)^2 & \text{if } 4 \le x \le 5. \end{cases}$$

Below is the graphical result. The spline S is the bold curve; the quadratic elements S_1–S_4 are shown extended beyond the knots to show how they fit together *at* the knots.

The picture is worth a careful look.

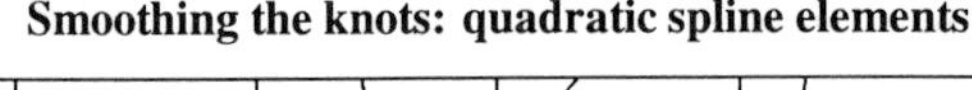

Smoothing the knots: quadratic spline elements

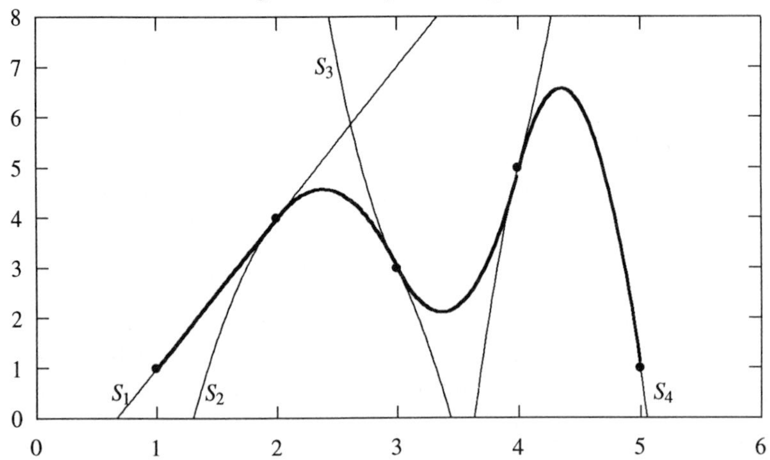

□

The example illustrates the formal definition:

> **Definition:** A **quadratic spline** is a continuous, **piecewise-quadratic** function S, whose first derivative S' is also continuous.

The definition may sound forbiddingly technical. Here it means, simply, that➠ incoming and outgoing quadratic elements "agree" at each knot—both in their values *and* in their first derivatives.

As we arranged.

Quadratic splining: the process in general

The technique just illustrated works for any collection $(x_0, y_0), (x_1, y_1), \ldots, (x_n, y_n)$ of knots, ordered from left to right. Here's the drill:

Start: Choose *any* quadratic curve S_1 joining (x_0, y_0) to (x_1, y_1). (A line segment is one possibility; other choices are possible.) For later use, calculate $m_1 = S_1'(x_1)$.

Fit the next parabola: Find a quadratic curve S_2 joining (x_1, y_1) to (x_2, y_2), such that $S_2'(x_1) = m_1$.➠ To do so, find coefficients a, b, and c so that $S_2(x) = a + b(x - x_1) + c(x - x_1)^2$. Then, for later use, calculate $m_2 = S_2'(x_2)$.

m_1 is the "incoming slope" at (x_1, y_1).

Continue: Proceed as above. For each successive pair of knots (x_i, y_i) and (x_{i+1}, y_{i+1}), choose a quadratic curve S_{i+1} joining the knots, with $S_{i+1}'(x_{i-1}) = m_i$.➠

m_i is the "outgoing slope" at (x_i, y_i).

How smooth are quadratic splines?

A quadratic spline S has a continuous *first* derivative. The graph of S, therefore, has no kinks or corners. The *second* derivative S'', on the other hand, is *discontinuous* at each knot.➠ This means, graphically, that the *concavity* of the S-graph can change abruptly at each knot. A close look at the previous graph shows this happening.➠ With *cubic* splines we'll smooth things even further.

Unless, by sheer coincidence, successive elements have equal second derivatives at a knot.

Imagine riding a roller coaster along a quadratic spline. What would you feel at each knot?

Counting the ways: degrees of freedom. There is just one line through *two* given points, or through *one* point with given slope. Either way, a straight line is completely determined by *two* conditions.

The reason, algebraically, is that the "generic" linear equation $y = a + bx$ involves *two* parameters, a and b—different choices of a and b give different lines. In mathematical language, we have **two degrees of freedom** in choosing a line; specifying two points (or one point and a slope) "uses up" both degrees of freedom.

By contrast, a *quadratic* polynomial $y = a + bx + cx^2$ involves *three* parameters. Thus *three* degrees of freedom are available when choosing quadratics. The practical result is that a quadratic spline element—a *parabola*—can be chosen to satisfy *three* conditions. Two degrees of freedom are used to hit the left and right knots, but the third degree of freedom remains available. Our method "spends" the extra degree of freedom in specifying a *derivative* at the left knot, thus "matching" incoming and outgoing slopes.

Cubic spline elements, of the form $y = a + bx + cx^2 + dx^3$, offers *four* degrees of freedom. As with linear and cubic elements, hitting the knots costs two degrees of freedom. We'll spend the remaining two on matching *two* derivatives of incoming and outgoing elements at the left knot.

Cubic splines: smoother still

A **cubic spline**, by definition, is a piecewise-cubic function S for which the *first two derivatives*, S' and S'', are continuous. Like linear and quadratic splines, cubic splines are constructed by piecing "elements" together, each element spanning two knots. With *cubic* equations we can assure that, at each knot, incoming and outgoing elements "agree" in their values and in their first *two* derivatives. By avoiding abrupt changes in concavity, cubic elements produce smoother, more pleasing splines than quadratic elements can achieve.

Cubic equations offer four degrees of freedom, one for each coefficient.

With quadratic splines we could manage just one derivative.

■ **Example 3.** Construct a cubic spline through the same knots:

x	1	2	3	4	5
y	1	4	3	5	1

Solution: Smoothness is no problem at the first knot. In theory, therefore, we can start by choosing *any* cubic curve S_1 that joins $(1, 1)$ to $(2, 4)$. Infinitely many possibilities exist—*any* values for $S_1'(1)$ and $S_1''(1)$ are possible.

In practice, some choices give better results than others. The resulting spline, moreover, depends *strongly* on how the first element is chosen. Here, for instance, are two different cubic splines through the same knots:

Two cubic splines through the same knots

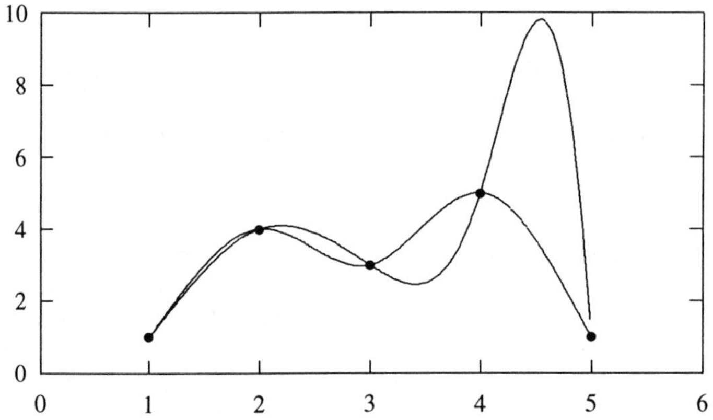

The two splines differ *only* in how the first element is chosen. As the picture shows, a tiny difference in the first element produces huge differences later on.

Faced with such exquisite sensitivity to initial choices, mathematicians have found systems for choosing the first cubic spline element. The **natural spline** method, for instance, arranges things so that $S''(x_0) = 0 = S''(x_n)$, i.e., so that S has *zero concavity* at the first and last knots. (The "tamer" curve above is a natural spline.) Full details on how natural splining works are beyond our scope. We'll simply remark that the unlikely-looking cubic

Natural and other splining methods are discussed in numerical analysis courses.

We used a computer to help find it!

$$S_1(x) = 1 + \frac{123}{28}(x-1) - \frac{39}{28}(x-1)^3$$

can be used to start things off. For use just below we notice that $S_1'(2) = 3/14$ and $S_1''(2) = -117/14$.

Check that $S_1(1) = 1$ and $S_1(2) = 4$.

For the next spline element, from $x = 2$ to $x = 3$, we need a cubic polynomial $S_2(x)$ that satisfies *four* conditions:

The arithmetic will soon get messy. Bear with us . . .

$$S_2(2) = 4; \qquad S_2'(2) = \frac{3}{14} = S_1'(2); \qquad S_2''(2) = -\frac{117}{14} = S_1''(2); \qquad S_2(3) = 3.$$

As before, writing S_2 in powers of $(x-2)$, like this—

$$S_2(x) = a + b(x-2) + c(x-2)^2 + d(x-2)^3$$

will simplify our search.

The coefficients a and b are chosen exactly as in Example 2. The expression above shows that $S_2(2) = a$, so $a = 4$. Similarly,

Just plug in $x = 2$.

$$S_2'(x) = b + 2c(x-2) + 3d(x-2)^2 \implies S_2'(2) = b \implies b = \frac{3}{14}.$$

To find c, we differentiate *again*:

$$S_2''(x) = 2c + 6d(x-2) \implies S_2''(2) = 2c \implies c = -\frac{117}{28}.$$

Now we know that $S_2(x) = 4 + \frac{3}{14}(x-2) - \frac{117}{28}(x-2)^2 + d(x-2)^3$; we need only find d. To do so we use the last remaining condition $S_2(3) = 3$:

Check the arithmetic if you like, but be sure to check the logic.

$$3 = S_2(3) = 4 + \frac{3}{14}(3-2) - \frac{117}{28}(3-2)^2 + d(3-2)^3 \implies d = \frac{83}{28}.$$

We're done at last:

$$S_2(x) = 4 + \frac{3}{14}(x-2) - \frac{117}{28}(x-2)^2 + \frac{83}{28}(x-2)^3.$$

For later reference, straightforward calculation shows that $S_2'(3) = 3/4$ and $S_2''(3) = 66/7$.

We'll need these numbers to fit the next element.

The remaining spline elements are found in the same way. The next one, S_3, must satisfy these four conditions:

$$S_3(3) = 3; \qquad S_3'(3) = \frac{3}{4} = S_2'(3); \qquad S_3''(3) = \frac{66}{7} = S_2''(3); \qquad S_3(4) = 5.$$

Calculations like those above reveal, when all the dust settles, that our desired spline has this piecewise-cubic form:

Checking all calculations isn't necessary; the idea's the thing.

$$S(x) = \begin{cases} S_1(x) = 1 + \frac{123}{28}(x-1) - \frac{39}{28}(x-1)^3 & \text{if } 1 \le x \le 2; \\ S_2(x) = 4 + \frac{3}{14}(x-2) - \frac{117}{28}(x-2)^2 + \frac{83}{28}(x-2)^3 & \text{if } 2 \le x \le 3; \\ S_3(x) = 3 + \frac{3}{4}(x-3) + \frac{33}{7}(x-3)^2 - \frac{97}{28}(x-3)^3 & \text{if } 3 \le x \le 4; \\ S_4(x) = 5 - \frac{3}{14}(x-4) - \frac{159}{28}(x-4)^2 + \frac{53}{28}(x-4)^3 & \text{if } 4 \le x \le 5. \end{cases}$$ □

Postscript and confession

The general idea of linear, quadratic, and cubic splines—our main interest in this section—is simple. Elements of the desired type are linked end to end; as many derivatives as possible are made to agree at knots.

The calculations involved, although routine, can be tedious and repetitive, especially when dozens or hundreds of knots are involved. In real-life practice, such calculations are left to machines. Specialized methods—based on but extending the ideas mentioned here—are used to speed up and simplify the machines' work.

Exercises

1. What does it mean for a function to be "piecewise-linear?" Explain briefly in words.

2. Describe (i.e., give a formula for) a piecewise-linear function whose graph passes through the points $(0, 0)$, $(1, 1)$, $(2, 4)$.

3. (a) Which upper-case letters of the alphabet could be graphs of piecewise-linear functions?

   (b) For two of the letters you chose in the previous part, describe (i.e., give a formula for) a piecewise-linear function whose graph has the right shape. (There are several ways to do this.)

4. Verify the last three lines of the multiline formula for the linear spline S in Example 1. [HINT: For each piece, start with the point-slope form of the line.]

5. A linear spline is given by the multiline formula below—one element is missing:

$$S(x) = \begin{cases} -2x + 7, & \text{when } 1 \le x \le 2 \\ \vdots & \vdots \\ -3x + 13, & \text{when } 3 \le x \le 4 \\ x - 3, & \text{when } 4 \le x \le 5 \end{cases}$$

   Draw the spline; then fill in the missing line of the formula.

6. In Example 2 we claimed that

$$S_4(x) = 5 + 9(x - 4) - 13(x - 4)^2 = -239 + 113x - 13x^2.$$

   satisfies the three conditions (i) $S_4(4) = 5$; (ii) $S_4'(4) = 9$; (iii) $S_4(5) = 1$. Verify that all three conditions really hold.

7. In each part below, find a quadratic polynomial that satisfies the three given conditions. Then plot each polynomial on an appropriate interval to *show* that the polynomial behaves as claimed.

   (a) $Q(0) = 0$; $Q'(0) = 3$; $Q(1) = 5$.

   (b) $Q(0) = 0$; $Q'(0) = 3$; $Q(10) = 5$.

   (c) $Q(1) = 0$; $Q'(1) = 3$; $Q(3) = 0$.

   (d) $Q(-17.3) = 11.1$; $Q'(-17.3) = -1.7$; $Q(-17.1) = 11.5$.

8. A picture on page 347 shows several quadratic curves, each joining $(0, 0)$ and $(1, 1)$, each labeled with its slope at $x = 0$. Find a quadratic *equation* for each curve.

9. Let (x_0, y_0) and (x_1, y_1) be any two points with $x_0 \neq x_1$, and let m_0 be any real number. Consider the quadratic function q defined by

$$q(x) = y_0 + m_0(x - x_0) + \frac{y_1 - y_0 - m_0(x_1 - x_0)}{(x_1 - x_0)^2}(x - x_0)^2.$$

   (a) Find $q(x)$ in the case $(x_0, y_0) = (2, 4)$, $(x_1, y_1) = (3, 3)$, $m_0 = 3$. Then check that $q(2) = 4$, $q(3) = 3$, and $q'(2) = 3$.

(b) Plot your function q from the previous part. How does the *graph* show that $q(2) = 4$, $q(3) = 3$, and $q'(2) = 3$?

(c) Show (work with the general formula above) that $q(x_0) = y_0, q(x_1) = y_1$, and $q'(x_0) = m_0$. What do these properties mean about the graph of q?

(d) Give an example in which $q(x)$ turns out to be a *linear* function. Interpret your example in graphical terms.

10. In each part below, find a quadratic spline S through the three knots

x	0	1	2
y	1	−2	3

(a) Choose the first element by assuming that $S'(0) = -3$.

(b) Choose the first element by assuming that $S'(0) = 0$.

(c) Below are graphs of the two splines described in (a) and (b). Which is which? Why?

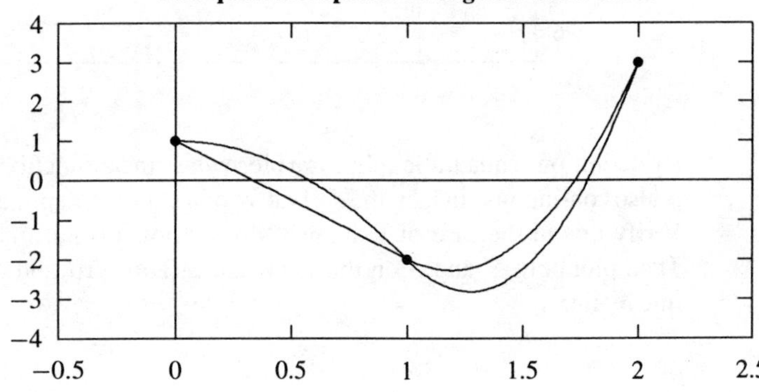

11. (For algebra buffs.) Let (x_0, y_0) and (x_1, y_1) be any two points with $x_0 \neq x_1$, and let d_1 and d_2 be any real numbers. Consider the cubic function c defined by

$$c(x) = y_0 + d_1(x - x_0) + \frac{d_2}{2}(x - x_0)^2 + \frac{y_1 - y_0 - d_1(x_1 - x_0) - \frac{d_2}{2}(x_1 - x_0)^2}{(x_1 - x_0)^3}(x - x_0)^3.$$

Show by (careful!) calculation that c satisfies the four conditions (i) $c(x_0) = y_0$; (ii) $c'(x_0) = d_1$; (iii) $c''(x_0) = d_2$; (iv) $c(x_1) = y_1$. (These four conditions mean that c is the "general" spline element joining (x_0, y_0) to (x_1, y_1) with first two derivatives d_1 and d_2 at (x_0, y_0).

12. Use the formula in the previous problem (even if you didn't *do* the previous problem) in each part below to find a cubic function with the given properties. Plot each result.

(a) $c(0) = 0$; $c'(0) = 0$; $c''(0) = 0$; $c(1) = 0$.

(b) $c(0) = 0$; $c'(0) = 0$; $c''(0) = 0$; $c(1) = 1$.

(c) $c(0) = 1$; $c'(0) = 0$; $c''(0) = -1$; $c(1) = 1/2$.

(d) $c(0) = 1$; $c'(0) = 1$; $c''(0) = 1$; $c(1) = 8/3$.

13. In each part below, find a cubic spline S through the three knots

x	0	1	2
y	1	-2	3

(a) Choose the first element by assuming that $S'(0) = -3$, $S''(0) = 0$.

(b) Choose the first element by assuming that $S'(0) = 0$, $S''(0) = 0$.

(c) Below are graphs of the two splines you just found. Which is which? Why?

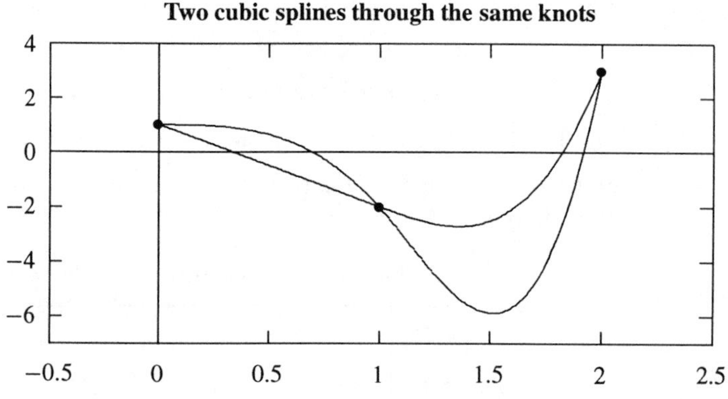

14. By definition, a quadratic spline is a piecewise-linear function whose derivative is also continuous. In fact, the derivative of a *quadratic* spline is a *linear* spline. Verify this in the case of Example 2 by writing a (multiline) formula for S'. Then plot both S' and S on the same axes. (Hint: To find S', differentiate S line by line.)

4.6 Calculus for money: derivatives in economics

Mathematics has been applied to finance for a very long time. A 3000-year-old Babylonian problem (quoted in *A History of Mathematics*, by Carl Boyer) asks:

> *Ten brothers received 1;40 minas of silver, and brother over brother received a constant difference. If the eighth brother received 6 shekels, find out how much each earned.*

(A mina is 60 shekels. The Babylonians used a base-60 number system, so the notation 1;40 means 1 mina plus 40 shekels, or 100 shekels.)

Much has changed since Old Babylon. Calculus and economics were invented, and base 60 disappeared from common use.➻ Financial applications of mathematics, however, remain very much alive, and calculus—the derivative, especially—is among modern economists' first tools of choice. In this section we hint briefly at one application of calculus to economics.

Ten-brother families are rare nowadays, too.

Derivatives in economics

Economics is full of *rates*—-rates of interest, tax, inflation, unemployment, return on investment, and many more. Most rates can be thought of, somehow, as derivatives. Naturally, therefore, many economic calculations involve calculus with derivatives.

Economic functions: functions of what?

To apply calculus we'll need *functions* to work with. Economics offers plenty. Here are just a few examples, informally described:➻

See the exercises for more details.

$$
\begin{aligned}
HW(t) &= \text{average U.S. hourly manufacturing wage at time } t;\\
U(t) &= \text{number of unemployed U.S. workers at time } t;\\
ND(t) &= \text{cumulative U.S. national debt at time } t;\\
C(q) &= \text{seller's total cost of } q \text{ bushels of soybeans;}\\
p(q) &= \text{price per bushel at which } q \text{ bushels of soybeans can be sold.}
\end{aligned}
$$

The first three functions above vary with *time*, so their derivatives measure rates with respect to time. To say that $U'(1993.5) = -50000$, for instance, could mean that halfway through 1993 the unemployment population was dropping at an instantaneous rate of 50000 people per year.➻

Notice the units of U': people/year.

The functions C and p are a little different: for them the independent variable represents *quantity*,➻ not time. Thus their derivatives measure rates of change with respect to quantity, not time. To say, for instance, that $C'(2000) = 5$ might mean that at 2000 bushels the seller's total cost was increasing at the rate of \$5 per bushel.➻ To put it another way, the 2001st bushel costs the seller \$5.➻

Here, the quantity of soybeans.

Notice the units of C': dollars/bushel.

See below for more on comparing these two interpretations of the derivative.

Discrete vs. continuous phenomena

Technically speaking, the functions C and p above accept only *whole-number* inputs q: grain traders sell only *whole* bushels. A variable that takes only isolated values (e.g., integers) is called a **discrete variable**; a **continuous variable** can take *any* real value. Although many financial functions involve discrete variables, it's common to approximate them—as we will below—with functions of continuous variables. Doing so makes the powerful tools of calculus available.

Modeling reality mathematically. To model any phenomenon—soybean sales on the Chicago Board, snowshoe hare and fox populations in the Arctic, heating requirements in Minnesota, demand for hard Montana wheat, the spread of AIDS—mathematically means to *describe* or *represent* the phenomenon quantitatively, in mathematical language.

Every mathematical model **simplifies**, to some extent, the phenomenon it describes. Economic models, for example, often involve "pretending" that a discrete variables is continuous. A useful model is simple enough to permit calculations, but detailed enough to capture essential qualities of the phenomenon studied.

Mathematical modeling involves three steps: (i) **describing** the phenomenon in mathematical terms, using functions, variables, equations, and other mathematical ingredients; (ii) **deducing** mathematical consequences of the model; (iii) **interpreting** mathematical results in terms of the phenomenon studied.

Mathematical economists use all sorts of functions. For simplicity, in this section we'll treat only functions that vary with quantity. Our first example shows several such functions in context.

Like C and p above.

■ **Example 1.** Lotta Mays, an experienced grain trader, wonders how many bushels of soybeans to buy—and then sell—on the Chicago Board of Trade. Lotta knows that the per-bushel price p (in dollars) she can get for her beans depends on the *quantity* q (in bushels) she wants to sell: too many beans on the market drives prices down. Here's her best guess for a **price function**:

$$p(q) = 8 - \frac{q}{1000}.$$

If Lotta sells q bushels at $p(q)$ dollars each, she'll raise a total of $q \cdot p(q)$ dollars. Thus her **total revenue function** has the formula

q is in bushels, R in dollars.

$$R(q) = q \cdot p(q) = q\left(8 - \frac{q}{1000}\right) = 8q - \frac{q^2}{1000}.$$

Before *selling* any beans Lotta must *buy* some. As a large wholesale customer Lotta can buy any amount of beans for \$5 a bushel—q bushels cost $5q$ dollars. In addition, Lotta has fixed expenses of \$1000 for buying and selling her beans (handling fees, taxes, commissions, etc.) Lotta's **total cost function**, therefore, has this formula:

$$C(q) = 5q + 1000.$$

How many bushels should Lotta buy and sell? At what price will she sell them? How much will she make?

Solution: Lotta wants to maximize her **profit**—the *difference* between revenue and cost—on the transaction. Like R and C, the **total profit** P depends on q:

$$P(q) = R(q) - C(q) = 8q - \frac{q^2}{1000} - (5q + 1000) = 3q - \frac{q^2}{1000} - 1000.$$

Lotta first plots P, R, and C together:

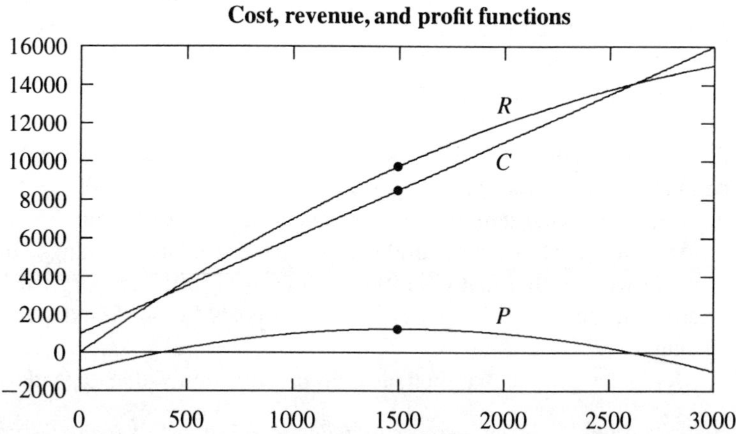

The bulleted point on the P-graph is clearly of interest: it suggests that the maximum possible profit—a little more than \$1000—occurs for $q = 1500$. The other two bulleted points are also important. They mark the spot at which the R-graph is *farthest above* the C-graph, i.e., where revenue most exceeds cost.

Symbolic calculations agree with the graphs. Differentiating our formulas for C, R, and P gives

$$C'(q) = 5; \qquad R'(q) = 8 - \frac{2q}{1000}; \qquad P'(q) = 3 - \frac{2q}{1000}.$$

Setting $P'(q) = 0$➻ gives $q = 1500$—as the graph shows. At this optimal quantity,

Check our work.

$$C(1500) = 8500; \quad R(1500) = 9750; \quad P(1500) = 1250; \quad p(1500) = 6.5.$$

All is revealed: Lotta earns the maximum profit, \$1250, by selling 1500 bushels at \$6.50 per bushel. □

On the margin: derivatives of revenue, cost, and profit

The derivatives R', C', and P' from the example above, though simple, deserve a look:➻

The term "marginal" is explained below.

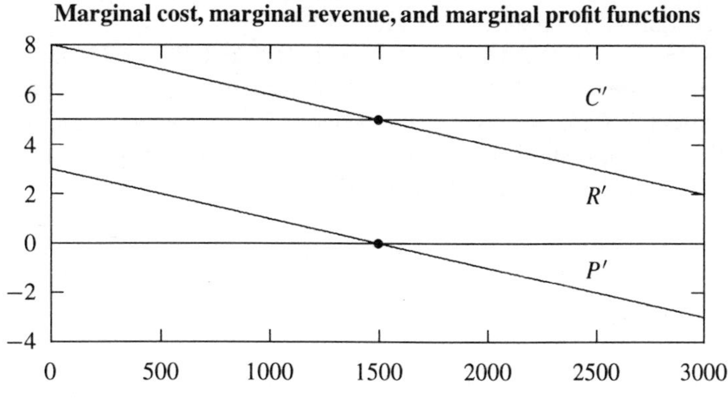

Again $q = 1500$ is the quantity of interest. As the bullets show,

$$C'(1500) = R'(1500) = 5; \qquad P'(1500) = R'(1500) - C'(1500) = 0.$$

At the critical value $q = 1500$, in other words, C and R increase at the *same* rate, and P is stationary.

Mathematicians usually interpret derivatives as rates of change. The statement $P'(1000) = 2$ means, in rate language, that after selling 1000 bushels, the trader is profiting at the rate of \$2 per bushel.

Economists often interpret such derivatives as R', C', and P' as **marginal** quantities. In this language, the statement $P'(1000) = 2$ means that after selling 1000 bushels, the trader makes \$2 profit on the *next bushel*. (The 1001st bushel is "on the margin.") For any q, **marginal profit at** q is defined as the additional profit to be made on the *next* (i.e., the $(q+1)^{\text{st}}$) item. That $P'(1500) = 0$ means, in the marginal sense, that *zero profit* will be made on the 1501st item.

As we found above.

A good point to quit the business.

Marginal cost and **marginal revenue** have similar meanings. In the previous example we saw that that $C'(1500) = 5 = R'(1500)$. In marginal language, this means that the 1501st bushel is a wash: it costs Lotta \$5 and sells for the same amount.

Here's the general marginal idea, for *any* function f that depends on quantity q:

Marginal f is the increase in f due to the $(q+1)^{st}$ item.

Marginals and instantaneous rates: economists vs. mathematicians

How different *are* the "marginal" and "rate" interpretations of the derivative? Are mathematicians and economists really at odds?

Not seriously. In practice "rates" and "marginals" seldom differ by much. A little symbolic algebra shows why. Suppose, say, that $P(q)$ describes the profit to be made on q items. Then the *marginal profit* function $MP(q)$ is defined by

$$MP(q) = \text{profit on } (q+1)^{\text{st}} \text{ item} = P(q+1) - P(q).$$

The *derivative* function $P'(q)$, by contrast, is defined by the limit

$$P'(q) = \lim_{h \to 0} \frac{P(q+h) - P(q)}{h}.$$

Setting $h = 1$ in the last expression gives

$$P'(q) \approx \frac{P(q+1) - P(q)}{1} = MP(q).$$

Thus $P'(q)$ and $MP(q)$ are at least approximately equal; mathematicians and economists are on the same wavelength.

In practice, the difference between MP and P' is seldom worth fretting over. One reason is that P, P', and MP are all mere models of reality, and so are inherently inexact. Another reason is that values of q are usually large, so setting $h = 1$ in the difference quotient gives a good approximation. If, say, P is the profit function in the example, and $q = 2000$, then

But not inherently useless.

As easy calculations show.

$$P'(2000) = -1; \qquad MP(2000) = P(2001) - P(2000) = -1.001.$$

The tiny difference isn't worth a fight.

Varying parameters

Economic strategies often depend sensitively on various *parameters*—the wholesale price of soybeans, the prime interest rate, the rate of inflation, etc—that change unpredictably from day to day. As parameters change, so do the *results* of economic calculations. The *form* of these calculations, however, may remain essentially the same.

■ **Example 2.** Lotta Mays (see Example 1) finds a new wholesale supplier, with soybeans at \$4.50 a bushel. What should Lotta do?

Solution: Lotta's price and revenue functions p and R are unchanged, but her cost and profit functions C and P are new. Here are full details:

$$p(q) = 8 - \frac{q}{1000}; \qquad R(q) = q \cdot p(q) = 8q - \frac{q^2}{1000};$$
$$C(q) = 4.5q + 1000; \qquad P(q) = R(q) - C(q) = 3.5q - \frac{q^2}{1000} - 1000.$$

We'll maximize P just as before:

$$P'(q) = 3.5 - \frac{2q}{1000} = 0 \implies q = 1750.$$

Since $P(1750) = 2062.5$ and $p(1750) = 6.25$, we have this result: Lotta should now sell 1750 bushels, at \$6.25 a bushel; she'll make \$2062.50. (Notice the bottom line: Lotta passed *half* her 50 cent per bushel savings on to her customers.) □

Treating the wholesale price simply as a parameter—without a specific value—can solve a whole lotta problems at once.

■ **Example 3.** The wholesale price of beans seems to change every day; Lotta's sick of doing the same problem again and again. How many beans should Lotta sell if the price to her is b dollars a bushel? At what price? How much will she make or lose?

Solution: For any value of b, our functions look like this:

$$p(q) = 8 - \frac{q}{1000}; \qquad R(q) = q \cdot p(q) = 8q - \frac{q^2}{1000};$$
$$C(q) = b \cdot q + 1000; \qquad P(q) = R(q) - C(q) = (8 - b)q - \frac{q^2}{1000} - 1000.$$

We'll maximize P in the usual way:

$$P'(q) = 8 - b - \frac{2q}{1000} = 0 \implies q = 4000 - 500b.$$

For this quantity the price formula gives

$$p(4000 - 500b) = 8 - \frac{4000 - 500b}{1000} = 4 + \frac{b}{2}.$$

A little algebra shows, too, that

$$P(4000 - 500b) = 15000 - 4000b + 250b^2.$$

Lotta has her general result: if beans wholesale for b dollars a bushel, she should sell at $4 + b/2$ dollars per bushel. Doing so, she'll sell $4000 - 500b$ bushels, for a total profit of $15000 - 4000b + 250b^2$ dollars. □

Exercises

1. In Example 1 Lotta Mays guessed that the formula

$$p(q) = 8 - \frac{q}{1000}.$$

might reasonably describe the selling price per bushel of q bushels of soybeans.

   (a) Plot p; choose *xrange* and *yrange* to make sense in context. What are the units on each axis?

   (b) State a sensible *domain* for the function p.

   (c) Using your answer from the previous part, state a plausible *range* for the function p.

   (d) The function p above is *decreasing*. Why would Lotta choose a *decreasing* function? Explain briefly in words.

   (e) The function p above is *linear*. Lotta chose a linear function purely for simplicity, but is that a good choice? Would you expect a *real* price function to be linear? If so, why? If not, sketch a more convincing price function and explain why it is a more realistic choice.

2. This problem is about several functions described informally in this section. In each part, first specify reasonable units for the input and output variables. Then give a plausible domain and range for the function, and draw a graph that could represent the function in question. (No special knowledge of economics is required—if in doubt, guess!)

   (a) $HW(t)$ = average U.S. hourly manufacturing wage at time t

   (b) $U(t)$ = number of unemployed U.S. workers at time t

   (c) $ND(t)$ = cumulative U.S. national debt at time t

3. What does "marginal tax rate" mean? Is this use of "marginal" consistent with those in marginal cost, marginal revenue, and marginal profit?

4. This problem refers to Example 2 in this section.

   (a) On one set of axes, plot the functions C, R, and P in Example 2. (A similar picture appears in Example 1.) What do the results show graphically about Lotta's maximum possible profit?

   (b) Calculate $C'(q)$, $R'(q)$, and $P'(q)$. Use the results to find the **marginal cost**, **marginal revenue**, and **marginal profit** at $q = 1500$. What does it mean, in context, that the marginal profit at $q = 1500$ is *positive*?

   (c) Find a value of q for which the marginal profit at q is *negative*. What are the marginal revenue and marginal cost at this q?

5. Consider again the situation in Example 1; use the functions C, p, R, and P given there.

   (a) Suppose that Lotta wants only to break even. What's the smallest quantity of soybeans she can sell? What's the greatest quantity? Explain your answers. (Hint: Look first at the P-graph on page 357.)

   (b) Suppose that Lotta wants to maximize her total revenue—regardless of profit. How many bushels should she sell? At what price? What is her bottom line?

6. Redo the previous problem in the situation of Example 2.

7. In Example 3 we concluded: if beans sell wholesale for b dollars per bushel, Lotta should sell $4000 - 500b$ bushels, at $4 + b/2$ dollars per bushel, for an optimal profit of $15000 - 4000b + 250b^2$ dollars.

   (a) What does our conclusion mean if $b = 5$? If $b = 4.5$? Do the results agree with earlier work?

   (b) What's Lotta's best strategy if $b = 7$?

   (c) Not all values for b make realistic sense. In this context, the sensible values for b lie between $b = 0$ and $b = 8$. (Prices can't be negative, and our price function says that nobody buys above \$8.) Among these possible values of b, what's the largest one for which Lotta can at least break even?

4.7 Related rates

Related amounts, related rates. Calculus was invented to describe and predict phenomena of change: planetary motion, objects in free fall, varying populations, etc. In many practical applications, several related quantities vary *together*; the rates at which they vary are also, naturally, related to each other. With calculus we can describe and calculate such **related rates.**

■ **Example 1.** A spacecraft travels directly toward Mars. Describe several amounts that vary with time. Interpret their derivatives as rates of change.

Solution: Many quantities vary with time. Among them: the spacecraft's distance from Earth, the spacecraft's distance from Mars, the distance and direction from Earth to Mars, the amount of fuel consumed, etc. These quantities are related to each other in various ways; at any time t, for instance, the third quantity depends on the first two.

Each such quantity is a *function* of time; its derivative, therefore, is the rate of change of the given quantity with respect to time. For the quantities above, the derivatives represent, respectively, the rocket's velocity away from Earth, its velocity toward Mars, Earth's velocity *relative* to Mars, and the rate of fuel consumption. These rates, like their corresponding amounts, are related to each other. □

Each rate's units depend on corresponding units of amount.

The following (more mundane) example illustrates the *technique* (as well as the idea) of related rates.

■ **Example 2.** A point P moves from left to right along the curve $y = x^2$, at a constant *horizontal* speed of 3 units/second. How fast does the y-coordinate of P increase at the moment when P passes through $(1, 1)$? When P passes $(2, 4)$?

The shadow P casts on the x-axis moves to the right at 3 units per second. Can you picture the situation?

Solution: As P moves, many different quantities vary with time. The two of interest here are x and y, the coordinates of P. Written as functions:

$$x(t) = x\text{-coordinate of } P \text{ at time } t; \quad y(t) = y\text{-coordinate of } P \text{ at time } t.$$

Because P moves along the parabola $y = x^2$, the functions x and y satisfy the equation

$$y(t) = \left(x(t)\right)^2. \tag{4.7.1}$$

Differentiating both sides of Equation 4.7.1 with respect to t gives

$$\frac{dy}{dt} = 2x(t)\frac{dx}{dt}, \tag{4.7.2}$$

or, more compactly, $y' = 2xx'$. With Equation 4.7.2 we can answer our questions. By assumption, $dx/dt = 3$, for all t. At the point $(1, 1)$, $x = 1$, so

$$\frac{dy}{dt} = 2x(t)\frac{dx}{dt} = 2 \cdot 1 \cdot 3 = 6 \text{ units per second.}$$

When $(x, y) = (2, 4)$,

$$\frac{dy}{dt} = 2x(t)\frac{dx}{dt} = 2 \cdot 2 \cdot 3 = 12 \text{ units per second.}$$

Notice, finally, that although x increases at the *constant* rate of 3 units per second, y increases faster and faster. □

Think again about the situation. Is it obvious that y should grow faster and faster?

What we just did: related rates in a nutshell. The "generic" related rates problem asks for one rate of change, given information about one or more others. *Solving* related rates problems can be hard, but the underlying idea is simple:

> *Start with an equation relating two or more quantities that vary with time. Differentiate both sides with respect to time, using the chain rule. The resulting equation relates the* rates *at which the quantities vary. Use it to solve for the desired rate.*

As usual with "story" problems, the first step—identifying the quantities in question and setting up the original equation—is often the hardest.

Textbook authors love related rates problems; the supply is almost inexhaustible. Many old favorites involve right triangles and the Pythagorean rule.➾

Lightly disguised, sometimes.

■ **Example 3.** (Pythagoras, Newton, and the state patrol.) It's spring break at Huxley College; the annual migration to Fort Lauderdale has begun. Hovering 1000 feet directly above the southbound interstate is the helicopter state patrol, Officer Ingkvist on the radar gun.

A car with Huxley decals passes underneath and continues south. Jason and Medea, fresh from their calculus midterm, aren't watching the speedometer.

Officer Ingkvist fires. In moments, the results are in: at the moment of firing the car was 2000 feet away from the helicopter, and *moving* away at 85 feet per second. "Got 'em!" mutters Ingkvist under her breath.

What happens next?

Solution: In traffic court Jason and Medea deny all wrongdoing. "The speed limit is 65 mph," they tell the judge. "We were clocked at 85 feet per second. But a simple calculation shows that 65 mph is 95 feet per second. Hence, clearly,➾ we couldn't have been speeding."

Under duress even students say "hence" and "clearly."

"Watch your language," replies the judge, "but what you say makes sense. Explain yourself, Ingkvist. Use that blackboard. Be clear. And cite your sources."

Officer Ingkvist rises calmly; she's been through this before. Do judges *never* learn? She draws this diagram:

Officer Ingkvist's diagram

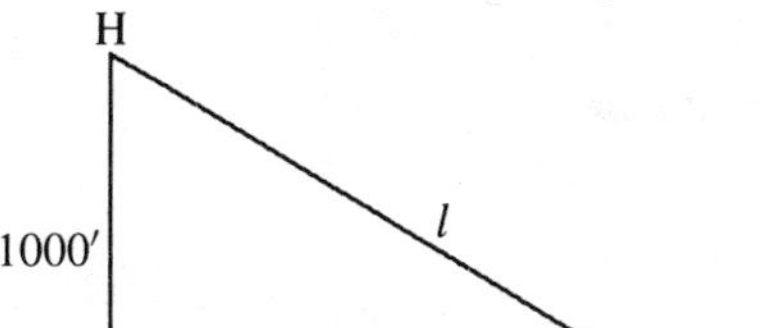

"In the diagram, your honor, H is the helicopter, C is the car, l is the straight-line distance from H to C, x is the horizontal distance from H to C, and 1000 feet is the constant height of the helicopter. The amounts x and l vary with time, of course. Pythagoras says, though, that at *any* time t, x and l satisfy the equation $l^2 = x^2 + 1000^2$. Newton says that differentiating this relation between l and x with respect to t relates the *rates* of change of l and x, as follows:

$$l^2 = x^2 + 1000^2 \implies 2l \cdot \frac{dl}{dt} = 2x \cdot \frac{dx}{dt} \implies \frac{dx}{dt} = \frac{l}{x} \cdot \frac{dl}{dt}.$$

At time in question, dl/dt was 85 and l was 2000, so➾ x was $\sqrt{2000^2 - 1000^2} =$

Here officer Ingkvist used the Pythagorean equation.

$1000\sqrt{3}$. At that moment, therefore, Jason and Medea's southward speed was

$$\frac{dx}{dt} = \frac{l}{x} \cdot \frac{dl}{dt} = \frac{2000}{1000\sqrt{3}} \cdot 85 \approx 98.1495457622 \text{ feet per second.}$$

Any questions?"

"Just one," says the judge. "Who are Pythagoras and Newton, and why won't they testify in person?"

"Never mind," say Jason and Medea. "We'll pay the ticket." □

Exercises

1. The width of a rectangle is increasing at a rate of 2 cm/sec, and its length is increasing at a rate of 3 cm/sec. At what rate is the area of the rectangle increasing when its width is 4 cm and its length is 5 cm?

2. Boyle's Law states that if the temperature of a gas remains constant, then the pressure P and the volume V of the gas satisfy the equation $PV = c$, where c is a constant. If the volume is decreasing at the rate of 10 in^3 per second, how fast is the pressure increasing when the pressure is 100 lbs/in^2 and the volume is 20 in^3?

3. It is a calm day in southern Neverland at the Erehwon air traffic control center. Only two aircraft are in the vicinity, Pachyderm flight 1003 from Celesteville to Paris is approaching from the south and Peterpan flight 366 from London to Wendytown is approaching from the east. Both are on paths that will take them directly over the air traffic control center.

   Suddenly the center is rocked by an earthquake. Conventional power is lost and the auxiliary generator fails to start. In desperation, a mechanic rushes outside and kicks the generator; it sputters to life. As the radar screens flicker on, the controllers find that both flights are at an altitude of 33,000 feet. The Pachyderm flight is 36 nautical miles from the center and approaching it at a rate of 410 knots. The Peterpan flight is 41 nautical miles from the center and approaching it at a rate of 455 knots. [NOTE: One **nautical mile** is equal to 1852 meters. One **knot** is one nautical mile per hour.]

   (a) How many minutes do the controllers have before the time of closest approach?

   (b) How close will the planes come to each other? Will they violate the FAA's minimum separation requirement of 5 nautical miles?

4. Sand is being dumped on a pile in such a way that it always forms a cone whose radius equals its height. If the sand is being dumped at a rate of 10 cubic feet per minute, at what rate is the height of the pile increasing when there is 1000 cubic feet of sand in the pile?

5. Digging in your backyard, you accidentally break a town water line. Water, bubbling up at a rate of 1 in^3/sec, is forming a circular pond of depth $\frac{1}{2}$ inch in your backyard. How quickly is this pond covering your lawn? (That is, how quickly is the surface area of this pond increasing?)

6. A tanker accident has spilled oil in Pristine Bay. Oil-eating bacteria are gobbling 5 ft^3/hour. The oil slick has the form of a circular cylinder. When the radius of the cylinder is 500 ft, the thickness of the slick is 0.01 ft and decreasing at a rate of 0.001 ft/hr. At what rate is the area of the slick changing at this time? Is the area of the slick increasing or decreasing?

7. Oil is leaking from an ocean tanker at the rate of 5000 liters per minute. The leakage results in a circular oil slick. The depth of the oil varies linearly from a maximum of 5 cm at the point of leakage to a minimum of 0.5 cm at the outside edge of the slick. How fast is the radius of the slick increasing 4 hours after the tanker started leaking? [NOTE: 1 liter = 1000 cm^3]

8. A spherical iron ball 8 in. in diameter is coated with a layer of ice of uniform thickness.

   (a) If the ice melts at the rate of 10 in^3/min, how fast is the thickness of the ice decreasing when it is 2 in. thick?
   (b) How fast is the outer surface area of the ice decreasing at this time?

9. Bazooka Joe is blowing a spherical bubble gum bubble. Let V be the volume of gum in the bubble, R the *inside* radius of the bubble, and T the thickness of the bubble. V, T, and R are functions of time t.

   (a) Write a formula for V in terms of T and R. [HINT: Draw a picture.]
   (b) Assume that the amount of bubble gum in the bubble is not changing. What is $V'(t)$?
   (c) After 5 minutes of blowing, the bubble is 3 feet in diameter and 0.01 feet thick. If the inside radius of the bubble is expanding at a rate of 0.5 feet per minute, how fast is the thickness changing? [HINT: Remember that the volume of gum in the bubble does not change over time.]

10. Two cars leave an intersection simultaneously. One travels north at 30 mph, the other travels east at 40 mph. How fast is the distance between them changing after 5 minutes?

11. At a certain moment, one bicyclist is 4 miles east of an intersection, traveling toward the intersection at the rate of 9 miles/hour. At the same time a second bicyclist is 3 miles south of the intersection, traveling away from the intersection at the rate of 10 miles/hour. Is the distance between the bicyclists increasing or decreasing at that moment? At what rate?

12. A radio transmitter is located 3 miles from a straight section of interstate highway. A truck is traveling away from the transmitter along the highway at a speed of 65 miles per hour. How fast is the distance between the truck and the transmitter increasing when they are 5 miles apart?

13. A baseball diamond is a square 90 ft on a side. A runner travels from home plate to first base at 20 ft/sec. How fast is the runner's distance from second base changing when the runner is halfway to first base?

14. A baseball diamond is a square 90 ft on a side. A batter hits a ball along the third base line at 100 ft/sec and runs to first base at 25 ft/sec.

    (a) At what rate is the distance between the ball and first base changing when the ball is halfway to third base?

(b) At what rate is the distance between the ball and the player changing when the ball is halfway to third base?

15. A highway patrol plane flies one mile above a straight section of rural interstate highway at a steady ground speed of 120 miles per hour. The pilot sees an oncoming car and, with radar, determines that the line-of-sight distance from the plane to the car is 1.5 miles and that this distance is decreasing at a rate of 136 miles per hour. Should the driver of the car be given a ticket for speeding? Tell it to the judge. (Assume the judge knows calculus.)

16. A coffee filter has the shape of an inverted cone. Water drains out of the filter at a rate of 10 cm^3/min. When the depth of water in the cone is 8 cm, the depth is decreasing at 2 cm/min. What is the ratio of the height of the cone to its radius?

17. An inverted cone has height 10 cm and radius 2 cm. It is partially filled with liquid, which is oozing through the sides at a rate proportional to the area of the cone in contact with the liquid. Liquid is also being poured in the top of the cone at a rate of 1 cm^3/min. When the depth of the liquid in the cone is 4 cm, the depth is decreasing at a rate of 0.1 cm/min. At what rate must liquid be poured into the top of the cone to keep the liquid at a constant depth of 4 cm?

18. The minute and hour hands on the face of a town clock are 7 feet and 5 feet long, respectively. How fast is the distance between the tips of the hands increasing when the clock reads 9:00?

19. A swimming pool is 15 feet wide, 40 feet long, 3 feet deep at one end, and 10 feet deep at the other end (see the sketch below). Water is being added to it at the rate of 25 cubic feet per minute.

    (a) How fast is the water level rising when there is 2000 cubic feet of water in the pool?

    (b) How fast is the water level rising when there is 3000 cubic feet of water in the pool?

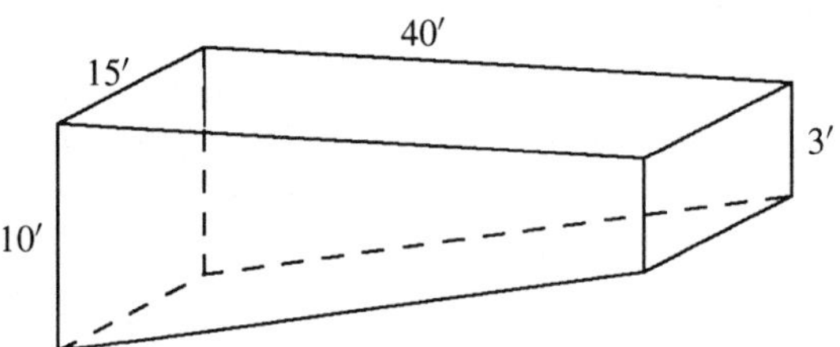

20. A rocket rises vertically from a point on the ground that is 100 m from an observer at ground level. The observer notes that the angle of elevation is increasing at a rate of 12° per second when the angle of elevation is 60°. Find the speed of the rocket at that instant.

21. A ferris wheel, 50 feet in diameter, revolves at the rate of 10 radians per minute. How fast is a passenger rising when the passenger is 15 feet higher than the center of the ferris wheel and is rising?

22. The ends of a horizontal trough 10′ long are isosceles trapezoids with lower base 3′, upper base 5′, and altitude 2′. If the water level is rising at a rate of 0.25″/min. when the depth is 1′, how fast is water entering the trough?

23. A railroad bridge is 20' above, and at right angles to, a river. A person in a train traveling at 60 mph passes over the center of the bridge at the same instant that a person in a motor boat traveling 20 mph passes under the center of the bridge. How fast are the two people separating 10 seconds later?

24. A ladder, 12 feet long, is leaning against a wall. If the foot of the ladder slides away from the wall along level ground, what is the rate of change of the top of the ladder with respect to the distance of the foot of the ladder from the wall when the foot is 6' from the wall?

25. An airplane, flying east at 400 mph, goes over a certain town at 11:30 a.m., and a second plane, flying northeast at 500 mph, goes over the same town at noon. How fast are they separating at 1:00 p.m.?

4.8 Parametric equations, parametric curves

A point P wanders about the xy-plane, tracing its path as it goes. As P travels, its coordinates $x = f(t)$ and $y = g(t)$ are *functions of time*. In this situation t is called a **parameter**, f and g are **coordinate functions**, and the figure traced out by P is a **parametric curve.**

Here the "parameter" is a variable—in other situations "parameters" are often constants.

Most plotting programs and graphing calculators handle parametric curves. Try yours.

Our first example illustrates the idea and some specialized vocabulary.

■ **Example 1.** At any time t with $0 \le t \le 10$, the coordinates of P are given by the **parametric equations**

$$x = t - 2\sin t; \qquad y = 2 - 2\cos t.$$

What curve does P trace out? Where is P at $t = 1$? In which direction is P moving?

Solution: The simplest way to draw a curve is to calculate many points (x, y), plot each one, and "connect the dots." The first step works as usual: for many inputs t, calculate the corresponding x and y. Here's a sampler of results, rounded to two decimals:

But most tedious.

I.e., the $y = f(x)$ case.

Check several entries.

Parametric plot points for $x = t - 2\sin t$, $y = 2 - 2\cos t$

t	0	0.1	0.2	0.3	0.7	0.8	0.9	1.0	...	9.8	9.9	1[illegible]
x	0	−0.10	−0.20	−0.29	−0.59	−0.63	−0.67	−0.68	...	10.53	10.82	11.[illegible]
y	0	0.01	0.04	0.09	0.47	0.61	0.76	0.92	...	3.86	3.78	3.[illegible]

Here's the result, a curve C:

The parametric curve $x = t - 2\sin t$, $y = 2 - 2\cos t$, $0 \le t \le 10$

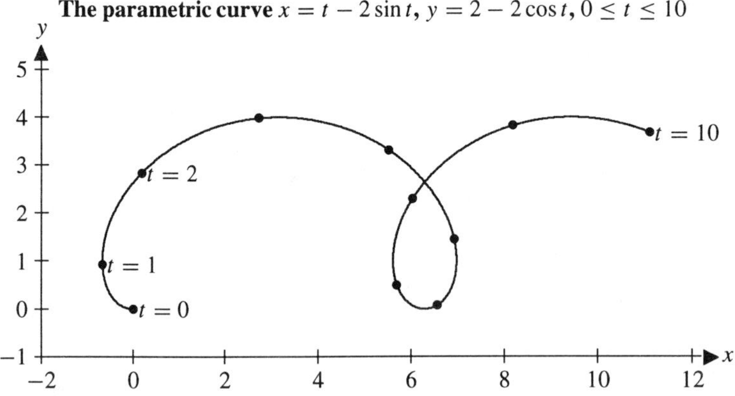

Notice:

- Points corresponding to *integer* values of t are shown bulleted. At $t = 1$, P has coordinates $(-0.68, 0.92)$; at this instant, P is heading almost due north.
- The full curve C is *not the graph of a function* $y = f(x)$—some x-values correspond to more than one y-value. Certain *pieces* of C, however, *do* define such functions. (The part of C from $t = 2$ to $t = 5$ does so.)
- The picture shows the x- and y-axes, *but no t- axis*: t-values are indicated only by the bulleted points. In most parametric curves t-values don't appear at all.

$x = 6$, for instance.

Most graphing calculators don't show t-values graphically, but some calculate t-values numerically.

- The bullets on the graph appear at equal *time* intervals, but not at equal *distances* from each other, because P speeds up and slows down as it moves. We'll see below how to *calculate* the speed of a parametric curve at a point.
- If t measures time we can visualize C *dynamically*, as a curve traced by a moving point. Curves defined by ordinary equations in x and y are *static* objects, lying passively on the page.

In this example, t represents time.

When is P moving fastest? Slowest?

A sampler of parametric curves

Parametric curves come in mind-boggling variety. *Any* choice of two equations $x = f(t)$ and $y = g(t)$ and a t-interval produces one. Surprisingly often the result is beautiful, useful, or interesting. The next several examples hint at some of the possibilities, and at connections between parametric curves and ordinary function graphs.

Or all three.

Example 2. Every ordinary function graph can be written in parametric form. To produce a sine curve, for example, we can use

$$x = t; \qquad y = \sin t; \qquad -2\pi \le t \le 2\pi.$$

Here's the graph; integer multiples of $\pi/2$ are bulleted:

The parametric curve $x = t$, $y = \sin t$, $-2\pi \le t \le 2\pi$

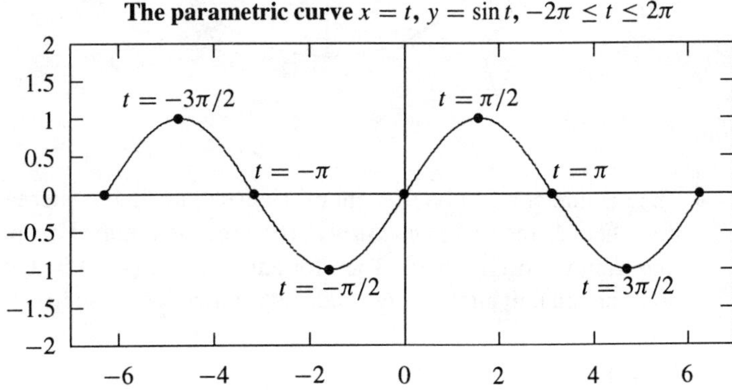

Example 3. Parametric curves may have loops, cusps, vertical tangents, and other peculiar features. Consider the curve

$$x = 2\cos(t) + 2\cos(4t); \qquad y = \sin t + \sin(4t); \qquad 0 \le t \le 5.$$

Here it is; bullets show the starting and ending points.

The parametric curve $x = 2\cos(t) + 2\cos(4t)$, $y = \sin t + \sin(4t)$, $0 \le t \le 5$

t = 5
t = 0

The previous example has this property.

■ **Example 4. The unit circle.** If a parametric curve's coordinate functions are periodic (i.e., repeat themselves), then the curve's shape reflects this fact. The simplest and most important such curve is the **unit circle**, often written in xy-form as $x^2 + y^2 = 1$. The simplest *parametric* description of the unit circle is this:

$$x = \cos t; \qquad y = \sin t; \qquad 0 \le t \le 2\pi.$$

Here's the picture; integer multiples of $\pi/2$ are bulleted:

The parametric curve $x = \cos t,\ y = \sin t,\ 0 \le t \le 2\pi$

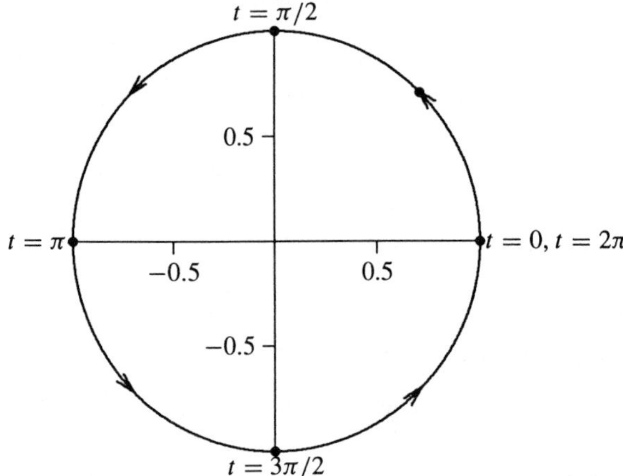

Notice:

- The parameter t *can* be thought of, as usual, as time. Alternatively, t can be thought of as the *radian measure* of the angle determined by the x-axis and the line from the origin to P. Then for any *angle* t, $(x, y) = (\cos t, \sin t)$ is the point on the unit circle lying t radians counterclockwise from $(1, 0)$.

- Because $x = \cos t$ and $y = \sin t$,

  $$x^2 + y^2 = (\cos t)^2 + (\sin t)^2 = 1.$$

  This shows that every point on our parametric curve satisfies the Cartesian equation $x^2 + y^2 = 1$, and so—as we intended—lies on the unit circle.

  "Reducing" two parametric equations to xy-form, as we just did, is called **eliminating the parameter**. (Doing so is sometimes possible, sometimes not.)

- The circle is traced *once* as t runs from $t = 0$ to $t = 2\pi$. With a larger t-interval the same circle would be traced *repeatedly*; with a smaller t-interval, the circle would be traced only partially.

■ **Example 5. Other circles.** The idea in the previous example extends to *all* circles. If (a, b) is any point in the plane, and $r > 0$ any radius, then the parametric equations

$$x = a + r\cos t; \qquad y = b + r\sin t; \qquad 0 \le t \le 2\pi$$

produce the circle with center (a, b) and radius r. (See the exercises for more details.)

■ **Example 6. Other curves with periodic coordinate functions.** Many curves defined by periodic coordinate functions have striking, beautiful shapes. A typical **Lissajou curve**, for instance, is defined by

I.e., repeating.

$$x = \sin(5t); \qquad y = \sin(6t); \qquad 0 \le t \le 2\pi.$$

(Replacing 5 and 6 above with other integers produces other Lissajou figures.) Here's ours:

The Lissajou curve $x = \sin(5t)$, $y = \sin(6t)$, $0 \le t \le 2\pi$

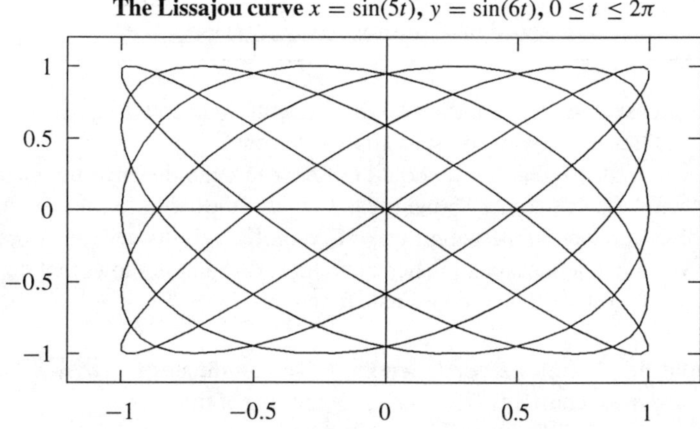

■ **Example 7. Same curve, different parametric equations.** Different pairs of parametric equations may produce exactly the same curve in the xy-plane. In such cases, labeling t-values can make differences appear. For example, setting

$$x = t; \qquad y = t^2; \qquad -1 \le t \le 1$$

produces a parabolic arc. So does

$$x = t^3; \qquad y = t^6; \qquad -1 \le t \le 1.$$

Here are both; the bullets mark 0.25-second time intervals:

The curve $x = t$, $y = t^2$, $-1 \le t \le 1$ **The curve** $x = t^3$, $y = t^6$, $-1 \le t \le 1$

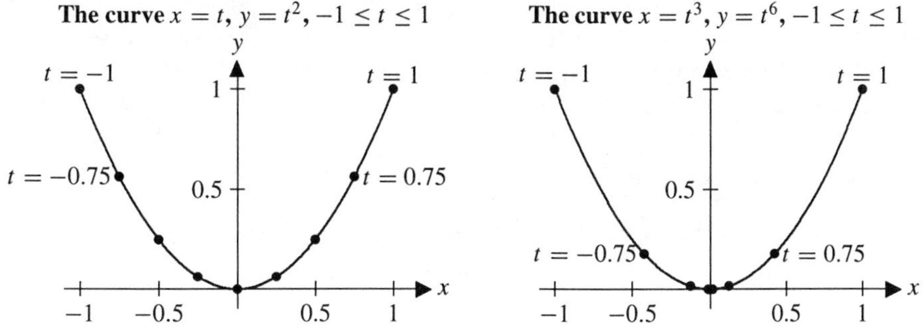

The curves are geometrically identical; they differ only in how they are traced out.

Calculus with parametric curves: speed and slope

Suppose that a parametric curve C has differentiable coordinate functions $x = f(t)$ and $y = g(t)$. What do the *derivatives* f' and g' say about the situation?

Speed

If t tells time, then $(f(t), g(t))$ gives P's *position* in the xy-plane at time t, and it makes sense to consider the **speed** of P at time t. Since the derivatives f' and g' tell, respectively, how fast x and y increase, their appearance below is no surprise:

As the bullets on some graphs above show, speed varies with time.

> **Definition:** Suppose that the position of a point P at time t, $a \leq t \leq b$, is given by differentiable coordinate functions $x = f(t)$ and $y = g(t)$. Then
>
> $$\textbf{speed of } P \textbf{ at time } t = \sqrt{f'(t)^2 + g'(t)^2}.$$

Making sense. Is the definition "right"? Definitions aren't subject to proof, but they *should* appeal to common sense. Does this one?

Speed, "properly" defined, should tell how fast the distance traveled by P increases with respect to time. Showing carefully that the definition above actually does so involves a rather subtle definition of **arclength**, i.e., distance measured along a curve. We won't define arclength here, but the next example shows that the definition makes good sense for *linear* coordinate functions.

■ **Example 8.** At time t seconds, a point P has coordinates $x = at + b$, $y = ct + d$; a, b, c, and d are constants. How fast is P moving at time t_0?

Solution: The definition says that the speed of P at *any* time t is constant:

$$\sqrt{f'(t)^2 + g'(t)^2} = \sqrt{a^2 + c^2}.$$

Let's see why this result makes sense.

Notice first that because P has *linear* coordinate functions, *P moves along a straight line.* When $t = t_0$, P has coordinates $(x_0, y_0) = (at_0 + b, ct_0 + d)$; by time t_1, P has moved to $(at_1 + b, ct_1 + d)$—a distance of

See the exercises for more on this point.

Check our algebra.

$$\sqrt{(at_1 + b - at_0 - b)^2 + (ct_1 + d - ct_0 - d)^2} = (t_1 - t_0)\sqrt{a^2 + c^2}$$

units. Therefore from $t = t_0$ to $t = t_1$, P has

$$\text{average speed} = \frac{\text{distance}}{\text{time}} = \frac{(t_1 - t_0)\sqrt{a^2 + c^2}}{t_1 - t_0} = \sqrt{a^2 + c^2}.$$

This shows that P has the same average speed—$\sqrt{a^2 + c^2}$—over *any* time interval. Thus the *instantaneous* speed of P at any time t_0 is also $\sqrt{a^2 + c^2}$, as the definition says. □

■ **Example 9.** Consider again the parametric curve

$$x = f(t) = t - 2\sin t; \qquad y = g(t) = 2 - 2\cos t$$

of Example 1, page 368. Find the speed at $t = 3$. When does P move *fastest*?

Look first at the picture; try to guess reasonable answers.

Solution: The definition says that at any time t,

$$\text{speed} = \sqrt{(f'(t))^2 + (g'(t))^2} = \sqrt{(1 - 2\cos t)^2 + (2\sin t)^2} = \sqrt{5 - 4\,\cos(t)}.$$

(The last step uses a trigonometric identity.)

Check for yourself.

The rest is easy. At $t = 3$ the speed is $\sqrt{5 - 4\,\cos 3} \approx 2.99$. The speed formula also shows—and the picture agrees—that the speed $\sqrt{5 - 4\,\cos t}$ is greatest when $\cos t = -1$, e.g., when $t = \pi$. □

Slopes on parametric curves

On an ordinary, $y = f(x)$-style curve, $f'(x)$ gives the slope at (x, y). Not surprisingly, slopes on parametric curves also involve derivatives.

Not all functions have derivatives; not all parametric curves have slopes. To avoid needless complications we'll work only with **smooth** parametric curves, defined as follows:

> **Definition:** The parametric curve C defined by
>
> $$x = f(t); \quad y = g(t); \quad a \le t \le b$$
>
> is **smooth** if f' and g' are continuous functions of t, and f' and g' are not simultaneously zero.

(The second requirement says that the moving point P *never stops*.)➡ For smooth curves the next theorem tells how to find the slope at a point.

See the exercises for more on this idea.

> **Theorem 3.** Let the smooth parametric curve C be defined as above. If $f'(t) \neq 0$, then the slope dy/dx at the point $(x, y) = (f(t), g(t))$ is given by
>
> $$\frac{dy}{dx} = \frac{g'(t)}{f'(t)} = \frac{dy/dt}{dx/dt}.$$

Before proving the theorem, let's use it.

■ **Example 10.** Consider the parametric curve

$$x = f(t) = t - 2\sin t; \qquad y = g(t) = 2 - 2\cos t$$

of Example 1, page 368. Find the slope at $t = 1$. Where is the curve horizontal? Where is it vertical?➡

Guess first, by looking at the picture.

Solution: The theorem says that

$$\text{slope at } t = \frac{g'(t)}{f'(t)} = \frac{2\sin t}{1 - 2\cos t},$$

unless $f'(t) = 0$.➡ Setting $t = 1$ gives

Where the denominator is zero.

$$\text{slope at time } 1 = \frac{g'(1)}{f'(1)} = \frac{2\sin 1}{1 - 2\cos 1} \approx -20.88.$$

The picture agrees: at $(f(1), g(1)) \approx (-0.68, 0.92)$, the curve has large negative slope.

The general slope formula

$$\frac{dy}{dx} = \frac{2\sin t}{1 - 2\cos t}$$

shows that the curve is *horizontal* only when the numerator is zero, i.e., when t is an integer multiple of π. Again the picture agrees. At $t = \pi$, for instance, $(x, y) = (\pi, 4)$. At this point the curve appears to be horizontal.

The curve C can be *vertical* only where the denominator above is zero,➡ i.e., when $\cos t = 1/2$. One such value is $t = \pi/3 \approx 1.05$; again the picture agrees. □

Otherwise, the slope of C is finite.

Proof of the theorem

Remember—we're assuming that f is smooth.

Denominators don't vanish unexpectedly.

Suppose that $f'(t_0) \neq 0$; then either $f'(t_0) > 0$ or $f'(t_0) < 0$. If $f'(t_0) > 0$, then continuity of f' implies that $f'(t) > 0$ for t *near* t_0, and therefore that $x = f(t)$ is *increasing* near $t = t_0$. If $f'(t) < 0$ then (by the same reasoning) $x = f(t)$ is *decreasing* near $t = t_0$. In either case it follows that if t is near t_0 but $t \neq t_0$, then $f(t) \neq f(t_0)$. This assures, in turn, that all of the following limit computations makes sense. Notice first that

$$\text{slope} = \left.\frac{dy}{dx}\right|_{t=t_0} = \lim_{t\to t_0} \frac{y - y_0}{x - x_0} = \lim_{t\to t_0} \frac{g(t) - g(t_0)}{f(t) - f(t_0)}.$$

A common sort of trick in proving calculus theorems.

Now for a little trick. We'll divide the numerator and denominator above by $(t - t_0)$, take limits of everything in sight, and see what happens. Here goes:

$$\left.\frac{dy}{dx}\right|_{t=t_0} = \lim_{t\to t_0} \frac{\frac{g(t)-g(t_0)}{t-t_0}}{\frac{f(t)-f(t_0)}{t-t_0}} = \frac{\lim_{t\to t_0} \frac{g(t)-g(t_0)}{t-t_0}}{\lim_{t\to t_0} \frac{f(t)-f(t_0)}{t-t_0}} = \frac{g'(t_0)}{f'(t_0)},$$

which is what we wanted to show. (The second last step is OK because, by assumption, the limit in the denominator is not zero.) □

Modeling with parametric equations

"Projectiles" could be baseballs, BB's, ballistic missiles, etc.

Parametric equations often help model physical processes that involve quantities varying in both time and space. Describing **trajectories**—paths taken by projectiles—is one such setting.

Major league batters don't ignore wind resistance. See the exercises for a more realistic example.

■ **Example 11.** A major league fastball leaves the pitcher's hand traveling horizontally, with initial speed 150 feet per second and initial height 7 feet. Ignoring wind resistance, describe the ball's trajectory. When, and at what speed, does the ball cross the plate, 60.5 feet away? Is the pitch a strike? If the batter, catcher, and umpire all miss the ball, where will it land?

Solution: We'll use an xy-coordinate system with origin at the pitcher's feet and home plate at $(60.5, 0)$; the ball starts at $(0, 7)$.

For more on falling objects, with and without air resistance, see pp. 93–95.

Recall: acceleration is the second derivative of position.

Why is the vertical acceleration negative?

Ignoring wind resistance means that the ball, once released, is influenced only by gravity. Thus the ball's horizontal acceleration is zero; its vertical acceleration, due to gravity, is -32 feet per second per second.

If $x = f(t)$, $y = g(t)$, and t measures time in seconds since the ball's release, then our information boils down to this:

$$f''(t) = 0; \quad f'(0) = 150; \quad f(0) = 0; \quad g''(t) = -32; \quad g'(0) = 0; \quad g(0) = 7.$$

These data lead to simple formulas for f and g. The argument for f goes like this:

$$f''(t) = 0 \implies f'(t) = a \quad \text{and} \quad f(t) = at + b,$$

where a and b are constants, as yet unknown. Finding them is easy: combining the facts that $f(t) = at + b$, $f(0) = 0$, and $f'(0) = 150$ gives $a = 150$ and $b = 0$, so $f(t) = 150t$. A similar argument applies to g—here's the result:

$$x = f(t) = 150t; \qquad y = g(t) = 7 - 16t^2.$$

These equations make sense, of course, only while the ball remains airborne, i.e., until $y = 7 - 16t^2 = 0$, or $t = \sqrt{7}/4 \approx 0.661$ seconds. Here's the parametric curve for $0 \le t \le 0.661$:

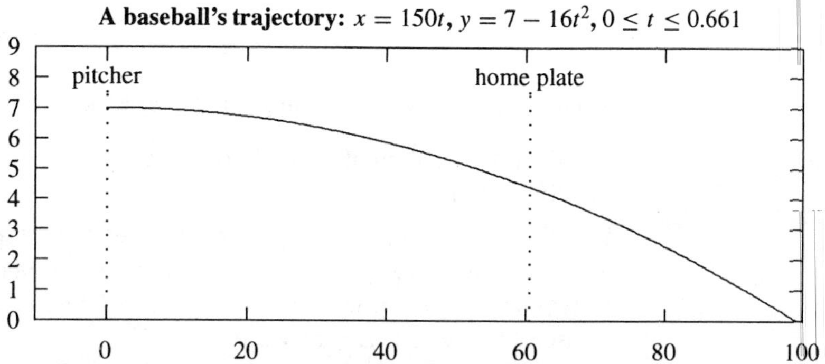

Notice the *parabolic* shape: in fact, *every* free-falling object either moves vertically or follows a parabolic trajectory.➻

See the exercises for more on parabolic trajectories.

Using the picture and the formulas we can answer our original questions. The ball crosses the plate when $x = f(t) = 150t = 60.5$, i.e., when $t = 121/300 \approx 0.4033$ seconds. At this time,➻

Check the arithmetic.

$$\text{speed} = \sqrt{f'(0.4033)^2 + g'(0.4033)^2} \approx 150.55$$

feet per second. At the same time, the ball's height is $y = g(0.4033) \approx 4.4$ feet—high but in the strike zone for an average batter. Left untouched, the ball hits the ground at $t = 0.661$; at this time, $x = f(t) = 150 \cdot 0.661 \approx 99.2$ feet—almost 40 feet behind home plate. □

Exercises

1. Plot each parametric curve below. (Using a machine is fine, but then draw or copy your own curve on paper.) In each case, mark the direction of travel and label the points corresponding to $t = -1$, $t = 0$, and $t = 1$.

   (a) $x = t,\ y = \sqrt{1-t^2},\ -1 \le t \le 1$

   (b) $x = t,\ y = -\sqrt{1-t^2},\ -1 \le t \le 1$

   (c) $x = \sqrt{1-t^2},\ y = t,\ -1 \le t \le 1$

   (d) $x = -\sqrt{1-t^2},\ y = t,\ -1 \le t \le 1$

   (e) $x = \sin(\pi t),\ y = \cos(\pi t),\ -1 \le t \le 1$

2. Each parametric "curve" below is actually a line segment. In each part, state the beginning point ($t = 0$) and ending point ($t = 1$) of the segment. Then state an equation in x and y for the line each segment determines.

   (a) $x = 2 + 3t,\ y = 1 + 2t,\ 0 \le t \le 1$

   (b) $x = 2 + 3(1-t),\ y = 1 + 2(1-t),\ 0 \le t \le 1$

   (c) $x = t,\ y = mt + b,\ 0 \le t \le 1$

   (d) $x = a + bt,\ y = c + dt,\ 0 \le t \le 1$

   (e) $x = x_0 + (x_1 - x_0)t,\ y = y_0 + (y_1 - y_0)t,\ 0 \le t \le 1$

3. A parametric curve $x = f(t)$, $y = g(t)$, $a \le t \le b$ has **constant speed** if—what else?—its speed is constant in t. Which of the curves in Problem 1 above have constant speed?

4. Show that if a curve C has *linear* coordinate functions $x = at + b$ and $y = ct + d$, then C has constant speed. (See the previous problem.)

5. Consider the curve C shown in Example 1; suppose that t tells time in seconds.

   (a) At which bulleted points would you expect P to be moving quickly? Slowly? Why?

   (b) Use the curve to *estimate* the speed of P at $t = 3$. (One approach: Estimate how far P travels—i.e., the length of the curve—over the one-second interval from $t = 2.5$ to $t = 3.5$. If d is this distance, then d distance units per second is a reasonable speed estimate at $t = 3$.)

   (c) Use the curve to estimate the speed of P at $t = 6$.

6. Plot the parametric curve

$$x = t^3; \qquad y = \sin t^3; \qquad -2 \le t \le 2.$$

   What familiar curve is produced? Why does the result happen?

7. Let (a, b) be any point in the plane, and $r > 0$ any positive number. Consider the parametric equations

$$x = a + r\cos t; \qquad y = b + r\sin t; \quad 0 \le t \le 2\pi.$$

   (a) Plot the parametric curve defined above for $(a, b) = (2, 1)$ and $r = 2$. Describe your result in words.

   (b) Show by calculation that if x and y are as above, then $(x-a)^2+(y-b)^2 = r^2$. Conclude that the curve defined above is the circle with center (a, b) and radius r.

   (c) Write parametric equations for the circle of radius $\sqrt{13}$, centered at $(2, 3)$.

   (d) What "curve" results from the equations above if $r = 0$?

8. Let a and b be any positive numbers, and let a parametric curve C be defined by

$$x = a\cos t; \qquad y = b\sin t; \quad 0 \le t \le 2\pi.$$

   The resulting curve is called an **ellipse**.

   (a) Plot the curve defined above for $a = 2$ and $b = 1$. Describe C in words. Where is the "center" of C? Why do you think the quantities $2a$ and $2b$ are called the **major and minor axes** of C.

   (b) What curve results if $0 \le t \le 4\pi$? Why?

   (c) Write parametric equations for an ellipse with major axis 10 and minor axis 6.

   (d) Write parametric equations for *another* ellipse with major axis 10 and minor axis 6.

   (e) Show that for all t, $\dfrac{x^2}{a^2} + \dfrac{y^2}{b^2} = 1$.

   (f) How does the "ellipse" look if $a = b$? How does its xy equation look?

   (g) How does an ellipse look if $a = 1000$ and $b = 1$?

(h) How does an ellipse look if $a = 1$ and $b = 1000$?

9. Consider the Lissajou curve in Example 6.

   (a) Label the points corresponding to $t = 0$, $t = 0.1$, and $t = \pi/2$. Add some arrows to the curve to indicate direction.

   (b) How often in the interval $0 \le t \le 2\pi$ does the tracing point P return to $(0, 0)$?

   (c) How would the picture be different if the t-interval $0 \le t \le 4\pi$ were used?

10. We stated in this section that if a parametric curve C has *linear* coefficient functions $x = f(t) = at + b$ and $y = g(t) = ct + b$, then C is a straight line (or part of a line). This problem explores that fact.

    (a) Plot the parametric curve $x = 2t$, $y = 3t + 4$, $0 \le t \le 1$. Where does the curve start? Where does it end? What is its shape?

    (b) Eliminate the variable t in the two equations above to find a single tion in x and y for the line of the previous part. e that the parametric curve is only part of this line.)

    (c) Find the slope at $t = t_0$ of the parametric curve $x = 2t$, $y = 3t + 4$, $0 \le t \le 1$. Why doesn't the answer depend on t?

11. This problem pursues the idea that if a parametric curve C has *linear* coefficient functions $x = f(t) = at + b$ and $y = g(t) = ct + d$, then C is a straight line (or part of a line).

    (a) Consider the parametric curve $x = at + b$, $y = ct + d$, $t_0 \le t \le t_1$. Where does the curve start? Where does it end?

    (b) Assume that $a \neq 0$. (Don't assume that $c \neq 0$.) Eliminate the variable t in the two equations above to find one equation in x and y. What line does it describe?

    (c) Assume that $c \neq 0$. (Don't assume that $a \neq 0$.) Eliminate the variable t in the two equations above to find one equation in x and y. What line does it describe?

    (d) What happens if a and c are both zero?

12. This problem explores the technical assumptions in the definition of *smooth* curves.

    (a) Consider the "curve" defined for all t by $x = 0$, $y = 0$. Plot C. Does C "deserve" to have a slope at $t = 0$? If so, what slope? If not, why not? Is C smooth in the sense of the definition?

    (b) Consider the curve defined for $-1 \le t \le 1$ by $x = t^3$ and $y = t^3$. Plot C. Does C "deserve" to have a slope at $t = 0$? What does Theorem 1 say in this case?

    (c) Consider the curve defined for $-1 \le t \le 1$ by $x = t$ and $y = t$. Plot C. Does this C "deserve" to have a slope at $t = 0$? What does Theorem 1 say about slope this time?

13. This problem concerns Example 11, p. 374.

    (a) How could the model be made more realistic? What additional information would be needed?

(b) Use the conditions $g''(t) = -32$, $g'(0) = 0$, and $g(0) = 7$ to show that $g(t) = 7 - 16t^2$, as claimed in the Example.

(c) Find a formula for $s(t)$, the ball's speed at time t. Plot $s(t)$ over an appropriate interval. How does the graph's shape reflect the physical situation?

14. Use parametric equations to describe the trajectory of a baseball thrown exactly as in Example 11, p. 374, except that this time the initial velocity is 100 feet per second. Plot the result over an appropriate interval. Is the pitch a strike? At what speed does it cross the plate? (The strike zone is roughly from 1.5 to 4.5 feet above the ground at home plate.)

15. Consider a baseball thrown horizontally, starting from height 7 feet (as in Example 11, p. 374), but with initial speed s_0.

(a) Explain briefly why the parametric equations

$$x = s_0 t, \quad y = 7 - 16t^2$$

describe the ball's trajectory (ignoring wind resistance).

(b) When does the ball reach home plate?

(c) Is the trajectory parabolic? Why?

16. (This problem is again about the situation in Example 11, p. 374, but takes wind resistance into account.) In practice, wind resistance *does* affect a baseball's trajectory. One possible model of wind resistance (we omit the details) leads to the parametric equations

$$x = \frac{\ln(150 \cdot k \cdot t + 1)}{k}; \quad y = 7 - 16t^2,$$

where the constant k can be thought of as the ball's "drag coefficient"—the smoother the ball, the lower the value of k. For a typical baseball, $k = 0.003$ is reasonable. With this value of k we get

$$x = \frac{1000 \ln(0.45t + 1)}{3}; \quad y = 7 - 16t^2.$$

The resulting trajectory is plotted below; the curve from Example 11 is also shown:

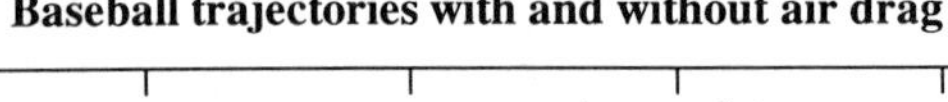

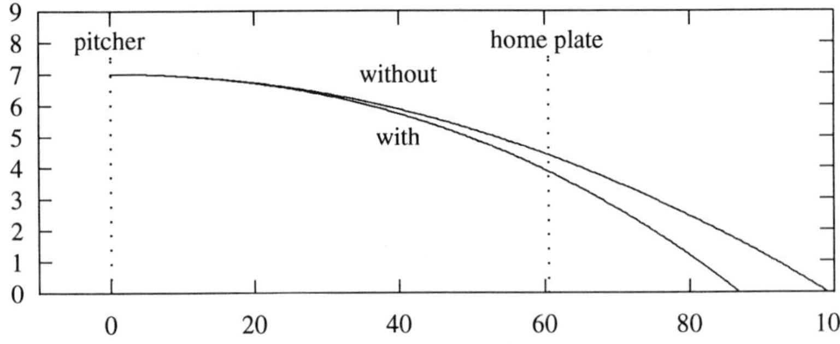

In each part below, use the graphs to give approximate answers; then use appropriate formulas to improve your results.

(a) At what *time* does the air-dragged ball cross the plate? (Note: the graphs don't show time.) How much longer does it take to reach the plate than the drag-less ball?

(b) At what height does the air-dragged ball cross the plate?

(c) At what speed does the air-dragged ball cross the plate?

(d) Where does the air-dragged ball land?

17. The situation is as in the previous problem, except that this time the ball is scuffed, so that its "drag coefficient" is 0.005, not 0.003. Plot the new trajectory. Then answer the same questions as in the previous problem.

4.9 Chapter summary

Chapter 4 offers a potpourri of applications of the derivative and antiderivative. (A skimpy one, unfortunately—these ideas have far more uses than any textbook could possibly cover.)

Yes, a function. Not a number!

Differential equations. A **differential equation** (DE) is any equation that involves derivatives. To **solve** a differential equation means to find a **function** that satisfies the DE.

Typical differential equations have **many solutions**. Every function of the form

$$y = Ce^x,$$

The world's most important DE.

for example, solves the differential equation

$$y' = y.$$

The world's most important IVP, perhaps.

Adding an **initial condition** to a DE creates a **initial value problem**, or IVP. IVP's typically have only **one solution**. The only solution of the IVP

$$y' = y; \qquad y(0) = 1,$$

for instance, is the function

$$y = e^x.$$

Sections 4.1 and 4.2 treat DE's, first briefly in theory and then, in more detail, in applications related to population growth.

Linear and quadratic approximation. The graph of any well-behaved function is approximated—more or less closely, and near the point of tangency—by its tangent line. This means, in functional language, that f is approximated well by the *linear function*, called the **linear approximation to f at** x_0, whose graph is the tangent line. Section 4.3 explores the meaning and ramifications of this fact, and takes matters one step further—to **quadratic approximation**. In graphical terms, the **quadratic approximation** to f at x_0 is the function whose graph is the **parabola** that "best fits" f at x_0. Going further still, Section 4.3 introduces **Taylor polynomials**, polynomials of *any* degree that approximate non-polynomial functions.

Newton's method. Finding roots of any but the simplest functions—e.g., linear functions—is difficult or impossible algebraically. **Newton's method** (like the **bisection method** of Section 3.6) offers a numerical alternative. To *estimate* a root of f near an initial guess x_0, Newton's method "rides the tangent line" from the f-graph at x_0 to the x-axis. The result is seldom *exactly* a root, but *repeating* Newton's method usually produces—remarkably quickly—a highly accurate approximation to a root. Section 4.4 treats the idea and typical applications of Newton's method—and suggests some ideas for "breaking" it.

Splines. Section 4.5 is about **splining**—"fitting" together pieces of simple curves (linear, quadratic, or cubic) to form larger curves of desired shapes. Derivatives are the basic tool: by matching one or more derivatives of "incoming" and "outgoing" functions at each "knot," curves of any desired smoothness can be constructed.

Optimization. Among the derivative's most important and useful applications is finding **extreme values**—i.e., maximum and minimum values—of functions. As Section 4.6 illustrates, solving optimization problems usually means identifying an appropriate function and then using the derivative to look for and classify its **critical points**. Problems posed in words are a special emphasis here: translating English descriptions into mathematically useful forms is important wherever mathematics is applied.

Economic applications. Calculus ideas apply to many areas, including economic measurement and prediction. In Section 4.7 we apply derivative ideas (using the **marginal** language economists favor) to maximize a grain trader's profit on various transactions.

Related rates. In practical situations, several quantities vary *together* in time; the *rates* at which these quantities vary are themselves related. The method of **related rates** is a technique for discovering such relationships.

A typical problem begins with an equation relating several quantities, all varying with time. Differentiating everything in sight—with respect to time, usually—produces a *new* equation, one that relates the *rates* at which the quantities vary.

Parametric equations and parametric curves. Many interesting plane curves—e.g., circles—are *not* graphs of functions, because they fail the vertical line test. Parametrically defined curves offer much more flexibility. Defining x and y *separately* as **coordinate functions** of another variable, say t, lets us draw all sorts of interesting, beautiful, and complicated curves. If the coordinate functions are differentiable in t, then calculus ideas apply; we use them to define and calculate slopes and speeds.

Chapter 5

The Integral

5.1 Areas and integrals

The **tangent line problem** and the **area problem** are the two big geometric problems of calculus. As we've seen, the idea of *derivative*, together with the rules for computing derivatives, solves the tangent line problem. For an impressive variety of functions, even complicated ones, it's by now a routine matter to calculate the slope of the tangent line at any point on the graph.

These problems have been big for many centuries: the Greeks worked hard, and ingeniously, at both. Had they had our algebraic advantages, they would have gone farther than they did.

The area problem and the integral

The general area problem asks how to measure the area of a plane region. For special regions—rectangles, triangles, squares, circles, trapezoids, etc.—well known formulas do the job.

And long known—the Greeks knew them.

Area problems are more challenging—and far more interesting—for regions bounded by less familiar curves, such as graphs of functions. The most important such area problem, phrased in calculus language, is to measure an area like that shown shaded in the "generic" picture below:

What's the shaded area?

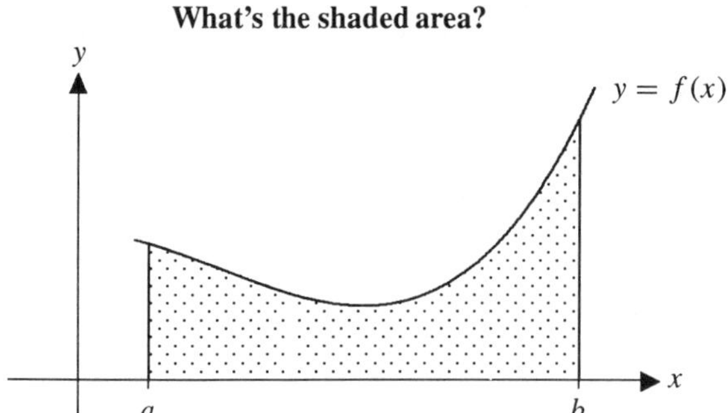

Stated carefully, the problem reads like this:

> *Find the area of the region bounded* above *by the graph of f,* below *by the x-axis, on the* left *by the vertical line $x = a$, and on the* right *by the vertical line $x = b$.*

That's a mouthful—we'll usually say just "the area under the graph of f from a to b."

The shorthand phrase is less tedious, but also less precise. If in doubt use the full form.

Signed area

In this chapter it will often be convenient to consider **signed area**, as opposed to area in the everyday sense. The adjective "signed" means that *area below the x-axis counts as negative.* (In the picture above all the shaded area is above the x-axis, so the question of sign doesn't arise.) We'll give more details below.

A compact notation for signed area is even more convenient:

> **Definition:** **(The integral as signed area.)** Let f be a function defined for $a \le x \le b$. Either of the equivalent expressions
>
> $$\int_a^b f \quad \text{or} \quad \int_a^b f(x)\,dx$$
>
> denotes the signed area bounded by $x = a$, $x = b$, $y = f(x)$, and the x-axis.

Note:

In words. For either $\int_a^b f(x)\,dx$ or $\int_a^b f$, read "the **integral** of f from a to b." The function f is the **integrand**.

Which is better? Both $\int_a^b f$ and $\int_a^b f(x)\,dx$ denote the same area. The first form looks simpler; for now, we'll usually choose it. The other ("dx") form has advantages that will sometimes matter later on.

Differences between the two forms are akin to those between the dy/dx and f' notations for derivative.

How to find it? We've defined the symbolic expression $\int_a^b f$ to *stand for* area. So far, that's all we've done. The problem of *calculating* areas remains.

■ **Example 1.** Several areas are shown below, labeled as integrals. Use familiar area formulas to evaluate each integral.

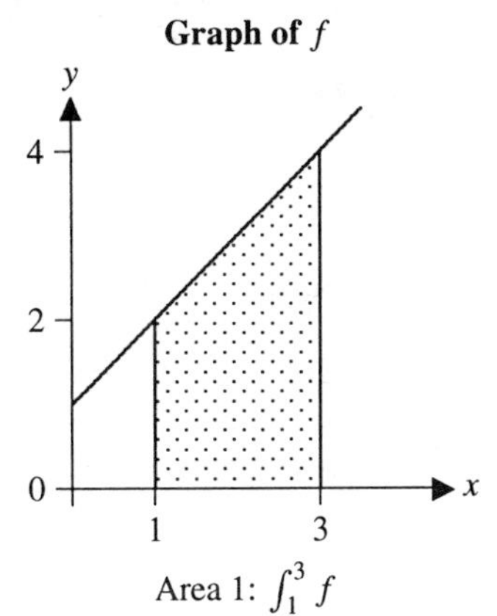

Area 1: $\int_1^3 f$

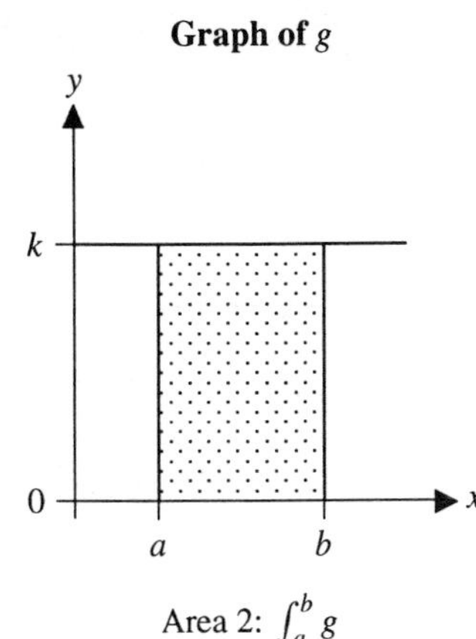

Area 2: $\int_a^b g$

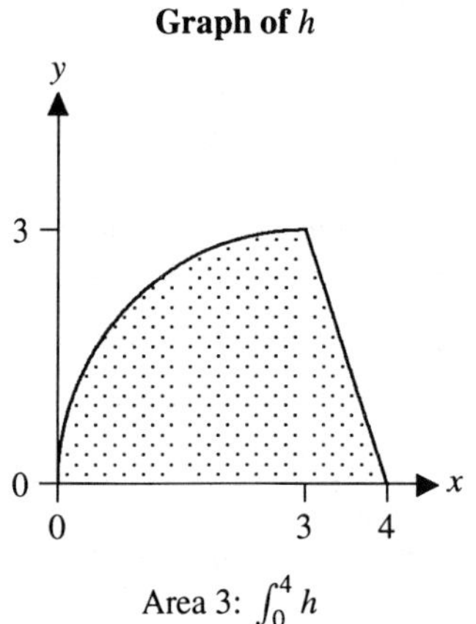

Area 3: $\int_0^4 h$

A trapezoid with base b and heights h_1 and h_2 has area $b(h_1 + h_2)/2$. Can you prove this?

base × height

Solution: All three areas are easy to find. Area 1 is a trapezoid, with base 2 and vertical sides 2 and 4—hence the area is 6. Area 2 is a rectangle; by the usual formula, its area measures $(b - a) \cdot k$. Area 3 is a quarter circle plus a triangle; a close look at these figures reveals a total area of $9\pi/4 + 3/2$, or about 8.569. In integral notation:

$$\int_1^3 f = 6; \qquad \int_a^b g = k(b-a); \qquad \int_0^4 h = \frac{9\pi}{4} + \frac{3}{2}. \qquad \Box$$

Signed area: positive and negative contributions

Integrals measure *signed area.* In calculating integrals, therefore, area *above* the graph of f and *beneath* the x-axis counts as negative. Thus if an *integrand* f takes negative values in an interval $[a, b]$, then so may the *integral* $\int_a^b f$.

■ **Example 2.** Let $f(x) = 1 - x^2$. Find (or estimate) values for the integrals $I_1 = \displaystyle\int_0^2 f$ and $I_2 = \displaystyle\int_{-2}^2 f$.

Solution: The areas in question look like this:

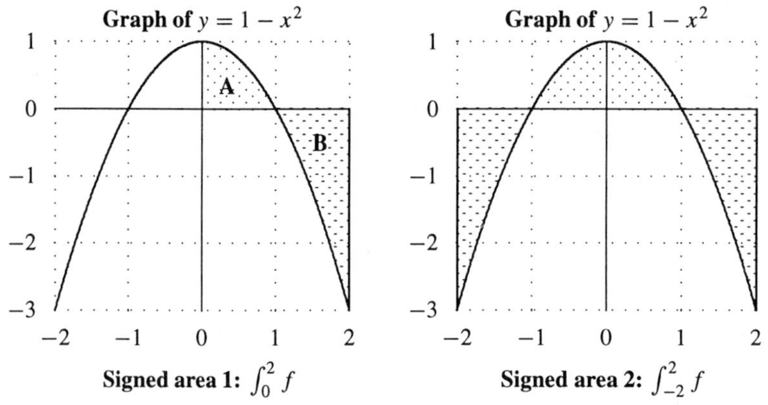

Signed area 1: $\int_0^2 f$ **Signed area 2:** $\int_{-2}^2 f$

Soon it will be easy.

Note that each square has area 1.

Computing I_1 and I_2 *exactly* is, for now, difficult. *Estimating* the integrals, on the other hand, is easy. Eyeballing general sizes suggests that A has area around $2/3$; similarly, B has area around $3/2$. From these guesses, we'd estimate (counting B as negative!)

$$I_1 = \int_0^2 f \approx \frac{2}{3} - \frac{3}{2} = -\frac{5}{6}.$$

How close is this estimate? We can't tell—yet—for sure, but it seems in the ballpark.➽ In any event, symmetry shows➽ that

It is in the ballpark; the exact answer turns out to be $-2/3$.

$$I_2 = 2 \cdot I_1 \approx -\frac{5}{3}.$$ □

Convince yourself; how is even-ness of f involved?

■ **Example 3.** Let $g(x) = x^3$. Find or estimate $\int_{-1}^{1} g(x)\,dx$ and $\int_{0}^{1} g(x)\,dx$.

Solution: Here's the graph:

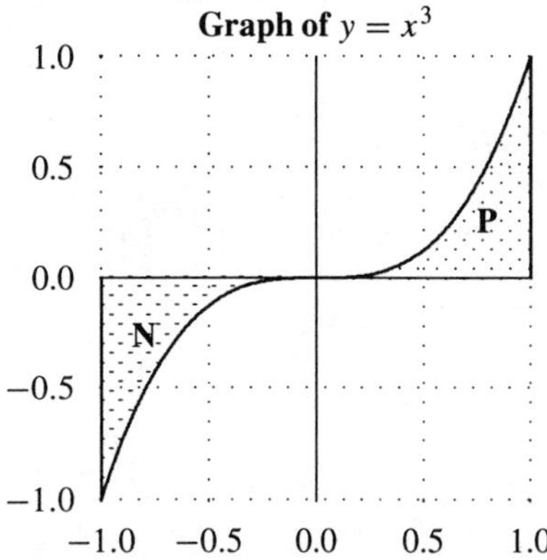

Because of the graph's symmetry➽ the positive and negative areas P and N cancel; hence

Or, equivalently, because g is odd.

$$\int_{-1}^{1} g(x)\,dx = 0.$$

(*Any* odd integrand over *any* interval that's symmetric about $x = 0$ behaves the same way.)

Symmetry is no help with $\int_0^1 g$. A close look suggests that P's area is about that of one small square, or 0.25. In other words,

$$\int_{0}^{1} g(x)\,dx \approx 0.25.$$

(We'll see soon that➽ this estimate is actually exact.) □

And why!

Properties of the integral

Viewing the integral as area makes many of the integral's important properties simple and natural. For example, this picture—

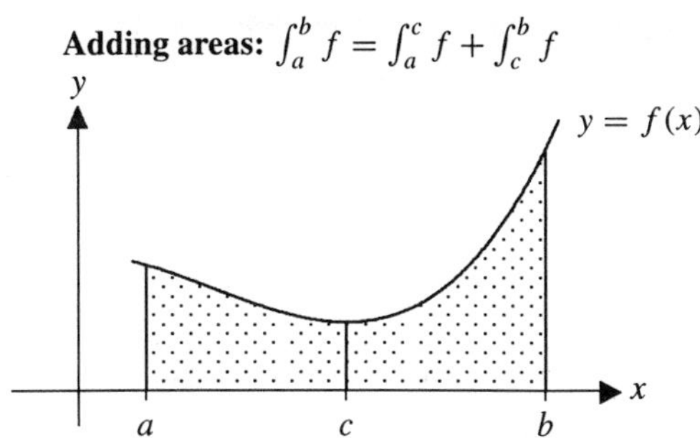

is a convincing illustration of the following simple➽ property of the integral:

But often useful.

$$\text{If } a < c < b, \text{ then } \int_a^b f = \int_a^c f + \int_c^b f$$

The next theorem collects several other properties of the integral, similar to the one above.

Requiring that f and g assures that all the integrals in question exist.

Theorem 1. (New integrals from old.) Let f and g be continuous functions on $[a, b]$; let k denote a real constant. Then

1. $\displaystyle\int_a^b (f(x) \pm g(x))\,dx = \int_a^b f(x)\,dx \pm \int_a^b g(x)\,dx.$
2. $\displaystyle\int_a^b kf(x)\,dx = k\int_a^b f(x)\,dx.$
3. If $f(x) \leq g(x)$ for all x in $[a, b]$, then
$$\int_a^b f(x)\,dx \leq \int_a^b g(x)\,dx.$$

Note:

Like the derivative. The first two properties above are akin to properties of the derivative: like the derivative, the integral behaves well with respect to sums and constant multiples. The following picture illustrates the **constant multiple rule** for integrals:

Constant multiple rule for integrals: why $\int_a^b 2f = 2\int_a^b f$

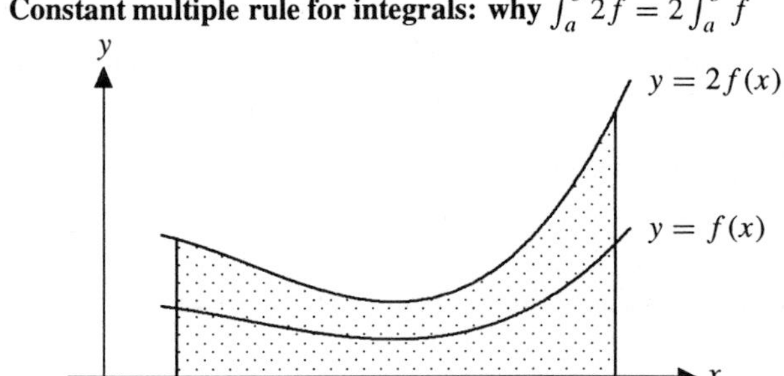

A useful case. The third property is often used in the case where either f or g is a constant. Here's one useful version:

Fact: (Bounding an integral.) Suppose that for some numbers m and M, the inequality $m \leq f(x) \leq M$ holds for all x in $[a, b]$. Then

$$m \cdot (b-a) = \int_a^b m\,dx \leq \int_a^b f(x)\,dx \leq \int_a^b M\,dx = M \cdot (b-a).$$

A picture best shows what's going on:

m and M are lower and upper bounds for f on $[a, b]$.

Bounding areas: why $m(b-a) \le \int_a^b f \le M(b-a)$

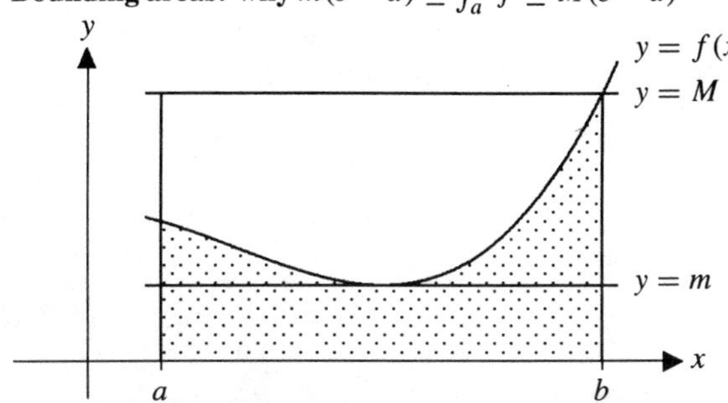

As the picture illustrates, the value of the integral (i.e., the area of the shaded region) lies between the areas of the smaller and the larger rectangles.

■ **Example 4.** Using the fact that $\int_0^\pi \sin x\,dx = 2$, find $\int_0^{\pi/2} \sin x\,dx$ and $\int_0^\pi (3\sin x + 2\cos x)\,dx$.

It is a fact—a remarkable one.

Solution: Symmetry of the sine and cosine graphs shows:

Draw them to convince yourself!

$$\int_0^{\pi/2} \sin x\,dx = \frac{1}{2}\int_0^\pi \sin x\,dx = 1; \qquad \int_0^\pi \cos x\,dx = 0.$$

Therefore, by the sum and constant multiple rules,

$$\int_0^\pi (3\sin x + 2\cos x)\,dx = 3\int_0^\pi \sin x\,dx + 2\int_0^\pi \cos x\,dx = 6 + 0 = 6.$$

A look at the graph should make the general size of the answer plausible:

Does it?

Why $\int_0^\pi (3\sin x + 2\cos x)\,dx = 6$

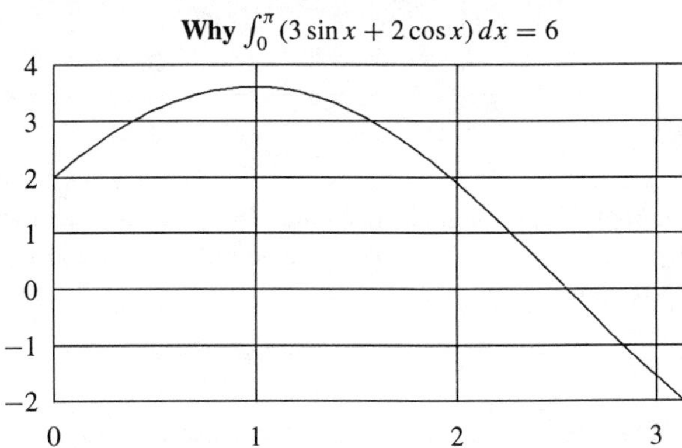

The "net area" *does* seem to be about 6. □

■ **Example 5.** For any positive constant b,

$$\int_0^b 1\,dx = b \qquad \text{and} \qquad \int_0^b x\,dx = \frac{b^2}{2}.$$

Explain why. Then use the theorem to find $\int_0^b (Cx + D)\,dx$, for any constants C and D.

Draw them!

Solution: Graphs of the functions $f(x) = 1$ and $g(x) = x$ over the interval $[0, b]$ show that the first two integrals have the claimed values. To finish, we use the sum and constant multiple rules for integrals:

$$\begin{aligned}\int_0^b (Cx + D)\,dx &= \int_0^b (Cx)\,dx + \int_0^b D\,dx \\ &= C\int_0^b x\,dx + \int_0^b D\,dx \\ &= C\frac{b^2}{2} + Db.\end{aligned}$$ □

Average value and the integral

In the picture below, the rectangle is chosen to have the same area as the shaded region:

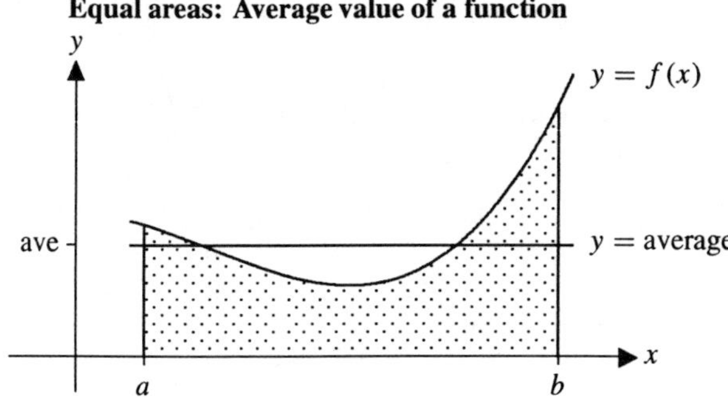

The *height* of that rectangle is, in a natural way, the **average value** of the function f over the interval $[a, b]$. The following definition restates in analytic language what the picture shows geometrically:

Definition: Let f be defined on an interval $[a, b]$. The quantity

$$\frac{\int_a^b f(x)\,dx}{b-a}$$

is the **average value of f over** $[a, b]$.

The ideas of integral and average value are very close cousins; understanding either helps with the other. The picture above summarizes this two-way relationship: either the integral defines the average value (as the *height* of a certain rectangle) or the average value defines the integral (as the *area* of the same rectangle).

■ **Example 6.** The graphs below show speed functions, $s_A t$ and s_B, for two cars A and B.

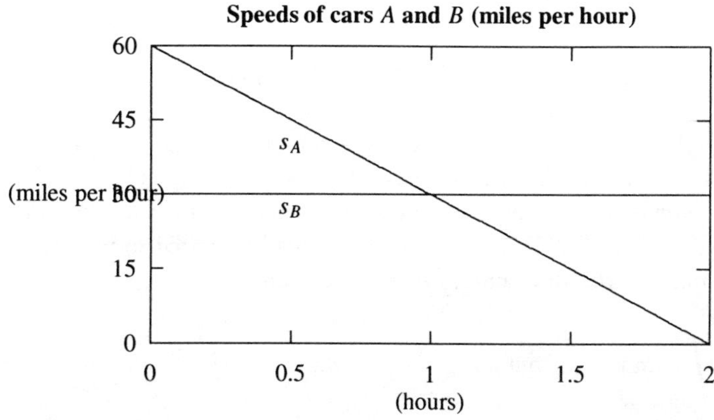

What's the average value of each function over the interval $[0, 2]$? What do the results mean in "car talk?"

Solution: Looking at areas shows readily➛ that

Convince yourself.

$$\int_0^2 s_A(t)\,dt = 60 = \int_0^2 s_B(t)\,dt.$$

Thus, using the definition above, *both* speed functions have average value 30 over the interval $[0, 2]$.

The answers make excellent sense automotively. The area under each graph represents the total distance—60 miles—that each car covers in the two-hour interval. Dividing the distance by the time elapsed gives an average speed of 30 mph for each car. □

Interpreting the integral

So far we've approached the integral $\int_a^b f$ only in geometric terms. Nevertheless, the integral has many *other* natural and important interpretations. We'll see several in this course. Here we mention just one.

Speed and distance

If a function $f(t)$ represents the *speed* of a moving object at time t, then $\int_a^b f(t)\,dt$ represents the *distance traveled* by the object over the interval $a \le t \le b$. Why?

If the speed function $f(t)$ happens to be a *constant*, say k, then➛

Draw a graph to convince yourself.

$$\int_a^b f(t)\,dt = k \cdot (b - a) = \text{speed} \cdot \text{time} = \text{distance},$$

as claimed. Remarkably enough, the same result holds even if $f(t)$ *isn't* constant. The previous example should make this plausible; in the next sections, we'll see exactly why it's true.

Velocity and net distance

Speed, by definition, is always positive. Velocity can be *either* positive or negative, depending on direction. As a result, integrating a velocity function $v(t)$ gives slightly different information from that above. If $v(t)$ tells the *velocity* of an object moving along a line at time t, then $\int_a^b f(t)\,dt$ represents the *net distance traveled* over the interval $a \le t \le b$. In particular, net distance, like velocity, can take either sign.

Integrating from right to left: a technicality

The variable name x isn't sacred—t is another popular choice.

The English description of $\int_a^b f(x)\,dx$—"the integral of f *from* $x = a$ *to* $x = b$"—suggests an implicit *direction* of movement: x *starts* at a and *ends* at b.

It's *almost* always natural to think of x as moving *from left to right.* Up to now, we've done just that: in every integral $\int_a^b f$ we've treated so far, we've assumed or stated that $a \le b$. For example, we've discussed

$$\int_0^\pi \sin x\,dx, \quad \text{but not} \quad \int_\pi^0 \sin x\,dx \quad \text{or} \quad \int_\pi^0 (3\sin x + 2\cos x)\,dx.$$

We'll see some in the next section.

Sometimes the latter sort of "right-to-left" integrals *do* arise. The following convention, based on signs, handles all the possibilities with a minimum of fuss and bother:

$$\int_a^b f(x)\,dx = -\int_b^a f(x)\,dx. \tag{5.1.1}$$

See Example 3.

The convention says, for instance, that since $\int_0^1 x^3\,dx = 0.25$,

$$\int_1^0 x^3\,dx = -\int_0^1 x^3\,dx = -0.25.$$

We saw it just above.

Why does Equation 5.1.1 make sense? The speed-distance context offers one answer:

> *If $f(t)$ represents speed at time t, and $a < b$, then $\int_a^b f(t)\,dt$ gives the (positive) distance traveled from time a to time b.*

Even if Equation 5.1.1 seems arbitrary now, it will prove useful, even natural, in later work.

It's physically reasonable, therefore, to consider as *negative* the distance covered over the *reverse* interval.

Integrals and areas: the story so far and a look ahead

In this section we defined the integral $\int_a^b f$ as a certain area. Then we observed some properties and uses of the integral, arguing mainly from geometric intuition.

What's missing, so far, is any really practical or effective method of *measuring* areas. In the simplest cases, as we saw, elementary area formulas (for squares, rectangles, etc.) are some help. For all *but* the simplest functions, however, such formulas are useless. We address the problem of *calculating* integrals, in two different ways, in the next three sections.

In Sections 5.2 and 5.3 we do so by relating the new idea of the integral to the older (and better-understood) idea of the derivative. This key connection between derivative and integral, known as the **fundamental theorem of calculus**, is among the most important results of mathematics.

In Section 5.4 we give *another* definition of the integral, this time as a limit of approximating sums. Logically, the situation resembles that for the derivative, which we defined informally as the slope of a line, but formally as a limit of *differences*.

(Must area exist?) There seems little question that areas under simple graphs—lines, parabolas, sinusoids, etc.—exist. Things are less clear for "not-nice" (e.g., discontinuous) functions, whose graphs may be extremely ragged. Consider, for instance, this graph:

The graph of $y = \sin(1/x)$

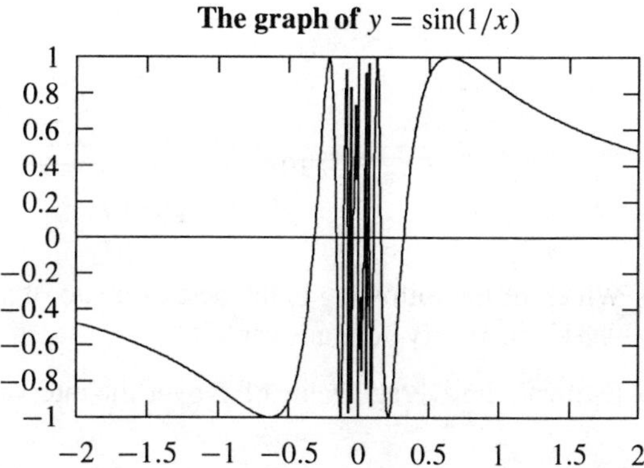

Can such a nasty curve sensibly be said to bound area?

The answer turns out (for this curve, anyway) to be yes. Defining area (let alone computing it) in such unpromising circumstances, however, requires special care. In Section 5.4 we'll redefine the integral, using limits, in order to handle cases like the one shown. In practice, there's no need to worry unduly; the vast majority of standard calculus functions behave nicely enough to accord well with our everyday intuition about area.

Exercises

1. Let g be the function shown graphically below. When asked to estimate $\int_1^2 g(x)\,dx$, a group of calculus students submitted the following answers: -4, 4, 45, and 450. Only one of these responses is reasonable; the others are "obviously" incorrect. Which is the reasonable one? Why?

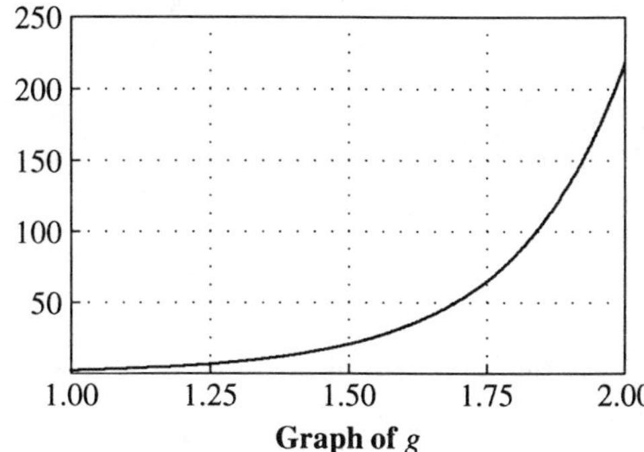

Graph of g

2. Let f be the function shown graphically below.

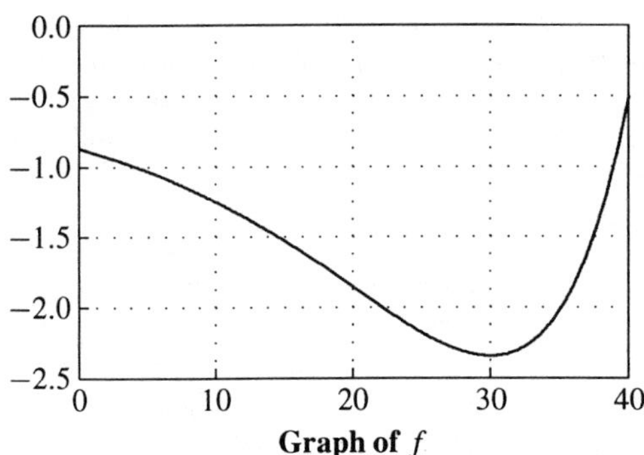

Graph of f

(a) Which of the following is the best estimate of $\int_0^{40} f(x)\,dx$: -65, -30, 0, 35, 60. Justify your answer.

(b) Estimate the average value of f over the interval $[10, 30]$.

3. Four students disagree on the value of the integral $\int_0^{\pi/2} \cos^8 x\,dx$. Jack argues for $\pi \approx 3.14$, Joan for $35\pi/256 \approx 0.43$, Ed for $2\pi/9 - 1 \approx -0.30$, and Lesley for $\pi/4 \approx 0.79$. Use the graph below to determine who is right. (One *is* right!) Explain how you know that the other values are incorrect.

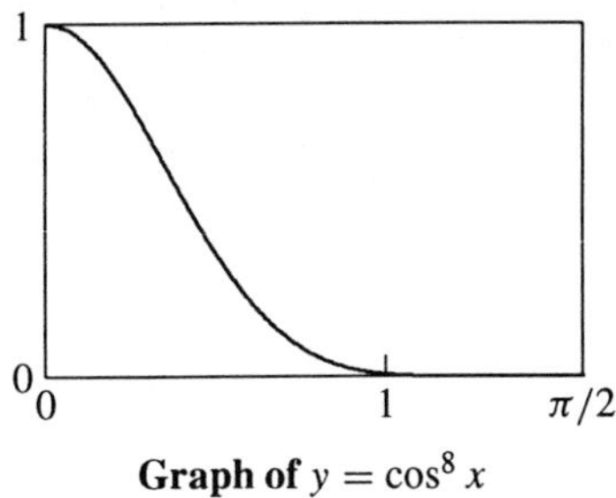

Graph of $y = \cos^8 x$

4. The graph of a function h is shown below.

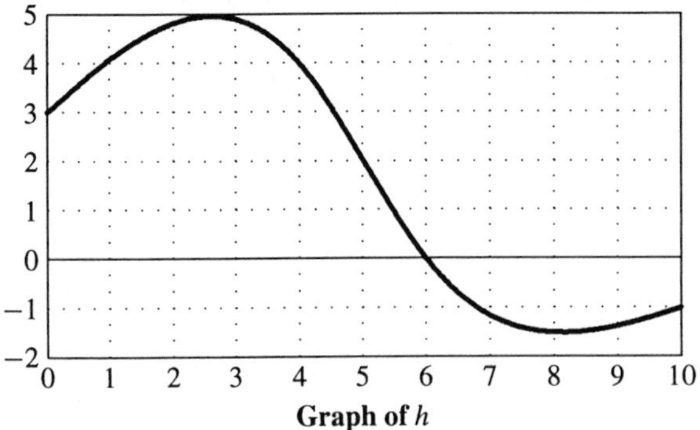

Graph of h

List, from smallest to largest: (i) $h'(5)$; (ii) the average value of h over the interval $[0, 10]$; (iii) the average rate of change of h over the interval $[0, 10]$; (iv) $\int_0^{10} h(x)\,dx$; (v) $\int_0^{5} h(x)\,dx$; (vi) $\int_6^{10} h(x)\,dx$.

5. Estimate each of the quantities (i)–(vi) listed in the previous problem.

6. Let h be the function shown graphically in Exercise 4 and suppose that $h(t)$ represents the *eastward* velocity (in meters/second) of an object moving along an east-west axis at time t seconds. Estimate each of the following quantities (use appropriate units!) and interpret in the language of velocity, distance, etc.

(a) $\int_0^{10} h(t)\,dt$

(b) $\frac{1}{10}\int_0^{10} h(t)\,dt$

(c) $\frac{1}{10}\big(h(10) - h(0)\big)$

(d) $|h(8)|$

(e) $\int_0^{10} |h(t)|\,dt$

(f) $\frac{1}{10}\int_0^{10} |h(t)|\,dt$

7. Suppose that a car travels on an east-west road with eastward velocity $v(t) = 60 - 20t$ mph at time t hours.

(a) Evaluate $\int_0^4 v(t)\,dt$. Interpret the answer in car talk.

(b) Find the average value of $v(t)$ on the interval $[0, 4]$. Show your result graphically.

(c) Let $s(t)$ be the car's speed at time t. Evaluate $\int_0^4 s(t)\,dt$ and interpret the answer in car talk.

(d) What is the car's average speed between $t = 0$ and $t = 4$?

8. Sketch the graph of a continuous function f such that $\int_{-2}^{3} f(t)\,dt = -10$ and

(a) $\int_{-2}^{3} |f(t)|\,dt = 10$.

(b) $\int_{-2}^{3} |f(t)|\,dt \neq 10$.

9. The graph of a function f is shown below.

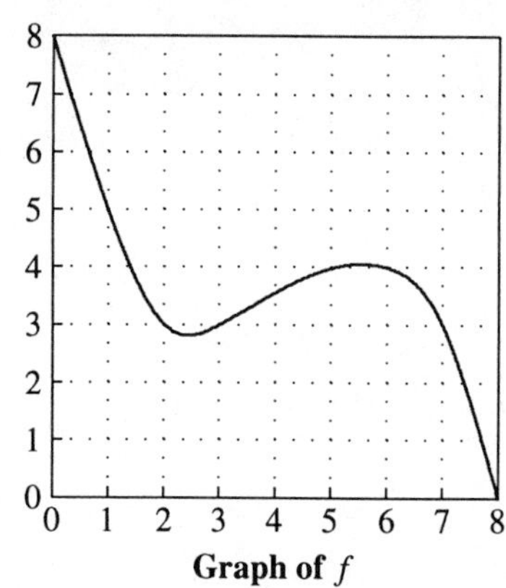

Graph of f

(a) Which of the following is the best estimate of $\int_1^6 f(x)\,dx$: $-24, 9, 20, 38$? Justify your answer.

(b) Find positive integers A and B such that $A \le \int_3^7 f(x)\,dx \le B$. Explain how you know that the values of A and B you chose have the desired properties.

(c) $\int_6^8 f(x)\,dx \approx 4$. Does this approximation overestimate or underestimate the exact value of the integral? Justify your answer.

(d) Estimate the average value of f over the interval $[0, 2]$.

10. For each function below, use a graph of f to evaluate $\int_0^2 f(x)\,dx$, $\int_1^4 f(x)\,dx$, $\int_{-5}^{-1} f(x)\,dx$, and $\int_{-2}^{3} f(x)\,dx$.

(a) $f(x) = 1$

(b) $f(x) = a$

(c) $f(x) = -a$

11. For each function below, use a graph of f to evaluate $\int_0^2 f(x)\,dx$, $\int_1^4 f(x)\,dx$, $\int_{-5}^{-1} f(x)\,dx$, and $\int_{-2}^{3} f(x)\,dx$.

    (a) $f(x) = 3x$

    (b) $f(x) = 2x + 5$

    (c) $f(x) = 5 - 2x$

12. The graph of a function f (shown below) consists of two straight lines and two quarter-circles.

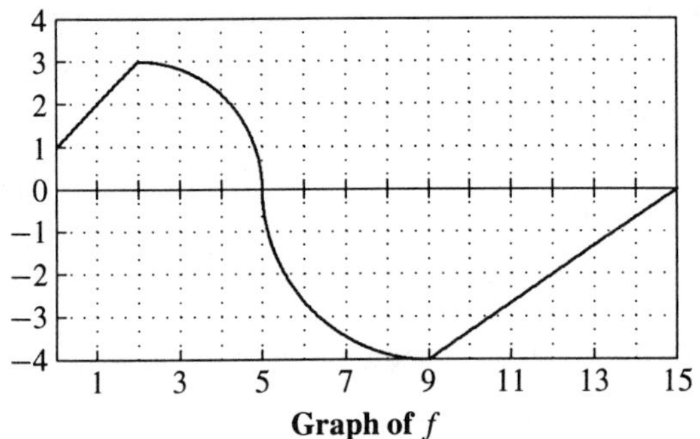

Graph of f

Evaluate each of the following integrals.

(a) $\int_0^2 f(x)\,dx$.

(b) $\int_2^5 f(x)\,dx$.

(c) $\int_0^5 f(x)\,dx$.

(d) $\int_5^9 f(x)\,dx$.

(e) $\int_5^5 f(x)\,dx$.

(f) $\int_0^{15} f(x)\,dx$.

(g) $\int_0^{15} |f(x)|\,dx$.

(h) $\int_{15}^{9} f(x)\,dx$.

(i) $\int_{12}^{15} f(x)\,dx$.

(j) $\int_9^{12} f(x)\,dx$.

13. Let f be the function shown graphically in the previous exercise.

    (a) Show that $\int_2^4 f(x)\,dx > 5$.

    (b) Show that $\int_6^9 f(x)\,dx < -9$.

    (c) Is $\int_0^6 f(x)\,dx < 10$?

    (d) Is $\int_2^7 f(x)\,dx$ positive or negative?

14. (a) Evaluate $\int_{-3}^{3} (x+2)\,dx$.

    (b) Evaluate $\int_{-3}^{3} |x+2|\,dx$.

    (c) Evaluate $\int_{-3}^{3} \big(|x|+2\big)\,dx$.

    (d) Evaluate $\int_{-3}^{3} \big(2-|x|\big)\,dx$.

15. Evaluate $\int_0^2 f(x)\,dx$, where $f(x) = \begin{cases} 1+x, & \text{if } 0 \le x \le 1 \\ 2-x, & \text{if } 1 < x \le 2. \end{cases}$

16. Evaluate $\int_0^1 \sqrt{1-(x-1)^2}\,dx$.

17. Evaluate $\int_1^3 \left(6 - \sqrt{4-(x-3)^2}\,dx\right)\,dx$.

18. Evaluate $\int_0^3 f(x)\,dx$, where $f(x) = \begin{cases} 1-\sqrt{1-x^2}, & \text{if } 0 \le x \le 1 \\ 1+\sqrt{4-(x-3)^2}, & \text{if } 1 < x \le 3. \end{cases}$

19. Explain why $\int_1^2 x^3\,dx = \int_3^4 (x-2)^3\,dx = \int_{-3}^{-2} (x+4)^3\,dx$.

20. Suppose that $\int_{-2}^5 f(x)\,dx = 18$, $\int_{-2}^5 g(x)\,dx = 5$, and $\int_{-2}^5 h(x)\,dx = -11$. Evaluate each of the following integrals.

(a) $\int_{-2}^5 \big(f(x)+g(x)\big)\,dx$

(b) $\int_{-2}^5 \big(f(x)+h(x)\big)\,dx$

(c) $\int_{-2}^5 \big(f(x)+g(x)-h(x)\big)\,dx$

(d) $\int_{-2}^5 3f(x)\,dx$

(e) $\int_{-2}^5 -4g(x)\,dx$

(f) $\int_5^{-2} f(x)\,dx$

(g) $\int_{-2}^5 \big(h(x)+1\big)\,dx$

(h) $\int_0^7 g(x-2)\,dx$

21. Suppose that (i) $\int_0^2 f(x)\,dx = 2$; (ii) $\int_1^2 f(x)\,dx = -1$; (iii) $\int_2^4 f(x)\,dx = 7$.

(a) Evaluate $\int_1^4 f(x)\,dx$.

(b) Evaluate $\int_0^4 3f(x)\,dx$.

(c) Evaluate $\int_0^1 f(x)\,dx$.

(d) Evaluate $\int_0^1 f(x+1)\,dx$.

(e) Evaluate $\int_0^1 \big(f(x)+1\big)\,dx$.

(f) Evaluate $\int_2^4 f(x-2)\,dx$.

(g) Evaluate $\int_2^4 \big(f(x)-2\big)\,dx$.

(h) Explain why f must be negative somewhere in the interval $[1,2]$.

(i) Explain why $f(x) \ge 3$ for some values of x in the interval $[2,4]$.

(j) Draw the graph of a function f with properties (i)–(iii).

22. Suppose that f is a function such that $\int_0^3 f(x)\,dx = -1$.

(a) Suppose that f is an *even* function. Explain why $\int_{-3}^3 f(x)\,dx = -2$.

(b) If f is an *odd* function, what is the value of $\int_{-3}^3 f(x)\,dx$? Explain.

23. Evaluate each of the following integrals using graphical arguments.

(a) $\int_0^\pi \cos x\,dx$

(b) $\int_{\pi/2}^{3\pi/2} \sin x\,dx$

(c) $\int_{-2}^2 \big(7x^5+3\big)\,dx$

(d) $\int_{-1}^1 \big(4x^3-2x\big)\,dx$

24. Evaluate each of the following integrals using graphical arguments and the fact that $\int_0^\pi \sin x\,dx = 2$.

(a) $\int_0^{2\pi} \sin x\,dx$

(b) $\int_0^{2\pi} |\sin x|\,dx$

(c) $\int_0^\pi (\sin x+1)\,dx$

(d) $\int_0^{\pi/2} \sin x\,dx$

(e) $\int_{-\pi/2}^{\pi/2} \cos x\,dx$

(f) $\int_0^{\pi/2} (\cos x + x)\,dx$

(g) $\int_0^{100\pi} \sin x\,dx$

(h) $\int_0^{100\pi} |\sin x|\,dx$

(i) $\int_0^{100\pi} \cos x\,dx$

25. Explain why $\displaystyle\int_1^3 \frac{1-x}{x^2}\,dx < \int_1^2 \frac{1-x}{x^2}\,dx$.

26. Is $\int_0^2 \left(2x^3 - x^2\right) dx$ greater than $\int_0^2 \left(3x^2 + x\right) dx$? Justify your answer.

27. Suppose that f is continuous and nonconstant on $[a, b]$. Show that if m and M are constants such that $m \le f(x) \le M$ when $x \in [a, b]$, then $m(b-a) < \int_a^b f(x)\,dt < M(b-a)$.

28. (a) Explain why $\int_0^{2\pi} (1 + \cos x)\,dx \ge 0$.

    (b) Show that $\int_0^{2\pi} (1 + \cos x)\,dx > 0$. [HINT: Consider the intervals $[0, \pi]$ and $[\pi, 2\pi]$ separately.]

29. Show that $0 \le \int_0^{\pi} x \sin x\,dx \le \pi^2/2$.

30. Show that $\pi/6 \le \int_{\pi/6}^{\pi/2} \sin x\,dx \le \pi/3$.

31. Show that $-\pi/3 \le \int_{2\pi/3}^{\pi} \cos x\,dx \le -\pi/6$.

32. (a) Prove that $2x/\pi \le \sin x \le x$ when $0 \le x \le 1$.

    (b) Use part (a) to show that $\pi/16 \le \int_0^{\pi/4} \sin x\,dx \le \pi^2/32$.

33. (a) Use the racetrack principle to show that $1 + x \le e^x \le 1 + 3x$ when $0 \le x \le 1$.

    (b) Use part (a) to find upper and lower bounds on $\int_0^1 e^x\,dx$.

34. (a) Show that $\pi(1 + 1/e) \le \int_0^{2\pi} e^{\sin x}\,dx \le \pi(1 + e)$.

    (b) Use the result in part (a) to find upper and lower bounds for $\int_0^{50\pi} e^{\sin x}\,dx$.

35. (a) Show that $\pi/6 \le \int_0^{\pi/2} \cos x\,dx \le 5\pi/12$. [HINT: $1/2 \le \cos x \le 1$ when $0 \le x \le \pi/3$.]

    (b) Using ideas similar to those in part (a), find upper and lower bounds on the value of $\int_0^{\sqrt{\pi/2}} \cos\left(x^2\right)\,dx$.

36. (a) Suppose that $f(x) \ge 0$ when $0 \le x \le 1$. Show that $\int_0^1 x^k f(x)\,dx \le \int_0^1 f(x)\,dx$ for all integers $k \ge 0$.

    (b) Does the result in part (a) remain valid if the assumption "$f(x) \ge 0$ when $0 \le x \le 1$" is not made? Explain.

37. Show that $\int_0^{\pi/4} \cos(2x)\,dx \ne \int_0^{\pi/2} \cos x\,dx$. Which integral is larger? Justify your answer.

38. Show that $\int_0^{\sqrt{\pi}} \sin\left(x^2\right)\,dx \ne \int_0^{\pi} \sin x\,dx$. Which integral is larger? Justify your answer.

39. Show that $\int_0^{\pi/2} \sqrt{1 + \cos(2x)}\,dx = \sqrt{2}\int_0^{\pi/2} \cos x\,dx$.

40. Show that $0 \le \int_0^{\sqrt{\pi/2}} \sin\left(x^2\right)\,dx \le \sqrt{\pi/2} - 1 + \frac{1}{2}\sin 1 \approx 0.674$.

41. Suppose that f is an odd function and continuous everywhere. Explain why the average value of f over any interval $[-a, a]$ is zero.

42. Suppose that f is an even function and continuous everywhere. Explain why the average value of f over the interval $[-a, a]$ is equal to the average value of f over the interval $[0, a]$.

43. Suppose that f is a continuous function and that $-2 \le f(x) \le 5$ when $1 \le x \le 3$. Show that the average value of f lies in the interval $[-2, 5]$.

44. Suppose that f is a continuous function. If the average value of f over the interval $[0, 1]$ is 2 and the average value of f over the interval $[1, 3]$ is 3, what is the average value of f over the interval $[0, 3]$?

45. Suppose that f is a continuous function. If the average value of f over the interval $[-3, 1]$ is 2 and the average value of f over the interval $[-3, 7]$ is 5, what is the average value of f over the interval $[1, 7]$?

46. Show that the expression $\int_a^b \left(f(x) - c\right)^2 dx$ assumes its minimum value when c is the average value of f on the interval $[a, b]$.

47. Suppose that f is continuous on $[0, 1]$. Explain why $\int_0^1 f(x)\,dx = \int_0^1 f(1-x)\,dx$.

48. Suppose that f is continuous on $[a, b]$. Show that $\left|\int_a^b f(x)\,dx\right| \le \int_a^b |f(x)|\,dx$. [HINT: $-|f(x)| \le f(x) \le |f(x)|$.]

49. Suppose that f and g are continuous on $[a, b]$ and $\int_a^b f(x)\,dx \le \int_a^b g(x)\,dx$.

    (a) Must $f(x) \le g(x)$ for every x in $[a, b]$? If so, explain why. If not, give a counterexample.

    (b) Must there be a number c such that $a \le c \le b$ and $f(c) \le g(c)$? If so, explain why. If not, give a counterexample.

50. Archimedes (ca. 250 B.C.E.) proved that the area under a parabolic arch is $2bh/3$ where b is the width of the base of the arch and h is the height. [NOTE: Archimedes actually proved a more general theorem about the area of any region cut off from a parabola by a line.]

    (a) Use Archimedes' result to show that $\int_{-a}^a x^2\,dx = 2a^3/3$. [HINT: Draw the curve $y = x^2$ and the line $y = a^2$.]

    (b) Use part (a) and the fact that x^2 is an even function to show that $\int_0^a x^2\,dx = a^3/3$. [HINT: $\int_{-a}^a x^2\,dx = \int_{-a}^0 x^2\,dx + \int_0^a x^2\,dx$.]

    (c) Use part (b) to show that $\int_a^b x^2\,dx = (b^3 - a^3)/3$. [HINT: $\int_a^b x^2\,dx = \int_0^b x^2\,dx - \int_0^a x^2\,dx$.]

51. Let $f(x) = 2x + 3$.

    (a) Sketch a graph of f in the viewing window $[1, 2] \times [5, 9]$.

    (b) Evaluate $\int_1^2 f(x)\,dx$. Shade the region of the part (a) graph represented by this integral.

    (c) Show that $f^{-1}(x) = (x-3)/2$.

    (d) Evaluate $\int_5^9 f^{-1}(x)\,dx$ and shade the region of the part (a) graph represented by this integral.

    (e) Verify that $\int_1^2 f(x)\,dx = 2f(2) - f(1) - \int_{f(1)}^{f(2)} f^{-1}(x)\,dx$.

52. Suppose that f is a continuous function and invertible on $[a, b]$. Then it can be shown that $\int_a^b f(x)\,dx = bf(b) - af(a) - \int_{f(a)}^{f(b)} f^{-1}(x)\,dx$.

(a) Give a graphical proof of this result when $0 < a < b$, and $0 < f(a) < f(b)$. [HINT: Draw a sketch of f in the viewing window $[0, b] \times [0, f(b)]$.]

(b) Show that $\int_1^e \ln x\, dx = e - \int_0^1 e^x\, dx$.

(c) Show that $\int_a^b \sqrt{x}\, dx = b^{3/2} - a^{3/2} - \int_{\sqrt{a}}^{\sqrt{b}} x^2\, dx$.

53. Use results stated in Exercises 50 and 52 to show that $\int_0^a \sqrt{x}\, dx = 2a^{3/2}/3$.

5.2 The area function

In the previous section we defined the integral $\int_a^b f$ to be the *signed area* of the region from $x = a$ to $x = b$, bounded above or below by the graph of f. For given f, a, and b, this area is a certain fixed *number*.➻

Positive, negative, or zero!

In this section we define and study a *function* based on the signed area bounded by the graph of f. This **area function**, which we'll denote A_f, is "built" from f, using the integral.

We've played the new-function-from-old game before. In the most important case, we built the *derivative* function f' from an "original" function f, and then studied what each tells about the other. Here we repeat the process, this time with f and A_f. The relationship between f and A_f will prove remarkably similar to that between f' and f.

Defining the area function A_f

First the formal definition:

> **Definition:** Let f be a function and a any point of its domain. For any input x, the **area function** A_f is defined by the rule
>
> $$A_f(x) = \int_a^x f(t)\,dt = \text{the signed area defined by } f, \text{ from } a \text{ to } x.$$

A "generic" picture illustrates the idea:

The area function: $A_f(x)$ = the shaded area

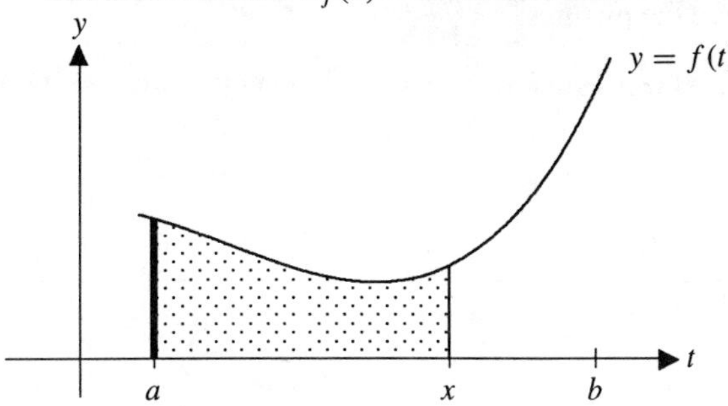

The idea is best understood through pictorial examples. First, three brief remarks:

Variable names: why so many? Why did we use another variable, t, in the defining expression $A_f(x) = \int_a^x f(t)\,dt$? Because x was already taken; we used it to denote the right-hand boundary of the defining region. To avoid using x in two different ways, we introduced another variable.

The domain of A_f. For which inputs x does the rule $A_f(x) = \int_a^x f$ make sense?

Barring bad behavior➻ of f, A_f has the same domain as f itself. In particular, $A_f(x)$ makes sense even if x is to the *left* of a; in this case we use the sign convention➻ $\int_a^x f = -\int_x^a f$.

E.g., discontinuities.

We discussed it in the previous section.

The choice of a. The role of a is to fix one edge (the *left* edge, in the picture above) of the region whose area gives $A_f(x)$—the other edge varies freely.

As the definition says, *any* a in the domain of f is a legal choice. We'll see below that different choices of a give different (but only slightly different) functions A_f.

■ **Example 1.** Let $f(x) = 3$ and $a = 0$. Describe the area function $A_f(x) = \int_0^x f(t)\,dt$ for positive inputs x. Does A_f have a simple formula?

A rectangle with height 3 and base x has area $3x$.

For now we ignore negative inputs x; we'll return to them later.

Solution: Because $f(x) = 3$, $A_f(x) = 3x$. The first picture below shows why; in the second, graphs of f and A_f appear together.

$A_f(x) = \int_0^x 3\,dt = 3x$

If $f(x) = 3$, then $A_f(x) = 3x$

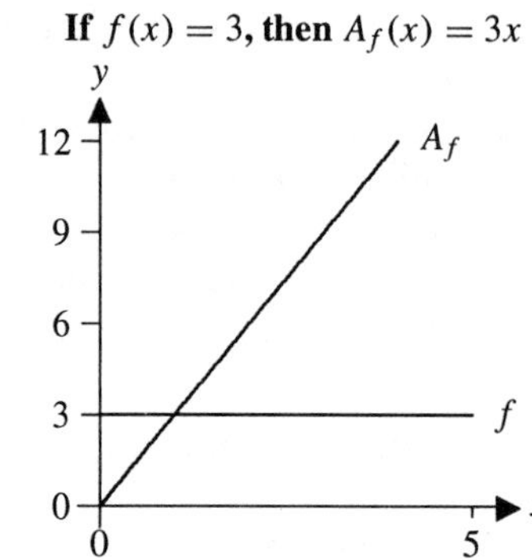

Notice too that $A_f(x) = 3x$ is an *antiderivative* of $f(x) = 3$. This result is no accident, as we'll see. □

We'll return to this important fact soon.

■ **Example 2.** As before, let $f(x) = 3$ and $a = 0$. Discuss the area function $A_f(x) = \int_0^x f(t)\,dt$ for *negative* values of x. Does the formula $A_f(x) = 3x$ still hold?

Solution: Yes—$A_f(x) = 3x$ for *all* values of x. The key step is a careful look at *signs*. Here are the pictures:

$A_f(x)$ for negative x

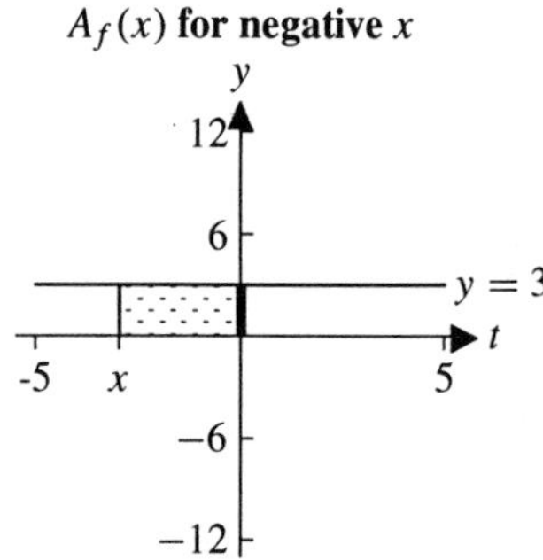

If $f(x) = 3$, then $A_f(x) = 3x$

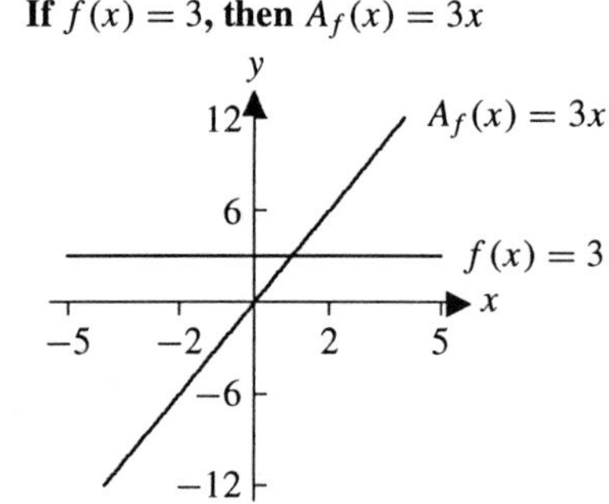

From the previous section.

To make sense of them, recall how we handle "right to left" integrals: Since $x < 0$,

$$\int_0^x f = -\int_x^0 f = -\text{(shaded area)}.$$

Since $x < 0$ and the rectangle has height 3, $3x$ is, just as claimed, *minus* the shaded area.

Combining this example with the last one leads to this conclusion:

If $f(x) = 3$ and $a = 0$, then $A_f(x) = \int_0^x f = 3x$ for *all* x.

□

See the first picture in this section if you've forgotten.

A happy moral. What $\int_a^x f$ means geometrically is clear if $x \geq a$. If $x < a$, things look trickier; the previous example was all about this possibility.

Working the previous example took some careful analysis of plus and minus signs. After the dust settled, though, the happiest possible outcome was revealed:

The same formula for $A_f(x)$ works for *all* x.

Thus the cases $x < a$ and $x \geq a$, though apparently different, lead to the same result.

This is evidence that our signed area conventions are not just convenient, but "right."

The same principle holds for any function f defined by a reasonable formula. Since it does, we'll seldom worry about (or even mention) the issue of whether $x < a$ or $x \geq a$.

■ **Example 3.** Consider the linear function $f(x) = x$ and the area function $A_f(x) = \int_0^x t\,dt$. What's A_f now?

Solution: As the left graph below shows, the region defining $A_f(x)$ for a positive input x is a *triangle*, with base x and height x. The formula for A_f, therefore, is

We'll skip the case of negative x, for reasons outlined above.

$$A_f(x) = \frac{\text{base} \times \text{height}}{2} = \frac{x^2}{2}.$$

Graphs of $f(x)$ and $A_f(x)$ appear together at the right.

$A_f(x) = \int_0^x t\,dt = x^2/2$

If $f(x) = x$, then $A_f(x) = x^2/2$

Again, A_f turns out to be an antiderivative of f. □

This is still no accident. Stay tuned.

■ **Example 4.** **(Another f, same a.)** Consider the new linear function, $f(x) = 2 - x$. Find the new area function $A_f(x) = \int_0^x f$. Is A_f again an antiderivative for f?

Solution: The usual area picture applies; area below the x-axis counts as negative.

Notice the different shadings above and below the t-axis.

$A_f(x) = \int_0^x (2 - t)\,dt$

If $f(x) = 2 - x$, then $A_f(x) = 2x - x^2/2$

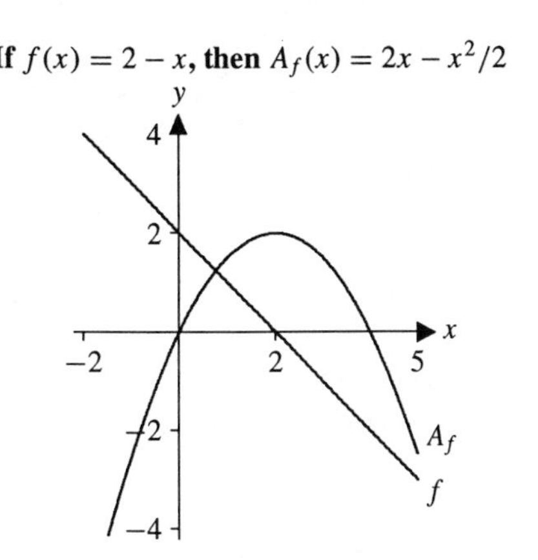

With a little care, one can use triangles to find the net shaded area. On the left-hand

Or trapezoids, if x < 2.

graph above the upper triangle has area 2; the lower triangle has area $(x-2)^2/2$. Thus the net area, for given x, is

Check the algebra.

$$A_f(x) = 2 - \frac{(x-2)^2}{2} = 2x - \frac{x^2}{2}.$$

(Note: The picture shows a value of x greater than 2. If $0 < x < 2$, the picture is different but the resulting formula is the same.) The graphs of both f and A_f appear at the right, above.

The exercises pursue this point further.

Another approach to the problem is to use additive properties of the integral and ideas from earlier examples:

Perhaps easier.

cf. Section 5.1.

$$A_f(x) = \int_0^x (2-t)\,dt = \int_0^x 2\,dt - \int_0^x t\,dt = 2x - \frac{x^2}{2}.$$

Either way the point is the same:

In all examples so far, the area function A_f is an antiderivative of f.

□

■ **Example 5.** **(Same f, another a.)** Consider the same linear function, $f(x) = 2-x$, this time setting $a=1$, so that $A_f(x) = \int_1^x f$. What's the area function now?

Solution: The only difference from the previous example concerns the lower endpoint of integration. Thus the new function A_f differs from the old one only by the *area of the trapezoidal region from $x=0$ to $x=1$.* In symbols:

This area is 3/2—convince yourself.

$$\begin{aligned} A_f(x) &= \int_1^x f(t)\,dt = \int_0^x f(t)\,dt - \int_0^1 f(t)\,dt \\ &= 2x - \frac{x^2}{2} - \frac{3}{2}. \end{aligned}$$

The graphs support all this:

$A_f(x) = \int_1^x (2-t)\,dt$

If $f(x) = x-2$ **and** $a=1$ **then** $A_f(x) = 2x - x^2/2 - 3/2$

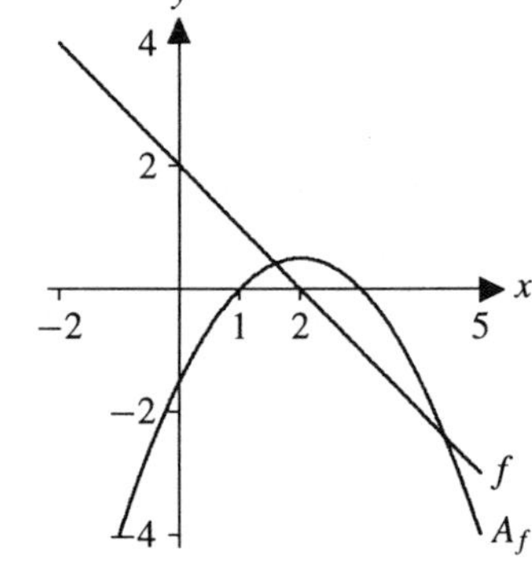

Yet again, A_f is an antiderivative of f; this time, the one for which $A_f(1) = 0$. □

Two antiderivatives of the same f can differ only by a constant, as they do here.

In each example above we've used an elementary area formula to find an explicit algebraic expression for the area function. In the next example, no such simple formula is available.

■ **Example 6.** Let $f(x) = 1/x$ and $A_f(x) = \int_1^x f(t)dt$. Discuss the area function A_f. Does it look familiar?

Solution: The graph below left shows $f(x)$; the shaded area represents $A_f(3)$:

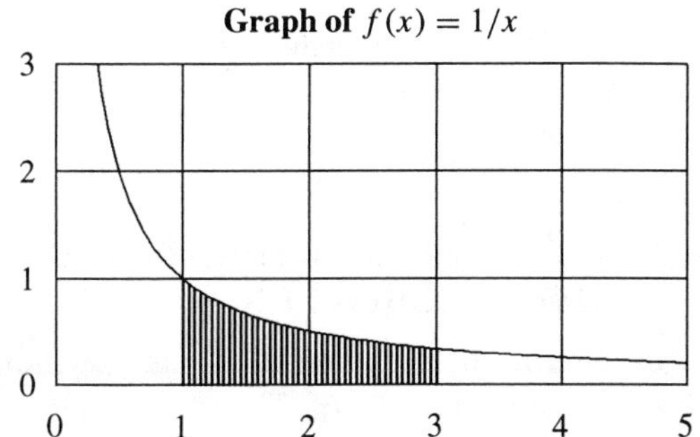

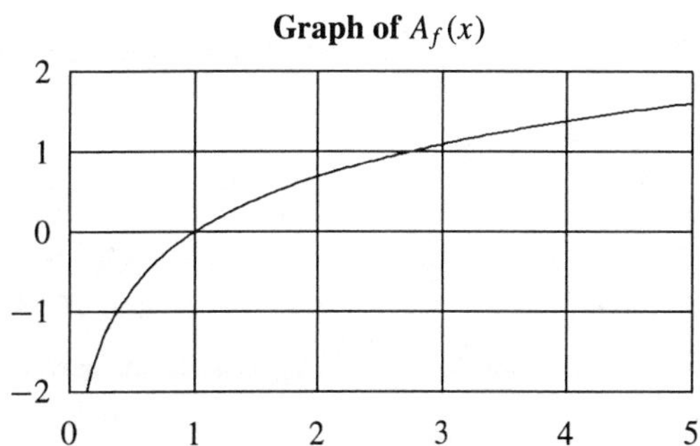

Values of A_f can be estimated, using the grid. The shaded area, for example, seems to be a little more than one unit. By plotting such estimates we can produce, at least approximately, a graph of A_f, like the one at upper right.➻

Note that $A_f(x) < 0$ for $x < 1$. Do you see why?

The graph of A_f should look familiar—in fact, it shows the natural logarithm function. We'll explain this striking result in the next section. □

Properties of A_f: what the examples show

In every example above, direct calculation showed the area function A_f to be an antiderivative of f. This was no accident. Quite the contrary:

> **Theorem 2. (The fundamental theorem of calculus, informal version.)** For *any* well-behaved function f and any "base point" a, A_f is an antiderivative of f.

We'll discuss and prove this important theorem➻ in the next section. In the rest of this section, we amass evidence for it.

One of the most important in mathematics.

To do so, we'll list various properties of A_f. Each follows directly from the definition, and each bolsters the claim that $A'_f = f$. Added to the concrete examples above, they build a strong case for the fundamental theorem of calculus.

Properties of A_f

Let f be a continuous function, a a point of its domain, and $A_f(x) = \int_a^x f(t)\,dt$. Then:

- $A_f(a) = 0$.
- Where f is positive, A_f is increasing.
- Where f is negative, A_f is decreasing.
- Where f is zero, A_f has a stationary point.
- Where f is increasing, A_f is concave up.
- Where f is decreasing, A_f is concave down.

Examples—in graphical form, especially—are the best evidence for each claim.➻ Each claim restates or sharpens the general principle of the fundamental theorem.

Use, e.g., the graphs in Example 5 to convince yourself.

Exercises

1. Let $f(x) = x$ and $A_f(x) = \int_0^x t\,dt$. It was shown in the text that $A_f(x) = x^2/2$ when $x > 0$. Show that this formula is correct even when $x < 0$.

2. Let $F(x) = \int_0^x f(t)\,dt$, $G(x) = \int_1^x f(t)\,dt$, and $H(x) = \int_{-2}^x f(t)\,dt$.

   (a) Suppose that $f(x) = 1$. Find symbolic expressions for the functions F, G, and H. Are F, G, and H antiderivatives of f?

   (b) Suppose that $f(x) = 3x$. Find symbolic expressions for the functions F, G, and H. Are F, G, and H antiderivatives of f?

   (c) Suppose that $f(x) = 3x+1$. Find symbolic expressions for the functions F, G, and H. Are F, G, and H antiderivatives of f? [HINT: Use your answers to parts (a) and (b).]

3. Let $F(x) = \int_0^x f(t)\,dt$, $G(x) = \int_2^x f(t)\,dt$, and $H(x) = \int_{-1}^x f(t)\,dt$.

   (a) Suppose that $f(x) = a$, a positive constant. Find symbolic expressions for the functions F, G, and H. Are F, G, and H antiderivatives of f?

   (b) Suppose that $f(x) = bx$ where b is a positive constant. Find symbolic expressions for the functions F, G, and H. Are F, G, and H antiderivatives of f?

   (c) Suppose that $f(x) = a + bx$ where a and b are positive constants. Find symbolic expressions for the functions F, G, and H. Are F, G, and H antiderivatives of f?

4. Let a be a constant, $f(x) = 2 - x$, and $A_f(x) = \int_a^x f(t)\,dt$.

   (a) Evaluate $A_f(a)$.

   (b) Find a symbolic expression for $A_f(x)$.
   [HINT: $\int_a^x (2-t)\,dt = \int_0^x (2-t)\,dt - \int_0^a (2-t)\,dt$.]

   (c) Show that A_f is an antiderivative of f.

   (d) On the same axes, plot f and A_f for $a = 0$, $a = 2$, and $a = -1$.

5. Let $f(x) = \sin x$ and $A_f(x) = \int_0^x f(x)\,dx$.

   (a) It can be shown that $A_f(\pi/2) = 1$. Use this fact to evaluate $A_f(\pi)$, $A_f(3\pi/2)$, $A_f(2\pi)$, $A_f(-\pi/2)$, $A_f(-\pi)$, $A_f(-3\pi/2)$, and $A_f(-2\pi)$.

   (b) Explain why A_f is a periodic function. [HINT: Use the fact that f is 2π-periodic function.]

   (c) Show that $0 \le A_f(x) \le 2$.

   (d) Sketch a graph of f and $A_f(x)$ on the same axes.

6. Use the fact that $\int_0^{\pi/2} \cos x\,dx = 1$ to show that $-1 \le \int_0^x \cos t\,dt \le 1$.

7. Suppose that f is a continuous function and that $\int_0^x f(t)\,dt = \sin\left(x^2\right)$.

   (a) Show that $\int_{\sqrt{\pi/2}}^x f(t)\,dt = \sin\left(x^2\right) - 1$.

   (b) Find an expression for $\int_{-\sqrt{3\pi/2}}^x f(t)\,dt$.

8. Let $F(x) = \int_a^x f(t)\,dt$ and $G(x) = \int_b^x f(t)\,dt$, where a and b are constants, and f is a continuous function. Show that $G(x) = F(x) + C$, where C is a constant.

9. Suppose that F is an antiderivative of a differentiable function f.

   (a) If F is increasing on $[a, b]$, what is true about f?

   (b) If f is negative on $[a, b]$, what is true about F?

   (c) If f' is positive on $[a, b]$, what is true about F?

   (d) If F is concave down on $[a, b]$, what is true about f'?

   (e) Suppose that G is another antiderivative of f. What relationship exists between F and G?

10. Let $f(x) = 2 - |x|$ and $A_f(x) = \int_0^x f(t)\,dt$.

    (a) Find a symbolic expression for A_f.

    (b) Plot f and A_f on the same axes.

    (c) Where is A_f increasing? What is true about f on on each of these intervals?

    (d) Where is A_f decreasing? What is true about f on each of these intervals?

    (e) Where does A_f have local extrema? What is true about f at each of these points?

    (f) Where is A_f concave up? What is true about f on each of these intervals?

    (g) Where is A_f concave down? What is true about f on each of these intervals?

    (h) Does A_f have any inflection points? If so, where are they located? What is true about f at each of these points?

    (i) How would your answers to parts (c)–(h) change if the definition of A_f were changed to $A_f(x) = \int_3^x f(t)\,dt$?

11. Let $A_f(x) = \int_0^x f(t)\,dt$ where f is the function graphed below.

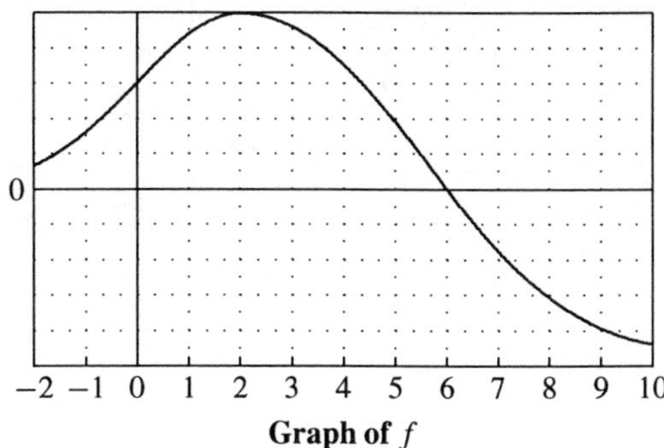

Graph of f

    (a) Which is larger: $A_f(1)$ or $A_f(5)$? Justify your answer.

    (b) Which is larger: $A_f(7)$ or $A_f(10)$? Justify your answer.

    (c) Which is larger: $A_f(-2)$ or $A_f(-1)$? Justify your answer.

    (d) Where is A_f increasing?

    (e) Explain why A_f has a local extremum at $x = 6$. Is this a local maximum or a local minimum?

(f) Let $F(x) = \int_{-2}^{x} f(t)\,dt$. Explain why $A_f(x) = F(x) + C$ where C is a negative constant.

(g) Rank the five numbers 0, $A_f(-1) - A_f(-2)$, $A_f(0) - A_f(-1)$, $A_f(1) - A_f(0)$, and $A_f(2) - A_f(1)$ in increasing order.

(h) The numbers $A_f(4) - A_f(3)$, $A_f(5) - A_f(4)$, $A_f(6) - A_f(5)$, $A_f(7) - A_f(6)$, and $A_f(8) - A_f(7)$ can each be interpreted as the slope of a secant line of A_f. What do these values suggest about the concavity of A_f on the interval $[3, 8]$?

12. Let $A_f(x) = \int_{c}^{x} f(t)\,dt$, where c is a constant and f is a continuous function.

(a) Prove that if f is positive on $[a, b]$, then A_f is increasing on $[a, b]$. [HINT: Let y and z be numbers such that $a \le y < z \le b$. Compare $A_f(y)$ and $A_f(z)$.]

(b) Use part (a) to show that if f is negative on $[a, b]$, then A_f is decreasing on $[a, b]$. [HINT: The function g defined by $g(x) = -f(x)$ is positive wherever f is negative.]

(c) Use parts (a) and (b) to show that A_f has a local extremum wherever f changes sign.

13. Let $A_f(x) = \int_{c}^{x} f(t)\,dt$, where c is a constant and f is a continuous function.

(a) Prove that if f is increasing on $[a, b]$, then A_f is concave up on $[a, b]$. [HINT: A function f is concave up on $[a, b]$ if and only if $\big(f(x) - f(a)\big)/(x - a) < \big(f(b) - f(x)\big)/(b - x)$ for every $x \in (a, b)$.]

(b) Use part (a) to show that if f is decreasing on $[a, b]$, then A_f is concave down on $[a, b]$.

(c) Suppose that f has a local extremum at a. Explain why A_f has an inflection point at a.

14. Let $G(x) = \int_{-3}^{x} f(t)\,dt$ and $H(x) = \int_{2}^{x} f(t)\,dt$ where f is the function graphed below. [NOTE: The graph of f is made up of straight lines and a semicircle.]

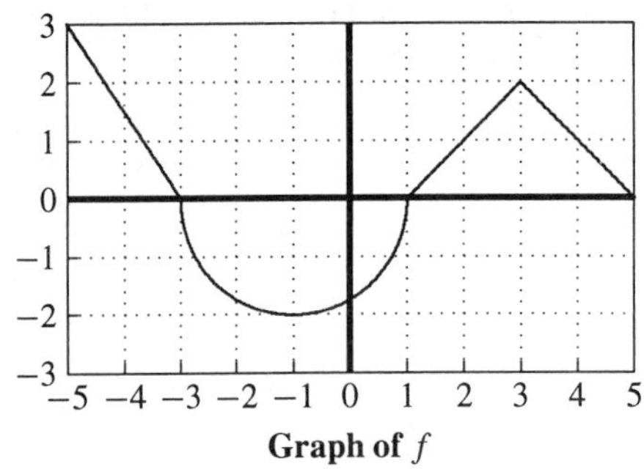

Graph of f

(a) How are the values of $G(x)$ and $H(x)$ related? Give a geometric explanation of this relationship.

(b) On which subintervals of $[-5, 5]$, if any, is H increasing?

(c) Explain why G has a local minimum at $x = 1$.

(d) Where in the interval $[-5, -2]$ does G achieve its minimum value? Its maximum value? What are these values?

(e) Where in the interval $[-5, -5]$ does H achieve its minimum value? Its maximum value? What are these values?

(f) On which subintervals of $[-5, 5]$, if any, is G concave down?

(g) Where does H have points of inflection?

15. Let $F(x) = \int_a^x f(t)\,dt$ and $G(x) = \int_b^x g(t)\,dt$, where f and g are continuous functions. Suppose that $F(c) = G(c)$ and $f(x) \le g(x)$ when $x \ge c$. Show that $F(x) \le G(x)$ when $x \ge c$.

16. (a) Use the figure below to show that $\int_0^x \sqrt{1-t^2}\,dt = \frac{1}{2}x\sqrt{1-x^2} + \frac{1}{2}\arcsin x$ when $-1 \le x \le 1$.

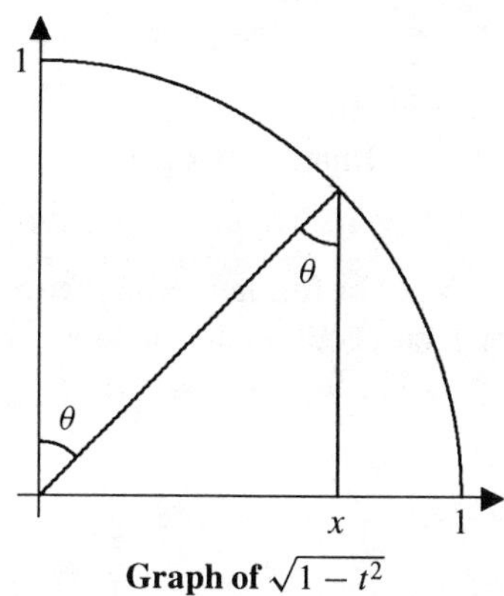

Graph of $\sqrt{1-t^2}$

(b) Let $f(x) = \sqrt{1-x^2}$ and let $A_f(x) = \int_0^x f(t)\,dt$. Show that A_f is an antiderivative of f.

17. Let $f(x) = \sqrt{1-x^2}$ and let $A_f(x) = \int_{-1/2}^x f(t)\,dt$.

(a) Use the result stated in part (a) of the previous exercise to find a symbolic expression for A_f.

(b) Is A_f an antiderivative of f? Justify your answer.

18. Let $a > 0$ be a constant. Use a sketch similar to that given in Exercise 16 to find an expression for $\int_0^x \sqrt{a^2-t^2}\,dt$ when $-a \le x \le a$. [HINT: Check that your expression produces the correct value when $x = a$.]

19. Let $f(x) = x^2$ and $A_f(x) = \int_0^x f(t)\,dt$.

(a) Use the result of Exercise 50 in the previous section to find a symbolic expression for $A_f(x)$.

(b) Is A_f an antiderivative of f? Justify your answer.

20. Let $f(x) = x^2$ and $A_f(x) = \int_{-3}^x f(t)\,dt$.

(a) Use the result of Exercise 50 in the previous section to find a symbolic expression for $A_f(x)$.

(b) Is A_f an antiderivative of f? Justify your answer.

5.3 The fundamental theorem of calculus

What the theorem says

In the last section we defined and studied the *area function* A_f, built from an original function f and a "base point" a. All evidence so far points irresistibly to this conclusion:

A_f *is an* antiderivative *of* f.

The formal statement of this fact is the most important theorem of our subject. Here it is, complete with mathematical fine print:

> **Theorem 3. (The fundamental theorem of calculus, formal version.)** Let f be a continuous function, defined on an open interval I containing a. The function A_f with rule
>
> $$A_f(x) = \int_a^x f(t)\,dt$$
>
> is defined for every x in I, and $\dfrac{d}{dx}\big(A_f(x)\big) = f(x)$.

Our shorthand.

We'll say much more about the FTC, and provide a proof at the end of this section. First, some remarks.

Why continuous? Requiring f to be *continuous* assures that the integral $\int_a^x f$ *exists*. If f is *discontinuous* (e.g., blows up somewhere) A_f may have problems, too.

Why is I open? Working on an *open interval* I is a technical convenience. Doing so avoids troubles that might occur if gaps and endpoints were permitted.

In other symbols. The last equation of the FTC is sometimes written as follows:

$$\frac{d}{dx}\left(\int_a^x f(t)\,dt\right) = f(x).$$

Which form is clearer?

This form avoids the symbol A_f, but requires more careful unpacking.

■ **Example 1.** Let $f(x) = 2x\sin(x^2)$ and let $A_f(x) = \int_0^x f(t)\,dt$. Find a symbolic formula for A_f; interpret results graphically.

For rectangles, triangles, trapezoids, etc.

Solution: For the simple functions of the last section, we used elementary area formulas to find explicit formulas for A_f. Here, simple formulas aren't enough. What, for instance, is $A_f(2)$, shown shaded below?

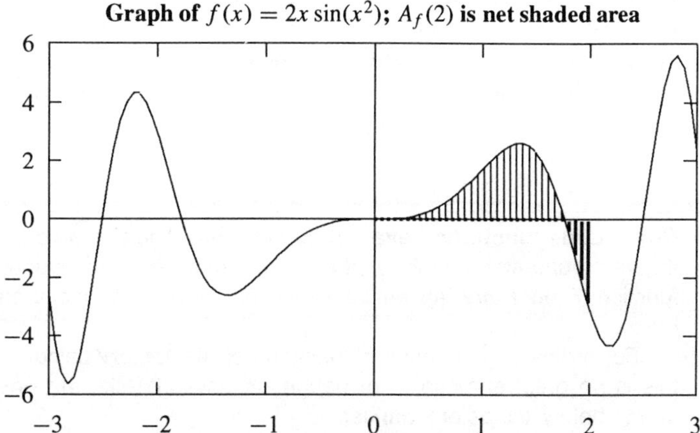

The FTC solves our problem. It says that A_f is *some* antiderivative of f; all we need do is find the right one.

Notice first that for any constant C, $F(x) = -\cos(x^2) + C$ is an antiderivative of $f(x) = 2x\sin(x^2)$. *Every* antiderivative of f—including A_f—has this form. Therefore for *some* constant C,

Differentiate to see for yourself.

See the fact that follows this example.

$$A_f(x) = -\cos(x^2) + C.$$

To choose the "right" value of C, we use the fact that $A_f(0) = 0$. In other words,

Why? Because $\int_0^0 f = 0$.

$$A_f(0) = 0 = -\cos 0 + C \implies C = 1.$$

We've found our formula: $A_f(x) = -\cos(x^2) + 1$.

The graphs below agree; the A_f graph seems, as it should, to describe the growth of signed area based at 0.

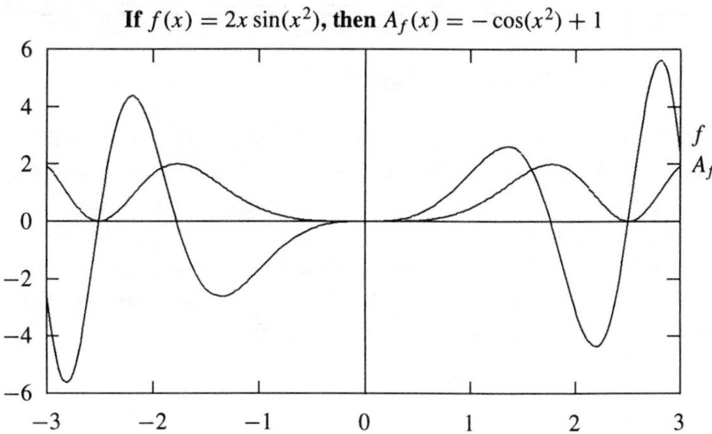

Notice, finally, that $A_f(2) = -\cos(4) + 1 \approx 1.65364$. □

Is this result reasonable, given the general size of units?

Finding *all* antiderivatives

In the previous example we claimed that any two antiderivatives of the function $f(x) = 2x\sin(x^2)$ may differ only by an additive constant. This important principle deserves specific mention:

> **Fact:** Suppose that $F'(x) = G'(x)$ for all x in an interval I. Then for some constant C, $F(x) = G(x) + C$ for all x in I.

The fact means, in practice, that finding *one* antiderivative for a function f on an interval I is (almost) tantamount to finding *all* antiderivatives: if $F(x)$ is *any* antiderivative, every other antiderivative is of the form $F(x) + C$.

This fact, although most useful for *integrals*, is really a property of *derivatives*; it follows from the mean value theorem.

We stated (and proved) it in Section 3.7. See page 298.

Continuous functions have antiderivatives. The fundamental theorem guarantees (among other things) that every continuous function f on I *has* an antiderivative on I—namely, the area function A_f.

For ordinary, well-behaved functions of elementary calculus, this is no great surprise. For naughtier functions, like the one shown below, things are murkier.

Does $f(x) = x\sin(1/x)$ have an antiderivative?

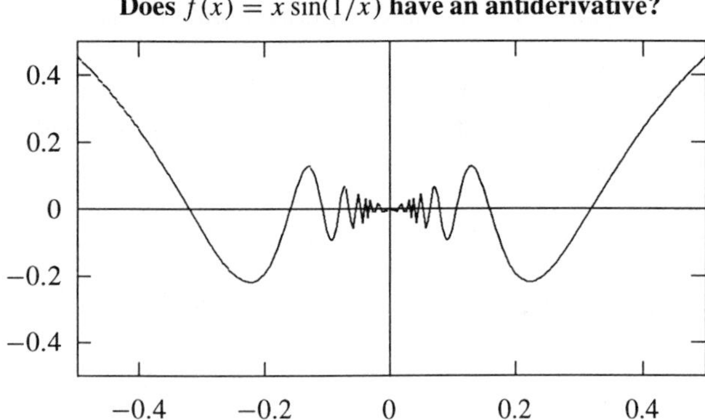

The fundamental theorem says that, naughty or not, f *has* an antiderivative. (*Finding* one in symbolic form may be difficult or impossible—the FTC offers no help there.)

Why the FTC is fundamental

The FTC deserves its high-sounding name for both theoretical and practical reasons. It's fundamental *theoretically* because it connects the two main concepts of the calculus: the derivative and the integral. In geometric terms, the FTC relates the tangent line problem to the area problem: each is a sort of inverse of the other.

The FTC's *practical* consequences are at least as important; implicitly or explicitly, we'll use them again and again. Most important of all, the FTC leads to a practical method of *calculating* specific integrals.

We don't have one yet. So far, we've relied entirely on elementary area formulas.

Using the FTC

Before proving the FTC, let's see it in action.

As a first use, we'll prove another theorem, closely related to the FTC above, but handier in computations:

Theorem 4. (Fundamental theorem, second version.) Let f be continuous on $[a, b]$, and let F be *any* antiderivative of f. Then

$$\int_a^b f(x)\,dx = F(b) - F(a).$$

Proof: This result follows readily from the original FTC. If F is any antiderivative of f, then $F(x)$ can differ from $A_f(x)$—another antiderivative of f, according to the FTC—only by some constant C. In other words, $F(x) = A_f(x) + C$. But then

$$\begin{aligned} F(b) - F(a) &= \big(A_f(b) + C\big) - \big(A_f(a) + C\big) = A_f(b) - A_f(a) \\ &= \int_a^b f - \int_a^a f = \int_a^b f, \end{aligned}$$

just as claimed. □

Calculating areas

■ **Example 2.** In Section 5.1 we claimed—but didn't show—that the regions N and P shown shaded have signed areas -0.25 and 0.25, respectively. Show it now.

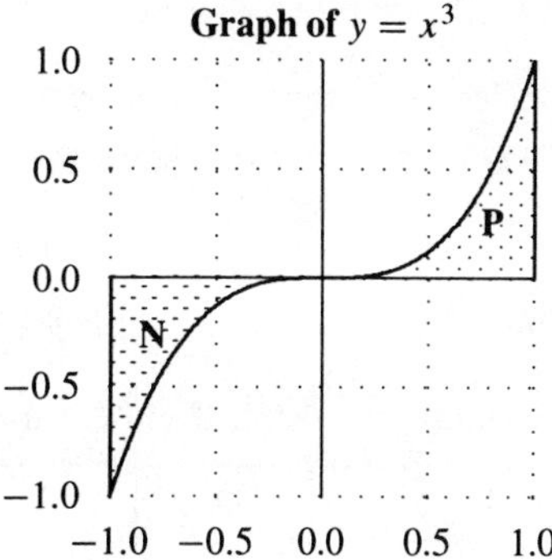

Solution: Let $f(x) = x^3$. The signed areas N and P are given by integrals:

$$\text{signed area N} = \int_{-1}^{0} f(x)\,dx; \quad \text{signed area P} = \int_{0}^{1} f(x)\,dx.$$

Because $F(x) = x^4/4$ is an antiderivative of $f(x)$, the previous theorem applies:

$$\int_{-1}^{0} f(x)\,dx = F(0) - F(-1) = -\frac{1}{4}; \quad \int_{0}^{1} f(x)\,dx = F(1) - F(0) = \frac{1}{4},$$

as we hoped. □

Bracket notation. The **bracket notation** offers a convenient shorthand for calculating integrals. For any function F,

$$F(x)\Big]_a^b \quad \text{means} \quad F(b) - F(a).$$

Watch for brackets in the next example.

■ **Example 3.** Evaluate $\int_0^1 x^2\,dx$ and $\int_0^1 x^{10}\,dx$. Interpret each integral as an area.

Solution: The previous theorem says that it's enough to find *any* antiderivatives, plug in endpoints, and subtract. We'll do just that:

$$\begin{aligned} \int_0^1 x^2\,dx &= \frac{x^3}{3}\Big]_0^1 = \frac{1}{3}; \\ \int_0^1 x^{10}\,dx &= \frac{x^{11}}{11}\Big]_0^1 = \frac{1}{11}. \end{aligned}$$

Each integral measures an area:

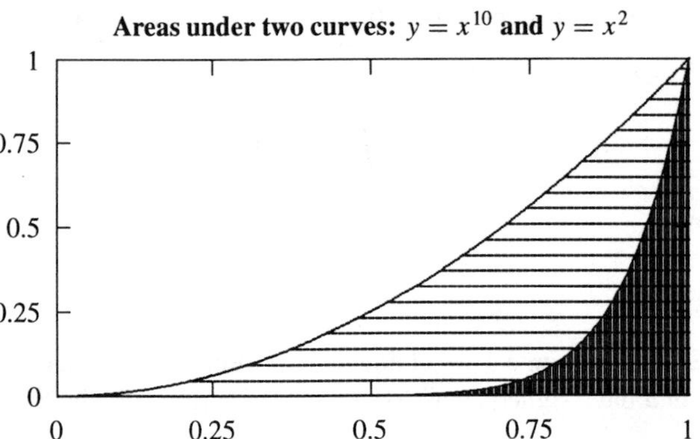

□

The light- and dark-shaded areas represent, respectively, the integrals $\int_0^1 x^2\,dx = 1/3$ and $\int_0^1 x^{10}\,dx = 1/11$. The picture shows that the answers are numerically reasonable.

■ **Example 4.** Calculate the area shown shaded below:

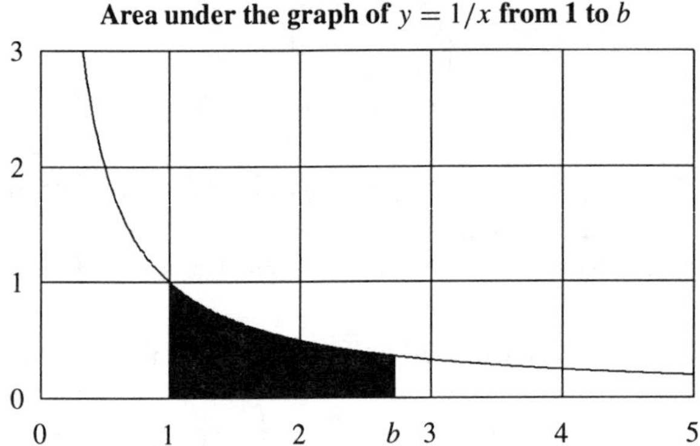

Which value of b makes the area 1?

Solution: The shaded area is the value of the integral $\int_1^b 1/x\,dx$. Since the function $\ln x$ is an antiderivative for $1/x$, the FTC says:

$$\int_1^b \frac{1}{x}\,dx = \ln x\big]_1^b = \ln b - \ln 1 = \ln b.$$

If $b = e$—as it is in the picture—then the area is $\ln e = 1$. □

From rate to amount

Restated slightly, the second version of the fundamental theorem reads like this:

> **Fact:** Let f be a well-behaved function on $[a, b]$, with derivative f'. Then
> $$\int_a^b f'(t)\,dt = f(b) - f(a).$$

In words:

Integrating f' (the rate *function) over $[a, b]$ gives the change in f (the* amount *function) over the same interval.*

This fact has important practical uses—with it, we can deduce *amount* information from *rate* information.

■ **Example 5.** Demand for electric power varies more or less predictably over the course of a day. Drawing on experience, engineers in one mythical small town (a bedroom suburb, perhaps) use the formula

$$r(t) = 4 + \sin(0.263t + 4.7) + \cos(0.526t + 9.4)$$

to model the *rate* of power consumption, in megawatts, t hours after midnight. A graph of r appears below. Is the model reasonable? What does the shaded area represent?

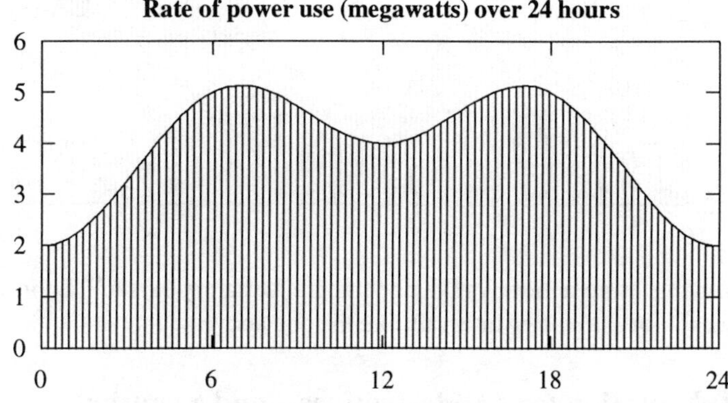

Solution: The graph looks plausible (though certainly oversimplified.) Residential power demand peaks in the morning, declines during working hours, and rises again in the evening. The formula for r is complicated, but the ingredients—periodic functions and various constants—look right.➻

Remember how additive and multiplicative constants affect periodic functions?

The shaded area is the *integral* $\int_0^{24} r(t)\,dt$. To understand it in the present context, let $a(t)$ be the total *amount* of power consumed up to time t, starting at midnight.➻ Then $a'(t) = r(t)$; by the fact above,

By definition, therefore, $a = 0$ when $t = 0$.

$$\int_0^{24} r(t)\,dt = a(24) - a(0) = a(24) = \text{total consumption, all day}\ .$$

With the "classic" FTC (and a little help from above in finding an antiderivative) we can *calculate* this amount. It's easy to *check*➻ that

But harder to guess!

$$4t - \frac{\cos(0.263t + 4.7)}{0.263} + \frac{\sin(0.526t + 9.4)}{0.526}$$

is an antiderivative for $r(t)$. The rest is straight calculation:

$$\begin{aligned}\int_0^{24} r(t)\,dt &= 4t - \frac{\cos(0.263t + 4.7)}{0.263} + \frac{\sin(0.526t + 9.4)}{0.526}\Bigg]_0^{24} \\ &\approx 95.781 \text{ megawatt hours.}\end{aligned}$$

□

When *not* to use the FTC

Beautiful, too.

The FTC, useful as it is, won't solve *all* our integral problems. Evaluating integrals by antidifferentiation means, first, *finding a usable antiderivative.*

For a surprising number of integrands, even apparently simple ones, finding a antiderivative formula is hard, or even impossible. None of the following functions, for instance, has an elementary antiderivative:

$$\sin(x^2); \qquad \frac{x}{\ln x}; \qquad 3 + \sin x + 0.3 \arcsin(\sin 7x)).$$

Nevertheless, all have perfectly sensible integrals over finite intervals. The picture below shows what $\int_0^{10} f$ means for the last function above:

An FTC-resistant integral: $\int_0^{10} \big(3 + \sin x + 0.3 \arcsin(\sin(7x))\big)\, dx$

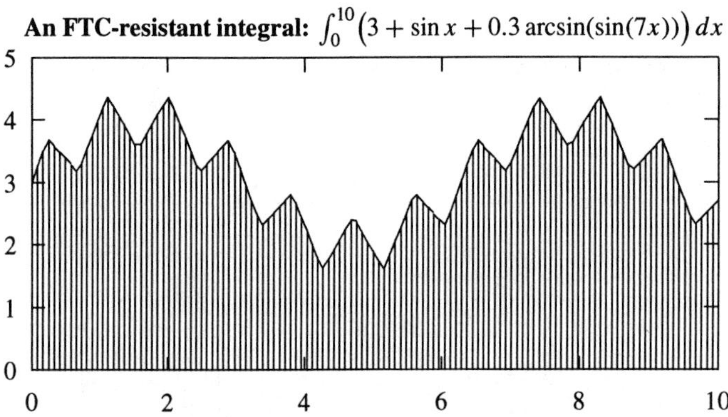

Can you estimate it? We get about 30.

Ones that don't *involve antiderivatives.*

Antiderivative or no antiderivative, the integral certainly exists. Soon we'll study techniques for *estimating* integrals like the one above.

A useful notation for antiderivatives—and a caution

The **indefinite integral notation** for antiderivatives, as in

$$\int x^2\, dx = \frac{x^3}{3} + C \quad \text{and} \quad \int \cos x\, dx = \sin x + C,$$

can be a convenient shorthand. It reflects, too, the fundamental connection between antiderivatives and integrals. A little care is necessary, however:

The whole family. $\int f(x)\, dx$ denotes a *family* of functions, one for each value of C.

Similar signs, different meanings. The **definite integral** $\int_a^b f(x)\, dx$ and the **indefinite integral** $\int f(x)\, dx$ have very different meanings: the first is a *number*, the second a family of *functions*.

Proving the FTC

The FTC is clearly *useful*. By now, we hope, it's *plausible*. But why is it *true*?

The idea of the proof

Recall the setup: f is a continuous function, defined on an interval I containing $x = a$, and

$$A_f(x) = \int_a^x f(t)\, dt.$$

The theorem claims that for x in I,

$$A'_f(x) = \lim_{h \to 0} \frac{A_f(x+h) - A_f(x)}{h} = f(x).$$

To show this, we'll work directly with the difference quotient.

Notice first that $A_f(x+h) - A_f(x) = \int_a^{x+h} f - \int_a^x f = \int_x^{x+h} f$. The pictures below shows why:

$A_f(x+h) - A_f(x) =$ **the shaded area**

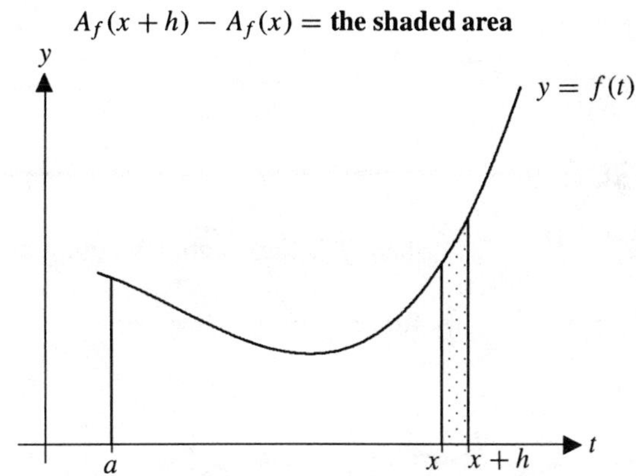

$A_f(x+h) - A_f(x)$**—a closer look**

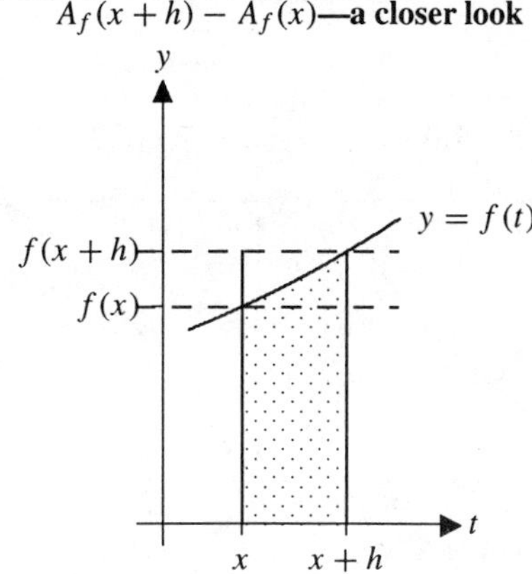

The picture just above shows that for small positive values of h,

$$A_f(x+h) - A_f(x) = \int_x^{x+h} f \approx f(x) \cdot h.$$

(The last quantity is the area of the shorter *rectangle*.) Thus for h near 0,

$$\frac{A_f(x+h) - A_f(x)}{h} \approx \frac{f(x) \cdot h}{h} = f(x).$$

Therefore, as $h \to 0$, the difference quotient tends to $f(x)$, as desired. $\square$

More on the proof: fine print

A rigorous proof can be constructed from the informal argument above. The missing ingredient is a precise, quantitative approach to the approximation $\int_x^{x+h} f \approx f(x) \cdot h$. It helps if f happens to be *increasing* near x—as it is in the figure above. In that case,➻

Draw a picture!

$$f(x) \cdot h \leq A_f(x+h) - A_f(x) = \text{shaded area} \leq f(x+h) \cdot h,$$

so

$$f(x) \leq \frac{A_f(x+h) - A_f(x)}{h} \leq f(x+h).$$

As $h \to 0$, the quantities on both left and right tend to $f(x)$. So, therefore, must the difference quotient.

(A similar idea works if f is not increasing, but some technical details are different.) □

Exercises

1. Let $F(x) = \int_0^x f(t)\,dt$ where f is the function whose graph is shown below.

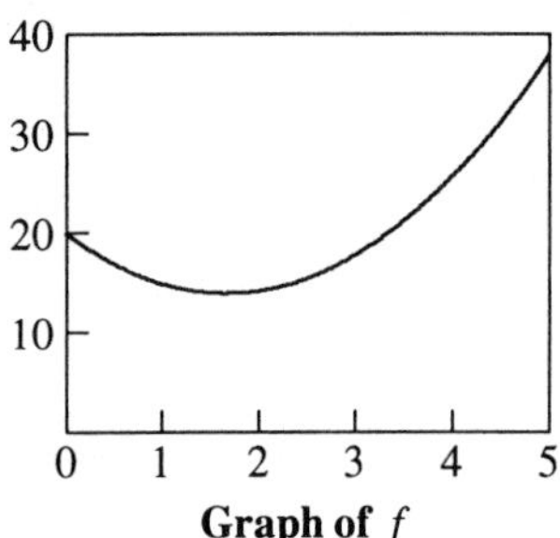

Graph of f

(a) Which of the following is the graph of F? Justify your answer.

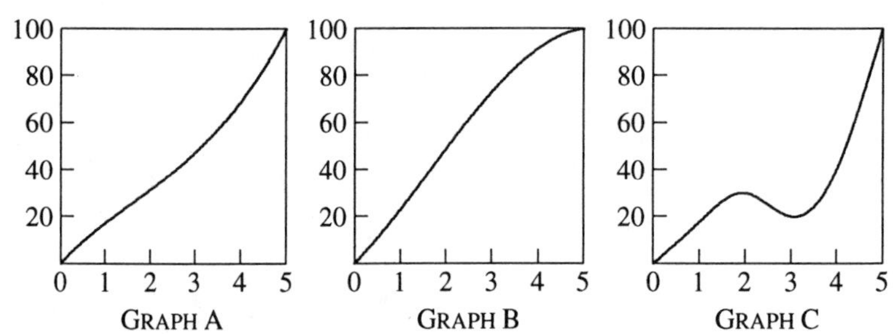

(b) Suppose that $g(0) = 2$ and $g'(x) = f(x)$ for all x. Explain how the graphs of F and g are related.

2. Let $F(x) = \int_0^x f(t)\,dt$ where f is the function graphed below. (The graph of f is made up of straight lines and a semicircle.)

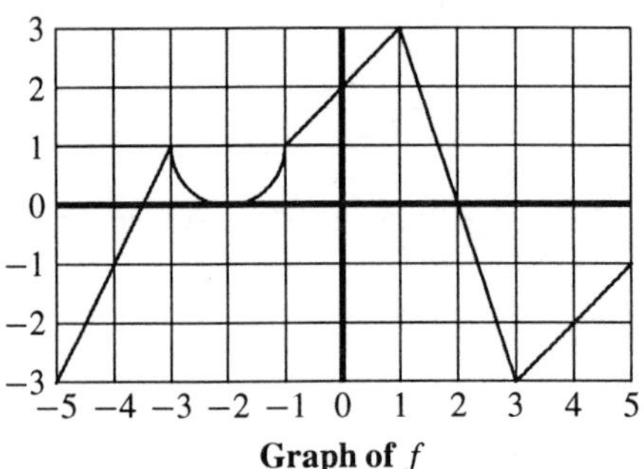

Graph of f

(a) Evaluate $F(-1)$, $F(0)$, and $F(2)$.

(b) Identify all the critical points of F in the interval $[-5, 5]$.

(c) Identify all the inflection points of F in the interval $[-5, 5]$.

(d) What is the average value of f on the interval $[-5, 5]$?

(e) Let $G(x) = \int_0^x F(t)\,dt$. On which subintervals of $[-5, 5]$, if any, is G concave upward?

3. Let $F(x) = \displaystyle\int_0^x f(t)\,dt$ where $f(t)$ is the function shown below:

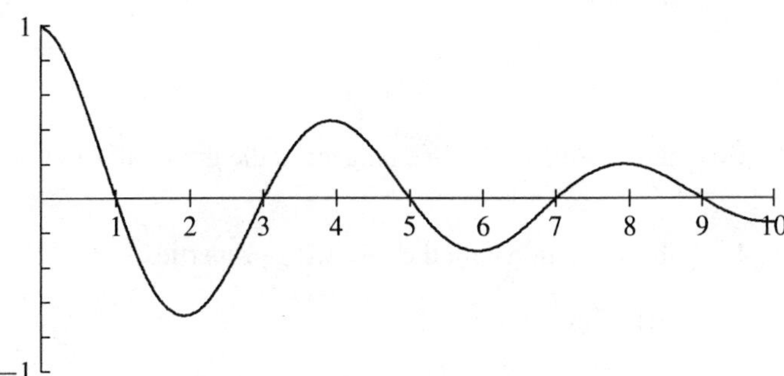

Graph of f

(a) Does $F(x)$ have any local maxima within the interval $[0, 10]$? If so, where are they located?

(b) At what value of x does $F(x)$ attain its minimum value on the interval $[0, 10]$?

(c) On which subinterval(s) of $[0, 10]$, if any, is the graph of $F(x)$ concave up? Justify your answer.

4. Let $G(x) = \int_0^x g'(t)\,dt$ where g is a differentiable function defined on the interval $[0, 10]$ such that the graph of g passes through the point $(5, 1)$ and the derivative of g is the function sketched below.

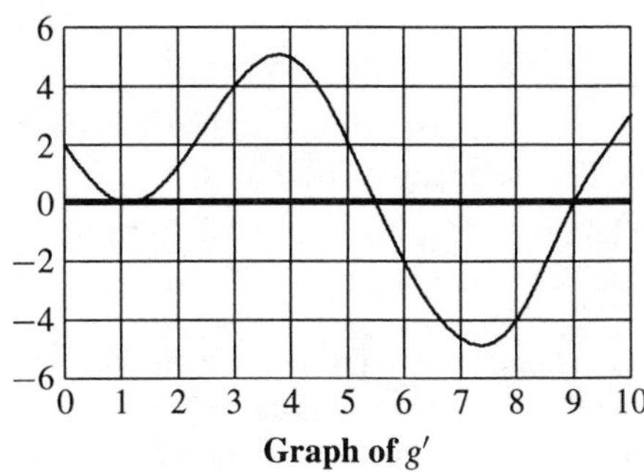

Graph of g'

(a) How are the graphs of g and G related? Explain.

(b) How many solutions of the equation $g(x) = 0$ exist in the interval $[0, 10]$? Explain.

(c) How many solutions of the equation $G(x) = 0$ exist in the interval $[0, 10]$? Explain.

5. Evaluate each of the following definite integrals using the Fundamental Theorem of Calculus.

(a) $\int_1^4 \left(x + x^{3/2}\right) dx$

(b) $\int_0^{\pi} \cos x \, dx$

(c) $\int_{-2}^{5} \frac{dx}{x+3}$

(d) $\int_0^b x^2 \, dx$

(e) $\int_1^b x^n \, dx \quad [n \neq -1]$

(f) $\int_2^{2.001} \frac{x^5}{1000} \, dx$

(g) $\int_0^{0.001} \frac{\cos x}{1000} \, dx$

(h) $\int_0^{\sqrt{\pi}} x \sin\left(x^2\right) dx$

6. Suppose that $\int_0^x f(t)\,dt = 3x^2 + e^x - \cos x$. Find $f(2)$.

7. Find an equation of the line tangent to the graph of $F(x) = \int_1^x \sqrt[3]{t^2+7}\,dt$ at $x = 1$.

8. Let f be a function with the following properties:

   (i) $f'(x) = ax^2 + bx$

   (ii) $f'(1) = 6$

   (iii) $f''(1) = 18$

   (iv) $\int_1^2 f(x)\,dx = 18$

   Find an algebraic expression for $f(x)$.

9. Let $f(x) = \begin{cases} -2, & \text{if } x < 0 \\ 1, & \text{if } x \geq 0 \end{cases}$ and let $F(x) = \int_{-2}^{x} f(t)\,dt$.

   (a) Evaluate $\int_{-1}^{1} f(x)\,dx$.

   (b) Sketch a graph of $F(x)$ and $f(x)$ on the same axes for $x \in [-2, 2]$.

   (c) Does $F'(1)$ exist? If so, evaluate it using the definition of the derivative. If not, explain why it doesn't exist.

   (d) Does $F'(-1)$ exist? If so, evaluate it using the definition of the derivative. If not, explain why it doesn't exist.

   (e) Explain why $F'(0)$ doesn't exist. Why doesn't this contradict the Fundamental Theorem of Calculus?

10. A company is planning to phase out a product because demand for it is declining. Demand for the product is currently 800 units/month and dropping by 10 units/month each month. To maintain customer and employee relations, the company has announced that it will continue to produce the product for one more year. At the present time, the company is producing the product at a rate of 900 units/month and 1680 units of the product are in inventory.

    (a) Give expressions for the demand and production rates as functions of time t (take $t = 0$ as the present).

    (b) Let $D(t)$ be the demand rate for the product. Explain why $\int_0^t D(s)\,ds$ is the total demand for the product in t months' time.

    (c) Give an expression for the inventory at time t. [HINT: The amount of the product in inventory is the difference between supply and demand at the end of t months.]

(d) The company would like to reduce production at a constant rate of R units/month, with R chosen so as to reduce its inventory to zero at the end of 12 months. What should R be to reduce the inventory to zero at $t = 12$?

11. The function $\ln x$ is sometimes *defined* for $x > 0$ by integration:

$$\ln x = \int_1^x \frac{dt}{t}.$$

Assume $a > 0$ and $x > 0$. Derive the identity $\ln(ax) = \ln a + \ln x$ by carrying out and justifying each of the following steps:

(a) Show that $\left(\int_1^{ax} \frac{dt}{t}\right)' = \frac{1}{x}$. [HINT: Use the chain rule.]

(b) Explain why the result in part (a) implies that that $\ln(ax) = \ln x + C$.

(c) By choosing an appropriate x, show that the value of the constant C in part (b) is $\ln a$.

5.4 Approximating sums: the integral as a limit

Remember what "signed" means? It's important.

The integral $\int_a^b f$, as defined so far, is the *signed* area of the region bounded by the graph of f from $x = a$ to $x = b$. In the last section we saw, in the fundamental theorem of calculus, the crucial inverse relationship between integrals and derivatives. According to the FTC, we can readily calculate any integral for which we can find an antiderivative.

Despite their close relationship, integration and antidifferentiation are *not* the same thing. For many integrals (even "nice" ones such as $\int_0^1 \sin(x^2)\,dx$) antidifferentiation is useless, because no usable antiderivative formula exists. Nevertheless, such integrals clearly exist, as graphs show.

We observed this for the integral $\int_0^{10}(3+\sin x+0.3\arcsin(\sin 7x))\,dx$ in the previous section. See the graph there.

In this section we take a new approach to the integral, defining it, this time, as a certain limit of "approximating sums." The limit definition offers new and useful perspectives on the integral and what it means. Equally important, it lends itself well to the problem of *estimating* integrals numerically.

The approach is new; the integral is the same!

Better than the FTC.

This section resembles Section 2.3, where we first met the limit definition of the *derivative*. There, as here, the general problem was to translate an intuitively reasonable geometric concept into precise analytic language. For both derivative and integral, the idea of limit proves crucial; it links *approximations* to *exact values*.

There, the slope of the tangent line; here, the area under a graph.

Estimating integrals by approximating sums

The formal definition of integral as a limit involves some formidable-seeming terminology and notation. The underlying ideas, however, are natural and straightforward—especially when thought of graphically.

To back up this claim, we'll approach the definition *via* a leisurely example, introducing terms and ideas as we go.

■ **Example 1.** Part of the graph of $f(x) = x^3 - 3x^2 + 8$ appears below; the shaded area is the integral $\int_{0.5}^{3.5} f(x)\,dx$. Use the FTC to evaluate the integral *exactly*. Then use approximating sums to *estimate* the same integral.

First of all, estimate the area roughly, by eye alone. Write your answer in the margin. Don't cheat.

What's the area?

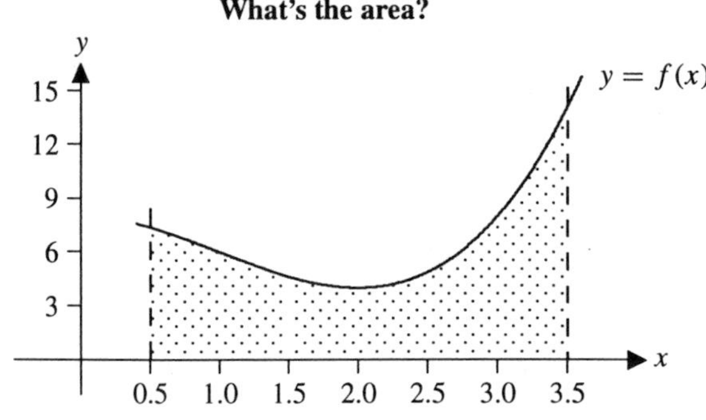

Solution: With the FTC, an exact answer is easy to find by antidifferentiation:

Check the steps; they're routine.

$$\int_{0.5}^{3.5}\left(x^3 - 3x^2 + 8\right)dx = \left(\frac{x^4}{4} - x^3 + 8x\right)\Big]_{0.5}^{3.5} = \frac{75}{4} = 18.75.$$

How might we *estimate* this area? The following figures suggest four plausible strategies:

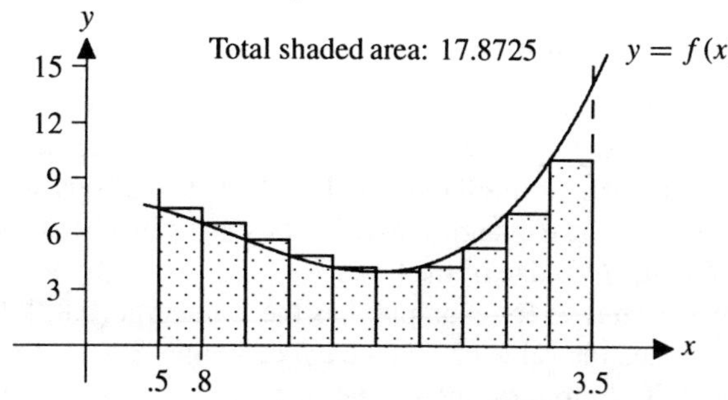

Right sum, 10 subdivisions

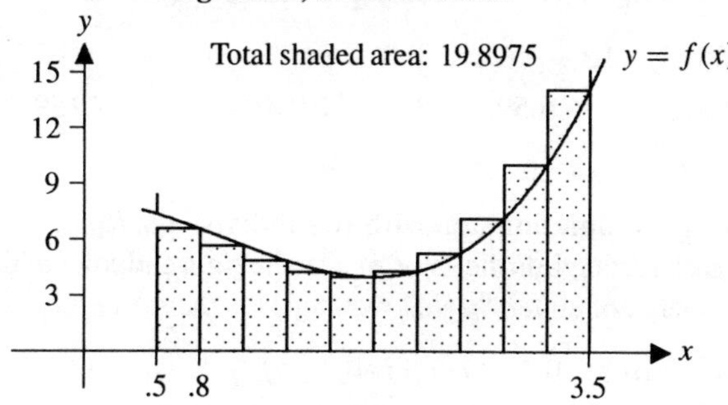

Midpoint sum, 10 subdivisions

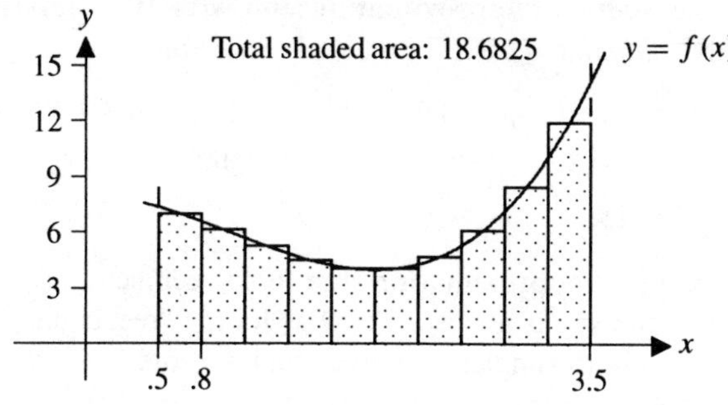

Trapezoid sum, 6 subdivisions

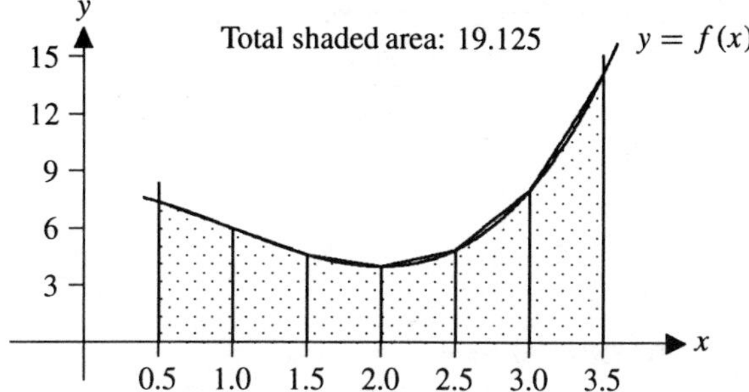

In each case we *approximated* the desired area by a sum of simpler areas—rectangles or trapezoids. (For trapezoids we used 6, not 10, subdivisions in order to show more clearly the difference between the integral and the trapezoid estimate.) Adding up the

We spare you—for the moment—all arithmetic details.

Study the pictures; which estimate looks best? Which is best?

areas of these simpler figures gives, in each case, a natural estimate to our desired area. □

Calculating approximate areas

How, exactly, did we calculate each area estimate given above?

A close look at each picture gives the answer. Consider first L_{10}, the **left approximating sum with 10 subdivisions**. The shaded area consists of ten rectangles; each has *base* 0.3. The rectangles' *heights* vary—the height of each is the value of the function f at the *left* edge of the base.

I.e., $(3.5 - 0.5)/10$.

Hence the name left sum.

The *second rectangle*, for example, has the x-interval $[0.8, 1.1]$ for its base; its height is $f(0.8)$, i.e., the value of f at the *left* endpoint. Since $f(x) = x^3 - 3x^2 + 8$, $f(0.8) = 6.592$. Therefore for the second rectangle,

$$\text{area} = 0.3 \cdot 6.592 = 1.9776.$$

The *total* area of all ten "left" rectangles, therefore, is the sum

$$\begin{aligned} L_{10} &= f(0.5) \cdot 0.3 + f(0.8) \cdot 0.3 + f(1.1) \cdot 0.3 + \cdots + f(3.2) \cdot 0.3 \\ &= 7.375 \cdot 0.3 + 6.592 \cdot 0.3 + 5.701 \cdot 0.3 + \cdots + 7.159 \cdot 0.3 + 10.05 \cdot 0.3 \\ &= 17.8725. \end{aligned}$$

The **right approximating sum with 10 subdivisions**, R_{10}, differs only slightly—the height of each rectangle is the value of f at the *right* endpoint of the base interval. Hence the total area of all ten "right" rectangles is the sum

Think this sentence through carefully. Do you see how the picture says the same thing?

$$\begin{aligned} R_{10} &= f(0.8) \cdot 0.3 + f(1.1) \cdot 0.3 + f(1.4) \cdot 0.3 + \cdots + f(3.5) \cdot 0.3 \\ &= 6.592 \cdot 0.3 + 5.701 \cdot 0.3 + \cdots + 10.05 \cdot 0.3 + 14.13 \cdot 0.3 \\ &= 19.8975. \end{aligned}$$

For M_{10}, the **midpoint approximating sum with 10 subdivisions**, heights are evaluated at the *midpoint* of each subinterval. Therefore

$$\begin{aligned} M_{10} &= f(0.65) \cdot 0.3 + f(0.95) \cdot 0.3 + f(1.35) \cdot 0.3 + \cdots + f(3.35) \cdot 0.3 \\ &= 7.007 \cdot 0.3 + 6.150 \cdot 0.3 + \cdots + 8.465 \cdot 0.3 + 11.93 \cdot 0.3 \\ &= 18.6825. \end{aligned}$$

Using a **trapezoid approximating sum** looks, geometrically, like a good idea. *Calculating* it, moreover, is almost as easy as for the "rectangular" sums above. A key idea makes things simpler: the area of a trapezoid is the average of the areas of the two rectangles determined by its shorter and longer sides. From this fact it follows:

A picture makes this clear; draw one.

> *The trapezoid approximation with n subdivisions is the* average *of the corresponding* left *and* right *approximations.*

For *our* trapezoid sum (we'll call it T_6):

Numerical details left to you.

$$\begin{aligned} T_6 &= \frac{1}{2}(L_6 + R_6) \\ &= \frac{1}{2}(17.4375 + 20.8125) = 19.125. \end{aligned}$$

Sigma notation; partitions

Sums with many terms are tedious to write. **Sigma notation** (*aka* $\sum$-notation) is more efficient than brute force—even better, it shows clearly the similarities and the differences among summands.

Those above, for instance.

■ **Example 2.** Discuss and evaluate each expression:

$$\sum_{k=1}^{4} k; \quad \sum_{j=1}^{4} j; \quad \sum_{i=1}^{10} 3i.$$

Solution: By definition, $\sum_{k=1}^{4} k = 1 + 2 + 3 + 4$, or simply 10. Although typographically slightly different, the second sum means *exactly* the same thing: $\sum_{j=1}^{4} j = 1+2+3+4 = 10$. The moral: *The name of the* ***index variable*** *doesn't matter.*

First it was k, then j; i through n are all popular choices.

The third expression is more complicated, but the ideas are the same:

$$\begin{aligned}\sum_{i=1}^{10} 3i &= 3\cdot 1+3\cdot 2+3\cdot 3+\cdots+3\cdot 9+3\cdot 10 = 3\cdot(1+2+\cdots+10)\\ &= 3\cdot 55 = 165.\end{aligned}$$

(Notice that the common factor can be pulled outside the sum: $\sum_{i=1}^{10} 3i = 3\sum_{i=1}^{10} i$. This is the Σ-version of the distributive law.) □

■ **Example 3.** Use sigma notation to rewrite the left, right, and midpoint approximating sums (L_{10}, R_{10}, and M_{10}) we calculated above.

Solution: All three approximating sums are based on subdividing the interval $[0.5, 3.5]$ into 10 equal subintervals, each of length $\Delta x = 0.3$. Here are their endpoints, listed in order:

Literally!

$$0.5 < 0.8 < 1.1 < 1.4 < \cdots < 3.2 < 3.5.$$

(This ordered set of 11 endpoints is called a **partition** of the x-interval $[0.5, 3.5]$.) For convenience, let's *name* these endpoints—in the same order—x_0, x_1, x_2, ... , x_{10}.

Now sigma notation is convenient:

$$\begin{aligned}L_{10} &= \sum_{i=0}^{9} f(x_i)\Delta x = f(0.5)\cdot 0.3 + f(0.8)\cdot 0.3 + \cdots + f(3.2)\cdot 0.3;\\ R_{10} &= \sum_{i=1}^{10} f(x_i)\Delta x = f(0.8)\cdot 0.3 + f(1.1)\cdot 0.3 + \cdots + f(3.5)\cdot 0.3;\\ M_{10} &= \sum_{i=0}^{9} f\left(\frac{x_i + x_{i+1}}{2}\right)\Delta x = f(0.65)\cdot 0.3 + f(0.95)\cdot 0.3 + \cdots + f(3.35)\cdot 0.3.\end{aligned}$$

The $\sum$ form makes the approximating sums appear simple and compact.

Why does the R_{10} sum run from $i = 1$ to $i = 10$?, not from $i = 0$ to $i = 9$?

If we'd rather see numbers than symbols, we can always use the fact that $x_i = 0.5 + 0.3i$ to rewrite our sums. Here are two of them:

It is a fact. Do you see why?

$$L_{10} = \sum_{i=0}^{9} f(x_i)\Delta x = 0.3\cdot\sum_{i=0}^{9} f(0.5 + 0.3i);$$

$$M_{10} = \sum_{i=0}^{9} f((x_i + x_{i+1})/2)\,\Delta x = 0.3\cdot\sum_{i=0}^{9} f(0.65 + 0.3i). \quad □$$

Getting better all the time

It stands to reason that an approximating sum—of any type—should do *better* at approximating an integral as the *number* of subdivisions increases. The following pictures (still pertaining to $\int_{0.5}^{3.5} f(x)\,dx$) agree:

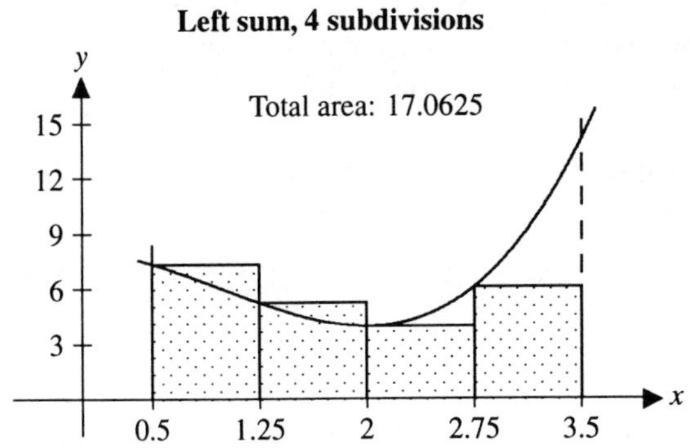

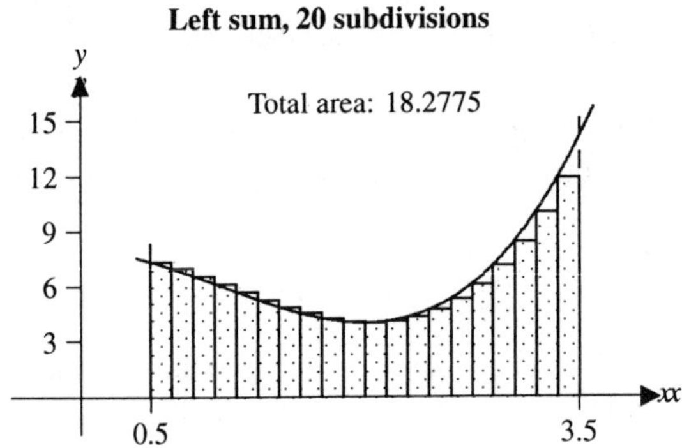

Neither left approximation appears perfect, but the error committed with 20 subdivisions seems much less.

All computed by machine, of course.

Numerical values of various sums show the same thing:

Approximating sums for the integral $\int_{0.5}^{3.5} f(x)\,dx$

n	left sum	right sum	midpoint sum	trapezoid sum
2	17.0625	27.1875	17.0625	22.125
4	17.0625	22.125	18.3281	19.5938
8	17.6953	20.2266	18.6445	18.9609
16	18.1699	19.4355	18.7236	18.8027
32	18.4468	19.0796	18.7434	18.7632
64	18.5951	18.9115	18.7484	18.7533
128	18.6717	18.8299	18.7496	18.7508
256	18.7107	18.7898	18.7499	18.7502

Riemann sums and the limit definition of integral

Riemann sums and their ingredients

Left, right, and midpoint approximating sums are all special types of **Riemann sums.** Roughly speaking, *any* "rectangular" approximating sum is a Riemann sum. Riemann's idea of an approximating sum to an integral $\int_a^b f(x)\,dx$ is very liberal. He allows rectangles with *unequal* bases; their heights can be determined anywhere—even randomly—within their respective subintervals.

After the great German mathematician G. F. B. Riemann, 1826–66; he gave the first modern definition of the integral.

Here, for instance, is the graphical version of a somewhat irregular Riemann sum for our by-now familiar integral:

A Riemann sum, 6 (unequal) subdivisions

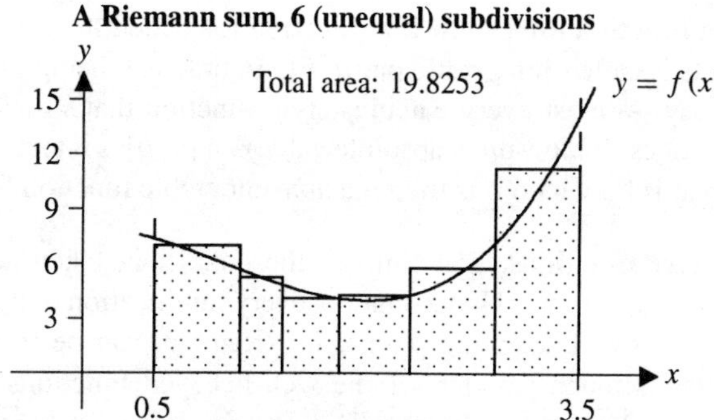

Not a *good* approximation perhaps, but a legitimate one.

We won't require such generality, but here, for the record, is the formal definition of Riemann sum. The necessary ingredients are a function f and an interval $I = [a, b]$.

> **Definition:** Let I be partitioned into n subintervals by any $n + 1$ points
> $$a = x_0 < x_1 < x_2 < \cdots < x_{n-1} < x_n = b;$$
> let $\Delta x_i = x_i - x_{i-1}$ denote the width of the i-th subinterval. Within each subinterval $[x_{i-1}, x_i]$, choose any point c_i. The sum
> $$\sum_{i=1}^{n} f(c_i)\Delta x_i = f(c_1)\Delta x_1 + f(c_2)\Delta x_2 + \cdots + f(c_n)\Delta x_n$$
> is a **Riemann sum with n subdivisions** for f on $[a, b]$.

Our left, right, and midpoint sums fit this definition with room to spare—each is built from a **regular partition** of $[a, b]$ (i.e., one with subintervals of equal length) and some simple, consistent, scheme for choosing the **evaluation points** c_i.

Or "sampling points."

(A *trapezoid* approximating sum, on the other hand, *isn't* quite a Riemann sum, since its approximating figures aren't rectangles. Nevertheless, trapezoidal sums do an excellent job of approximating the integral.)

The integral defined as a limit

Graphical intuition suggests that all of our various approximating sums—L_n, R_n, M_n, T_n—should "converge" toward the true signed area $\int_{0.5}^{3.5} f(x)\,dx$ as n increases. Numerical evidence argues irresistibly for a value somewhere near 18.75.

See the table to dispel any lingering doubts.

The limit definition of integral makes these ideas precise:

> **Definition:** Let the function f be defined on the interval $I = [a,b]$. The **integral of f over I**, denoted $\int_a^b f(x)\,dx$, is the number to which all Riemann sums S_n tend as n tends to infinity and as the widths of all subdivisions tend to zero. In symbols:
>
> $$\int_a^b f(x)\,dx = \lim_{n\to\infty} S_n = \lim_{n\to\infty} \sum_{i=1}^{n} f(c_i)\,\Delta x_i\,,$$
>
> if the limit exists.

Note:

When is a function integrable? A function for which the limit in the definition exists is called **integrable** on $[a,b]$. In practice, being integrable on $[a,b]$ is easy—almost every calculus-style function that's defined and *bounded* (i.e., doesn't blow up in absolute value) on $[a,b]$ is integrable. The surprise, rather, is how hard it is to find a *non*-integrable function.

Here's one: $f(x) = 1$ if x is rational; $f(x) = 0$ if x is irrational.

Well-behaved functions. The limit in the definition, taken at face value, is a slippery customer. Understanding every ramification of permitting arbitrary partitions and sampling points, for example, can be tricky. Luckily, the matter is much simpler for the well-behaved functions (e.g., continuous functions) we typically meet in calculus. For such functions, almost any respectable sort of approximating sum does what we'd expect—approaches the true value of the integral as n tends to infinity.

Notes on notation

The limit definition helps explain the otherwise mysterious dx in the notation $\int_a^b f(x)\,dx$. Consider, e.g., the case of a *right* approximating sum with n *equal* subdivisions, each of length $(b-a)/n = \Delta x$. Then, by definition,

$$\int_a^b f(x)\,dx = \lim_{n\to\infty} \sum_{i=1}^{n} f(x_i)\,\Delta x.$$

Now the left side looks much like the right; "dx" on the left corresponds, in a natural way, to "Δx" on the right.

We've seen this before: $dy/dx = \lim_{\Delta x\to 0} \Delta y/\Delta x$.

Approximating sums and computers

Approximating sums offer simple, effective, and accurate approximations to almost any integral. Simple for a computer, anyway—calculating approximating sums *by hand* is impractical except for simple integrands and few subdivisions. Calculating approximating sums is the sort of bureaucratic task computers do best–simple, repetitive, and tedious.

Exercises

1. Let g be the function graphed below. Estimate the value of $\int_{-5}^{5} g(x)\,dx$ by evaluating left, right, and midpoint sums each with 5 equal subintervals, then draw sketches that illustrate these sums geometrically.

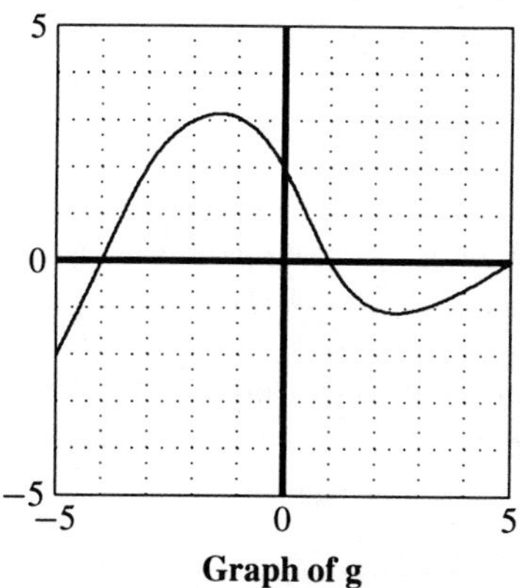

Graph of g

2. Let f be the function graphed below.

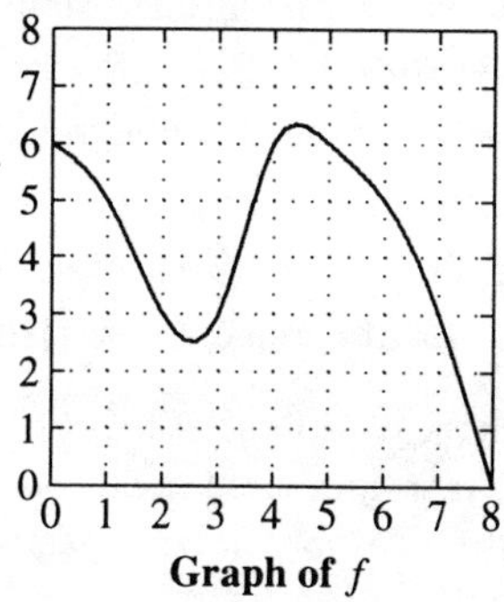

Graph of f

(a) Is $22 < \int_1^7 f(x)\,dx$? Justify your answer.

(b) Estimate the value of $\int_1^7 f(x)\,dx$ using a right sum with three equal subintervals.

(c) Estimate the value of $\int_1^7 f(x)\,dx$ using a left sum with three equal subintervals.

(d) Estimate the value of $\int_0^8 f(x)\,dx$ using a right sum with four equal subintervals.

(e) Estimate the value of $\int_0^8 f(x)\,dx$ using a left sum with four equal subintervals.

3. Let $I = \int_0^5 \sqrt[3]{2x}\,dx$. Use sigma notation to write the left, right, and midpoint approximations to I. (Assume that N = 10 equal subintervals are used.)

4. Let $I = \int_0^5 \sqrt{3x}\,dx$. Use sigma notation to write the left, right, and midpoint approximations to I. (Assume that N equal subintervals are used.)

5. Find a definite integral that is approximated by the midpoint sum

$$\frac{2}{10}\sum_{k=1}^{40}\cos\left(\frac{2k-1}{10}\right).$$

What is the value of this integral? [HINT: Write out the first few terms of the sum.]

6. Find a definite integral that is approximated by the right sum $\frac{2}{100}\sum_{k=1}^{100}\sin\left(\frac{2k}{100}\right)$. What is the value of this integral?

7. At time t (measured in hours), $0 \le t \le 24$, a firm uses electricity at the rate of $E(t)$ kilowatts. The power company's rate schedule indicates that the cost per kilowatt-hour at time t is $c(t)$ dollars. Assume that both E and c are continuous functions.

   (a) Set up an N-term left sum that approximates the cost of the electricity consumed in a 24-hour period.

   (b) What definite integral is approximated by the sum you found in part (a)?

8. The table below contains values of a continuous function f at several values of x.

x	1	2	3	4	5	6
$f(x)$	0.14	0.21	0.28	0.36	0.44	0.54

   (a) Estimate $\int_2^5 f(x)\,dx$ using a left sum with 3 equal subintervals. (Be sure to show your work.)

   (b) Do the same using the trapezoid rule.

   (c) Draw a sketch that illustrates the computations you did in parts (a) and (b).

   (d) Show that $f(2)\cdot 2 + f(4)\cdot 3$ is a Riemann sum approximation to $\int_1^6 f(x)\,dx$. Justify your answer. [HINT: Draw a picture.]

9. The rate at which the world's oil is being consumed is continuously increasing. Suppose that the rate (measured in billions of barrels per year) is given by the function $r(t)$, where t is measured in years and $t = 0$ is January 1, 1990.

   (a) Write a definite integral that represents the total quantity of oil used between the start of 1990 and the start of 1995.

   (b) Suppose that $r(t) = 32e^{0.05t}$. Find an approximate value for the definite integral from part (a) using a right sum with $n = 5$ equal subintervals.

   (c) Interpret each of the five terms in the sum from part (b) in terms of oil consumption.

   (d) Evaluate the definite integral from part (a).

10. Evaluate $\displaystyle\lim_{n\to\infty} \frac{1}{n}\sum_{j=1}^{n}\left(\frac{j}{n}\right)^3$ by expressing it as a definite integral and then evaluating this integral using the Fundamental Theorem of Calculus.

11. Evaluate $\displaystyle\lim_{n\to\infty} \frac{2}{n}\sum_{j=1}^{n}\left(\frac{2j}{n}\right)^3$ by expressing it as a definite integral and then evaluating this integral using the Fundamental Theorem of Calculus.

12. (a) Write the sum $\frac{5}{2}(2.3)^2 + \frac{5}{6}(2.8)^2 + \frac{5}{12}(3.3)^2 + \frac{5}{20}(3.8)^2$ using sigma notation.
    [HINT: $2 = 1\cdot 2$, $6 = 2\cdot 3$, $12 = 3\cdot 4$, and $20 = 4\cdot 5$.]

    (b) Is the sum in part (a) a Riemann sum approximation to $\displaystyle\int_0^4 x^2\,dx$? Explain.

13. For each of the following definite integrals, draw a sketch illustrating the approximations L_4, R_4, M_4, and T_4. Then compute each approximation and compare it with the exact value of the integral computed using the FTC. How could you have used the sketches to predict the results of these comparisons?

(a) $\int_{-2}^{2} x^2\,dx$

(b) $\int_{-2}^{2} x^3\,dx$

(c) $\int_{-2}^{2} (x+1)\,dx$

(d) $\int_{-\pi/2}^{\pi/2} \sin x\,dx$

14. The table below gives speedometer readings at various times over a one-hour interval.

Speed readings over one hour							
time (min)	0	10	20	30	40	50	60
speed (mph)	42	38	36	57	0	55	51

(a) Plot a plausible speed graph for the one-hour period.

(b) Estimate the total distance traveled using

(i) A trapezoid approximating sum, 6 subdivisions

(ii) A left approximating sum, 6 subdivisions

(iii) A midpoint approximating sum, 3 subdivisions

Which answer is most convincing? Why?

(c) Plot a plausible distance graph for the one-hour period.

5.5 Approximating sums: interpretations and applications

In the previous section we defined the integral as a limit of approximating sums. In symbols:

$$\int_a^b f(x)\,dx = \lim_{n\to\infty} \sum_{i=1}^{n} f(c_i)\,\Delta x_i .$$

The limit itself involves some technical subtleties, but the basic idea of sums (left sums, right sums, midpoint sums, etc.) approximating an integral is natural and straightforward—especially if thought of graphically.

In this section we look more closely at approximating sums. In the process we'll both see the integral itself in another light and apply the idea of approximating sums to several problems of measurement.

Different views of approximating sums

Approximating sums are **discrete** (i.e., stepwise) approximations to integrals of **continuously** varying functions. This important relationship can be interpreted in several useful ways. We discuss three.

Approximating sums and simpler areas

The simplest and most natural view of approximating sums is geometric; geometrically, approximating sums represent simpler versions (polygons, usually) of "curvy" regions. The shaded region below, for example, might be called a **polygonal approximation** to the area from a to b under the graph of f.

Most of the pictures in this section and the last reflect this point of view.

A polygonal approximation to a curved area

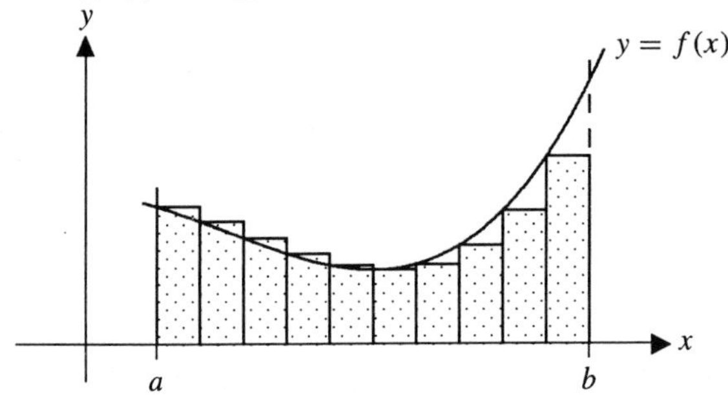

The total *area* of the polygonal region is (in the case shown) the value of a *left* sum; it's evidently a reasonable approximation to $\int_a^b f$, the "true" area under the graph.

Approximating sums and simpler functions

Another view of approximating sums for an integral $\int_a^b f$ concerns the function f. From this point of view an approximating sum amounts to *replacing the original function f with a new, simpler function*, one that's linear on each subinterval of the partition in question. In the graph below, for example, the function f of the previous

I.e., a "piecewise linear" function.

picture was "replaced" with a 6-step linear approximation.

Replacing f with a piecewise-linear function

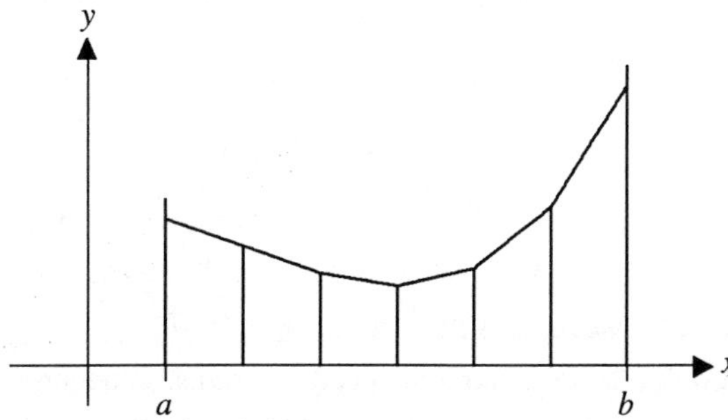

The area underneath is the value of the trapezoid approximating sum T_6.

Weighted sums

A Riemann sum for $\int_a^b f$ has the form

Left, right, midpoint, or any other kind

$$\sum_{i=1}^{n} f(c_i)\,\Delta x_i = f(c_1)\Delta x_1 + f(c_2)\Delta x_2 + \cdots + f(c_n)\Delta x_n.$$

In other words, an approximating sum is a **weighted sum** of values of f at various points c_i (the **sampling points**) in the interval $[a, b]$. The exact choice of sampling points, and the weights attached, depend on the type of approximating sum chosen.

An ordinary average is another type of weighted sum.

■ **Example 1.** Let $I = \int_0^1 \sin x\,dx$. Let R_4 and M_4 be the midpoint and right approximating sums for I, each with 4 subdivisions. What are the sampling points? What are the weights? What are the weighted sums?

Solution: Calculating M_4 and R_4 is routine:

Convince yourself that the forms are correct.

$$\begin{aligned} R_4 &= \sin(0.25)\cdot 0.25 + \sin(0.5)\cdot 0.25 + \\ &\qquad \sin(0.75)\cdot 0.25 + \sin(1)\cdot 0.25 \approx 0.56248; \\ M_4 &= \sin(0.125)\cdot 0.25 + \sin(0.375)\cdot 0.25 + \\ &\qquad \sin(0.625)\cdot 0.25 + \sin(0.875)\cdot 0.25 \approx 0.460897. \end{aligned}$$

The sampling points for R_4 are 0.25, 0.5, 0.75, and 1—the *right* endpoints of four equal subintervals. For M_4, the sampling points are 0.125, 0.375, 0.625, and 0.875, the midpoints of the same subintervals.

The weights in an approximating sum are the coefficients of the sample values $f(c_i)$. In the sums above, every sample value has weight $1/4$, the length of the subinterval it comes from. This result seems just; there's no obvious reason to favor one value over another. The weighted sums are the numerical values of R_4 and M_4, shown above. □

Unequal subintervals would give unequal weights.

Applications of approximating sums

Approximating sums are good for more than formally defining the integral. Indeed, compared to symbolic integrals, approximating sums are often simpler conceptually, handier in applications, and much, much easier to calculate. For integrals that involve complicated formulas, or no formulas at all, approximating sums may be the *only* practical resort.

For machines, especially.

Such integrals are common in practice.

Beyond formulas—integration with tabular data

Integration is important in the real world. Alas, real-world functions seldom come with handy formulas attached. The FTC, for all its other glories, is not much good without symbolic formulas to act on. Approximating sums are the answer.

■ **Example 2.** If $v(t)$ is the speed (in mph) of a car at time t (in hours), then $\int_a^b v(t)\,dt =$ miles traveled from $t = a$ to $t = b$. To measure distance traveled from $t = 0$ to $t = 1$, "all" we need is the integral $\int_0^1 v(t)\,dt$.

Real cars don't adhere to explicit speed formulas. What *can* be observed, practically speaking, are numerical speed data, like those below. (Notice the irregular time intervals; real data sets often have gaps.)

Speed readings over one hour

time (min)	0	5	10	15	20	30	35	40	45	55	60
speed (mph)	35	38	36	57	71	55	51	23	10	27	35

How far did the car travel in one hour?

Solution: Without more information (e.g., about speeds *between* the times measured), we'll never know exactly. All we can do is use approximating sums to estimate $\int_0^1 v(t)\,dt$ as best we can.

Our discrete speed data are mathematically compatible with many possible speed functions. The simplest possibility, probably, is drawn by "connecting the dots" (first figure below):

We converted time from minutes to hours.

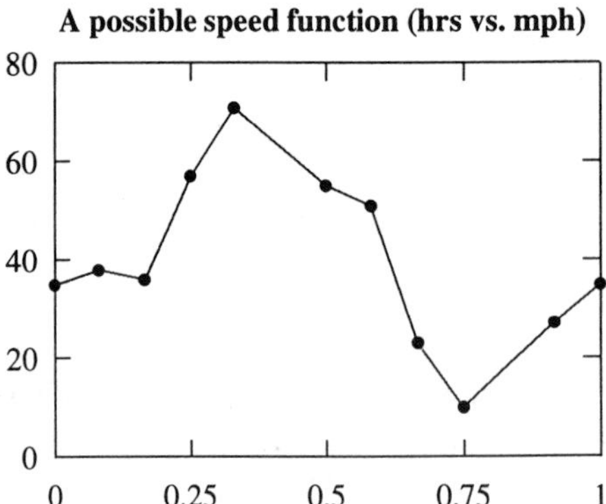

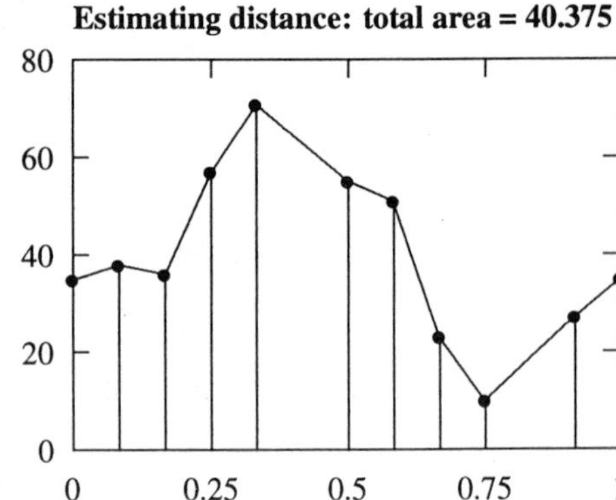

The total bounded area (above right) is easily computed using ten trapezoids; we got 40.375—a reasonable estimate for distance traveled over the hour.

We'll spare you the arithmetic.

The speed function plotted above isn't the only possibility. *Any* curve through the known data points makes mathematical sense. The important point is that the trapezoid estimate depends *only* on the 11 observed data—not on the particular curve drawn through them. The picture below illustrates this idea: it shows a *new* speed function, but the *same* trapezoid estimate (40.375 miles) for distance.

Some curves are physically more likely than others.

Better or worse than the old? What do you think?

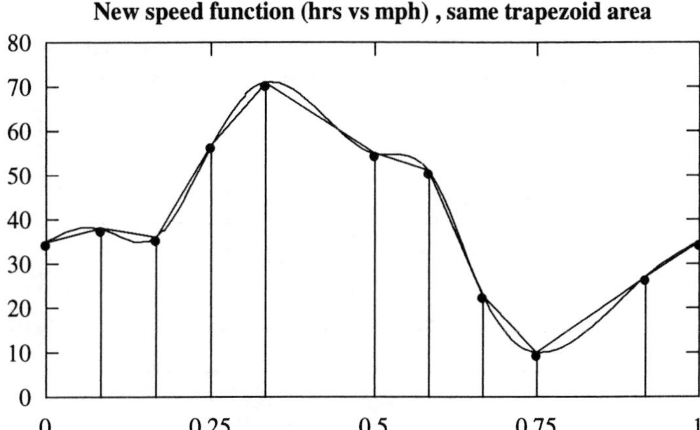

□

Areas in the plane; measuring by slicing

We first defined the integral in terms of area bounded by the graph of one function. Not surprisingly, integrals can also be used to measure areas of more general plane areas, e.g., areas bounded by two or more graphs. Approximating sums help show how and why.

■ **Example 3.** Using an integral, measure the area shown below. (It's bounded by the graphs of $y = \sin x$ and $y = \cos x$.)

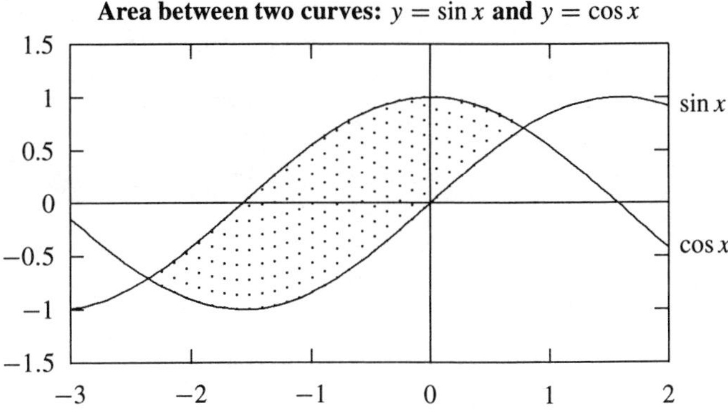

Solution: The picture itself suggests an approximate solution. We'll *slice* the area into vertical strips, approximate each strip by a *rectangle*, and add up the rectangles' areas. Here's the picture for 10 rectangles:➡

The first rectangle has height 0.

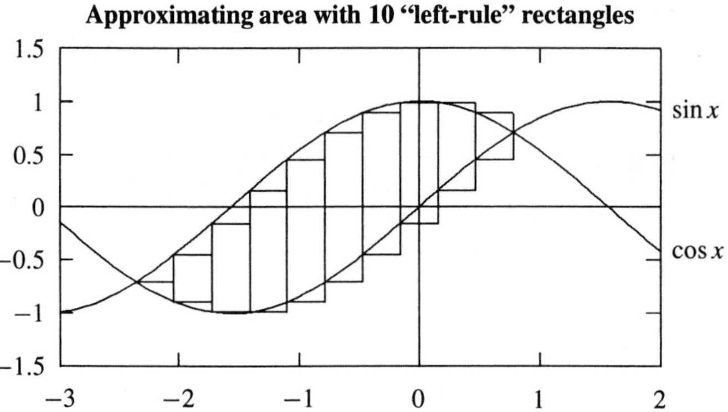

Look carefully:

Do you see why?

- The curves intersect at $x = -3\pi/4$ and $x = \pi/4$. (Because $\cos x - \sin x \geq 0$ over the interval $[-3\pi/4, \pi/4]$, the integral gives the true shaded area desired—even though part of the area lies below the x-axis.)

- The height of each rectangle is determined at its *left* edge $x = x_i$; the height itself is $\cos(x_i) - \sin(x_i)$.

- The total area of all ten rectangles is L_{10}, the *left sum* with 10 equal subdivisions for the function $\cos x - \sin x$ on the interval $[-3\pi/4, \pi/4]$. (It isn't necessary to solve our problem, but by machine, calculating L_{10} is easy; we get 2.80513.)

Geometric intuition says that as $n \to \infty$, the area L_n tends to the exact area we want. By the limit definition of integral, L_n *also* tends to the integral in question. We conclude:

$$\textit{Our desired area is the integral } \int_{-3\pi/4}^{\pi/4} (\cos x - \sin x)\, dx.$$

But check the details.

Finding an exact answer is now easy, thanks to the FTC:

$$\begin{aligned} \text{area} &= \int_{-3\pi/4}^{\pi/4} (\cos x - \sin x)\, dx \\ &= \sin x + \cos x \Big]_{-3\pi/4}^{\pi/4} \\ &= 2\sqrt{2} \approx 2.82843. \end{aligned}$$

□

Draw a general picture to illustrate.

A more general fact applies:

> **Fact:** Let f and g be any continuous functions. Let R be the region bounded above by g, below by f, and on the left and right by $x = a$ and $x = b$. Then R has area $\int_a^b (g - f)$.

Two basic area formulas

The simplest plane regions, from our point of view, are bounded *above* by the graph of one function, below by the x-axis, and on the left and right by vertical lines, like this:

Area at its simplest

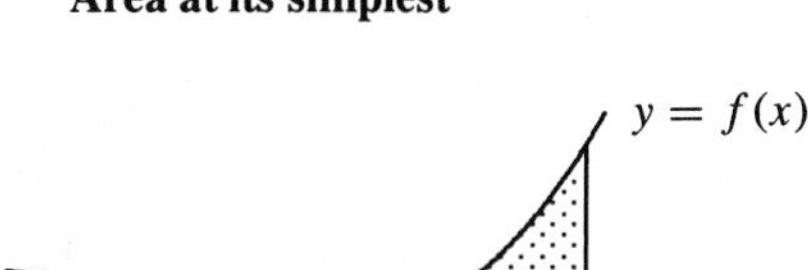
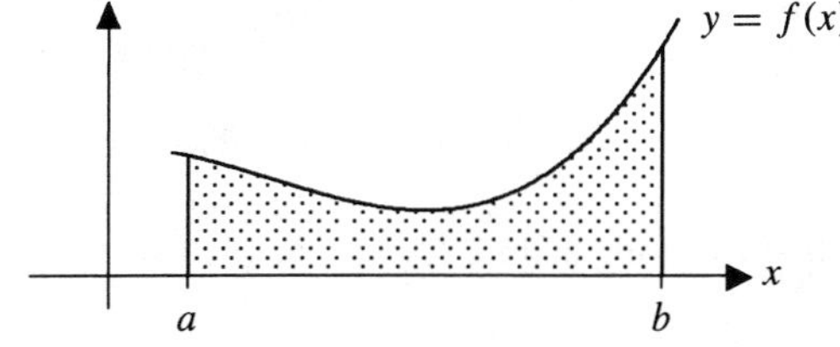

In this simplest case, the integral $\int_a^b f(x)\,dx$ measures the shaded area.

More interesting, but slightly more complicated, regions may be bounded by various types of curves—not necessarily all graphs of functions. Two common types appear below:

Some plane regions are of neither *type shown. However, many regions, even quite complicated ones, are combinations of regions of the two types below.*

Region 1: top and bottom curves

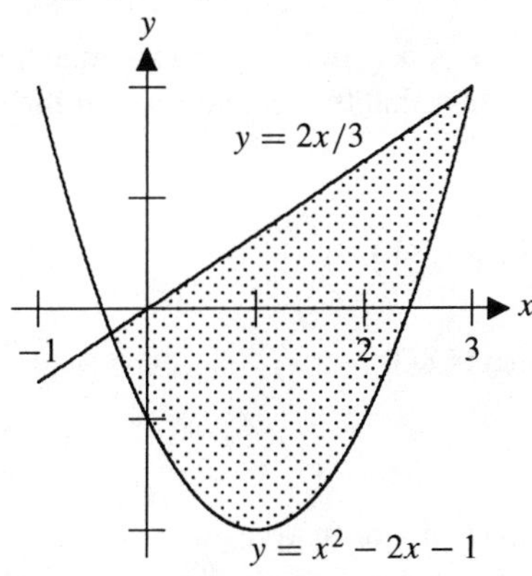

Region 2: right and left curves

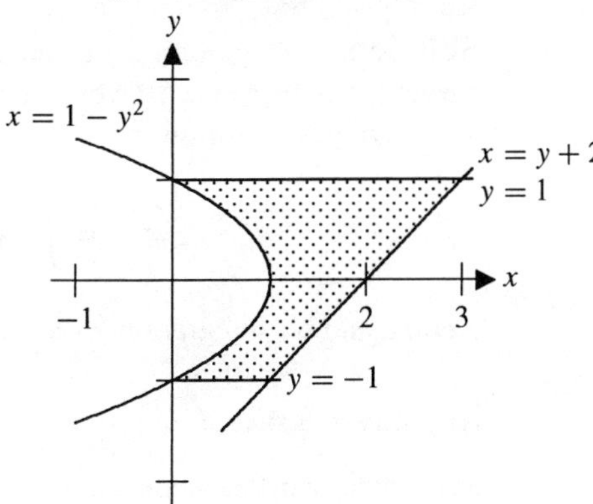

The following rules apply to finding areas like those above:

> **Fact:** Let f and g be continuous functions.
>
> **Integrating in x.** Let R be the region bounded *above* by $y = g(x)$, *below* by $y = f(x)$, on the *left* by $x = a$, and on the *right* by $x = b$. Then R has area
>
> $$\int_a^b \big(g(x) - f(x)\big)\,dx.$$
>
> **Integrating in y.** Let R be the region bounded on the *right* by $x = g(y)$, on the *left* by $x = f(y)$, *below* by $y = c$, and *above* by $y = d$. Then R has area
>
> $$\int_c^d \big(g(y) - f(y)\big)\,dy.$$

For Region 2 above, and others like it, integrating in y may be much simpler.

Using the rules

Using the rules effectively may require a combination of graphical, algebraic, and symbolic operations. We illustrate by example.

■ **Example 4.** Find the area of Region 1 above.

Convince yourself of this!

Solution: The graphs *appear* to intersect at $x = 3$. Indeed they do. By the quadratic formula,

$$\tfrac{2}{3}x = x^2 - 2x - 1 \iff x = 3 \text{ or } x = -\tfrac{1}{3}.$$

(This shows, in fact, that the two graphs intersect also at $x = -1/3$, to the left of the shaded region.)

Now, by the first rule (and a close look at the picture):

$$\text{area} = \int_0^3 \left(\tfrac{2}{3}x - \left(x^2 - 2x - 1\right)\right)\,dx.$$

A simple antiderivative calculation shows the result to be 6. □

■ **Example 5.** Find the area of Region 2 above.

Solution: Integration in x seems impractical, since defining upper and lower curves is troublesome. However, a close look shows that the second form of the rule above applies, as follows:

$$\text{area} = \int_{-1}^{1} \left(y + 2 - \left(1 - y^2\right)\right)\,dy.$$

In the variable y, this time.

Another simple integration shows that the area is 8/3. □

Any way you slice it

Some areas can be calculated by integration either in x or in y.

■ **Example 6.** Find the area of the region R bounded by the curves $x = 0$, $y = 2$, and $y = e^x$.

Solution: Here's the picture:

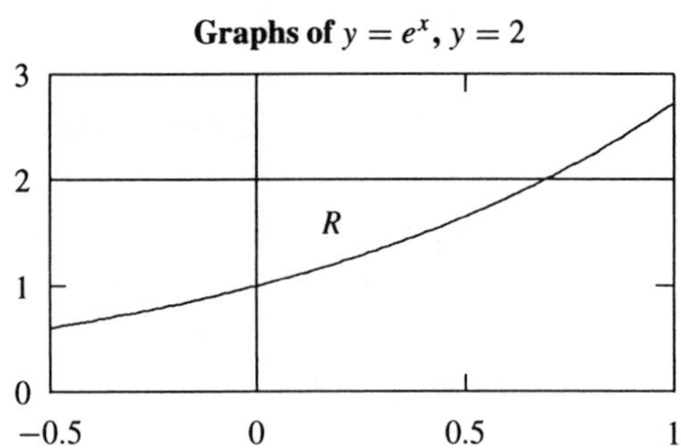

The two curves intersect where $e^x = 2$, i.e., at $x = \ln 2$. Therefore

$$\text{area of } R = \int_0^{\ln 2} \left(2 - e^x\right)\,dx.$$

Why is this legitimate?

To find the same area in terms of y, we rewrite the equation $y = e^x$ in the equivalent form $x = \ln y$; the associated curve becomes our *right* boundary. Then

$$\text{area of } R = \int_1^2 \ln y\,dy.$$

Either integral is easy to calculate. For the last one (recalling that $y \ln y - y$ is an antiderivative of $\ln y$, we get

$$\text{area} = y \ln y - y]_1^2 = 2 \ln 2 - 1 \approx 0.3863.$$

□

Exercises

1. Let A be the region between the curves $y = x$ and $y = x^2$.

   (a) Draw a sketch of the region A.

   (b) Use 5 left rule rectangles to approximate the area of A. (Give a numerical answer.)

   (c) Draw a picture (similar to the one on p. 434) that illustrates the sum you computed in part (b). Use this picture to decide whether your answer overestimates or underestimates the area of A.

   (d) Find the area of A *exactly* by integration.

2. Find the area of the region bounded by the curves $y = \sin x$ and $y = \cos x$, and the lines $x = 1$ and $x = 3$ *exactly* (i.e., express your answer in terms of values of elementary functions rather than as a decimal number.)

Sketch the region bounded by the given curves and find the area of the region *exactly*.

3. $y = x^4, \quad y = 1$
4. $y = x, \quad y = x^3$
5. $y = x^2, \quad y = x^3$
6. $y = x^2 - 1, \quad y = x + 1$
7. $x = y^2 - 4, \quad y = 2 - x$
8. $y = \sqrt{x}, \quad y = 0, \quad x = 4$
9. $y = \sqrt{x}, \quad y = x^2$
10. $y = 9(4x + 5)^{-1}, \quad y = 2 - x$
11. $y = 9\left(4x^2 + 5\right)^{-1}, \quad y = 2 - x^2$
12. $y = \sin x, \quad y = \cos x, \quad x = 1, \quad x = 3$
13. $y = 2 + \cos x, \quad y = \sec^2 x, \quad x = -\pi/4, \quad x = \pi/6$
14. $y = e^x, \quad y = 0, \quad x = 0, \quad x = 1$
15. $y = 2^x, \quad y = 5^x, \quad x = -1, \quad x = 1$

5.6 Chapter summary

Chapter 5 introduces the **integral**. The derivative and the integral are the two most important concepts of calculus. Remarkably, they're closely related: the **fundamental theorem of calculus** describes how and why.

The integral as signed area. In Section 5.1 the integral is introduced graphically, as measuring in terms of **signed area**. ("Signed" means that area below the x-axis counts negatively.) The graphical viewpoint, though insufficient for *exact* calculations, explains clearly what the integral is, and why some of its elementary properties hold.

The area function. Given a function f and "starting point" $x = a$, we define the related **area function** A_f:

$$A_f(x) = \int_a^x f = \text{signed area bounded by } f \text{ from } a \text{ to } x.$$

Once its peculiar-looking definition is understood, the area function is easy to understand. Simple examples suggest, moreover, that the area function is an **antiderivative** for f. This idea, suitably embellished, is the simplest form of the **fundamental theorem of calculus**.

The fundamental theorem. Put more formally, the fundamental theorem says that if A_f is defined as above, then

$$\frac{d}{dx}\big(A_f(x)\big) = f(x).$$

This result connects derivatives and integrals—the two main calculus ideas. For that reason, it's deservedly called fundamental.

The same idea, restated in another form, is called the **second version of the fundamental theorem**:

If F is *any* antiderivative of f, then

$$\int_a^b f(x)\,dx = F(b) - F(a).$$

In other words:

To find $\int_a^b f$*, find* any *antiderivative, plug in endpoints, and subtract.*

As one useful consequence, the theorem permits easy calculations of certain areas.

The integral as a limit of approximating sums. Like the derivative, the integral must be defined rigorously as a limit—of approximating sums. Section 5.4 describes the procedure. Although symbolically messy, approximating sums make good graphical sense. Several varieties are introduced, compared, and calculated. (With computers, calculating approximating sums is easy; without, it's almost impossible.)

Approximating sums and applications of the integral. Thinking of the integral as a limit of sums suggests a variety of applications. Several are presented; the main point is that the integral is capable of various interpretations.

One application of the integral concerns rates and amounts:

> *If $f(t)$ tells the* rate *at which a quantity varies at time t, then $\int_a^b f$ tells the* amount *by which the same quantity varies over the interval from $t = a$ to $t = b$.*

Another application of the integral is to calculating areas of plane regions defined by graphs of functions. Such regions come in many shapes and forms. Choosing exactly the right integral to calculate a given area can be a challenging problem. We illustrate various techniques for doing so.

Appendix A

Real numbers and the coordinate plane

The real numbers might seem, at first glance, almost *too* familiar. What is there to say? Surprisingly, a great deal—far more than a calculus course could cover.

Here's just one hint at the subtleties: It's been known since Pythagoras (*ca.* 500 B.C.) that some numbers, such as $\sqrt{2}$, are **irrational**—that is, they can't be written as *ratios* of integers. But how *thickly scattered* are the irrationals among the reals? Are "most" real numbers rational or irrational? The answers are remarkable, even mysterious: "most" real numbers are irrational; a dart thrown randomly at a number line will almost always hit an irrational. Yet plenty of rational numbers exist; in any interval, no matter how small, there are *infinitely many* rational numbers! Resolving these tantalizing mysteries must wait for a later mathematics course. For us, a brief, brisk, selective review of the properties of real numbers will suffice.

Isaac Newton himself did quite well without a fully rigorous development of the real numbers. The first mathematically satisfactory *definition* of the real numbers was given by Richard Dedekind, over 130 years after Newton's death.

The real number line

The real numbers are really no more *real*, in an existential or philosophical sense, than the integers, the rationals, or even the complex numbers. The best reason for the adjective "real" may be that the set of real numbers can be thought of naturally as an unbroken, unending *line*. Once an origin and a unit of distance are fixed, every point has its own number and every number its own point. Here is the usual picture:

Order. The best feature of the line is that it shows nicely how the reals are **ordered**: *as we move to the right on the line, real numbers increase.* This is important, so we restate it as an inequality:

$$a > b \text{ if and only if } a \text{ is to the right of } b.$$

At the risk of redundancy, we'll say it one last time: for real numbers, "greater than" means "to the right of." Thus, for example, $-3 > -4$, even though -4 has greater *magnitude* than -3.

Subsets of the reals, subsets of the line

The set of real numbers, like any infinite set, has a gigantic infinity of possible subsets. Some have fiendishly complicated structures. ("Fractals," for example, are sets that are irregular or ragged at any scale. The most spectacular fractal sets are usually shown in two dimensions, but many fractals have one-dimensional forms.) In calculus, luckily, most subsets of interest are easily understood.

Intervals. Intervals are "pieces" chopped from the real line. They are the simplest and most useful subsets of the reals. Intervals come in various styles: they can be bounded or infinitely long, and they may or may not include their endpoints. (**Closed intervals** contain their endpoints, **open intervals** don't.➽) The table of examples below illustrates the full taxonomy. It also shows that every interval can be defined by one or more inequalities:

Calculus inevitably requires that some mathematical language (closed, open, infinite, bounded, etc.) be learned, and then used carefully. The work may be hard, but the rewards are great.

Taxonomy of intervals

Interval	*Description*	*Inequality form*
$(-2, 3)$	an *open* interval	$\{x \mid -2 < x < 3\}$
$[a, b]$	a *closed* interval	$\{x \mid a \le x \le b\}$
$[2, b)$	a half-open interval	$\{x \mid 2 \le x < b\}$
$(5, \infty)$	an infinite interval	$\{x \mid x > 5\}$
$(-\infty, \infty)$	another infinite interval	

More subsets of $\mathbb{R}$. Below are more examples of subsets of the reals. Notice carefully our use of various mathematical *notations*, especially $\mathbb{R}$, $\mathbb{Q}$, and $\mathbb{Z}$ for the sets of reals, rationals, and integers. These notations are standard in mathematical writing; we will use them often.

Subsets of the reals

Set	*Explanation*	*Alternative notation(s)*
$\mathbb{R}$	the real numbers	$(-\infty, \infty)$
$\mathbb{N}$	the natural numbers	$\{1, 2, 3, \dots\}$
$\mathbb{Z}$	the integers	$\{0, \pm 1, \pm 2, \pm 3, \dots\}$
$\mathbb{Q}$	the rationals	
$\{0, 2, 5\}$	a finite set	$\{x \mid x = 0 \text{ or } x = 2 \text{ or } x = 5\}$
		$\{x \mid x(x-2)(x-5) = 0\}$
$(1, 4) \cup (5, 6)$	*union* of two intervals	$\{x \mid 1 < x < 4 \text{ or } 5 < x < 6\}$
$(1, 6) \cap [4, 7]$	*intersection* of two intervals	$\{x \mid 1 < x < 6 \text{ and } 4 \le x \le 7\}$,
		$\{x \mid 4 \le x < 6\}$
		$[4, 6)$

Pictures of subsets. Uncomplicated subsets of the reals are easy to "draw" on the real line. Intervals are nicest of all: they appear as line segments, including some, all, or none of their endpoints. Errors of approximation are inevitable in *all* pictures, but for most sets they do no harm. Several straightforward examples appear below; a *closed* dot indicates an *included* point; an *open* dots indicates an *excluded* point.

For example, because ideal "points" on a line, unlike pencil points, have zero thickness. Errors of omission are also inevitable; no picture can show everything.

Drawing Sets

Set	*Picture*
$(-2, 3)$	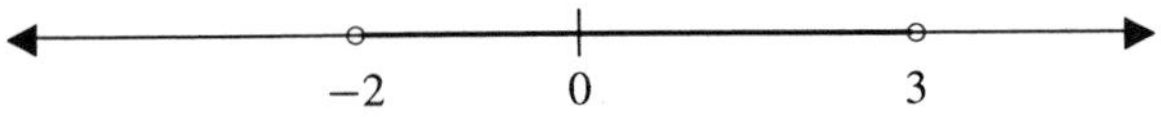 −2 0 3
$[3, \infty)$	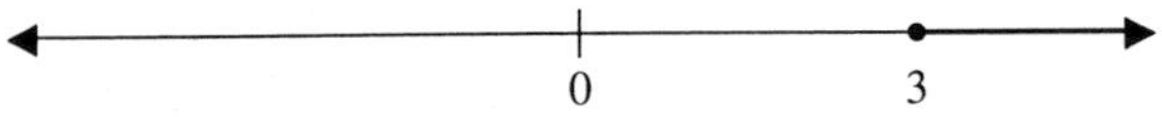 0 3
$(-3, 2]$	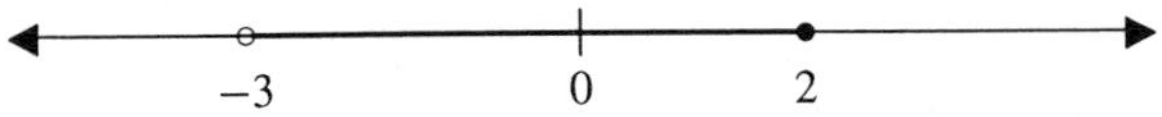 −3 0 2
$\mathbb{Z}$	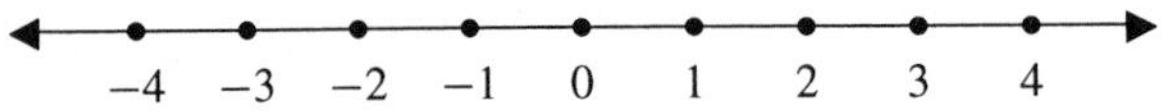 −4 −3 −2 −1 0 1 2 3 4
$[-4, -2) \cup (1, 3)$	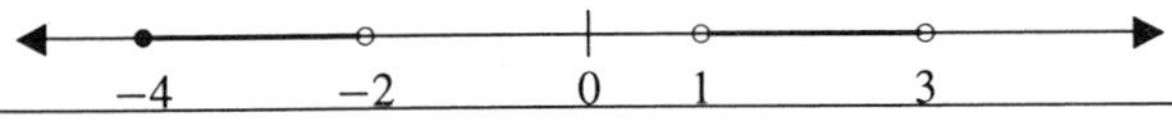 −4 −2 0 1 3

The symbol ∞: *not* a number

Every real number corresponds to a unique point on the real line. The symbol ∞ does not; ∞ *is not a real number.*

What *is* ∞, if not a number?

That's a thorny question indeed, in a league with "What is truth?" A fully rigorous answer is very far beyond the scope of this book. A good enough answer for us (and for most working mathematicians, most of the time) is that the ∞ symbol represents the idea of *unboundedness*, or *endlessness.* When we say that the real line has *infinite* length, for instance, we mean that the line goes on forever.

The ∞ symbol is a useful, convenient, and suggestive shorthand for the idea of "without bound." Use it sparingly and with care; ∞ is *not* a number and seldom behaves like one. In particular, "algebra" with the infinity symbol takes special care.

For more on "algebra with ∞," see Section 2.6.

Absolute value, distance, and inequalities

The idea of **absolute value** (or **magnitude**) should be familiar from long experience. Its use in simple expressions like these—

$$|-3| = 3; \qquad |\sin x| \le 1; \qquad \sqrt{x^2} = |x|$$

will cause no trouble. What absolute value means is usually clear in context, but sometimes a formal definition is helpful. Here it is:

$$|x| = \begin{cases} x & \text{if } x \ge 0 \\ -x & \text{if } x < 0 \end{cases}$$

Familiar as all this is, absolute values can still be sticky in practice—especially if inequalities are involved. Two useful tricks of the trade often help.

If you learn nothing else about absolute values, learn these facts.

- **Interpreting absolute value as distance.** For *any* numbers a and b, $|a-b|$ can (and should!) be thought of as the *distance from a to b.* Thinking of absolute value as distance helps us visualize algebraic expressions geometrically. For example, the absolute value equation

Perhaps we should say the distance between a and b, *since the distance in both directions is the same. The equation $|a-b| = |b-a|$ says the same thing.*

$$|x+2| = 3$$

isn't hard to solve algebraically, but the algebraic solution doesn't provide us with much insight. Distance brings the situation to life. Because

$$|x+2| = |x-(-2)| = \text{distance from } x \text{ to } -2,$$

the equation $|x+2| = 3$ says that *x lies 3 units away from* -2. Clearly, $x = -5$ and $x = 1$ are the only solutions of the equation.

- **Trading absolute values for inequalities: two for one.** In calculus, inequalities often involve absolute values. Here's one:

$$|x+2| < 3$$

Solving such inequalities requires care. Here's the key idea: *One absolute value inequality corresponds to two ordinary inequalities.*

To solve an inequality involving a variable x means to find—and describe concisely—the solution set, the set of values of x for which the inequality holds.

The inequality above is equivalent to these two:

$$-3 < x+2 \quad \textbf{and} \quad x+2 < 3$$

or, more succinctly, $-3 < x+2 < 3$. Now it's easy find the solution set: $-5 < x < 1$. In other words, the inequality $|x+2| < 3$ holds precisely for those x that lie in the interval $(-5, 1)$; the set of points that lie within 3 units of -2.

More generally, for *any* quantities x and b:

$$|x| < b \quad \text{if and only if} \quad -b < x < b$$
$$|x| > b \quad \text{if and only if} \quad -b > x \ \textbf{or} \ x > b$$

(Similar rules hold for $\le$ and $\ge$ inequalities.)

■ **Example 1.** Any open or closed finite interval can be described in terms of its **midpoint** and **radius**; absolute value inequalities help. The open interval $(-3, 5)$, for instance, has midpoint $x = 1$ and radius 4 because the distance from every point in the interval to 1 is less than 4. Therefore, $(-3, 5)$ corresponds naturally to the inequality $|x - 1| < 4$. In formal language:

$$(-3, 5) = \{ x \mid |x - 1| < 4 \}$$

□

■ **Example 2.** Solve the inequality $|2x + 3| \le 5$.

Solution: By the second fact above, the inequality

$$|2x + 3| \le 5$$

is equivalent to

$$-5 \le 2x + 3 \le 5$$

Now the usual algebraic rules for inequalities apply:

$$-5 \le 2x + 3 \le 5 \iff -8 \le 2x \le 2 \iff -4 \le x \le 1$$

(The symbol $\iff$ means "if and only if"; it indicates that either side implies the other.) We conclude that the inequality holds if and only if x lies in the interval $[-4, 1]$. □

■ **Example 3.** Solve $|x - 2| > |x + 3|$.

Solution: Having absolute values on *both sides* of the inequality complicates things. A workable—but tedious—strategy is to look separately at several cases: $x < -3$, $-3 \le x < 2$, and $x \ge 2$.

An easier approach is to interpret *both sides* as distance. If we do, the given inequality says simply:

Convince yourself of this—it's easy but important.

x is farther from 2 than from -3.

Now the solution set is easy to visualize; it's everything to the *left* of $-1/2$, the point halfway between 2 and -3. In interval notation, the solution set is $(-\infty, -1/2)$. □

Draw yourself a picture!

Most absolute value inequalities arise in richer contexts. Here is one in its natural habitat.

■ **Example 4.** Solve the inequality $|x - \sin(x)| < 0.1$.

Solution: How might such an inequality arise? Why does an answer matter? Consider these graphs of two functions:

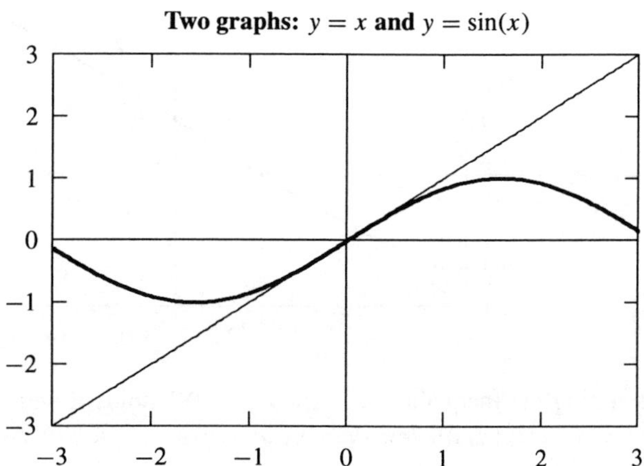

The picture shows that $\sin(x) \approx x$ if $x \approx 0$. This approximation has practical value, but only if we know something of *how* closely x approximates $\sin(x)$. Thus we might ask: for which values of x do x and $\sin(x)$ differ (in either direction) by less than 0.1? That's exactly what our original inequality, $|x - \sin(x)| < 0.1$, asks.

We'll solve our inequality graphically. Here's a piece of the graph of $y = x - \sin(x)$:

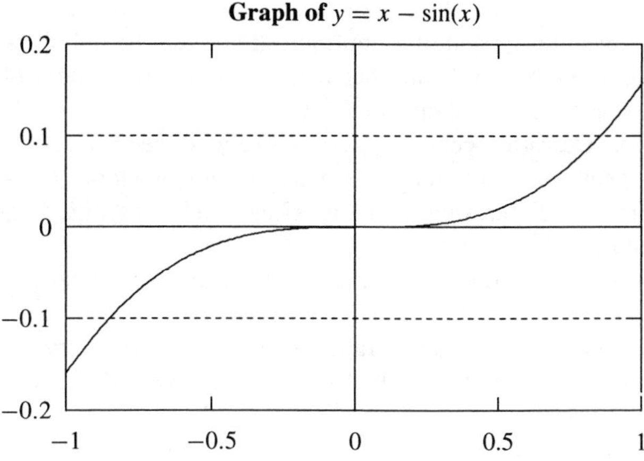

For what values of x does the inequality $-0.1 < x - \sin(x) < 0.1$ holds? The graph shows➽ that this occurs for $-0.8 < x < 0.8$. *Approximately, of course.*

Further graphical insight is available. Here's a closer look at the two original graphs:

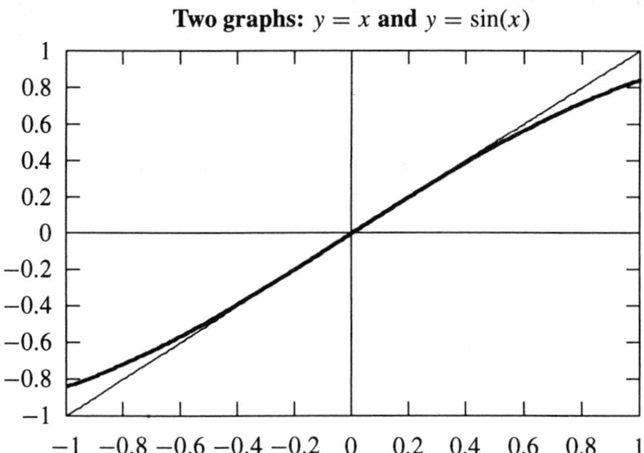

In this setting the inequality $|x - \sin(x)| < 0.1$ holds if and only if *the graphs of* $y = x$ *and* $y = \sin(x)$ *are less than* 0.1 *unit apart, vertically.* As we've already seen, this occurs for $-0.8 < x < 0.8$.

Approximately!

The coordinate plane

The real numbers correspond to points on a *line*. In much the same way, *pairs of real numbers* correspond to points in the *coordinate plane.*

Dearly beloved . . .

The idea of attaching numerical coordinates to points in the plane is credited to the French philosopher René Descartes (1596–1650). It is no exaggeration to describe Descartes's idea, natural as it seems in hindsight, as one of the most powerful in intellectual history.

Descartes's idea is powerful because it links *geometry* with *algebra* and *analysis.* Geometry is the study of figures—lines, curves, circles, etc.—in the plane. Algebra studies operations—addition, multiplication, etc.—on numbers and on functions. Analysis is harder to define, but it includes the main ideas of calculus, such as function, derivative, and integral.

Before Descartes, geometry was relatively isolated from other branches of mathematics; geometers used compasses and other drawing tools to construct and measure plane figures. Figures *not* based on circles and lines were harder to describe and manipulate.

The *parabola*, for instance, was described geometrically as the set of points equidistant from a fixed point and a fixed line. Properties of the parabola (such as the *reflection property*: all rays parallel to the axis of symmetry "bounce" to the same point, the *focus*) were hard to understand and prove with purely geometric tools and ways of thinking.

The great advantage of Cartesian coordinates is that they allow *algebraic* descriptions of geometric figures in the plane. The algebraic equation $y = x^2$, for example, describes a parabola in a far simpler and, for many purposes, more convenient fashion than its geometric properties.

When geometric figures are described algebraically the powerful tools and ideas of algebra and analysis kick in. The connection, moreover, goes both ways: geometric intuition sheds light on algebraic and analytic problems.

This link is the essence of the field of mathematics known (logically enough) as **analytic geometry**. In its most familiar form, analytic geometry studies properties of lines, circles, ellipses, parabolas, and hyperbolas. Collectively, these figures are called **conic sections**, because each can be thought of, *geometrically*, as a slice (i.e., *section*) of a **cone**. (The "cone" in question is hollow, and may be "double," as in the case of a hyperbola.)

The key idea for us is that the conic sections can be described *algebraically*, as graphs of quadratic equations. (The equation $x^2 + 2y^2 = 1$, for example, describes an ellipse.) Thus, properties of quadratic equations are, from another point of view, properties of conic sections, and *vice versa*. Knowledge of either tells us something of the other.

Throughout calculus, linking geometric, algebraic, and analytic ideas is absolutely crucial to understanding; it is the most important theme of this course.

Amen. Back to work.

Coordinates

A **rectangular coordinate system** in the plane has three parts: two perpendicular *axes*, with scales, and an *origin* at their intersection. By convention, the x-axis is horizontal and numbered from left to right; the y-axis is vertical and numbered from bottom to top. (These are *only* conventions. "Tilted" axes, other numbering schemes, and other variable names are all possible.)

With a coordinate system in place, every point's coordinates are defined. Here is the familiar picture; several points have coordinates labeled:

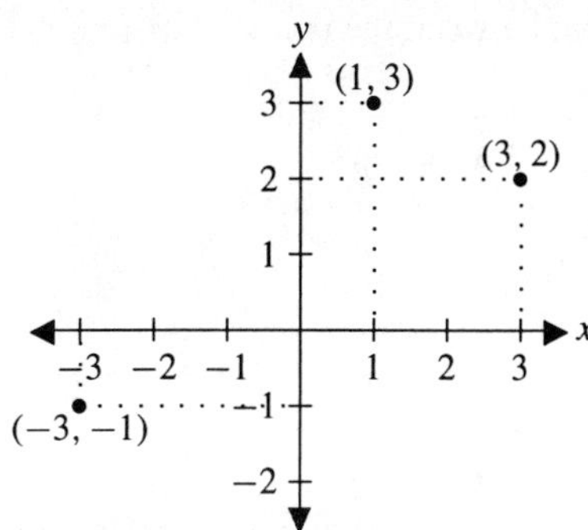

A coordinate system defines a one-to-one correspondence between points in the plane and pairs of real numbers: each point corresponds uniquely to its two coordinates.

Cartesian addresses. The coordinates of a point are, in a sense, the point's "address"—they *locate* the point in the plane. A point's Cartesian address, moreover, gives *explicit directions for getting there*: To reach (a, b), from the origin, go a units "east" and b units "north." This is more than can be said for typical street addresses—123 Elm Street, for instance. (Some cities, of course, do use Cartesian-style numerical addresses.)

Calculating with coordinates: distance and midpoint

Using Cartesian coordinates, many questions about points in the plane can be reduced to straightforward, direct calculations.

The midpoint formula. Recall the situation in *one* dimension: If x_1 and x_2 are points on the real *line*, their midpoint, m, is just their average: $m = (x_1 + x_2)/2$.

A similar situation holds in the plane. To find the midpoint, M, of the segment joining points $P = (x_1, y_1)$ and $Q = (x_2, y_2)$, we average their x- and y-coordinates *separately*:

$$M = \left(\frac{x_1 + x_2}{2}, \frac{y_1 + y_2}{2} \right)$$

A picture makes everything plausible:

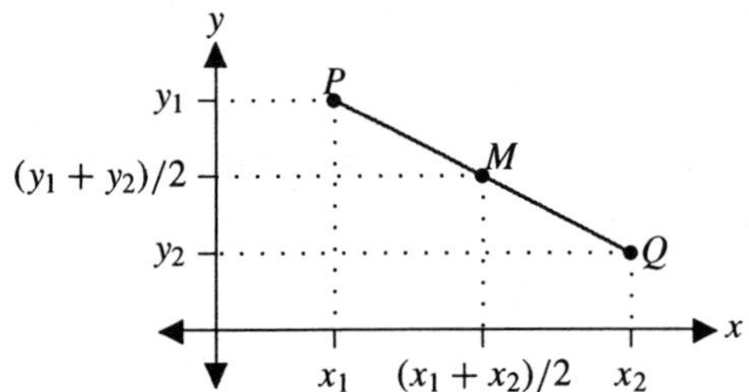

In particular, the coordinates of M are, respectively, midpoints of intervals on the two axes.

Distance. On the *line* the situation is simple: the distance between x_1 and x_2 is $|x_2 - x_1|$. The distance formula in the *plane*, like the midpoint formula, derives from the one-dimensional situation.

What's the distance between the points $P = (x_1, y_1)$ and $Q = (x_2, y_2)$? Here's the picture:

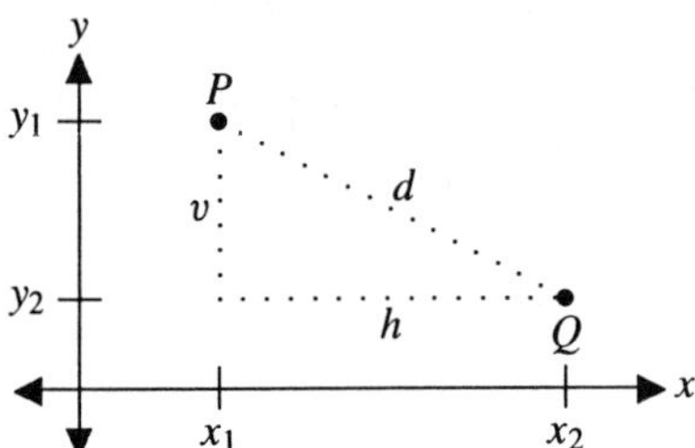

As the picture shows, the distance from P to Q (labeled d) is the hypotenuse of a right triangle, with sides (labeled h and v) parallel to the axes. We'll use the Pythagorean theorem to find d, but first we need values for h and v. By the *one*-dimensional formula:

$$h = |x_2 - x_1| \quad \text{and} \quad v = |y_2 - y_1| .$$

Notice where (and why!) the absolute value signs conveniently vanished.

The distance formula now follows easily:

$$d = \sqrt{h^2 + v^2} = \sqrt{|x_2 - x_1|^2 + |y_2 - y_1|^2} = \sqrt{(x_2 - x_1)^2 + (y_2 - y_1)^2}$$

The last form is standard. To summarize:

> **Fact:** The distance from $P = (x_1, y_1)$ to $Q = (x_2, y_2)$ is given by $d(P, Q) = \sqrt{(x_2 - x_1)^2 + (y_2 - y_1)^2}$.

Elementary properties of distance in the plane follow from this formula:

The same distance either way. Intuition says that the distance from P to Q should be equal to the distance from Q to P. All is well (but check the equation carefully to see why):

$$\begin{aligned} d(P,Q) &= \sqrt{(x_2-x_1)^2+(y_2-y_1)^2} \\ &= \sqrt{(x_1-x_2)^2+(y_1-y_2)^2} \\ &= d(Q,P). \end{aligned}$$

Finding the midpoint. It stands to reason that the **midpoint** M between $P = (x_1, y_1)$ and $Q = (x_2, y_2)$ should be equidistant from both. An ugly computation (check the details, as an algebra exercise!) shows that this is indeed so. Squaring everything in sight helps a little:

$$\begin{aligned} d(P,M)^2 &= \left(\frac{x_1+x_2}{2}-x_1\right)^2+\left(\frac{y_1+y_2}{2}-y_1\right)^2 \\ &= \frac{(x_2-x_1)^2}{4}+\frac{(y_2-y_1)^2}{4} \\ &= \frac{(x_1-x_2)^2}{4}+\frac{(y_1-y_2)^2}{4} \\ &= \left(\frac{x_1+x_2}{2}-x_2\right)^2+\left(\frac{y_1+y_2}{2}-y_2\right)^2 \\ &= d(M,Q)^2. \end{aligned}$$

Using the distance and midpoint formulas

Simply finding distances and midpoints is neither very edifying nor, fortunately, very common in calculus. More often, such calculations arise in more interesting contexts.

Circles. A circle is, by definition, the set of points at some fixed distance, say r, from a center, say $C = (a, b)$. The distance formula puts all this conveniently and simply, in algebraic form:

> *The point* $P = (x, y)$ *lies on the circle if and only if* $d(P, C) = \sqrt{(x-a)^2+(y-b)^2} = r$.

It's equivalently to say that the circle has equation $(x-a)^2 + (y-b)^2 = r^2$.

■ **Example 5.** Find an algebraic equation for the circle of radius 5, centered at $C = (3, 2)$.

Solution: A point $P = (x, y)$ lies on this circle if and only if $d(P, C) = 5$. Thus,

$$\sqrt{(x-3)^2+(y-2)^2} = 5$$

is an algebraic equation for this circle. We're done; we've found a perfectly acceptable algebraic equation. For anyone squeamish about square roots, there are other, equivalent, forms:➻

The $\Longleftrightarrow$ symbol means "if and only if."

$$\sqrt{(x-3)^2+(y-2)^2}=5 \iff (x-3)^2+(y-2)^2=25$$
$$\iff x^2+y^2-6x-4y-12=0$$
$$\iff x^2+y^2-6x-4y=12 \qquad \square$$

■ **Example 6.** Is $x^2+4x+y^2-2y=10$ the equation of a circle? If so, which one?

Solution: Let's *complete the square* in both x and y:

$$x^2+4x+y^2-2y=10 \iff \left(x^2+4x+4\right)+\left(y^2-2y+1\right)=10+4+1$$
$$\iff (x+2)^2+(y-1)^2=15$$

The answer can now be read off: the equation is that of a circle of radius $\sqrt{15}$ centered at $(-2,1)$. □

■ **Example 7.** It's well known among those who know such things that *the segment joining the midpoints of two sides of a triangle is parallel to the third side, and half its length.* Classical geometers would have proved this "constructively," with drawing tools. With coordinates the proof is an easy calculation.

Here's a picture; we arranged things to simplify calculations, but convince yourself that we did nothing illegal:

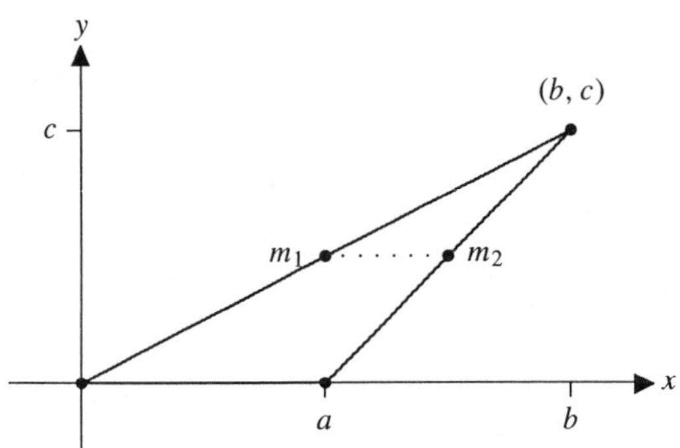

To prove our first claim—that the segment joining m_1 and m_2 is horizontal—it's enough to show that m_1 and m_2 have the same "height." By the midpoint formula,

$$m_1=(b/2,c/2) \qquad \text{and} \qquad m_2=\big((a+b)/2,c/2\big).$$

Thus m_1 and m_2 have the same y-coordinate, as claimed. We leave the remaining claim (about lengths) as an exercise. □

Exercises

1. Express each of the following intervals using absolute value inequalities.

(a) $(0,10)$
(b) $[-\pi,\pi]$
(c) $(-2,4)$
(d) $(2,8)$
(e) $[-3,7]$
(f) $[-10,-2]$

2. Express each of the following sets using absolute value inequalities.

(a) $\{x \mid x < -3 \quad \text{or} \quad x > 3\}$

(b) $\{x \mid x < -5 \quad \text{or} \quad x > 3\}$

(c) $\{x \mid -7 < x \quad \text{and} \quad x < 7\}$

(d) $\{x \mid -7 < x \quad \text{and} \quad x < 5\}$

3. Express each of the following sets using interval notation.

(a) $\{x \mid -10 < x \leq 15\}$

(b) $\{x \mid -6 \leq x < 4\}$

(c) $\{x \mid -13 < x < 17\}$

(d) $\{x \mid |x| \leq 3\}$

(e) $\{x \mid |x-2| \leq 5\}$

(f) $\{x \mid |x+3| \leq 4\}$

(g) $\{x \mid |x-a| < b\}$

(h) $\{x \mid |x-a| < a\}$

4. Explain why each of the following statements is true for every real number r such that $3 < r < 7$.

(a) $|r| < 7$

(b) $|r| > 3$

(c) $|r-5| < 2$

5. Suppose s is a real number and that $-2 \leq s \leq 1$.

(a) Must $|s| \leq 1$ be true? Justify your answer.

(b) Must $|s| \leq 2$ be true? Justify your answer.

(c) Must $|s| < 10$ be true? Justify your answer.

6. Which of the following statements is true for every real number x such that $-3 \leq x \leq 11$? Justify your answers.

(a) $|x| < 12$

(b) $|x| > -1$

(c) $|x| \geq 2$

(d) $|x| > 4$

(e) $|x-4| < 7$

(f) $|x-7| < 4$

7. Suppose $|x - 11| \leq 0.02$. Find real numbers L and U such that $L \leq x \leq U$.

8. Express each of the following inequalities in the form $|x - A| \leq B$.

(a) $-3 \leq x \leq 9$

(b) $2 \leq x \leq 10$

(c) $-7 \leq x \leq -4$

(d) $5.9999 \leq x \leq 6.0001$

9. Suppose $L \leq x \leq U$. Show that $\left|x - \frac{1}{2}(L+U)\right| \leq \frac{1}{2}(U-L)$. [HINT: Draw a picture.]

10. Suppose $|x-3| \leq 0.005$ and $|y-2| \leq 0.003$. Find real numbers A and B such that $\left|(x+y) - A\right| \leq B$. [HINT: Draw a picture.]

11. Find the distance between each of the following pairs of points.

(a) $(0, 0)$ and $(2, 3)$

(b) $(1, 2)$ and $(3, 4)$

(c) $(-4, 2)$ and $(-7, -4)$

(d) $(-5, -2)$ and $(2, 5)$

12. Find the points in the xy-plane that are at distance 13 from the point $(1, 2)$ and have y-coordinate equal to -3. [HINT: Draw a picture.]

13. Find an algebraic equation for the circle of radius 4 centered at $(-3, 7)$.

14. Is $x^2 + y^2 - 6x - 8y = -9$ the equation of a circle? If so, which one?

15. Show that $3x^2 + 3y^2 + 4y = 7$ is the equation of a circle. Find the radius and center of this circle.

16. Show that the line segment joining the midpoint of two sides of a triangle is half the length of the third side.

Appendix B

Lines

Manipulating lines and linear functions is important throughout calculus. In this appendix we review the rudiments of lines: algebra, definitions, and techniques.

Slope

Slope measures a line's *steepness* (i.e., the *rate* at which a line rises or falls). Before reviewing the formal definition, study the picture below. Several lines appear, each labeled with its slope.

The letter m almost invariably stands for slope. Perhaps from the French monter–*to climb.*

Lines with various slopes

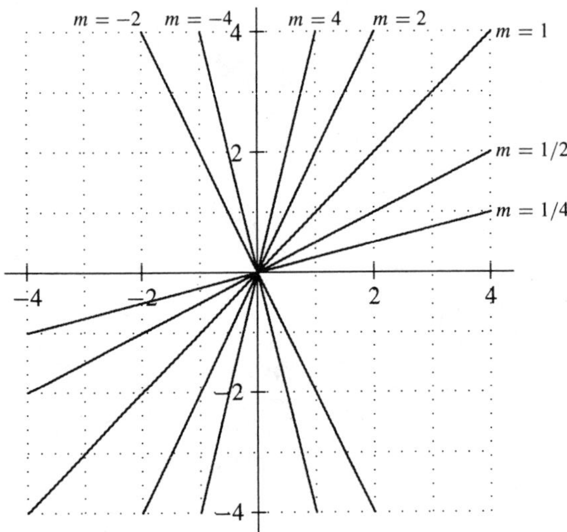

The picture illustrates the general situation:

> *Lines with* positive *slope* rise *(from left to right); lines with negative slope* fall. *The steeper the line, the larger the* absolute value *of its slope.*

> **Definition:** The **slope of a line** is the *ratio*
>
> $$\frac{y_2 - y_1}{x_2 - x_1}$$
>
> where (x_1, y_1) and (x_2, y_2) are *any* two points on the line.

Note:

- A line has the same slope everywhere; *any* two points on a line give the same slope. *Order* doesn't matter either—the slope from P to Q is the same as the slope from Q to P. In algebraic language,

  $$\frac{y_2 - y_1}{x_2 - x_1} = \frac{y_1 - y_2}{x_1 - x_2}.$$

Keeping the same order in numerator and denominator does matter, of course.

- Lines with equal slope are *parallel*. The slopes of *perpendicular* lines are negative reciprocals (i.e., their product is -1.)
- *Horizontal* lines have slope 0; slope is undefined for *vertical* lines. The definition shows why.
- It's easy to see that the line $y = x$ has slope 1. How steep the line *looks*, on the other hand, depends strongly on the size of units (i.e., the **scales**) on the x- and y-axes. To see the effect of scales, consider these three graphs of the line $y = x$:

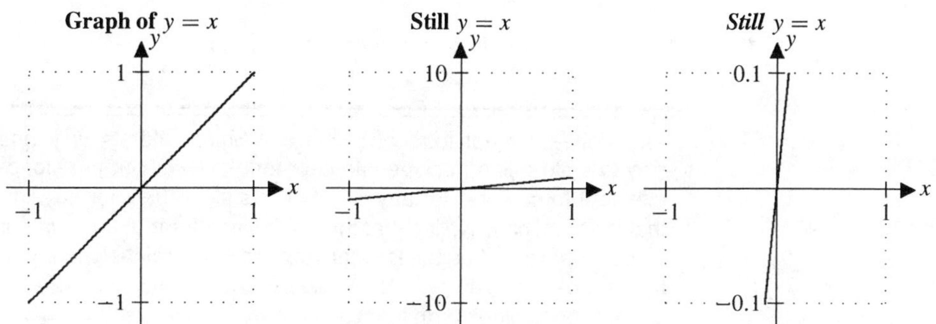

  If—but only if—identical scales are used on both axes, the line $y = x$ makes a 45° angle with the x-axis.

- The formula for slope is sometimes written as $\Delta y/\Delta x$, or as *rise/run.*

  The Δ-notation is a convenient shorthand. Invariably, Δ*anything* refers to a *change* in *anything*; it's usually calculated as the *difference* between a final value and an initial value. *Which* values these are must be made clear from context. For lines, things are simple: Δx is a *run*, or *horizontal* change; Δy is a *rise*, or *vertical* change. Either or both can be negative.

Convince yourself that these alternative versions really say the same thing.

- Slope is defined as the ratio $\Delta y/\Delta x$. Slope, therefore, is a *rate of change*—the rate of change of y with respect to x. The *straightness* of a line means that this rate is constant.

Lines, equations, and functions

A line is completely determined by two bits of information. It's enough to know either (1) two points on the line, or (2) just one point and the slope. With either sort of information, several simple algebraic descriptions of a line are possible. Here are two:

> **Definition: Point-slope form**: The line through (a, b) with slope m has equation $y = m(x - a) + b$.
>
> **Slope-intercept form**: The line with slope m and y-intercept b has equation $y = mx + b$.

■ **Example 1.** Consider the lines

$$\ell_1\text{: through } (0,1) \text{ and } (2,5);$$
$$\ell_2\text{: through } (-1,3)\text{, with slope } -2.$$

Describe each in point-slope form and in slope-intercept form.

Solution: The line ℓ_1 has slope $(5-1)/(2-0) = 2$. Now we know both the slope and (at least) one point on each line. Hence, in point-slope form:

$$\ell_1\colon\ y = 2(x-2)+5 \qquad \text{and} \qquad \ell_2\colon\ y = -2(x+1)+3$$

"By inspection" is the mathematician's grandiloquent way of saying "just by looking."

Now for slope-intercept forms. By inspection, ℓ_1 has slope 2 and y-intercept 1. Thus, ℓ_1 has slope-intercept equation $y = 2x+1$. How about ℓ_2? Its slope is -2, so the slope-intercept equation looks like $y = -2x+b$. But what's b? Well, since ℓ_2 passes through $(-1,3)$, those coordinates must satisfy the equation. In other words,

$$3 = -2\cdot(-1)+b = 2+b\,.$$

Clearly, $b = 1$. Therefore the slope-intercept equation is $y = -2x+1$. □

The slope-intercept form of a line is *unique*—there's *only one* way to write a line in slope-intercept form. Moreover, the slope-intercept form works for any line that *has* slope (i.e., for any line that isn't vertical). Notice that the point-slope form of a line is not unique—*any* point on the line can appear in the point-slope equation. Since, for example, $(10, 21)$ lies on ℓ_1, $y = 2(x-10)+21$ is *another* point-slope form for ℓ_1.

■ **Example 2.** Write an equation in slope-intercept form for the line ℓ through two given points (a,b) and (c,d). Where does ℓ intersect each axis?

Solution: If $a = c$, then ℓ is vertical; its equation is just $x = a$.

If $a \neq c$, ℓ has slope $(d-b)/(c-a)$, and the point-slope form applies:

$$y = \left(\frac{d-b}{c-a}\right)(x-a)+b\,.$$

More algebra yields this (slightly clumsy) equation for ℓ in slope-intercept form:

$$y = \left(\frac{d-b}{c-a}\right)x + \left(b - a\left(\frac{d-b}{c-a}\right)\right).$$

Check it, please.

The y-intercept can now be read off; it's the second summand on the right. To find the x-intercept, we set $y = 0$ and solve for x. The result:

$$x = a - b\left(\frac{c-a}{d-b}\right).$$

□

■ **Example 3.** How many lines do the equations

$$y+2x = 6, \qquad y = -2(x+2)+6, \qquad \text{and} \qquad y = -2(x-5)-8$$

represent? Why?

Solution: Putting everything in slope-intercept form gives

$$y = -2x + 6 \qquad y = -2x + 2 \qquad y = -2x + 2$$

This shows that the *three* equations represent *two* different lines. □

Exercises

1. A line L passes through the points $(1, 2)$ and $(-2, 0)$.

   (a) Find an equation for the line L in slope-intercept form.

   (b) Does the line L pass through the point $(\pi, 2\pi)$? Explain your answer.

2. Find an equation of the line through $(2, 1)$ that has slope $2/3$.

3. Find equations in slope-intercept form for

   (a) the line that is parallel to the x-axis and passes through $(-3, 2)$.

   (b) the line that is parallel to the y-axis and passes through $(2, 4)$.

   (c) the line that is parallel to the line $y = x$ and passes through $(-3, 1)$.

   (d) the line through $(-3, 1)$ that is perpendicular to the line $y = 5x + 7$.

4. Find the x- and y-intercepts of the following lines

   (a) $3x + 4y = -12$

   (b) $y = m(x - a) + b$

5. For each condition below, find **all** values of k, if any, for which the line $2x + ky = -4k$ satisfies the condition.

   (a) The line has slope 3.

   (b) The line has slope $m \neq 0$.

   (c) The line passes through the point $(0, 4)$.

   (d) The line is horizontal.

   (e) The line is vertical.

Appendix C

Polynomial algebra: a brisk review

Polynomials are among the simplest and most useful calculus functions. In this appendix we offer a brisk review of the *pre-calculus* of polynomials: basic ideas, terminology, techniques, and algebra. First, the definition:

> **Definition:** A **polynomial** in x is an expression of the form
>
> $$a_0 + a_1 x + a_2 x^2 + a_3 x^3 + \ldots + a_n x^n,$$
>
> that is, a sum of *constant* multiples of *nonnegative integer* powers of x.

■ **Example 1.** Each of the following expressions

$$5x + 2, \qquad -x + 5x^{17}, \qquad \text{and} \qquad (x+3)(\pi x^{17} + 7)$$

Use algebra to write the last example in standard form.

is a polynomial in x. (*Linear* functions, in particular, are polynomials—among the simplest ones.) None of

$$3 - \frac{1}{x}, \qquad \sqrt{x}, \qquad \text{and} \qquad \frac{x+3}{\pi x^{17} + 7}$$

is a polynomial. □

Basic facts, terms, and techniques. As an aid to recalling basic polynomial properties and concepts, we offer a brief glossary of polynomial language:

Degree. The **degree** of a polynomial is its largest power. Constant polynomials, for instance, have degree *zero*. The polynomials $x^3 + 5x^2 + 1$, $-x + 5x^{17}$, and $(x+3)(\pi x^{17} + 7)$ have degree 3, 17, and 18, respectively.

Learn and use such names; they make sense, and they're part of mathematical "culture."

Polynomials of *small* degree have useful, suggestive nicknames. Polynomial functions of degree one are called **linear**, those of degree two **quadratic**, or **parabolic**. The naming sequence goes on: cubic, quartic, quintic, sextic . . . .

Factoring and expanding. To **factor** a polynomial is to write it as a product of lower-degree polynomials. To **expand** is to multiply out. The table below illustrates both the **factored form** and the **expanded form**:

Polynomials	
Expanded form	**Factored form**
$x^2 + 3x + 2$	$(x+1)(x+2)$
$(x^4 - 1)$	$(x+1)(x-1)(x^2+1)$
$x^4 + 6x^3 + 11x^2 + 6x$	$x(x+1)(x+2)(x+3)$

Roots. A number r is a **root** of a polynomial➳ p if $p(r) = 0$. Graphically speaking, real roots and x-intercepts are the same thing.

The idea of root makes sense for any function f. The number r is a root of f if $f(r) = 0$. Finding roots of arbitrary functions is an important, and sometimes difficult, problem. We'll return to it.

The previous graph nicely shows the connections among real roots, intercepts, and factors. So does the one below, this time for the polynomial expression $y = x^5 - x = x(x+1)(x-1)(x^2+1)$.

Graph of $y = x^5 - x$

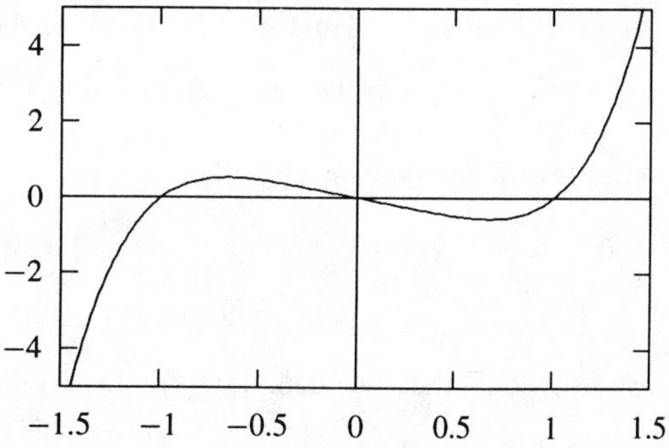

Notice, in particular, the *number* of real roots. Each linear factor contributes one root, in the obvious place. The remaining quadratic factor, $x^2 + 1$, is always positive, so it contributes no real roots.

How many roots? A polynomial of degree n can have *at most* n real roots. Geometrically, this means that the graph of a polynomial of degree n crosses the x-axis at most n times.➳

Here's one consequence: The sine function isn't a polynomial. Can you think of any other reasons why sine can't possibly be a polynomial?

As we've seen, some polynomials of degree n have fewer than n real roots; *any* number up to n is possible. Want a polynomial of degree 43 with 27 real roots? Here's one of many:

$$(x-1)(x-2)\cdots(x-27)(x^2+1)^8.$$

Roots and factors. Roots and factors have an important algebraic relationship:

> *$(x - r)$ is a* factor *of the polynomial $p(x)$ if and only if the number r is a* root *of p.*

The connection between roots and factors leads to a simple strategy for factoring polynomials: Somehow find (graphically, by guessing; whatever works) a root; then divide out the corresponding linear factor.➳

This strategy seldom works in real life. In calculus courses, it seldom fails—the problems are rigged to make it so.

Can every polynomial be factored? No. For *linear* polynomials there's nothing to do; they're *already* factored. Factoring a *quadratic* polynomial p is either impossible or easy, depending on whether p has real roots. The **quadratic formula**

$$r = \frac{-b \pm \sqrt{b^2 - 4ac}}{2a}$$

finds the roots—if any exist—of the quadratic function $ax^2 + bx + c$.

Polynomials of degree three and higher are stickier. For the record, abstract theory (well beyond this course) says that *every* polynomial of degree three or higher has at least *some* lower-degree factors. In other words, *every* nonconstant polynomial can be written as a product of *linear* and *quadratic* factors; *finding* these factors can be hard.

Completing the square. It's sometimes convenient to rewrite a quadratic polynomial in the general form $a(x+b)^2+c$; doing so is called **completing the square**. The following example illustrates the technique.

■ **Example 2.** Let $p(x) = 2x^2 + 8x + 1$. Complete the square; use the result to find all roots of p.

Solution: We want to write $p(x)$ in the form $p(x) = 2(x+b)^2 + c$. Here goes—follow each algebra step closely:

$$2x^2 + 8x + 1 = 2(x^2 + 4x) + 1 = 2(x^2 + 4x + 4) + 1 - 8 = 2(x+2)^2 - 7.$$

The *third* equation explains the name. Adding 4 to $x^2 + 4x$ "completed" the perfect square $(x+2)^2$.

We "paid" for doing so by subtracting 8 at the end.

The roots of p can now be read off:

$$p(x) = 0 \iff 2(x+2)^2 - 7 = 0 \iff 2(x+2)^2 = 7 \iff (x+2)^2 = \frac{7}{2}$$
$$\iff x + 2 = \pm\sqrt{7/2} \iff x = -2 \pm \sqrt{7/2}.$$

(It's easy to check that the quadratic formula gives the same roots.) □

Do so!

Exercises

1. Let p, q, r, and t be the polynomials

$$p(x) = 2x^3 + 5x^2 - x \qquad r(x) = 5x^{12} - 123x^8 + 47$$
$$q(x) = 4x^5 - 6x^3 \qquad t(x) = 17x^{123} - 26x^{19} + 71x^5$$

   (a) What is the degree of each polynomial?
   (b) Which polynomials are *even* functions? *Odd*? *Neither*?

2. Find a polynomial of degree 5 with $x = -2$, $x = 1$, and $x = 3$ as its *only* real roots. Sketch its graph.

3. The graphs below show (i) a quadratic polynomial with two real roots, (ii) a quadratic polynomial with no real roots, (iii) a cubic polynomial with only one real root, and (iv) a cubic polynomial with three real roots.

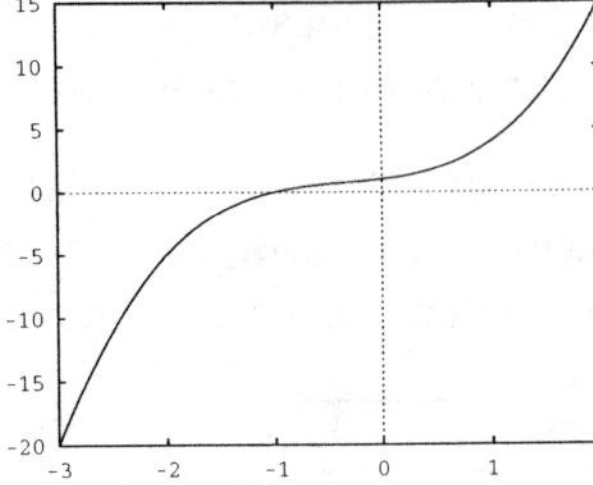

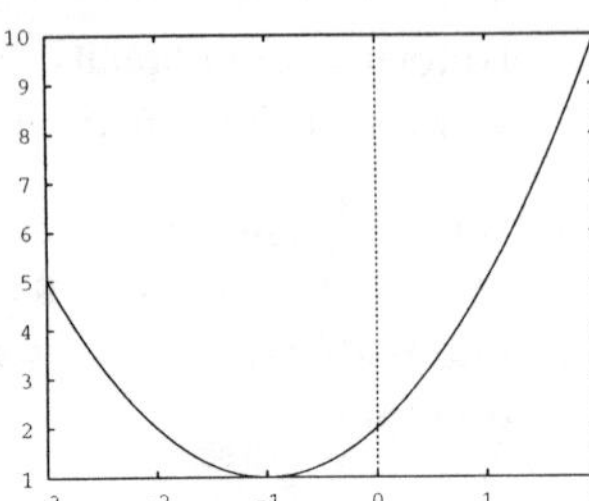

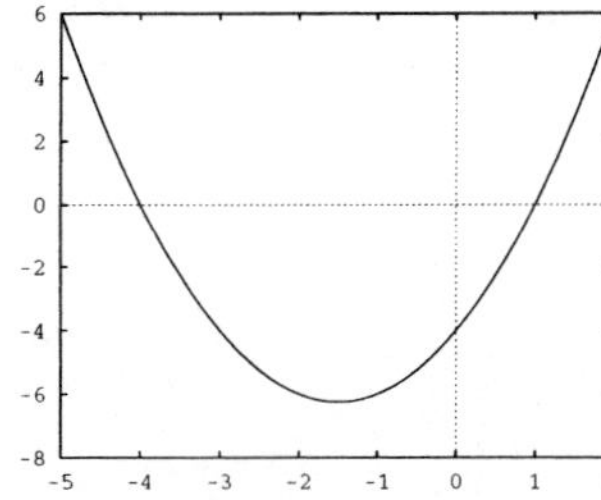

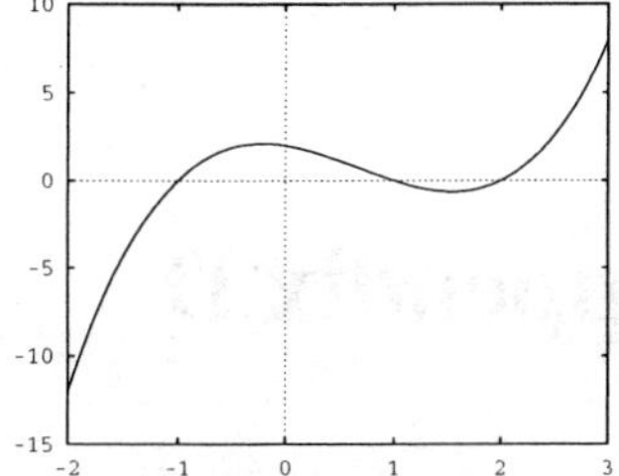

(a) Find an equation for the quadratic polynomial with two real roots.

(b) Find an equation for the cubic polynomial with three real roots.

(c) The cubic polynomial with only one real root can be written in the form $p(x) = (x + r)(x^2 + s)$. Find the values of r and s.

(d) Find an equation for the quadratic polynomial with no real roots.

4. Match each of the functions

(i) $f(x) = (x - 1)(x + 2)$.

(ii) $g(x) = \dfrac{x + 3}{(x - 1)^2}$

(iii) $h(x) = \dfrac{2x^2 + 3x - 1}{x^2 - 2x - 8}$

to one of the graphs below. Then determine all values of x for which each function is positive.

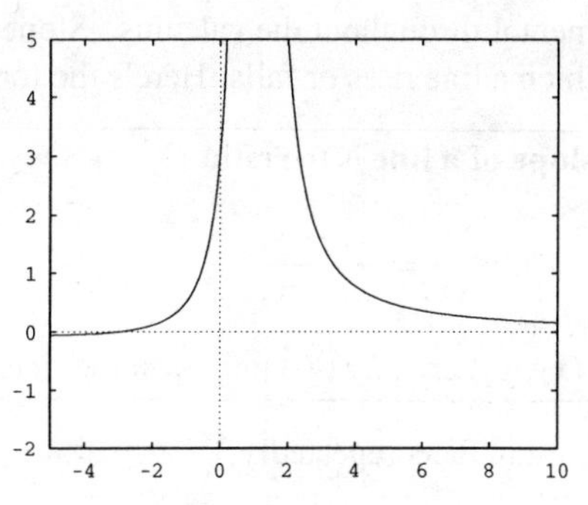

Graph (a)

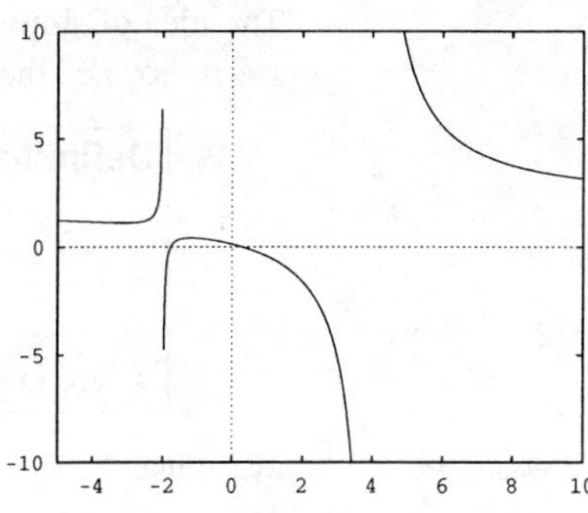

Graph (b)

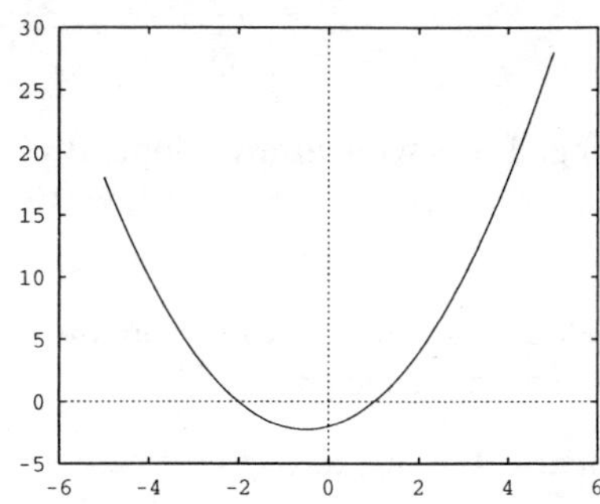

Graph (c)

Appendix D

Linear, polynomial, and rational functions

Lines and linear functions

Lines and linear functions are, above all, *simple*—geometrically, algebraically, and as functions. Nevertheless they're *vitally* important in calculus; a ready understanding of the terminology and technical aspects of linear functions is crucial to understanding calculus itself. For a thorough review of lines—terminology, techniques, and graphical aspects, all with examples—see Appendix B.

Slope

The idea of **slope** is fundamental throughout the calculus. Slope measures a line's *steepness*, i.e., the *rate* at which a line rises or falls. Here's the formal definition:

> **Definition:** The **slope of a line** is the ratio
>
> $$\frac{\Delta y}{\Delta x} = \frac{y_2 - y_1}{x_2 - x_1},$$
>
> where (x_1, y_1) and (x_2, y_2) are *any* two points on the line.

For more details, see Appendix B.

We'll use the following important facts repeatedly:

One slope. A line has the same slope everywhere; *any* two points give the same slope. *Order* doesn't matter either: in algebraic language,

$$\frac{y_2 - y_1}{x_2 - x_1} = \frac{y_1 - y_2}{x_1 - x_2}.$$

Rising, falling. Lines with *positive* slope *rise* (from left to right); lines with negative slope *fall*. The steeper a line, the larger the *absolute value* of its slope.

I.e., their product is -1.

Parallel lines. Lines with equal slope are **parallel**. The slopes of **perpendicular** lines are negative reciprocals.

Different forms. The line through the point (a, b) with slope m has **point-slope** equation $y = m(x - a) + b$. The **slope-intercept** equation $y = mx + b$ describes a line with slope m and y-intercept b.

Zero slope. *Horizontal* lines have slope zero. Slope is undefined for *vertical* lines.

Rates of change. The slope of a line measures the *rate of change* of y with respect to x as we move along the line. This rate is constant because a line is *straight.*

The following example takes a typical calculus-style point of view.

■ **Example 1.** Find an equation in point-slope form for the line ℓ that meets the graph of $y = \sin x$ at $x = 1.3$ and at $x = 1.5$. (A line that "cuts" a graph at two prescribed points is called a **secant line.**) Here's a picture:

Need details on point-slope form? See Appendix B.

From the Latin, secare: to cut.

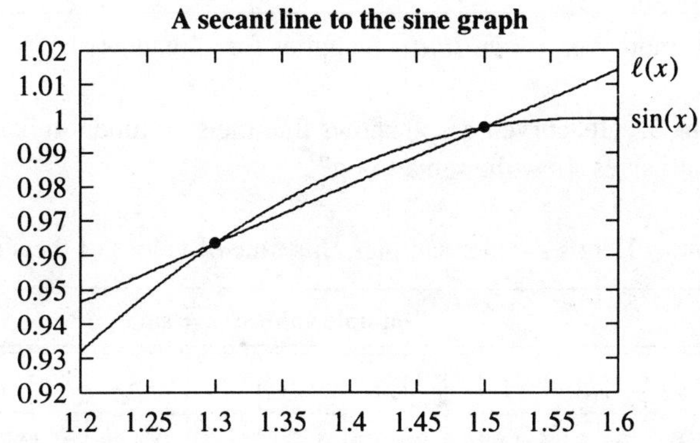

Solution: First let's find the slope of ℓ. Any two points on ℓ will do. As the graph shows, ℓ passes through $(1.3, \sin(1.3))$ and $(1.5, \sin(1.5))$. The slope of ℓ is, therefore,

$$m = \frac{\sin 1.5 - \sin 1.3}{1.5 - 1.3} \approx \frac{0.9975 - 0.9636}{1.5 - 1.3} = 0.1695\,.$$

Hence an equation for ℓ is

$$y = m(x - 1.3) + \sin(1.3) \approx 0.1695(x - 1.3) + 0.9636\,.$$

□

Linear functions

The line with equation $y = 5x + 2$ can be thought of in various ways: as a geometric figure, as an algebraic equation, or—more typically in calculus—as the *function* $f(x) = 5x + 2$. Functions whose graphs are lines are called, naturally enough, **linear functions**. Such functions have an especially simple algebraic form:

Unfortunately, the word "linear" is used in more than one way in mathematics; confusion can result.

> **Definition:** A **linear function** is one whose rule can be written in the form
> $$f(x) = Ax + B$$
> where A and B are constants.

A crucial property of linear functions, from our point of view, is that they "grow" at *constant* rates. In geometric terms, graphs of linear functions are *straight.* The numerical interpretation is also important.

■ **Example 2.** The graph of the linear function $f(x) = 5x + 2$ is a line with slope 5. Interpret this slope *numerically* as a *rate of change.*

Solution: Here's a sampler of x- and y-values:

Sample values: $y = f(x) = 5x + 2$											
x	1.2	1.3	1.4	1.5	1.6	...	−3.4	−3.3	−3.2	−3.1	−3.0
y	8.0	8.5	9.0	9.5	10.0	...	−15.0	−14.5	−14.0	−13.5	−13.0

Notice what the numbers say: whenever x increases by 0.1, y increases by 0.5 (i.e., 5 times as much). In symbols: $\Delta y = 5\Delta x$. In words:

The Δ symbol denotes a change, or increment, in a variable. We'll use it repeatedly.

Along the line $y = 5x + 2$, y increases 5 times as fast as x.

This rate, moreover, is *constant*—it applies for all values of x. □

■ **Example 3.** Its curved graph shows that the sine function is *not* linear. How do numerical values show the same thing?

Solution: Here's another sampler, this time of values of the sine function:

Sample values: $y = \sin x$										
x	1.2	1.3	1.4	1.5	1.6	...	−3.4	−3.3	−3.2	−3.1
y	0.932	0.964	0.985	0.997	1.00	...	0.256	0.158	0.0584	−0.0416

The *non-linearity* of the sine function shows clearly in the numbers. This time there's no regular "growth" pattern: increasing x by 0.1 produces varying increases—or even decreases!—in y. □

As opposed to the previous table.

Lines in calculus: why they matter

Lines are important throughout calculus—perhaps surprisingly so, given that most functions of interest *aren't* linear.

Local straightness. The key idea, and the link to linear functions, is that a typical calculus function is "locally straight," i.e., it "looks straight at small scale" near every point of its domain.

An idea we'll return to repeatedly.

We'll return repeatedly to this subtle but important idea. Rough synonyms for "locally straight" include "almost linear" and "locally linear."

The next (important) example explores what local straightness means.

■ **Example 4.** In what *graphical* sense is the sine function "locally straight" near $x = 1.4$? *Which* line does the sine graph resemble near $x = 1.4$? What does all this mean *numerically*?

To choose a function at random.

To choose a domain point at random.

Solution: "Locally straight" means that the sine graph *looks* straight near the point $(1.4, \sin 1.4)$ if viewed in a small enough window—i.e., after enough "zooming in." One view of the graph appears in Example 1. Here are two successively closer views:

Zooming is easy with a graphing calculator. As always, a graph's appearance depends on the x- and y-scales.

A closer view: $y = \sin x$

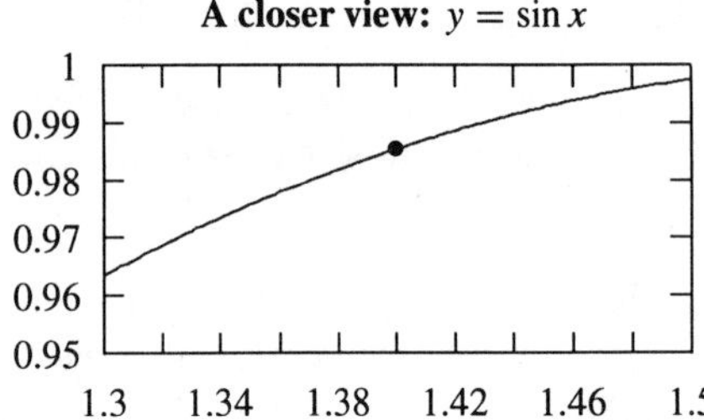

Closer still: $y = \sin x$

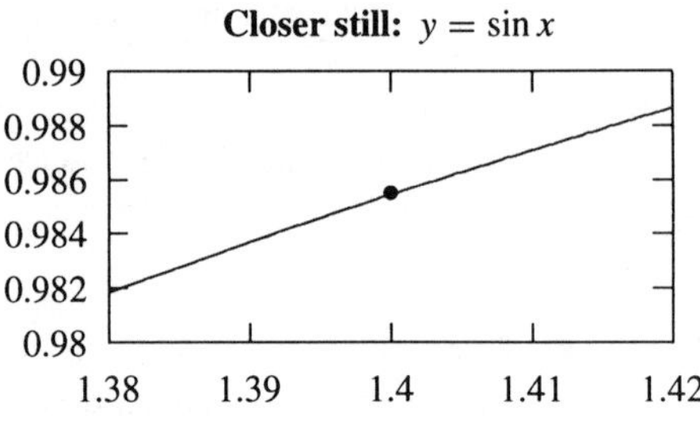

The last view makes our point: the sine graph is all but indistinguishable from a straight line.

Which straight line? Because our graph passes through (1.4, sin 1.4) with slope $\approx$ 0.17, the line we want has equation

To estimate slope accurately, read values from the graph at $x = 1.38$ and $x = 1.42$.

Allowing for some estimation.

$$y = \ell(x) = \sin 1.4 + 0.17(x - 1.4) = 0.17x + 0.7474.$$

What all this means is that $\sin x$, although *not* a linear function, behaves *similarly* to $\ell(x)$ for x near 1.4. Numerical data support this conclusion:

If $x \approx 1.4$, $\sin x \approx \ell(x)$

x	1.380	1.385	1.390	1.395	1.400	1.405	1.410	1.415	1.420
$\sin x$	0.9819	0.9828	0.9837	0.9846	0.9854	0.9863	0.9871	0.9879	0.9887
$\ell(x)$	0.9820	0.9829	0.9837	0.9846	0.9854	0.9863	0.9871	0.9880	0.9888

□

The next example illustrates an entirely different use of linear functions.

■ **Example 5.** Are hardness of water and central nervous system (CNS) disorders in infants related, as some health researchers suspect? Below are some relevant data; hardness is measured in parts per million, the disorder rate in malformations per 1000 births. [These data come from *Biostatistics: A Foundation for Analysis in the Health Sciences*, 2nd ed., Wayne W. Daniel (Wiley, 1978).]

Hard Water: Good or Bad?

hardness	50	25	15	75	100	150	180	250	275	220
disorder rate	7.2	8.1	11.2	9.3	9.4	5.0	5.8	3.3	3.6	4.8
hardness	160	50	45	60	100	155	200	240	40	65
disorder rate	6.3	12.5	15.0	6.5	8.0	10.0	5.3	4.9	7.2	11.9

Is there pattern in the data? It's hard to tell from the table. Let's plot the data:

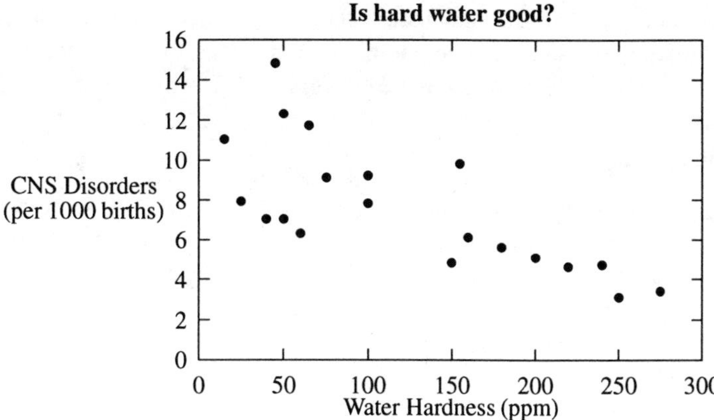

What *does* the picture show? The data don't lie on any obvious curve or line, but they suggest a general tendency—with harder water, the CNS disorder rate seems to *decrease*.

Can we describe this situation mathematically? One possibility is to "fit" a reasonable *line* to the data, perhaps something like this:

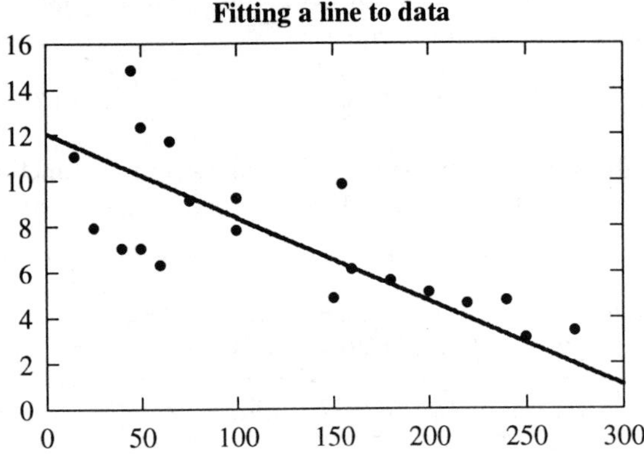

The picture raises obvious questions: How was the line chosen? Is it a "good" fit? Might another line fit better? What does the line mean about CNS disorders? Does *any* line really fit this situation?

We chose the line entirely by appearance—it just *looked* right. Having confessed this, let's find an equation for the line. The y-intercept, 12, can be read directly from the graph. Reading from upper left to lower right shows a *rise* of -11, a *run* of 300, and hence a *slope* of $-11/300 \approx -0.0367$. A suitable equation, therefore, is

$$y = -\frac{11}{300}x + 12 .$$

What good is such an equation? If $x = 125$, then

$$y = -\frac{11}{300} \cdot 125 + 12 \approx 7.4 .$$

This means, in context, that in an area with water hardness 125 ppm we'd predict about 7.4 CNS disorders per 1000 births.

How trustworthy is such a prediction? The answer depends both on the philosophy and on the mathematics of mathematical modeling. □

Polynomials

We assume, here and in the remainder of this book, that the reader is generally familiar with the *pre-calculus* of polynomials: basic ideas, terminology, and algebra. For a quick review of these topics, see Appendix C.

Algebraic functions

An **algebraic function** is one defined using only the ordinary algebraic operations: addition, multiplication, division, and raising to powers. Polynomials are the *simplest* algebraic functions; their rules require only multiplication and addition.

Roughly speaking, algebraic functions are those a $2.98 calculator can handle. Non-algebraic, or "transcendental" functions, such as sine, start at $3.98.

Positive integer powers of x can be found by repeated multiplication.

Definition: A **polynomial** in x is an expression that can be written in the form

$$a_0 + a_1x + a_2x^2 + a_3x^3 + \ldots + a_nx^n ,$$

that is, a sum of *constant* multiples of *nonnegative integer* powers of x.

■ **Example 6.** Each of the expressions

$$5x + 2, \qquad -x + 5x^{17}, \qquad \text{and} \qquad (x+3)(\pi x^{17} + 7)$$

is a polynomial in x.➻ (*Linear* functions are the simplest polynomials.) None of

Use algebra to write the last example in standard form.

$$3 - \frac{1}{x}, \qquad \sqrt{x}, \qquad \text{and} \qquad \frac{x+3}{\pi x^{17} + 7}$$

is a polynomial. □

Polynomials as functions. The polynomial *expression* $2x^3 + 5x$ corresponds naturally to the *function* $p(x) = 2x^3 + 5x$. *Any* function defined by a polynomial expression is called a **polynomial function**. In practice the technical distinction between *polynomial* and *polynomial function* is seldom important. We'll use the terms interchangeably.

Domain and range. Because polynomials involve only multiplication and addition, every polynomial function has the same *domain*: all real numbers.

Polynomials' *ranges* vary drastically. The range of $p(x) = 3$ is $\{3\}$, a set with just one member. By contrast, the range of $q(x) = x^2 + 3$ is $[3, \infty)$, an infinite interval. The range of $r(x) = x^3 - 7x^2$ may not be obvious from the formula. Here's a graph:

Graph of $y = x^3 - 7x^2$

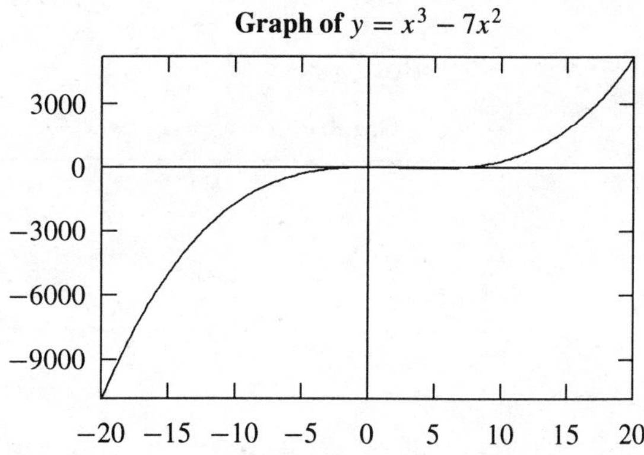

The picture shows how r behaves "in the long run." It "blows up" (tends to ∞) as $x \to +\infty$ and "blows down" (tends to -∞) as $x \to -\infty$. Therefore, apparently, r "hits" all real values; its range is $(-\infty, \infty)$.

Polynomial-speak. Polynomials have their own specialized vocabulary. We'll assume familiarity with such words as **root**, **degree**, **factor**, and **expand**, and with the **quadratic formula**. (Forgotten any of these words? All are defined in Appendix C.)

All these important words crop up in the next examples.

■ **Example 7.** Find the roots of the 4th-degree polynomial $p(x) = x^4 + 6x^3 + 11x^2 + 6x$; interpret results both graphically and algebraically.

Solution: In its expanded form, the formula for $p(x)$ is unhelpful. The factored form➻ reveals much more:

Could you have found it? If not, see Appendix C.

$$p(x) = x^4 + 6x^3 + 11x^2 + 6x = x(x+1)(x+2)(x+3).$$

It's clear now that p has *four* real roots, and also where they are. The following picture tells the same story:

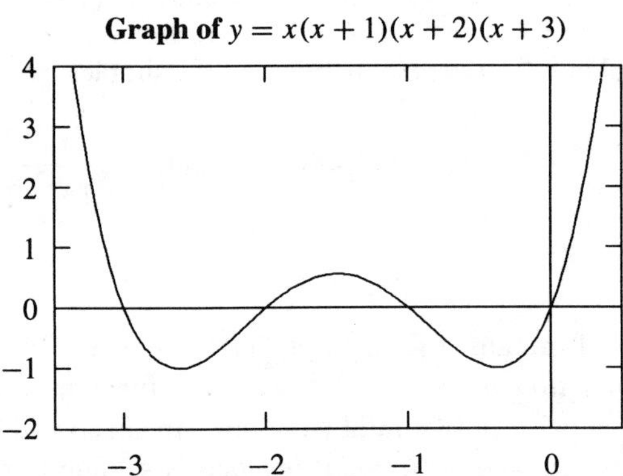

Whether a factored or expanded form of a polynomial is "better" depends on what we're doing. Here the factored form was preferable; the expanded form, on the other hand, may be handier for such symbolic operations as differentiation and integration.◂ □

As we'll see!

Some polynomials have *fewer* real roots than their degrees allow.

■ **Example 8.** Consider the cubic polynomial polynomial $p(x) = x^3 - 2x^2 + x - 2$. Factor p as much as possible; find all of p's real roots.

Solution: Here's a graph of p:

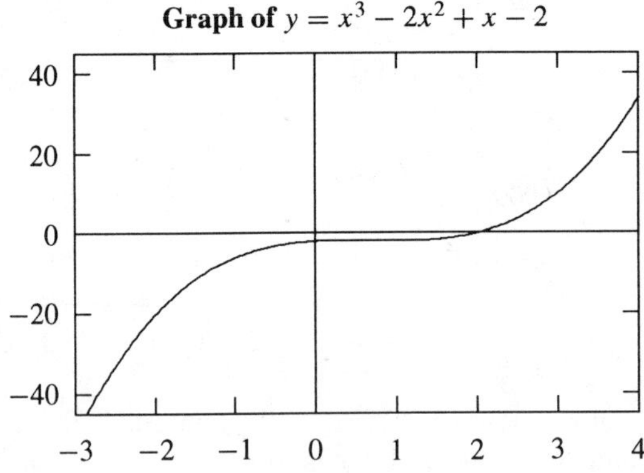

The graph suggests that 2 is a root; a simple check confirms that, indeed, $p(2) = 0$. Therefore $(x - 2)$ is a factor of p. By long division,

$$p(x) = x^3 - 2x^2 + x - 2 = (x - 2)(x^2 + 1).$$

Is further factorization possible? No. Additional factors, if any, would come from $x^2 + 1$. But $x^2 + 1$ has no real roots◂ and hence no linear factors.

Why not?

Note that the factored form $p(x) = (x - 2)(x^2 + 1)$ tells us something new: $p(x) = 0$ *only if* $x = 2$. In other words, 2 is the *only* real root. No graph could tell us this, because we can never see *all* of any polynomial's graph. □

Why polynomials matter

Polynomial functions are simple but surprisingly useful. They lurk in calculus problems ranging from the sublime:

Show that among all rectangles of given perimeter, the square encloses the most area.

to the ridiculous:

Design the most spacious possible rectangular pigpen, using 100 feet of fence. One side abuts a river . . . .

A subtler but equally important use of polynomials is in *approximating* less convenient, non-polynomial functions. For example, the graphs below show that, for x near 0, the polynomial function $x - x^3/6$ does a good job of approximating the sine function, which *isn't* a polynomial.

Can you tell which is which?

Unlike the sine, polynomials can't have infinitely many roots.

Two graphs: $y = x - x^3/6$, $y = \sin(x)$

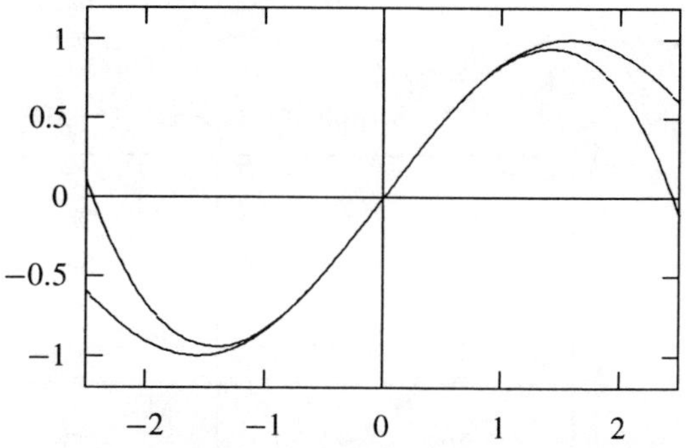

This is worth knowing. It suggests how a calculator—even a budget model—might compute numerical values for non-algebraic functions like sine.

Rational functions

Adding or multiplying two polynomials creates a new polynomial. *Dividing* two polynomials doesn't (usually) give another polynomial; it gives a **rational function**. Formally:

Is this really obvious? Think about it; try some examples.

> **Definition:** A **rational function** is a function that can be written as the quotient, or "ratio," of two polynomials.

■ **Example 9.** Each function below is rational:

$$f(x) = \frac{1}{x} \qquad g(x) = \frac{x^2}{x^2+3}$$

$$h(x) = \frac{x^7 + x^6 + x^5 - x^4}{x+1} \qquad k(x) = \frac{2}{x} + \frac{3}{x+1}$$

The function $m(x) = \sqrt{x} = x^{1/2}$ is not rational because it involves a *fractional* power of x.

The function k may look suspicious. It's certainly the *sum* of two rational functions, but is k *itself* rational? The answer is yes, because we can *rewrite* $k(x)$ in the form:

$$k(x) = \frac{2}{x} + \frac{3}{x+1} = \frac{2(x+1)}{x(x+1)} + \frac{3x}{x(x+1)} = \frac{5x+2}{x(x+1)}. \qquad \square$$

This computation illustrates a more general fact:

> **Fact:** Let r and s be rational functions. The sum, difference, product, and quotient of r and s are all rational functions—each can be written as the ratio of polynomials.

Graphs of rational functions

Unlike polynomials.

Rational functions have an important new feature: the possibility of **horizontal** and **vertical asymptotes**. Asymptotes are straight lines toward which a graph "tends."

■ **Example 10.** Consider the rational function

$$r(x) = \frac{x^2}{x^2 - 1} = \frac{x^2}{(x-1)(x+1)}$$

and its graph:

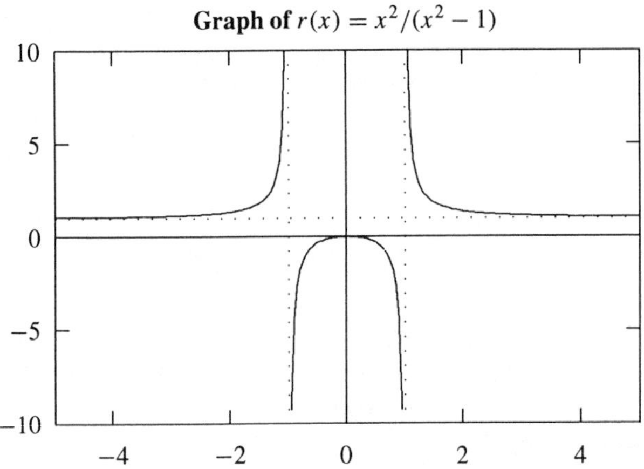

Technicalities aside, it's evident graphically that this function has three asymptotes: the *vertical* lines $x = -1$ and $x = 1$, and the *horizontal* line $y = 1$.

In Section 1.5, page 57, we show these facts carefully, relating them to infinite limits and limits at infinity. □

Asymptotes and limits

The ideas just illustrated—horizontal and vertical asymptotes, tending to infinity, etc.—are clumsy to express in ordinary words. The language of limits lets us say clearly and concisely what we mean. In that language, the full story of r's asymptotes reads like this:

Economy and clarity are the proper uses of technical language in any field. Technical language that doesn't serve these purposes is jargon.

$$\lim_{x\to\infty} r(x) = 1 \qquad \lim_{x\to 1^+} r(x) = \infty \qquad \lim_{x\to 1^-} r(x) = -\infty$$

$$\lim_{x\to -1^-} r(x) = \infty \qquad \lim_{x\to -1^+} r(x) = -\infty \qquad \lim_{x\to -\infty} r(x) = 1$$

Comparing each limit statement above to the appropriate part of the graph should make its meaning clear. For example,

$$\lim_{x\to\infty} r(x) = 1$$

restates the fact that $r(x) \to 1$ as $x \to \infty$, or, equivalently, that the line $y = 1$ is a horizontal asymptote. Similarly,

$$\lim_{x\to 1^+} r(x) = \infty$$

says that $r(x)$ blows up to the *right* of $x = 1$, so $x = 1$ is a vertical asymptote.

Asymptotes and limits: how they're related

The connection between asymptotes, limits at infinity, and infinite limits is easily summarized:

Horizontal asymptotes; limits at infinity. The horizontal line $y = L$ is an asymptote to the graph of f if (and only if) f approaches L as $x \to \pm\infty$—that is, if

$$\lim_{x\to\infty} f(x) = L \qquad \text{or} \qquad \lim_{x\to-\infty} f(x) = L.$$

In either case, L is a **limit at infinity**.

Vertical asymptotes; infinite limits. The vertical line $x = a$ is an asymptote to the graph of f if (and only if) f "blows up" (or "blows down") at a—that is, if

$$\lim_{x\to a^-} f(x) = \pm\infty \qquad \text{or} \qquad \lim_{x\to a^+} f(x) = \pm\infty.$$

In any of these cases, f has an **infinite limit at** $x = a$.

Exercises

1. Consider the curve shown below.

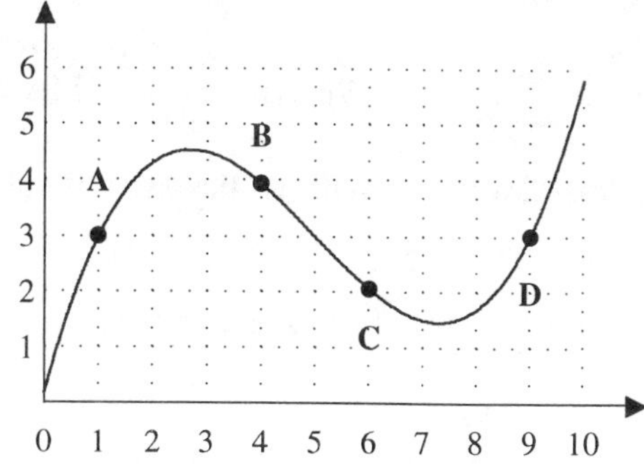

For each of the following pairs of points, find the slope of the secant line passing through the points and an equation of this line. [HINT: Draw the secant lines on this page.]

(a) **A, B**

(b) **A, C**

(c) **B, D**

(d) **C, D**

2. Consider the curve shown below:

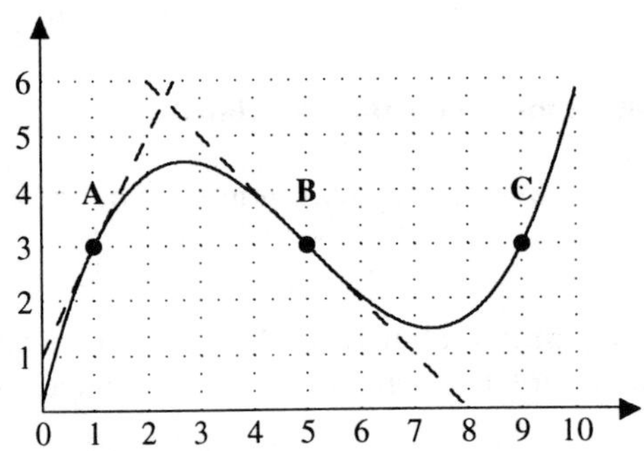

(a) What is the slope of the line tangent to the curve at **A**? Find an equation of this line in slope-intercept form.

(b) What is the slope of the line tangent to the curve at **B**? Find an equation of this line in slope-intercept form.

(c) What is the slope of the line tangent to the curve at **C**? Find an equation of this line in slope-intercept form.

3. Find a rational function with *vertical* asymptotes at $x = -1$ and $x = 2$, and has the line $y = 3$ as a *horizontal* asymptote. Sketch a graph of this function.

4. Shown below is the graph of a rational function k. Use it to answer each of the following questions about k.

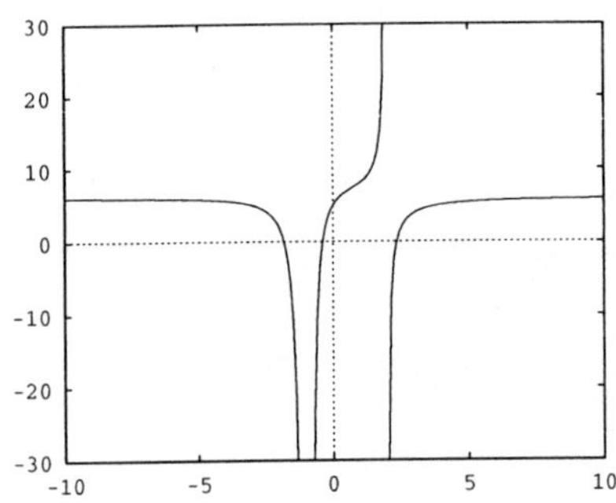

(a) What is $\lim_{x \to -1^-} k(x)$? What is $\lim_{x \to -1^+} k(x)$? Explain why $\lim_{x \to -1} k(x) = -\infty$.

(b) What is $\lim_{x \to 2^-} k(x)$? What is $\lim_{x \to 2^+} k(x)$? Explain why $\lim_{x \to 2} k(x)$ doesn't exist.

(c) What is $\lim_{x \to -\infty} k(x)$? What is $\lim_{x \to \infty} k(x)$?

5. Suppose that the lines $y = 3$ and $y = -3$ are horizontal asymptotes of a continuous function f and that f has no vertical asymptotes.

(a) Explain why f cannot be a polynomial function.

(b) Can f be a rational function? Justify your answer.

Appendix E

Algebra of exponentials

Exponential functions (i.e., functions defined by exponential expressions) are among the most important in both the theory and the applications of calculus. Indeed the exponential function $f(x) = e^x$ has been called the most important function in all of mathematics. To understand and use such functions effectively requires a basic familiarity with the algebra of such expressions.

Where $e \approx 2.71828$.

Exponential expressions

An **exponential expression** is any algebraic expression that contains exponents. Each of the following expressions is exponential:

$$2^x, \quad 3^{x+h}, \quad b^3, \quad 2^{x^2}, \quad \frac{2^x}{3^x}, \quad \left(\frac{2}{3}\right)^x, \quad \left(1+\frac{1}{n}\right)^n.$$

In any expression of the form b^x, b is the **base** and x is the **exponent**.

The natural exponential function

The base-e exponential function $f(x) = e^x$ is called the **natural exponential function** or simply **the exponential function**. (The definite article in the latter name is slightly unfortunate. Expressions with *other* bases—2^x, 10^x, etc.—also deserve the name "exponential.") Various notations are used for the natural exponential function:

$$\exp(x), \qquad \exp x, \qquad \text{and} \qquad e^x$$

all mean the same thing.

Basics of exponential algebra

The basic algebraic rules for exponential expressions are few and simple. Know (at least) these:

$$\text{(E.1)} \qquad b^x b^y = b^{x+y}$$

$$\text{(E.2)} \qquad \frac{b^x}{b^y} = b^{x-y}$$

$$\text{(E.3)} \qquad \left(b^x\right)^y = b^{xy}$$

$$\text{(E.4)} \qquad a^x b^x = (ab)^x$$

$$\text{(E.5)} \qquad b^0 = 1$$

$$\text{(E.6)} \qquad b^{-x} = \frac{1}{b^x}$$

We'll see below why $b > 0$ matters.

In each case, b can be any *positive* number; x and y can take any real values. Memorize these rules if necessary. Better still, learn to derive them. What each says is straightforward if the exponents are positive integers.

The "addition rule."

■ **Example 1.** Explain Rule E.1: $b^x b^y = b^{x+y}$, assuming that x and y are positive integers.

Solution: If x and y are positive integers, then

$$b^x = \overbrace{b \cdot b \cdot b \dots b}^{x\text{-times}} \quad \text{and} \quad b^y = \overbrace{b \cdot b \cdot b \dots b}^{y\text{-times}}.$$

Therefore

$$b^x b^y = \overbrace{b \cdot b \cdot b \dots b}^{x} \cdot \overbrace{b \cdot b \cdot b \dots b}^{y} = \overbrace{b \cdot b \cdot b \dots b}^{x+y} = b^{x+y}.$$ □

■ **Example 2.** Make sense of the "zeroth power" rule: $b^0 = 1$.

Solution: Rule E.5 follows directly from the addition rule: If b is any positive number, then

$$b \cdot b^0 = b^1 \cdot b^0 = b^{1+0} = b^1 = b.$$

Thus $b \cdot b^0 = b$; dividing through by b gives $b^0 = 1$. □

■ **Example 3.** Rule (E.6) tells how to switch the sign of an exponent. It helps with calculations like this:

$$\left(\frac{1}{2}\right)^{-17} = \frac{1}{2^{-17}} = 2^{17}.$$ □

■ **Example 4.** Derive Rule (E.6) from the other rules.

Solution: Use Rules (E.1) and (E.5) to convince yourself of each equality below:

$$b^{-x} \cdot b^x = b^{x-x} = b^0 = 1.$$

Dividing the first and last quantities by b^x gives Rule (E.6). □

■ **Example 5.** Let k be any constant, and define the function f by $f(x) = 3^{kx}$. Show that

$$\frac{f(x+h)-f(x)}{h} = f(x)\cdot\frac{f(h)-f(0)}{h}.$$

This example is algebraically tricky, but it shows one way exponential algebra is really used in calculus.

Solution: Watch carefully—we'll use several of the rules cited above:

$$\begin{aligned}\frac{f(x+h)-f(x)}{h} &= \frac{3^{k(x+h)}-3^{kx}}{h} = \frac{3^{kx+kh}-3^{kx}}{h}\\ &= \frac{3^{kx}\cdot 3^{kh}-3^{kx}}{h} = 3^{kx}\cdot\frac{3^{kh}-1}{h}\\ &= 3^{kx}\cdot\frac{3^{kh}-3^0}{h} = f(x)\cdot\frac{f(h)-f(0)}{h}.\end{aligned}$$

□

Thinking of positive powers: why $b > 0$ is best

Exponential expressions with negative bases can cause trouble. To see how, consider the expression $(-8)^x$ for various values of x:

$$(-8)^2 \qquad (-8)^{-2} \qquad (-8)^{1/2} \qquad (-8)^{1/3} \qquad (-8)^{3/2} \qquad (-8)^{4/3}$$

The first two make good sense:

$$(-8)^2 = 64 \qquad \text{and} \qquad (-8)^{-2} = \frac{1}{64}.$$

The third, $\sqrt{-8}$, isn't a real number, but the fourth, $(-8)^{1/3}$, has a real value. The fifth expression is meaningless (it involves $\sqrt{-8}$) but the sixth makes good sense:

What is this value?

$$(-8)^{4/3} = (-8)\cdot(-8)^{1/3} = (-8)\cdot(-2) = 16.$$

Faced with such difficulties, we retreat. In calculus, we'll take the base b of every exponential expression b^x to be positive.

Transcendental meditations on exponential functions (optional)

The *exponential* function $f(x) = 2^x$ differs from the *power* function $g(x) = x^2$ far more than typography would suggest. One important difference is that the expression x^2 is an *algebraic* formula (i.e., an explicit recipe for computing output values). If, say, $x = 2.3$, it's easy, even without a calculator, to compute the output: $2.3^2 = 5.29$.

The expression 2^x, by contrast, is not algebraic. Finding the output value $2^{2.3}$ by hand is almost impossible. For this reason, exponential functions (and other "non-algebraic" functions) are referred to as **transcendental.** We explore some ramifications of the non-algebraic character of exponential functions below.

Do you see why? Try it.

A curious word. It suggests that exponential functions somehow float above, or transcend, the mundane world of algebra.

Fractional and irrational exponents: abuse of powers?

What does b^x really mean if the exponent x isn't an integer? What if x is irrational?

■ **Example 6.** Find (or estimate) decimal values for

$$2^{1/3}, \quad 1.6^{11/13}, \quad \text{and} \quad \pi^{-2/3}.$$

Solution: $2^{1/3}$ is the *cube root* of 2. According to any scientific calculator,

$$\sqrt[3]{2} \approx 1.25992104989.$$

For *any* integer $n > 0$,

$$b^{1/n} = \sqrt[n]{b}.$$

Is it obvious that every positive number b has a positive n-th root? How would one estimate, say, the 11th root of 13?

The connection between roots and powers suggests how to estimate $1.6^{11/13}$ numerically:

$$1.6^{11/13} = \left(1.6^{1/13}\right)^{11} \approx 1.03681563373^{11} \approx 1.4883905652\,.$$

Similarly,

$$\begin{aligned} \pi^{-2/3} &= \frac{1}{\pi^{2/3}} = \frac{1}{\sqrt[3]{\pi^2}} \approx \frac{1}{\sqrt[3]{9.869604401089}} \\ &\approx \frac{1}{2.14502939711} \approx 0.466194077036\,. \end{aligned}$$

□

So far so good: the examples show how to handle *rational* exponents. How about *irrational* exponents?

■ **Example 7.** Estimate the value of $\pi^{\sqrt{2}}$.

Solution: The "obvious" approach—to approximate everything in sight with rational numbers—works:

Decimal numbers are rational, aren't they?

$$\pi^{\sqrt{2}} \approx 3.1415^{1.4142} \approx 5.0472\,.$$

□

Fair questions

Does all this approximation really work? Is it really OK to approximate *both* b and x with convenient decimal numbers before computing b^x?

The short answer to all of these good questions is "yes." In mathematical language, the fortunate fact is that

$$\text{if } a \approx b \text{ and } x \approx y, \text{ then } b^x \approx a^y.$$

Reasonable as this seems, a rigorous proof is subtle; we'll omit it.

Exercises

1. Evaluate 64^x when x equals

(a) 0
(b) 1
(c) 1/2
(d) −1/2
(e) 2/3
(f) 5/6

2. Express each of the following numbers as 4^x for a suitable exponent x.

(a) 16
(b) 2
(c) 8
(d) $1/\sqrt{2}$
(e) $4\sqrt{2}$
(f) 16^{35}

3. Let a be a positive number. Rewrite each of the following expressions in the form a^x.

(a) $(\sqrt{a})^2$
(b) $1/a^2$
(c) 1
(d) a^3/a^4
(e) $(a^3/a^5)^{10}$
(f) $a/\sqrt[3]{a}$

4. Here's further evidence for the fact that $b^0 = 1$:

$$b^0 \cdot b^0 = b^{0+0} = b^0.$$

Therefore, b^0 *is its own square.* Does it follow that b^0 must be 1? Explain.

5. Let f be the function $f(x) = 5^{2x}$. Show that

$$\frac{f(x+h) - f(x)}{h} = f(x) \cdot \frac{f(h) - f(0)}{h}.$$

6. Mimic the arguments given for the "addition" rule in Example 1 to show that each of the following rules are "obvious" for positive integer powers.

(a) Rule (E.2)
(b) Rule (E.3)
(c) Rule (E.4)

Appendix F

Algebra of logarithms

Logarithm *functions* (i.e., functions defined by logarithmic expressions) are important in both the theory and the applications of calculus. To understand and use such functions effectively requires a basic familiarity with the algebra of such expressions.

Logarithms and exponentials: how they're related

Logarithmic expressions like these—

$$\log_2 x, \qquad \log_{10} t, \qquad \log_e z, \qquad \ln w, \qquad \text{and} \qquad \log_b x$$

may be mystifying at first glance. What does "$\log_b$" *mean*? What is the role of b? Who is "ln?" Some mystification is natural: Like "sin," "cos," and "exp," "$\log_b$" is the *name* of a function—not a recipe for computation.

Demystifying logarithms means, first and foremost, understanding how they're related to exponentials. For us, this relation *defines* the idea of logarithm.

Definition: For any suitable **base** b and positive number x, the expression $\log_b x$ is defined by the condition

$$y = \log_b x \iff x = b^y$$

(Note: "Suitable" means $b > 0$ and $b \neq 1$.)

■ **Example 1.** Use the definition to simplify the expressions

$$\log_2 8, \qquad \log_{10} 100, \qquad \log_e e^{25}, \qquad \text{and} \qquad \log_b \frac{1}{b^3}.$$

Solution: By definition,

$$y = \log_2 8 \iff 8 = 2^y.$$

It's clear from the second equation that y must be 3; hence $\log_2 8 = 3$. By similar reasoning,

$$\begin{aligned} y &= \log_{10} 100 &\iff& 10^y = 100 &\iff& y = 2; \\ y &= \log_e e^{25} &\iff& e^y = e^{25} &\iff& y = 25; \\ y &= \log_b \tfrac{1}{b^3} &\iff& b^y = b^{-3} &\iff& y = -3. \end{aligned}$$

□

Logarithms and exponentials as inverses

The relation

$$y = \log_b x \iff x = b^y$$

means that the logarithm function $\log_b x$ and the exponential function b^x are *inverses*. For any two functions f and g to be inverses means that each function "undoes" the other: the equations

$$f(g(x)) = x \qquad \text{and} \qquad g(f(x)) = x$$

hold for all sensible inputs x.

This general fact, applied specifically to the logarithm and exponential functions with base b, looks like this:

$$\log_b b^x = x \qquad \text{and} \qquad b^{\log_b x} = x\,.$$

These equations hold for all x in the respective domains of $\log_b$ and b^x.➸

Forgotten these domains? See Section 2.6.

Basics of logarithmic algebra

A few algebraic rules for logarithmic expressions go a long way. Here are four to know:

(F.1) $$\log_b xy = \log_b x + \log_b y$$

(F.2) $$\log_b x/y = \log_b x - \log_b y$$

(F.3) $$\log_b x^r = r \log_b x$$

(F.4) $$\log_b 1/x = -\log_b x$$

(Note: $b > 0$ and $b \neq 1$.)

Using the rules

The rules simplify computations that involve logarithms—and even some that don't seem to.

■ **Example 2.** Just before it died, your calculator said that $\log_{10} 2 \approx 0.301$ and $\log_{10} 3 \approx 0.477$. You *really* need to know

$$\log_{10} 6, \qquad \log_{10} 1/18, \qquad \log_{10} 2000, \qquad \text{and} \qquad \log_{10} 0.003\,.$$

What can you do?

Solution: With the rules there's no problem:➸

But watch closely, and check the results with your own (live) calculator.

$$\begin{aligned}
\log_{10} 6 &= \log(3 \cdot 2) = \log_{10} 3 + \log_{10} 2 \approx 0.301 + 0.477 = 0.778 \\
\log_{10} 1/18 &= -\log_{10}\left(2 \cdot 3^2\right) = -\log_{10} 2 - 2\log_{10} 3 \approx -1.255 \\
\log_{10} 2000 &= \log_{10} 1000 + \log_{10} 2 = 3 + \log_{10} 2 \approx 3.301 \\
\log_{10} 0.003 &= \log_{10} 0.001 + \log_{10} 3 = -3 + \log_{10} 3 \approx -2.523
\end{aligned}$$

□

■ **Example 3.** Solve (for x) each of the equations

$$200 \cdot 1.05^x = 375 \qquad \text{and} \qquad \ln x + \ln x^2 = 5\,.$$

Solution: For the first equation we'll take the natural logarithm of both sides, and then use rules (F.1) and (F.3):

$$200 \cdot 1.05^x = 375 \iff \ln 200 + \ln\left(1.05^x\right) = \ln 375$$
$$\iff x \ln 1.05 = \ln 375 - \ln 200$$
$$\iff x = \frac{\ln 375 - \ln 200}{\ln 1.05} \approx 12.8839$$

To solve the second equation we'll first use rules (F.1) (in "reverse") and (F.3), and then apply an exponential function to undo the logarithm. Notice first that

$$\ln x + \ln x^2 = \ln x^3 = 3 \ln x.$$

Therefore,

$$\ln x + \ln x^2 = 5 \iff 3 \ln x = 5$$
$$\iff \ln x = 5/3$$
$$\iff x = e^{5/3} \approx 5.2945\,.$$

□

Why the rules hold: translating between logarithms and exponentials

The familiar properties of logarithms listed above are, in a sense, disguised versions of similar rules for exponentials. Properties of logarithms can be "translated" into properties of exponentials, and *vice versa.*

■ **Example 4.** Explain, in terms of exponentials, rule (F.1):

$$\log_b xy = \log_b x + \log_b y\,.$$

Solution: What does rule (F.1) really say? The equation $\log_b xy = z$—where z is *any* real number—means that $b^z = xy$. Therefore rule (F.1) really says that

$$b^{\log_b x + \log_b y} = xy.$$

Now *exponential algebra* comes in:

$$b^{\log_b x + \log_b y} = b^{\log_b x} \cdot b^{\log_b y} = xy,$$

just as we wanted. □

Why does the last equation hold? Because logs and exponentials are inverses.

Which base?

The general ideas of logarithm and exponential functions are the same for *any* base b. In practice, though, either $b = 10$ or $b = e \approx 2.71828$ is almost invariably used. Logarithms with these bases are known as the **common logarithm** and the **natural logarithm**, respectively. The natural log function, usually written as $\ln x$, is for many good reasons the favorite in calculus. We'll use base e almost exclusively.

For at least one good reason see Section 2.6.

Moving around the bases: two key identities

To exploit the advantages of base e—for both logarithm and exponential functions—we'll need to move easily from *any* base b to the special base e. Two key identities

Puckett-like

tell how. For any base b and input x,

$$\begin{aligned} b^x &= e^{x \cdot \ln(b)}; \\ \log_b(x) &= \frac{\ln(x)}{\ln(b)}. \end{aligned}$$

Why do these equations hold? Both follow from the fact that logarithm and exponential functions are inverses, and from basic properties of logarithms. For the first:

$$b^x = \left(e^{\ln(b)}\right)^x = e^{x \cdot \ln(b)},$$

as claimed➻. The second identity is similar:

Why does $b = e^{\ln(b)}$?

$$\begin{aligned} x = b^{\log_b x} \quad &\Longrightarrow \quad \ln(x) = \ln\left(b^{\log_b x}\right) = \log_b x \, \ln b \\ &\Longrightarrow \quad \log_b(x) = \frac{\ln(x)}{\ln(b)}. \end{aligned}$$

■ **Example 5.** Rewrite the exponential function 3^x in base e.

Solution: From the first identity above,

$$3^x = e^{x \ln(3)} \approx e^{1.09861228867x}.$$

□

■ **Example 6.** Rewrite $\log_5 x$ in terms of the *natural* logarithm.

Solution: From the second identity above,

$$\log_5 x = \frac{\ln x}{\ln 5} \approx \frac{\ln x}{1.60943791243}.$$

□

Exercises

1. Translate each of the following equations into the language of logarithms.

   (a) $8^{2/3} = 4$

   (b) $10^3 = 1000$

   (c) $10^{-4} = 0.0001$

   (d) $\left(\frac{1}{2}\right)^{-2} = 4$

2. Translate each of the following equations into the language of exponentials.

   (a) $\log_2 7 = x$

   (b) $\log_5 \frac{1}{25} = -2$

   (c) $\log_{10} 1000 = 3$

   (d) $\log_{64} 128 = 7/6$

   (e) $\log_{\frac{1}{2}} (1/4) = 2$

3. Evaluate each of the following expressions *exactly*.

(a) $2^{\log_2 16}$
(b) $2^{\log_2 1/2}$
(c) $10^{\log_{10} 7}$
(d) $\log_6 \sqrt{6}$
(e) $\log_5 5^3$
(f) $\log_3 (1/27)$

4. If $\log_4 A = 2.1$, evaluate each of the following expressions *exactly*.

(a) $\log_4 A^2$
(b) $\log_4(1/A)$
(c) $\log_4 16A$
(d) $\log_2 A$
(e) $\log_{16} A$

5. Interpret rules (F.2) and (F.3) in exponential language.

6. Explain why $\ln\left(x^2 - x - 2\right) = \ln(x-2) + \ln(x+1)$.

7. Describe how the graph of each of the following functions is geometrically related to the graph of $y = 2^x$. [EXAMPLE: The graph of $y = 2^{-x}$ is the reflection of the graph of $y = 2^x$ about the y-axis.]

(a) $(1/2)^x$
(b) $(1/2)^{-x}$
(c) -2^{-x}
(d) 2^{x-1}
(e) $2 - 2^x$
(f) $2 \cdot 2^{x-1}$

8. Find an equation for the graph that results from each of the following operations on the graph of $y = e^x$.

(a) Reflection about the x-axis.
(b) Reflection about the y-axis.
(c) Reflection about the line $y = 4$.
(d) Reflection about the line $x = -1$.
(e) Reflection about the y-axis, then a reflection of the resulting graph about the x-axis.

9. (a) Explain how to obtain the graph of $y = 2e^{x+3}$ from the graph of $y = e^x$ using *only* vertical stretching.
(b) Explain how to obtain the graph of $y = 2e^{x+3}$ from the graph of $y = e^x$ using *only* horizontal translation.
(c) Can the graph of $y = 2e^{4x+3}$ be obtained from the graph of $y = e^x$ using only the operations of vertical stretching and horizontal translation? Explain.

10. (a) Explain how to obtain the graph of $y = 2 + \ln(3x)$ from the graph of $y = \ln x$ using *only* vertical translation.
(b) Explain how to obtain the graph of $y = 2 + \ln(3x)$ from the graph of $y = \ln x$ using *only* horizontal stretching.
(c) Can the graph of $y = 2 + \ln(3x + 4)$ be obtained from the graph of $y = \ln x$ using *only* the operations of vertical translation and horizontal stretching? Explain.

11. Let $f(x) = 20e^{0.1x}$.

    (a) Find an x for which $f(x) = 20$.
    (b) Find an x for which $f(x) = 40$.
    (c) Find an x for which $f(x) = 80$.
    (d) Find an x for which $f(x) = 10$.

12. Let $g(x) = Ae^{0.2x}$ where A is a real number.

    (a) Suppose that $g(0) = 5$. Find A.
    (b) Suppose that $g(1) = 5$. Find A.
    (c) Suppose that $g(-1) = 5$. Find A.

13. Let $h(x) = 20e^{kx}$ where k is a real number.

    (a) Suppose that $h(1) = 20$. Find k.
    (b) Suppose that $h(1) = 40$. Find k.
    (c) Suppose that $h(1) = 10$. Find k.

14. Let $j(x) = Ae^{kx}$ where A and k are real numbers.

    (a) Suppose that $j(0) = 5$ and $j(3) = 10$. Find A and k.
    (b) Suppose that $j(1) = 5$ and $j(3) = 10$. Find A and k.

15. In each part below, plot *both* graphs on the same axes. Explain what you see, referring to properties of exponential and logarithm functions.

    (a) $y = 2^x, \qquad y = 4^{x/2}$
    (b) $y = \ln\left(\exp(x^2)\right), \qquad y = x^2$
    (c) $y = \ln\left((\exp x)^2\right), \qquad y = 2x$
    (d) $y = \exp(\ln x), \qquad y = x$
    (e) $y = \exp(2 \ln x), \qquad y = x^2$
    (f) $y = \exp(\frac{1}{2} \ln x), \qquad y = \sqrt{x}$

Appendix G

Trigonometric functions

The six trigonometric functions are introduced and defined in Chapter 1, Section 5. Start there for definitions and basic properties.

In this Appendix we collect a variety of information, in more detail, on trigonometric functions, their properties, their graphs, and their importance in calculus.

Trigonometric function notation

And a few others.

Trigonometric functions are often typeset without the customary $f(x)$-style parentheses. It's standard to write

$$\sin t, \qquad \cos t, \qquad \text{and} \qquad \tan t$$

rather than

$$\sin(t), \qquad \cos(t), \qquad \text{and} \qquad \tan(t).$$

But not slavishly.

We'll generally follow this convention, though a bit reluctantly—parentheses remind us that *functions* are involved. Whenever confusion seems possible (e.g., with the expression $\sin(t+1)$) or we want to emphasize the functional point of view, we'll use parentheses.

When in doubt, sacrifice elegance for clarity.

Other quirks of trigonometric notation involve *powers* of trigonometric functions. It's conventional, for instance, to write

$$\sin^2 t + \cos^2 t = 1 \quad \text{instead of} \quad (\sin(t))^2 + (\cos(t))^2 = 1,$$

Other powers are handled similarly—e.g., $\sin^{17} x$ means $(\sin x)^{17}$.

though both mean the same thing. *Neither* of these equations should *ever*, of course, be confused with

$$\sin t^2 + \cos t^2 = 1 \quad \text{or} \quad \sin(t^2) + \cos(t^2) = 1,$$

which are equivalent to each other, but *false*.

Sines, cosines, angles, and triangles

Any real number is a legitimate input to the sine or cosine function. So far we've interpreted such an input as the *signed length of an arc*. Thus $\cos(2) \approx -0.42$, because -0.42 is (approximately) the x-coordinate of the point 2 *units of distance* counterclockwise from $(1, 0)$ on the unit circle. (The same units of distance are used both on the circle and on the axes.) Here's the picture for $\cos(2)$:

Convince yourself carefully that all the quantities shown are plausible.

Why $\cos(2) \approx -0.42$

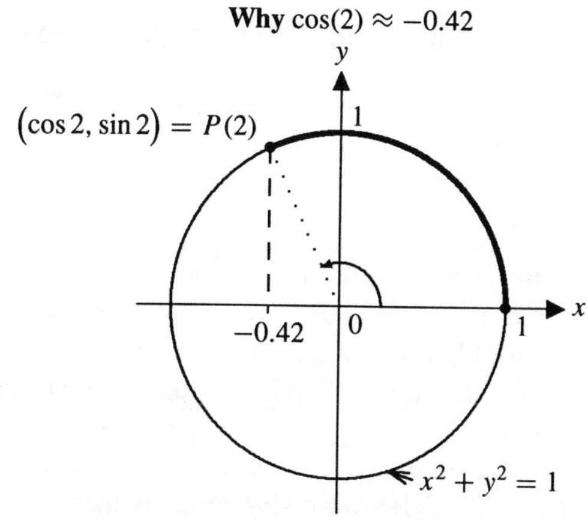

Sometimes we prefer to interpret inputs to the sine and cosine functions as *angles*, not arclengths. Any arc on the unit circle determines an obvious angle: the one between the two line segments joining the origin to the ends of the arc. (See the picture above.) From this point of view, $\cos 2$ is the cosine of the *angle* determined by an arc of length 2.

From radians to degrees and back. Two standard units—**radians** and **degrees**—are used to measure angles. Radian measure will prove far more convenient for us; we'll use it consistently. To convert between radians and degrees, use these formulas:

So should you. So should your calculator. Lock it in radian mode and throw away the key.

Radians ⇄ Degrees		
radian measure	=	$\dfrac{\pi}{180} \times$ degree measure
degree measure	=	$\dfrac{180}{\pi} \times$ radian measure

(Both follow from the fact that 2π radians $= 360°$.) In particular, the angle shown above is

$$2 \text{ radians} = 360/\pi \approx 114.6°\,.$$

Right triangles. "Trigonometry" refers, etymologically, to *measuring triangles*. Our "circular" viewpoint on trigonometric functions is easily linked to right triangles; doing so sometimes aids intuition.

If $P(t)$ lies in the first quadrant, i.e., if $0 \le t \le \pi/2$, then $P(t)$ naturally determines, as shown below, a right triangle with unit hypotenuse, one of whose angles measures t radians:

Triangles and trigonometric functions

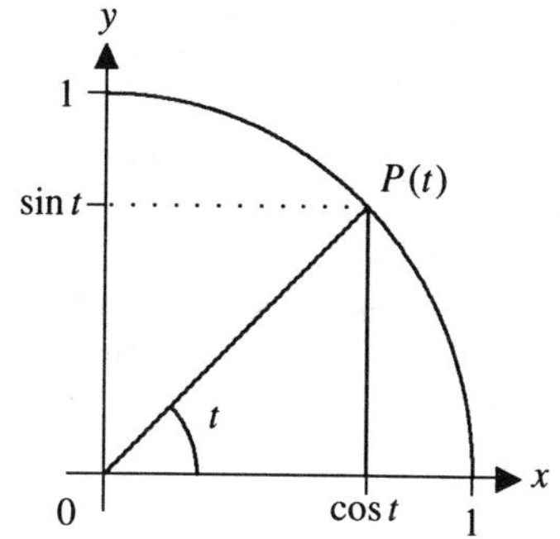

It's easy to see that this triangle has the "right" trigonometric properties. For example:

$$\sin t = \frac{\text{opposite}}{\text{hypotenuse}} = \frac{y}{1} = y; \qquad \cos t = \frac{\text{adjacent}}{\text{hypotenuse}} = \frac{x}{1} = x.$$

Famous sines and cosines

Isn't it? If not, review the definitions to convince yourself. It may also help to review the definition of "evident."

We've already violated our prohibition against degree measure! Maybe we should have said $\pi/6$–$\pi/3$–$\pi/2$ and $\pi/4$–$\pi/4$–$\pi/2$.

It's evident from the definitions of the sine and cosine functions that $\sin 0 = 0$ and $\cos(\pi/2) = 0$. Other important sines and cosines, such as $\sin(\pi/4) = \sqrt{2}/2$ and $\cos(\pi/3) = 1/2$ are well known but less obvious. All the well-known values can be computed as ratios of sides of the 30–60–90 and 45–45–90 right triangles. Know these important values:

Celebrated sines and cosines

t	0	$\pi/6$	$\pi/4$	$\pi/3$	$\pi/2$
$\cos t$	1	$\sqrt{3}/2$	$\sqrt{2}/2$	1/2	0
$\sin t$	0	1/2	$\sqrt{2}/2$	$\sqrt{3}/2$	1

In daily practice one needs to know sines and cosines of *all* integer multiples of $\pi/4$ and $\pi/6$. This is easier than it seems. Given the values above for angles in the *first quadrant* we can use the symmetry of the unit circle to find these values.

■ **Example 1.** Use symmetry to find $\sin(7\pi/6)$ and $\cos(7\pi/6)$.

Solution: This picture—

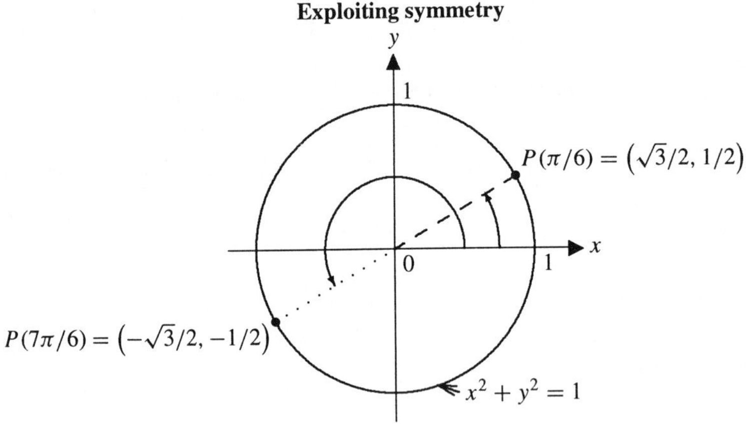

shows that

$$\sin\left(\tfrac{7\pi}{6}\right) = -\sin\left(\tfrac{\pi}{6}\right) = -\tfrac{1}{2} \quad \text{and} \quad \cos\left(\tfrac{7\pi}{6}\right) = -\cos\left(\tfrac{\pi}{6}\right) = -\tfrac{\sqrt{3}}{2}.$$

□

Obscure sines and cosines

For most inputs, precise values of the trigonometric functions are far from obvious. For example, what are $\sin(1)$ and $\cos(13)$? We could estimate values graphically using a unit circle, but, as it turns out, there is *no* simple algebraic formula for computing *exact* values of trigonometric functions. Fortunately, calculus offers methods of *approximating* values of these functions.

Other trigonometric functions

Four additional trigonometric functions are defined in terms of the sine and cosine functions.

> **Definition:** For real numbers t,
>
> $$\tan t = \frac{\sin t}{\cos t} \qquad \cot t = \frac{\cos t}{\sin t}$$
>
> $$\sec t = \frac{1}{\cos t} \qquad \csc t = \frac{1}{\sin t}$$

Graphs of all these functions appear in Section 1.5, page 67.

How many trigonometric functions are there? Cosine, sine, tangent, secant, cosecant, and cotangent make six. From another point of view, there are only two—sine and cosine—from which all the others are derived.

If we were serious about this numbers game, we could count at least *ten* trigonometric functions: the familiar six and their justifiably obscure relatives *exsecant*, *versine*, *coversine*, and *haversine*. Taking the opposite tack, we might argue for only *one* trigonometric function, say cosine, from which sine, and hence all the others, can be derived.

In the end, the number of trigonometric functions is a matter more philosophical than mathematical. What's important is that, whatever their number, *all* trigonometric functions are closely related to each other and to the unit circle.

More on the tangent function

Among the "other" trigonometric functions, the tangent function arises often enough to deserve special attention. To start, here's a close look at its graph, bristling with asymptotes (shown dotted):

Graph of $y = \tan x$

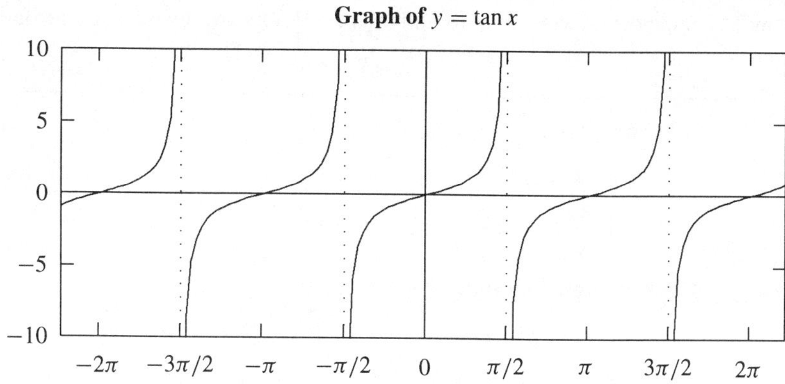

Many properties of the tangent function follow easily from its definition:

Domain and range: The tangent function accepts all real inputs t *except* those for which $\cos t = 0$ (i.e., $t = \pm\pi/2, \pm 3\pi/2, \pm 5\pi/2$, etc.). The domain of the tangent function, therefore, consists of all real numbers *other* than these obvious offenders. The graph reflects these troubles. The range is the *full* set of real numbers.➸

The graph shows this, too.

Periodicity: The tangent function (like the sine and cosine functions) is 2π-periodic. A simple calculation shows why:

$$\tan(t + 2\pi) = \frac{\sin(t + 2\pi)}{\cos(t + 2\pi)} = \frac{\sin t}{\cos t} = \tan t .$$

The graph reflects the same property.

Look at it. Do you agree?

More on periodicity—a surprise: Look again. The tangent function's graph repeats its basic shape on intervals of length π—*twice as often* as the computation above suggests. In other words, the tangent function appears to be π-periodic. Is something wrong?

No. Every π-periodic function is *also* 2π-periodic, automatically. The tangent function repeats itself on intervals of length π for the following reason:

$$\tan(t + \pi) = \frac{\sin(t + \pi)}{\cos(t + \pi)} = \frac{-\sin t}{-\cos t} = \tan t.$$

The second equality is the key. It holds because $\sin(t + \pi) = -\sin t$, and $\cos(t + \pi) = -\cos t$.

Are these equalities plausible? Are they obvious? If not, draw the points $P(t)$ and $P(t+\pi)$ on the unit circle. How are they related?

Trigonometric identities

Equations like

$$\sin^2 t + \cos^2 t = 1, \quad \sin(t + \pi/2) = \cos t, \quad \text{and} \quad \tan^2 t + 1 = \sec^2 t,$$

that relate various trigonometric functions to each other are known as **trigonometric identities**. A great many such relations exist—not surprisingly, because all six trigonometric functions spring from the same unit circle idea.

Some trigonometric identities, like the first one above, follow directly from the definitions. Others are far subtler. Memorizing every trigonometric identity is out of the question. It's wiser to memorize a few truly basic identities.

The three above enjoy this exalted status.

Other—less obvious but still useful—trigonometric identities exist; one should know *that* they exist and *where* to find them. Below are several such second-rank identities.

At least.

Addition formulas

$$\sin(s + t) = \sin s \cos t + \cos s \sin t$$

$$\cos(s + t) = \cos s \cos t - \sin s \sin t$$

Double-angle formulas

$$\sin(2t) = 2 \sin t \cos t \qquad \cos(2t) = \cos^2 t - \sin^2 t$$

$$\sin^2 t = \frac{1}{2}\big(1 - \cos(2t)\big) \qquad \cos^2 t = \frac{1}{2}\big(1 + \cos(2t)\big)$$

The double-angle formulas are junior-grade versions of the addition formulas; the former are readily derived from the latter.

■ **Example 2.** Derive the formula for $\cos(2t)$.

Solution: Using the addition formula,

$$\begin{aligned}\cos(2t) &= \cos(t+t)\\ &= \cos t\cos t - \sin t\sin t\\ &= \cos^2 t - \sin^2 t.\end{aligned}$$ □

Exercises

1. The angle drawn within the unit circle shown below measures 1.2 radians. The tick marks around the circumference of the circle indicate tenths of a radian.

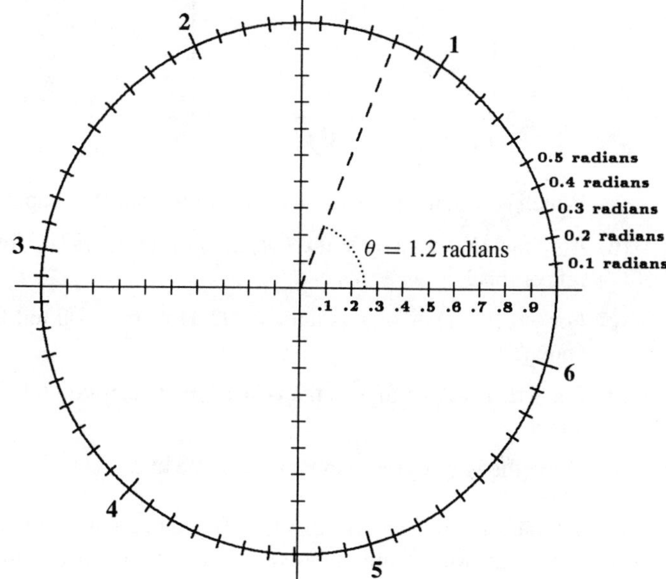

Use this diagram to estimate each of the following values:

(a) cos(1.2)
(b) sin(0.5)
(c) tan(2.8)
(d) cos(0.2)
(e) sin(4.5)
(f) cos(13)

2. Use the diagram above to estimate each of the following. (Then check your answers with a calculator.)

(a) Two values of x such that $\sin x = 1/2$.
(b) Two values of x such that $\tan x = 5$.

3. Let $P(t)$ be the point t units counterclockwise from $(1, 0)$ on the unit circle. Explain in words:

(a) How $P(t)$ and $P(t+\pi)$ are related.
(b) Why $\cos(t+\pi) = -\cos(t)$.
(c) Why $\sin(t+\pi) = -\sin(t)$.
(d) Why $\tan(t+\pi) = \tan(t)$.

4. Find the domain of each of the following functions.

(a) $\cot x$

(b) $\sec x$

5. Graphs of $y = \sin x$ and $y = \cos x$ are shown below.

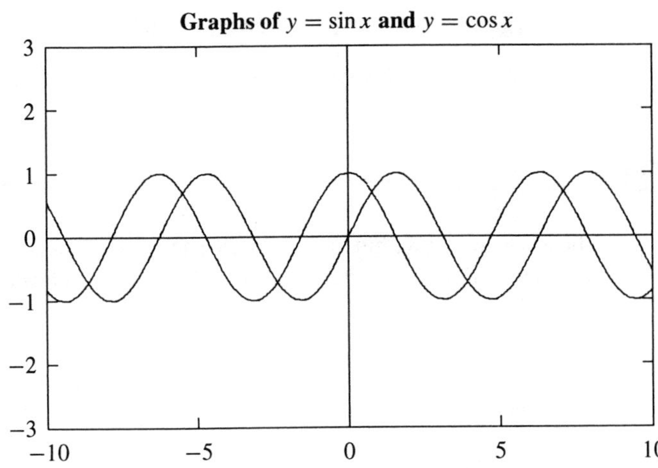

(a) Which is which? Trace these graphs onto a sheet of paper and *label* them.

(b) It's a fact that $\cos x = \sin(x + \pi/2) \approx \sin(x + 1.57)$. How do the graphs reflect this?

(c) For which values of x is $\tan x = 0$? How can you tell from the graphs above?

(d) For which values of x is $\tan x = 1$? How can you tell from the graphs above?

(e) Draw the graph $y = 3 \sin x$ on the same axes.

6. Suppose that $\sin a = b$ and $\cos c = 0.3$. Evaluate each of the following expressions. (Your answers should involve only real numbers and the constant b.)

(a) $\sin(-a)$

(b) $-\sin a$

(c) $\cos(-c)$

(d) $\sin c$

(e) $\sin^2 a$

(f) $\sin(2a)$

7. Evaluate each of the following expressions *exactly*. (No decimal approximations allowed!)

(a) $\cos\left(\frac{5\pi}{6}\right)$

(b) $\sin\left(\frac{2\pi}{3}\right)$

(c) $\tan\left(\frac{3\pi}{4}\right)$

(d) $\cot\left(\frac{4\pi}{3}\right)$

(e) $\sec\left(\frac{5\pi}{3}\right)$

(f) $\csc\left(\frac{7\pi}{4}\right)$

(g) $\sin\left(\frac{257\pi}{3}\right)$

(h) $\tan\left(\frac{-2000\pi}{3}\right)$

8. Use the addition formulas for sine and cosine to evaluate each of the following expressions *exactly*.

(a) $\cos\left(\frac{5\pi}{12}\right) = \cos\left(\frac{\pi}{4} + \frac{\pi}{6}\right)$

(b) $\sin\left(\frac{19\pi}{12}\right) = \sin\left(\frac{3\pi}{4} + \frac{5\pi}{6}\right)$

(c) $\sin\left(\frac{\pi}{12}\right) = \sin\left(\frac{\pi}{4} - \frac{\pi}{6}\right)$

(d) $\tan\left(\frac{7\pi}{12}\right) = \tan\left(\frac{5\pi}{4} - \frac{2\pi}{3}\right)$

9. Which of the following pairs of expressions define the same function?

(a) $\sec^2 x$ and $1 + \tan^2 x$

(b) $\cos^2 x$ and $1 - \sin^2 x$

(c) $\cos x$ and $\sin\left(x - \frac{\pi}{2}\right)$

(d) $\sin x$ and $\cos\left(x + \frac{\pi}{2}\right)$

10. Find subtraction formulas for sine and cosine similar to the addition formulas.

(a) $\sin(s - t) = ???$

(b) $\cos(s - t) = ???$

Appendix H

Real-world calculus: from words to mathematics

Translation. Calculus is more than a brilliant theoretical invention. It is also a practical tool—among the most powerful ever discovered—for posing and solving important real-world problems. Real-world problems seldom arrive as neat mathematical packages. More common are untidy bundles of questions, assumptions, information, and (sometimes) disinformation. Important parts may be missing; useless extras may be included.

The first (and sometimes hardest) step in tackling such problems is to translate them, as concisely as possible, into mathematical language. Since calculus operates mainly on functions, "translation" in calculus usually means interpreting a problem in *functional language.*

To understand real phenomena—the Consumer Price Index, gravitational forces, population growth, planetary motion etc.—we must be able to *predict* their behavior. Useful predictions, moreover, must be *quantitative*, not merely qualitative. Mathematics is the only route to quantitative results.

Different areas of mathematics are best suited to describe and predict different sorts of phenomena. Describing phenomena of *change* is the special genius of calculus; calculus offers both language in which to describe changing quantities, and rules with which to *predict* their behavior.

Story problems: you may feel a little discomfort ... Mathematics has been compared (in jest, of course) to dentistry. "Story problems," in particular, sometimes elicit emotions normally associated with the whine of an approaching high-speed drill.

Such fear and loathing, though common, can be alleviated—without pharmaceutical intervention. This is not to deny the difficulty. Translation of any sort is expert work, combining both technical and "literary" expertise.

In our case, mathematical.

Learn the words by heart. The essential point is that progress is possible. Handling story problems is no more a "knack" than speaking French. Indeed, the brevity, bluntness, and precision of mathematical language make mathematical translation simpler and more straightforward than it would otherwise be. For the same reason, mastering basic mathematical vocabulary and "grammar" is especially important. Calculus has its own recurring key words and phrases—**proportional**, **parameter**, **domain**, **maximum**, **increasing**, and many others. An important goal of this appendix is to review several important mathematical terms and techniques and to illustrate their uses in calculus-style applications.

■ **Example 1.** As a rocket rises, the force earth's gravity exerts on it decreases. This *qualitative* observation, although perfectly true, is utterly useless in practice.

It doesn't take a rocket scientist to see why. Without more information, we can't *compute* anything: how much fuel to load, how much thrust is needed, how long anything will take.

Newton's law of universal gravitation➻ describes gravity's effect *quantitatively*. It says that for a 1000-lb. rocket d miles from the center of the earth, the approximate force (in pounds) of earth's gravity is given by the function

We'll discuss it more fully later. See p. 498.

$$F(d) = \frac{1.6 \times 10^{10}}{d^2}.$$

With the formula, predictions are possible. If, say, d =20,000 miles,➻ then the force of gravity is only

A reasonable distance for a communications satellite.

$$F(20000) = \frac{1.6 \times 10^{10}}{20000^2} = 40 \text{ pounds.} \qquad \square$$

Garden-variety optimization

Many real-life problems boil down to finding the largest or smallest value of some function. Finding the *right* function hidden in the verbiage, may be the main challenge.

■ **Example 2.** Gardener Alpha plans a rectangular lettuce patch; 100 feet of rabbit-proof fencing is available. What are the best dimensions?

Translating Alpha's problem. "Best" can mean different things; we'll take it to mean "largest in area."➻ The problem, then, is to find the largest rectangle with perimeter 100 feet.

Could "best" possibly mean anything else? Probably so. For real lettuce patches, "best" would involve harvesting convenience, ease of watering, etc.

The answer—a square—isn't surprising; translation corroborates our intuition. Thus, let x and y represent the lengths of the "vertical" and "horizontal" sides of the garden:

Alpha's garden

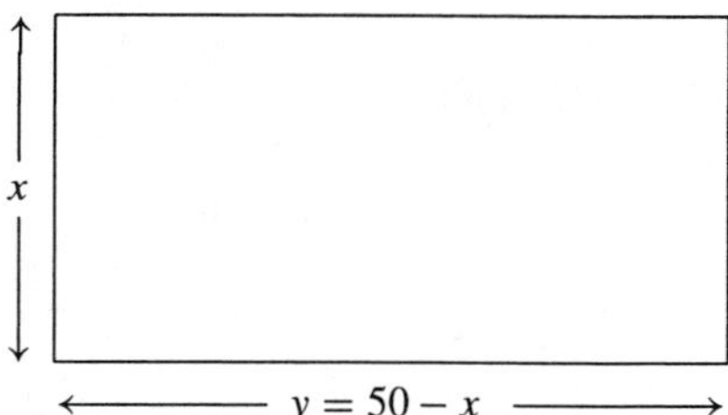

(That 100 feet of fence is available says, algebraically, that $100 = 2x + 2y$.)➻ The crucial point is that the area A, given by

Equivalently, that $y = 50 - x$.

$$A = \text{length} \times \text{width} = xy = x(50 - x),$$

is a function of the variable x.

The rule $A(x) = x(50 - x)$ makes *algebraic* sense for any real number x. *In context*, though, both x and $50 - x$ must be nonnegative, because each represents a physical length. Thus the "feasible" input set, or domain, is the x-interval $[0, 50]$.

We've arrived at an optimization problem:

Find the maximum value, and where it occurs, of the function

$$A(x) = x(50 - x)$$

on the interval $[0, 50]$.

Solution: The area A is a *quadratic* function of x, so its graph is (part of) a parabola:

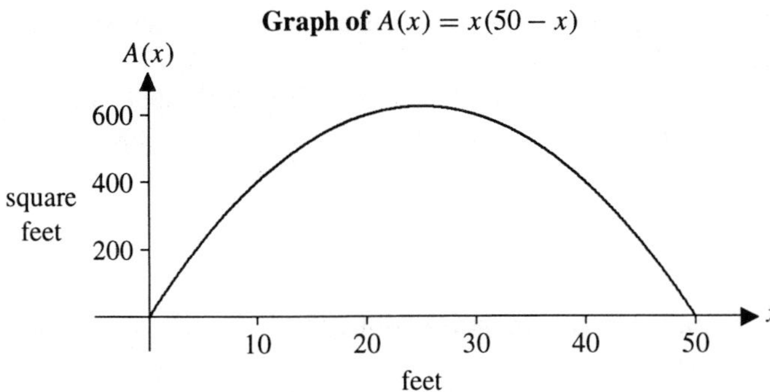

The graph suggests that the maximum value of A occurs at $x = 25$, where the area is $A(25) = 625$ square feet. Graphical guesses are often imperfect, but this time we're right: symmetry guarantees that the vertex of a parabola lies *exactly* midway between the two roots.

In the original language of the problem:

> *Alpha's lettuce patch should be square, 25 feet on a side, with area 625 square feet.*

□

■ **Example 3.** Beta too has 100 feet of fence. Beta's barn will form one side of a rectangular patch. (The barn is long enough so that its length isn't a constraint.) Which dimensions are best now?

Over 100 feet, say.

Solution: This time, the answer *isn't* obvious; *posing* the problem mathematically will help us solve it.

Another "generic" picture applies:

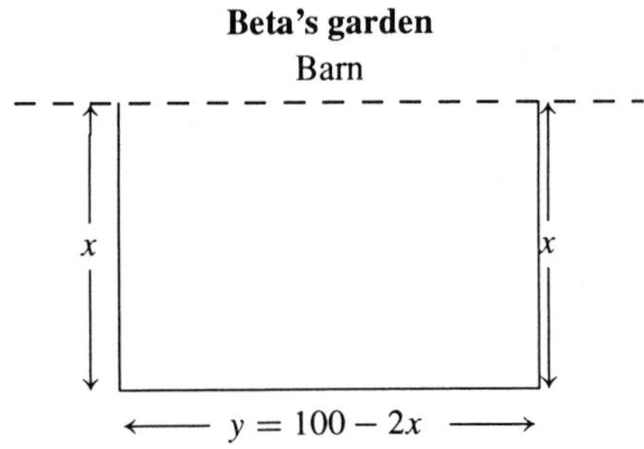

As before, area is a quadratic function of the side we called x:

Convince yourself that $y = 100 - 2x$.

$$A(x) = xy = x(100 - 2x) = 100x - 2x^2 = 2x(50 - x).$$

The feasible domain is (again) the interval $[0, 50]$. In functional language, the problem is to *maximize the function A over its domain.*

Because x and y represent physical lengths.

The area function A is again quadratic, so its maximum value occurs midway between the two roots, at $x = 25$. The graph of A agrees:

Graph of $A(x) = 2x(50 - x)$

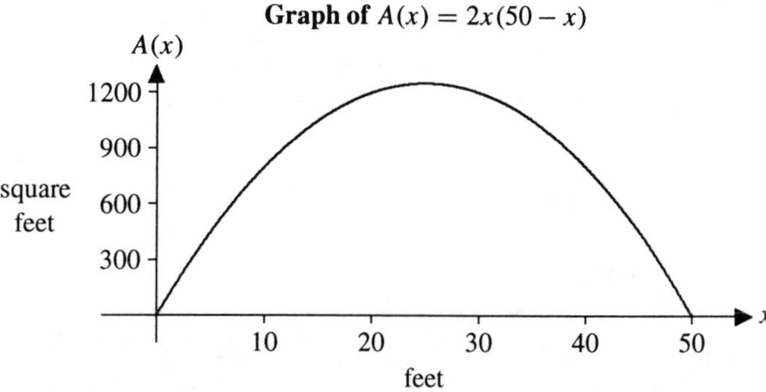

In barnyard language:

> *The largest such garden has dimensions* $25' \times 50'$ *and area* $A(25) = 1250$ *square feet.*

□

■ **Example 4.** Gardener Gamma plans to fence exactly 1000 square feet of land. *Any* rectangular shape will do. For convenience in watering, one side will lie along a (straight) river. How much fencing will Gamma need for the other three sides?

Notice the new twist: Alpha and Beta aimed to *maximize area, for a fixed perimeter.* Gamma wants to *minimize perimeter, for a fixed area.* Optimization problems often come in such pairs.➻

Paired optimization problems are known as "duals" of each other. This problem might be called a fencing dual.

Solution: A familiar picture applies:

Gamma's garden

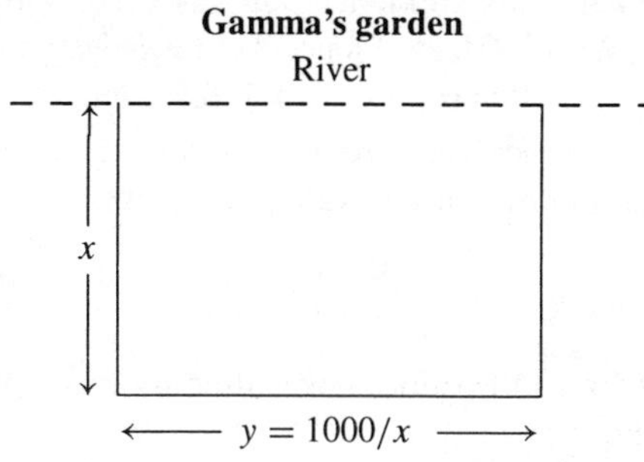

Using it, let's find our function. Let x and y be the lengths shown, and let L denote the total length of the fence. By assumption, $xy = 1000$, so

$$L = 2x + y = 2x + \frac{1000}{x}.$$

There's our function.

The domain of L: a subtlety. What is L's "natural" domain? Technically, *any* positive number is a feasible input—a fence a mile long and 2.27 inches wide makes mathematical sense. Since no such ridiculously oblong design could possibly be most economical, we can safely ignore very large and very small positive inputs x. Given the general size of the numbers, the domain $5 \le x \le 50$ leaves plenty of room.

Here, finally, is our problem:

> *Find the minimum value, and where it occurs, of the function* $L(x) = 2x + 1000/x$ *on the interval* $[5, 50]$.

Solving the problem without calculus is hard, so we'll work approximately, with graphics. Here's a look:

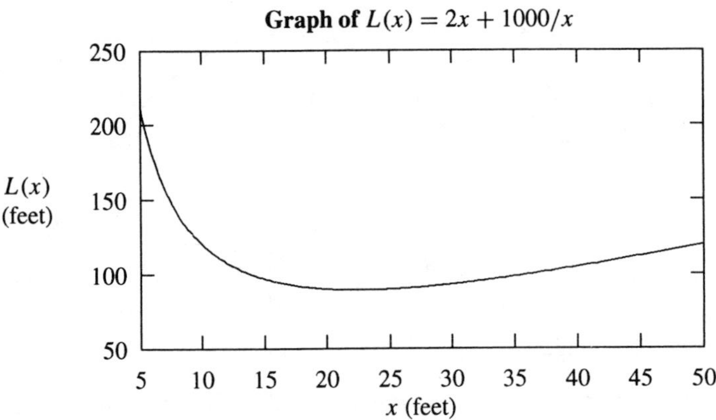

The graph shows that L attains its minimum value (about 90 feet) around $x = 22$. In agricultural terms:

With a bit of calculus, we can find exact answers: $x = \sqrt{500} \approx 22.3607$ *and* $L(\sqrt{500}) \approx 89.4427$.

Gamma needs 90 feet of fence; the garden should have approximate dimensions $22.5' \times 45'$. □

Parameters

We assumed earlier that Alpha and Beta each had 100 feet of fencing; our answers, naturally, reflected that assumption. But was the number 100 essential in either problem? Hardly. With 200 feet of fence we'd *still* design a square garden for Alpha, and a rectangular one, with proportions 1:2, for Beta.

Such "accidental" aspects of a problem are conveniently handled using **parameters**—symbols that stand for *any* constant value. The next example illustrates a simple use of parameters.

■ **Example 5.** Delta and Epsilon, horticulturally incompatible, agree to "divorce" their gardens as shown:

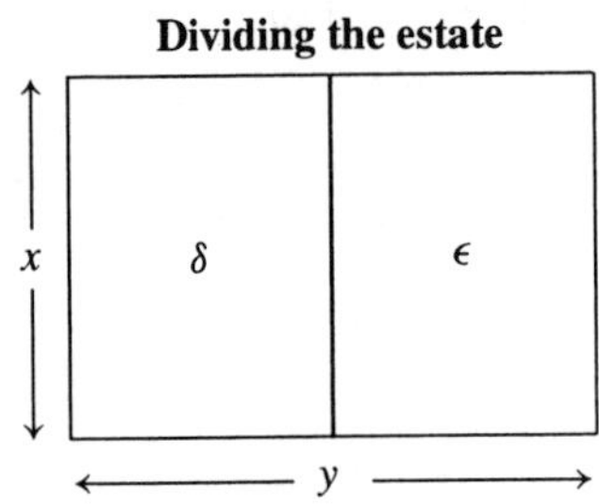

They have L feet of fence. What shape is best? Note:

- In this problem, the parameter is perimeter.

Sorry; it just worked out that way.

- Before proceeding, *guess* an answer. Should the total garden be square? Vertically oblong? Horizontally oblong?

Solution: Let x and y be as shown. As before, the area A satisfies the equation $A = xy$. The garden's peculiar design dictates that the total length of fence needed is $L = 3x + 2y$, so➻

$$A(x) = xy = \frac{x(L-3x)}{2}.$$

Solve this equation for y to get $y = (L - 3x)/2$.

In context, both x and $L - 3x$ must be nonnegative, so $0 \le x \le L/3$ must hold. Our problem, then, is to maximize A for x in the interval $[0, L/3]$.

The presence of the parameter L now complicates life slightly. We'll show two possible strategies.

Maximizing A with algebra. For *any* nonnegative number L the function

$$A(x) = \frac{x(L-3x)}{2}$$

is quadratic in x. Its graph is a parabola, opening *downward.* Symmetry guarantees that the vertex of a parabola lies midway between its two x-intercepts. From the formula above it's clear that $A(x) = 0$ if $x = 0$ or $x = L/3$. Therefore the largest value of A occurs halfway between, at $x = L/6$.

Maximizing A with graphics. Another strategy is to plot $A(x)$ for *several* reasonable values of the parameter, and look for pattern:

Graphs of A for various lengths L

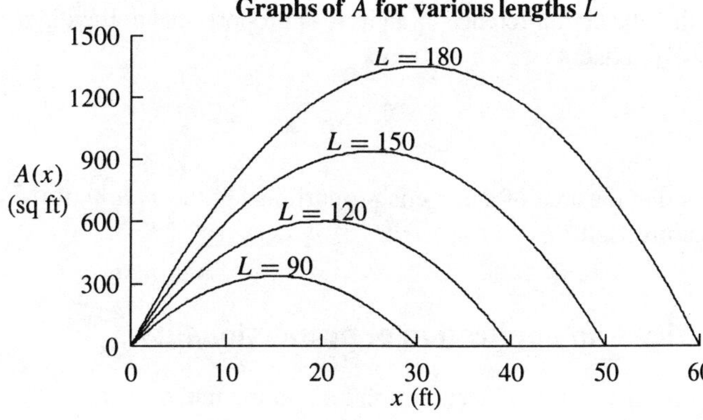

The picture shows that for each value of L, the maximum area occurs at $x = L/6$, the *midpoint* of the domain $[0, L/3]$.

Conclusion. The most spacious double garden uses $L/6$ feet of fence for each of the three "vertical" runs. The remaining $L/2$ feet is divided equally for the two "horizontal" runs.➻ The result, drawn proportionately to scale, looks like this:

Again, half the fence runs in each direction. Is this coincidence or is something happening here?

Biggest gardens with perimeter L

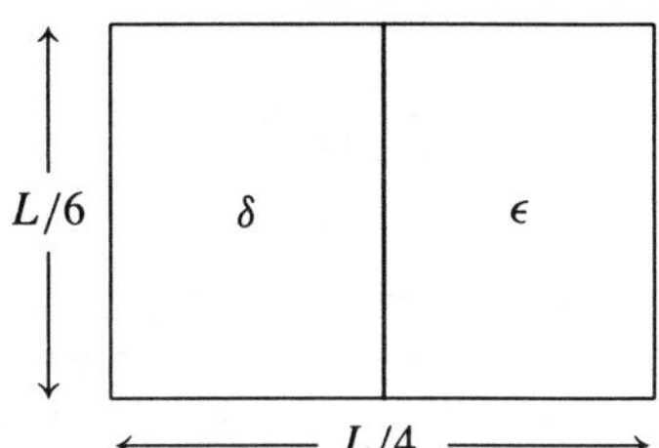

□

Taking leave of our fences

Fencing problems, although unglamorous, illustrate nicely the standard and important process of defining a pertinent function on a sensible domain, finding maximum or minimum values, and then interpreting the results.

Proportionality

Proportionality and inverse proportionality are relationships between varying quantities:

> **Definition:** Let A and B be quantities which vary together. A is **proportional** to B if, for some nonzero constant k, the equation
>
> $$A = k\,B$$
>
> holds for *all* values of A and B.
>
> A and B are **inversely proportional** if
>
> $$A = \frac{k}{B}.$$

Although familiar, this formula is not trivial. That the same constant, π, appears here and in the area formula is a remarkable fact.

■ **Example 6.** The formula

$$C = \pi\,d$$

says that the circumference of a circle is proportional to the diameter, with **proportionality constant π**. The formula

$$A = \pi\,r^2$$

shows that the area of a circle is proportional to the *square* of the radius, but not to the radius itself. □

Gravity—an application of proportionality

It's well known that objects weigh less on the moon than on the earth. How much less? Why?

Newton's law of universal gravitation describes the relationships among quantities involved in gravitation:

Our words—Newton wrote in Latin.

> *The force of gravity exerted on one object by another is proportional to the mass of each, and inversely proportional to the square of the distance between them.*

In each case all other quantities are held constant.

In algebraic form, Newton's law says that

$$F = k\frac{M_1 M_2}{d^2},$$

where F represents gravitational *force*, M_1 and M_2 are the objects' *masses*, d is the *distance* between the objects' centers of gravity, and k is a constant of proportionality. The numerical value of k depends on the units chosen. In the metric system (using kilograms, meters, etc.), $k \approx 6.7 \times 10^{-11}$. In the British system (miles, pounds, etc.), $k \approx 3.82 \times 10^{-17}$.

For a sphere the center of gravity is the ordinary (geometric) center.

We'll choose our problems to minimize fuss over units.

■ **Example 7.** How much less does an object weigh on the moon than on Earth? What would the same object weigh on Jupiter?

Solution: An object's *weight* is defined as the force gravity exerts on it.

According to Newton's law, the "earth-weight" F_e of an object with mass M, at the surface of the earth, is

$$F_e = k\frac{MM_e}{{R_e}^2},$$

where M_e is earth's *mass*, and R_e is earth's *radius*. Similarly, the same object's "moon-weight" and "Jupiter-weight," are, respectively,

$$F_m = k\frac{MM_m}{{R_m}^2} \quad \text{and} \quad F_j = k\frac{MM_j}{{R_j}^2},$$

where M_m and M_j are the masses, and R_m and R_j are the radii, of the moon and Jupiter.

Our problem is about the ratios F_m/F_e and F_j/F_e. By easy algebra,

$$\frac{F_m}{F_e} = \frac{M_m {R_e}^2}{M_e {R_m}^2} \quad \text{and} \quad \frac{F_j}{F_e} = \frac{M_j {R_e}^2}{M_e {R_j}^2}.$$

Remarkably enough, every constant above is known—physics and astronomy textbooks have tables like this one:

Celestial Constants		
Object	*Mass (kg)*	*Radius (km)*
Moon	7.35×10^{22}	1740
Earth	5.98×10^{24}	6378
Jupiter	1.90×10^{27}	71398

Now only simple arithmetic remains:

$$\frac{F_m}{F_e} \approx 0.165; \qquad \frac{F_j}{F_e} \approx 2.535.$$

In human terms, an astronaut weighing 160 pounds on earth weighs only $0.165 \cdot 160 \approx 26.4$ pounds on the moon. On Jupiter, the astronaut weighs a staggering 405.6 pounds. □

Mass or weight? Physicists distinguish between an object's *mass* and its *weight*. An object's weight can vary (as our example shows) but its mass is the same everywhere. In the metric system, the standard unit of force (and therefore of weight) is the *newton*. At the surface of the earth an object with *mass* 1 kilogram has *weight* 9.8 newtons. (Actually, since the earth is not perfectly spherical, an object's weight is slightly different at different points on the earth's surface.)

Exercises

1. Zeta plans to fence off a rectangular field along the bank of a river; no fence is needed along the river. Fencing costs \$2 per foot for the ends and \$3 per foot for the side parallel to the river. Zeta's budget is \$900.

   (a) Let x be the length of the side of the field that lies along the river. Explain why the formula
   $$A(x) = x(225 - 0.75x)$$
   describes the area of Zeta's field.

   (b) What is the domain of A? Why?

   (c) What are the dimensions of Zeta's *largest* field?

   (d) If given twice as much money, can Zeta enclose twice as much area? Why or why not?

2. Water is flowing into a cubical tank. Each side of the tank is ten feet.

   (a) Write a formula for V, the volume of water in the tank, as a function d, the depth of water in the tank.

   (b) What is the domain of V? What is the range of V?

   (c) Write a formula for d as a function of V.

3. Guido's pizza is delivered in square boxes formed from 20 cm by 40 cm rectangular pieces of cardboard. The boxes are made by cutting out six squares of equal size, three from each of the 40 cm edges (one square at each corner, and one in the middle of the edge), then folding in the obvious way. (If it isn't obvious, order one with sausage and mushrooms to investigate.)

   (a) Find the volume of the box as a function of the length of the side of the square cut-outs.

   (b) How large should the cutouts be to maximize the volume of the box?

   (c) How large should the cutouts be to maximize *area*? Why?

4. Suppose that A and B are *directly* proportional, but A and C are *inversely* proportional. Suppose, further, that if $A = 1$, then $B = 2$ and $C = 3$.

   (a) What are the values of B and C if $A = 10$?

   (b) Are B and C directly proportional? Inversely proportional? Explain.

   (c) Suppose that $B = 10$. Find values for A and C.

5. Is the volume of a sphere proportional to its radius? Explain.

6. The weight of an object is inversely proportional to the square of its distance from the center of the earth. A satellite weighs 200 pounds when 10,000 miles from the center of the earth.

   (a) Express the weight of the satellite as a function of d, its distance from the center of the earth.

   (b) At what distance from the center of the earth does the satellite weigh 100 pounds?

7. An open box with a capacity of 36,000 cubic inches is needed. The box must be twice as long as it is wide. The material out of which the box is to be constructed costs \$0.10 per square foot. Find the cost of the material for the box as a function of the width of the box.

8. A Norman window is a rectangle surmounted by a semicircle. The rectangle is of clear glass while the semicircle is of rose-colored glass (the better for seeing the world) that transmits only half as much light per square foot as clear glass does. The total perimeter is fixed. Express the amount of light transmitted by the window as a function of the radius of the semicircle.

9. It's 9:30 p.m. Your snowmobile is out of gas and you are 3 miles due south of a major highway. The nearest service station on the highway is 6 miles east of your position; it closes at midnight. You can walk 4 miles per hour on roads, but only 3 miles per hour through snowy fields.

   Express the time to reach the service station as a function of the distance r you walk along the roads. [HINT: You could walk on roads all the way, straight through the fields, or partway through the fields, then on the road.]

Appendix I

Selected proofs

This Appendix contains careful proofs of various results, more or less in order of subtlety. The proofs are intended to be read "as needed," as particular questions arise. Alternatively, some readers may enjoy reading proofs for their own sake, as an introduction to the formal ideas and methods of analytic mathematics.

A challenging limit

Many limits that arise in calculus courses can be evaluated either by "inspection" (i.e., at a glance) or with elementary algebra. All of the following limits are of these type:

$$\lim_{x\to\infty} \frac{1}{x} = 0; \quad \lim_{x\to 3}(x+2) = 5; \quad \lim_{x\to 2} \frac{x^2-4}{x-2} = 4.$$

Only the last one requires any argument, and simple algebra is all that's needed:

$$\lim_{x\to 2} \frac{x^2-4}{x-2} = \lim_{x\to 2} \frac{(x-2)(x+2)}{x-2} = \lim_{x\to 2}(x+2) = 4.$$

One of the 2 or 3 most important in calculus.

The important limit

$$\lim_{t\to 0} \frac{\sin t}{t} = 1$$

is different. Because $\sin t$ is *not* an algebraic expression, the usual proof tricks—factoring, expansion, etc—are useless. A rigorous proof must take another tack.

Before beginning a rigorous proof, we remark that overwhelming *circumstantial* evidence—in graphical and numerical forms—that $\sin t/t \to 1$ is available. (See, e.g., Example 4, page 153.) Still, pictures and numbers aren't proofs. On the contrary, what a computer or calculator "understands" about the sine function probably depends implicitly on some "knowledge" of the very limit in question.

A proof. Because $\sin t$ and t are both *odd* functions of t, their ratio is *even*. Thus it's enough to consider only *positive* values of t, i.e., to show that

$$\lim_{t\to 0^+} \frac{\sin t}{t} = 1.$$

The following unit-circle diagram describes the situation:

Why $\sin t \approx t$

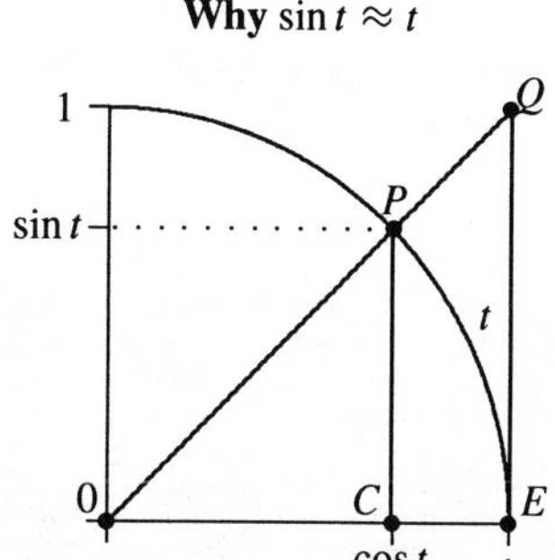

The diagram supports three key claims:

(i) $\sin t \le t$; (the segment CP is shorter than the arc EP)

(ii) $t \le \sin t + 1 - \cos t$; (the arc EP is shorter than EC+CP—the route traveling *west*, then *north*)

(iii) as $t \to 0^+$, $\dfrac{1-\cos t}{t} \to 0$.

Claim (iii) requires some support. Here's an an airtight proof, based on (i):

$$\begin{aligned}\frac{1-\cos t}{t} &= \frac{1-\cos t}{t}\cdot\frac{1+\cos t}{1+\cos t} = \frac{1-\cos^2 t}{t(1+\cos t)} = \frac{\sin^2 t}{t(1+\cos t)}\\ &= \frac{\sin t}{t}\cdot\frac{\sin t}{1+\cos t} \le \frac{\sin t}{1+\cos t}.\end{aligned}$$

Now it follows that

$$0 \le \frac{1-\cos t}{t} \le \frac{\sin t}{1+\cos t}.$$

As $t \to 0^+$, the right side tends to 0. By the squeeze principle, (iii) holds as claimed.

To finish our proof we'll use the squeeze principle again. From (i) and (ii) we have

$$t - 1 + \cos t \le \sin t \le t.$$

Dividing through by t gives

$$\frac{t-1+\cos t}{t} = 1 - \frac{1-\cos t}{t} \le \frac{\sin t}{t} \le 1.$$

Taking limits gives

$$1 - \lim_{t\to 0^+}\frac{1-\cos t}{t} \le \lim_{t\to 0^+}\frac{\sin t}{t} \le 1.$$

From (iii), the first limit is 1; we're done. □

Another proof. Another "squeeze" proof of the same limit can be based on areas. The same picture shows the following area relation:

$$\text{area(OCP)} \le \text{area(OEP)} \le \text{area(OEQ)}.$$

Here OCP and OEQ are triangles; OEP is a circular sector. *Calculating* these three areas gives

$$\begin{aligned}
\text{area(OCP)} &= \frac{\text{base} \times \text{height}}{2} = \frac{\cos t \, \sin t}{2}; \\
\text{area(OEP)} &= \pi \times \text{fraction of circle} = \pi \times \frac{t}{2\pi} = \frac{t}{2}; \\
\text{area(OEQ)} &= \frac{\text{base} \times \text{height}}{2} = \frac{\tan t}{2}.
\end{aligned}$$

Thus

$$\frac{\cos t \, \sin t}{2} \le \frac{t}{2} \le \frac{\tan t}{2}.$$

A positive number!

If $t > 0$, then multiplying through by $2/\sin t$ gives

$$\cos t \le \frac{t}{\sin t} \le \frac{1}{\cos t}.$$

As $t \to 0^+$ the left and right quantities tend to 1; so, therefore, does the middle. □

Proving the product rule

Recall the product rule:

> **Fact:** **(The product rule.)** Suppose that u and v are differentiable at x. If $p(x) = u(x) \cdot v(x)$, then p is differentiable at x, and
>
> $$p'(x) = \big(u(x) \cdot v(x)\big)' = u'(x) \cdot v(x) + u(x) \cdot v'(x).$$

In Section 3.3 we argued the case informally. Below is a formal proof; notice that it shows—rather than assumes—that the product uv is differentiable.

Proof. Let u and v be differentiable functions. By definition,

$$(uv)'(x) = \lim_{h \to 0} \frac{u(x+h)v(x+h) - u(x)v(x)}{h}.$$

We need to show that this limit exists, and equals $u'(x)v(x) + u(x)v'(x)$.

An algebraic trick—subtracting and adding the same quantity in the numerator—does the job:

Check each step.

$$\begin{aligned}
(uv)' &= \lim_{h \to 0} \frac{u(x+h)v(x+h) - u(x)v(x)}{h} \\
&= \lim_{h \to 0} \frac{u(x+h)v(x+h) - u(x)v(x+h) + u(x)v(x+h) - u(x)v(x)}{h} \\
&= \lim_{h \to 0} \frac{u(x+h)v(x+h) - u(x)v(x+h)}{h} + \lim_{h \to 0} \frac{u(x)v(x+h) - u(x)v(x)}{h} \\
&= \lim_{h \to 0} \frac{u(x+h) - u(x)}{h} \cdot \lim_{h \to 0} v(x+h) + u(x) \cdot \lim_{h \to 0} \frac{v(x+h) - v(x)}{h} \\
&= u'(x)v(x) + u(x)v'(x).
\end{aligned}$$

We're done. □

An $\epsilon - \delta$ limit proof

Recall the $\epsilon - \delta$ definition of limit:

Definition: Suppose that for every positive number ϵ, no matter how small, there is a positive number δ so that

$$|f(x) - L| < \epsilon \quad \text{whenever} \quad 0 < |x - a| < \delta.$$

Then

$$\lim_{x \to a} f(x) = L.$$

Recall, too, this plausible-seeming property:

Fact: Suppose that

$$\lim_{x \to a} f(x) = L \quad \text{and} \quad \lim_{x \to a} g(x) = M,$$

where L and M are finite numbers. Then

$$\lim_{x \to a} [f(x) + g(x)] = L + M.$$

(Other limit properties, in the same spirit, appear in Theorem 1., page 170.)

A rigorous proof must use the rigorous definition. Here's how:

Proof. We need to show that for any number $\epsilon > 0$ there's a corresponding number $\delta > 0$ such that

$$0 < |x - a| < \delta \implies |(f(x) + g(x)) - (f(a) + g(a))| < \epsilon.$$

Let $\epsilon > 0$ be given. To find the desired δ we'll first set $\epsilon_1 = \epsilon_2 = \epsilon/2$. Since ϵ_1 and ϵ_2 are positive, there exist, by our assumption, other positive numbers δ_1 and δ_2 such that

$$\begin{aligned} 0 < |x - a| < \delta_1 \quad &\implies \quad |f(x) - f(a)| < \epsilon/2; \\ 0 < |x - a| < \delta_2 \quad &\implies \quad |g(x) - g(a)| < \epsilon/2. \end{aligned}$$

If we now set δ to be the smaller of δ_1 and δ_2, then we have what we want:

$$0 < |x - a| < \delta \implies 0 < |x - a| < \delta_1 \quad \text{and} \quad 0 < |x - a| < \delta_2,$$

so

$$\begin{aligned} |(f(x) + g(x)) - (f(a) + g(a)| &\leq |f(x) - f(a)| + |g(x) - g(a)| \\ &< \epsilon/2 + \epsilon/2 \\ &= \epsilon. \end{aligned}$$

□

Appendix J

A graphical glossary of functions

Graphical reasoning—representing functions and their derivatives graphically—is an invaluable skill in calculus. This appendix offers a brief "atlas" of representatives of the most important classes of calculus functions. Each function is shown together with its derivative.

A linear function and its derivative

Graph of $f(x) = x$ **Graph of $f'(x) = 1$**

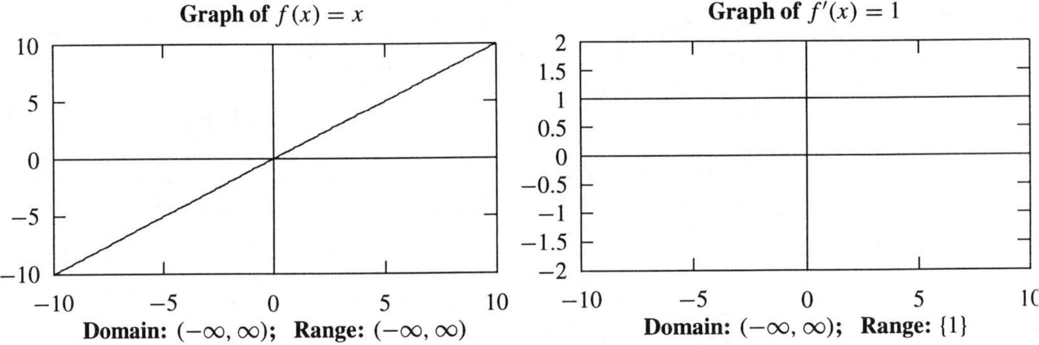

Domain: $(-\infty, \infty)$; **Range:** $(-\infty, \infty)$ **Domain:** $(-\infty, \infty)$; **Range:** $\{1\}$

Notes. The derivative of a linear function is a constant function.

A quadratic function and its derivative

Graph of $f(x) = x^2$ **Graph of $f'(x) = 2x$**

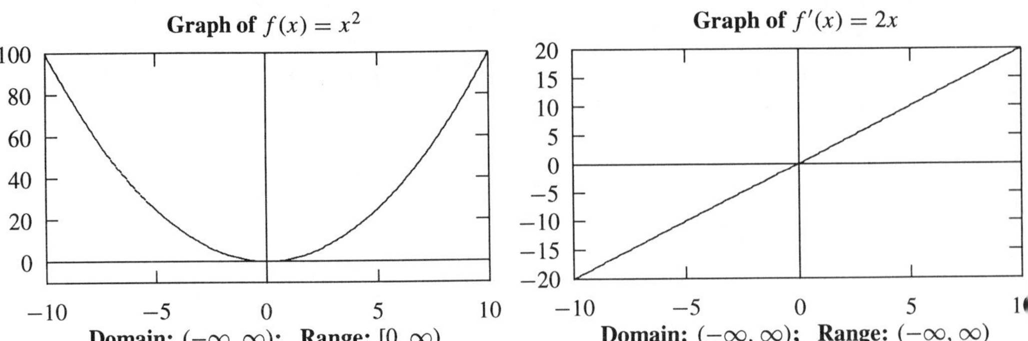

Domain: $(-\infty, \infty)$; **Range:** $[0, \infty)$ **Domain:** $(-\infty, \infty)$; **Range:** $(-\infty, \infty)$

Notes. The derivative of a quadratic function is a linear function. The quadratic function's vertex corresponds to a root of the derivative.

A rational function and its derivative

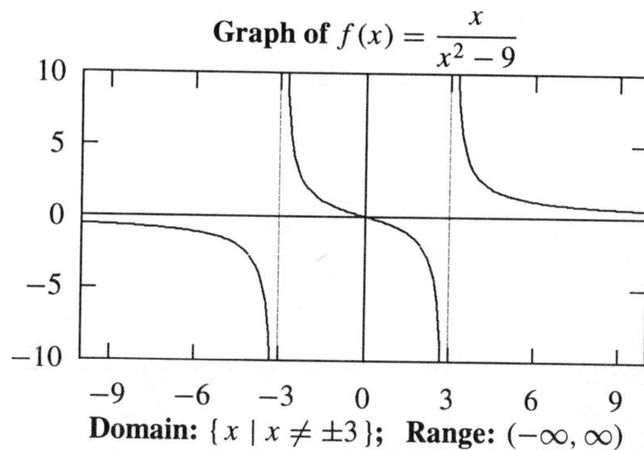

Domain: $\{x \mid x \neq \pm 3\}$; **Range:** $(-\infty, \infty)$

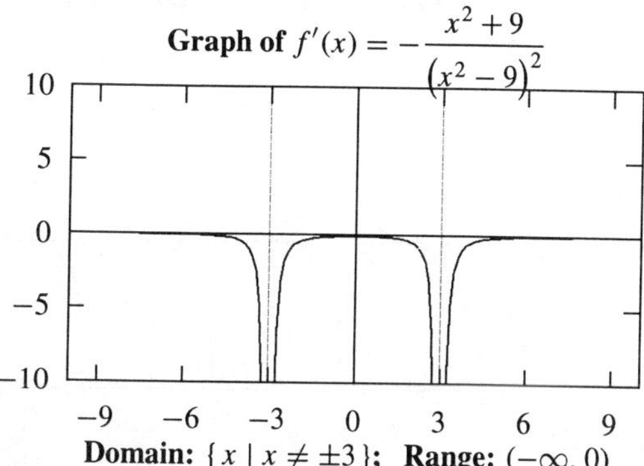

Domain: $\{x \mid x \neq \pm 3\}$; **Range:** $(-\infty, 0)$

Notes. The derivative of a rational function is another rational function. Notice the behavior of asymptotes: If f has a *vertical* asymptote at $x = a$, then so does f'. If f has a *horizontal* asymptote at $y = b$, then f' has a horizontal asymptote at $y = 0$.

The sine function and its derivative

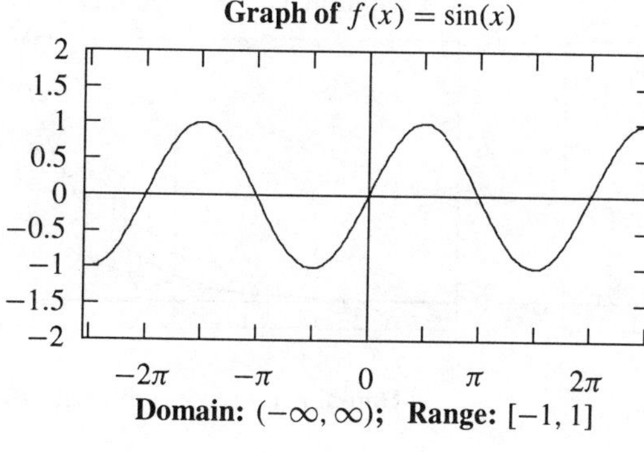

Domain: $(-\infty, \infty)$; **Range:** $[-1, 1]$

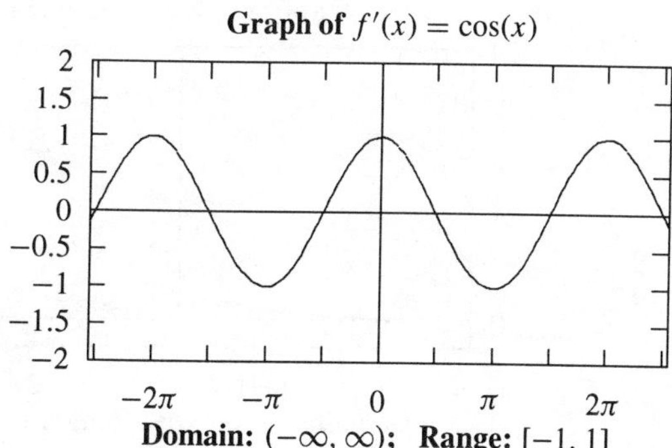

Domain: $(-\infty, \infty)$; **Range:** $[-1, 1]$

Notes. The sine function is 2π-periodic; so, therefore, is its derivative. Both the sine function and its derivative oscillate between -1 and 1. At the origin, the sine graph has slope 1.

The cosine function and its derivative

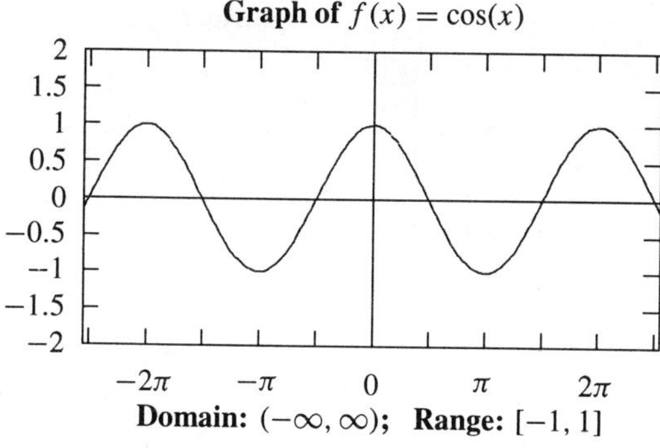

Domain: $(-\infty, \infty)$; **Range:** $[-1, 1]$

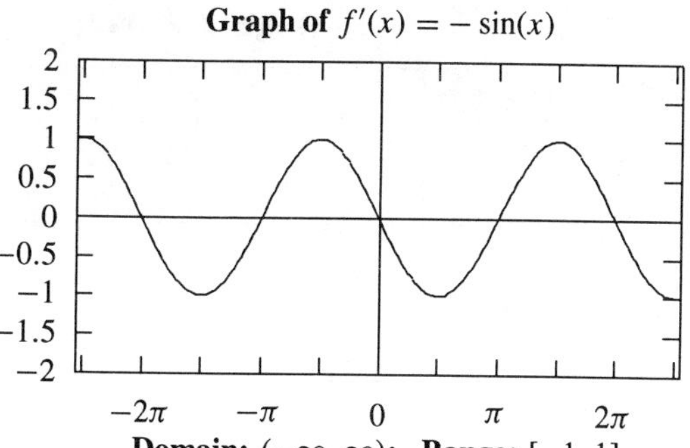

Domain: $(-\infty, \infty)$; **Range:** $[-1, 1]$

Notes. The cosine function is 2π-periodic; so, therefore, is its derivative. Both the sine function and its derivative oscillate between -1 and 1. At the origin, the cosine graph is horizontal.

The tangent function and its derivative

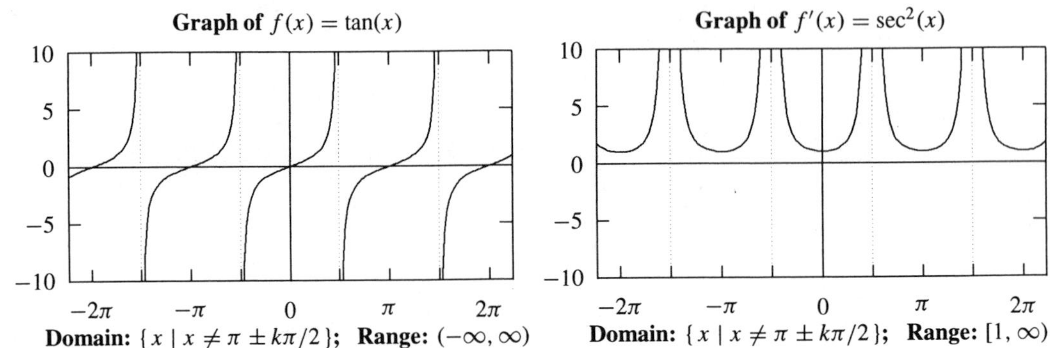

Notes. The tangent function is π-periodic; so is its derivative. Unlike the sine and cosine functions, the tangent function and its derivative have vertical asymptotes. At the origin, the tangent graph has slope 1.

Exponential functions and their derivatives

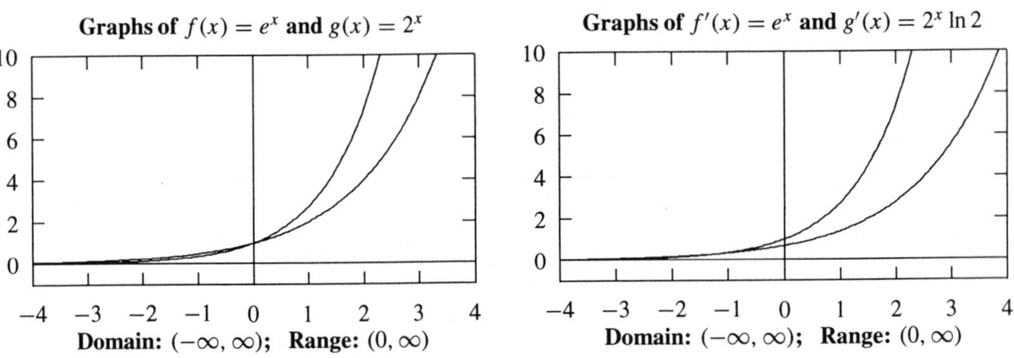

Notes. The natural exponential function $y = e^x$ is its own derivative. Other exponential functions, such as $y = 2^x$, are *proportional* to their own derivatives. The $y = e^x$ graph has slope 1 at $x = 0$; the $y = 2^x$ graph has slope $\ln 2$ at $x = 0$. All exponential functions have horizontal asymptotes; so do their derivatives.

The natural logarithm function and its derivative

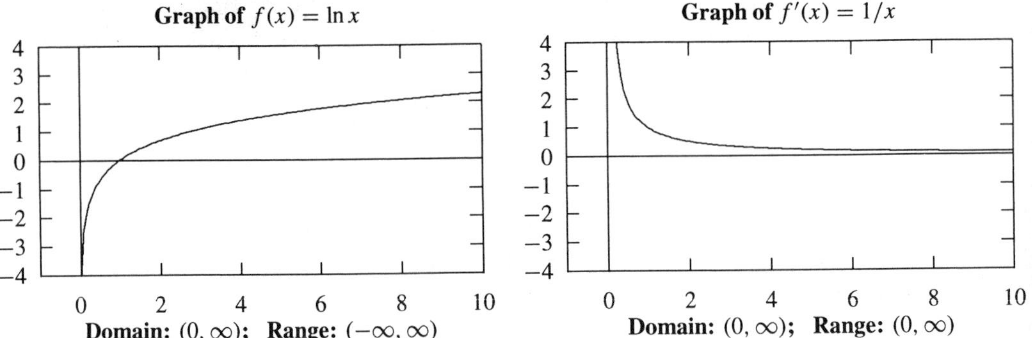

Notes. The natural logarithm function $y = \ln x$ is the inverse function to $y = e^x$. It is defined only for positive inputs. The graph of $y = \ln x$ has slope 1 at $x = 1$.

Index